1,000,000 Books

are available to read at

---◆---

www.ForgottenBooks.com

---◆---

**Read online
Download PDF
Purchase in print**

ISBN 978-1-333-50048-1
PIBN 10512246

This book is a reproduction of an important historical work. Forgotten Books uses
state-of-the-art technology to digitally reconstruct the work, preserving the original format
whilst repairing imperfections present in the aged copy. In rare cases, an imperfection in
the original, such as a blemish or missing page, may be replicated in our edition. We do,
however, repair the vast majority of imperfections successfully; any imperfections that
remain are intentionally left to preserve the state of such historical works.

Forgotten Books is a registered trademark of FB &c Ltd.
Copyright © 2018 FB &c Ltd.
FB &c Ltd, Dalton House, 60 Windsor Avenue, London, SW19 2RR.
Company number 08720141. Registered in England and Wales.

For support please visit www.forgottenbooks.com

1 MONTH OF
FREE
READING

at

www.ForgottenBooks.com

By purchasing this book you are eligible for one month membership to ForgottenBooks.com, giving you unlimited access to our entire collection of over 1,000,000 titles via our web site and mobile apps.

To claim your free month visit:
www.forgottenbooks.com/free512246

* Offer is valid for 45 days from date of purchase. Terms and conditions apply.

English
Français
Deutsche
Italiano
Español
Português

www.forgottenbooks.com

Mythology Photography **Fiction**
Fishing Christianity **Art** Cooking
Essays Buddhism Freemasonry
Medicine **Biology** Music **Ancient**
Egypt Evolution Carpentry Physics
Dance Geology **Mathematics** Fitness
Shakespeare **Folklore** Yoga Marketing
Confidence Immortality Biographies
Poetry **Psychology** Witchcraft
Electronics Chemistry History **Law**
Accounting **Philosophy** Anthropology
Alchemy Drama Quantum Mechanics
Atheism Sexual Health **Ancient History**
Entrepreneurship Languages Sport
Paleontology Needlework Islam
Metaphysics Investment Archaeology
Parenting Statistics Criminology
Motivational

THE GROWTH

of

ENGLISH INDUSTRY

and

COMMERCE

IN MODERN TIMES.

London: C. J. CLAY AND SONS,
CAMBRIDGE UNIVERSITY PRESS WAREHOUSE,
Ave Maria Lane.

CAMBRIDGE: DEIGHTON, BELL AND CO
LEIPZIG: F. A. BROCKHAUS.

THE GROWTH

OF

ENGLISH INDUSTRY

AND

COMMERCE.

IN MODERN TIMES.

BY

W. CUNNINGHAM, D.D.

VICAR OF S. MARY'S THE GREAT, FELLOW AND LECTURER IN TRINITY COLLEGE, CAMBRIDGE;
TOOKE PROFESSOR IN KING'S COLLEGE, LONDON.

CAMBRIDGE:
AT THE UNIVERSITY PRESS
1892

[*The Right of Translation and Reproduction is reserved.*]

𝕮𝖆𝖒𝖇𝖗𝖎𝖉𝖌𝖊:

PRINTED BY C. J. CLAY, M.A. AND SONS,

AT THE UNIVERSITY PRESS.

PREFACE.

THE present volume treats of a clearly marked episode in English economic history; it deals, not indeed with the origins, but with the rise and fall of the Mercantile System. The sketch of this portion of the subject in my First Edition was so slight, that it has hardly served even as a scheme for arranging the mass of material that had to be dealt with.

There is no lack of excellent books on different parts of the subject, like those of Chalmers, Tooke, Macculloch, Roscher, Thorold Rogers and Toynbee; but I know of none that treats it as a whole, or that carefully combines the study of economic aims and opinions, with an examination of the events of our commercial history. This is the characteristic feature of the method I have adopted, and to it I have sedulously adhered. My primary aim has been to understand the economic policy of Englishmen in past days; the logic of events has already subjected it to crushing criticism. There is much in the past which we cannot but condemn, especially in the light of after events; we need not condemn it less decidedly when the reasons which brought it about become intelligible. But we cannot understand the economic measures of bygone days, unless we examine the evidence patiently, and try to read it in the light of contemporary thought and opinion. We are doomed to failure if we are content to take the attitude of *doctrinaire* economists, and explain the course of our history on the assumption that it has been dominated by the economic

motives of self-interested individuals. Until we are prepared
to look behind the 'greed' of capitalists and the 'tyranny' of
landlords, potent though these may have been, we cannot
hope to understand the steps by which English Industry and
Commerce attained supremacy. There always have been
landowners and monied men, and even magistrates and
members of Parliament, who tried to do their duty, and
who were not without influence on the course of our national
life. It is easy to play the part of a shallow cynic and
ignore these elements, as if they had never existed. It is by
no means so easy to try and take systematic account of all
the various factors that have combined to shape the course
of our economic progress, and to assign to each its due
importance; this is the problem towards the solution of
which I have made my contribution.

It was obvious from the first that if the work was to
be kept within reasonable compass it would be impossible
to attempt an exhaustive treatment, but I trust I have
been able to indicate the main lines of development, clearly
and distinctly, and to bring them into due prominence.
Again and again, I have had to resist the temptation of
enlarging unduly on some topic which interested me specially,
and I have been obliged to discard some of the material I
had collected, in order to preserve a proper proportion in the
space allotted to different parts of the subject. As my friend
Professor Foxwell most kindly allowed me constant access
to his magnificent library of Economic books, the resources
at my command have been very large; and it has been by
no means easy to make a wise selection.

There are several other friends to whom I am deeply
indebted, and from whom I have received constant and
unwearied assistance in my attempt. Miss E. A. McArthur
of Girton College has aided me in verifying the references
and dates. About some such matters it is difficult to be
right, about others it is impossible. The Record Commission
Edition of the Statutes is not to be trusted for the dates
at which they were passed. Again, the pagination of the
Parliamentary Papers is put in by hand, and is by no means
identical in all the copies of the same volume. The author-

ship of pamphlets opens up a vast field for patient research, and the bibliographical index, which Miss McArthur has compiled, as well as the statistical tables and diagrams which she has contributed, are considerable additions to the usefulness of the volume.

Mr Hubert Hall of the Record Office, and Professor Gonner of University College, Liverpool, have been kind enough to read the proofs; to each of them I am indebted for very valuable aid. Mr G. Townsend Warner, Fellow of Jesus College, had seen the whole in an earlier stage, as he read the manuscript, and I was able to make substantial additions in accordance with his suggestions. I have also had valuable assistance on special points from Professor Sir T. Wade, Fellow of King's College, and from Mr Archbold, of Peterhouse.

The friend to whom I owe most has not lived to see the publication of a volume in which she was keenly interested. Both in collecting materials and in the arrangement and composition of the book I had constant assistance from Miss Lamond of Girton College. I think she knew I was not ungrateful, but I only learned to appreciate her help aright when I lost it. She had a wonderfully high standard of accuracy and thoroughness in work of every kind, and an infinite capacity for taking pains to "finish things off properly." Twenty sheets were printed off some time before the rest of the book, but no portion of the proofs had the advantage of her care in revision.

W. C.

TRINITY COLLEGE, CAMBRIDGE,
14 *July*, 1892.

CORRIGENDA AND ERRATA.

p. 18, l. 5. *For* martins *read* martens.
p. 36, n. 4. *For* Boy's *read* Boys.
p. 37, n. 8. *For* XLVII. *read* XLIII.
p. 39, n. 1. *For* Hansard *read* Parl. Debates.
          For Davis *read* Davies.
p. 44, n. 3, l. 9. *For* mystery *read* mistery.
p. 52, n. 2. *Read* Handelspolitik II. 671.
p. 52, n. 3, l. 3. *For* 1609 *read* 1607.
p. 52, n. 3, l. 6. *For* 1607 *read* 1602.
p. 52, n. 3. *Read Parl. Hist.* I. 899.
p. 52, n. 4, l. 4. *For* f. 219 *read* f. 219.
p. 56, l. 19. *For* bye-avocations *read* by-avocations.
p. 59, l. 27. *After* work *for* , *read* ;
p. 59, l. 31. *For* bear-traders *read* bear-leaders.
p. 60, n. 4, l. 18. *For* Olliver *read* Oliver.
p. 69, l. 8. *For* resume *read* résumé.
p. 75, margin. *Delete* 1665
p. 79, l. 23. *For* published *read* written.
p. 80, n. 1. *For* 17 *read* 173.
p. 81, n. 3, and p. 86, l. 31. *For* Molina *read* Molinaeus.
p. 86, l. 30. *For* divine *read* authority.
p. 90, l. 32. *For* borne *read* born.
p. 91, l. 32. *After* corn *for* , *read* ;
p. 95, n. 3. *For* Hendricks *read* Hendriks.
p. 95, n. 4. *For* vessel *read* vessels.
p. 100, l. 4. *For* first *read* fifth.
p. 114, l. 22. *After* Tunis *supply* in.
p. 115, n. 3. *For* Reynal *read* Reynel.
p. 120, n. 4. *For* Trevor's *read* Trevers'.
p. 121, n. 4, l. 2. *For* Criticism *read* criticism.
p. 124, n. 3. *After* Vol. II. *supply* Bk. v.
p. 126, l. 2. *For* Polaroon *read* Polaroon.
p. 135, nn. 4, 5. *For* Hibernica *read* Hibernia.
p. 136, n. 4. *For* Knowler *read* Knowler.
p. 136, nn. 2, 5. *For* Hibernica *read* Hibernia.
p. 142, n. 1, l. 7. *After* § 9 *supply* (Irish).
p. 147, n. 6. *For* IV. *read* Series III. Vol. III. p. 55.
p. 154, n. 1. *For* 1607 *read* 1655.
p. 158, l. 2. *After* discomfort *for* , *read* .
p. 159, n. 4. *Supply* (Irish).
p. 171, l. 1. *For* time *read* tune.
p. 176, l. 5. *For* divided *read* decided.
p. 178, l. 21. *For* Britanny *read* Britanny.
p. 190, l. 35. *For* bushel *read* quarter.
p. 202, l. 22. *For* and *read* and.
p. 205, n. 1, 4 and p. 209, n. 3. *For* Stowe *read* Stow.
p. 222, n. 2. *After* 655 *delete* !
p. 229, n. 3. *For* Fauc *read* Fabic.
p. 245, n. 3. *For* Trades *read* Trade.
p. 264, n. 1, 5. *After* Survey II. *supply* Bk. v.
p. 272, n. 4. *For* Geo. II. *read* Geo. I.

CONTENTS.

INTRODUCTION.

BOOK VI.

THE ELIZABETHAN AGE.

CHAPTER I. POLITICAL SURVEY.

CHAPTER II. SHIPPING.

CHAPTER III. PLANTATIONS.

CHAPTER IV. INDUSTRY.

CONTENTS.

BOOK VII.

THE STUARTS.

BOOK VIII.

THE STRUGGLE WITH FRANCE.

CHAPTER I. THE FALL OF THE MERCANTILE SYSTEM.

PART I. 1689—1776.

CHAPTER II. COMMERCE.

CHAPTER III. PLANTATIONS.

CHAPTER IV. INDUSTRIAL PROGRESS.

PART III. 1815—1846.

INTRODUCTION.

160. IF the history of the world is looked at as a whole, *The special importance of England in the history of the world is due to her* it seems that each of the great civilisations, which have risen in different ages, has had a special character of its own. Some one side of human life has come into prominence in each, and each has made its particular contribution to the heritage of human culture which after-ages appropriate and make their own. Philosophy and sculpture are the imperishable monuments of the best days of Greece, while Roman law has affected the development of all modern polities. In the same way we may see that modern English civilisation has its own special character, and that the influence it is exercising on the destinies of the race differs markedly from the part that was played either by Greece or Rome. We are apparently a nation of shop-keepers, continually pushing our commerce; but we are pre-eminently a nation of artisans, busily engaged in producing all sorts of goods. England's place as a leader in the history of the world is chiefly due to her supremacy in Industry and Commerce. The arts, which the citizens of Greece and Rome despised, have become the foundations of her pride; and the influence which she exercises on the world at large is most clearly seen in the efforts, which other nations make, to follow the steps by which she has attained this supremacy.

It is not a little curious to remember that this supre- *commercial and industrial supremacy.* macy is of very recent growth; in the great period of English literary effort it was undreamt of; England seemed to be far behind. There was no question of taking a first place in the world, but there was much reason to fear that she could not maintain an independent position in Europe. The country was only beginning to enter on a course of industrial and commercial success. In the fourteenth century the whole of the external, and much of the internal, trade of the country had been in the hands of foreigners; in the fifteenth our merchants began to push their way from point to point in the Mediterranean and the Baltic; in the sixteenth they followed slowly in the wake of other adventurers, or tried to establish themselves in unkindly regions which had attracted no one else. When Elizabeth ascended the throne England appears to have been behind other nations of Western Europe in the very industrial arts and commercial enterprise on which her present re-putation is chiefly based. The economic side of English History is of special interest, because it is on this side of human activity that our country has attained pre-eminence; the modern economic history of England is of special im-portance, because this industrial and commercial supremacy is of recent growth.

Complexity of the sub-ject and necessity of selection. 161. At the same time the extent and complexity of the subject may well force us to pause before we attempt to enter on it at all. It would be difficult even to chronicle the series of changes in commercial enterprise, or to de-scribe the steps in industrial progress, within reasonable limits. It is not easy to become fully acquainted with the changes in any one industry,—say the worsted manufacture or any other single branch of the textile trades; the litera-ture which deals with the coal and iron trades in all their ramifications is enormous; there can be no hope of treating such topics exhaustively; and after all, they only form a portion of one part of our subject. There has been an agricultural as well as an industrial revolution in modern times; the steps, by which new markets have been opened, or new supplies of raw produce obtained as our commerce expanded, could not be fully treated without entering on the domain of universal history, and sketching the physical geography of the whole earth. The mere enumeration of technical improvement, and of the triumphs of mercantile enterprise in any detail, would be impossible if that were all we attempted; but the object of the present volume is more ambitious, as it aims not merely at stating what has occurred, but at exhibiting how it has come about. We wish to reach not a mere description but an explanation. The secret springs of our industrial supremacy lie deeply hidden; some of it can be traced to national characteristics, much of it is indirectly due to political institutions which led to the consolidation of the national life at an early date, or tempted skilled workmen to immigrate from continental towns; while the equable climate, mineral resources and maritime situation have afforded unexampled opportunities for successful industry and world-wide commerce. There have been moral forces, in human skill and foresight; and there have been favourable physical conditions; but it would be no easy task to trace the genesis of the various kinds of skill, or to show how far personal qualities and how far physical environment have respectively contributed to national success in any one direction. The range is so wide, the complexity is so great, that if we are to survey it intelligently, a vast mass of the material must be deliberately rejected and laid aside; and we cannot begin our task till we have settled on some principle of selection, which may help us to discriminate what is of primary importance from such other phenomena as must be left out of sight for fear they should confuse the mind, and which may be left out of sight with comparatively little loss. They may have been very important in many ways, even of great interest for the study of particular departments, but they are relatively unimportant to us, if they do not help us to get a clearer view of the growth of English Industry and Commerce as a whole.

162. It is perhaps unnecessary to insist here that we cannot draw a rough and ready division which will isolate economic from other phenomena. To understand the changes that have taken place in material wealth we must take into account the indirect effects of many events on the national life. Constitutional changes and international relations, religious enthusiasms and scientific discoveries, have

Economic growth must be viewed not apart from but in connection with

all played their part in aiding, or at least in affecting, material progress; and we cannot hope to understand it at all, if we leave any of these deliberately on one side. Indeed one might almost say, paradoxical as it appears, that we can only explain economic changes, when we get outside the circle of prices and market values to the political and moral and intellectual forces which make themselves felt in changes of supply and demand. The economic history of a nation cannot be clearly followed unless it is habitually regarded as a subordinate aspect of the political life of the people. As a matter of fact, the economic development has been consciously and deliberately controlled in the supposed interest of the polity; sometimes for good and sometimes for evil there has been interference, but the rate of growth and the directions of growth have been constantly affected by legislative or administrative interference. It is impossible to understand the stimulus that was given in one case, or the lethargy that affected other branches of business, unless we understand the aims of the Government for the time being. They had the power to exert great influence on commerce; they were anxious according to their lights to promote material prosperity. Hence if the course of material progress is to be intelligible, we must try to view it in connection with political projects and aims. This is obviously true in regard to the period of the Mercantile System, and it is also true even when politicians decided that it was wisest to abstain from direct interference with the course of any business. The advocates of Free Trade insisted that greater political advantages would flow from adopting it, than from continuing to maintain the Corn Laws. The repeal was a great economic change, but it was brought about by a great political agitation.

political projects and aims: The nation and its dependencies and relationships give the limits of the subject; the nation and its ambitions and policy did much to determine the direction of development; while the Government is, both by means of legislation and by its fiscal arrangements, a constant controlling force. On every side political considerations are of primary importance

in tracing industrial and commercial history, and they supply
the framework and chief divisions of the subject.

163.   As we are concerned with growth, and all growth *the study of the beginnings of changes;*
means change, we must concentrate our attention on the
beginning of each change, especially of changes which have
continued to operate for any considerable number of years,
and of which the accumulated effects are very great.   The
impetus may originate within the country or it may come
from without.   The importation of precious metals from
Spanish America altered the value of silver in England, and
set agoing a movement in prices which continued for nearly
a century; all sorts of fiscal, social and industrial readjust-
ments followed as the consequences of this change.   The *improved skill;*
immigration of skilled workmen from abroad, and the inventions by which we have acquired new power to direct and
control such physical agents as water, in canals, or as steam,
in all its applications to machinery, have had even greater
results.   Increased knowledge of natural resources has given
increased power of using them to advantage.   The progress
of invention and discovery is progress in human ability and
human acquaintance with nature; the changes, when once
begun, have continued with accelerated velocity; but the
first beginnings of these changes, so far as we can trace them,
demand our closest attention.

164.   But great as have been the changes in industrial *foresight.*
intelligence and skill since the time of Elizabeth, they are as
nothing compared with the new development of human foresight in saving up funds of wealth, and in applying the
wealth thus saved in directions which might yield an annual
income.   Capital had been employed in commerce from time
immemorial, and it had begun to make itself felt as a power
in the cloth manufacture in England during the fifteenth
century; but from the time of Elizabeth onwards the formation of capital, and the application of capital to industry,
and to developing the resources of England and her dependencies, went on with increasing rapidity.   The obvious
symptom of this change is seen in the rise of a class of
monied men, who even in the later Elizabethan Parliaments
began to attract attention as a political power.   The gold-

*Monied
men.* smiths of the seventeenth century show us the increasing
prominence of this class; and the facilities which have been
given by the later developments of credit put new powers
into their hands. From the beginning of the eighteenth
century onwards the monied interest has overbalanced the
landed interest, and we find many analogies with the capitalistic economy of the Roman Republic rather than with the
landed economy of mediæval England.

The formation of capital by monied men has given the
material facilities for carrying out improved methods of
industry and agriculture. Money has flowed into any district where it could be used with advantage, and it has been
the means of introducing machinery of every kind. Poor
men cannot afford to invest a large amount of wealth as
fixed capital, and the industrial revolution could never have
occurred unless there had been considerable accumulations
of wealth. But capital has also been useful for developing
the special advantage which any district possesses, and thus
leading to the centralisation of different industries in the
localities where they could be prosecuted to greatest advantage. The water power of Lancashire and Yorkshire could
be utilised so as to undersell the textile industries of the
eastern counties. The Sheffield grindstones were set working in greater numbers, and Hallamshire secured a practical
monopoly in an art for which it had long been famous. The
migration of industry, and the extraordinary development of
the north of England, bear witness to the effectiveness of
capital as an agent in production; and it had a similar success, when sunk in plantations abroad, in laying the foundations of colonial prosperity. The formation and application
of capital, with which credit is closely connected, has been a
second great factor in English industrial progress in modern
times.

*Specially
important
factors.* 165. The preceding paragraphs may serve to show what
we mean by particularising any one factor as especially important. It is of course true that all the conditions which
precede any phenomenon are its cause, and that all are
concerned in producing the result. But when we are viewing a series of phenomena ranging over a long period of time,

and find one condition which is an antecedent of great changes in all of them,—more especially when we can note its influence in very many different directions,—we are justified in saying that this factor is of great importance, because it brought about such striking results, for so long a time and in so many places. It demands the attention of the student—→ of history because it effected so much; and whenever we can assign a factor that produced many or rapid changes we come on something of the first importance.

From this it seems to follow that a period when there *Periods of* have been no changes, or only minor modifications in indus- *stagnation of less im-* trial and commercial affairs, is relatively unimportant for our *portance for the* purpose; it is one of stagnation when there are no new *under-* developments and no striking departures. It may be a *standing of history.* period of general comfort and prosperity, or it may be a time of great privation and misery; but it is a time when all goes on regularly and steadily with no new impulse from without and no new developments within. There may be, as a matter of speculation, interest in discussing why this stagnation occurred,—why the scheme of life and industrial habits which had been inherited from a preceding generation lasted on without change; but when the conditions which thus continued for so long have once been described, there is no need to dwell on them; interest will be concentrated, not on the periods of regularity and stagnation, but on the disturbing causes which did at last assert themselves and initiated a new era of change. These periods of stagnation, whether happy or unhappy, are relatively unimportant in the history of industry and commerce; but they must not be left out of sight, and in such periods, if long continued, there may be a formation of deep-seated customs, so that the change when it does come will be very violent. Long restricted in its earlier phases, because of the strength of habit it had to oppose, the new factor must carry all before it like a flood when once it has made itself felt as an effective force.

This statement as to the nature of the influences which *The formu-* are of primary importance in history and of those which are *lating of Economic* relatively unimportant appears to be almost a truism; condi- *laws.* tions which remained unaltered and the periods which were

practically stationary may be happy and peaceful, but they
have no history. In such periods all proceeds with regularity, and the "laws" in accordance with which the phenomena
are regulated can be stated with more or less exactness. If
the conditions for the production of corn remain the same, it
is easy enough to formulate a law of the supply of corn, and
there may be purposes for which it is convenient to do so.
But the fact that you can formulate a law, which describes
the phenomena for a long period, only shows that there was
little if any change in the conditions under which industry
was carried on; the whole was regular, the old conditions
lasted, the old equilibrium continued; no readjustment was
needed, it was all normal and so there is nothing to attract
attention. There was stagnation, not necessarily because
the conditions of production were specially good, or specially
wise, but merely because there was nothing to disturb the
balance, and therefore nothing to explain. In the present
volume attention will be constantly turned to change, to
disturbing forces, and to the description of what was new at
any time. In so far as what was once new became habitual
and regular and normal, it may be surely left out of sight,
until it is necessary to describe the operation of some new
factor which introduced disturbance and effected a change.

The chief source of information is　　166. The mass of evidence which might be brought to
bear on these various topics is very large; so much is already
printed that it has only seemed necessary to consult unpub-
lished sources of information on special points here and
there. Some use has been made of the considerable mass
of pamphlet literature which survives; in many cases these
pamphlets are of high value as evidence, as they throw a
fresh light on the practices and projects of the Government
which might otherwise have been unintelligible. For
certain developments of commerce the records of special
companies, like the Merchant Adventurers, or the East India
Company, are of the highest authority. But the existence
the pro- ceedings of Parlia- ment.　of a great representative body like Parliament gives much
assistance to those who wish to follow any side of our
national life. In its debates and its legislation, the course of
contemporary affairs is reflected in the light of contem-

porary opinion, and the inquiries which it instituted resulted
in a marvellous body of well-selected evidence. Matters in
regard to which there were no complaints in the Commons,
and no attempts at legislation, have for the most part been
neglected. Not of course always; we may find as we look back
on some forgotten pamphlet, that attracted no attention at
the time, the first symptom of a great movement. But since
selection must somehow be made, it seems wisest to take
Parliamentary proceedings in regard to industry and commerce as the basis for the whole fabric, though many sorts of
incidental evidence have been drawn on; the proceedings of
Parliament have also been carefully sifted, as there may be
little interest in tentative and experimental legislation, and
still less in projects which died at their very birth.

VI. THE ELIZABETHAN AGE.

I. Political Survey.

A.D. 1558
—1603.
*The change
from medi-
æval to
modern life
marked by*
167. THE great dispute as to the precise epoch which
marks the close of mediævalism and the rise of modern
society is never likely to be finally settled; the change must
be placed comparatively early by those who are thinking
chiefly of intellectual life, and for whom the decline of
scholasticism and renaissance of the study of classical models
are the main events; but the structure of society was not so
readily susceptible of rapid change as the enthusiasms of
students and patrons. For our immediate purpose it is convenient to take the accession of Elizabeth as marking the
crisis; from that time we can see that the struggle was
really over, and that industry and commerce were organised
in complete accordance with modern political conditions and
social ambitions. The growth of nationalities was proceeding
apace; and in England, an active middle class was coming to
the front, well able to insist on having a say in the direction
of affairs.

*the acces-
sion of
Elizabeth.*
Elizabeth has earned the reputation of being a successful
diplomatist, and earned it chiefly by being completely unscrupulous. She did not attempt the higher wisdom of
forming a deeply conceived scheme and gradually carrying it
out as circumstances enabled her; but she rarely made up
her mind at all, and therefore never committed herself. In
her case, to avoid signal failure was to score a complete success, and she did not fail. She played on chivalrous and

national sentiments, and she tried to avoid levying taxes, so she A.D. 1558 was popular. Under her administration England prospered, —1603. and no one need grudge her the credit of the achievement.

The consolidation of the nations was not accomplished *Disaffected elements* without a struggle where municipal life had been healthy and *and national consoli-* vigorous, or where great vassals had enjoyed independence; *dation.* it was no easy matter to force them into a subordinate position, as mere elements in the nation of which they formed part; and Elizabeth, despite her strong views on the wickedness of disaffection on the part of Roman missionaries or the Scottish queen, had no scruple in fomenting disloyalty among the subjects of foreign powers. She would not fight her enemies openly, but she could do them much mischief indirectly by aiding and abetting the schemes of traitors; this was the sort of strategy that suited her best, and in which she was fitted to succeed. The Scottish crown had never been in a position to curb the great feudatories; the French communes obtained little encouragement either from the nobles or the barons, and Philip had to deal with a little federation of separate republics in the Netherlands. In every case there were elements which prevented the consolidation of these realms and the establishment of a firm government which should be free to organise a regular attack on England.

The fierce religious passions of the age gave these various *Religious* civil wars the character of crusades. Some men conscien- *differences.* tiously believed perhaps, that it was a duty to slay those who were propagating soul-destroying error; and this motive might appeal either to the conscientious Romanist or the conscientious Calvinist. It is useless to record the horrors which were everywhere enacted, and which were bitterly recounted among the friends of the sufferers to goad them to cruel retaliation. The national sentiment in England was already strong, and the papal jurisdiction and papal taxation had long been unpopular; hence Elizabeth was able to rally around her men of both communions from all parts of the country, when the Spanish Armada was sent out, and to show to an astonished Europe the spectacle of a nation that was practically at one; while other rulers were distracted by dissensions caused by men who were ready to sacrifice their

A.D. 1558
—1603.

country for the sake of their party[1]. As the storm passed 2 England afforded an asylum to vigorous elements of industrial and commercial life that proved incongruous with the new order in their native lands.

The influx of American silver to Spain.   168.   The reign of Elizabeth is also marked as the beginning of a new era for England from the fact that the results of American discovery began to be felt; for a share of the silver which poured from the new world found its way to England as well as to other European countries. The total amount obtained in the first half century after the discovery of the new world was not so very large; the adventurers rightly argued that there must be masses of silver which could be rendered accessible, but they were wrong in supposing that the inhabitants possessed large quantities, or had had great success in mining. They wore their entire hoards as personal ornaments, and they parted with them readily for novel trinkets like hawkbells; but the tyrannies of the conquerors could not wring a regular and constant supply even from the people of Mexico or Peru. The regular flow of silver to Europe began after the mines of Potosi were opened up; and as a stimulus was also given to the efforts of miners in different parts of Europe, there was an enormous increase in the quantity of silver bullion[2] which was available for amass-

---

[1] Condé in his agreement to give Havre as a pledge for the restoration of Calais. Froude, *History* (1872), VI. 579.

[2] A careful discussion of various estimates of the quantities of gold and silver obtained from the New World has been given by Humboldt (*Essai Politique*, II. 519, 616). The results of Humboldt's enquiry have been summarised by Jacob, who places the average annual importation of treasure from 1492 to 1521 at £52,000; from 1521 to 1545 at £630,000; from 1556 to 1578 at £440,000; and during the rest of the century at £280,000 (*History of Precious Metals*, II. 53, 58, 60). Mr Jacob thinks Humboldt's estimate for 1545 to 1556 too large, and that the rate during these years was similar to that from 1556 to 1578. To estimate the difference the treasure made in European prices is however a very different matter: the attempt made by Mr Jacob (cc. XVIII. and XIX.), is not so successful as to deserve special attention. The quantity of coinage in Europe in 1490 is wholly unknown, though Mr Jacob hazards an approximation; his estimates of the quantity used in manufacture and sent to India are, as he allows, "in the absence of precise data," quite hypothetical; his conclusion that before 1545 the mass of bullion in Europe had increased not quite 50 per cent. on the amount in 1490, and had in 1599 quadrupled, is perhaps as good a guess as any other—but not obviously any better. According to Roscher, the quantity of bullion which got into circulation before 1545 was inconsiderable (*Political Economy*, I. 408).

ing as treasure, for purposes of coinage, or for use in the arts. A.D. 1558
—1608.
Charles V. endeavoured to retain all the silver that came to
Europe from Spain under his own control: it served as a
medium for trading with the East[1], but the export to any
part of Christendom was strictly forbidden, and he hoped to
amass a treasure which should far exceed that of any of his
rivals and should give him an impregnable position in
Europe; but the defects of his administration, and the wars[2]
in which he engaged, rendered his scheme abortive. But
there were circumstances, other than the Spanish enactments,
which prevented England from sharing in the bullion that *and to England.*
was flowing into Europe. It had been asserted both in the
twelfth[3] and the fifteenth century[4] that England received large
payments in bullion from abroad; and the development of
the cloth manufacture ought to have tended to the increase
of the balance in favour of England. But the debasement of
the coinage would effectually prevent merchants from bringing pure silver to England, so long as base metal served to
make their payments; not till the coinage was restored could
trading relations re-adjust themselves. After 1561 silver
found its way to England in large quantities, and the rise of
prices which had already begun went on with unexampled
rapidity. In 1549 the price of wheat shot suddenly upwards[5]; -
only in exceptional years did it fall back to anything like the
previous level, and during the century preceding the Great
Rebellion, ordinary prices of commodities were quadrupled. *Rise of*
Professor Thorold Rogers has summarised the results drawn *prices and*
from his examination of the prices actually paid for different
classes of goods, and if we take grains of all sorts[6] as on the
whole the most accurate measure of value for long periods,

---

[1] Blanqui, *History of Political Economy*, p. 213. The Portuguese trade had
been similarly organised with gold from the Guinea coast. Heyd, *Geschichte des
Lerantehandels*, II. 525.

[2] C. Marchand, *Charles Ier de Cossé*, p. 272. The expense of keeping the
French armies in the field is well discussed, 159. M. de Brissac was in frequent
difficulties from want of money, p. 273, and the frauds of officials, p. 586.

[3] Henry of Huntingdon, *Historia Anglorum*, I. 5.

[4] Sir John Fortescue, *Comodytes of Englond*, in *Works* (1869), I. 551.

[5] Thorold Rogers, *Agriculture and Prices*, IV. 290.

[6] Wheat was not during some part of the period the chief food of the poorer
classes. Harrison, *Description of England*, in Holinshed, p. 283.

the ratio of rise appears to have been 2·40 from 1540 to 1582[1] and 2·23 from 1582 to 1642[2].

The increasing quantities of silver favoured the rapid progress of industry and commerce in two ways; prices were rising steadily, and therefore all business was conducted at a very high rate of profit[3], for the expectations of merchants or manufacturers as to the terms on which they could sell *formation of capital.* would be more than fulfilled. But not only was business attractive by its success, but the formation of capital was rendered easier by the mere fact that so much silver was in circulation. It is possible to lay up corn in store against time of famine, but no kind of produce can be hoarded for an indefinite period without loss in bulk or quality, and such stores cannot be used for the production of other forms of wealth unless they are realised. But when bullion became plentiful and passed freely from hand to hand, a larger number of people had opportunities of forming a little hoard which could eventually be used as capital. Statisticians have recently called attention to the large amount of capital in co-operative and other societies, which has been formed by the facilities afforded to the working classes for investing their savings; and the more plentiful circulation of bullion gave similar facilities to the Elizabethan farmers; in the beginning of the century the tenants rarely possessed more than a few shillings of ready money, but at its close, despite the enhanced rents, they were able to lay by very considerable sums[4]. The importance of capital, as an agent in industry and commerce, had been felt before[5]; but the increased supply of bullion in England rendered the formation of capital easy and general. Manufactures introduced and managed by capitalists, and even capitalist agriculture, were becoming practicable; while there was plenty of money available for merchants who wished to engage in foreign trade.

Effects on persons with fixed incomes. This formation of capital, unlike the hoarding of treasure, would not however keep money altogether out of circulation

---

[1] Thorold Rogers, *Agriculture and Prices*, IV. 725.   [2] *Ib.* v. 789.
[3] Walker, *Money*, p. 79, where the opinions of Hume and Alison on this point are reviewed at length. Compare Hall, *Elizabethan Society*, p. 41.
[4] Harrison, *Description of England*, 318.   [5] See above, Vol. I. pp. 392, 466.

or depress prices; even if the rise of prices stimulated the A.D. 1558 —1603. operations of the capitalist alike in industry and trade, it pressed heavily on other classes of the community. Those who had fixed incomes were forced to pay more for all they bought, and therefore they found the times very hard; many of the landed gentry could scarcely maintain their establishments[1] while they suffered from the independence of their tenants; the crown revenues did not increase, and there was little rise in labourers' wages, since the latter were regulated if not fixed. The very causes that made industry and commerce active, rendered the position of the country gentleman more difficult and the lot of the labourer harder. We may find an instructive contrast in the story of the last twenty years, when there has been a gradual fall of prices; the capitalist has complained of continued depression, but the man with £1000 a year can probably live as well as one with £1100 did twenty years ago, and the artisan can get more of the comforts of life for his wages than in former days.

169. Though the Elizabethan age was a time of rapid *Eliza-* industrial and commercial development, it was also an era *bethan legisla-* of systematic and effective legislation; at first sight it *tion.* might appear that these two things are hardly compatible, and that legislative enactments, if they are to be executed and to mould society, imply stability and fixity rather than rapid changes and growth. But the striking success of the Elizabethan laws is due to this very thing,—that they instituted a system of regulation which was so far flexible that there was scope for constant modification and change. The whole experience of many years of tentative legislation was gathered and embodied in a great system of national commerce and industry; Parliament did not merely lay down a set of hard and fast rules, but created a national machinery for the regulation of industry and commerce. So wisely was this machinery framed, that all through the seventeenth century and the greater part of the eighteenth it reigned unquestioned, and was only slightly modified from time to time; the Elizabethan navigation laws, and corn laws, the

[1] Rogers, *Agriculture and Prices*, IV. 739, 750. Norden, *Surveyor*, 17.

Elizabethan regulations for industry and wages, the Elizabethan incorporations of new manufactures and new companies for trade, the Elizabethan system for the relief of
the poor, held their ground all through the struggles of
Royalist and Roundhead, of Tory squires and Whig principles, through the growth of our first colonial empire and
the rise of the monied men. Expansion and development
were noticeable on all sides, but the great system of regulation was maintained; it broke down at last under the
combined strain of a great political struggle and of unexampled seasons of distress together with a rapid migration
of industry.

The
Mercantile
system.
In preceding chapters attention has been directed to the
first beginnings and gradual growth of this great system
of national regulation of industry and commerce, which is
generally spoken of as the Mercantile system[1]. We have
found it in germ as far back as the reign of Richard II.,
when the London merchants obtained distinct political influence[2]; it had been partially and fitfully maintained and
had grown in definiteness, as well as completeness; under
Edward VI. the main points of the policy had been neglected,
but under Elizabeth the whole was taken up again, and
worked out in a complete and systematic form.

National
power
The rationale of the whole was the deliberate pursuit
of national power; the means of attaining this end had
been made the subject of repeated experiment, and now
they were organised by statute. Treasure was the direct
means of securing power, and industry and trade were to
be so managed that treasure might be obtained; but the
power of the English nation was almost equally dependent
upon shipping; hence the navigation laws, and the care for
fisheries and for the supply of naval stores. The management of industry, especially the planting of new manufactures, rendered our trade more profitable for the purpose

---

[1] This name may be conveniently applied retrospectively, though in a narrower
sense it is restricted to the views of those who opposed the bullionist methods of
regulating commerce, and argued that the export of bullion might under certain
circumstances be advantageous. See below, p. 211.

[2] § 117 above, Vol. I. p. 350.

of acquiring treasure; together with tillage, it gave em- ployment and the necessary conditions for regular life to the population, and thus favoured the security of the realm from internal disorder. The Corn Laws, by encouraging tillage, had similar effects; they also helped to provide suitable conditions for constant supply of food. The punishment of those who would not work, and the support of those who could not, were subordinate points in this great scheme of national regulation, which aimed at directing the industry and trade of each so as to promote the power of the nation as a whole.

Since the time of Adam Smith it has been the fashion *success-* to decry this policy; but we may notice that the wisdom *fully pro-moted.* of the whole scheme is apparently justified by the striking development of national power which took place during the period when it lasted. England first outstripped Holland, and then raised an empire in East and West, on the ruins of French dependencies. Its wisdom also seems to be justified from another side, by the misery which came on the masses of the population towards the end of last century, when the system of industrial regulation proved unworkable and the repeal of the old laws became inevitable. But, even though the logic of facts seems to tell in its favour, there is a danger of fallacy; success was attained, but how far was it due to the working of coal, and the age of mechanical invention, and how far to the policy pursued? We need only say that under the Mercantile system, Englishmen attained those objects which the Elizabethan statesmen had in view, both in regard to securing a great position among political powers and to the maintenance of social order at home.

170. There is however only one important new de- *Emigra-* parture during this Elizabethan period; it saw the be- *tion and Plantation.* ginning of emigration for purposes of plantation. A field was opened up in the New World, but efforts were also made to repair the neglects of bygone days and develop the resources of Ireland. From the time of Elizabeth onwards Ireland begins to have a real place in the story of English industry and commerce.

C. II. 2

A.D. 1558
—1608.
Ireland
In the fifteenth century[1], Ireland was for commercial purposes a foreign country, and an entirely undeveloped country; its principal products were obtained from its wastes and rivers and the surrounding seas. Rabbits and deer, otters and squirrels and martins, salmon and herrings, were objects of merchandise; while there was also some cloth[2] and hides and woolfels. The author of the *Libel* urges in impassioned language that the lordship of such a country should be made a reality, that the wild Irish should be reduced from barbarism, and that its rich resources, both in mineral wealth and in the fertility of its soil, should be developed. Even while he wrote the fatal effects of the Hundred Years War were telling on the English nobility, and the 'wild Irish' were becoming bolder and recovering some of the ground they had lost[3]. When the Wars of the Roses drew still further upon the English gentry resident on their Irish estates, the 'wild Irish' descended from the mountains, and lands which had been occupied by settlers were "shortly displanted[4]." And where the 'wild Irish' encroached, the possibility of industrial life was lost. They reverted at once to the nomadic type, moving from place to place to pasture their cattle, and subsisting chiefly upon their milk[5]. This roving mode of life gave abundant opportunity for the harbouring of thieves or the retaining of stolen cattle and for disorders of every kind. The chief article of their attire was a mantle or plaid, which served as a "fit house for an outlaw, a meet bed for a rebel, and

and the
Irish.
an apt cloak for a thief[6].", The feuds of different septs rendered the country a constant scene of civil war, and gave excuse for the maintenance of galloglasses and kerns whose "common trade of life[7]" was to oppress all men. "They spoil as well the subject as the enemy, they steal, they are cruel and bloody, full of revenge and delighting in deadly execution, licentious, swearers and blasphemers, common

[1] *Libel of English Policy* in *Political Songs*, II. 186.
[2] See below, p. 295, n. 1.
[3] *Libel of English Policy*, in *Political Songs*, II. 189.
[4] E. Spenser, *View of the State of Ireland*, *Works* (ed. Todd), VIII. 315.
[5] *Ib.* 363.   [6] *Ib.* 367.   [7] *Ib.* 392.

ravishers of women and murderers of children." The general A.D. 1558 —1603.
uncertainty of life was particularly inimical to tillage; as
among the border reevers[1], so among the Irish, corn was
only to be had in small quantities[2]: neither the landlord
nor the tenant would have long leases,—the tenant because
the "landlords there used most shamefully to rack their
tenants, laying upon them coigny and livery at pleasure,
and exacting of them (besides his covenants) what he
pleaseth. So that the poor husbandman either dare not
bind himself to him for longer term or thinketh by his
continual liberty of change to keep his landlord in awe from
wronging of him[3]." Such continual disorder and uncertainty rendered industry and commerce impossible, and
the work of civilisation had to begin over again. It is
unnecessary to examine the precise reasons of the failure of
the various monarchs who, from the time of Henry II. onwards, had endeavoured to evolve order from this chaos; it
is enough to mark the chequered success which attended
subsequent efforts.

Either of two distinct policies might have been pursued; *Mili-*
one was the Roman method of establishing a strong mili- *tary rule.*
tary rule and forcing the natives to abstain from constant
pillage so as to give the opportunity for the development
of some sort of civilised life, for settled homes, and at all
events for tillage. This was the scheme of Spenser, as of
the author of the *Libel.* Had it been followed, a real Irish
nation might have at last grown up out of the rival septs,
under this protecting and civilising despotism; the Brehon
laws might possibly have given birth to an Irish common law,
and the poetry of the bards to a wealth of Irish literature.
This was the statesmanlike scheme, and the scheme which is
being now followed in India; but it appeared to involve
an enormous expenditure in maintaining a military establishment, and Elizabeth could not be expected to adopt it.

On the other hand it might be possible to establish *Plantation.*
successive bodies of settlers who should be strong enough
to hold their own in a considerable territory, and thus bit

---

[1] Scott, *The Monastery*, c. 23.   [2] Froude, *History* (1872), x. 220.
[3] Spenser, *View*, *Works*, VIII. 404.

A.D. 1558
—1603. by bit to plant the whole country, till those Irishmen who
were not willing to take a servile position among the settlers
should be gradually ousted, and should, after maintaining
an ineffective struggle for existence, miserably perish before
an advancing civilisation, as native races have fared before
the white man in America and Australasia. This was the
miserable policy on which the Elizabethan rulers entered;
but it was never pursued so deliberately or so ruthlessly
as to obtain the success which has attended the efforts of
New England statesmen in dealing with the red man. From
a purely economic point of view, either method might have
answered the purpose of developing the resources of the
Emerald Island, and raising up a prosperous and civilised
community there: in one case it would have been Irish,
in the other Saxon. The folly of successive generations of
English statesmen has been shown in the way in which
they have changed from one of these lines of policy to the
other, and have thus failed to obtain the economic results
which might have been secured by pursuing either one plan
or the other, steadily and patiently.

II. Shipping.

Navigation Act.   171. The traditional policy of encouraging English shipping, especially in the wine trade, had been discarded under
Edward VI.[1], possibly because the navy of England was so
far reduced in his reign that it did not suffice to serve the
merchants properly; in the first year of Elizabeth however
something was done to restore the old rule and at the same
time to increase the customs revenue. It was asserted that
foreign powers had retaliated on England by enforcing a
strict navigation policy of their own, and a remedy was
provided by charging the customs due from aliens in the
case of those subjects who shipped goods in foreign bottoms.
Thus the differential rate was in favour of the employment
of English ships; but since foreign ships could be used if the

---

[1] 5 & 6 Ed. VI. c. 18.

higher rate was paid, there was less danger of reducing the A.D. 1558 —1608. volume of trade and thus of affecting the customs revenue[1] or of provoking retaliation. The Merchants of the Staple and the Merchant Adventurers were exempted from the operation of this act at the time of their regular shippings, as well as the Merchants of Bristol who had suffered severely from losses at sea[2]. A few years later however the more stringent policy was adopted again in regard to the Gascony trade, and the use of foreign ships in the wine trade with England was forbidden[3].

172. Elizabethan efforts to develop the English naval *Fishery.* power were chiefly directed to the encouragement of subsidiary callings, and especially of the fishing trades[4]. The great act passed in 1563[5] of "politic constitutions for the navy" shows how carefully the bearing of other trades on the development of shipping was taken into account. Fish caught by subjects in the ships of subjects might be exported without the payment of customs; no tax or toll might be levied on the landing of fish so taken; and the exactions of purveyors were restricted so far as this article was concerned. The arrangements for the political Lent[6] were elaborated, Wednesday was added to the two fish days already enjoined; but wealthy persons might obtain licences to eat flesh, on contributing six and eightpence yearly for the relief of the poor; or they might have one dish of flesh on Wednesdays if they had also three of fish[7]; invalids might have licences for a limited period granted by their parish priest. Care was taken to reiterate that this was simply intended politically,

---

[1] See above, § 139. Vol. I. p. 434.
[2] 1 Eliz. c. 13.   [3] 5 Eliz. c. 5, § 11.
[4] Some idea of the current opinions in 1580 on the development of fishing as an industry may be gathered from *The Politic Plat*, in Arber's *English Garner*, II. 133. It contains an elaborate scheme for diminishing the number of idle vagabonds, and increasing the prosperity of decayed towns. Its author, Robert Hitchcock, had served in the Low Countries, and had, while there, seen how profitable an industry fishing could be. His scheme was not adopted, although it was laid before Parliament, but his tract gives an interesting account of the fishing trade during this period.
[5] 5 Eliz. c. 5.   [6] § 142. Vol. I. p. 443.
[7] On the enforcing of fish days in 1585 at Leicester, see Leicester Corporation Records in *Hist. Manuscripts Commission*, Report VIII. 432, February 1585; also for privileged persons, *Ibid.* p. 433, 16 January 1598.

A.D. 1558
—1603.
for the increase of mariners and fishermen and repairing of port towns and navigation; and any one who asserted that it had spiritual importance, for saving souls or the service of God, was to be punished as a spreader of false news.

Restrictions were also placed on the pressing of fishermen to serve in the navy; fishermen were not to be pressed for soldiers but only as mariners; the commission was only to be executed through the Justices of the Peace, and this proviso, while it would enable the admiral to pick better men, would also give the fishermen security against being taken away suddenly and arbitrarily for the public service.

Hemp-growing and export of corn. The same statute, though primarily designed for the encouragement of navigation, touches also on two agricultural matters, which were closely connected with its main object; the law of Henry VIII.[1] about the sowing of hemp was revived, and the scope of the measure was extended, as the new act required that a whole acre, and not merely a rood, should be devoted to this kind of culture. On the other hand the existing restrictions on the export of corn were modified; and we get an insight into the fact that the corn laws of this reign had a double bearing and were meant to be "for the better increase of tillage and the maintenance and increase of the navy and mariners of this realm[2]." These measures in all probability had more result in promoting agriculture, than all the penal laws against grazing ever accomplished[3].

Iceland Trade. The Iceland trade in cod, and the herring fishery[4], were the branches of the fishing business which Parliament specially tried to encourage[5]; the latter was protected in the usual

[1] 24 H. VIII. c. 4.   [2] 13 Eliz. c. 13.   [3] See below, p. 52, n. 4.
[4] The first effect of these statutes was good, if we may judge from the following certificate from Trinity House, Jan. 26, 1580. "We the masters, wardours, and assistants of the Trinitie house at Deptford Strond made dilligent enquirie of all the costmen that be here at this instant at the cyttie of London, what fisher boates have been encreased sythence the last parliament as by particulers may appear. That is to say from Newcastle to Portsmouth 114 sayle betwene 15 & 40 tonne a piece. Which boates doe maintaine for every 20 tonne 8 men and a boy at the least which are betwene 1000 men ready to serve in her majesties shippes." Record Office, *State Papers, Dom., Eliz.* CXLVII. 21.
[5] Hitchcock wished to see Whale-fishing established. "There is another exercise to breed profit, called the hunting of the whale, which continueth all the summer. The whale is upon the coasts of Russia towards Muscovy and Saint

way, by giving facilities for export, and by conferring a _{A.D. 1558} monopoly of the home market for salt fish. On the pretext ^{—1608.} that cod and ling were badly packed in barrels by aliens, the importation was wholly forbidden in 1563[1], but permission to import them was afterwards accorded to English subjects "using uprightness and truth in the barrelling of such fish[2]." The English merchants took advantage of this permission. and "for their private gain" engrossed salt fish in foreign countries, though it was inferior in quality, and "great masses of money" were sent abroad to pay for it[3]; by reason of which "unnatural dealings" of merchants and fishmongers, the shipping of the realm had suffered to the extent of 200 sail and more of ships, which had once found employment in the Iceland trade. No salt fish was now to be imported, unless from Iceland or Newfoundland, except on the payment of additional duties corresponding to those charged by the different foreign countries on the importation of English-cured herrings; and it was expected that English fishermen and English skippers would be able to supply the whole of the home demand. But these hopes were doomed to disappointment; protection did not serve to call forth enterprise, and it was stated in 1597[4], as the result of experience, that "the navy is no whit bettered by the means of that act, nor any mariners increased nor like to be increased by it; but contrariwise, the natural subjects of this realm, not being able to furnish the tenth part of the same with salted fish of their own taking," the trade had really fallen into the hands of strangers and aliens, who had much enriched themselves, greatly increased their navigation and had extremely en-

Nicholas. The killing of the whale is both pleasant and profitable, and without great charges; yielding great plentie of oil, the tun whereof is worth ten pound." (*Politic Plat*, p. 158.)

[1] 5 Eliz. c. 5, § 10. Licences to export were obtainable however (*State Papers, Dom. Eliz.* xxxv. 36).

[2] 13 Eliz. c. 11, § 3.

[3] 23 Eliz. c. 7. "The Flemings and other Nations...seeing our careless dealing, have not only taken this beneficial Fishing from us, but very warily doeth sell the same commodity unto us; and thereby carrieth out of this land both Gold and silver and a marvellous quantity of double double beer, and other thynges satisfying us with these fishes, which, through our owne slothe, we lose." (Hitchcock, *Politic Plat* in Arber's *English Garner*, II. 144.)

[4] 39 Eliz. c. 10.

A.D. 1558
—1608. hanced the price of fish; while the shipping of England had rather suffered than otherwise. The trade was consequently allowed to revert to the same condition in which it had been when English merchants had practised their unnatural dealings, but had at least done active and remunerative business in the importation of foreign cured fish. Almost a century was to elapse before the continual struggle was to be crowned with success and Englishmen were to oust their foreign rivals[1] from this branch of maritime trade.

Merchant Companies. 173. But though Englishmen had not yet obtained any pre-eminence in the new trades which were being opened up, they were gaining very decidedly in the struggle with their old rivals. The Merchant Adventurers and the Eastland Company, were succeeding to the business of the Hanse League; and the Turkey Company were carrying on a direct trade that had formerly been conducted by way of Venice and in Venetian galleys. The changes were partly due to the political complications of the times. The English rovers had persistently pillaged the Spanish fleets; though Philip, whose dread of French influence rendered him unwilling to quarrel with England, ignored these repeated injuries, he was unable to maintain his apparent indifference, when Elizabeth connived at the seizure in 1568 of treasure ships which were taking money to Alva for the payment of his soldiers in the Netherlands[2]. The commercial relations which had been maintained for so long were rudely broken; all English ships and traders in the parts of Spain and Flanders were arrested, and Elizabeth retaliated on such of Philip's subjects as were within her reach. England was the gainer in the amount of the prizes which were thus seized; *Sea Rovers.* and the channel rovers[3] had a merry time for some months

---

[1] See below, pp. 111, 115.

[2] Froude, viii. 486. Wheeler, *Treatise of Commerce* (1601), 55.

[3] A question which was discussed in one of the earlier meetings of the committee of East India governors shows the manner in which sailors regarded these opportunities for gain. "Wheras this assemblie were acquainted that ther hath bene some question made by some of the mariners what allowaunce they should have uppon such reprisalles as may happen in the voyage, it is uppon that question aunswered, that there is noe intention to make anie attempte for reprisalles, but only to pursue the voyage in a merchauntlike course." Stevens, *Dawn*, p. 118. This is a marked difference from the time of Chaucer and a contrast with the

to come, in scouring the seas for trading ships which were A.D. 1558
brought into Dover, where the cargoes were disposed of, and —1608.
the Spanish grandees were auctioned off to any one who liked
to keep them in irons on the chance of a ransom[1]. The
heroes of maritime warfare in the Elizabethan age carried on
the African slave trade with reckless boldness, in defiance of
the laws which closed the Spanish colonies against them,
and their slave market at Dover had no parallel in Christendom. When Englishmen pride themselves over their efforts
to put down the horrors of the middle passage, they may do
well to remember that they were merely demolishing the
great monument of the vigour of Elizabethan sailors who
broke down the monopoly which Spaniards and Portuguese
had hitherto enjoyed[2].

The breach with Spain and the interruption of the
Netherlands' trade, led to the transference of the Merchant
Adventurers' factory from Antwerp to Hamburg, where the
trade was carried on successfully[3] for some ten years, till the *Hanse*
Hansards drove them out; Elizabeth retaliated in 1578[4], by *League.*
abrogating all the special privileges which the men of the
Hanse enjoyed in England and placing them on the same
footing as other aliens, as well as by granting a charter
to the Prussian or Eastland Company[5], who were competitors in the Baltic trade: she gave them a more complete
organisation than they had possessed under the patent of
Henry IV.[6]

The Venetian trade had been gradually declining since *Venetian*
Trade.

practice of Hawkins. The founders of our modern trade were the London merchants who formed these companies and not the gentlemen privateers who merely
preyed on the commerce of other nations. The East India Company were prepared to defend their ships from attack, but they were able to distinguish between
legitimate trading and mere piracy; they had probably no great sympathy with
the exploits of the channel rovers. This seems to come out in their determination
" Not to employ any gentleman in any place of charge or commandment in the
said voyage, for that beside their own mislike of the imploying of such they know
the generality will not endure to hear of such a motion, and if they should be
earnestly pressed therin they would withdraw their adventure." They wished " to
sort ther business with men of ther owne quality." Stevens, *Dawn,* 28.

[1] Froude, IX. 486. [2] *Ib.* VIII. 476. [3] *Ib.* IX. 29, 42.
[4] Macpherson, *Annals,* II. 161.
[5] 17 Aug. 1579. Stow, *Survey,* II. bk v. p. 262.
[6] Vol. I. p. 371.

the old routes to the East were superseded, and in 1587 it came to. an end; as the last of the argosies sent out to Southampton was totally wrecked off the Needles; Sir William Monson gives a graphic description of a disaster of which he was an eye-witness[1]. On the suggestion of London merchants, Elizabeth had already sent an emissary to try to open up direct commercial communication with the subjects of Amurath III. the Sultan[2]; and in 1581 the Levant Company was regularly incorporated. In 1584 they pushed by the Persian Gulf to Goa[3]. The transference of this trade from Venetian to English merchants had another ultimate result; Southampton, which had been the Italian depot, declined and London was enriched, as the Eastern trade was now drawn into the Thames. Besides forming these new companies, Elizabeth showed some care for the interests of the Muscovy Merchants, who had been already incorporated, and who had pushed their trade by means of the Russian river system eastward into Persia[4]. The Company had had many difficulties to contend with[5], but they were able to maintain their position. An attempt was also made by some London merchants to organise a trade with Barbary, and a company was formed, but not apparently with much result[6].

All of these companies were regulated companies; each member traded with his own capital, but according to rules that were laid down for the common convenience of all who were carrying on a legitimate trade with these regions; the *East India Company* which was incorporated in 1600 was originally similar in form, but each voyage was on a separate joint stock, to which such of the members as wished might contribute. Its early history shows us an interesting transition; for the members at first took shares in each voyage, just as merchants had combined for shipping ventures from time immemorial. Each separate voyage was on a joint stock, and the members were very particular in framing rules against private trading by any of

East India Company.

Common Stock.

---

[1] Sir W. Monson, *Naval Tracts*, IV., in Churchill's *Collection* (1732), III. 400.
[2] Macpherson, *Annals*, II. 165.   [3] *Ib.* II. 198.
[4] Camden, *Elizabeth*, anno 1569 (ed. 1688), p. 124.
[5] *Ib.* anno 1583, p. 285.   [6] *Ib.* anno 1585, p. 325.

their factors[1]. But in 1612 a change took place, which increased the importance of the Directors[2]; instead of having
different funds, separately subscribed to and managed, for each
voyage, the Company determined to have one joint stock only,
and that the aggregate fund then subscribed should be managed
officially by the Governor and Directors. This was an important change in form, but no encouragement had ever been
given to individual or private trading. The subscription list
for shares of £200 and upwards in the first voyage amounted to
£30,133. 6s. 8d. and the first call was 1s. in the £100[3]. Very
great difficulty was found in getting the subsequent calls paid,
and the Lords of the Privy Council were requested to put
pressure on the members to pay up their promised shares[4]:
while some additional capital was obtained by borrowing a
pro rata contribution from the members of the company[5].
Altogether there was great difficulty in financing the scheme,
though the promoters calculated on a return of from 100 per
cent. to 400 per cent. on the capital employed[6]. There were
many delays before the ships could actually start, and much
uncertainty as to the best cargo with which to lade them; a
considerable amount was taken in *reals* and they also took

---

[1] "It is ordayned and decred that all the preparation of moneis, merchandizes
and other provisions for this present voiadge, and all commodityes, moneis,
jewells and other merchandize retourned in the saide voiadge shalbe holden,
reputed and accompted, and be carried, mannaged, ordered and handled as one
entyre joynte and common stock of adventure wherein no private traffique, barter,
exchange or merchaundizinge shalbe used, practized or admytted by any particuler Governor, Capten, Merchaunte factor, Master Marinner, officer or other
person whatsoever imployed in the saide voiadge, or permitted to go in the same
vppon payne of the losse and forfeiture to thuse of the Generall Companie and
Adventurers in this voiadge of all sommes of money, jewells, warres, goodes or
merchandizes which shalbe founde in the saide shippes or elswhere, carried forthe
or retourned home by any private or particuler man, and not contayned and
brought into general and common accompte and joynte adventure of the saide
voiadge. And to the end this prejudice of private traffique may the better be
avoyded it is alsoe ordayned and appointed that due inquisicion be made in all and
everie the several shippes of the saide voiadge and elswhere by serche of all such
chestes, boxes, packes, packetts, books, wrytinges. and other meanes whereby
discoverie may be made of the breache of this present ordinaunce." H. Stevens,
The Dawn of the British Trade to the East Indies, p. 130.

[2] Mill, *History of British India*, I. 22.

[3] Stevens, *Dawn of British Trade*, pp. 4, 17. This volume is a careful reprint
of the minutes of the Company, and gives most interesting details of the purchase,
fitting and victualling of the ships for the first voyage.

[4] Stevens, *Dawn*, 165.   [5] *Ib*. 110.   [6] *Ib*. 152.

A.D. 1558
—1608. some handsome presents in plate[1] to propitiate oriental princes.

*The North-
West Pas-
sage.*   The objection to exporting bullion was very strongly felt, and the committee of governors were ready to listen to a proposal for obviating this difficulty. Mr George Waymouth[2] had inherited the enthusiasm for forcing a north-west passage to the East, and it was argued that in northern climates it would be possible to find a market for English cloth, and that therefore trade could probably be carried on with China without any export of bullion. "Whereas this society in the setting forth of their late voyage by the Cape of Bona Esperanza towards the Island of Sumatra, Java, and the other parts thereabout intending to trade those islands and places for pepper, spices, gold and other merchandises which are likest yield the most profitable return for the adventurers in the same voyage have set forth the greatest part of their adventure in English money coined of purpose for the said voyage, and other foreign coin current in these islands, which moneys and coin they could not prepare but with great difficulty and trouble, and not without some mislike of the transportation of treasure out of land. They therefore being desirous to use the privileges to others granted rather for the good of the commonweal of their country than for their private benefit and to maintain the trade of the East Indies if it be possible by the transportation and vent of cloth and other the native commodities of this realm, without any money at all or else so little as may be conveniently tolerated, do resolve to attempt the discovery of a passage by seas into the said East Indies through some part of America, which if they shall find navigable then shall they by that passage arrive in the countries of Cathay and China being the east part of Asia and Africa, climates of that temperature which in all likeliehood will afforth a most liberal vent of English cloths and kersies to the general advancement of the traffic of merchandise of

---

[1] Stevens, *Dawn*, 151.

[2] *Ib.* 188. Compare an earlier attempt by John Davis; Camden, *Elizabeth*, anno 1585, p. 324. A similar idea struck the Dutch and led to a north-east passage expedition being sent out by merchants of Amsterdam. Davies, *History of Holland*, II. 291. On the N.W. passage see A. Markham, *Voyages of John Davis*, 197.

this realm of England[1]." The scheme for forcing a north- A.D. 1558
—1603.
west passage was therefore taken up originally from a desire
to save the export of bullion and to find a new market for
English goods. There were some difficulties with the Muscovy Company who claimed that their existing patent for
river trade with the East gave them a prior claim to the
fruits of the north-west trade also ; eventually the voyage took
place under the joint management of the two companies ;
but its failure contrasted strongly with the success which attended the Cape of Good Hope voyage, and the Company
wisely threw their strength into this route. It is to be
noticed, however, that all these new associations, whether
regulated or joint stock, were aiming at a share of the trade
in spices ; the Muscovy Company by Moscow, the Levant
Company by Bagdad, the East India Company by the
Cape of Good Hope, and if possible by a more direct route
of their own in the north-west.

III. PLANTATIONS.

174. When traders frequented a country where there *Colonies as* *centres for* was a settled government, it was possible to enter on diplo- *trade.* matic relations, and to secure a footing in a factory, and
this would amply suffice when they came into communica-
tion with peoples who had regular trade, or whose cities
were depots for foreign produce. But in the New World
it was different ; there were no public authorities among
the North American Indians from whom it was possible
to procure grants, or to sue for privileges ; while the articles
in which they traded could be best obtained by settling in
the country and developing its resources. Though little
success attended the attempts of the first planters, they set an
example which led to the growth of a great colonial empire.

The first attempt at settlement took place in connexion *Newfound-* *land.* with the fisheries of Newfoundland. From Parkhurst's
memoir on the subject it appears that the English autho-
rity was recognised among the fishing fleets off that coast in

---

[1] Stevens, *Dawn*, 198.

A.D. 1558
—1603.
1578[1], though they only sent some fifty sail, while the Spaniards had over a hundred and the French a hundred and fifty. They could obtain sea-salt in plenty and become the lords of the fishing if they were settled there, while there was always a chance of mining, and furs might be had from the adjoining mainland. Just before the Bristol merchant[2] had urged his scheme, however, a patent had been granted to Sir Humphrey Gilbert[3] "for the inhabiting and planting of our own people in America," couched in the widest terms and empowering Gilbert to settle in America, to take out subjects there and to exercise jurisdiction over them. The difficulties which attended this ill-fated expedition "in which Sir Humphrey consumed much substance and lost his life at last," have been related in detail by Mr Edward Hayes one of his companions. In sending it out, Elizabeth had evidently been actuated by the hope of obtaining precious metals, for she had reserved a right to one-fifth of all the minerals discovered; the Saxon refiner who accompanied the expedition declared that certain ores they discovered in Newfoundland contained silver, but this proved to be an error. The chief cause of failure, however, lay in the vagueness of the enterprise; it was Sir Humphrey's intention to take possession of the whole coast from Florida to Newfoundland and grant assignments to settlers who chose to occupy some particular points. But in order to found a colony it was necessary to fix on some definite place of settlement which should be chosen for clear and intelligible reasons and concentrate the enterprise on that point[4].

Gilbert
1578.

Raleigh
1584.

Sir Walter Raleigh[5] who received a very similar patent in 1584, did not fall into the same error, but expended his efforts on special points in Virginia. The settlers wrote enthusiastically of the fertility of the soil and the excellence of the grapes and maize it produced, but they had to contend with many difficulties; their stores failed them before they reaped their harvest, and after ten months' residence they returned to England, with the assistance of Sir Francis

---

[1] Hakluyt, *Voyages*, III. 184, also III. 150.
[2] 13 Nov., 1578.   [3] June 11, 1578. Hakluyt, III. 185.
[4] Hayes in Hakluyt, III. 160.   [5] Hakluyt, III. 243.

Drake[1]. Raleigh shortly afterwards sent out an expedition; A.D. 1558 —1603. fifteen men, with stores for two years, were left in the deserted colony, and in 1587 an expedition was sent out on a much larger scale. Raleigh obtained a charter of incorporation for the Virginia Company, and appointed Mr John White governor, with twelve assistants, to carry on the affairs *White.* of the colony[2]. But disaster still dogged the attempt; it was found necessary to move the colony inland, and the vessels, which came from England after a long delay, were unable to follow the settlers to their retreat, where they at last perished miserably.

175. The distance from the mother country and the lonely and defenceless position of colonists in America was certainly a grave disadvantage; Camden remarks[3] that such undertakings were too much for private persons to attempt; and some who might otherwise have adventured in these expeditions preferred if possible to try their fortune nearer home.

The idea of establishing plantations in Ireland was talked *Plantations* of as early in the reign as 1560 when Sussex who was then *in Ulster* Deputy proposed it[4]. In 1567 a definite plan was arranged; Sir Humphrey Gilbert and other west-country Englishmen undertook to plant crown lands in Ulster; and an elaborate plan was drawn up by which every two parishes in England were to provide a man, and £9. 2s. to keep him[5]. It was also suggested that some of the refugees from Flanders, who were coming to England in great numbers, should be sent there[6]: the scheme however fell through.

Two years later the Devonshire men offered to plant *and Mun-* Munster, a scheme of which Cecil did not altogether ap- *ster.* prove[7]. The Earl of Desmond had surrendered his large territory in Munster, and it was proposed that the whole should be declared forfeit, and granted to these gentlemen of Devonshire, who would proceed to carry England into Ireland; they were ready to transport labourers, and artisans

---

[1] Hakluyt, III. 263.   [2] Ib. III. 280.   [3] Elizabeth, anno 1583, p. 287.
[4] Calendar of State Papers, Carew, (1515 to 1574), p. 302.
[5] Froude, x. 225.   [6] State Papers, Ireland, xxi. 48, July, 1567.
[7] Froude, x. 292. State Papers, Ireland, xxviii. 2, 3, 4, 5, 9.

from their own neighbourhoods, and they were prepared to proceed to extremities with any of the native Irish, who would not suffer themselves to be absorbed in the new social system : they hoped after three years to be able to pay a regular rental to the Queen. The scheme was too bold and thoroughgoing to commend itself either to Elizabeth or to Cecil; and any prospect of its being carried into effect was wrecked by Sir Peter Carew and others of the projectors, who attempted to enforce claims to landed possessions to which they had legal claims under ancient deeds[1], though they had been re-occupied by the Irish during the fifteenth century. The whole of Ireland was set in a blaze by their proceedings, and the project of planting the Desmond estates was deferred. It was revived in 1584, under specially favourable circumstances, as the country was so entirely waste that there was no reason to fear difficulties with the native inhabitants[2]; but between the dilatoriness of the commissioners who surveyed the estates, and the recklessness of the undertakers who occupied them, the whole proved a miserable failure.

Ardes.   Meanwhile the scheme for planting lands in Ulster[3] had been kept in view; Sir Thomas Gerrard undertook it in 1570[4], but the attempt was first really made by the son of Sir Thomas Smith[5]. When the Irish heard of the scheme the country was in an uproar[6]; and Smith was killed in a fray soon after his arrival[7]. Sir Thomas Smith did not relinquish the effort, however, to which he had given

---

[1] Froude, x. 234.   [2] Dunlop in *English Historical Review*, III. 250.

[3] Cox, *Hibernia Anglicana*, I. 393 : Camden, *Elizabeth*, 190.

[4] *State Papers, Ireland*, xxx. 32.

[5] (Sir Thomas Smith) has " sithens his returne tolde me divers times that he thought Irelande once inhabited with Englishemen and polliced with English lawes, would be as great commoditie to the Prince as the realme of England, the yearly rent and charges saved that is now laide out to maintaine a garrison therein, for there cannot be (sayeth he) a more fertile soile thorowe out the worlde for that climate than it is, a more pleasant, healthful, full of springs, rivers, great fresh lakes, fishe and foule, and of most commodious herbers, England giveth nothing save fine woole, that will not be had also moste abundantly there, it lacketh only inhabitants manurance and pollicie......To inhabit and reforme so barbarous a nation as that is, and to bring them to the knowledge and law, were both a godly and commendable deede, and a sufficient worke for our age." Letter of T. B. Gent. to his friend Master R. C. in Hill, *Macdonnells of Antrim*, p. 406.

[6] *Calendar of State Papers, Carew*, 1515—1574, p. 419.

[7] Strype, *Life of Sir T. Smith*, 133.

much thought, and his nephew William Smith endeavoured to carry on the undertaking after his death; but he had no success, and his heirs failed to establish a claim to the lands on which so much had been spent[1]. About the time when Sir Thomas Smith was planning the undertaking, Essex obtained a grant of Clandeboy, and many gentlemen joined with him to establish a settlement[2], but after a fruitless attempt he gave up the enterprise and resigned his grant. The Elizabethan planters had but little success either in America or Ireland, but subsequent generations profited by the experience which they had purchased so dearly, and accomplished what they had attempted.

IV. INDUSTRY.

176. It is unnecessary to describe in any detail the *Protective Legislation.* industrial policy which Elizabeth pursued; in its main outlines it was protectionist, and utilised the various expedients which had been already tried and had been deemed successful.

a. The importation of finished goods from abroad was *Import of manufactures prohibited.* prohibited early in her reign; the list of articles to be excluded is not as lengthy as that in the statutes of Edward IV. or Richard III., and consists for the most part of cutlery and small hardware goods; but the principle of action is precisely similar to that of preceding monarchs, and the preamble urges the old pleas, in the encouragement given to the artisans abroad and the consequent enrichment of other realms while our own workmen were unemployed[3].

b. The exportation of unmanufactured products, which *and export of raw materials.* might be worked up at home, was also restricted. The English wool was of course the mainstay of the manufactures of the realm, and it was desirable to retain the English breed of sheep; in consequence a very severe measure was passed in 1566, and those who exported sheep or lambs alive were

---

[1] Strype, *Life of Sir Thomas Smith*, p. 137.
[2] *State Papers, Ireland*, XL. 59–71 (May, 1573).
[3] 5 Eliz. c. 7. Compare also on Wool cards, 39 Eliz. c. 14.

A.D. 1558
—1603.

liable to lose a hand for the first offence, while a second was adjudged felony[1]. At the same time it was enacted that no Kentish or Suffolk cloth was to be exported unless it was wrought and dressed, and that for every nine unwrought cloths sent from other parts of England, one dressed cloth should be sent abroad[2].

Encourage-
ments to
consump-
tion of
native
goods.

c. Another mode of encouraging native industry was by trying to promote the consumption of English manufactures. During the whole of the Tudor period there was frequent interference in regard to the cappers. Henry VIII. had tried to regulate the trade[3]; while Elizabeth insisted that her subjects should wear English made caps. The trade had apparently been very extensive: London alone had maintained 8000 workers[4], and it had also been practised in Exeter, Bristol, Monmouth, Hereford, Bridgnorth, Bewdley, Gloucester, Worcester, Chester, Nantwich, Alcester, Stafford, Lichfield, Coventry, York, Richmond, Beverley, Derby, Leicester, Northampton, Shrewsbury, Wellington, Southampton, Canterbury, and elsewhere; the division of employment had been carried very far in this science of capping, for carders, spinners, knitters, parters of wool, forcers, thickers, dressers, walkers, dyers, battelers, shearers, pressers, edgers, liners, and bandmakers are all mentioned; but it was alleged that people had left off wearing caps, that many who had been busily occupied were thrown into beggary, and that there were fewer personable men to serve the Queen in time of war. On every Sunday and Holy Day every person of six years and upwards, with some few exceptions, was to wear on his head one cap of wool fully wrought in England, and if he neglected to do so, was to pay a fine of three and fourpence for each offence.

Patents.

d. Attention was also directed to the introduction of new industries, and in 1565 an exclusive patent[5] for the produc-

Brimstone. tion of brimstone was given to two men named Wade and

---

[1] 8 Eliz. c. 3.   [2] 8 Eliz. c. 6.

[3] 3 Hen. VIII. c. 15. He subsequently limited the prices charged for foreign caps. 21 Hen. VIII. c. 9.

[4] 13 Eliz. c. 19.

[5] On the constitutional character of these patents see below, p. 157.

Herlle, for thirty years[1]. Very important mining rights were *A.D. 1558 —1603.* conceded in the same year to certain German adventurers, and in conjunction with the Lord Keeper Bacon and others they formed a company which introduced considerable improvements in wire-drawing and other manufactures in the *Wire-drawing.* Forest of Dean[2]. But one of the most remarkable inventions of the age was due to Mr William Lee, of S. John's College, Cambridge, who in 1589 constructed a stocking frame, and *Frame-work knitting.* thus gave rise to a new and important branch of industry. *knitting.* He is said to have been much put out, when paying his addresses to a young lady, by the sedulous interest she gave to her knitting[3], and he determined to find a mechanical means for doing such work. The public, and the Queen in particular, regarded his ingenuity as so perverse that he found it impossible to work his machine in England. Under the patronage of Sully he successfully established a business at Rouen, but his Protestantism prevented him from carrying it on without disturbance. Before his death more successful efforts were made to work his invention in Nottinghamshire, but he died, like most of his race, a disappointed man.

Another trade, which was naturalised, was the manufac- *Salt.* ture of salt; besides the salt obtained from Droitwich[4], a great deal had been imported, and treasure was conveyed to foreign parts, so that a patent was given to the Earl of Pembroke and others for twenty years, for the sole right to use a new process in the manufacture of white salt and bay salt. This patent was perfectly satisfactory according to modern ideas, for it did not interfere with the existing arts, and the new process was not protected against foreign importers; it simply was assigned to the inventor and certain capitalists who might make the most of it[5]: on the other hand Sir John Pakington's patent for the manufacture of starch[6] brought *Starch.* him into serious conflict with the Grocers in 1595; they had recently introduced this article from abroad and had a large sale for it, and the patentee and his assigns claimed a right

---

[1] Rymer, *Foedera*, xv. 650.   [2] Macpherson, *Annals*, II. 142.
[3] *Reports*, &c. 1845, xv. p. 15.   [4] Harrison in Holinshed, I. 403.
[5] 8 Eliz. c. 22.   [6] Stow, *Survey*, Vol. II. bk. v. p. 177.

to seize and destroy all foreign starch. Less success attended the manufacture of glass[1], which seems to have been hampered by want of fuel; but paper making was introduced and prosecuted with advantage[2]. Efforts were also made to introduce the making of sailcloth of good quality, for which we had hitherto depended on France[3].

England was also favoured by a great influx of manufacturing skill from abroad during this period through a fresh immigration of artisans from Flanders. They were driven out by the rigorous measures of Alva, and came to England, bringing their own ecclesiastical discipline with them. The

first settlement of these strangers was at Sandwich, to which town license was given in 1561 to receive from twenty to five-and-twenty master workmen with their families and servants, who were to exercise there "the facultie of making saes bay or other cloth," and for fishing in the seas[4]. In 1565 the Mayor and Corporation of Norwich asked and obtained leave to have some of these strangers in their town, where the weaving industry was decaying[5]. Thirty householders, some of whom were Dutch, and others Walloon, settled there, and by their skill and industry the town soon regained prosperity. They met with some opposition from jealous natives, particularly the dyers[6], but after the space of ten years the town could recount more than one benefit it had received from the strangers; they gave employment not only to their own people but to the inhabitants of Norwich and the country round about; the increase of dwellers had occasioned the repair of old houses and the building of new,

and the rents had increased in value[7]. The cloth made by the settlers soon became known as the 'new drapery'; and as early as 1578 they had a most elaborate system for searching the work at every stage of the manufacture[8]. They also introduced linen-weaving[9] into the city and the making of gallipots[10]; their work and trade was regulated by the Corporation[11].

1 Ellis, *Original Letters*, II. Series. III. 157.
2 Dowell, *History of Taxation*, I. 204.
3 1 James I., c. 24. Dowell, *History of Taxation*, I. 205.
4 Boy's *History of Sandwich*, p. 740.
5 Moens, *The Walloons* (Huguenot Society), p. 18.   6 *Ib*. 79.
7 *Ib*. 264.   8 Stow, Vol. II. bk. v. p. 299.   9 *The Walloons*, 76.
10 Stow, Vol. II. bk. v. p. 300.   11 *The Walloons*, 28, 255.

Other towns saw what good results might be obtained from an infusion of foreign skill, and Southampton and Maidstone petitioned to have strangers allotted to them, in 1567[1]; the requests of both were acceded to; the industry established at Maidstone was the making of thread[2].

Their most celebrated settlement however was at Col- *Colchester.* chester, where eleven households arrived in 1570. About fifty, out of the two hundred persons who had fled from Flanders to Sandwich, had come on hoping to obtain leave to reside and ply their trades at Colchester. They wished to make needles and parchment, and weave sackcloth and fine cloths known as bays. None of these arts were commonly practised in the town at the time, and the bailiffs, who did not like to act on their own responsibility, wrote to the Lords of the Privy Council asking that they should be allowed to remain and settle. The Council were much pleased at the manner in which the Colchester burgesses had received the Flemings, as they were engaged in allotting the immigrants to different towns. The burgesses were to protect them in the exercise of their crafts as long as they conducted themselves well, and to give them facilities for buying and selling[3]. The Flemish colony appears to have flourished on the whole, *Jealousy* though the English weavers were somewhat jealous of them, *of other inhabitants in* and complained that they assembled as a Company in their *Colchester,* Hall, and made ordinances in an illegal fashion[4]. But James I. continued their privileges, and they were protected both in the exercise and regulation of their trade[5].

Other settlements were at Stanford, Halstead, Yarmouth, Lynn[6] and Dover[7]. At Stanford, Cecil gave the immigrants a house of his own to live in[8]; at Halstead the strangers started weaving as an industry, and when they tried to leave in order to join their fellow countrymen at Colchester, the inhabitants petitioned that they should be compelled to

[1] *State Papers, Dom., Eliz.* xiv. 43 and xx. 19. Pennant, *Journey,* i. 104, appears to ascribe a great improvement in gardening to the Flemings who settled in Kent.
[2] Hasted's *History of Kent,* ii. 109. [3] Morant, *Essex,* i. 75.
[4] See above, Vol. i. p. 454. [5] Morant, *Essex,* i. 77.
[6] About 40 settled there in 1568. Record Office, *State Papers, Eliz.* lxxviii. 18.
[7] *Strangers at Dover* in *Huguenot Society* (1890), iii. 111. *State Papers, Eliz.* lxxviii. 19. [8] *Ib.* xlvii. 11.

A.D. 1558
—1603.

return[1]; but at Yarmouth the Dutch settlement was a failure; there were Scots and French in the town, and many Zealanders had recently come[2]; the Dutch after a trial were

in London. expelled[3]. In London and its suburbs many refugees found homes and exercised various callings, and excited much jealousy and opposition, and in 1592 it was ordered that every foreigner should serve an apprenticeship of seven years[4].

Silk-
weaving.

In 1582 when the fortunes of the French Huguenots became desperate, there was a considerable immigration of foreign silk-weavers; they did not meet with a very friendly reception when they plied their craft in London[5]; but they succeeded before very long in driving a flourishing trade[6], and others carried on a prosperous business at Coventry and at Canterbury.

The other attempts at introducing new industries appear to be of a capitalistic character, but the migration of the Flemings and Huguenots was really a transference of artisans; the Dutch Bay-makers of Colchester originally formed an association which was similar in type to a fourteenth century craft gild. The trade prospered under their management, till the time of Queen Anne, when the Spanish war ruined it, and the association was shortly afterwards broken up.

Statute of
Appren-
tices, 1563.

177. The most monumental work of the Elizabethan age, so far as economic legislation was concerned, was the great code of industrial regulation which was passed in the fifth year of her reign[7]. Taken in conjunction with the poor law of the same year, which however was subsequently modified, it forms a great system for controlling both the employed and the unemployed; all the experience of preceding reigns is gathered together, and the principal statute was so well framed that it continued to be maintained for more than two centuries, while the disorganisation which forced on its

---

[1] *State Papers, Dom., Eliz.* CXLVI. 63.

[2] Record Office, *State Papers, Dom., Eliz.* LXXVIII. 10.

[3] *Hist. MSS. Commission Report,* IX. Ap. 1, p. 306 (e), 316 (k, l, o).

[4] *Ib.* III. Ap., p. 6.   [5] Stow, *Surrey,* Vol. II. bk. v. p. 219.

[6] They were made a fellowship under James I., and incorporated in 5 Ch. I. Stow, *Surrey,* II. bk. v. p. 233.

[7] 5 Eliz. c. 4.

repeal[1] was a matter of great regret to some of our acutest statesmen, and was entirely contrary to the views of the artisan classes[2].

A.D. 1558 —1603.

The preamble states the reason for enacting a new 'statute of labourers'; the need of amending the old laws was "chiefly for that the wages and allowances limited and rated in many of the said statutes are in diverse places too small and not answerable to this time respecting the advancement of prices of all things belonging to the said servants and labourers, the said laws cannot conveniently without the great grief and burden of the poor labourer and hired man be put in good and due execution." This is a remarkable sentence, for all previous statutes on the subject from the time of Edward III. onwards, had been deliberately framed with the view of reducing excessive wages to a lower level[3]; this statute was devised as a means of adjusting wages so that they might be sufficient for the labourer to live on, in times when prices were high. Elizabeth's advisers too, were well aware that prices were fluctuating, and varied from place to place, so that instead of trying to frame a hard and fast rule to hold good in all places and in every year, they devised a machinery which, as they hoped, might "yield unto the hired person both in time of scarcity and in the time of plenty a convenient proportion of wages." Unfortunately they were at no sufficient pains to interpret this very vague instruction, for the words "and other circumstances necessary to be considered" do not render it much more explicit. It could hardly mean that wages were to be raised in exact proportion to a rise in the price of corn; as the only result would be that the effective demand of well paid labourers would drive the price still higher[4]. The failure of the crops was regarded as a public evil, and no class could be entirely exempt from feeling it. On the other hand, the possibilities of eking out wages by domestic manu-

Objects in view.

---

[1] See the speeches by Whitbread, Fox and Pitt, *Parl. Hist.* xxxii. 700, xxxiv. 1426. The repeal took place in 1813, by 53 Geo. III. c. 40. Hansard, xxv. 594. Compare the excellent discussion of the policy of the Act by Davis. *Case of Labourers,* (1795) 106.

[2] See below, § 320. [3] See above, Vol. i. pp. 306, 477.

[4] Sir T. Bernard in the *Reports of the Society for bettering the condition of the poor,* v. 27. (Brit. Mus. 288 g. 12.)

A.D. 1558
—1603.
factures, or from common rights, were surely meant to be taken into account; the justices had to consider the possibility of maintaining a family, and individual earnings were only one element in a complex problem.

*Compari-
son with
previous
measures.*
This final statute of labourers, as we may call it, offers some interesting points of comparison with the measures that had preceded it. It begins by defining those to whom it applies and who might be forced to work; those who neither had lands of the annual value of forty shillings, nor who had ten pounds' worth of personal property, and who were not retained in the household of any noble or gentleman, and who were not tenants of a farm holding, who also were unmarried and of less than thirty years of age must accept offers of work at the trade in which they had been brought up. If not otherwise employed they were to serve in husbandry, and all persons up to the age of sixty were liable to be compelled to labour at tillage; this is very similar to the ordinance which was issued in 1349 during the pressure of the difficulties caused by the Black Death.-

*Period of
service.*
Artisans in several leading employments were to be hired by the year, and there were severe penalties for leaving service or dismissing a servant before the time was out; labourers and artisans were to have testimonials from their last employers whenever they left their parish, and could not obtain fresh employment without presenting such letters, so that the general purpose of the measure was to give stability to society by insisting on long engagements for artisans, and by checking the migration of servants in husbandry and other artificers and labourers, as those employed in the building trades who were commonly hired by the day or week.

*Hours of
labour and
rates of
wages.*
The hours of labour are defined in very similar terms to those which have been quoted from other Tudor laws[1], but there was a real improvement in the machinery for settling the rates of wages. Every year in each locality and each corporate town the justices were to assemble before June 10th, "and calling to them such discreet and grave persons......as they shall think meet and conferring together respecting the plenty or scarcity of the time, and other

[1] See above, Vol. I. p. 477.

circumstances necessary to be considered" should limit and ^{A.D. 1558}—1603. appoint the wages for every kind of manual labour, skilled or unskilled, by the year, week or day, and with or without allowances of food. Six weeks after they might revise their decision as to wages for the year if they thought fit to do so. As every effort was thus made to assess wages fairly, there were severe penalties on giving more than the rate thus settled.

Having thus provided for the terms of employment, and made special exemptions for the necessity of field labour in harvest, the legislators turned their attention to the rearing *Apprenti-* of future generations of labourers, and passed the apprentice- *ces* ship clauses. Anyone who had half a plough-land in tillage might take a lad to serve as an apprentice in husbandry till his twenty-first year. As a scheme of technical education the regulations for artisans were admirably suited to the needs of the times. Seven years' apprenticeship was required for all artisans; if any master had more than three apprentices he was required to have one journeyman for every extra appren- tice, and this would give some security against over-stocking with apprentices and facilitate their receiving suitable in- struction; this was a general requirement for the whole country, and extended the regulations which had been en- forced by the craft gilds in cities, so as to ensure a fair standard of skilled labour both in towns and villages; as other clauses embodied the experience of previous legislators, this embodied the experience of the craft gilds. There was however a curious system of limiting the range from which *in different* apprentices to any trade might be drawn; those who were *towns.* engaged in employments which were subsidiary to agricul- ture, smiths, wheelwrights and so forth, or which were ordi- narily combined with agriculture, like linen weaving and weaving household cloth[1], might take any apprentice they could get; artisans in corporate towns might take any apprentice who was the son of a freeman and who was not withdrawn from agriculture, and the inhabitants of market towns were under similar restrictions: merchants or shop- keepers in corporate towns might take the sons of forty- shilling freeholders, but in market towns they were restricted

---

[1] § 23, it appears to be further restricted by § 25.

to the sons of sixty-shilling freeholders. It is curious to
compare these limitations with the apprenticeship statute of
Henry IV.[1]; that made a hard and fast line which pressed
severely on the towns in order to facilitate tillage. These
regulations encourage agriculture chiefly, but they give a
preference to the old corporate towns over others, and perfect
freedom in regard to the ordinary village arts of life. But
while there was this variety in the precise regulations for
different localities, a similar period of apprenticeship, involving similar opportunities of acquiring the trade, was
enforced on all, though the period of apprenticeship to
husbandry was longer and was not definitely settled.

*Flexibility
of system.*
It may thus be said that this Act gathers up the experience derived from many previous measures, but the system
that was now introduced, though applicable everywhere
was wonderfully flexible. This flexibility served to maintain it as an effective system of industrial regulation till
the time when the introduction of machinery so revolutionised the conditions of production that the old scheme was
no longer applicable.

*Incorpor-
ated trades.*
There were indeed a considerable number of trades in
England in the eighteenth century which never came under
the Act at all; for it only applied to those crafts which were
actually practised at the time it was passed: those that were
subsequently introduced had grown up outside the range of
the operation of this labour law. They were commonly
spoken of as the incorporated trades which were regulated
under patents granted to those who started or improved
the manufacture. Thus the Framework-knitters, and the
Bay-makers[2] of Colchester were the incorporated trades, but
industries already in vogue in England in 1563 came under
the Act.

*Alleged
effects of
this mea-
sure, on
the assump.*
178. This Elizabethan measure has been subjected to
an immense amount of hostile criticism at different times,
and especially it has been maintained that it handed the
working classes over to the tender mercies of the justices and

[1] 7 Hen. IV. c. 17.

[2] Their cloth was regarded as quite a distinct make by the deputy aulnager, who
contrasts it with our heavy cloth and praises their system of search. J. May, *Declaration of Estate of Clothing,* (1613) p. 7.

gave them power to oppress them and drive down their A.D. 1558 —1603. wages. There is indeed no very good evidence that this part *tion that* of the measure was ever strenuously enforced, or that it *it was en-forced.* made any very considerable differences in wages one way or another; we can at best only discuss its tendency rather than its results. On the face of it there seems to be some ·justification for this charge, as real wages were exceedingly low during the latter part of the sixteenth and early part of the seventeenth century. But this fall in real wages was chiefly due to the great rise of prices which was now beginning to be constantly felt; wages did not rise *pari passu* with the *The rise of prices.* price of food and the labourers may have suffered greatly. But in the presence of an unexampled rise, the causes of which were entirely misunderstood, the administrators could hardly be expected to foresee the course which affairs were taking; each rise would seem abnormal, and so long as the high prices were supposed to be due to the excessive demands of different classes of the community there would be great hesitation in raising the statutory rates. If there was grave moral blame in the matter, and not a mere error of judgment, that blame must rest with the administrators of the law rather than with those who framed it. It may be safely said that under any economic conditions, with free competition or calculated rates, it would have been hardly possible for the labourers to maintain their old standard of comfort through such a long period of steadily rising prices. The preamble of the statute of 1604 complains that the Act had proved ambiguous and had practically remained a dead letter since, the rates of wages of the poor labourers had not been proportioned according to the plenty and scarcity of the times[1]. Penalties were imposed for paying less than the assessed wages, but none for paying more, so that the system as reorganised by James and continued by Charles[2] could scarcely tend to depress wages, in so far as it ever became a reality[3].

After the rise of prices was checked however, there is *Wages in the 18th century.* reason to believe that the Act was distinctly favourable to

---

[1] 1 James I. c. 6. In the corresponding measure for Scotland the Justices of the Peace were instructed to enforce the rate they assessed, neither more nor less. *Acta* 1617, c. 8, §§ 14, 17.

[2] 3 Charles I. c. 4; 16 Charles I. c. 4.   [3] See below, § 266, p. 199.

A.D. 1558
—1603.
the labourer; by far the greatest industrial evils of which we read during the eighteenth century took place in connection with incorporated trades, and not in those crafts which were under this statute. Again at the time when the whole system was becoming impracticable, the labourers looked to the method embodied in this measure as the great means which would protect them[1]; and it is generally believed that 1815—25. the condition of the manual labourer was never worse than in the years when it had fallen into desuetude, when no attempt was made to regulate industry, and when the men were not free to combine and demand their own terms jointly.

How far do money wages serve as a good measure of the standard of comfort?

Professor Thorold Rogers, who condemns the Act most strongly as positively injurious to the artisans, seems inclined to take for granted that the condition of the labourer at any time can be told by comparing the rates of wages and price of food at a given date, so as to estimate the purchasing power of labour in terms of food. This involves very large assumptions however; it implies that we know the nature and the quality of food, in what proportions for example wheat, rye, and flesh made up the food of different classes at different dates[2]; it implies that we know how far individual earnings at any date represent the family income from all sources; it implies farther that we know the conditions of employment, especially are fully informed as to the constancy or inconstancy of employment. Lower rates of wages may give a far larger income if employment is more constant. Recent discussions as to the comfort of the working classes in the nineteenth century show the extreme difficulty of getting any accurate means of comparison, and our data for comparing the conditions of the labourer as he was in 1563 and 1662 are far less complete than those which lie at hand for a similar comparison of his condition in 1832 with that of 1882.

Constancy of employment and bye occupations.

The most variable element and the one which seems almost incalculable is the precise opportunities for employment, and the earnings that could be made from bye employments at different times: the greatest fall in the standard of comfort among the English peasantry was not due to a fall in the rates of rural wages, but to changes in the methods of

---

[1] See below, p. 469.   [2] Pitt in *Parl. Hist.* xxxii. 706.

agriculture and the loss of domestic industries; there is every reason to believe that during the reign of Elizabeth and the Stuart period there was on the whole a more general diffusion of these industries; and in so far as this was the case, the standard of comfort need not have fallen greatly even though the rates of wages did not increase so rapidly as the price of food.

179.   The statute could make no adequate provision for *Super-* supervising the quality of wares; and experience seemed to *vision of the qual-* show that it was necessary for the Crown to devise some *ity of* machinery for the purpose.   In some cases authority was *wares by patentees* granted to an individual and his assigns; but more commonly companies were organised which somewhat resembled, and occasionally really continued the old craft gilds.   These gilds had for the most part received their death blow under Edward VI.[1], but yet they were not actually broken up[2]. They doubtless fared differently in different towns, but it appears that during the earlier part of Elizabeth's reign they were quite effete and failed to exercise a real influence on the trades in which they were formed[3].   They had been

---

[1] This statement has been called in question by Dr Lambert, *Two Thousand Years of Gild Life*, p. 8, but the evidence he has himself printed from Hull serves to confirm the opinion expressed in the text.   It is still further confirmed if we compare the history of craft gilds (or incorporated trades) in Scotland, where the Acts of Edward VI. did not extend; see below, p. 353 n.

[2] A strenuous effort was made by the members from Lynn and Coventry to prevent gilds from being included in the Act (1 Ed. VI. c. 14) which confiscated the property of the chantries (Burnet, *Reformation*, by Pococke, II. 101), but without success; though the craft gilds were formally excluded (§ 7) they suffered like the rest.   The Tailors of Hull seem to have lost their hall (Lambert, p. 232): and such of the London companies as had attempted to conceal their lands were forced to give them up or pay heavy fines at a later date.   The London Grocers suffered specially in this way (Stow, *Survey*, II. 253), and the records of the London Ironmongers contain much information about the proceedings (Nicholl, *Ironmongers*, 136).

[3] This is the substance of the complaint in a petition sent in by fourteen of the London crafts in 1571 (Clode, *Early History of Merchant Taylors*, p. 204).   It is implied in the constant complaints of decay in the trade in connection with the reorganisation of Companies at Hull in 1598; the very form of the grants, as compared with that to the Tailors, seems to show that they had no regularly elected officers and that the companies had practically to be called into being anew (Lambert, pp. 236, 273); see especially the Cordwainers who were empowered "to be a company of themselves" in 1564 (*Ib.* 316).   Indirect evidence of the decay of gilds may be derived from the cessation of the mystery plays in Coventry; they were revived (Sharp, *Dissertation on Pageants*, 39) about the time when several of the

objects of suspicion before[1], and when the Government, instead of reforming and supporting them turned round and
attacked them[2], they were not able to make an effective
stand[3].

*and re-
organised
companies*
Very early in the reign of Elizabeth however there are
signs of a reaction; the pretext for reorganising the companies, as they were now called, was of course the alleged

companies were resuscitated in 1586. In Norwich the gilds had been very active
under Henry VIII., but they took no part in the pageants when Queen Elizabeth
visited the town in 1578 (Blomfield, II. 148). For the reorganisation at Shrewsbury
see Hibbert, p. 77.

[1] 19 Henry VII. c. 7; 22 Henry VIII. c. 4; 28 Henry VIII. c. 5.

[2] The combination Act of Edward VI., though specially directed against the
building trades and victuallers, must have seriously hampered all craft gilds in
trying to enforce their rules (2 and 3 Ed. VI. c. 15).

[3] In London the Merchant Taylors had encroached on the sphere of the Clothworkers, and flooded them with apprentices; the Clothworkers failed to secure
redress or to enforce a limitation or secure supervision (Clode, p. 199). The same
process was taking place in other trades, and persons who had been apprenticed
in one trade were following others. As a remedy it was proposed on one side,
that the supervision of the trade should be retained by the company with the
right of search, but that those who had served their time in one trade and were
freemen, might have liberty to carry on any craft, so long as they submitted to the
rules of that craft (see the petition in Clode, p. 205); this policy was embodied in
a Bill *That all the Freemen of the City of London may use the Mysteries and
Trades within the same City lawfully*, which passed the Commons (*Journals*, I.
105, 106, 107), and was read a second time in the Lords on 9th March, 1576
(*Journals*, I. 734, 745), but which proceeded no farther. This measure would
apparently have defined and given greater scope for a practice as to apprenticeship which rested on ancient custom in the City, and which was not touched by
5 Eliz. c. 4; see § 33. The citizens of London continued to exercise their ancient
freedom despite the statute (*Remembrancia*, 91). There was a decided effort however to extend the provisions of 5 Eliz. c. 4 to the City, and to prevent anyone from
working at a trade to which he had not been apprenticed; this was embodied
in certain ordinances (*Remembrancia*, p. 154), and apparently in *A Bill prohibiting
the Exercise of any Art or Mystery saving to such as have been Apprentice to
the same*, mentioned in Stow, *Survey*, II. bk. v. p. 252; according to this scheme
each calling would be confined to those who had served their time in that trade;
it maintained the trade monopoly of each company more stringently than ever.
According to the other policy the freemen would be permitted to exercise any
trade, but the monopoly of the freemen was maintained against outsiders. Though
not sanctioned by any Act either of Parliament or of the Common Council so far
as I can learn, that was the policy which gradually triumphed. Even those companies which were able, by charter or statute or prescription, to exercise an
effective supervision over the men who worked at a trade would not necessarily
bestir themselves to exclude a freeman, who submitted to their regulations, from
carrying on a business to which he had not been regularly apprenticed. The
custom of Chester in the seventeenth century was of the stricter type; no one
might exercise a craft unless he had the freedom of the 'company whereof he
desires to trade' as well as of the city. Gross, I. 118, n. 2.

necessity for supervising the quality of work; but the motive A.D. 1558 was a desire to exclude aliens. The new companies were —1603. apparently devised as means for protecting the freemen against the intrusion of foreign artisans[1]. The jealousy of aliens was a matter of long standing[2], but it was stimulated by the immigration from Flanders. As the immigrants formed companies and met in their halls[3], it was only natural that Englishmen born should claim similar privileges and should obtain them from the Crown. The revived life of these companies lasted during the whole of the seventeenth century; they sank into unimportance, not so much through actual changes in trade, as through the growth of public sentiment in favour of the general naturalisation of foreign protestants.

These reorganised companies differed from the craft gilds *which differed much from the craft gilds they superseded.* which they superseded in three ways. (i) They were directly or indirectly[4] authorised by the Crown, if not by Parliament, and they did not derive their authority from the municipal government[5]. The Newcastle cooks, who could not claim this source for their 'incorporation' were disallowed[6]; the Hull Mayor alleged that he had the right to authorise such bodies[7]

[1] See the Hull Cordwainers. Lambert, p. 316. Compare the Mayor's proclamation to the London Gilds in 1581. Clode, 199 n. In London the opposition to foreigners was particularly strong; the Londoners obtained the repeal (3 and 4 Ed. VI. c. 20) of the clause in Edward VI.'s Combination Law (2 and 3 Ed. VI. c. 15, § 3) which allowed native or naturalised workmen to practise certain crafts in corporate cities where they were not free and did not inhabit. The Common Council passed acts against them in 1606 and 1712 [Brit. Mus. 816, l. 3 (25, 26)] also in regard to their dealings in Cloth Halls [Brit. Mus. 712, g. 16 (22)]. The City authorities also demanded in 1662 that all trades should be managed by regulated companies, so as to exclude foreigners from commerce. *Petition for reducing all foreign trade under government* [Brit. Mus. 517, k. 16 (2)].

[2] In 1481 the Mercers of Shrewsbury refused to receive any alien as an apprentice. Hibbert, p. 82. [3] Morant, *Essex*, i. 77.

[4] The Carlisle Burgesses reorganised the crafts in 1564, but their proceedings were subsequently confirmed by the Crown. Ferguson and Nanson, *Municipal Records*, 29. Queen Elizabeth's Charter to Winchester empowered the Mayor and Burgesses to create companies (Lambert, p. 382).

[5] Mr Hibbert points out that at Shrewsbury the rights of the municipality were carefully guarded in the patents to companies (p. 85), but this was not always the case. The complaint of the Lord Mayor of London about the Tallow Chandlers (Stow, *Survey*, ii. bk. v. 210) recalls the complaints of an earlier date. See above, Vol. i. p. 397. [6] Merewether and Stephens, 1323.

[7] Lambert, p. 241. The bricklayers could not enforce their privilege against an Englishman from Amsterdam who professed to rectify smoking chimneys. (Lambert, 273, 275.)

A.D. 1558
—1603.
but apparently on no very good grounds. So far as these companies had legal and effective powers they were constituted from outside, and not from inside the town. (ii) They were obliged to pay for their patents or charters, and they were, as Mr Hibbert points out, associations of capitalists rather than craftsmen[1]. The London Upholsterers were prepared to pay Elizabeth £100 for a grant of privilege, though there were only six of them who were "men of any sub-stance[2]." (iii) So many different callings were amalgamated in the new companies that there could be no pretence of that effective supervision of wares, for which the old craft gilds had been called into being; a single organisation of many trades would serve equally well for excluding aliens[3]. There had been a tendency to combine trades in one company before[4], but it now became more obvious.

Companies empowered by statute. In some few cases the companies were empowered by statute to exercise supervision over the quality of goods. Thus the wardens of the London Haberdashers[5] were to have a right of search in regard to the hats and caps which required so much oversight. So too in regard to the trades which worked on leather; all men living within three miles of the city of London and working at these crafts were to make their payments to the London Companies, and to be under the survey of the wardens: the Companies of the Curriers, Saddlers and Shoemakers were recognised as the proper authorities for seeing into these matters[6]. In a similar fashion when a series of disgraceful frauds was discovered on the part of the Goldsmiths in 1574[7] the wardens and fellowships of the Company were made liable for any loss that occurred if plate which bore their mark was not of the proper touch[8].

---

[1] Hibbert, p. 75.   [2] Stow, *Survey*, II. bk. v. 229.

[3] The Goldsmiths' Company in Hull included in 1598 the goldsmiths, smiths, pewterers, plumbers, glaziers, painters, cutlers, musicians, stationers, bookbinders and basketmakers. (Lambert, 262.) At S. Albans the various trades were combined in four, and eventually the Mercers and Innholders absorbed all the rest. (Gibbs, *Corporation Records*, 10.)

[4] Gross, I. 118.   [5] 8 Eliz. c. 11.

[6] 5 Eliz. c. 8, § 31. There was a very severe struggle shortly after the passing of this Act, as to the respective rights of the London Company and the Westminster Company of Cordwainers. Stow, *Surrey*, Vol. II. bk. v. p. 213.

[7] Stow, *Surrey*, Vol. II. bk. v. p. 184.   [8] 18 Eliz. c. 15.

In some cases indeed the gilds had urged that they could A.D. 1558 —1603. fulfil this duty, but were not entrusted with it: thus the *Failure of* Drapers of Shrewsbury complained that certain dealers in- *some Companies to* fringed their privileges, and that as a consequence the public *justify* were defrauded by having defective Welsh cloth brought for *their claims.* sale[1]: their privileges were at first reaffirmed, but no real gain accrued to the public from re-establishing this monopoly and it was rescinded after a short experiment[2]. Still more curious was the petition of the London House-painters, who had long been a brotherhood, but had never been incorporated, and who were annoyed by the way in which plasterers 'intermeddled with their science.' The consequence was that "much slight work went off, as pictures of the Queen and other noblemen and others and all manner of work which shewed fair to sight, and the people bought the same being much deceived, for that such pictures and works were not substantially wrought, a slander to the whole company of Painters, and a great decay of all workmanship in the said science, and also a great discouragement to diverse forward young men very desirous to travail for knowledge in the same[3]." The painters did not get supervision in this matter of portraits however: perhaps the Queen had no desire that her pictures should be substantially wrought unless they were also fair to see.

On the whole it seems that in London at all events the companies of craftsmen secured very real power for searching out badly made goods and maintaining the quality of wares. In rural districts there was much more diffi- culty in exercising such supervision, and there was a strong *Dislike of* feeling in many quarters that the clothiers should be forced *rural artisans.* to carry on their trade in populous places where they could be supervised. A statute of Philip and Mary[4] had confined the cloth manufacture to the inhabitants of market towns, as it was supposed that some supervision would be exercised there. John Coke, the Secretary of the Merchant Adven- turers[5], was in favour of this regulation, and Hales[6], the most

---

[1] 8 Eliz. c. 7.   [2] 14 Eliz. c. 12.
[3] Stow, *Survey*, II. bk. v. p. 214.
[4] 4 and 5 P. and M. c. 5, § 21.   [5] *Debate betwene the Heraldes* (1550).
[6] *Briefe Conceipt, Harleian Miscellany*, IX. 188.

judicious economist of his time, was in sympathy with it. Special acts were passed however to amend this measure, so as to allow the manufacture of cloth to continue at Coggeshall and some other places in Essex[1] which were not of the rank of market towns, and to enable the clothiers in the West of England to practise their calling in villages as well as in market towns; they were scattered about near Frome, and Kingswood and Stroud, and other places in Wiltshire, Gloucestershire and Somerset. The attempt to force them into towns would have been attended with great difficulty, and they were allowed to continue in rural districts[2].

Patentees with rights of search, &c. over all England. On the other hand the granting of patents to individuals was sometimes adopted as the best means for regulating industry in out of the way districts where no gild could exercise supervision[3]. Sir Edward Darcy had a patent in 1592 for the sealing and searching of leather throughout the whole of England[4], and a very good thing he seems to have made of it; his exactions were quite intolerable as he sometimes took as much as 33 % on the value of the skin for his trouble in the matter. A still more curious proposal was the offer of a certain Mr Edward Dymoch, and again of Sir Thomas Mildmay, to supervise all the strangers in England; the tragedies of Evil May Day had been re-enacted in 1586, and there were very general complaints of the number of aliens and of the way in which they retailed goods; a roll was to be kept of them with full details of their names, families, occupations, time of residence and so forth. But Cecil was opposed to any unnecessary restrictions on the foreign refugees and no action was taken in the matter[5].

Supervision implies Most of these attempts at regulating industry necessarily implied that the exercise of certain callings should be con-

---

[1] 1 Eliz. c. 14.

[2] 18 Eliz. c. 16. This contains a curious proviso that no clothier shall have more than 20 acres of land; it testifies to the combination of rural and artisan employment. See below, p. 480.

[3] In London it brought the patentees into direct conflict with some of the Companies; Vintners in 1594 (Stow, *Survey*, II. bk. v. 196), Brewers in 1580 and 1586 (*Ib.* 202), Distillers in 1596 (*Ib.* 237), Fletchers in 1570 and 1576 (*Ib.* 217).

[4] Stow, *Survey*, Vol. II. bk. v. p. 205.

[5] Stow, *Survey*, bk. v. c. 21. This chapter contains an excellent history of these immigrants, not only in London, but in other parts of the country.

fined to particular persons whose work or whose dealings A.D. 1558
—1603.
*limits and
tends to
monopoly.* might be effectively supervised. The action of the Crown in creating such monopolies raised very important constitutional questions, which Elizabeth's parliament discussed with much vehemence, and considerable surprise at their own temerity[1]. In the case of the monopoly of tin[2], the question was complicated by the special rights of the Crown in the Duchy of Cornwall; and on the whole it appears to have been the general feeling that there should be proof of a real grievance on the part of consumers—through the enhancing of the price of an article of common consumption—before they were justified in taking a stand against the practice.

V. RURAL ECONOMY.

180. The prosperity of agriculture was closely connected *Reasons for the encouragement of tillage.* with the population and therefore with the power of the English realm; it gave a supply of food for victualling the armies, and it gave men a healthy busy life which fitted them for service in the field[3]; we need not be surprised that such constant efforts were made to develop it, or rather to prevent its decline. For the much deplored increase of grazing land at the expense of tillage still continued. It had in all probability begun soon after the Black Death, and had made considerable progress, as noted in the earlier part of this work, during the fifteenth century. Two important pieces of evidence connected with that period may be added *Evidence of decay in 1459* here; in 1459, John Ross presented a petition to the parliament of Coventry on the subject of the increase of pasture farming in Warwickshire; this has been lost but he fortunately introduced the main points of his grievances, à propos of the New Forest, as a digression in his history of the Norman Kings. He compares the county as he knew it with the records given in the *Hundred Rolls*, and shows how

---

[1] *Parliamentary History*, I. 923.

[2] In 1646, a *Declaration of Sundry grievances* [Brit. Mus. 669, f. 10 (45)] blames the patentees for the decay of trade, but a later writer asserts that the quality of tin and pewter suffered when the restrictions were removed. W. Smith, *Essay for recovery of Trade* (1661), p. 31.

[3] Bacon's Essay on the *Greatness of Kingdoms* (1612), *Works*, VI. 588.

A.D. 1558
—1608.
many villages had been depopulated; while he complains of the inconvenience and danger to travellers, and of the trouble they were put to in getting off their horses to open the gates in these enclosed districts[1]. Even more interesting

and 1517. is the inquisition which was taken in 1517, by Henry VIII., as to the enclosures which had occurred since the first Act of his fathers on the subject. It is somewhat surprising to see that at this period, the change was going on so slowly, and that in the Isle of Wight, so many of the new enclosures were made not by one great landowner, but by yeomen who took in little parcels of seven or eight acres each[2]. However this may be, there can be little doubt that enclosures for sheep farming accompanied by eviction took place on a large scale in the last years of Henry VIII. and under Edward VI.

*Decrease
in time of
Edward
VI.*
Hales' Commission, as well as his dialogue[3], are conclusive on this point. The evil of turning arable land into pasture was kept constantly in view, and during the greater part of Elizabeth's reign the measures which had been in vogue under Henry VIII.[4] against turning arable land into pasture were revived and kept in force till 1592 when they were allowed to drop[5]: at this date there appears to have been an opinion

*Apparent
cessation of
evil,* 1592.
that the mischief was a thing of the past. Bacon, writing in 1592, speaks of the abundance of grain; so that "whereas England was wont to be fed by other countries from the East, it sufficeth now to feed other countries....Another evident proof thereof may be that the good yields of corn which have been, together with some toleration of vent,

---

[1] J. Ross, of Warwick, *Hist. Regum Angliae*, p. 120. It must be remembered, however, that the depopulation may have been chiefly due not to enclosures but to the Black Death, and that enclosing was the method adopted to utilise land which could no longer be tilled. Cullum, *Hawsted*, p. 217, gives evidence of the change before 1387.

[2] British Museum, Lansdowne 1, f. 153: see abstract in Schanz, *Handels-politik*, 671.

[3] Curiously enough he also refers to the region round Coventry, where according to Ross enclosing had been so much carried out a century earlier. Mr Hubert Hall, who has examined the returns of the Commission in 1609 informs me that there were more recent and extreme cases of depopulation in Warwickshire than elsewhere. At Hillmorton 15 houses of husbands, each able to maintain a plough, had been decayed by the conversion of 250 acres of arable to pasture in 1607. (*Petty Bag. Depopulation Returns*, Record Office).

[4] 4 Hen. VII. c. 19, 7 Hen. VIII. c. 1, and 27 Hen. VIII. cc. 22, 28. 5 Eliz. c. 2.

[5] 35 Eliz. c. 7.

hath of late time invited and enticed men to break up more ground and convert it to tillage, than all the penal laws for that purpose made and enacted could ever by compulsion effect. A third proof may be that the prices of grain and of victual were never of late years more reasonable[1]." But the repeal of restrictions which had been in force in one form or another for more than a century[2] was premature, for it was followed by a rapid increase in the depopulations and turning of tillage into pasture. Accordingly in 1597 a new Act was passed embodying the substance of former measures, but allowing for the changes which were requisite if the improved system of husbandry was to be carried on. This measure was introduced by Bacon in a speech[3] which shows that he had found reason to modify the opinion he expressed five years before. All land in specified counties which had been employed in tillage at the beginning of Elizabeth's reign was to be restored and was to continue to be used for arable purposes though it might be laid down with grass for a time to recover strength; and the Act was not to be so enforced as to prevent the employment of the course of husbandry which the occupier found convenient.

Its sudden re-appearance 1597.

On the whole it appears that this decade marks the turning point, when the evil, which had occupied so much attention for so many years, ceased to be of practical importance; the enquiry in 1607[4] seems to confirm this view. The years between 1593 and 1597 were part of a short period when the price of wool was specially high; but in the seventeenth century it did not advance, or even

Price of wool.

---

[1] Spedding, *Letters and Life*, I. 158.   [2] 1488. 4 Hen. VII. c. 19.
[3] *Parl. Hist.* I. On the distress in Oxfordshire, *State Papers, Domestic, Eliz.* 1597, Vol. CCLXII. 4. For Durham, *Ib.* 10.
[4] There were riots in Northamptonshire about enclosures, and a proclamation on the subject was issued on May 30 [*Book of Proclamations* (1609), p. 139]. The matter came before the council, for whom a careful paper was prepared [Brit. Mus. *Cotton MSS.*, Titus F. IV. f. 219]. July 5, 1607. A proclamation explaining the policy of the government and treating the outcry about enclosures as a pretext, was issued July 9, 1607 (*Book of Proclamations*, p. 140), and a pardon was proclaimed on 24 July (*Ib.* p. 146). The Council then sent commissioners of enquiry to several shires (Aug. 20), with instructions to report before the end of October. The returns are in the Record Office. *Petty Bag. Depopulation Returns.*

A.D. 1558
—1603.
remain quite so high as it had done from 1540 to 1600; the
price of corn improved, and on the whole the profit of the
plough became as good as the profit of the flock. James I.
did indeed continue this statute, but there is evidence that the
encroachments on tillage which had lasted during the fifteenth
and sixteenth centuries practically ceased in the seventeenth.

*Encourage-
ment to
corn-grow-
ing.*

181. Great pains were also taken to remove the temptation to increase grazing, by rendering the cultivation of corn
more profitable. Obstacles had been put in the way of the
export of corn under Philip and Mary[1], as the legislators supposed the high price at home was due to excessive exportation
to foreign markets; exportation was allowed when the price
was 6s. 8d.; Elizabeth in the fifth year of her reign permitted
it at a price of 10s.[2], and the limit was fixed at 20s. in 1592[3].
At the same time, though the Parliament of Philip and
Mary were trying to restrain exportation, and Elizabeth's
measures seemed at first sight to render it more difficult, we
must remember that the great rise of prices was taking
place. This rise of the price of corn, which was the one
change that could effectually check the increase of grazing
and the consequent depopulation, was however viewed with
much suspicion. In Harrison's *Description of England* there

*Internal
trade.*

is a most interesting account of the internal corn trade[4],
from which we see that he had the strongest view that the
engrossers and large farmers were able to raise prices for
their own profit, to the disadvantage alike of the consumer
and the small farmer. He would have taken measures to
check the market operations of "Bodgers" or middlemen, as
the best means of securing that there should be plenty of
corn in the market at a reasonable price[5]. Others were
bitterly opposed to the permission which was given to the
export of corn. But on the whole this line of policy was
falling into discredit; it may be possible to keep a note of
the stacks of corn and to force men to sell at a low price on

[1] 1 and 2 Philip and Mary, c. 5.   [2] 5 Eliz. c. 5, § 17.   [3] 35 Eliz. c. 7, § 5.
[4] Compare also Mr E. Green's admirable paper *On the Poor and some attempts
to lower the price of Corn*, in *Proceedings of Bath Nat. Hist. Club*, IV. 6. On restrictions on the internal corn trade in early times, see Faber, *Die Entstehung des
Agrarschutzes in England* (*Abhand. staatswiss. Seminar Strassburg*, V.), p. 66.
[5] *England*, II. 18 in Holinshed, *Chronicles* (1807), I. 340.

some occasions, but it is not possible to induce them to pro- A.D. 1558 —1603. duce corn regularly and constantly unless they are to be free to sell it at a remunerative price. The measures that were proposed in order to induce an immediate supply at a low rate, would be most unfavourable to the development of arable farming as a regular and permanent source of supply. Elizabeth's advisers were fully aware of the great stimulus *More free-* that would be given to tillage if the farmer was able to find *dom for export.* a market for his corn in foreign lands, and they empowered the justices to settle in each locality how far the export of grain might be permitted at any time[1]. The Act was intended to provide for the increase of tillage and maintenance of the navy, so that we may see that the double benefits of the export of corn as encouraging tillage, and as supplying a commodity for trade, were clearly kept in view. The flexibility of the method of regulating export, so that the system might be adapted to the differing needs of different localities is very characteristic of the Elizabethan legislature and in some degree resembles the provisions for the assessment of wages. The necessity of maintaining a high price of corn, if *Higher* arable farming was to be profitable and to be continued, was *prices maintained.* clearly perceived; but laws for raising the price of corn would be most unpopular even if they were clearly politic[2]. The legislators had this object in view, but they were forced to proceed cautiously. Still it appears that they were successful, for Dymock writing about 1650, remarks that in "Queen Elizabeth's days good husbandry began to take place[3]." There is indeed only one product which was cultivated during this reign on a far larger scale than before. Hops proved a very profitable if somewhat speculative crop; and the agriculturists of the seventeenth century have a great deal to say about them; but on the whole it certainly appears that the long depression which had attended tillage and caused the area of arable land to shrink more and more was really coming to an end.

Other measures were taken to secure the prosperity of *Subsidiary* tillage; the statute of apprentices is obviously framed with *measures.*

---

[1] 13 Eliz. c. 13.

[2] Compare Hales' *Briefe Conceipt*, in *Harleian Miscellany*, IX. 164.

[3] *Samuel Hartlib, his Legacy*, p. 52 (1651).

the view of forcing all surplus labour into agricultural employment, and in times of emergency such as harvest, artificers were to assist in saving the crops[1]. Serious efforts were also made to protect the farmer from loss through the depredations of crows, rooks and various sorts of vermin; the damage done to grain is specially mentioned, and the churchwardens were required to assess the farmers and spend the money raised in giving rewards for the heads and eggs of the birds which did most damage to the crops[2].

Dairy Farming.   182. It may seem strange at first sight that the increase of pasture should have been accompanied by a decline of dairy farming; but there was at all events a general impression that the two changes had gone on together. And this is not unlikely; sheep farming enabled the landlord or tenant to dispense with labour and to depopulate his farm; for dairy farming and poultry farming constant care and attention was requisite; when the households of husbandmen were broken up there was no one left who could manage the cows, or the poultry; these were really bye-avocations which were actually combined with arable farming. It was commonly asserted that eggs and dairy products had become specially dear, even though other things were rising in price also. A statute of Philip and Mary insisted that a cow should be kept and a calf reared for every sixty sheep[3], this *Woad.* regulation was continued under Elizabeth[4]. In 1585 a proclamation was issued against the increasing growth of woad at the expense of arable and of pasture ground. It was said that this practice was to the great prejudice of "the countrymen which fed on white meats made of milk[5]." It would not have been possible to allege this reason if there had not been a general opinion that dairy farming was declining, but it can hardly have had much weight with any one. The proclamation referred to the country within eight miles of the Queen's houses, or four miles of towns; and there was a general impression that the Queen objected to the smell of the plant. On the great debate on monopolies in

---

[1] 5 Eliz. c. 4, §§ 15, 16.
[2] 24 Hen. VIII. c. 10, and 8 Eliz. c. 15.   [3] 2 and 3 Philip and Mary, c. 3.
[4] 13 Eliz. c. 25.   [5] Camden, *Elizabeth*, anno 1585, p. 325.

A.D. 1558
—1603.

1601 Elizabeth agreed to withdraw this prohibition, adding a request that "when she cometh in progress to see you in your counties, she be not driven out of your towns by suffering it to infect the air too near them[1]."

183. One other statute on rural matters deserves special attention as it is the first of a long series of efforts that were made to reclaim the great marshes and fens. This work of improvement was by no means popular; as the fishers and fowlers who had enjoyed a free but hardy life had the strongest objections to the draining of marshes which supplied them with the means of livelihood. The undertaking was prosecuted with much energy in the seventeenth century and there were many feuds between the Fenmen and the Dutch drainers[2], but the Act of Elizabeth shows that the matter was already engaging attention. When people were ready to go and plant new and distant settlements, it was well worth while to try and make more room for profitable cultivation at home. The Act for the recovery of many thousands of acres of marshes and other grounds[3] in the Isle of Ely in Cambridgeshire, Norfolk, Leicester, Huntingdon-

Reclaiming the Fens.

Popular feeling and legal difficulties.

---

[1] *Parliamentary History*, I. 985.

[2] One Thomas Lovell undertook to drain the fens near Market Deeping at his own expense. He began the work and spent all his fortune to the amount of £12,000 on it, but the fenmen broke down his bank and destroyed his works, and he gave up the attempt. Wheeler, *History of the Fens*, p. 122.

[3] 43 Eliz. c. 11. There had been a previous attempt to legislate, and a summary of the Act presented in 1585, intitled "An Act for the recovery and inning of drowned and surrounded grounds" will be found in *State Papers, Domestic, Eliz.* CLXXVI. 74. Other projects during this interval were as follows:

1592. Guillaume Mostart to Lord Burghley. Has undertaken to drain the fens of Coldham in Cambridgeshire, bought by John Hunt, of London, on assurance that they can be drained. The work will be a great encouragement and example to the draining of other fens in the kingdom, &c. *State Papers, Domestic, Eliz.* CCXLI. 114.

1593. Humfrey Bradley to Lord Burghley. Sends a project for draining the fens......Considering the diversity of the tenures and leases of the fens, and the opinions of men, the most expedient way will be by Act of Parliament, &c. *State Papers, Domestic, Eliz.* CCXLIV. 97.

1598. Note of the course to be taken for recovering surrounded grounds until the late intended Act is established. Information is to be made by the Attorney General in the Star Chamber of the loss to the Commonwealth by continuing those grounds under water, and the loss and decay of outfalls to the sea; of the rich profit which would arise from their recovery, and the multitude of people which might be relieved and nourished thereby. *State Papers, Domestic, Eliz.* CCLXVIII. 102.

shire and other counties, was intended to remove the pre-
liminary difficulty which lay in the way of all such undertakings; the common rights on those wastes could not be
extinguished by any process of law, and the statute was
passed to enable the Lords of Manors and Commoners to
make terms with undertakers for improving the property by
drainage.   The measure is of little importance as an enacting statute, but it marks the beginning of the great work of
improvement which occupied much attention in subsequent
years, and to which Englishmen were incited by the example
of the Dutch.

*For
pasturage.*
    The actual attempts which were carried out in this reign
had no direct bearing on the increase of tillage ; so far as we
can gather they only tried to prevent the inundations of the
sea[1] on certain low grounds so as to obtain additional grazing
for their cattle[2], and even under James I. they only aimed at
making the fens sufficiently dry in summer to serve a similar
purpose.   They did not attempt to keep them free from
floods in winter and bring them under crop till a later date[3].

VI. The Poor.

*Charity
organisa-
tion and
compulsory
contribu-
tions.*
    184.   The Act of the 43rd of Elizabeth for the relief of
the poor was the last of a series of experiments which
occupied the attention of Parliament throughout the whole
reign.   The existing measures for organising charity under
the force of moral suasion had not proved effective, and in
1563 we have the beginning of a compulsory provision for
the poor.   If the Bishop found that his exhortations failed
and that he had to deal with a man who "with a froward
and wilful mind, obstinately refused to give to the relief of
the poor according to his ability," he was to bind him over to
appear before the justices[4] who had power to assess the pay-

---

[1] A serious inundation occurred in the neighbourhood of Lynn in 1569.
Mackerell, *Kings Lynn*, 228.

[2] *Samuel Hartlib, his Legacy*, 52.

[3] Vermuïden, *Discourse touching the drayning the great Fennes*, 2.

[4] 5 Eliz. c. 3.

ment which such a person should make to the poor and to A.D. 1558 —1603. imprison him if he failed to comply. In this way the duty of aiding the distressed came to have quite a new character; it was no longer an act of charity to be done out of love to God and pity to man, but it became a sort of tax demanded by public authority, to ameliorate a public nuisance, and the payment of which could be enforced under pain of imprisonment. As it lost the character of a voluntary gift, it was no longer an evidence of mercy, it failed to bless those who paid their poor rates, and it called forth little gratitude from those who obtained relief.

The next step in advance was in complete accord with *Assessment by the Justices.* this new view of the problem; the justices of the peace were required, not merely to punish those who refused to give, but to take the initiative in the matter[1]; they were to ascertain the number of the impotent poor, born or resident for three years in the district, and to keep a register of them; they were also to erect convenient habitations for them, and to appoint overseers to see after them. They were to calculate the amounts required for the support of these poor folk, to make the necessary assessment, and provide for the collection of rates. In 1597 the system of compulsion was rendered complete, as the authorities in each parish were empowered to distrain the goods of those who did not pay their rates[2].

185. Simultaneously with these measures for the sup- *Vagrancy.* port of the impotent, additional efforts were made to set all vagrants at work, they were strangely varied people for whom order was taken; people who used subtle, crafty and unlawful games and plays, or who feigned a knowledge of Physiognomy and Palmistry, all those who had no apparent means of support and who were fit for work, all fencers, beartraders, jugglers, pedlars, tinkers, petty chapmen and strolling players, all unlicensed scholars or shipmen who were caught begging, were considered to be rogues and sturdy beggars. Mere punishment did little to reduce the evil; the real difficulty was to find work for them to do; in 1572 the *Stock for employment.* justices were empowered to employ any surplus that remained over after providing for the impotent poor in setting

[1] 14 Eliz. c. 5.   [2] 39 Eliz. c. 3, § 3.

A.D. 1558
—1603.
the vagrants to work[1] and in 1576 there were some very
remarkable provisions for rendering this possible[2].   The
justices were required to provide a stock of hemp, wool, iron
and other materials so as to find employment for vagrants,
they were to be housed and paid for their work, so that no
one who was able to work need go begging for lack of employment[3]. This provision probably remained a dead letter,
though there were some attempts to provide employment
Lynn and for the poor in various places, for example at Lynn[4] and at
Leicester. Leicester[5]. Certainly the difficulty of organising such estab-
Adminis- lishments as were here designed would be very great; officials
trative dif-
ficulties. could not be trusted in all cases to administer the funds

---

[1] 14 Eliz. c. 5, § 23.   [2] 18 Eliz. c. 3.

[3] To the intent youth may be brought up in labour......also that rogues may not
have any just excuse in saying they cannot get any service or work......and that
other poor needy persons being willing to work may be set on work. 18 Eliz. c. 3, § 4.

[4] "This year (1581) a great deal of money was laid out about S. James's Church,
in fitting it up and preparing it for a Workhouse, for the employment of the poor
in making of Bays, &c., which not answering the charge was in a short time disused.
...Divers poor people were this year (1586) set to work at the new building at
S. James's in dressing of Hemp and making Strings and Tows for Fishermen."
This whole attempt must have come finally to an end when the church was pulled
down in 1623. Mackerell, *History of Kings Lynn*, 229.

A poor house at Waltham Cross was undertaken, and John Stinton a chap-
man was empowered to collect benevolences for it. His wife got leave to pass
through the country at the time the plague was raging in Leicester (1593). *Hist.
MSS. Com.* VIII. App. 432.

At a later time we hear of similar efforts in Beverley. In 1599 it was stated
that the town had become impoverished by the removal of the staple to Hull, that
four hundred tenements were utterly decayed and uninhabited, and that the town
expended the annual sum of £105 in support of the poor, besides the charge of
maintaining and educating eighty orphans, in knitting, spinning and other works
of industry, according to the provisions of an Act of Parliament passed 39 Eliz.
(Olliver, *Beverley*, 192.)

[5] *Leicester Corporation MSS.* in *Hist. MSS. Com. Report* VIII. Ap. I., pp. 430-432.

(VII.) 2 June, 1584. Letter from Thomas Clarke, Mayor of Leicester, to the
Earl of Huntingdon, respecting an arrangement for setting the poor of Leicester
to work on spinning. Also two other letters touching a proposal to entrust Blase
Villers, gent., a merchant of the staple, and one of our company, with £100 of the
common charge of our town, who therewith will set the poor to work on spinning.

(I.) 22 Feb., 1591. Letter from the Earl of Huntingdon to the Mayor, Re-
corder and Aldermen of Leicester. About "a note of receit of coles" for the
benefit of Leicester, and about the relief of the poor of the same town.

(V.) 2 June, 1592. Letter from the Earl of Huntingdon to the Mayor of
Leicester. For the payment of £70 of "the cole money" to one Thomas Elkington
of Langar, County Nottingham ; the same to be used "to the benefit of the poor of
Leicester, by setting them aworke about clothing."

(XIII.) 9 Feb., 1596. Mem., that, by the appointment of the Earl of Hun-

honestly[1], and the permission for benevolent persons to A.D. 1558
—1608. found hospitals[2] did not meet with such a general response that the evil sensibly abated. The want of some such system of providing employment has been the weak point of the whole English Poor Law. The Act of 1601, which held its ground for so long, with but trifling modifications, suffered from the same defect; it was meant to provide work for those who could work, relief for those who could not, and punishment for those who would not; but the local administrators never set themselves seriously to fulfil the first of their duties and raise a fund, to provide work[3] for the unemployed, and from which loans might be made to the deserving[4]. The duty of *Appren-* training children to work has been performed, though some-*tices.* times in a fashion that gave rise to grave scandal, through the gross mistreatment of parish apprentices; but I cannot find that many attempts were made at this time to raise such a fund in each parish as might provide employment for "all persons married or unmarried having no means to main-*Providing* tain themselves and who used no ordinary and daily trade of *work.* life to get their living by." The history of such experiments as were made, could it be recovered, would be of great interest in times like ours when so many are inclined to insist that there is a right to work, and that the State is bound to provide employment.

VII. FINANCE.

186. The first years of Elizabeth's reign were marked by *The re-* a great financial operation; she was able to carry through a *coinage.* scheme which had been in consideration for some time, and

tingdon, the Mayor and burgesses of Leicester have lent to Thomas Moseley, of Leicester, the sum of ten pounds, wherewith to "sett and keepe poor children in Leicester on worke in knitting of Jersey stockings."

(XVI.) 28 July. Letter from the Earl of Huntingdon to the Mayor and others. Recommending to them Thomas Clarke and Margaret his wife, as competent persons to receive a loan of money for setting the poor to work.

See also p. 433. (XVII.) 12 Sept., 1598, and (XXIII.) 7 Jan., 1599.

[1] 39 Eliz. c. 4, § 13.　　　[2] 39 Eliz. c. 5.　　　[3] 43 Eliz. c. 2, § 1.
[4] Toulmin Smith, *The Parish* (1857), 433.

A.D. 1558
—1603.
restore the coinage to something very like the old standard of fineness. In the unsettled state of public feeling there was real courage in facing such a difficult task, and in taking a course which was sure to cause general inconvenience and arouse discontent.

Calling down debased money.

The first step was to issue a proclamation calling down the current coins to their actual value in fine silver[1]; the testoon (a sixpence) was to pass as fourpence halfpenny, except some which bore special marks and were only to pass for twopence farthing. These last were all to be called in, the Queen promised to supply money of fine silver coined at her own charges to those who brought them in. There was some reason to fear that prices would be raised when the nominal value of the coins was thus altered; though if the coins were already circulating at their value as commodities there was no excuse for such a movement; the proclamation insisted that no one should be permitted to ask higher rates on the pretext of this change.

Reasons for re-coinage.

Having thus entered on this difficult undertaking, Elizabeth proceeded in a second proclamation[2] to explain the reasons which had rendered the step necessary. This document urged that the reputation of the nation was at stake, as England had always been distinguished above other countries by the fineness of the coinage; further it pointed out that merchants brought base money into the realm, and thus got our rich commodities of coal, cloth and tin on very easy terms; and that there was a strong temptation to export the precious metals. In fact, as Sir Thomas Gresham had expounded, experience had proved that when good and bad money are in circulation together, base money will drive out the good, but good money will not drive out the bad.

Effects on prices.

It was also explained that the circulation of base money had brought about a great rise of prices, and a hope was expressed that the recoinage would bring things to the former level; if this were so the benefit would be felt by all labourers who lived on wages, by all soldiers who lived on pay, and

[1] 27 Sept., 1560. Ruding. *Annals*, 1. 333.
[2] 29 Sept., 1560. Ruding. *Annals*, 1. 334.

gentlemen who had pensions[1]. Within the country the A.D. 1558 —1603.
poorer classes would be the chief gainers by the change,
while it would also bring about a favourable re-adjustment of
our commerce with other countries[2], and foreign commodities
would be imported at easier rates.

The scheme thus fully explained was rendered unneces- *Change in the currency.*
sarily burdensome by a miscalculation; the testoons were
really undervalued in the proclamation, and many persons
collected them in order to export them and pass them off at
a better rate; by a subsequent proclamation these practices
were declared to be felony, and rigid restrictions were enforced to prevent the coins from being taken beyond the
seas. As the new money began to get into circulation, the
base money was called in[3] and the authorities offered to take
it at the mint as bullion up till the 9th of April; a little
more grace was given by the Exchequer to her Majesty's
tenants, but a proclamation was issued on June 12th, 1561,
which declared that the base moneys were no longer current.

Such were the public proceedings; there was consider- *Machinery employed*
able difficulty in organising the machinery by which this
important change was successfully effected. Some pre-
liminary investigation had been made in the time of
Edward VI.[4], but the scheme as eventually carried through
was entirely organised under Elizabeth; it seems that she
took a keen personal interest in the matter and drafted some
papers on the subject with her own hand. A mass of base
money amounting to 631,950 lbs. was collected, which yielded
244,416 lbs., it was recoined into £733,248, and as only
£638,113 had been paid for it, the Crown was a gainer by the
transaction: after the cost of collection had been paid and
the expenses of recoinage (£12,983. 4s. 3d.) a handsome

---

[1] On the grievances of the poor through tampering with the coinage, see
Cooper's *Chronicle*, in 1552 (ed. 1565, f. 351).

[2] This was a far more important point than appears in the proclamation.
Elizabeth at the commencement of her reign owed some £200,000 to Jews in
Flanders, and had to pay interest at 14 or 15 per cent. (Froude, vi. 118.) This
rate would be greatly increased to her by an unfavourable state of the exchanges.
It has been pointed out that in 1696, William III. was paying 20 or 30 per cent.
on all sums remitted to Flanders for the wars, and that the rectification of the
coinage enabled him to remit at par. Thorold Rogers, *First Nine Years*, 43.

[3] 19 Feb., 1561. Ruding, *Annals*, i. 340.   [4] Ruding, *Annals*, i. 321.

A.D. 1558
—1603.
and gain
by the
trans-
action.

balance remained to the Queen as the profit of the transaction. Such successful management reflects the greatest
credit on those who accomplished this difficult work[1]; the
chief refiner employed was Daniel Wolstat of Antwerp who
was engaged by Sir Thomas Gresham, and who was to receive 5 per cent. on the value of the re-issued coinage[2]; the
rapidity with which the work was executed may have been
facilitated by means of a sum of 200,000 crowns which were
borrowed about this time by the same financier.

*Main-
tenance of
treasure.*

187.   There were no new expedients, with the doubtful
exception of some patents and monopolies, for raising revenue
during this reign; but the Commons were fully alive to the
importance of maintaining the treasure of the realm, if the
nation was to hold its position as an independent power.   In
the first Parliament of the reign they granted a subsidy, as
well as two-fifteenths and a tenth.   They expressed their
grief at the decay which had taken place in many things, and
especially in "these three, first, wasting of treasure, abandon-
ing of strength, and in diminishing the ancient authority of.
your imperial crown," and they proceeded thus:—"we do
most earnestly and faithfully promise to your Highness that
there shall lack no good will, travail, nor force on our behalf
to the redress of all this, but we shall be ready with heart,
will, strength, body, lives and goods, not only to recover
again that which is thus diminished, but if need be to recover farther (as far as right, and the will and pleasure of
God shall suffer), the old dignity and renown of this realm,
the time and place whereof doth not rest in us, but, as
most reason is, in your most noble Majesty with the advice
of your honourable Council.   Nevertheless since it doth so
manifestly appear to us all, what inestimable wasting and
consumption of the treasure and ancient revenues of this
realm hath been of late days, and what great new charges
and intolerable expenses your Highness is forced now to
sustain, by reason of the decay and loss of parcel of your
ancient crown, so being not ignorant that no worthy enterprise, no noble attempt, no not so much as the prosecu-

---

[1] £14,079. 13s. 9d.   Froude, vii. 9.   [2] Burgon's *Gresham*, i. 344.

tion of a strong and puissant estate may be without some mass of treasure, presently to be had, and ready against all occurrents[1]," and then the grant is made. Now while we may make all allowance for the obsequiousness of Tudor Parliaments and may remember that the nation was at this time smarting under the loss of Calais, and eager to reassert that the Pope had no jurisdiction in an Imperial realm, there can be no doubt that the Commons were thoroughly loyal to Elizabeth, and continued to act on the feeling they expressed in this preamble.

At the same time the calls which Elizabeth made on *Elizabeth's parsimony.* them were comparatively small. She must indeed have often been in great straits from want of money, for the rise of prices, first through the debasement of the coinage, and then by the influx of silver, seriously diminished the permanent revenue; but many of the expenses of her court fell on the nobles whom she honoured by being their guest[2], and even the defence of the realm at the critical juncture when the Armada was threatening our shores was effected by the munificence of private individuals rather than at the public expense[3]. The pressure of taxation must have been comparatively slight, at least on some classes of the subjects, for *General prosperity and slight pressure of taxation.* the great graziers, and the clothiers were rapidly becoming rich. There is abundant evidence of prosperity in the Elizabethan mansions and manor houses which are found in many parts of England; and the complaints of general poverty which have come down to us from this date are curiously diversified by indignant diatribes against the increase of extravagance and luxury[4]. And it is easy to see that those tenants who, whether as leaseholders or copyholders, had agreement for a long term of years must have prospered greatly as their rents could not be raised, while they could take advantage of higher prices. There were other symptoms of the general increase of comfort among the humbler classes; there were far more chimneys than formerly; the bedding was far better than in bygone days, and the furniture was very much superior, while most farmers had some ready

[1] 1 Eliz. c. 21. [2] Dowell, *Sketch*, I. 296. [3] Froude, *History*, XII. 434.
[4] Harrison, *Description*, cc. VI., VII. in Holinshed, I. 278.

money and were able to put something by[1]. This statement as to increasing comfort, which seems to apply to the
farmers, is borne out on the whole by evidence as to the
long time which elapsed in many cases before landowners
were able to obtain much additional income by raising
rents[2]. There is accordingly every reason to suppose that
the clothiers and many of the farmers were prospering during
this reign, as well as the graziers, even though the labourer
and the owner of arable land were alike suffering from high
prices. Had the general subsidies been collected on a new
assessment the revenues would have increased as the industrious prospered; but, as has been pointed out above, the
general subsidy was really collected as a sort of fixed charge,
amounting to about £80,000; indeed while personal property
was so generally increasing, the amounts of the subsidies
declined to some extent through the carelessness or dishonesty of collectors[3].

*Diminu-
tion of
customs.*
Allusion has been made above to the losses which the
Crown suffered from this cause in regard to the customs;
but the revenue from this source showed some signs of declining from other causes. The very success of the economic
policy for rendering England more self-sufficing tended to
diminish the revenue that could be procured from trade.
The prejudicial manner in which the Navigation Acts affected
the receipts on imported wine has been noted above[4], and as
weaving was successfully planted in England by the immigrants, the customs on exported wool and imported cloth
declined, while the new manufactures did not at once supply
any considerable quantity of goods for export. The planting
of these trades was a statesmanlike proceeding, but it was
not a very popular one, and it was not accomplished without
some immediate loss to the Crown[5].

*Frauds by
officials.*
A temporary loss of this kind was, however, the merest
trifle, as compared with the constant drain from the bare-

---

[1] Harrison in Holinshed, I. 318. Hall, *Elizabethan Society*, p. 41.
[2] Thorold Rogers, *Agriculture and Prices*, IV. 135, 750. This was while they
continued to let the land for arable purposes: eviction and the formation of
pasture farms at high rents was another matter.
[3] Dowell, *History*, I. 199.   [4] § 189, Vol. I. p. 435.
[5] Sir T. Smith in Stow, *Survey*, II. bk. v. p. 297.

faced dishonesty of officials. Sir Thomas Smith, who had A.D. 1558 —1603. detected the goldsmiths' frauds[1], was forced to refund some of the money which had passed into his hands, when he farmed the revenue[2]. Sir Thomas Gresham was only able to retain his illgotten gains by ingenious tricks, and successful use of court influence, which procured the Queen's signature to his unaudited accounts[3]. Sir George Carey appears to have been even more unscrupulous[4]. Nor was it only the great ministers of the time who yielded to temptation to defraud the public purse. The army contractors, who supplied clothing for the troops in Ireland, were quite as barefaced, and only delivered half the quantity of goods for which they were paid[5].

VIII. Economic Opinion.

188. In the preceding pages the current economic doctrines have been clearly stated in language drawn from public documents, and illustrated from the measures which attempted to reduce them to practice. The Elizabethan legislation forms a sort of systematic code, for each single statute is obviously part of a great economic system which was generally accepted as the right mode of treating the resources of the nation. The close interconnection between the development of agriculture and the prosperity of commerce comes out again and again, while the intimate relationships between industry and foreign trade in these regulations, are everywhere patent. Nor can we miss the object with which all these minute ordinances were framed, the mediate end was treasure in most cases, but the ultimate aim was the increase of national power. *Current Economic doctrine in documents*

We might find much additional illustration in the literature of the day but one work stands out pre-eminently among all the writings of the period which deal with economic matters. The *Brief Conceit of English policy* was published in 1581, and it purports to have been written by W. S. *and literature.*

---

[1] Stow, *Survey*, II. bk. v. p. 184.   [2] Dowell, *History*, I. 167.
[3] Hall, *Elizabethan Society*, 68.   [4] *Ib.* 124.   [5] *Ib.* 126.

A.D. 1558
—1608.

Hales 1549.

in regard to whose identity there has been much dispute. I take it as proved, however[1], that the work was written by John Hales as early as 1549, and that it was issued in 1581 with some slight[2] emendations. The revision might have been due to Hales himself who lived till 1577, but on the whole this seems unlikely and there is no sufficient clue to the identity of W. S. who has been successful in securing the credit of authorship for so many years.

In form it is a dialogue, and the remarks of the various speakers give a very vivid picture of the common causes of complaint; but as a description of England it has far more importance for the time of Edward VI. than for the reign of Elizabeth. Most of the definite allusions refer to the earlier time and we can only say that in all probability there had been no such obvious changes as to render the language of the tract glaringly inapposite. This must be borne in mind in regard to his estimates as to the extent of the rise in prices[3]; but there can be no doubt that there was a continuous rise of prices and that it was mainly due, as the Doctor notes, to a fall in the value of silver coins, which affected all callings, though it did not affect all alike. Some, as merchants, who could raise their prices and recoup themselves soon when they paid more, were neither better off, nor worse off for the change. Some, as farmers with long leases positively gained, as they could get higher prices, but need pay no more rent; while some, like landlords who had granted long leases, lost terribly, for they paid more for everything, and could not recoup themselves. Hales shows how the rapid rise began with the debasement of the coinage

Mercantile Doctrine.

[1] Miss E. Lamond in *English Historical Review*, vi. 284. Compare also the Introduction to the Cambridge University Press Edition.

[2] A long passage on debased currency is omitted, while on the other hand there is an insertion about the continued high prices under Elizabeth. It is interesting to compare this tract with the *Discours sur les causes de l'extrême cherté qui est aujourdhuy en France* (1574), Cimber et Danjou, *Archives*, Série I. vi. p. 428. This was probably written by Bodin and contains one of the earliest references to the influence of American silver in raising prices. Compare his *Discours sur le rehaussement des monnoyes* (1578). The same influence is noticed in the insertion in Hales' dialogue, but the passages are so distinct that there is no reason to suppose the insertor had come across the French tract.

[3] *Harl. Misc.* ix. 173. Professor Thorold Rogers holds that no rise took place before 1541, and that the nominal increase then was merely proportional to the debasement of coin. *Agriculture and Prices*, v. 780.

under Henry VIII.; he thinks that the real enhancing which A.D. 1558 —1608. then took place would render it impossible to return to the old level of prices, even if it were wise to attempt it. The main interest of the treatise, however, does not lie in the description it contains, but in the arguments which are put into the mouth of Dr Pandotheus; and which form a very remarkable body of economic doctrine. It contains an excellent resumé of principles which were generally accepted till the time of Adam Smith, and which just because they were so commonly recognised, were often assumed rather than stated, especially by writers who were discussing some particular practical project.

It is, of course, clear on every line that he regards the *State and Individual.* power of the country as a whole as the great object towards which all efforts should be directed; but he also sees that the resources of government are drawn by taxation[1] from the pockets of the people, and that the aggregate of individual wealth is the fund from which supplies must come.

Knight. "I have heard oftentymes much reasoning in this matter, and some in maintenaunce of these inclosures would make this reason; every man is a member of the commonweale, and that which is profitable to one man may be profitable to another, if he would exercise the same feate. Therefore, that which is profitable to mee and so to another, may be profitable to all, and so to the whole commonweale; as a greate masse of treasure consisteth of many pence, and one peney added to another and so to the thirde and fourth, &c. maketh up a greate somme; so doth each man added one to another make up the whole body of a common weale."

Doctor. "That reason is good, adding some what more to it; true it is, that that thing which is profitable to each man by himselfe, so it be not prejudicial to any other, is profitable to the whole commonweale, and not other wise: or else stealing or robbing which percase is profitable to some men, were profitable to the commonweale, which no man will admit. But this feate of inclosing is so, that where it is profitable to one man it is prejudiciall to many; therefore I thinke that reason sufficiently aunswered[2]."

[1] *Harl. Misc.* IX. 155. [2] *Ib.* 161.

We consequently find a remarkable change in tone from
the language that had been usually employed under Henry
VII. and Henry VIII. Then writers usually implied that
Private gain. /the pursuit of private gain was necessarily hurtful and that
·men ought to be consciously public-spirited[1] in their mode
of doing their business; but while Hales did not palliate
the moral evil of self-seeking, he recognised that it might be
directed so as not to work serious mischief to the community.

Doctor. "To tel you plaine," he says, "it is avarice that I
take for the principall cause thereof: but can we[2] devise that
all covetousnes can be taken from men? No, no more then
we can make men to be without wealth, without gladnes,
without feare, and without all affections: what then? we
must take away from men the occasion of their covetousnes
in this part: what is that? the exceeding luker that they se
grow by these inclosures more then by their husbandry.
And that may be done by any of these two meanes that I will
tell you. Either by the minishing of the luker that men
have by grasing; or els by advaunsing of the profite of
husbandry, til it be as good and as profitable to the occupiers
as grasing is: for every man (as Plato saith[3]) is naturally
covetous of luker. And that wherein they see most luker,
they will most gladly exercise."

He reiterates over and over again that it is possible to
modify circumstances so that private gain shall guide him to
take the course that is favourable to the public weal. It was
Sheep farming and tillage. easy to lament the decline of tillage and to condemn the
avarice of graziers, but no real remedy was to be found by
merely appealing to the personal patriotism or charity of
sheep farmers. The important thing was "to make the
profit of the plough as good, rate for rate, as the profit of the
grazier or sheep master[4]," and this might be done by putting
heavier taxes on the exportation of unwrought wool, which
would diminish the sale without diminishing the Queen's

---

[1] See Statute on Worcester Clothiers, above Vol. I. p. 461.
[2] It is interesting to compare this passage with Sir James Steuart (see below, p. 430) who may be regarded as the last of the mercantilists.
[3] *Hipparchus*, 232 c.
[4] *Briefe Conceipt*, in *Harleian Miscellany*, IX. 184.

customs, and by giving facilities for the export of corn[1]: A.D. 1558 —1608.
there was no danger of any great dearth in the home market
as men "provoked with lucre[2]" would prefer to sell in this
country rather than have the expense of carriage across the
sea, and would keep some store of corn as a speculation on
the chance of a dear year. This is thoroughly characteristic
of the Mercantilist period, in its view of the position to be
assigned to the individual desire of wealth; in mediæval
times it was only recognised to be condemned as immoral;
in our own day it is sometimes spoken of as though there
were a pre-arranged harmony which made private self-seeking tend unconsciously to public good[3]. Hales and many
subsequent writers fully recognised the effectiveness of the
force of the self-interested desire of wealth, but they believed
that a little management was needed in order to direct it
into channels where it should bring about public gain, rather
than public loss. It may be necessary to say some words of
criticism on this doctrine of private interest below[4]; for the
present it may suffice to say that this principle was constantly acted upon by the legislature during the seventeenth
and eighteenth centuries and that it is clearly recognised in
Hales' dialogue.

The importance of so managing trade as to procure the *Treasure.*
import of treasure from abroad and to discourage the export
was, of course, a mere commonplace at the time when he
wrote; the Doctor is opposed to allowing the importation of
things which we could make at home, and is eagerly anxious
to have greater freedom for the migration of industry and
very jealous of the craft[5] exclusiveness; he thinks strange

---

[1] Compare the measures actually in force in the eighteenth century. See
below, p. 371.   [2] *Briefe Conceipt,* in *Harl. Misc.* IX. 165.
[3] Bastiat.   [4] See below, p. 431.
[5] At the same time he evidently assumes that each town should control and set
the work of suburban workmen. "But where other cities do allure unto them good
workemen, ours will expell them out: as I have knowen good workemen, as well
smythes as weavers, have comen from straunge parties to some cityes within this
realme, entending to set up theyr craftes; and because they were not free there
(but specially, because they were better workemen then were any in the towne)
they coulde not bee suffered to worke there. Such incorporations had those mis-
teries in those townes, that none might worke there in their faculty, except they
did compounde with them first."

Capper. "And doe you thinke it reasonable, that a straunger should bee as

workmen may improve the trade of a town if they are allowed to settle there; but his scheme for developing an

free in a city or towne, as they that were prentises there? then no man would bee prentice to any occupation, if it were so."

Doctor. "I sayde not, that they shall have commonly lyke liberty or fraunchise; but as one crafte makes but one particuler companie of a towne or city, so I would have the weale of the whole city rather regarded, then the commodity, or fraunchise, of one craft or mistery: for though commonly none should be admitted there to worke but such as are free; yet when a singuler good workeman in any mistery comes, which by his good knowledge might both enstructe them of the towne, being of the same faculty, and also bringe into the towne much commodity beside; I woulde, in that case, have private liberties and privileges gieve place to a publique weale, and such a man gladly admitted for his excellency to the freedome of the same towne, without burdening of him with any charge for his first entry or setting up. Yea, where a towne is decayed and lackes artificers to furnish the towne with such craftes, as were either sometimes exercised well there, or might bee, by reason of the situation and commodity of the same towne; I woulde have such craftesmen allured out of other places where they bee plenty, to come to those townes decayed, to dwell; offering them theyr freedome, yea, theyr house rente free, or some stocke lent them, of the common stocke of such townes: and when the towne is wel furnished of such artificers, then to stay the comming in of foreners. But while the towne lackes enhabitauntes of artificers, it were no policy for the restauration of the towne to keepe of any straunge artificers: for the most parte of all townes are mainteyned by craftes men of all sortes, but specially by those that make any wares to sell out of the countrey, and brynges therefore treasure into the same; as clothiers, cappers, worstedmakers, hatmakers, poyntmakers, pinners, painters, founders, smythes of all sortes, cutlers, glovers, tanners, parchment-makers, gyrdlers, poursers, makers of paper, thredmakers, turners, basketmakers, and many other such. As for the mercers, and haberdashers, vintners and grocers, I cannot see what they doe to a towne, but fynde a livinge to v. or vi. householdes; and in steade thereof, empoverish ten times as many. But since men wil needes have silkes, wine and spice; it is as good that men do spend theyr money upon such in their owne towne, as to be dryven to seeke the same further. As for the rest of the artificers, like as I said before, even as they take no money out of the countrey, so they bryng none in; as taylours, shoemakers, carpenters, joyners, tylers, masons, bouchers, vittailers, and such like. Also, an other thinge I recken woulde helpe much to relieve oure townes decaied: if they would take order that al the wares made there, should have a speciall marke; and that marke to be set to none, but to such as be truely wrought. And also that every artificer dwelling out of all townes (such as cannot for the commodity of their occupations, be brought to any towne to enhabite, as fullers, tanners, and clothiers) should bee limitted to bee under the direction of one good towne or other; and they to sell no ware, but such as are first approved and sealed by the towne that they are lymited unto. And by these two meanes; that is to say, fyrste by staying of wares wrought beyond sea, which might be wrought within us, from comming in to be sold. Secondly, by restraining of our wolles, tinne, felles, and other commodityes, from passing over unwrought: And thirdly, by brynging in (under the correction of good towns) artificers dwelling in the countreies; making wares to be solde outward, and these wares to be viewed and sealed by the towne seale, before they shoulde bee solde: I woulde thynke oure townes myght be soone restored to theyr auncyent wealth, or farre bettered if they would follow this." *Harl. Misc.* IX. 187.

A.D. 1558
—1608.

try rests on a very interesting classification of employ-
. Vintners, haberdashers, or mercers who sell wares
beyond the seas are really engaged in sending coinage >
f the realm: bakers, brewers, builders, saddlers and
th who supply the home market only, neither bring
ye in, nor send it out: but clothiers and others who
wares for export help to bring treasure into the realm[1].
ivision corresponds roughly with that in the Elizabe-
'Statute of labourers and apprentices," but the general
of that measure is physiocratic. Hence it leans to
:velopment of agriculture, while the whole preference
s dialogue is given to the trades which manufactured
hing that we might sell to other nations. High tariffs
ported "trifles" would give more employment as they
give the manufacturers of thread prints the command
: home market and save a drain of treasure. But
er principle comes in to justify a restraint on certain
s of imports; we ought to procure such goods as "serve
ity," not those that "serve pleasure," we should procure _Thrifty_
which as they are consumed give opportunity for the _goods._
cing of more wealth. This is illustrated by the story
: Welsh town of Caermarthen, "When there came a
n vessel thither out of England, all laden with apples,
aforetime was wont to bring them good corn, the
commanded that none should buy the said apples upon
at pain, and so the boat stood so long in the haven
ut sale or vent, till the apples were putrified and lost.
when the owner demanded of the bailiff of the town why
d stayed his sale and vent, the bailiff answered again
the said vessel came thither to fetch the best wares
had in the country as friezes, broad cloths and wool and
d thereof he should leave them in their country but
: that should be spent and wasted in less than a week;
aid, 'Bring us corn or malt, as ye were wont to do (and
of the country hath need) and ye shall be welcome at
1es, and ye shall have free vent and sale thereof in our
" This Welsh bailiff evidently regarded apples as the
n economist does pine apples as a typical extravagance,

---

[1] _Briefe Conceipt_, in _Harleian Miscellany_, IX. 186.

A.D. 1558
—1603.
and he desired to have goods that were suitable for the support of labourers or as we may call them articles of productive consumption. It is important to notice, however, that the classification of employment has clear reference to the aim of obtaining treasure; it is not a division into productive and unproductive labour, but rather into profitable, non-profitable and unprofitable labour, according as any craft facilitated the import of bullion or had no favourable effect on foreign trade.

Commercial Morality as exhibited in 189. This plain recognition of the fact that the State might be economically justified in allowing free play to individual self-interest marks a distinct departure from the commercial morality which had held its ground from time immemorial. But the completeness of the change is more clearly seen when we turn to the subject which formed the very foundation of the traditional doctrine on all other points, and note the progress of a revolution in public opinion about monetary transactions.

It has been noticed above[1] that there were, during the thirteenth century, so many recognised pleas which entitled men to take 'interest,' that the whole doctrine might have broken down if it had not been for the constant support it received from public opinion. But during the sixteenth century public opinion underwent a change; (*a*) the law was modified *successive Statutes* so as to permit practices which had hitherto been condemned, (*b*) the changed circumstances of trade affected the attitude taken by practical men, while (*c*) the phalanx of theological authority was broken, and (*d*) the arguments from expediency were no longer convincing. It is important to follow out these changes in some detail, for the doctrine of the moralists about the nature of money and price affected practical life in many ways; and till it lost its hold there was little opportunity for a clearer understanding of the nature of exchange[2], or for an improved analysis of value.

(*a*) The first sign of this change so far as the law is concerned is to be found in a statute passed in 1545. This condemns all 'usury' or payments for the mere *use* of money,

---

[1] § 84. Vol. i. p. 238.   [2] See below, § 239.

d been done from time immemorial, and specifies one of A.D. 1558—1603.
ɿost common evasions of the law[1]; but its main object
limit the rate of 'interest' which was allowable, that is
the payments which might be received on the definite
that had always been recognised,—such as delay in
ment (*poena conventionalis*). According to the old view
might be special grounds for claiming more than the
y lent, and it was fair to take something (*id quod
st*) under such special circumstances, but unfair to
payment for the mere use (*usuria*), if no such special
nstances could be proved. The practical effect of this
e was to abolish this distinction; it aimed at limiting
itant claims though made on good grounds, but it 1565?
ed in giving lenders facilities for claiming a moderate
n cases, where according to the old way of thinking,
should have been paid. By limiting excessive 'interest'
ct opened the way for moderate 'usury.' That this was
fect may be gathered from the statute of 1552 which
bits interest as well as usury[2]; but this act cannot have
d satisfactorily for it was repealed in 1571, and the act
45 was revived[3]. Despite the strong verbal condemna-
of usury there can be little doubt that the practical
of the Elizabethan measure was to render usury legal,
g as it was moderate. This becomes perfectly clear in
atute of 1624; although entitled 'an Act against Usury,'
really directed against excessive rates, and 'usury' is
itly permitted so long as it does not exceed eight *per*
; there is a mere tribute to the older opinion in the
clause which forbids that this act shall be construed so
"allow the practice of usury in point of religion or
ience."

urrent opinion as to right and wrong is embodied in the
f the land, and the modifications which were introduced
ccessive statutes give us the most precise means for

y the fictitious sale of goods which were repurchased at a later date for less

and 6 Ed. VI. c. 20.
Eliz. c. 8. This statute makes an exception in regard to the Orphans' fund
lon. Mosse, *Arraignment* (1595), 159.
James I. c. 17.

A.D. 1558
—1603.

1624.

*Changed
conditions
of trade.*

tracing the change in public sentiment. This is also reflected in the pamphlet literature of the time[1]; the facts
stated, the tone taken by the controversialists on each side,
the manner in which old arguments are re-stated, and the
very language employed, will all serve to indicate the direction, and even the rate of change.

190. (*b*) This great revolution of general feeling was not
merely due to the diffusion of new opinions on the subject:
that was an important element, but there were widespread
changes that rendered men more ready to accept, and more
anxious to propound these new doctrines; the most important factor was the revolution in English commerce which
occurred during the sixteenth century; for various circumstances had combined to bring about an entire recasting of
the ordinary business system of the country. For one thing,
the exclusive trading of the great gilds had suffered a
series of severe blows, and it was open to any one to engage

[1] Thomas Rogers, who published translations of P. Caesar, entitled a *General
Discourse against the damnable sect of usurers* and of Nicolas Hemming's *Lawful
use of Ritches* (1578), deplores the change of sentiment. "If but a probable suspicion
rose of a man to occupie that filthie trade, he was taken for a devill in the likeness
of a man * * But goode Lorde, how is the Worlde chaunged? That which Infidels
cannot abide, Gospellers allowe, that which the Jews take onlie of straungers, and
will not take of their owne Countreimen for shame, that doe Christians take of
their deare freindes, and thinke for so doing they deserve greate thankes" (Epist.
Ded.). Richard Porder in his *Sermon* (1570) connects the growing practice of
lending money to the rich with engrossing, as this could be done by men who had
the use of large capital (p. 59). Miles Mosse in dedicating his *Arraignment and
Conviction of Usurie* (1595) to Archbishop Whitgift assigns as one of his reasons,
—" your Grace is reported to bee one who neither lendeth, nor taketh upon usurie,
which is not in this age every such mans commendation."

That moderate usury is right, was commonly assumed in the early part of the
xviith century by writers, who discuss what the rate of usury should be, see below,
§ 243. The men who opposed all usury, on theological and legal grounds, in
the seventeenth century write as if they were conscious that public opinion is
against them. Among them we find Bishop Andrews who maintained the thesis
Usuras legitimas esse illicitas when proceeding his degree as Bachelor of
Divinity, *Opuscula Posthuma*, 119, Sanderson, Blaxton and Holmes. Fenton's
Treatise of Usury was the most celebrated and called forth a reply from Sir
Robert Filmer, *Quaestio Quodlibetica* (1653), which came to be the classical expression of the opinion then current among well-doing men that only 'biting'
usury was unlawful. Before the close of the century however the controversy was
practically over, and though Mr David Jones, *Farewell Sermon* (1692), p. 84, at
S. Mary's Woolnoth roused passing excitement, it was treated with contemptuous
ridicule; see *The Lombard Street Lecturers late Farewell Sermon answered, or
the Welsh Levite Toss'd De Novo* (1692) [Brit. Mus. T. 752 (2)].

in commerce and to win its rewards. The great improve- A.D. 1558 —1608.
ments in the management of estates—as well as the planting of new industries—brought much wealth into the hands
of many citizens all through the country. But almost equally *Formation of Capital.*
important was the fact that owing to the supplies of silver
from America this easily acquired wealth took the form of
bullion, so that it could both be easily stored and easily
transferred for purposes of profit. For the first time in the
history of England the circumstances were present which
rendered the general formation of capital possible.

At the same time the very conditions which had contributed to the formation of private capitals, opened new
opportunities for their employment even without breaking
the laws of Henry VIII. and Elizabeth. If men cared to take
shares in trading enterprises, these enterprises were more *Opportuni-ties for in-vestment.*
frequent and successful than ever before, and the gain from
ventures or loans on bottomry would be large. If the purchase of rents was not such a wise investment under the circumstances, it was one to which no objection would be raised;
while the pleas of incidental loss and cessation of gain
would serve to justify the payment of interest for sums lent in
other ways. We may thus say that the English law as it stood
permitted a sufficient freedom of investment for an immense
extension of transactions to take place under the new social and
monetary conditions, without any modification of the old rules.

But one thing was noticeable now. Plenty of people
had capital to invest, and others could tell of means to
employ it, but the two did not always come in contact: it
was convenient to many people to lend their money to a
merchant or goldsmith who should for his part look out for *The Gold-smiths.*
opportunities of trading with it. In this way the transactions of the capitalist with the goldsmith were strictly
usurious according to the old definitions, while those of the
goldsmith with the shipowner were not. In the one case a
man bargained for a payment for the mere loan of money, in
the other he got interest, or payment for risk undertaken or
loss endured. Yet after all, if the goldsmiths' loans were
justifiable, those of the capitalist were hardly to be condemned. He enabled the goldsmith to carry on a lawful

calling; he did indirectly what the goldsmith did directly, and though, according to the form of the bargain he was undoubtedly guilty of usury, it was impossible to pronounce a condemnation without including in it much that had been deemed lawful, time out of mind. Moralists might be suspicious of the motives which tempted men to regard what they found so profitable as fair; divines might quote the words of Scripture, and civilians descant on points of law, but common opinion found itself in a dilemma. If the old view was to be maintained, it was imperative either to prohibit what had always been allowed, or else to condemn a man for doing through an agent what he might do freely *Was all* on his own account. The logic of common sense decided *usury still* that the old view should not be maintained. The learned *wrong?* might adduce authorities without end to show that men of all ages had condemned it; but if they were asked to show why it was wrong then and there, they could only fall back on this general consent of men in times bygone.

No man who took 6% from a goldsmith felt he was gaining at his expense or doing a wrong to him—or any one else, and the attempt to maintain the old objection failed, not because it had always been futile, but because the change of conditions had removed all its force. Indeed it is to be noticed that the change of conditions has not everywhere taken place; there are many lands where bullion is scarce, and those who have the command of it possess a monopoly of the means of saving capital; there are many lands where social barriers have prevented the general diffusion of wealth; in such cases there is no concourse of would-be investors, and there are few openings for profitable ventures. In them the evils of usury may become as rampant as ever, the moral objection is as strong as ever, and the need for the state to interfere to regulate the bonds of debtors and to prevent remorseless distraint may be as necessary as in the time of Edward I.

Justifica-
tion of
interest
from
circum-
stances.
We speak airily about the freedom of the individual to get what he can for the use of his money—but it is desirable that we should recognise that only under very special conditions is such freedom at all tolerable. It is not a question of

the use for which a man's money is lent—whether productive A.D. 1558 —1608. or unproductive. He may lend to a farmer on terms which absorb the whole or more than the whole profit accruing from the land; and such a contract is usurious as much as that of the money-lender who supplies an "infant" with the means of gratifying every caprice. Nor is it a question of felt oppression by the borrower, for his need may be so great that any extortion is a less evil than the failure to obtain immediate supplies entails. The freedom for individuals to make the most they can of their money only ceases to be a danger when much capital is being formed and is ready for investment, and when that capital is in many hands. The one necessary condition is that the society should have reached a stage of economic development in which there is capital seeking investment, and where the competition of many owners tends to prevent any from securing exorbitant terms.

191. (c) Circumstances alter cases, but when there is *Wilson* 1569. such an extraordinary change of circumstances we cannot be surprised that a great difficulty was felt in applying the old principles to the changed conditions. Instead of the old unanimity, we find a perfect chaos of conflicting judgments which are excellently portrayed in Wilson's *Discourse upon Usurie.* This was published in 1569, that is to say before the Statute of Henry VIII. was re-enacted by Elizabeth, and it gives us a very vivid picture of London opinion on the subject as represented by a merchant, his apprentice, a preacher, a lawyer, and a doctor of laws. It may perhaps be most convenient for our purpose, however, to discuss the various conflicting opinions which were put forward by the different religious parties.

First of all we must notice the line taken by Puritanism, and by this I mean an opinion which rested on the letter of the Bible, as interpreted by private judgment. Texts could be found in the Old Testament which prohibited the taking *Henry* of any increase for money—that is to say, which prohibited *Smith.* interest or recompense of any kind as well as usury. This view was maintained by the silver-tongued lecturer at S. Clement Danes in two of the discourses which attracted so much attention in London at one time; and he inveighs strongly[1] against the "evasions" of this scriptural prohibition by men who bought an interest in some estate, or lent money on mortgage, or gave advances in partnership with merchants, or were concerned in other such transactions to which no exception had ever been taken before. This very rigid doctrine found expression in the measure passed under

1552.
Edward VI. which simply condemns increase of every kind[2]—interest and usury and all else—under the same penalties.

Jewish and Puritan morality
Here then at last we have a case of that blind following of the Old Testament rules which has been ascribed to the Church—but mistakenly ascribed. The Church condemned all greed of gain, and condemned any increase that seemed to be clearly due to greed of gain; but the doctrine which was now enforced was Jewish and Puritan, but certainly not Christian. It was the outcome of a mode of thought which treated the moral precepts of the Old Testament as binding in all countries and for all time, and which neglected the existence of a living power to provide against new forms of evil in some new way. It regarded the Old Testament Scriptures not as the revelation of God's dealings with His ancient people, but as a code of commands which should be constantly enforced; and thus it shifted the foundation on

as opposed to Christian teaching.
which the whole structure of Christian morality had been reared, by appealing to the letter of an ancient code instead of trusting to the utterances of a divinely-instructed Christian Consciousness.

The immediate effect of the new doctrine however must have been very serious, especially on conscientious Englishmen who sought to do their duty. They were now told by the preachers that practices which had been approved in all ages, and which they and their fathers had practised without scruple, were condemned by God's law; that no true distinction could be drawn between fair increase and heinous usury, because the Old Testament made none. The overstrained interpretation of these texts brought the preachers into direct conflict with the old Christian opinion as to right and wrong in these matters; they held that all modes of obtain-

---

[1] Henry Smith, *Examination of Usury* (1591), p. 17.
[2] 5 and 6 Ed. VI. c. 20.

ing increase were equally wrong, but they forged a weapon for those who were ready to argue that all were equally right.

But the Puritans were by no means unanimous in adopting this interpretation, there were some who regarded it as "overprecise," and who were tempted by stress of circumstances to act on their laxer opinion. The Marian exiles were in many cases reduced to great want, and those who had escaped with their possessions were fain to make the most of them. Some of these refugees during their residence *Calvin.* in Geneva and elsewhere had been therefore drawn into transactions that had hitherto been stigmatised as usurious[1], and Calvin, Bucer, and others were forced to appear as their apologists. The former expressed an opinion hesitatingly and reluctantly; for he evidently regarded usury as an evil,— but felt unable to draw the line between transactions that were admittedly fair and those that had hitherto been condemned. He saw dangers on both sides:—" Si totallement nous defendons les usures nous estraignons les consciences dun lien plus estroict que Dieu mesme. Si nous permettons le moins du monde plusieurs aincontinent soubs ceste couverture prennent une licence effrenee dont ils ne peuvent porter que par aulcune exception on leur limite quelque mesure[2]";—and it seems strange that his very hesitating pronouncement should have attained such celebrity as a justification of money-lending. But it had a very real importance, not as a learned discussion of the difficulties in the light of patristic teaching and ecclesiastical decisions, but because it disposed once and for all of the new-fangled Puritan doctrine and the overstrained interpretation of the Bible which had made itself felt under Edward VI. Calvin regarded the passage in S. Luke as rhetorical and as referring to an excellent ideal, not to actual practical life[3]; it gives a counsel of perfection. Again, the command in Deuteronomy was treated as binding on us, only so far as equity and human reason reiterate it; and the denunciations of the prophets

---

[1] Wilson, *Discourse*, f. 179. Fenton, *Treatise of Usurie*, p. 60.

[2] "Corpus Reformatorum." Calvini *Opera*, x. i. 244.

[3] Molina argued that it prohibited such rates of interest as were oppressive, but that it enjoined lending as an act of charity and without expecting even the return of the principal. *Tract. Contract. et Usurarum*, 11.

were viewed as directed against the Jews, because usury was forbidden to them, while all usury is not forbidden us.

He takes his stand on the fairness of such transactions as the buying of rents; it is as fair to lend a rich man money on interest, as to take his estate on pledge and profit by it; and to condemn the one and allow the other is mere playing with words. On the other hand, the danger of oppression and of covetousness, the duty of doing as one would be done by, the necessity of being guided by public good not by our own gain, are all noted; and the custom of the country is not to be taken as relieving our own consciences; moreover, he could not allow that anyone should practise usury as a calling.

Calvin then agreed with men like Henry Smith in disregarding the old distinctions in this matter, but he completely undermined the position from which they had so solemnly warned citizens against evading God's law, by lending on mortgage. Calvin held that lending on mortgage was obviously fair and right; and the differences of opinion between these teachers produced their necessary result, and by rendering men doubtful as to the right and wrong of the matter, tempted them to regard the whole discussion with indifference, and to enter on any contract that gave them a prospect of gain.

Subsequent Puritan writers[1] appear to have followed the line which Calvin took, and to have trusted to the private consciences of interested dealers to decide cases that proved *No positive doctrine on the subject.* too hard for learned doctors in their studies. Nor is there any attempt to reconstruct a third doctrine of fair dealing, out of the ruins of the Puritan prohibition, on the space from which the canon law had been cleared. The preachers were a great power in all the reformed countries, and they do not appear to have made much use of their influence in upholding a new standard of commercial morality. The "Pope's laws" were treated with contempt, as containing much that was evil, in all countries where the Reformation had made any way; and when the leaders of the Calvinistic and Zwinglian parties explained away the Scriptural prohibitions, there was no firm ground which could be taken for reproving

---

[1] Pearson, *Theories of Usury*, p. 79, and Haweis's *Reformation Sketches*, c. 12.

any usurious practices that were permitted by civil or muni- cipal law[1]. The strict ecclesiastical discipline which was reared in Scotland does not appear to have been much concerned with attempting to check extortion or greed of gain: its authors were so eager to root out witchcraft[2] that they had little time to attack covetousness, and were more ready to put down promiscuous dancing[3] than to prevent usurious contracts.

The combined influence of capital in altering the conditions of commercial life and of Puritanism in overstraining and undermining the restrictions which were contained in the Jewish Law are sufficient to account for the revolution in public opinion. The old Christian doctrine was not without its defenders indeed: Nicholas Sanders wrote a little *Sanders.* tract on the subject in which, besides adducing many forcible considerations, he dwells on an argument that came into little prominence till this period, and that did not do much to support the cause he had at heart. You have no right to sell Time, since it is not a human possession at all, but something that lies in God's power alone; the portion of time granted "was not of your gift to your neighbour but of God's gift to you both[4]." But where there is a constant market for capital a man cannot be condemned for charging according to the length of time, for he is kept from making use of other opportunities of profit during all that time. He does not sell the Time itself, but he calculates the fair remuneration for *lucrum cessans* in terms of time.

192. (d) When we turn to consider the attitude of other English writers during the reigns of Elizabeth and James we find two different lines of argument used by those who desired to maintain the old Christian standpoint.

Several writers argued on political grounds against allow- *Political danger.* ing the practice of usury. They held that it was injurious to the State, because men were tempted to leave off undertaking the risks of trade or the toil of labour, if they could gain from letting out their money on good security[5]. Now,

---

[1] This is the gist of the celebrated treatises of Salmasius.
[2] *Acts of Assembly*, 44, 216.   [3] *Ib.* 201, 311.
[4] *Briefe Treatise of Usurie* (Louvain, 1568), 49. Cf. *Opusc. de usuris*, 8.
[5] Wilson, *Discourse upon Usurie*, 1569, f. 184 *seq.*

A.D. 1558
—1608.

while this was true of the Roman Empire, and may be true of
many lands, it was not, generally speaking, true of England, as
events proved: and therefore the historical proof, of the same
thesis which other writers put forward, is not convincing to
our minds.   It may be true that Rome and countless other
empires have been destroyed by usury, but to argue that it
is therefore proved that usury is always a danger to the
State, is only to give an excellent example of that false
induction which lurks in all generalisations from history[1].
Calvin, and writers of all schools, call attention to the political danger of usury; but without attempting a general
argument on the point, it is sufficient to state that in
England, according to the common opinion of men, the
liberty to lend freely has been generally beneficial, and not
the reverse.   As the growth of capital has continued, the
rate at which men could lend it declined, and experience
proved abundantly that facilities for borrowing at a low rate
of interest were beneficial as developing the resources of the
country[2].   We need not follow out this line through the
writings of Bentham and the abolition of the usury laws;
though it is worthy of notice that a practical man of business
like Cobden did not seem to be completely convinced as to
the wisdom of this course[3].

*City
opinion.*

The other line of argument was taken chiefly by traders
and City men, as we may infer from its being put forward by
men of this type in Wilson's dialogue, and from its occurrence
in a merchant's chapters on the subject.   They held that
only "biting" usury was oppressive, if you lent to a merchant who made gain with your money, it was fair to charge
him for the use of it; but if you lent to the poor husbandman
it should be as a gratuitous kindness[4].   The Puritans repudiated this doctrine as lax and unworthy,—any usury was
sin against God whether it was "biting" or not; while they
insisted that all usury was biting, and the difference was one

[1] See however the recent argument on this line by the French banker, A.
Bouron, in his *Guerre au Crédit.*

[2] See below, § 244, p. 251.

[3] Cobden's *Political Writings; What next and next?* p. 294.

[4] Wilson, *Discourse,* f. 139.   Malynes, *Lex Mercatoria,* pt. ii. c. 10.

of degree only[1]. And it may be questioned whether this distinction is so clear as to be satisfactory. Can a man— especially an interested man—be trusted to decide rightly whether bargains are fair or not? Are there not cases where the most moderate charge for the use of money may be oppressive, as when it is applied to improving poor soils? or when a needy man is glad to get money at rates that are really oppressive, because money is needed to deliver him from worse oppression, as *e.g.* when a peasant is glad to bargain for money at an exorbitant rate so that he may pay a rack-rent? Oppressiveness is not a decisive mark by which conduct should be tried *in foro interno*, as it is the greed that is to be condemned, not its evil effects.

Now though this is true, it is also true that oppressive- *Oppressiveness as* ness may serve usefully as a negative test. We cannot say *a test.* all pecuniary transactions that are not oppressive are right, and may be done with a clear conscience; but we can say all transactions that are oppressive are wrong in some way or other, and therefore are to be condemned. And we cannot venture to neglect the importance of this distinction, and of the consideration of the consequences of actions, because it does not give us a complete solution of all the difficulties. Indeed the same objection might be urged in regard to any suggested criterion of right and wrong in actions. We can only point out that certain things are wrong, but never give a man an assurance that in pursuing a certain line of conduct he is sure to be right. Absolute rules cannot be laid down to tell us what our conduct ought to be, but only to condemn what ought not to be done. And the argument which had commended itself to practical minds was at last adopted by theologians: it is well stated by Peter Baro[2], who for a long time was Lady Margaret Professor at Cambridge:—

"The last verse containeth yet two things, whereof the *Baro.*

---

[1] "There is difference in deed between the biting of a dogge and the biting of a flea, and yet, though the flea doth the lesse harm, yet the flea dooth bite after hir kinde, yea, and draweth blood too. But what a world this is, that men will make sinne to be but a flea biting, when they see God's word directly against them." Wilson, *Discourse*, f. 66.

[2] For an account of him see Fuller's *History of the University of Cambridge*, Section vii. 10, 21, 22.

first is, that he giveth not his money to Usurie: touching which pointe, many thinges were to be spoken, if the time would suffer: but we must be content with a fewe. This then is the meaning of the Prophet, that albeit in the Common weale by reason of the sundry affaires and dealings of men among themselves, and the use of money so manifold, and necessary for the trafficks of men, and that almost in every contract and bargaine: albeit, I say, for these and such other like causes, it is plaine and evident, that all gaine, which is gotten by money is not to be condemned, yet a godly man must take diligent heed sith there is also so great and many abuses of money, least he abuse his moneye to the hurt of his neighbour: as it is a usual practice among rich men and some of the greater sort, who by lending, or by giving out their money to usurie, are wont to snare and oppress the poore and needier sorte: as they commonly are wont to do, who sitting idle at home make marchandise only of their money, by giving it out in this sort to such needy persons, altogither for gaines sake, without having any regard to his commoditie, to whome they gave it, but onely of their owne gaine. For by this craft they easily get many into their snares whome they do not only bite, which is meant by the noune נשׁך nashac, which David useth, but also devoure and spoyle. But the true worshippers of God are far from this wickednes, seeing they embrace others with true brotherlye love, neither will they do that to any which they would not have done to themselves. Which rule in human affaires and contractes, is diligentlye of us evermore to be observed if we will live uprightly as becommeth us[1]."

Holden. Baro was not the only French divine who took this view of the subject: Molina had advocated it, and it was clearly put by Henri Holden, who wrote in 1642, "Ubi praeceptio lucri ex mutuo proximum non laedit illicita forsitan et injusta non erit, quamvis propriam cujusdam usurae naturam participet[2]." The doctrine which was somewhat of a novelty

---

[1] *Fowre Sermons and two Questions as they were uttered and disputed ad clerum in S. Maries Church and Schools in Cambridge.* Sermon II. on Ps. xv. p. 419. Appended to *Special treatise of Gods Providence.*

[2] Quoted by Marin-Darbel, *L'usure, sa définition*, p. 178.

at that date has come to be very generally adopted by Roman divines since[1]. (This too appears to be the ordinary English view in the present day; as we find the word usury in common conversation implies oppressive interest, and has lost the signification which attached to it when there was no real market for capital; it had then meant payment for the use of money when the charge was not justified by any real risk undertaken or inconvenience sustained by the lender. Perhaps it already bore this modern and popular sense rather than the ancient and technical one when it was condemned by the CIX. Canon of 1604.

193. Many illustrations of these changes of opinion may be found in the information we have as to alterations in commercial practice and in the conduct of business. The formation of capital and the opening up of facilities for employing it were, as has been noted above, conditions which brought about the change in opinion, and this change reacted on the habits of business men. As trading on borrowed capital became profitable, it also became more general; as it became more general, and the strong feeling in regard to the morality of such transactions was gradually modified, the practice of lending money for usury was not merely permitted under exceptional circumstances but was recognised as legitimate, so long as the rate demanded was not excessive[2].

The opportunities which were thus opened up for trading on borrowed capital seem to have exposed the old-established merchants to unwonted competition: in the fifteenth and earlier part of the sixteenth century the Merchant Companies had become somewhat exclusive corporations, and young men had difficulty in obtaining entrance to them; in the end of

Marginal notes: A.D. 1558 —1608. *Commercial practice and excessive rates.* *Competition of new men.*

---

[1] Mastrofini, *Discussion sur l'usure*, and compare Funk, *Zins und Wucher*, p. 6.

[2] The moral influence of prohibitive statutes must have been weakened by the necessity of making exemptions. The Statute of 5 and 6 Ed. VI. had forbidden the taking of usury and interest, but it was continually set aside and increase permitted by royal license.

License by the queen to Sir Wm Garrard and others to receive 10% on their loan of £30,000 to the Crown without incurring the penalties of the statute against usury. Sept. 1561. *State Papers, Dom., Eliz.* XIX.

Gresham raised money for the queen at 12% and 6% in 1570, the lenders having discharges from the statute of usury. Ellis, *Orig. Letters*, 2^d *Series*, II. pp. 316, 319.

A.D. 1558
—1603.
Elizabeth's reign we hear new complaints. Men who had made money at retail trades were forcing their way into foreign commerce, not always with profit to themselves, and sometimes to the loss of other traders, whose market they spoiled[1]. Others who were apprenticed were able to borrow money and deal on a large scale before they had really learned their business: the opportunity of borrowing "caused many apprentices to become untimely masters, when as swimming with other men's bladders they are soon drowned[2]." Some of them, however, were sharp enough to take good care of themselves, and to prosper at the expense of easy-going masters[3].

From these two different sides their unwonted competition was bringing disorder into the old-established trade usages; these younger merchants who recklessly pursued their own gain with little regard to the good of the trade introduced *Well-ordered trade.* a new and as it seemed unwholesome competition. The old practice had been to have the whole carried on by rule, as to the times of sailing, terms of purchase and so forth: the very necessity of sailing under convoy led to the formation of merchant fleets, and the desire of gain prevented competition between those who sailed together. The organisation of the Flanders Galleys[4] at Venice, when the number of galleys was voted by the Senate according to the state of the markets and the entire regulations were a matter of public concern, may be taken as typical of mediæval commerce, and Elizabeth created new organisations for regulating *Merchant Adventurers.* various branches of trade. Despite the opposition of the tailors, the Merchant Adventurers of Exeter were empowered to carry on the cloth trade with France[5]. A Spanish company, with a branch at Exeter was also formed[6], though it did not have a very long life, as it was dissolved in 1606 and the trade was thrown open[7]. The discussions of that year show how competition was breaking up well-ordered trade; but it held its own in the Baltic. The doings of the 'straggling' merchants at Narva[8] led to the extension of the powers of the

---

[1] Wheeler, *A Treatise of Commerce* (1601), 78. Compare Bagehot, *Lombard Street*, p. 9.　　[2] Malynes, *S. George* (1601), 39.
[3] Hall, *Elizabethan Society*, p. 50.　　[4] Brown, *Calendar*, I. lxii.
[5] Cotton, *Elizabethan Guild*, 3, 25.　　[6] *Ib.* 78.
[7] 3 James I. c. 6.　　[8] Stow, *Survey*, II. bk. v. p. 268.

Muscovy Merchants in 1566 and subsequently to the incorpora- *A.D. 1558 —1608.* tion of the Eastland Company, who argued effectively about the advantages of regulated trade in 1689[1]. The strong view *East India Company.* which is expressed in the minutes of the East India Company's Court about the evils of private trading serves as another illustration, and they were probably right in supposing that the only complete security for the maintenance of a well-ordered trade lay, not in any regulations as to the stint·or any rules of trading, but in working with a joint stock and only dividing the profits. It is curious that the form of trading which they eventually adopted to maintain well-ordered trade against "interlopers," who made use of free competition, should be now turned into the agent by which the severest competition is brought to bear on old-established firms.

194. Besides these alterations in the methods of con- *Facilities for inter-communication.* ducting foreign trade, there were great changes in the internal trade of the country. Authorities seem to agree that the roads and means of intercommunication were in a very bad state, and there may have been greater physical obstacles to internal trade than in some earlier ages[2]; but so far as laws and institutions were concerned there was a very marked change. It seems as if the national organisation was really becoming complete, as if the local barriers were at last broken down, and each locality was treated not as an inde- *Municipal barriers broken down.* pendent body to be cherished for its own sake, but as a member which ought to contribute to the general prosperity of England. Municipalities had still a useful part to play for purposes of police, but they, and the institutions they had brought into being, were ceasing to be of importance for trade purposes. Where local companies exercised an important influence on any branch of trade, they generally claimed to exercise powers granted by the Crown, and not merely to act in the name of local authorities.

The story of the various patentees and their projects *Fluidity of Capital.* shows that there was a free flow of capital to any part of the

---

[1] Stow, *Survey*, II. bk. v. 263. See also *Reasons humbly offered by the Merchants of Hull* (1661). [Brit. Mus. 816 m. 11 (100).]

[2] Thorold Rogers, *Agriculture and Prices*, IV. 217.

A.D. 1558
—1603.
country. Wherever there was a chance of starting a new industry the capitalist would settle, and bring the hands who were necessary to carry on the trade. Thus there was a ready flow of capital into any direction where it could be used to advantage, while the accounts we read of the gold-smiths' trade give the impression that men from all parts of the country were ready to make deposits in London. Both in regard to the accumulation and the employment of capital we can see how easily it flowed throughout the whole land.

Fluidity of labour

The old restrictions on the fluidity of labour were also at an end. So far as rural districts are concerned villeinage had probable ceased to have any influence in hampering the labourer's movements. It might be a serious matter so far as the tenure of land was concerned, for the man might be called upon to forfeit his holding[1] on very trivial grounds, or there might be disputes about the customs by which he was bound, and manumission was a formal privilege which Eliza-

in country districts

beth conferred on many of her tenants[2]. Villeinage might possibly be of some importance in legal proceedings, as the right of certain persons to plead might turn upon the point[3]. But it was no longer in all probability a real hindrance to personal movement; the *nativus* who left his native estate was not sought for or fetched back, and this great barrier to the fluidity of labour was practically at an end.

and in towns.

In the towns there was something similar; the exclusive rights of freemen of a town, or members of a company in a town, to ply their trade appear to have been set aside by the Act of Edward VI.[4] It was then ordained that "no person shall interrupt, deny, let or disturb any Freemason, rough mason, carpenter, bricklayer, plasterer, joiner, hardhewer, sawyer, tiler, pavier, glasier, limeburner, brickmaker, tile-maker, plumber, or labourer, borne in this realm or made denizen to work in any of the said crafts in any city, borough or town corporate," although the said person did not dwell in the City where he worked, and was not free of the same. This clause was subsequently set aside so far as London was con-

---

[1] Norden, *Surveyor's Dialogue*, 60.   [2] Rymer, *Foedera*, xv. 731.
[3] Hall, *Elizabethan Society*, 35.
[4] 2 and 3 Ed. VI. c. 15, § 3. Compare Sheppard, *Of Corporations*, § 8.

cerned[1]; this may be a sign of the jealousy which was so *A.D. 1558 —1603.* generally felt of the growth of the City, a feeling which found expression in Elizabethan proclamations[2]; but it bore on the face of it that it was intended to favour and protect the heavily taxed citizens. Exclusive claims were created in certain cases where trades were incorporated, or where special measures were passed by Parliament; but municipal privileges appear to have been set aside very completely, so far as the exercise of any trade, and the supervision over that trade was concerned. There was at all events a decided step in the direction of fluidity of labour, even if many practical obstacles remained partly through customary privileges which no one questioned, and partly through new grants from Parliament or the Crown.

The fluidity of capital and the fluidity of labour, with a com- *National Economic Organism.* mon law throughout any area, were noted by Bagehot[3] as the marks of a nation for economic purposes; and we may certainly say that in the time of Elizabeth there was a national economic life in this country such as had never been known before.

The decline of local economic authority is seen in another *Forestall-ing and Engrossing at Local Markets.* way; the laws against forestalling and engrossing[4] were first rendered nugatory by a system of licences and then allowed to drop. They had been made for the most part in the supposed interest of small local markets; no one was to monopolise the supply coming to any town and make goods dearer in that market. If he claimed that he was going to sell the products in a distant place where they were badly off, he would not be excused; why should corn be made unnecessarily dear here, in order that some other place might be more plentifully supplied[5]? But in the time of Elizabeth, this local exclusiveness was breaking down, and bodgers[6] were busily engaged in buying up corn, they would raise prices in local markets, but the practice probably tended to the advantage of the realm as a whole, and certainly to the encouragement of the agricultural interest.

---

[1] 3 and 4 Ed. VI. c. 20.   [2] See below, p. 172.
[3] *Economic Studies*, 40, 41.   [4] 5 and 6 Ed. VI. c. 14, and 5 Eliz. c. 12.
[5] Common buying on behalf of a town corporate was allowed, however, 5 and 6 Ed. VI. c. 14, § 5.   [6] Harrison, in Holinshed, I. 340.

A.D. 1558
—1603.
Justices of
the Peace.
Even when it was impossible to frame general regulations and some local administration was required, we may notice that the old institutions are to some extent set aside. The justices of the peace, exercising the queen's commission, come to the front, the manorial courts sink into the background. So too with regard to the poor; it was here that the conflict between a local and a national system[1] of administration was most obvious and most disastrous. The whole was based on the parochial system; but it could not be worked effectively in all parishes without the occasional interference of the justices; and the tendency of subsequent legislation has been to diminish the importance of the parochial authorities and to rely more and more on centralised administration.

Bankrupts 195. Keen competition and speculative trading seem to have had their natural result in an increase in the number of 1543. bankrupts[2]. The first Act on this matter[3] seems to be directed against men who indulged in very prodigal expenditure and then made off, and the curious statute which insists on cash payments for foreign apparel and wares, except in the case *through ex-* of purchasers who had £3000 a year[4], was probably aimed at *travagance.* the same class of dishonest but "delicate livers," but the Act of 1571 is specially intended to apply to traders[5], and it ordains that anyone who exercised his trade by way of bargaining, exchange, rechange, bartering or otherwise, in gross or retail, and who fled the country, or took sanctuary should be reputed bankrupt, and his estate should be administered for the benefit of his creditors by commissioners appointed by the Lord Chancellor. It is not unlikely too that the increase *Borrowed* of bankruptcy was due to other causes also: as the practice *Capital.* of lending money for usury became common, those who were in temporary difficulties would be less likely to obtain gratuitous loans from their friends. All the literature of the day is full of complaints about the decline of this kind of charity[6], while the resources of the gilds were no longer available for helping men to live down some unexpected misfortune. In *Gratuitous* the present day people are inclined to doubt whether such *Loans.*

---

[1] Compare Massie, *Plan*, 108. [2] Wilson, *Discourse on Usurie*, f. 31 b.
[3] 34 and 35 H. VIII. c. 4. [4] 5 Eliz. c. 6.
[5] 13 Eliz. c. 7. [6] Harrison in Holinshed, *Chronicles*, I. 189.

gratuitous lending was ever done even by charitable people, A.D. 1558 and such may esteem Sir Thomas Whyte's benefaction a real —1608. curiosity. He died in 1592 and provided a sum of money which should afford every year a free loan of £25 to each of four young freemen and occupiers to set them up in trade; they were to find sureties for the return of the money at the end of ten years, when it could be lent out to others: twenty-four towns were to share in the benefit of this fund in turn, but if the burgess of any town and his sureties failed to repay the loan, that town was to be struck out of the list for the future[1]. There were very many similar benefactions for gratuitous loans, and parochial authorities endeavoured to grant temporary assistance, under the powers given them by the Act of 1601, by loans out of the parish stock. The accounts for thirty-five years of the fund at Steeple Ashton in Wilts, where loans were made at 10 %, have been printed by Mr Toulmin Smith[2], and give an excellent illustration of the working of such a public friendly society. This must have been a real boon to many young traders, and the change of circumstances which rendered such loans less frequent, and enabled them to try and start with capital borrowed at— 10 per cent. was a doubtful boon and one that may have had something to do with the increased number of bankrupts.

196. Several transactions which had been on the border *Insurance* line, according to the old habit of thought, now became quite common. From time immemorial there had been a method of relieving merchants from the sole responsibility for losses at sea by loans on bottomry[3]. An investor would lend a merchant a certain sum to fit and freight his vessel[4] or pur-

---

[1] Cole MSS. XII., 124, 121. On the mismanagement of this charity by the Corporation of Warwick, see Park's *Charter of Warwick*, p. 26. See also Stow, *Survey*, II. bk. v. p. 62. Similar benefactions occur in many towns.

"Indenture 13 Sept. 1574 of the gift of £20 by Rose Bloyze, widow, to the bailiffs and burgesses of Ipswich, to be employed in loans to four young and poor tradesmen." *Hist. MSS. Com. Rep.* IX. 247.

"Several accounts touching the fund of John How which was confided by him in trust to the Mayor and Corporation of Plymouth, for making loans of money to indigent and worthy persons. Made in the years 1567, 1570, 71, 81, 83, 84, 86, 87, 88, and 1613. *Ib.* 263.   [2] Toulmin Smith, *The Parish*, p. 626.

[3] Hendricks, *Contributions to the History of Insurance*, p. 7.

[4] For an excellent account of the practice in regard to fitting fishing vessel see Hitchcock's *Politic Plat* in Arber, II. 165.

chase a return cargo, on the understanding that he would receive his money back when the ship came in with a definite sum to reimburse him (or a *premium*). This had been
against risks at sea.
regarded as a fair transaction because the lender undertook a considerable risk and was entitled to a profit; he did not bargain for a certainty. In the sixteenth century the more modern form of insurance seems to have become common; the premium was paid in advance and the principal sum only changed hands if the ship was lost, and a claim arose. This mode of insurance became possible when merchants had large capitals of their own or could borrow on their personal credit, but it lent itself to frauds more readily than transactions of the older type. Bacon alludes to it as a familiar practice when he asks, "Doth not the wise merchant in every adventure of danger, give part to have the rest assured?[1]"

Fund for orphans
The great practical difficulty in the old days had been that of making provision for a family in case of death. It was not easy to find trustees, and trustees could not find suitable investments. Public bodies assumed the guardianship of orphans; this system was in operation under Richard II. in London[2] and a similar practice is mentioned in the Custumel of Rye[3]. So long as the City acted as a trustee, and took charge of the orphans' inheritance it was an obvious boon; but a practice seems to have been in use in Elizabeth's time about which casuists were more doubtful. "A merchant lendeth to a corporation or company an hundred pounds, which corporation hath by statute a grant that whosoever lendeth such a sum of money and hath a child of one year, shall have for his child, if the same child do live till he be full fifteen years of age, £500 of money, but if the child die before that time, the father to lose his principal for ever. Whether is this merchant an usurer or no? The law saith, if I lend purposely for gain, notwithstanding the peril or hazard, I am a usurer[4]."

in London.
In the reign of Edward VI. the city of London made elaborate ordinances[5], chiefly intended to prevent the orphans

---

[1] *Parl. Hist.* I. 1558. See below, § 258, p. 289.   [2] Stow, II. bk. v. p. 372.
[3] Lyon, *Dover,* II. 367.   [4] Wilson, *Discourse upon Usurie,* f. 104 b.
[5] Stow, *Survey,* II. bk. v. p. 322.

of freemen from marrying vain and light persons who squan- A.D. 1558
dered their portions; but the whole system was called in —1603.
question in 1586, and the Mayor and Corporation wrote in
defence of the custom to the Privy Council. "The Court of
Orphans[1]," they said, "taketh care for their reasonable maintenance and virtuous education, forseeth that they be not
defrauded by their executors, by concealment, or mispraising
the goods or by false account; nor abused by disparagement
in marriage; provideth safeguard for their portions. So that
neither themselves nor others may misspend the same. And
in the behalf of the orphans do prosecute suits for recovery
or defence of their right. Which provident care had of the
orphans, as aforesaid, doth not only extend to their benefit,
but stretcheth farther to the good of the Widows, Creditors
and Legatories of the Dead, who might, by sinister practice
of the executors be greatly prejudiced if such exact care were
not had. And that which is more, there be a great number
of young and towardly merchants and occupiers within the
City, relieved and profited by the use of orphans' portions,
yielding but an easy allowance to the orphans for their competent maintenance." On this method of managing the
orphans' money Wilson spoke with no uncertain sound.
"Neither do I allow of your order in London for orphans'
money, because it hath no ground upon God's word, but
rather utterly forbidden[2]." The system appears to have continued in successful operation till the time of the Great Fire,
when the fund became bankrupt; the wrongs of these widows
and orphans were at length redressed by Parliament[3].

197. The influx of silver from the new world had *Money and
Price's.*
caused extraordinary changes in prices and fluctuation
in the exchanges, and we need not be surprised that
practical men were unable to account satisfactorily for these
unwonted phenomena. In this respect the editor of John
Hales' book showed himself most clear-sighted. Some
opinions were set forth in the last years of Elizabeth's reign

---

[1] Stow, *Survey*, II. bk. v. p. 373.   [2] Wilson, *Discourse upon Usurie*, f. 70.
[3] Stow, *Survey*, II. bk. v. p. 373. 5 and 6 W. and M. c. 10. The Speaker of the
House obtained a gratuity of a thousand guineas on this occasion, and was
expelled in consequence. *Parl. Hist.* v. 906.

by the leading commercial writer of the day: they eventually aroused a good deal of controversy, and the discussion though confused and difficult to follow did something to clear the way for a sounder theory of money. Gerard Malynes' *Treatise of the Canker of England's Commonwealth* (1601) is chiefly instructive from the light which it throws on the conditions of commerce at the time.

Malynes' curious doctrine of   He appears to hold that the price of commodities depends on their relation to money, but that the value of money depends simply upon public authority. Money "must still be the measure, and is valued by public authority at a certainty, whereby it doth not only give or set a price unto all other metals but received as it were by repercussion a price in itself and ruled at all times the course of commodities. For albeit that plenteousness or scarcity of commodities doth alter the price of commodities yet with money it is otherwise, notwithstanding the course of usury or exchange devised thereupon, whose operation falleth in effect upon the commodities and valuation, and alteration of money concerneth only the sovereignty and dignity of the prince or governor of every country, as a thing peculiar unto them[1]." His doctrine thus entirely ignores the cost of producing the precious metals as an element to be taken into account at all, and holds that money has an intrinsic value assigned by the prince.

the Exchanges.   This might be admitted for any one country, but one would suppose that something else was needed to explain the monetary relations of one country with another. Here too Malynes insists that the terms of exchange can be laid down by public authority, having reference simply to the fineness of the current coin of different countries and the actual cost of coinage; he therefore held that the prince should insist on fixing the rate of exchange with each country, and that his officers at the public exchange should see that this rate was kept. The constant variations from this fair and definite rate seemed to him to be due to the speculative operations of monied men who took advantage of the requirements of merchants and arbitrarily altered their rates. His theory thus ignores the fact that "grains of silver" of

---

[1] Malynes, *Canker*, p. 14.

given fineness may have a different purchasing power in different countries, and that the exchanges between countries are ultimately regulated by the purchasing power of silver (*e.g.*) in each country at that particular time.

His theory derived plausibility, however, from the fact *Plausibility of these opinions owing to* that large quantities of the precious metals were engrossed in the hands of certain continental bankers, and that they seemed to be able to rule the course of the exchange for their own advantage. This view was consonant with the current opinion which attributed the high price of wool to a ring of graziers, and the high prices of other commodities to the avarice of the person who owned them and set such high prices on them. The facts as to continental banking which gave some colour to the view are in themselves so little known that the statements may be quoted at length.

" It behoveth us to speak somewhat of the commanders *the operations of bankers* or rulers of this exchange through all Christendom, which in effect are the bankers, and therefore shall we declare what the nature of a bank is, from whence the name banker is derived."

" A bank is properly a collection of all the ready moneys of some province, city, or commonwealth, into the hands of some persons licensed and established thereunto by public authority of some prince, erected with great solemnity in the view of all the people and inhabitants ; and with an ostentation in the open market place upon a scaffold, of great store of money, of gold and silver as (belonging unto the persons so established) which is unto them an attractive matter to persuade and allure the common people to bring their moneys into these bankers' hands, where at all times they may command it and have it again at their own pleasure, with allowing them only a small matter of five upon every thousand ducats or crowns, when any man will retire or draw his money into his own hands again : which although it be once but in twenty years, yet during all that time they are to have no more : so that these persons or bankers do become (as it were) the general servants or cashiers of that province, city, or commonwealth.

" These bankers, as they have their companies, factors, or

A.D. 1558
—1608.
.
correspondents in the chief places of trade in Christendom: so must they also keep account with every man, of whom they have received any money into their bank, out of which number no man of that jurisdiction is almost exempted. But generally all men are desirous to please them, and to bring their ready money into their bank, as also such money as they have in foreign parts: in regard whereof these bankers do give them great credit: for if any man have occasion to bestow in merchandise or to pay in money three or four thousand ducats, and have but one thousand ducats in the bank, the bankers will pay it for him more or less, as the party is well known or credited, without taking any gain for it, although it be for three, four, six, or more months.

"This seemeth to be a great commodity (as no doubt it is to men in particular:) but being well considered of, it will be found a small friendship, and no more in effect than if a man did participate the light of his candle unto another man's candle: for what is this credit? or what are the payments of the banks: but almost or rather altogether imaginative or figurative? As for example: Peter hath two thousand ducats in the bank, John hath three thousand, and William four thousand, and so consequently others more or less. Peter hath occasion to pay unto John one thousand ducats, he goeth to the bankers at the hours appointed (which are certain both in the forenoon and afternoon) and requireth them to pay one thousand ducats unto John, whereupon they presently make Peter debtor for one thousand ducats, and John creditor for the same sum. So that Peter having assigned unto John one thousand ducats, hath now no more but one thousand ducats in bank, where he had two thousand before. And John hath four thousand ducats in the same bank, where he had but three thousand before. And so in the same manner of assignation. John doth pay unto William and William unto others, without that any money is touched, but remaineth still in the bankers' hands, which within a short time after the erection of the bank, cometh to amount unto many millions. And by their industry they do incorporate the same, which may easily be understood, if we do but consider what the ready money and wealth of London would come unto, if it were gathered in some one man's hands, much more if a great deal of riches of other countries were added thereunto, as these bankers can cunningly compass by the course of the exchange for moneys: the ebbing and flowing whereof, is caused by their motion from time to time, as shall be declared.

"But some will say or demand, Cannot a man have any ready money out of the bankers' hands, if he have occasion to use it?

"Yes that he can: but before he have the same, they will be so bold, as to know for what purpose he demandeth the same, or what he will do with it.

"If it be to pay any man withal, they will always do that for him, as having account almost with all men, for he is accounted to be of no credit, that hath not any money in bank.

"If he do demand it for to make over by exchange in some other country, they will also serve his turn in giving him bills of exchange, for any place wheresoever, because they have their companies or correspondents in every place.

"If he do demand it for his charges and expenses, it will be paid him forthwith, because it is but a small sum, and in the end the money cometh into their hands again.

"If they pay out money to any man, that having money in bank, will bestow the same in purchase of lands, they will still have an eye to have it again in bank one way or another, at the second and third hand. So that they once being possessed of moneys, will hardly be dispossessed. And their payments are in effect all by assignation and imaginative.

"And if they have any money in bank, belonging unto orphans or widows, or any other person, that hath no occasion to use the same, they will allow them interest after four or five upon the hundred in the year at the most, and upon especial favour; for every man seeketh to please them, as in matters where *commodum privatum* beareth the rule: for they can easily please men in particular, in giving them some credit, of that great credit which they have obtained in general.

"The money then remaining in the bankers' hands, is - employed by them to other uses and purposes.

7—2

"First, they deal with princes and potentates, that have need of money, for the maintenance of the wars, as the Geneuoises and Germans did with the Emperor Charles the first during the wars in Germany, taking an exceeding gain for it. And as of late years the Florentines and others have done with Philip the second king of Spain, during his wars with France and the Low-countries, causing him to engage the revenues of his dominions, and territories, and of the customs, and notwithstanding to pay them exchange, rechange, and interest of 25, 30, yea, 50 upon the hundred, devouring a great part of his Indian treasure, as might at large be declared.

"Secondly, they do engross the commodities and merchandise of their own country, and of other countries many times also: so that none can be had but at the second hand, and at such prices as they think fit to sell them: and that to England's great prejudice, as shall be declared.

"Thirdly, whereas it is a maxim in matters of exchange, that plenty of money beyond the seas, maketh the price of the exchange to rise, and scarcity of money likewise beyond the seas, maketh the price to fall: and so on the contrary with us here in England, plenty of money maketh the price to fall, and scarcity of money maketh the price to rise. And that for places for the which the head of the exchange resteth with us, and on the contrary, for places where the head resteth with other nations; hereupon I say it is an easy matter for these bankers with the money to rule the same at their pleasure, from place to place, causing (as it were) ebbings and flowings, as shall be declared[1]."

On the whole the banking system seems to have been very considerably developed before the close of Elizabeth's reign.

---

[1] Malynes, *Canker*, p. 20.

VII. THE STUARTS.

I. Political Rivalries and Changes.

198. The seventeenth century is associated in our minds A.D. 1603 —1689. *Constitutional struggles had but little direct effect on*
with most violent political and religious struggles. A civil
war, waged on broad issues of principle, and not on personal
attachments and preferences, was a new thing in our history;
the earnestness of personal loyalty, and of public spirit,
which characterised the combatants on either side, have
no parallel in the chronicles of other ages. It might have
been supposed that these great struggles in the national
life would have made great changes in the means that were
taken for maintaining the national power; but this was
hardly the case. The same industrial and commercial prin- *Economic Policy.*
ciples hold good during the whole of this period; throughout
the wars of Personal Government and the Great Rebellion,
the Commonwealth and the Restored Monarchy, the same
mercantile scheme was maintained; the pursuit of national
power was put in the forefront, and the accumulation of
treasure, the increase of shipping and management of industry and trade, were the means of pursuing it. The main
lines had been laid down in Elizabeth's reign, and though
many particular pieces of policy were modified, they were for
the most part modified in a similar direction; as the commercial ambition of all the various rulers was the same, they
wished to overtake and outdo other nations, and especially
the Dutch.

A.D. 1603
—1689.
*Rivalry
with
Holland.*

The rise of the Dutch Republic was the great event in northern Europe at the close of the sixteenth century; and the marvellous success of the Dutch had awakened the jealousy of other powers. Holland seemed to have succeeded to the Eastern trade of Venice, as well as to much of the continental trade of the Hanse Towns. The Dutch had obtained a footing in the new world, and their fishing fleet secured large supplies from the coast of England, as well as from more distant waters. The success with which they had held their ground against the Spaniards and the suddenness with which they had risen into great commercial note[1] fixed attention upon them; and the one dominant idea of our economists and statesmen seemed to be to learn lessons from the Dutch,—to imitate their practice, and if possible to outvie them[2]. The age of the Stuart kings was governed by this policy, and also served to show its success. When James I. ascended the throne, Holland was ahead of England in all matters connected with navigation and trade; her commerce[3], her fleets, her factories, her fisheries, were superior: but before the flight of James II., Englishmen were beginning to see that their great commercial ambition was already gratified; in America as in the East Indies, they were more firmly fixed; they had got a large proportion of the fishing trade, and as Sir William Temple noted[4], the maritime greatness of Holland was beginning to wane. It is on the whole true to assert that while there was the direst confusion in church and state, the course of industry and commerce was marked by steady and little interrupted progress.

It may indeed be said that this was due to the fact that the issues about which the seventeenth century struggles were waged were so fundamental; they had reference to the nature of Sovereignty, to the basis on which political authority rested, and the grounds on which civil obedience might be demanded; but Englishmen all desired that whether as a monarchy or a commonwealth, their land should be great

---

[1] Davies, *Holland*, II. 199.   [2] Raleigh, *Observations* in *Works*, VIII. 355.

[3] This was disputed, as the Dutch did not organise so many companies as the English; and many writers thought the English system better; the Dutch gradually adopted it. Misselden, *Free Trade*, 82.

[4] *Observations upon the United Provinces*; in *Works*, I. 80.

among the countries of Europe; the means which would A.D. 1603 —1689.
render her a great monarchy, were precisely the same as *The means*
those which would render her a great commonwealth; and *for*
acquiring
hence, so far as the means for acquiring power were con- *power*
cerned, both parties were at one; though one set of men
desired that the power should be exercised as a divinely
committed trust by the king, and the other that it should be
held by the nominees of the army or the representatives of
the people.

This is an interesting fact with reference to the history
of the time, but it is of still greater importance with reference to the history of Economics; a national scheme of commercial and industrial policy was so far formulated that it
maintained itself in practice, through the gravest constitutional and ecclesiastical convulsions. Not merely did certain
localities escape because the struggle did not reach them,
but there was one side of the national life which the
struggle did not touch; the pursuit of wealth, as a means to *in the*
national power, was keenly desired by all alike and the steps *pursuit of*
wealth.
that would lead to the attainment of this object, were eagerly
considered. And thus we may see that there was a preparation for the great revolution of the eighteenth century, when
public opinion began to look on national wealth not as a
means for procuring power, but as an object which might be
pursued for its own sake, and without conscious reference to
any ulterior object. The seventeenth century showed that
national wealth might be pursued in common, and on the
same lines, by Royalist and Republican, however diverse
their ulterior aims might be; and hence the times were
ripening for the acceptance of the doctrine that it was an
error to complicate the pursuit of wealth by deliberate reference to the ulterior object of power, but that the means of
obtaining wealth might be discussed, and the principles of
accumulating it formulated, without any reference to matters
of state. The practice of the seventeenth century was reflected
in the doctrine by which Adam Smith constructed a new
science, which took the place of the mercantile system.

199. Such then is the general character of this time; *Conscious*
the Elizabethan policy was steadily pursued, and pursued *imitation*

A.D. 1608
—1689.
of the Dutch

in *Finance.*

*Embarrass-
ments of
the Stuarts.*

*Restora-
tion
Finance.*

with intelligence which was quickened by constant examination and imitation of the doings of the Dutch; there were, however, certain directions in which the economic life and the constitutional changes of the time were closely connected. This is more especially true with regard to finance; the great rise of prices had affected all those who had fixed incomes; among them may be included the Crown, as a very large proportion of the revenue came from sources or 'funds' which practically yielded a fixed amount. The rents of the crown lands could not be readily raised[1], the feudal fines could not be augmented, the assessment of the subsidies did not rise as the wealth of the country increased; it was only by successfully combining personal popularity and public parsimony that Elizabeth was able to make the revenue suffice. The Stuarts were neither popular nor parsimonious, and they found themselves dependent on parliamentary grants in a way that no other monarchs had been; they were forced to make unheard of demands from parliament, and thus the breach between the Crown and the parliamentary party was widened more and more. The continual rise of prices even rendered it difficult to carry out any scheme within the estimated cost; and there can be little doubt that the constitutional crisis was hurried on by the embarrassments which were due to the fall in the value of silver, since this rendered the ancient revenue of the Crown totally inadequate. Nor did Oliver and the Majors General find it easy to make both ends meet.

When the revenue was settled after the Restoration, it was put on an entirely different basis; the feudal dues were abolished, and a land tax levied in its stead; and there were a considerable number of financial expedients. In fact the arrangements which had been devised by parliament for meeting the expenses of their army were now incorporated in the permanent financial system of the country. It is worth noting that in their monthly assessments and excise, the parliamentary party were following the example of the Dutch; and thus in the reconstruction of taxation, as in so many

---

[1] On the diminution of revenue from this source, see H. Hall on *Crown Lands* in *Antiquary*, Jan. 1886.

other matters during this period, Englishmen introduced the A.D. 1603
plans which had answered well in Holland. —1689.

There is another important matter of finance in which a *Banking.*
great advance was made during these reigns; the whole
nature of commercial and public credit came to be better
understood than ever before in England. There was no great
bank, like that of S. George at Genoa, or the Bank of
Amsterdam, but there were a number of goldsmiths who
received money on deposit from the public and lent it to private individuals, or to the government on the assignment of
certain taxes. They were becoming a very important element
in city life, but they did not enjoy undisturbed prosperity.
Their wealth had proved a temptation to Charles I. when it was
deposited in the mint; and Charles II., by stopping his repayments to them, took a step which led eventually to the creation
of a National Debt. These new expedients in taxation, and
experiments in regard to credit, are the most important new
developments which are to be noticed during this century.

200. The great constitutional change did not perhaps
produce much direct effect on industry and commerce; but the
literature which deals with these subjects illustrates in a very
remarkable manner the nature of that fundamental change
in our polity. The claim of the king to exercise an office to *The Divine*
which he was called by God and for which he was responsible *right of*
to God, was in complete accordance with the mediæval view *kings*
that all authority emanated from God, and that all power
over human beings which could not claim a divine warrant
was but a usurped and tyrannous power. The Stuart theory
seems to have been that it was wise for the king to have councillors, to call in the representatives of his subjects to tender
advice and let him know of any mischief from which they
suffered, but that he was himself responsible for acting in
any matter, and that the initiative should come from him.
If he failed in the high task to which God had called him,
then his punishment at the hands of God would be dire
indeed; but it was not for the subjects to attempt to control
the Lord's anointed. They might tender advice, and give
information, but he, and he only was responsible to God for
the government of the realm committed to his charge.

A.D. 1603
—1689.
illustrated
in regard to
monopolies.

The practical bearing of this doctrine is illustrated by the action of James I. in regard to monopolies: it was the duty of the king to do his best for industry and trade, and to organise it as wisely as he could; and therefore he gave patents to those who seemed able to improve it. If however experience showed that his expectations had failed, he was ready to withdraw the rights which had been given to men who had been proved to misuse them. The prerogative was undoubted, in regard to foreign trade; and in regard to internal trade, the supporters of the Crown argued that the really important point was that as to the extent of the grievance. The whole nature of monopolies, the rights of subjects in regard to trade of all kinds, and the powers of the Crown to regulate this department of national life, were fully discussed and very clearly defined before the century closed.

The social
influence of
Puritan-
ism.

201. So far we have noted the new relationships of the country, and the change in its constitutional framework; we must also take account of the current morality[1]; and this is specially important in a century which saw the rise and temporary triumph of a great religious movement like Puritanism. Of the real earnestness and personal piety of these men, of the energy with which they devoted themselves to the work they took in hand, and the strictness of their own code of personal morality, there need be no doubt; all this may be fully and frankly recognised, but it should not lead us to prejudge the question as to the influence of Puritanism on commercial and social morality. A very little consideration serves to show that its social influence was most mischievous, and that the whole tone of industrial and commercial life was lowered, as it gradually attained to greater and greater power. What we find is, not the failure of individuals to live up to a Christian standard, but the deliberate acceptance of a lower tone of social duty.

Jewish not
Christian
morality in
regard to

The general tendency of Puritanism was to discard Christian morality and to substitute Jewish habits in its stead: the Old Testament rather than the New was appealed to, and there was in consequence a retrogression to a lower type of social morality which showed itself both at home and abroad.

[1] § 7. Vol. I. p. 9.

The effects of Puritan teaching in undermining the old A.D. 1603 teaching about the lawful use of riches has been already —1689. discussed; but the mischievous influence it exercised is seen *the use of* in other directions. There are three positive evils where its *money,* tendency can be most clearly traced; (*a*) in degrading the condition of the labourer, (*b*) in reckless treatment of native races, and (*c*) in the development of the worst forms of slavery.

(*a*) It is of course true that during the years of Puritan ascendancy there was a sudden and substantial rise of wages. The outbreak of the civil war caused a demand for all sorts of military stores and equipment, which gave an impetus to some branches of industry, while many labourers must have been drafted into the army. It was natural that wages should rise, and the complaints which were made in Cromwell's third parliament[1] show that they continued at this higher level; but the real influence of Puritanism on the labourer's condition was exerted long before, when the worker was deprived of all the old holidays, as opportunities of rest and recreation. Much had been lost at the Reformation; the destruction of the gild festivals had been an irreparable loss, but it was Puritanism which changed the character of the days that were left. The Sunday Festival was, so far as possible, remodelled on the lines of the Jewish Sabbath: not only was work rendered more monotonous and unbroken, but the strict notions of parliamentary piety succeeded in stamping out all recreation on Sundays[2]. The barrier which was thus raised between religion and innocent amusement has had many pernicious effects; Puritan ascendancy rendered the lot of the labourer hopelessly dull,

---

[1] Inderwick, *Interregnum*, 115. The Puritan policy about wages is most clearly seen in New England. In 1633 a statute was passed for limiting wages when a penalty was prescribed on those who gave or received higher wages. In 1634, the penalty for paying was abolished, but that for receiving was retained and enforced by prosecutions that are recorded. Weeden, *Economic and Social History of New England*, I. 83, 104, 173. The whole was short-lived, but may be fitly contrasted with the tone of King James' legislation.

[2] The attitude of the Puritans is clearly indicated in James' *Declaration of Sports* (1618). "Whereas we did justly in our progress through Lancashire rebuke some puritans and precise people, and took order that the like unlawful carriage should not be used by any of them hereafter, in the prohibiting and unlawful punishing of our good people for using their lawful recreations, and honest exercises upon Sundays after the afternoon sermon or service." Wilkins, *Concilia*, IV. 483.

and by cutting down his opportunities for wholesome recreation, forced him to find relief in dissipation. The reigns which saw these unsuccessful attempts to revive the old sports were marked by a series of statutes intended to check the increase of drunkenness[1].

(b) The time of Puritan ascendancy was marked by a change in the attitude of English merchants and settlers in foreign lands. Traders like the East India Company appear to have been more fully alive to their Christian responsibilities in 1619[2] than in 1656[3]. Again, the appointments made by the Levant Company show that they were most careful for the spiritual requirements of the residents at their factory[4]; they appear to have succeeded in maintaining their accustomed arrangements abroad, even when the influence of the sectaries was dominant at home. But the deterioration of moral and religious feeling comes out most clearly in connection with the plantations, and the treatment which English settlers showed to the native races.

The first English colony which was settled in America was in Virginia; and there is ample evidence that the enterprise was undertaken and carried out in a thoroughly missionary spirit, and with a distinct desire to civilise and Christianise the native population[5]. The documents issued by the Company at home, as well as the conduct and letters of their officials abroad, show that they had a keen sense of their responsibility in this matter. Very different was the attitude of the Puritan founders of Connecticut, who claimed to be the divinely-favoured conquerors of a New Canaan. "The heathen," they boasted, "are driven out, and we have their lands in possession; they were numerous and we are few; therefore hath the Lord done this great work, to give his beloved rest[6]." In all the terrible story of the dealings of the white man with the savage, there are few more miserable instances of cold-blooded cruelty than the wholesale de-

---

[1] See below, p. 169.   [2] Anderson, I. 377.   [3] *Ib.* II. 108.
[4] Pearson, *Biographical Sketch of Chaplains to Levant Company.*
[5] See below, p. 144.
[6] *General History of Connecticut,* attributed to Rev. Samuel Peters (1781), p. 31. The same writer calculates that within fifty years from this time the English had killed 86,000 Indians. See also *News from New England,* 1676. Hooker, *History of New England,* III. 117, also 17, 51.

struction of the Pequod nation men, women and children A.D. 1608 —1689.
by the Puritan settlers[1].

(c) The great blot upon all the European nations at this
time was their recklessness in regard to the traffic in slaves.
Individuals in many countries raised their voices against it[2],
but there is no one Christian nation which can afford to
condemn another in this matter; still there was a special
callousness in the development of slavery during Puritan as- *and slavery.*
cendancy.   There was a popular prejudice against subjecting
Christians to slavery[3] or selling them into foreign parts, but
Cromwell did not draw any such distinctions.   Not only did
his agents systematically capture Irish youths and girls for
export to the West Indies[4], all of the garrison who were
not killed in the Drogheda massacre were shipped as slaves
to Barbadoes[5], and a most touching petition has been preserved of seventy Englishmen who had been shipped to the
West Indies from Plymouth and sold for "1550 pound weight
of sugar a piece, more or less[6]."   It is unnecessary to dwell
on the tale of cruelty, but it is not unnecessary to call attention to the source of so many of the worst evils of our
modern English civilisation.   Neither the personal character
nor the political success of the Puritans need lead us to
ignore their baleful influence on society.

---

[1] Bancroft, I. 401, 402.

[2] Ximenes did his utmost to prevent the king of Spain from permitting
this trade. Robertson, *America*, (1808) I. p. 319. The opinion of a canonist
is worth quoting. Quod si libere veneunt non est cur mercatura illa crimine
ullo denotetur. Veruntamen si, quae jam percrebuit, vera est fama, diversa est
ferenda sententia. Sunt enim qui affirmant fraude et dolo calamitosam gentem
seduci....Quae si vera est historia, neque qui illos capiunt, neque qui a captoribus
coemunt, neque illi qui possident, tutas habere unquam conscientias possunt quo-
usque illos manumittant, etiam si pretium recuperare nequeant. D. de Soto,
Libri X. de Just. et Jure, l. iv. q. ii. c. 2, p. 103.

[3] On the detrimental effect of this opinion, see below, p. 316.

[4] Prendergast, *Cromwellian Settlement*, 89.   [5] Carlyle's *Cromwell*, I. 457.

[6] M. J. Rivers, *England's Slavery* (1659), p. 5. He continues: "being bought
and sold still from one Planter to another, or attached as horses and beasts for the
debts of their masters, being whipt at their whipping posts, as Rogues, for their
master's pleasure, and sleep in styes worse than hogs in *England*, and many other
wayes made miserable, beyond expression or Christian imagination." For this
condition, and the account is fully confirmed by other evidence, slavery is not too
strong a term; the conditions of servitude are described by N. D. Davis, *Cavaliers
and Roundheads*, p. 82, and E. Eggleston, *Century Magazine* (October 1884), N. S.
Vol. VI. p. 853 f.

II. Commerce.

A.D. 1603
—1689.

*Navigation
Acts.*

202. The policy of encouraging native shipping as a security for the realm and the means of bringing in wealth had engaged attention more or less since the time of Richard II.; it was embodied in a very strict form by the Rump ˙Parliament and perpetuated in the Navigation Act of 1660. Elizabeth had found some difficulty in enforcing the existing regulations[1] and James I. had specially directed a commission to enquire into the manner in which the laws were being worked[2] in 1622; and Charles I. insisted that they should be more vigorously executed, with special reference to the Baltic trade, in 1629[3]. What was novel about the Acts of the

1651.

Rump and the Restoration Parliament was that they were √ deliberately directed against the Dutch, and that they were not only Acts for encouraging English commerce but for striking a blow at Holland. Elizabeth had modified the existing Act rather than provoke hostility with foreign powers; but the form of the measure of 1651 was intended to provoke the Dutch, and did lead to more than one open rupture. It was passed immediately after the murder of Dr Dorislaus at the Hague, and apparently with the view of putting pressure on the Dutch to give satisfaction; when they sued for its repeal, they were met by a claim for arrears of fishing tribute, for the punishment of those who were implicated in the murder of the English at Amboyna, as well as a demand for £1,700,000 for damage done to English shipping[4]. The immediate result was the naval war of 1652, when a frightful amount of mischief was done to the shipping of each nation, and when Van Tromp, after a success over Blake, sailed down the channel with a broom at his mast-head in contempt of the English claim to the sovereignty of the sea.

*Carrying
trade of
Holland
attacked
in 1651.*

The Dutch at this time almost monopolised the carrying trade from distant lands and between different countries of Europe, and the Navigation Act was intended to get the

---

[1] See above, p. 20.

[2] *Ib.* xix. 130.

[3] Rymer. *Foedera*, xvii. 414.

[4] Macpherson, *Annals*, ii. 443.

portion of the trade which concerned England out of their A.D. 1603 —1689. hands[1]; it forbade importation or exportation of goods be-tween Asia, Africa and America, and England, except in English ships that were manned with English crews, and thus it secured that the whole trade between England and the plantations as well as the Levant trade and the East India trade fell into the hands of Englishmen. The Act of 1660 was even more sweeping than that of 1651, as it insisted 1660. that the shipping should be English-built as well as owned by Englishmen, and it prohibited aliens from being merchants or factors in our plantations; admirals and governors of the plantations were enjoined strictly to use every endeavour to enforce the Act and drive out the Dutch from taking any part in our colonial trade[2]. The colonies had been intended to strengthen the mother country, and in so far as their trade enriched foreign merchants they did not serve the original purpose. Another clause of these Acts excluded the Dutch from a carrying trade between England and the Mediterranean ports; since goods of foreign growth and manufacture were only to be imported in English ships, English-built and English-manned; and they might not be brought from Dutch depots, but only direct from the countries which produced them. There was an exception allowed in 1651 in the case of silk or silk goods; these might be imported from Holland and Flanders if the owners made oath that they had been brought overland from Italy.

While thus attacking the Dutch colonial trade and carry- *Fisheries.* ing trade, the Act of 1651 also aimed a blow at their fisheries; it prohibited importation under pain of forfeiture; this penalty was relaxed in 1660, but double alien customs were imposed on all ling, cod, herring, whalebone or blubber imported into England, as a merchant's speculation, and not by the owners of the ship who had themselves prepared the cargo.

There can be no doubt that this Act was in many ways *Disadvan-* prejudicial to commerce and to the colonies; English ship- *tages due to these measures.*

---

[1] 1651, c. 22. Scobell, *Acts*, II. 176.

[2] "When the Civil War broke out in England, the Dutch managed nearly the whole trade of the English West Indian Colonies." N. D. Davis, *Cavaliers and Roundheads*, p. 70.

ping was not sufficient at first to carry on the whole of English trade, and as a consequence of the great demand, the cost of ship-building was said to increase enormously so as to render some established trades unprofitable[1], while the plantations, and even English producers, were restricted in their dealings and unable to obtain the best market for some of their products[2]; but these disadvantages were clearly understood by the men who passed the Acts, and who believed that the benefit to the power of the country would far outweigh the immediate inconvenience of any individual.

Counter-railing advantages in

It did inflict great hardship on the planters and tended to raise prices to English consumers, but it was argued that there were great benefits too. The whole is discussed with judgment by Sir Josiah Child[3], who strongly advocated the policy of the Acts, and believed that it had doubled our mercantile marine before 1668. But the best proof that it attained its object, of enabling us to overtake and outrun the Dutch, is to be found in the strong feeling it excited in Holland. This was not only shown in actual warfare, but it is reflected in the literature of the day; De Witt, who saw the measure come into operation, complained that it was so devised, "that it is much to be feared the English merchants may in time bereave the Dutch of *enabling us* much of their trade[4]." In this, Englishmen have eventually *to overtake* succeeded; they have not only got the whole of their own *the Dutch.* trade into their hands, but have rendered this country an emporium for the trade of the world, in a way that would have astonished the merchants who advocated some attempt of the kind in 1641[5]. Relatively to the Dutch the power of the country was increased by the policy pursued; and while

---

[1] Roger Coke, *A treatise wherein is demonstrated that the Church and State of England are in equal danger with the Trade*, I. p. 36. He alludes especially to the impossibility of providing wood for ship-building, but points out many evils from the Act.

[2] The complaints of the planters are stated and discussed by Child (*New Discourse*, p. 115). The author of *Britannia Languens* (1680) complains that the Act gives English merchants a monopoly, and that if it were repealed there would be a far larger export of English cloth.

[3] *New Discourse of Trade* (1694), p. 112.

[4] De Witt, *Interest of Holland*, pt. i. c. 22.

[5] H. Robinson, *England's Safety in Trades Encrease*, pp. 20, 23.

it did not serve to develop the resources of the colonies so A.D. 1603 —1689. rapidly as might have been done by other schemes, it did strengthen the political ties between the mother country and the plantations[1], and thus it helped to secure the ulterior aim which its authors had in view, since the commerce of the country was so regulated that its power was increased.

203. Besides these Acts for the encouragement of mer- *The Royal Navy.* chant shipping, more direct steps were taken, especially, for increasing the maritime strength of the realm. The naval commission of 1608 had revealed a terrible amount of mismanagement in the dockyards; the expense attending the maintenance of a fleet was enormous, and yet the number, if not the tonnage, of the available ships declined under James I. Nottingham, the High Admiral succeeded in resisting the proposed reforms in 1608[2], and in shelving further enquiries; but the day of reckoning came at last, and the report of the commission of 1618 made it necessary that some attempt should be made to obtain efficiency and if possible to diminish the expenses. The commissioners reported that though the present expenditure was more than £53,000 per annum, better results might easily be obtained with an outlay that did not exceed £30,000[3]. The Duke of Buckingham was made head of the department, and he obtained the appointment of a permanent naval commission in 1619[4]; but the change did not secure the improvement that was hoped for[5].

There was plenty of scope for the useful employment of a *Pirates of Barbary.* fleet even in times of peace with the other continental powers. The Dey of Barbary, over whom the Sultan of Turkey held a nominal suzerainty, allowed Algiers to be the headquarters of gangs of pirates, in whose booty he shared. They ravaged the seas for prizes, pillaged the ships and carried off the men into lifelong slavery. Ruffians from every European country were ready to join in these expeditions, and among the most notorious leaders were Sir Francis Verney and another Englishman named Ward[6]. The evil was not really new, for

---

[1] L. v. Ranke, *History of England*, III. 68.
[2] Gardiner, *History*, III. 203. *State Papers, Domestic*, XLI.
[3] Gardiner, *History*, III. 204. [4] *Ib*. III. 206.
[5] See the account of the fleet prepared against Rochelle, Gardiner, VI. 228.
[6] *Ib*. III. 65.

we read of somewhat similar cases under Edward IV.[1] and during the Tudor reigns, from the briefs which were issued for collections in church to obtain the freedom of slaves among the Turks or on the North African coast[2]. But it would certainly appear to have been on the increase; James was eager to secure the growing commerce of England in the Mediterranean, and several schemes were planned for destroying the nest of pirates[3]; but it was a formidable task, and the jealousy of other powers prevented him from carrying his proposals into effect. The Dutch protected themselves and had no interest in stopping depredations on other nations[4], while the Spaniards disliked having English fleets off their shores.

Charles I.   Charles I. gave considerable attention to the matter, after the breach with Spain. In 1626 an expedition was fitted out under Captain John Harrison; attempts were to be made to effect an exchange of prisoners, and by presents to induce the princes and governors of Barbary and Sallee to deliver up English captives[5]. The mission was so far successful that Harrison was employed on a similar voyage in 1628[6]. But there could be no hope of really stopping the piracy by bargaining with the pirates, and the matter was so important that it could be put in the forefront and treated as a national danger when Charles attempted to levy shipmoney under *Shipmoney.* Noy's advice[7]. He was not able to make an attack upon them however, and the evil continued; the subject was frequently before the Long Parliament[8]; though Blake had some success at Tunis 1655[9], and the cession of Tangier to Charles II. on his marriage limited the sphere for these depredations, the mischief continued during the whole of this period. The chief evidence is found in the continued charitable contributions for this purpose. Bishop Cosin devoted money to this purpose in his will[10], and charity sermons on

---

[1] Ellis, *Original Letters, II. Series*, I. p. 268.   [2] Strype's *Whitgift*, II. 334.
[3] Gardiner, *History*, III. 68, 106, 288, 375. The expedition of 1621 seems to have done more harm than good. Macpherson, II. 309 and refs.
[4] De Witt, *True Interest*, 159.   [5] Rymer, *Foedera*, XVIII. 793, 807.
[6] *Ib.* XIX. 27.   [7] Dowell, *History*, I. 263.
[8] 17 Charles I. c. 31. Scobell, I. 22, 96, II. 111, &c.   [9] Thurloe, III. 390.
[10] Anderson, *Colonial Church*, II. 100.

behalf of this object were preached by Fitz Geffrey[1]. With A.D. 1608 —1689. the extension of the power of civilised nations this form of charity which was so prominent both in early and mediæval times has come to be a thing of the past.

204. [?] While this rivalry with the Dutch in the colonial *Fishing as a school for seamanship.* and carrying trade was being pushed on, attention was directed more and more closely to the possibility of ousting them from the fishing trade, which was said to be the very foundation of their prosperity[2]. The reasons for pursuing this policy, so as to monopolise a branch of industry which formed a school for seamanship, have been stated above[3]; and allusion has been made to the importance attached to it in the Navigation Acts; but it is also worth while to call attention to the mass of pamphlet literature on the subject. Cursory reference to a few examples serves to show how keenly and how widely the importance of the matter was felt. Some laid stress on the sovereignty of the sea, with reference to the treatise of Grotius, and deplored the encroachments of the Dutch on our herring fisheries[4]. Others insisted that Englishmen should build ships of the Dutch pattern for this trade[5], or gave other suggestions from practical experience[6]. In 1677 a joint stock company was incorporated, but, as their busses were destroyed by the French, the scheme failed.

Several writers insist on the expediency of maintaining *Political Lent.* the political Lent[7], and others advise the granting of bounties to encourage fishing[8]. While most of these writers deal specially with the herring fishery, there was also a good deal of interest in the developing of the English cod fishery off Newfoundland[9]. Before the close of the century, both of

[1] *Compassion towards captives* (1637). Compare also Andrews, *Works*, III. 230, and Dean Sherlock's *Exhortation* in S. Paul's, 11 March, 1702.

[2] John Smith, *England's Improvement Revived* (1673), p. 262. Motley, *Dutch Republic*, I. 43.   [3] § 142, I. 443.   [4] Misselden, *Free Trade* (1622), p. 35.

[5] *Britain's Busse* (1615), *Politic Plat* in Arber's *English Garner*, II. 142.

[6] *England's way to win wealth* (1614), by Tobias Gentleman.

[7] H. Robinson, *England's Safety in Trades Encrease* (1641), p. 16. Numerous *Proclamations* in *Foedera*, XVII. 131, 134, 661, XVIII. 268, 822, 961, XIX. 116, 329, 376. On the strictness with which it was enforced at Hull; Andrews, *Curiosities of the Church*, 71. E. Jennings, *Brief discovery of the damages that happened to this realm by disordered and unlawful diet* (1593).

[8] C. Reynal, *The True English Interest* (1674), p. 28.

[9] John Hagthorpe, *England's Exchequer*, p. 31.

these branches of trade were being worked by the English to the partial exclusion of the Dutch, while on the other hand the whale fishery remained almost entirely in their hands[1].

Commis-
sions on
Trade 205. Very full information as to the designs for encouraging commerce, which were then being tried, may be obtained by examining the letters which appointed commissioners to enquire into the state of trade at different dates.

1622. In 1622 the Lord President of the Council and fifty commissioners were appointed to enquire into the decay of the clothing trade, and the various mischiefs which followed from this cause. The king had taken some obvious measure at once by proclamation, but he adds, " because we found that the occurrents of the trade are variable, and must be directed and governed as times and occasions shall serve or do vary, and that it is impossible to foresee what may be the future event of these things or to set down such constant rules for trade as shall not require an addition or alteration upon just reasons and grounds "; he therefore determined to appoint a standing commission which might certify their suggestions to the Privy Council, " to the end that thereupon the king might give such order for remedies as might be for his own honour and for the wealth and prosperity of his people."

Points for
special con-
sideration The commissioners were to consider, (1) Why wool had fallen in price, and how the price might be restored. (2) How all the export of English, Scotch and Irish wools to foreign parts, as well as of yarn, fuller's earth and wood ashes, might be prevented, and whether there is any danger of a glut of wool in England, if this policy be pursued. (3) As to the laws for regulating the manufactures of cloth, could they be amended or codified? could rules for the new drapery be devised? could the laws be better enforced? (4) Were the brokers who collected small quantities of wool and interposed between the grower and the clothier necessary or hurtful, and should their calling be regulated? (5) What were the causes why dyeing stuffs had become dear? (6) Was the suspicion that was felt of the ordinances of Merchant Companies and of Industrial Companies well grounded? Did they limit

---

[1] Child, *New Discourse of Trade* (1694), Preface.

the number of traders, and would it be well to render trade A.D. 1608
—1689. free from their interference? Also should merchants be re-tailers as well? (7) Why was money so scarce? By what means might bullion be bought in greater quantities and the exportation prevented? (8) They were to diligently observe the true balance of the trade of the kingdom, lest the importation of merchandise from foreign parts exceed the exportation of our own native commodities, and consider of some fitting course to reduce the same to more equality, and to think upon the gain or loss that comes to our kingdom by the course of exchange now used by merchants.

They were also to turn their attention to (9) general *and of general policy.* questions connected with the trade and the improvement of the resources of the realm, they were (like the Caermarthen bailiff)[1], to see how to prevent vain and unprofitable returns and to see which English commodities were in such demand abroad that they could insist that they should be paid for, at least in part, in coin. (10) Special attention was to be given to the maintenance of shipping, as a principal means to advance the honour, strength, safety, and profit of the kingdom, and as to a supply of qualified sailors, and of course the encouragement of fishery, the Navigation Acts are particularly mentioned. (11) So too are the statutes of employment and the best returns for English exports.

The conduct and prospects of several particular companies *Mercantile Companies.* were also to engage their attention, the Eastland Company, which had exported corn and brought in raw flax and hemp, to the benefit of agriculture and the employment of the poor, no longer exported any corn and brought in manufactured or dressed hemp and flax. The complaints about the East India Company and the export of bullion were also to be examined, as well as the possibility of planting a linen manufacture and supplying home-grown hemp and flax; while the commissioners were to consider how to stimulate the home consumption of English cloth[2].

Whatever results this commission may have secured, it *Subsequent Commissions.* could not have had a very long life; Oliver Cromwell ap-

---

[1] See above, p. 73.   [2] Rymer, *Foedera*, XVII. 414.

A.D. 1608
—1689.
pointed a commission of enquiry on trade concerns in 1655[1];
and a standing committee was formed by Charles II. in 1672,
with special reference to the encouragement, protection and
defence of the colonies[2], but this project fell, stillborn, and
the king depended for advice on special and occasional enquiries. In the time of William III. the scheme of establishing a permanent Board of Trade was really carried through.
The king appointed commissioners in 1696[3], to promote the
trade of the kingdom, and to inspect and improve the plantations in America and elsewhere; they thus combined the
special objects which had been put forward in the schemes
of James I. and Charles II. respectively.

Companies for
206. One of the points to which King James's commissions on trade were specially to direct their attention was the
character of merchant companies. A suspicion had arisen
that they put in execution various rules for the ordering of
trade, which were of no public benefit, though the merchants
were themselves enriched. On any complaint the commissioners were to enquire what the constitutions of these companies were; and also to see whether business would not be
done on a larger scale, and the volume of trade increased, if the
opportunity of trading was opened to anyone, and not confined
to the members of companies. " We will and require you to
consider whether it be necessary to give way to a more open
and free trade or not ? and if it be, then in what manner it is
fittest to be done ? wherein we would always have you take
government and order in trades.
care that government and order in trade may be preserved
and confusion avoided, and that to be done which may be
best for us and our people, and among other things which we
consider to be hindrances of a fair and free trade, we will and
require you to consider how far it shall be fit to admit of a
joint stock in companies or societies of merchants."

A principle is here assumed as axiomatic, which later
economists were inclined to discard altogether: the idea of a
laissez faire policy in foreign trade had scarcely dawned on

[1] Thurloe, *State Papers*, IV. 177. See also the earlier commission in 1650,
Inderwick, *Interregnum*, 74.   [2] Macpherson, *Annals*, II. 564.
[3] *Ib.* 681 n. There had been some difference of opinion as to whether they
should be appointed by the Crown or by Parliament. *Parl. Hist.* v. 977.

anyone[1]; if mere wealth had been the object in view, then it might have been recognised that what was most profitable to the merchant would also be most profitable to the State as a whole. But the men of the time desired that trade should be subservient to power, that it should bring in those kinds of wealth which did work for the security and strength of the realm, and that it should be so managed as to bring about the steady development of national resources. This was an axiom which was, so far as I see, generally accepted by seventeenth century pamphleteers; all the disputes turned on the best means for procuring and executing wise regulations. It might conceivably be sufficiently regulated by the government, who should appoint consuls for the protection of subjects in foreign parts, and define the conditions on which export and import might take place; this was the mode of regulation which eventually triumphed. Or the arrangement as to all details of life and commerce might be committed to particular companies to deal with for a definite period, but subject to the chance of having their ordinances overhauled and their privileges rescinded if it appeared they had been abused. In other words the question was, whether trade should be directly or only indirectly regulated by the State.

The loss of Calais practically extinguished the trade of the *The Staplers* Staplers. The ancient fellowship still exists, but its glory has departed, and it had no effective position in the beginning of the seventeenth century; the Merchant Adventurers, on the *and Merchant Adventurers.* other hand, were in great force; expelled from the Empire in 1582, they had established their factory at Middelburg in Holland, and their *Lawes, Customes and Ordinances*, have survived to give us a very fairly clear insight into their mode of operation. The regulations for the life of the merchants and apprentices in their factory are particularly curious; they formed an Adventurers' College[2], and the discipline about giving 'full banquets, dinners and suppers' was similar to college discipline at Oxford or Cambridge. No apprentice

---

[1] It is equally far from the views of Cromwell in appointing commissioners in 1650; while investigating the societies and companies they are to "take care that government and order in trade may be preserved and confusion avoided." Inderwick, *Interregnum*, 75.   [2] Wheeler, *Treatise of Commerce*, 117.

might play at cards or dice for higher points than fourpence a game[1].

For the rest the rules were meant to secure fair play among the merchants; no one might trade at odd times or in secret places, but fairly and openly; a minimum price was fixed, and no one was to spoil the market by taking less; but if he failed to get the price, other merchants could be required to take the goods off his hands; only when the market was regularly glutted and after consultation with others did they come down; thus one man did not try to undersell *The stint.* others. Similarly the "stint" was intended to prevent any one dealer from engrossing the whole trade[2]. The adventurers contended that these regulations benefited merchants, as they ensure a steady trade with no violent fluctuations, and thus their rules really conduced to the public weal; while they denied that there was any monopoly, as the merchants competed with one another within the prescribed limits, and the whole body was subject to competition with the Hanse and other alien merchants[3].

Vicissitudes in their trade. This company suffered a very severe blow in 1608, when James I. endeavoured to develop the arts of dressing and dyeing cloth; their charter was seized[4], though the company was not broken up. When the failure of that project was demonstrated, their powers were again revived (1615) and they settled themselves at Hamburg and Dort. Parliament found that the Dutch were developing a cloth manufacture of their own[5], and in the hope of stamping out the new industry, they adopted a free trade policy and passed a resolution to reduce the fines and amend the restrictions of the company[6]; but in 1634 their privileges were again confirmed though the fines

---

[1] *Lawes of Merchant Adventurers* (in Brit. Mus. Add. ms. 18,913), p. 31.

[2] *Lawes*, p. 51 (1609). Wheeler, *Treatise*, 79. See below, § 318 on the 'Vend.'

[3] Wheeler, *Treatise of Commerce*, 143.

[4] Macpherson, *Annals*, ii. 301. Gardiner, *History*, ii. 386. They had been very seriously attacked in 1605 in the Commons. The arguments for and against the Company then will be found at some length in a ms. in the British Museum (Cotton, Titus F. iv. f. 259—285).

[5] This was attributed by R. Coke (*Detection of the Court and State of England*, i. 358), to the migration of 140 Walloon families from Canterbury and other towns to Holland, as they found themselves aggrieved by Laud's measures. See Gardiner, *History*, viii. 121. Compare the curious poem, in J. Trever's *Essay* (1677).

[6] Macpherson, *Annals*, ii. 327.

for admission were definitely fixed[1]. They were continued by an ordinance of the Long Parliament in 1643[2].

After the Restoration they had factories at Dort and Hamburg, and besides the principal court at London, they had courts at York, Newcastle and Hull. The society was hardly represented at Exeter, where the merchants had an incorporation of their own, and there was much complaint of them from the West of England clothiers[3]: they were accused of using their command of the Dutch market in such a fashion, that they were able to oppress the clothiers and to force them to sell at very low rates. Apparently the answer of the company to these complaints was deemed satisfactory, for they continued to retain their privileges, and drove a flourishing trade at Hamburg in the earlier part of the eighteenth century.

This company had exclusive privileges for the export of cloth between the Somme and the Skaw—the northern point of Jutland; but while on the whole their privileges were maintained, there were periods when the trade was thrown open, and the interlopers and 'straggling' merchants were allowed to deal at towns within these bounds. It is impossible to judge of the rights or wrongs of the matter, or to trace the different effect of differing ordinances. On the whole it may be supposed that the company justified their pretensions, since they held their ground; but on the other hand we may notice that Malynes and other Staplers, who approved of regulated trade, were yet very bitter about their exclusiveness[4]. On the face of it we might have believed that a regulated company, which any merchant in the kingdom could join if he wanted to engage in this trade, would not prove a serious obstacle to the growth of trade; but they may have put on such heavy fines on entrance as to become exclusive and to inflict a real grievance by their "stint."

[1] Rymer, *Foedera*, xix. 583.

[2] Scobell, *Acts*, i. 58. Its validity and policy were vigorously criticised. *A discourse for enlargement of Trade engrossed by Merchant Adrenturers* (1645).

[3] *Reasons humbly offered* (167—) [Brit. Mus. 712 g. 16 (8)], that Merchant Adventurers are detrimental to England and especially to Devonshire.

[4] Malynes, *Maintenance of Free Trade* (1622), 50, 68 ; *Center of Circle* (1623), 87. See Misselden's *Criticism* in *The Circle* (1623), p. 52. Malynes complained that the Merchant Adventurers had become a practical monopoly; he had not made this charge in 1603 (*England's View*), 84.

English trade with every part of the world was carried on by such companies; most of them were regulated companies, but all of them were at constant feud with interlopers. The Levant Company, connected as it was with overland trade to India[1], was the great rival of the East India Company, and these merchants contended that they were able to obtain Eastern goods by the sale of English cloth, and that their trade could be easily maintained without the export of bullion: they had succeeded, in part at all events, to the trade which had at one time been done by the Venetians. After two temporary grants of privileges had expired, they obtained a permanent charter in 1605; any subject under twenty-five years of age could obtain admission on a payment of £25. The fellowship of merchants trading to the Levant seas was continued and made a corporation by the Long Parliament in 1644 with very extensive powers of self-government[2]; as a regulated company it was open to all English subjects[3].

Another regulated company of a similar type was the Eastland Company which traded with the Baltic; it had obtained a charter from Queen Elizabeth which was confirmed in 1629[4]; but in 1672 full liberty of trading to the Scandinavian Peninsula was given to all English subjects; and the fine for admission to the company was reduced to forty shillings[5]. At the same time, the company zealously maintained that great advantages followed from their regulations for the export of woollen cloth to the ports on the south of the Baltic; their governor, Nathaniel Tench, wrote a pamphlet in defence of their privileges, while in his place in parliament he advocated the lowering of the fine for admission to the Muscovy Company to forty shillings, so that the trade might practically include all merchants, while at the same time due regulation should be enforced[6]. Both the

A.D. 1603
1689.
Regulated companies.

Levant.

Eastland.

---

[1] *The Allegations of the Turky Company*, Brit. Mus. 522 l. 5 (8), p. 2.
[2] Scobell, *Acts*, I. 65.   [3] Eton, *Survey of Turkish Empire*, 451.
[4] Rymer, *Foedera*, XIX. 129.   [5] 25 C. II. c. 7.
[6] Stow's *Survey*, II. bk. v. c. 17, p. 261. Compare also *Reasons for passing the Bill for encouraging Trade to Russia*, also *Some Considerations relating to the enlarging the Russia Trade*. This last deals especially with the large market for tobacco which might be found in the Czar's dominions. Brit. Mus. 8223 e. 1 (19—20).

Eastland and the Muscovy[1] Companies were regulated, not A.D. 1603 —1689. *Russia.* joint stock companies, but the fines of admission to the Muscovy Company were so high as to be practically exclusive: the Eastland merchants desired that the payments should be merely nominal, so that anyone might be really free to engage in trade, but that the trade itself should still be conducted according to the rules of the company.

These associations were composed almost entirely of *The Exeter Merchant Adventurers.* London merchants, though the Merchant Adventurers boasted that they were a national body; another side of their life is brought out however by the curious Act which confirmed the former privileges of the Merchants of Exeter. Elizabeth determined in acknowledgment of services rendered by the citizens, "as also for the taking away, abolishing and convoying of many and sundry absurdities and inconveniences which within the said city and county did increase by reason of the excessive number of artificers and other inexpert, ignorant and unworthy men which did take upon them to use the art, science and mistery of merchandise and traffic of merchant wares to the great detriment of the commonwealth of this realm of England, and to the manifest impoverishment of the said city, to incorporate certain merchants named therein and their successors," as the Governor, Consuls and Society of the Merchant Adventurers of the city and county of Exeter. In King James's time it was alleged that this incorporation had been very serviceable to the state in general and to the advancement of the customs in particular; according to this statement they also constantly "relieved twelve poor men with gowns, money, and other necessaries, to their great comfort, and do yearly so apparel and comfort them and by their charter are to continue and keep the same for ever; and likewise they have and do not only charitably from time to time set up sundry young merchants with the loan of money at their first entrance into trade, but also have raised and also do raise divers ancient merchants who by losses at the sea have been decayed, by means whereof they have proved afterwards profitable both

---

[1] The Russian Company becomes the official name after 1698, when the fines on admission were reduced to £5. 10s. 10 Will. III. c. 6.

to the king in custom and other payments, and good members
to the commonwealth of the said city, and for that, many
particular merchants of the said corporation have in time of
dearth and scarcity of corn adventured great sums of money
out of their own private stocks for corn into foreign kingdoms
for the relief of the poor as well of the said city as of the
county of Devon, to whom they have sold the same corn in
time of great dearth and necessity, sometimes for two shillings and sixpence, three shillings and three and fourpence
less than the prices in the market have been." A statute in
the preceding year had opened the trade with France to all
subjects, but this was not to be interpreted as meaning that
this Exeter Corporation should be dissolved.

*Joint Stock
Under-
takings.*
207. These were regulated companies, into which any
English subject could obtain admission on understood terms,
and the various members of which traded, each with his
own capital, but according to the regulations of the company;
but there were also other societies of merchants which traded
on a joint stock[1]; each member subscribed so much to the
common fund and obtained a share in any profits that were
made. For very distant trades, or undertakings on a very
large scale, this may have been the best method of working;
there had been a joint stock bank of the Levant Company
Morea. for trading to the Morea[2]. The Canary Merchants incorporated by Charles II. also had a joint stock; and the whale
fishery gave rise to several attempts of this kind: but the
two great companies which enjoyed this constitution were
the Royal African Company and the East India Company.

Guinea. The Guinea Company never obtained parliamentary
sanction, but it had an important place in the history of
English commerce: it imported the gold of which guineas
were coined, and it exported great quantities of negroes for
the supply of our American plantations, by whose labour and
the planter's industry the king and his subjects were much
enriched[3]. The merchants maintained forts and factories at

---

[1] The regulated companies corresponded to such bodies as Lloyd's or the Stock
Exchange; the joint stock to the London and North Western or any other railway
company.

[2] Macpherson, *Annals*, II. 202.   [3] Stow, *Survey*, Vol. II. c. 13, p. 269.

great expense, but they never succeeded in excluding inter- A.D. 1608
—1689.
lopers, and they complained that their trade had been entirely
ruined more than once by the unscrupulous dealings of private
individuals.   They obtained a charter from Charles II.[1], but
as they had no parliamentary status, the trade in which they
were engaged was thrown open by the Declaration of Right,
and this liberty was practically affirmed in 1697[2], though the
company were allowed to exact a $10°/_0$ duty on the exports
of interlopers: but the company were unable to maintain
their footing, though in the eighteenth century Parliament
subsidised them on more than one occasion. As they brought
gold to the country, exported cloth suitable for the climate,
and facilitated the working of the plantations, the trade in
which they were engaged was regarded with great favour,
but there was difficulty in convincing the public that it could
not be carried on by separate traders as successfully as by a
joint stock and monopolising company[3].

Of far greater interest, from the great success which *The East* *India* *Company.*
eventually attended it, is the story of the East India Com-
pany; in 1653 the experiment was tried of throwing the trade
open to all, but Europe was glutted with Indian goods, and
the private traders also lost much in India[4], so that it was
thought necessary to reestablish the company as a joint stock
affair in 1657. King Charles II. gave them every encouragement; he granted them the island of Bombay "to be held in
free and common socage" at an annual rent of £10, and in
successive charters gave them ample privileges, which included the power to suppress interlopers and to exercise
government in India.

The company obtained factories at Surat (1603), Madras *Rivalry* *with the* *Dutch.*
(1620), Hooghly near Calcutta (1642), and Bombay (1668),
and the English power has gradually extended over the
whole of Hindustan; but they were not equally successful in
maintaining themselves in the Spice Islands: the Dutch had

---

[1] Macpherson, II. 569.

[2] Stow, Vol. II. bk. v. p. 270.

[3] It was forcibly attacked by Roger Coke, *Reflexions upon the East India and Royal African Companies*, 1695, where the case against monopolies is well stated.

[4] The author of *Britannia Languens*, however, held that the experiment was successful. *Select Tracts on Commerce*, 337.

been before them[1], and eventually drove them out altogether.
The massacre at Amboyna[2] in 1622, and the loss of Poleroon
in 1664, were the two chief incidents which marked the
rivalry of English and Dutch merchants in the East; as
well as the disputes at Bantam, by which the English were
forced to retire, and establish themselves at Bencoolen in
1682; but if they were confined in this one direction, their
trade was opened up in many others: they had obtained
privileges in Persia, in 1622, and sent ships to China before
1680. The rivalries of Europeans resulted in their taking
different sides in the quarrels of native princes, and in this
way the East India Company began to change its character
and to become a great political power, as well as a company
for carrying on foreign trade.

At the same time, the East India Company never showed
themselves anxious to increase their political responsibilities;
and one of their reasons for their strenuous efforts to put
*Inter-
lopers.* down interlopers was the allegation that these private traders
embroiled them with native princes. The exclusive rights[3]
granted to them in 1609, were confirmed in 1661, despite the
strong grounds on which the claim of the interlopers was
based. The interlopers admitted the king's right to restrain
any of his subjects from going out of the kingdom, and also
the royal right to restrain subjects to one particular place, as
in time of plague; but Pollexfen argued that it could not be
claimed on this account that the king had power to grant to
any subject or corporation a sole right to trade to one particular
place for ever, to the exclusion of all his other subjects[4]. The
precise form of all these constitutional questions was altered
not long after the Revolution. When at length the company
held their position by parliamentary enactment, the question of
the royal prerogative and the common law right of the subject
was no longer of primary importance; but so far as the sub-

---

[1] On James's policy about E. I. commerce and the Dutch see Gardiner. iv. 408.
[2] Gardiner. v. 242.
[3] On their exercise of jurisdiction in Skinner's case, and the quarrel between the Houses in 1666, see below, p. 270. n. 1, also *Parl. Hist.* iv. 423.
[4] See the *Argument of a learned Counsel,* p. 10. in defence of Sands. an interloper who was sued by the company, appended to his *Discourse of Trade, Coyn and Paper Credit* (1697).

stance of the companies' claim was concerned, they were able to hold their own; and the temporary expedient of forming a regulated company[1] had no better success than had been afforded by the four years of free competition.

While these two companies were alike engaged in a *Gaining and losing trades.* struggle with interlopers, and while the constitutional points in the two cases were similar, there was curious difference in the current opinion about the trades in which they were respectively engaged. The African trade was generally approved; but in regard to the East India Company there was a good deal of division of opinion, as many persons maintained that the operations of the company were really injurious to the wealth and power of the kingdom. This is one of the clearest cases for noting what was meant by the contention so frequently urged, e.g. in regard to dealings with France, that a certain trade was hurtful to the country, and that England lost by permitting the trade to continue at all. If we merely look at the wealth of the country, this would be difficult to maintain; and no economist does maintain it in the present day; the trade will not continue unless merchants gain by it, and if they gain by it individually, the aggregate wealth of the country in which they are citizens is *Private gain not necessarily conducive to national power.* increased; this is practically certain and may be admitted at once. But even though all this be granted, it does not follow that there is any addition to those kinds of wealth which give rise to national power. It is conceivable that there may be gain accruing to private traders, and better sources for levying taxation, while the shipping and the treasure, and the industrial capacity of the realm are declining, or stationary; or at least are making less progress than they might, if the energies of the merchants were employed in other directions. As there was no direct political rivalry with the powers of Hindustan, the contention that the trade was hurtful to the nation while beneficial to the shareholders, rested on the allegations that the trade was not duly regulated so as to subserve political ends, and even that this trade could not be made to subserve these ends at all.

It is unnecessary to attempt to follow a controversy

[1] See below, § 252, p. 271.

which raged at intervals throughout the whole Stuart period, and broke out with renewed vehemence in the time of William III., but some few notes may be made of the principal points on which it turned. The arguments *pro* and *con* are weighed by Sir Thomas Mun in his *Discourse of*

Treasure. *trade from England unto the East Indies*[1]. The chief objection was based on the quantity of gold[2] and silver which was exported to the East: but it was asserted in reply that the spices taken in return were got with far less outlay than when they were obtained by an overland route and through the intervention of Venetian and Egyptian merchants; while there was also a vent for some English goods in the East, and a profitable coasting trade to be done there; but the principal point was that by the sale of Indian products in Europe, England obtained far more of the precious metals in return than the sum that was needed to purchase them in the East; the coin sent to India was but the seed which brought back a large balance in coin by the sale of spices to other European nations[3].

Again it was urged that the shipping and seamen of the realm were employed, and sometimes lost, in a distant trade, where they were of no avail for purposes of defence in case
Shipping. need for them should arise. But it was asserted in reply that the East India Company by providing employment for shipping and seamen were giving an encouragement to all the maritime trades, and were thus indirectly promoting the naval strength of the realm. This objection was more especially heard in the early days of the company, when the total shipping of the country was but small, and when the length of the voyage and the losses that occurred seemed to some

---

[1] Printed in Purchas's *Pilgrimes* (1625), I. 732.

[2] Compare the heavy fines imposed on foreign merchants in 1619 for this practice. Gardiner, *History*, III. 323.

[3] This point is much discussed in a contemporary controversy on the course of the foreign exchanges. Misselden argues for the reality of the gain which accrued through the East India trade as a balance from the sale of Eastern goods in Europe (*Circle of Commerce*, 1623, p. 34), while Malynes held that this gain was illusory, unless there were a statute enforced for actually bringing in bullion in return for spices exported to other parts of Europe (*Center of Circle*, 1623, p. 114). The argument for the company on this point is well put by Robinson, *England's Safety in Trades Encrease* (1641), p. 24.

to be out of all proportion to the gain[1]. The company did A.D. 1608
—1689.
indeed provide for the wives and children of those who were
lost in its service, and "a thousand widows and some hundreds of blind and lame" joined in petitioning Parliament
against the suppression of the company[2].

Another objection was very generally made: it is difficult
to estimate what amount of force there may have been in it;
but one may remember that all sorts of projects for the
improvement of England were being brought out, and that
there was no very great mass of capital available for carrying
them through. Roads were bad, much land was waste that
could be drained and tilled, and many manufactures could
be set agoing if there were funds for the purpose; such was
the general cry, and as banking was in its infancy, the capital *Capital mis-*
which did exist was not so fully utilised as would now be *directed.*
done under our modern system of credit. There were some
who complained that the East India Company diverted
capital that would be more prudently employed at home[3];—
and as the company became more successful, and was
able to borrow money to a very large amount at three per
cent., there were serious forebodings that any mischief
which happened to the company would entail ruin on large
classes throughout the nation; just as eventually happened
at the time of the failure of the Scottish Darien Company,
and the bursting of the South Sea Bubble.

It was also argued that this trade was hurtful on the *Employ-*
further ground of its effects on the employment of English *ment.*

---

[1] Compare the objections printed in Sir D. Digges' *Defence of Trade* (1615), p. 16.

[2] *Petition of Margaret Walker*, Brit. Mus. 8223, e 1 (47).

[3] Misselden, who was ready to defend the East India Company at other times,
writes, "The special remote cause of our want of money is, the great want of an
East India Stock here at home: for the stock of the East India Company, being of
great value, and collected and contracted from all the other particular trades of the
Commonwealth; and a great part thereof having been embargued and detained
now for more than five years past; * * * this loss I say * * * is the more intolerable,
in that the Commonwealth hath lost the use and employment of the stock itself,
and all the increase of Trade which the same might have produced in the several
trades of the subjects, whereby abundance of treasure might have been brought
into this land in all this time." *Free Trade*, 1622, p. 13. The frequent discussions
as to whether the Merchant Adventurers possessed sufficient capital to develope
their trade is another illustration of the difficulty which was felt from the scarcity
of capital in these times.

labour; the act of 1663, which permitted the exportation of
bullion without a license, gave a great impulse to the East
India trade; but the Company continued to import drugs and
spices as their chief returns till about 1670, when a considerable quantity of textile goods was brought over, and some
artisans were sent out to introduce patterns suitable for sale
at home. So great was their success that a few years later
it was alleged that "from the greatest gallants to the
meanest cook maids nothing was thought so fit to adorn
their persons as the fabrics of India, nor for the ornaments
of chambers like Indian screens, cabinets, beds and hangings,
nor for closets, like china and lacquered ware[1]." It thus appeared that the field for the employment of English subjects
was becoming restricted through the importation of commodities manufactured abroad; it was argued that to divert
employment from Englishmen to Hindus was distinctly
prejudicial to the good of the realm[2], and that though the
East Indian trade might have been profitable as long as it
was confined to the importation of Eastern products like
spices, it became distinctly hurtful when it consisted largely
of importing textile fabrics and other goods, which took the
place in the home market of articles already made in
England[3].

*Fanmakers
and
Clothiers
demand
protection.*
There was a great outcry from the fan makers, who seem
to have been a numerous class[4], but the chief complaint
arose in connection with the clothing trades. The company
"finding the advantage they had of having their goods
wrought cheap by the wretched poverty of that numerous
people, have used sinister practices to betray the arts used
in their native country such as sending over artificers[5] and

[1] Pollexfen, *A Discourse of Trade, coin, and paper credit* (1697), p. 99.

[2] This was another point argued in the attack made by the Turkish Company
on the East India Company in 1681. *Allegations* [Brit. Mus. 522, 1, 5 (8), p. 4].

[3] Compare *A memento to the East India Companies* (1700), p. 19. This consists
of a reprint of a remonstrance presented by the East India Company to the House
of Commons in 1628 with animadversions upon it showing how much the character
of their trade had altered since that time and that it could no longer be defended
upon the same grounds.

[4] *The Fann Makers Grievance* [Brit. Mus. 816 m. 12 (97)].

[5] This was denied, except as regards one or two dyers, by the E. I. C. in their
answer to the *Allegations* of the Turkey Company, p. 12.

goods to instruct them in the way of making goods, and A.D. 1603 —1689. mercers to direct them in the humour and fancy of them to make them fit our markets"; this had affected not only the silk weavers at home, but the Norwich clothiers also[1]. It was argued that the employment of 250,000 manufacturers would be injuriously affected by allowing this trade to continue, and that this must react on the price of wool and the prosperity of the landed interest[2]. The case of the company *Davenant.* was powerfully stated by Davenant; he showed that "the importation of East India and Persia wrought silks, stained calicoes, though it may interfere with the manufactures of Norwich, Bristol and other particular places, yet that such importation adds to the kingdom's main stock and wealth, and is not prejudicial to the general woollen manufacture of England[3]." But he did not succeed in convincing the general public that the trade was not hurtful to the employment of our own people. The reply was put thus,—"Suppose a 1697. merchant send £10,000 to India and bring over for it as much wrought silks and painted calicoes as yield him here £70,000, if they be all worn here in the room of our own silk and woollen manufactures, the nation loses and is the poorer £10,000, notwithstanding the merchant has made a very profitable adventure, and so proportionably the more and oftener he sends, the faster he grows rich, and the more the nation is impoverished[4]." The attempt to argue the question without reference to the export of Indian silks to other countries in Europe was unfair to the company: but the arguments are of interest as they proved convincing, and the objectors were successful in carrying their point, for they obtained an act of Parliament in 1700 to restrict the trade *Prohibition* so far as the home market was concerned[5]. It was alleged *Act.*

---

[1] *The great necessity and advantage of preserving our own manufactures* by N. C. a weaver of London (1697), pp. 7, 13.

[2] *Reasons humbly offered for the passing a Bill for the hindering of the Home Consumption of East India Silks* by T. S. a weaver of London (1697), 19.

[3] An *Essay on the East India Trade* (1696), p. 33.

[4] *Great necessity and advantage of preserving our own manufactures*, N. C., p. 6.

[5] 11 and 12 W. III. c. 10. "Whereas it is most evident that the continuance of the trade to the East Indies in the same manner and proportions as it hath been for two years past, must inevitably be to the great detriment of the kingdom by

after a brief experience that the results were most satisfactory; Canterbury "was become desolate, they are now returned to their homes, as before they left them in shoals and companies.   Their houses and their bellies are full; they rather want hands than work, and there is at this day neither complaint nor decay among them for lack of employment," while Norwich and London weavers were flourishing too[1]. It has been necessary, in order to follow out this episode clearly, to refer to events which fell within the succeeding period, but the whole story serves to illustrate what was meant by those who insisted that certain trades were hurtful.

III.   PLANTATIONS.

208.   Sir John Davies, the Attorney General of Ireland under James I., wrote an interesting tract entitled *A discoverie* *of the true causes why Ireland was never entirely subdued.* He pointed out that the English settlers had really been absorbed by the native population, and asserted that a very large proportion of the people outside the pale were, partly at least, of English descent.   He found great fault with the scope which had been given for the survival of Irish customs, more especially tanistry and others which interfered with the settled occupation of the land.   But he also criticised the schemes of colonisation which had been set on foot in previous reigns[2]; the Irish had been driven to fastnesses in the hills and the settlers had occupied the plains without sufficient protection; the grants had been so large that there could be no effective management.   The plantation of Ulster under James I. took place while he was in office and in accordance with the views he expresses in this tract; its success as a prosperous colony may perhaps be ascribed to the wisdom

exhausting the treasure thereof and melting down the coin, and taking away the labour of the people whereby very many of the manufacturers of this nation are become excessively burdensome to their respective parishes and others are thereby compelled to seek employment in foreign parts," East India goods were to be warehoused for re-exportation and not sold within the country.

[1] *Reflections on the Prohibition Act* (1706), p. 8.

[2] Ed. 1612, p. 168.

of his advice; on the assumption that there could be no A.D. 1608 —1689.
civilisation in Ireland, unless it were of an English pattern,
it was necessary to reconstruct the whole social fabric, to —
give a new title to those of the Irish who were still
allowed to hold lands, and to intermingle them with English
so that there might only be one law for the whole country and that they might have no excuse for maintaining
a separate system of jurisprudence among themselves. Sir
Arthur Chichester was the main instrument in carrying
out this scheme[1].

The plantation of the escheated lands in the six counties *Scots in Ulster.*
of Ulster was carefully devised; the country was to be
divided into parishes of from 1000 to 2000 acres, a church
built and a glebe assigned in each case; there were besides
to be three sorts of undertakers,—English or Scottish settlers,
who were to plant their proportions with English or Scottish
tenants; servitors[2] in Ireland, who might take British or
Irish tenants as they pleased; and native freeholders. Both
classes of British settlers were to reside for five years and to
build substantial dwellings, which could be held effectively;
but those who were allowed to take Irish tenants were to
pay £8 per 1000 acres, and not £5. 16s. 0d. as the other
undertakers did. There were also to be market towns
erected, and corporations for the settling of tradesmen and
artificers, as well as a free school in each county for the
education of youth[3].

The whole scheme was one for the foundation of a mili-
tary colony, as may be clearly seen from the survey which *Survey in 1619.*
was taken in 1619 by Captain Pynnar. An extract from
Portlough in Donegal[4] may suffice as an illustration of the
whole.

"LXXXV. 1000 acres. James Cunningham 1000 acres

---

1 The plantation which he devised in Wexford was devised on a system that is
said to have been somewhat more favourable to the natives. Gardiner, *History*,
VIII. 1. But compare Prendergast, *Cromwellian Settlement*, 46.

2 This term Petty understood as applying to anyone who had land given him
in reward for his service in a rebellion or insurrection. Petty, *Anatomy of Ireland*
(1691), 108.

3 Harris, *Hibernica* (Dublin, 1770), 123—130.

4 Pynnar's *Survey* in Harris' *Hibernica*, 177.

called Moyegh. Upon this there is a Bawne of Lime and
Stone, sixty feet square with two flankers; the walls are
fourteen feet high. Within the Bawne there is a good stone
house three stories high, himself and his family dwelling
therein.

I find planted and estated upon this land of British
families,

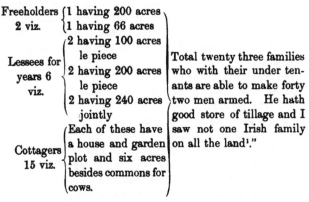

From the point of view of the project, this was a model
estate, but Nicholas Pynnar was not able to report so favourably of the whole scheme. "Many of the English tenants,"
he said, "do not yet plough upon the lands neither use
husbandry; because I conceive they are fearful to stock
themselves with cattle or servants for those labours. Neither
do the Irish use tillage, for that they also are uncertain of
the stay upon the lands; for that by this means the Irish
ploughing nothing, do use grazing, the English very little, and
were it not for the Scottish tenants, which do plough in many
places of the country, those parts may starve." The Irish
graziers paid the best rents, and the undertakers or their
agents preferred to have them as tenants. The twelve
London Companies, each of which had an estate of over 3000
acres, were subsequently reported to be the greatest defaulters
in this respect[2]. Their agents found the Irish "willing to

London Companies in 1628.

---

[1] Pynnar's *Survey* in Harris' *Hibernica*, 286.
[2] On the proceedings against them, see Gardiner, *History*, VIII. 59.

overgive rather than remove"; and that they "could not A.D. 1608 —1689.
reap half the profit by the Irish, whom they use at their
pleasure, never looking into the reasons which induced the
natives to give more than indeed they could well raise, their
assured hope, that time might by rebellion relieve them of
their heavy landlords.... So as the covetousness of the Londoners, meeting with the rebellious hopes of the Irish, has
bred the danger which his prudent Majesty sought to avoid[1]."
While from one side great complaints were made of the
injustice done by the commissioners in seizing lands, and of
the small proportion they allotted to the ancient inhabitants[2],
it was said on the other side that the Irish would not take to
tillage, even on their diminished lands, but continued pasture
farming; also that an essential part of the scheme had been
omitted, since no attempt had been made to transport the
Irish swordsmen and soldiers into Connaught[3], and that
these unruly elements of population, which could not be
absorbed in civilised employments, were still engaged in
robbery and ready for rebellion. There was another element
of uncertainty, in the fear that the patents would be revoked
in the case of those who had failed to fulfil all the conditions
on which they were granted[4]. The statement of those difficulties makes one feel that if success was to attend the effort
to plant English civilisation in Ireland, it was necessary that
the execution of the scheme should be *thorough*.

Whatever may be truthfully alleged against the Earl of *Strafford's*
Strafford it cannot be said that he failed in this respect; *Planta-tions.*
he planned a new plantation on the Shannon[5]; he set himself to clear Connaught of the old proprietors, by asserting
the ancient and disused rights of the crown and cancelling
the patents granted by a commission under James I.[6] He
intended to found a noble English plantation there: but his
grand inquisition of 1635 only resulted in sowing the seeds
which bore fruit in subsequent rebellions, and the great

---

[1] Sir T. Phillips' *Letter* in Harris' *Hibernica*, 247.
[2] Prendergast, *Cromwellian Settlement*, 44.
[3] *Observations* in Harris' *Hibernica*, 122.
[4] Instructions to Lord Falkland. R. Cox, *Hibernica Anglicana*, II. 50.
[5] Gardiner, *History*, VIII. 55.   [6] Cox, *Hibernica Anglicana*, II. 56.

A.D. 1608.
—1689.
*Linen
Manu-
factures.*
scheme was soon abandoned[1]. He had more success in developing the linen manufacture: he reported to the council that he had sowed £1000 of Holland flax seed and set up six or seven looms and that the Irish could undersell France and Holland by 20%[2]. He tried to insist on a high standard of quality in the manufacture, according to the usual practice of the time in the planting of any new industry; and it was made a complaint against him in the Bill of Attainder that he had issued proclamations on this subject "prescribing and enjoining rules and methods of making yarn and thread, which the unskilful natives could not practise," while he seized all badly made linen whereby multitudes were undone and starved[3]. He also procured Privy Seal letters to super-sede the chief grievances of the English settlers, who had had to pay 4s. a ton on imported coal, and excessive customs on the transportation of horses, and 3s. 4d. per head on the exportation of live cattle[4]; he secured that the English settlers in Ireland should no longer be treated as aliens. In all these efforts to develop the resources of Ireland by plant-ing English settlers, Strafford avoided doing anything that would compete with English trade and diminish English revenue, and he took credit for having discouraged the woollen manufacture[5]. By this he did not mean the domestic weaving of freize which the people made for their own use. Twelve sheep sufficed to keep a family in clothing; it was made in widths of about 20 inches, and dyed by the women with madder; very little of it was exported, but the industry continued to flourish till the rebellion of 1641[6]. What Strafford referred to were the attempts to introduce the English industries of manufacturing the old and the new drapery into Ireland. In 1615 Mr Talbot moved in the Irish Parliament that "cloth might be made in this realm[7]";

*English
Settlers
cease to be
Aliens.*

*Dis-
couraged
attempts to
plant
drapery
manu-
facture.*

---

[1] Gardiner, *History*, x. 45.

[2] Cox, *Hibernica Anglicana*, II. 57.

[3] *Ib.* 69.   [4] *Ib.* 57.

[5] Compare his own explanation of the reasons of State for this; Knowles. *Strafford Letters*, i. 193; Cox, *Hibernica Anglicana*, II. 57.

[6] Petty, *Political Anatomy*, 98, 112.

[7] *Irish Commons Journals* (11 May, 1615), I. 52. The substance of this para-graph has already appeared in the *Eng. Hist. Review*, I. 279.

and Mr Dallaway followed him with a proposal that cloth-_{A.D. 1603} workers might be sent for out of England, and " every one to ^{—1689.} be free in each corporation." The subject seems to have been dropped at once and the proposal was not even referred to a committee. Twenty years later the matter was mooted again, and a bill for freedom for working up native materials was introduced and made some little progress in 1634[1]. Strafford may have been successful at that time in intervening against the migration of the staple English trade; the new industry could not be planted unless skilled artisans were allowed to migrate from England; and in 1640 the Council in London gave an unfavourable opinion of the scheme. They did not see how to enforce the seven years' apprenticeship and other rules which were supposed to be necessary for the due regulation of the broad cloth trade[2].

209. With the fall of Strafford, the steady prosecution *Rebellion* of the scheme for carrying on the planting of Ireland came *and Re-* *conquest.* to an end; the rebellion of 1641 and the reconquest by Cromwell interrupted all the industrial life that was beginning to appear; and the scheme for the settlement which commended itself to the wisdom of Parliament was different in kind from that which had been adopted by James and Charles.

It was devised by Parliament chiefly as a means of *The Crom-* *wellian* getting rid of that pressing difficulty, the victorious army, to *Settlement.* which such large arrears of pay were now due; this could be most easily done by giving them allotments of land as 'servitors' in Ireland; and for this purpose a great project of transplantation was carried out. All who had not shown *Transplan-* *tation of* constant good faith to Parliament were to be forced to mi- *proprietors* grate from their lands to new possessions in Connaught, where they could be hedged in by the rivers and a few forts[3], and this transplantation was to apply to Englishmen who had recently settled as well as to the men who had Irish blood in their veins; the grandson of Edmund Spenser suffered the confiscation of the estates which had descended

[1] *Irish Commons Journals* (19 Nov., 1634), I. p. 82.
[2] 25 March, 1640. *Ib.* p. 124.
[3] They were also cut off from the coast. Stokes, *Pococke's Tour*, Introduc. p. 5.

A.D. 1603
—1689.
to him and failed in his plea for exemption[1]. The project
was devised so as to produce the greatest possible shock to
property; labourers were allowed to remain, that they might
till and herd for those to whom the lands were newly assigned,
but the old proprietors were to go[2]; and this ukase applied

*and
burgesses.*
not only to landowners, but to the citizens of Waterford, Kil-
kenny and Galway. The inhabitants of these towns were
English in every respect, but they had not shown active
sympathy in the proceedings of the Puritan Parliament, and
hence the towns were cleared of English merchants and
artisans; some continued to pick up a miserable existence
in the neighbourhood, and some were driven beyond the seas
to Ostend, S. Malo and Nantes[3]; but the deserted towns did
not attract new settlers either from among foreign protestants

*Kidnap-
ping and
traffic in
slaves.*
or from the American plantations. The clearing of the country was carried out ruthlessly; thousands of women, girls and
boys were sent as slaves to Barbados and Jamaica[4]. A careful survey of the districts thus evacuated was made by
Petty[5]; but the repeopling was not easily effected, and at

---

[1] Prendergast, *Cromwellian Settlement*, 116.   [2] *Ib.* 98.   [3] *Ib.* 299.

[4] Thurloe writes to Henry Cromwell:—"I did hope to have given your lordship
an account by this post of the young wenches and youths in Ireland to be sent
into the West Indies; but I could not make things ready. The Committee of the
Council have voted 1000 girls and as many youths to be taken up for that purpose,
and that there be a sum of money allowed for each head for the clothing of them,
and other necessaries to the water side." (Thurloe, *State Papers*, IV. 75.) The
similar project for Scotland met with little favour from the authorities there; it
would set the country in a flame (*Ib.* 41), but Henry Cromwell in Ireland had
readily fallen in with the scheme "despite more than ordinary cross providences
in the undertaking." "Concerning the young women although we must use force
in taking them up yet it being so much for their own good" he was ready to send
as many as were wanted (*Ib.* 23); while he also expressed the opinion that "it
might be of like advantage to your affairs there, and to ours here, if you should
think to send 1500 or 2000 young boys of twelve or fourteen years of age to the
place aforementioned. We could well spare them, and they would be of use to
you, and who knows that it would be a means to make them Englishmen, I mean
rather Christians" (*Ib.* 40). The merchants of Bristol had regular agents for
treating with the Irish Government for slaves for the sugar plantations. Prendergast, *Cromwellian Settlement*, 90, and there seems to have been a good deal of kid-
napping for the same object. E. Eggleston in *Century*, N. S. VI. 854.

[5] He was Professor of Anatomy at Oxford and Gresham Lecturer, and was
sent to Ireland to attend to the Army Medical arrangements; but he soon found
other departments which required to be overhauled. His Survey is distinguished
as the 'down' Survey, apparently because everything was measured and laid down
in maps, instead of being roughly estimated. See Weale's *Letter* in Petty's *History
of the Down Survey* (edited by Larcom for Irish Archaeological Society), p. vii.

the time of the Restoration the country was little better *A.D. 1608 —1689.*
than a wilderness. No social reconstruction of any sort had
been effected, but the claims of the Cromwellian assignees
presented a formidable barrier against any attempt to replace
the former inhabitants in their homes[1]. The 'innocents'
and 'ensigns' who had been dispossessed were not restored,
and gradually sank into utter misery as outcasts who still
hung about the neighbourhood of the lands of which they
and their fathers had been deprived.

The best possibility of turning the miseries of this dis- *Pasture-farming.*
tressful country to good account lay in the development of
pasture farming; for this the climate and soil were alike
suited, and it had been carried on largely in the time of
James I[2], but the possibility of prosperity in Ireland was *1620.*
again sacrificed by the English House of Commons. This
time the pressure came, not from demands of the army, but
from the alleged necessities of the landed interest in some
counties in England[3]. Rents were falling, and it seemed
impossible to raise the supplies which were necessary for the
conduct of the war, if there was any further diminution of
the available resources at home; the importation of Irish *Prohibition of import of Irish cattle.*
cattle was said to be the chief reason of the fall of rents[4],
and though a temporary prohibition did nothing for the
English farmers, the House of Commons persisted in
passing a measure which was fatal to the success of the Irish
graziers. Charles was too much afraid of losing the supplies
on which he counted, to take a decided stand upon the
matter[5]; no similar restriction was placed on Scotland; and
the eagerness of the House of Commons was perhaps to be
partly accounted for by a fear, that if Ireland became too *Motives and*

---

[1] Prendergast, *Ireland from the Restoration*, 15.

[2] It was estimated in 1620 that 100,000 head of cattle were annually imported from Ireland and from 40/- to 60/- a piece paid in bullion for them, *Parl. Hist.*, I. 1195. On the Trade in 1664 see Petty, *Political Anatomy* (1691), 71.

[3] *Parl. Hist.*, IV. 337. There was considerable personal jealousy of the Duke of Ormonde (*Ib.* 340). The Lords held out against the Bill for some time, and many parts of England were opposed to it (*Ib.* 345), but the Commons forced it on.

[4] This is discussed and controverted by Temple, *Works*, III. 19.

[5] The point which was most keenly debated was as to describing the trade as a 'nuisance': the insertion of this word made it impossible for the King to render the Act a dead letter by granting licenses for occasional shipments. Carte, *Ormonde*, II. 334.

prosperous, or prospered more rapidly than England, Charles would, through the influence of the Duke of Ormonde[1], become practically independent of the English parliament.

Effects of the measure on In so far as this political aim underlay their action, the House of Commons were undoubtedly successful: Ireland under their management did not become so prosperous as to furnish the King with independent power; the effects in Ireland were remarkable, and in some ways unexpected. The Irish graziers, debarred from cattle breeding, turned their attention to the growing of wool: for this they found a considerable market on the continent[2]. The main trade of Ireland had hitherto been with England, but now a considerable intercourse sprang up with France and other European countries; and foreigners utilised the materials so well that they became formidable rivals to the cloth manufactures of England[3].

the English in Ireland, The immediate sufferers by the restriction were the English settlers who had devoted themselves to cattle breeding; but their ruin was probably the salvation of the labourers and husbandmen who had escaped transportation when the landowners were turned out to make room for the disbanded army. The English in Ireland were sacrificed to the English at home, and as the cattle ranches no longer paid, there was less excuse for driving out the peasantry. Hence it was that those, who were interested in the preservation of the native Irish, looked back with little dissatisfaction on a measure which ruined the great graziers, but left room for the humbler cultivators. It seems possible too that the prohibition of exportation rendered the price of meat and *and on the cost of living.* cost of living rather lower in Ireland. This is shown by the complaint that ships could be more cheaply victualled in Irish than in English ports[4].

Immigration of English Clothiers. This state of things attracted artisans to that country; at any rate we see signs of a steady immigration of English

---

[1] Carte, *Life of Ormonde*, II. 317—338.

[2] J. Trevers, *An Essay to the restoring of our decayed trade, wherein is detected the Smugglers' Lawyers' and Officers' Frauds* (1677), p. 19.

[3] Carte, *Ormonde*, II. 337.

[4] *Britannia Languens*, 53, 164.

clothiers[1] and a development of the manufacture of drapery
during this period. The cheapness of wool and of living favoured the experiments which were made at different times; and about 1665 or a little later, some "Western Clothiers finding, so early and upon other reasons that are now suborned, that Trade decaying, and many of them reduced to extreme Poverty, removed themselves and their families over into Ireland, invited by the cheapness there of Wool, and of Livelihood. These erected then a Manufactory (great in respect to Ireland) at Dublin which hath been carried on ever since and increases daily. There came also over much about the same time sixty families from Holland, setting up another at Limerick; which, by occasion of the succeeding wars decayed. But, after these more of the English clothiers came and fixed about *Corke* and *Kinsale*, where they continue and are grown not inconsiderable. Some *French* have since resorted to *Waterford* to make druggets there, and other Commodities of their Fashion. And about a year or two ago, some Merchants of *London* raised another Manufacture at *Clonmel*, managing it by their Agents. . . . There is more cry than Wool in this matter: For I dare and do assure you that, modestly speaking, the whole Quantity of what we work up in Ireland amounts not to the Half of what any one Clothing County in England does[2]."

The author of this letter, writing in 1677 to allay his brother's fear of Irish rivalry in the English woollen manufacture, gives us a brief sketch of the attempts that had been made to introduce the trades of making the old and new drapery. The experiments were made by settlers from the west of England and abroad, who roused some opposition, as the English manufacturers were afraid of being undersold by Englishmen in Ireland, who had cheaper material and cheaper food. But the ancient native manufacture of freize is not mentioned at all in this connection, for it did not compete with west of England cloth or Colchester bays. We have here a further indication, if any were needed, that there

---

[1] Walloon clothiers were introduced by the Duke of Ormonde at Clonmel to make Norwich stuffs for the Spanish trade. Carte, *Ormonde*, II. 342.

[2] '*A Letter*,' § 4, quoted in Smith's *Chronicon-Rusticum*, I. chapter lix. p. 303.

was little, if any, export of Irish freize to England at this time, and that it was a distinct manufacture which did not interfere with English trade.

The policy, which was then pursued with regard to the manufacture of drapery in England, was soon applied to the English manufacture which had been newly planted in Ireland. A guarantee of the quality of goods is now afforded by trade marks; but as the woollen manufacture was entirely a domestic industry, it was hardly to be expected that the name and workmanship of any of the hundreds of English handloom weavers should be known abroad. Accordingly, the

The Aulnager. state undertook to give a guarantee that the pieces of English cloth were of a certain size and quality; and it was the business of the *aulnager* to see that this was attended to, and to seal the cloth in regard to which he was satisfied. If Irish drapery was to compete in the English and foreign markets with English drapery, it was desirable that there should be no misunderstandings in regard to size and quality. Accordingly, in 1665 a statute was passed which instituted the office of aulnager[1], and defined the sizes to which the cloth should be woven.

The intention of this act was evidently to improve and foster the art of woollen manufacture in Ireland; but, as was often the case with similar enactments, it did not serve its purpose. In 1695, the Irish Commons condemned it as "impracticable and prejudicial," and proceeded to prepare "the heads of a bill for the better making and regulating" of the woollen manufacture[2]. But no further progress appears to have been made in the matter.

Ireland was thus beginning to make some steps towards

Effects of the Navigation Act. recovery, but there were other restrictions which greatly hampered her. The Navigation Act was so interpreted as

---

[1] "For the more orderly managing the trade and mystery of making and working of woollen cloth, and all other sorts of clothes of the natures and kinds aforesaid, and for the better ascertaining of the length, breadth, and weight of all such clothes to be made within the realm of Ireland ... and that the buyers thereof may have just commerce and trade without deceit or fraud, may it please your majesty, that there shall be and hereby is constituted and appointed an office, called the Alnage Office, &c." (17 & 18 C. II. c. 15, § 9.)

[2] *Irish Commons Journals* (16 Oct. 1695), II. i. 95.

to exclude her from direct trade with the American planta- _{A.D. 1603} tions[1]; little progress was made in shipping, and the colonial _{—1689.} markets were practically closed to her manufactures. In fact the principal grievances which Strafford had endeavoured to remove were re-imposed by Parliament; the policy which they pursued in regard to all colonies was to prevent them from injuring the mother country in any way, as they had been called into being to give support to her power. But Ireland was placed at a distinct disadvantage as compared with other dependencies[2]; tobacco growing was forbidden that the development of Virginia might not be arrested; while disabilities were imposed on the export of cattle to England, which did not affect trade from Scotland. The general subordination of colonial interests to those of the mother country is easily explained; and the special jealousy of Ireland was probably due to the fear which the Commons entertained of Popery, and their suspicion that Charles was ready to avail himself of any aid to render himself absolute; while there was not the same employment for English ship- ping in running across the Channel, as in carrying on more distant trades.

210. While the Irish plantations were struggling with *North* such difficulties, attempts to colonise in North America were *America.* being pushed on with some success; more than one group of settlers obtained a permanent footing, and though the ulti- mate development of their enterprise has far exceeded their wildest expectations, it has in no case been carried out on the precise lines the first founders had devised.

In 1606 serious efforts were made to renew the experi- *Virginia* ments which had ended so disastrously in the time of Elizabeth, *Company* and to colonise the large region which was then known as *1606.* Virginia. Powers were granted simultaneously to a London, and to a West of England or Plymouth Company. Their limits seem to overlap, but they were to keep out of each

---

[1] For disastrous effect on trade of Galway, see *Pococke's Tour*, 104.

[2] Petty calculated that ½d of the imported manufactures might be made in Ireland and ½d of the remainder obtained from foreign parts more easily than from England; it was not necessary to receive anything from England, and not convenient to receive more than ⅓th of the imported goods. *Anatomy*, 126.

other's way and the Londoners were to settle on the southern
portion of the coast while the West of England men were to
occupy the region we know as New England.   They made
some gallant but unsuccessful efforts to colonise, and eventually a portion of their territory was occupied without formal
permission by the emigrants in the May Flower.   Far more
interest attaches to the proceedings of the London Company
which was managed by Hakluyt[1] and other men[2] who had a
real enthusiasm for diffusing a thoroughly Christian civilisation in the newly discovered lands.   Neither the desire for
treasure, nor even the wish to promote the power of England,
appears to have been the chief object of this undertaking.

Its aims. They set about their adventures in the hope that it would
"hereafter tend to the glory of his Divine Majesty in propagating of Christian religion, to such People as yet live in
Darkness and miserable Ignorance of the true Knowledge
and Worship of God, and may in time bring the Infidels and
Savages living in those Parts to human Civility, and to a
settled and quiet Government[3]."   The Company endeavoured
to be careful in the selection of the men who were to emigrate and to refuse "idle and wicked persons such as shame
or fear compels into this action: and such as are the weeds
and rankness of this land": they issued a *Declaration* to show
the persons they would accept both as regards religion and
conversation and faculties arts and trades[4].   They also made

---

[1] Richard Hakluyt in his dedicatory letter to Sir W. Raleigh writes as follows:
"A wise philosopher, noting the sundry desires of diverse men, writeth that if an
ox be put into a meadow he will seek to fill his belly with grass, if a stork be cast
in, she will seek for snakes, if you turn in a hound, he will seek to start a hare: so
sundry men entering into these discoveries propose unto themselves, several ends.
Some seek authority and places of commandment, others experience by seeing of
the world, the most part worldly and transitory gain, and that oftentimes by dishonest and unlawful means, the fewest number the glory of God, and the saving
of the souls of the poor and blinded infidels.   Yet because diverse honest and well
disposed persons are already entered into this business, and that I know you mean
hereafter to send some such good churchmen thither, as may truly say with the
Apostle to the savages, We seek not yours but you, I conceive great comfort of
the success of this your action; hoping that the Lord, whose power is wont to be
perfected in weakness will bless the feeble foundations of your building." Hakluyt,
III. 302.   Compare also *Nova Britannia* by R. I., ff. 6, 7.

[2] Peckard's *Life of Ferrar*, 86, 107; Purchas, *Pilgrimes*, IV. 1777.

[3] King James' first Charter, 10 April, 1606; Stith, *Virginia*, Ap. p. 1.

[4] The persons required for the plantation in 1609 were as follows:—Foure
honest and learned Ministers, 2 Surgeons, 2 Druggists, 10 Iron men for the

careful provision for the maintenance of the religious habits they prized so highly; churches were built with such elabo- ration as their means allowed[1], and the practice of attending the daily services there was carefully enforced[2]. The whole work of colonisation was treated as an enterprise in which it was a work of piety to engage[3], and collections were made in parish churches for the college that was planned, for English and Indians, at Henrico[4]. The work continued with fair success despite many difficulties of every kind. Not- withstanding the efforts of the company the colony had been the refuge of a certain number of dissolute adventurers from the first; there had been much difficulty in keeping them in order, and in preserving friendly relations with the natives, while there had been many quarrels among the officials. Still on the whole the colony prospered. In 1619 a representative assembly was formed of the Boroughs and *Representa-* *tive As-* Townships in Virginia[5], who were to carry on the govern- *sembly* ment in conjunction with the Council of the Company at home. *1619.*

This divided responsibility did not answer well[6], and

Furnace and Hammer, 2 Armorers, 2 Gunfounders, 6 Blacksmiths, 10 Sawyers, 6 Carpenters, 6 Shipwrights, 6 Gardeners, 4 Turners, 4 Brick makers, 2 Tilers, 10 Fishermen, 6 Fowlers, 4 Sturgeon-dressers, and preservers of the Caueary, 2 Salt-makers, 6 Coopers, 2 Coller-makers for draught, 2 Plow-makers, 4 Rope- makers, 6 Vinedressers, 2 Press-makers, 2 Ioyners, 2 Sope-ash makers, 4 Pitch- boilers, 2 Minerall men, 2 Planters of Sugar-cane, 2 Silke-dressers, 2 Pearle- drillers, 2 Bakers, 2 Brewers, 2 Colliers. Anderson, *History of Church of England in Colonies,* I. 224.

[1] "The Captain Generall (Earl De la Warr) hath given order for the repairing of the Church at Jamestown, and at this instant many hands are about it. It is in length threescore foote, in breadth twenty foure, and shall have a chancel in it of cedar, and a Communion Table of the Blake Walnut, and all the Pewes of Cedar, with faire broade windowes, to shut and open as the weather shall occasion, of the same wood, a Pulpet of the same, with a Font hewen hollow, like a Canoa, with two Bels at the West end. It is so cast, as it be very light within, and the Lord Gouernour and Captaine Generall doth cause it to be kept passing sweete, and trimmed up with divers flowers, with a Sexton belonging to it; and in it every Sunday wee have sermons twice a day, and every Thursday a sermon, having true preachers, which take their weekly turnes; and every morning at the ringing of a bell, about ten of the clocke, each man addresseth himself to prayers, and so at foure of the clocke before Supper." Purchas, IV. 1753.

[2] Smith, *Advertisements,* c. xiv., *Works,* p. 957; and in Bermuda, Purchas, *Pilgrimes,* IV. 1746.

[3] Sermons by Crashay and Whitaker, quoted by Anderson, I. 194, 237.

[4] Anderson, I. 255.

[5] Stith, p. 160. W. N. Sainsbury, *On the first Parliament in America, Anti- quary* (July 1881), Vol. IV. p. 8.

[6] Smith, *Advertisements* in *Works* (English Scholar's Library), 927.

A.D. 1603
—1689.

Penal
Settlement
1620.

Slave
Trade.

Spanish
jealousy.

Company
dissolved.

New
England.

Plymouth
1620.

almost immediately afterwards various occurrences took place which entirely changed the character of the undertaking. In 1620 James determined to turn the plantation into a penal settlement to which dissolute persons might be transported[1]; and in the same year a Dutch vessel introduced the first cargo of negro slaves[2]. The company were in grave difficulties with the Crown at the time; as their enterprise was regarded with the greatest jealousy by the Spaniards, with whom James desired to be on friendly terms. Raleigh's name was intimately associated with their undertaking and he had returned in disgrace from his ill-judged expedition to Guiana. The main product of the colony was tobacco, which had been hitherto imported from the Spanish colonies. There need be no wonder that the Spaniards were uneasy about this plantation, or that James was willing to play into their hands at this juncture. In 1622, when all appeared to be on a friendly footing, the English were massacred by the Indians; but for the warning given by a convert, hardly one would have escaped; in the consequent disorganisation, there must have been grave difficulties in carrying on the government of the plantation, and Smith lays great blame on the management in London. In 1624 the Virginia Company was dissolved; and the affairs of the colony were left to be governed by the Assembly in Virginia, subject to the approval of the Crown.

211. The Pilgrim Fathers, when they landed in New England, were able to profit by the experience that had been won in Virginia. They had obtained a patent which was confirmed by the London Virginia Company and gave them permission to plant within their limits, but they found it convenient to settle to the north of Cape Cod[3], and thus within the limits not of the London Company, but of the Plymouth Company from whom they some years later received a patent, which was not however confirmed by the Crown[4]. Plymouth was the name which they gave to their settlement. On their arrival they had no definite relation with the authorities at home but formed themselves by mutual

---

[1] Stith, 168.

[2] A few years later (1623) we hear of the entrapping of English emigrants as bondmen to the Company, *Manchester Papers*, 818, 325 in *Hist. MSS. Commission Report* VIII. Ap. ii. pp. 39, 40.   [3] Gardiner, *History*, IV. 168.

[4] Story, *Commentaries on Constitution*, I. 31.

compact[1] into a civil body politic; they thus enjoyed a position of independence which gave them a free hand in the management of their own affairs. The advantage they possessed, from the experience gained by others in Virginia, was specially clear when the Company of Massachusetts *Massa-chusetts* Bay was founded in 1628, and Salem was built. Smith, who *1628.* was a veteran planter, watched the new attempt with much sympathy, and embodied his advice in *Advertisements for the Inexperienced*[2]; his own operations had been hampered by the London governors, and he would strongly approve of the provision in this case that the government should be in America and not in London[3]. Hence there were no practical means of enforcing compliance with the terms of the charter[4], nor of preventing encroachments upon the neighbouring proprietary colonies at Maine, New Hampshire and Connecticut[5]. The progress of the New England settlements was very rapid; they avoided the difficulties to which Virginia had been exposed from the intrusion of criminals, by establishing a very strict discipline; temporal privileges were dependent *Strict* on church-membership. "Most of the persons at New *discipline.* England are not admitted of their church and therefore are not freemen; and when they come to be tryed there, be it for life or limb, name or estate or whatsoever, they must be tried and judged too by those of the church, who are in a sort their adversaries[6]." They sought out witches, and banished Antinomians; they even expelled and shipped off two members of the Council who were caught using the Prayer-Book[7]: but they succeeded in forming a flourishing community. Though they had traded with the Indians, they had made no serious efforts to civilise them[8], and had been careful to keep

---

[1] Story, *Commentaries on Constitution*, i. 50.
[2] *Works* in *English Scholar's Library*, p. 926.
[3] *Advertisements*, c. ii., *Works*, p. 931; Gardiner, *History*, vii. 155, 156.
[4] Anderson, ii. 139. [5] *Ib.* 143, 148, 175.
[6] Lechford, *Plaine Dealing* (1642), 23, (*Mass. Hist. Soc.* iv.).
[7] Anderson, i. 362. These acts contrast curiously with their professions before leaving England (Baird's *Religion of United States*, 107), with the terms of the Massachusetts Charter (*Ib.* 105), and with the impression they made on Smith, who regarded them, not as Brownists, but "good Catholic protestants, according to the Reformed Church of England," *Works*, 926.
[8] Lechford seemed to think that the form of church government which existed

A.D. 1608
—1689.

*Extermina-
tion of
Pequod
nation.*

*United
Colonies*
1643.

them at arm's length. The war of extermination, **waged** against the Pequod nation alarmed all the neighbouring tribes; and some of the colonies found it wise, in 1643, for their own security to consolidate themselves into "The United Colonies of New England." Massachusetts, Plymouth, Connecticut and New Haven were the first members of this Union[1]; it was the beginning of that federation which has proved such a convenient system for governing a growing nation. Owing to the disturbances in England they were left uncontrolled by English statesmen, and they successfully avoided the difficulties which had proved so injurious in the case of the Virginia Company.

*Practical
independ-
ence and
nominal
subjection.*

At the same time while effectually asserting this practical independence, they professed to be subject to England[2]. This was embodied in all the charters which had been granted to them by the Crown, and it was a view which the Parliamentary Party at home were prepared to enforce. "There hath been and are colonies and plantations which were planted at the cost and settled by the people, and by the authority of this nation, which are and ought to be subordinate to and dependent upon England[3]." But the tie between the mother country and these northern colonies was always of the slightest; they continued to maintain the character they had had from the first; and even commercially they were less indebted to English capital and less favoured by legislation than the sugar colonies.

*Other
Colonies.*

212. Other plantations on the mainland had their special characters stamped on them by their respective founders. Maryland was planted by a conscientious Romanist, Sir George Calvert, in 1632; he had previously endeavoured to

in New England was incompatible with systematic efforts for the conversion of the natives (*Plaine Dealing*, 31—35). There were however some heroic and earnest individuals who did what they could; Henry Demster, a schoolmaster of Cambridge (*Ib.* 53), Roger Williams (Neal, *New England*, I. 160), and Eliot (*Ib.* 242), were remarkable examples of what might be done by men who gave themselves to this work. A Society which was formed in 1649 (Scobell, *Acts*, II. c. 45) to publish Eliot's translation of the Bible, was reorganised through Boyle's influence by charter (7 Feb. 1662); and led to the formation of the Society for the Propagation of the Gospel in 1701. Anderson, II. 410, 496.

[1] Bancroft, *History of the United States*, I. 420.

[2] *Declaration of Pilgrim Fathers* in Anderson, I. 359.

[3] 3 Oct. 1650, c. 28; Scobell, *Acts*, II. 132.

occupy Newfoundland with a settlement which he named A.D. 1608 —1689.
Avalon. Rhode Island was planted by Roger Williams, after
being obliged to leave New England in 1636; farther north a
company was empowered to carry on trade and discovery
near Hudson's Bay, and Rupertland bears the name of the
prince who was one of the prime movers in the speculation.
William Penn obtained a patent in 1680 and was enabled to
provide an asylum for his co-religionists in Pennsylvania.

Meantime the English were also establishing themselves *Bermudas*
on the American islands. The history of the Bermudas is *1609.*
closely connected with that of Virginia, as it was first
occupied by Englishmen who were wrecked there in 1609[1],
while on their way to that plantation. Barbados was inha- *Barbados*
bited by settlers in 1614; but though the soil was fertile they *1614.*
did not turn it to much account till some thirty years later,
when the cultivation and manufacture of sugar were first
introduced. In 1627 the rights of the Earl of Carlisle, who
had received a patent from James I., were recognised over
Barbados and the rest of the Carribee group. Soon after the
introduction of sugar, the West Indian planters began to
realise enormous fortunes. Cheap labour was obtained by
importing negroes and Irish; and there was a sufficient
demand for English goods to make a lively trade with Bristol
and London, which were the principal European depots for
colonial sugar. These islands, like the southern colonies, were
decidedly royalist in their sympathies, and in 1650 Parliament found it necessary to take active steps to reduce them
to obedience. They were quite incapable of offering any
effective resistance to the force sent against them under
Ayscue, though Lord Willoughby was not inclined to give in.

The islands were a centre of royalist influence; but Cromwell seems to have had far larger schemes in view than the
reduction of the whole of the British dominions; he saw that *Cromwell's*
by attacking the Spanish possessions in the New World he *designs against*
could undermine the sources of her strength in the Old. It *Spain.*
was pointed out during negociations with the Dutch in 1653[2],
that the Spaniards had used the wealth of America to further
the designs of the Papacy, and England and Holland might
join in conquering Spanish America. The combined fleets

---

[1] Purchas, *Pilgrimes*, IV. 1737.   [2] Thurloe, II. 126.

would serve to conquer Spanish America one year and Brazil
the next: the allies might thus divide the spoils; England
would relinquish the East India trade to the Dutch, if they
would leave America to us. " By this conquest England may
very well enjoy such a revenue as to discharge all taxes of the
subjects of England and to pay all the navy and forces by sea
and land, by the customs of America, besides the great trade
and riches the subject shall have thereby." The Protector
had no scruple about a right to tax the colonists; and he
seems to have adhered to the narrow view of the New World,
which was even then out of date[1]; and to have valued these
plantations not for the sake of the products that might be
developed, but for the treasure that could be extracted from
them. He undoubtedly had, however, a very clear notion as
to an effective method of wounding Spain. He was not very
successful when he attempted to put it into execution, however. Penn and Venables failed in their attack on Hispaniola[2],
which was a Spanish stronghold, though they managed to
cover their discomfiture by seizing Jamaica,—a valuable possession but one that did little to further the large scheme
of conquest.

*New
Holland.*
    The Dutch had been less successful in America than in
any other field of enterprise; their *forte* lay in trade, rather
than in colonisation. Hudson had been in their employ; and
after one of his failures to find a N. W. passage, he had hit
upon the river, which bears his name, as a possible channel
for river communication with the Pacific. Dutch settlers had
occupied Manhattan Island, and had held their own, despite
the prior claims alleged in 1613 by Argall, the high-handed
governor of Virginia. The colony was not of much importance however, and was easily reduced by the Duke of York
when he attacked it in 1664. The chain of English settlements was complete, and New Amsterdam became New
York.

*The French
in Acadie
1605.*
    There were also some anticipatory symptoms of the great
struggle which raged during the eighteenth century between
the French and English in America. The French had taken
possession of Acadie in 1605, before the issue of the charter
under which the English claimed it[3]. Argall's attempt to

---

[1] See below, p. 152.   [2] Thurloe. IV. 40.   [3] Anderson, I. 246.

oust them was a gratuitous impertinence; but it was not the last time when the conflicting claims of the two rivals under vaguely worded charters came into collision. Early in the century there were disputes with the French as to their right to fish off the coast of Newfoundland and to dry their fish on the shore.

213. As colonisation was the fresh development of *Colonial policy* English enterprise which characterised the seventeenth century, it is perhaps worth while to look more closely at the political objects with which it was undertaken, and the principles on which it was managed.

The Spaniards, in their conquest of the New World, were *of the Spaniards.* undoubtedly attracted by the desire to procure silver and gold; they saw in these new lands a source from which the treasury of their monarch might be filled to repletion, so that the realm might be raised to the highest point of power. The main, if not exclusive, object which they had in view was the procuring of the precious metals; and it has been some-times assumed that the adventurers of other nations were influenced by the same motive. Adam Smith has expressed this opinion[1]; the greed of gold undoubtedly influenced many of the men who joined the expeditions[2], and it seems to have weighed with Raleigh, when he set out on his last voyage to Guiana. Still, even in his case, there was not that devotion to mineral wealth which characterised the Spaniards; and the men who formed the Virginia Company under James I. were bent on developing the resources of the land, and not merely on extracting bullion from the mines. Bacon's advice in his *Essay on Plantations* expresses the *Bacon 1625.* view on which they acted. "Moile not too much under Grounde; For the hope of mines is very uncertain, and useth to make the Planters lazie in other things." Iron indeed he

---

[1] *Wealth of Nations*, 231, but compare the criticism in Roscher, *Zur Geschichte der Eng. Volkswirthschaftslehre*, p. 22.

[2] "The worst was our guilded refiners with their golden promises made all men their slaves in hope of recompences; there was no talke, no hope, no work, but dig gold, wash gold, refine gold, load gold, such a bruit of gold, that one mad fellow desired to be buried in the sands, lest they should by their art, make gold of his bones." Smith, *History of Virginia*, III. 3; *Works*, 407.

A.D. 1603
—1689. regarded as "a brave commodity where wood aboundeth," but the precious metals held no undue place in his remarks. Still more decided expressions of opinion occur in other *John Smith* tracts, especially in the writings of John Smith[1], whose life *1630.* was spent in giving effect to these schemes, and who was the true founder of our colonies; his work in Virginia was a turning point in colonial history. When Englishmen determined to settle in the new land and develop its resources, instead of merely visiting it for trade or to obtain the pre- *Developing* cious metals, they took the first step towards developing the *the re-* *sources of* resources of the great continent and making it the seat of a *New* *Lands,* flourishing civilisation.

That some of them entertained very high views of their mission we have already seen; but in so far as these schemes were adopted and pushed as a piece of English statecraft, we *so as to* may say that politicians hoped to supplement the resources of *supplement* *those of the* the mother country in every way, and not merely to add to its *mother* *country.*

[1] *Advertisements*, cc. i, ix; *Works*, 929, 945. Compare also "But what are those riches where we heare of no Gold nor Silver, and see more impoverished here than thence enriched, and for Mines we heare of none but iron? Iron mindes! Iron age of the world! who gave Gold or Silver the monopoly of wealth, or made them the Almighty's favourites? Precious perils, speecious punishments whose originall is neerest hell. * * Penurious mindes! Is there no riches but Gold Mines? * * But let us consult the wisest Counsellour. *Canaan, Abraham's* promise, *Israel's* inheritance, type of heaven and joy of the earth! What were her riches? Were they not the Grapes of *Eshcol*, the balme of *Gilead*, the Cedary neighbourhood of *Libanus*, the pastury vale of *Jericho*, the dewes of heaven, fertility of soile, temper of climat, the flowing (not with Golden Sands, but) with Milke and Honey (necessaries, and pleasures of life, not bottomeless gulfes of lust), the commodious scituation for two seas and other things like (in how many inferior?) to this of *Virginia*. * * That then is the richest land which can feede most men, Man being a mortall God, the best part of the best earth, and visible end of the visible World. What remarkable Gold or Silver Mines hath *France, Belgia, Lumbardy*, or other the richest peeces of *Europe?* * * The *Spaniards* old Mynes made them the servaunts of *Rome* and *Carthage:* and what their Mynes and mindes doe now I leave to others. * * Neither let any thinke that I pleade against the sourness of the grapes like the fox which could not reach them: but I seriously shew that they are calves and not men, which adore the Golden Calfe, or *Nabuchadnezzars* great golden statue, as if the *body* were not *more than raiment*, and those thinges to be preferred to money, for whose sake mony (the creature of Man; base Idolatry where the Creator worships his Creature!) was first ordained and still hath both use and being." *Virginias Verger* in Purchas's *Pilgrimes*, IV. p. 1814. See also *Nova Britannia* by R. I., f. 23. "The abundance of King Solomon's gold and silver did not rain from heaven upon the heads of his subjects, but heavenly providence blessed his navigations and public affairs, the chief means of their wealth."

treasure. The failure of the Spaniards to retain the wealth they imported, or to profit by it, was becoming manifest; their colonial policy was really bullionist in character, since they tried to amass treasure by obtaining possession of mines. In so far as the Jacobean statesmen took account of *Treasure sought by* treasure in connection with these colonies, they seem to have *mercanti-* expected that the imported commodities would alter our *list rather* trading relations with other countries, and thus affect the *bullionist* balance of trade[1]. They did not confine their attention to *measures.* the prospects of treasure, and they hoped to secure it by mercantilist, rather than bullionist methods.

At the same time, while they desired to develop the resources of the new lands, they desired to do it in such a way as to supplement, and not to compete with, the resources of the mother country. The general character of the policy, which was deliberately pursued towards the colonies, has been indicated above in discussing the Navigation Act; indeed it may be said at once that no English statesman could have seriously proposed to plant and develop distant lands to become our own rivals in trade. There were some who looked *Jealousy* on the plantations with much jealousy. Some maintained *of Plan-* *tations.* that they drained away population we could ill spare[2], and others felt that there was no real gain in diverting English capital to such distant regions[3]. If they competed with merchants at home or industries at home, so as to divert wealth from England[4], they were simply increasing their private lucre; while the power of England was no whit advanced and there was a smaller fund available for its support. Anything that diverted trade from the mother country, or reduced employment in the mother country, was to be deprecated; and the development of the plantations was carefully watched, and their trade managed, so that it might always tend to the aggrandisement of the power of

---

[1] Sandys, *Parl. Hist.* i. 1195, 1197. [2] *Britannia Languens* (1680), 173.
[3] The objection is stated and effectively answered by William Penn. *The benefit of Plantations* in *Select Tracts relating to Colonies* (Brit. Mus. 1029 e. 15).
[4] The North American Colonies were soon able to compete with England for the supply of certain goods to the West Indies. C. Reynel, *The True English Interest*, p. 91. Similar objections are stated and answered by Child, *New Discourse of Trade* (1694), p. 178.

A.D. 1603
—1689.
the realm.　The general scheme for carrying out this plan is well delineated by a Bristol merchant named Cary[1].

in public, not in private, interest.
At the same time it must be noticed that, so far as this general policy was concerned, it aimed at the good of the realm as a whole, and the increase of English power; there was no deliberate intention to subordinate the good of the plantations to the 'private lucre' of any class at home[2]—only to prevent them from tapping the source from which the expenses of the foreign wars were ultimately defrayed.　This may be made clearer by noting one case where a different line was taken, and the 'private lucre' of individuals at home was set aside in order that the products of a colony might be encouraged.　This apparent exception will serve to illustrate the real nature of the rule.

Tobacco introduced.
Tobacco appears to have been introduced into England about the year 1585[3], and the taste for it grew very rapidly. Tobacco shops soon became as common in London as taverns, and great quantities were imported from Spain, where the produce of her colonies was sent; the value of the imports

---

[1] *Essay on State of England* (1697), p. 71.

[2] Pollexfen, *Discourse of Trade and Coyn* (1697), p. 86. "Our *Trade* to our Plantations or *West-India* Collonies takes off great quantities of our Products and Manufactures, as well as Provisions and Handicraft Wares, and furnishes us with some Goods for a further Manufactury, and others in great abundance to be Exported to Foreign Nations, especially of *Sugar* and *Tobacco*. And although some Objections may be made against the use and necessity of those Commodities, yet being so introduced amongst us as it may be impossible to prevent our having them from other Countries, and being a *Trade* which imployes vast numbers of Ships and Seamen, ought to be incouraged; for having lost so great a part of our *Fishing Trades*, these *Trades*, and that to *Newcastle*, are now become the chief support of our Navigation, and Nursery for Seamen. And if all back doors could be shut, that all the Products Exported from those Collonies might without diminution be brought to *England*, that what are not spent here, might be Re-exported from hence; and those Collonies, as the proprietors are *English*, made to have their whole dependance on *England*, the fruits of their labours to be as much for the advantage of *England*, as of those that stay at Home, then all incouragement by easie Laws, Regulations and Protection, should be given to them, they having more opportunities, and being under a greater necessity of gaining more Laborious People, (from whence Riches must arise) to help to make great improvements than *England*, or any other of the Dominions belonging to it: And if it be considered what Forests and Deserts have been improved, and Riches acquired, in some of those Collonies, in so short a time, as the Age of a Man, it must be agreed what hath been asserted, *That the Original of moveable Riches is from Labour*, and that it may arise from the Labour of Blacks and Vagrants, if well managed."

[3] Camden, *Elizabeth*, 324.

of this commodity was estimated at £120,000 per annum, in 1620[1]; it was soon found however, that it could be grown in Virginia, and those, who were interested in the success of the colony, agitated for encouraging the British product, so that we might be able to supply ourselves and not to depend on Spain. The Crown viewed the new luxury as an excellent source of revenue, and levied a heavy duty, and subsequently took the whole crop in charge as a monopoly[2]. James was by no means inclined to encourage this product; partly because he was not unwilling to sacrifice Virginia in order to keep on good terms with Spain, partly because he thought the colonists had better devote their energies to other products[3], and partly because he was strongly prejudiced against the use of tobacco. Under his son however, and after the breach with Spain, there was no hesitation about giving *Virginia protected against* protection to the produce of our own colonies as against *Spanish com-* Spain; under James I.[4], Charles I.[5], the Commonwealth[6], and Charles II.[7] protective measures were passed, for en- *petition* couraging tobacco planting in Virginia and the Bermudas. This was natural enough so long as the competition came from Spanish colonies; but it is surprising to find that the colonial planters were protected against the possible rivalry *and against tobacco* of tobacco growing in England and Ireland[8]. One motive *growing at* lay in the alleged unwholesomeness of British tobacco, *home.* and another in the desire to maintain a source of revenue which gave a considerable yield, as it would have been practically impossible to levy an excise on home-grown tobacco. But these could hardly have been the sole motives; Parliament was jealous of any revenue that came from sources which it did not control[9], and there can be but little doubt that the Acts of Charles II. express the genuine *Summary of Colonial* motives of Parliament, when they say that it is of great *Policy.*

---

[1] Sir E. Sandys, *Parl. Hist.* I. 1195, 1197.   [2] Rymer, *Foedera*, XVII. 190, 233.
[3] This opinion was strongly expressed by John Smith, *History*, IV. in *Works*, 616.
[4] Rymer, *Foedera*, XVII. 621, 668.   [5] *Ib.* XIX. 235.
[6] Scobell, *Acts*, II. 238; Macpherson, *Annals*, II. 448.
[7] 12 C. II. c. 34; 15 C. II. c. 34; 22 and 23 C. II. c. 26.
[8] The Tobacco Monopoly was one of the grievances alleged by the Irish Parliament against Strafford (Cox, II. 62) and 12th article of the impeachment in Rushworth. *Historical Collections*, VIII. 66.   [9] See below, p. 295.

"concern and importance that the Colonies and Plantations
of this Kingdom in America be defended, protected, maintained and kept up, and that all due and possible encouragement be given unto them, and that not only in
regard great and considerable dominions and countries have
been thereby gained and added to the Imperial Crown of this
Realm, but for that the strength and welfare of this kingdom do very much depend upon them in regard of the
employment of a very considerable part of its shipping and
seamen, and of the vent of very great quantities of its
native commodities and manufactures, as also of its supply
with several considerable commodities, which it was wont
formerly to have only from foreigners, and at far dearer
rates, and forasmuch as tobacco is one of the main products
of several of those plantations, and upon which their welfare
and subsistence and the navigation of this kingdom and
vent of its commodities thither do depend," &c.[1] As a consequence, tobacco growing in England and Ireland, with all the
prospective gain to the landed interest, was sacrificed to
develop a colony. The very existence of the colony seemed
to be at stake; and Parliament determined to take a line
which maintained the distant colony, rather than allow the
grower in England to attempt to compete with the planter
in Virginia.

IV. INDUSTRY.

*Industrial
policy
maintained
and de-
veloped*
214. The seventeenth century furnishes a large number
of additional illustrations of the industrial system which has
been already described in connection with the reign of
Elizabeth. The same sort of policy was continued on every
side, and it was only in one direction that there was any
fresh departure which calls for special attention. There were
new developments however in the regulation of industry,—
the one subject on which Elizabeth's action was wholly
tentative, and did not come to be embodied in any great
legislative measure. It is also a subject which presents

---

12 C. II. c. 34. See also 22 and 23 C. II. c. 26.

special difficulties to the student; we have so entirely discarded all attempts of the sort that we are apt to regard all
such efforts at regulation as being mischievous and oppressive; we fail to discriminate between them. To contemporaries, however, it appeared that the regulation of industry
was necessary and right for many purposes; the only question
with them was as to the manner in which it should be done.
There is no topic on which it is more necessary to divest
ourselves of our habitual modes of thought, and to adopt the
standpoint of bygone politicians, if we really wish to understand their actions and the occurrences of the time; and
there are few subjects in regard to which it is so hard to
grasp the current view exactly.

The regulation of industry was universally regarded as *in regard*
right and necessary for certain distinct objects. It might be *to the regu-*
lation of
desirable (1) for political purposes or as they said for ' Rea- *industry*
for political
sons of State'; how far this should include fiscal reasons was,
as we shall see, a point that gave rise to much dispute; but if
the political reasons were good, then the regulation of trade
needed no defence. There was also a widely recognised *and other*
justification for regulation in order (2) to maintain the quality *public pur-*
poses.
of goods, and to keep up the standard and reputation of
English manufactures; and (3) to reward those who introduced some new trade or improved process. No one of these
is wholly left out of sight in the present day; there are
government secrets in our arsenals which it is deemed inex-
pedient to publish to possible foes; and opium is an important fiscal monopoly in India. Quality is regulated by
parliamentary authority in many adulteration acts, and
inventions are secure by patents. But whereas such regulation is exceptional and occasional with us, it was frequent and habitual in many trades to which we should
never think of applying it. There are indeed Socialists
who would carry State or Municipal regulation of industry
much further than was attempted under the Stuarts, in the
hope of getting rid of the evils of competition altogether;
the experience of the seventeenth century will at least
serve to illustrate the extreme difficulty of any similar
attempt in the present day.

(1) Political excuses were clearly forthcoming for one grant which must have caused much discomfort, Saltpetre was needed for the manufacture of gunpowder, and had to be procured at any cost; the patent was not discontinued in 1601 ; Cecil said of it, " There is another patent for saltpetre that hath been both accused and slandered ; it digs in every man's house, it annoys the inhabitant and generally troubleth the subject, for this I beseech you to be contented.......Her Majesty means to take this patent unto herself and advise with her Council touching the same, for I must tell you the kingdom is not so well furnished with powder now as it should be[1]." The House appeared to be perfectly satisfied with this arrangement, and the exemption was retained in the Act of 1624 ; although the practical inconvenience caused by the operations of the saltpetre-men must have been very hard to tolerate[2]. The East India Trade, by bringing in a sufficient supply for the manufacture of powder, rendered the minute regulations, such as those about the paving of stables, unnecessary. The monopoly of the patentees was set aside in 1641[3], so that there might be free importation and unrestricted manufacture of gunpowder; but the practice of allowing patentees to dig for saltpetre was revived by Parliament during the Civil War[4].

Similarly the patent for ale-houses was intended to restrict their numbers and promote temperance : it did not have this result, and gave rise to scandalous exactions and abuses; but the granting of these letters commended itself to the House of Commons as wise, since this patent also was exempted at the time of the general repeal. Like Sir Walter Raleigh's patent for taverns[5] it helped to secure a sort of police supervision, and the same motive was at work in other cases; great abuses were found to exist in common bowling alleys, dicing houses and tennis courts, erected and frequented by many persons of mean quality ; and the whole responsibility for the supervision and regulation of such places of amusement in London and the neighbourhood was

---

[1] S. D'Ewes' *Journals*, 653.   [2] *Foedera*, xviii. 23.   [3] 17 Charles I. c. 21.
[4] 1644, c. 35, Scobell, i. 68.   Gardiner, iv. 2—6.   [5] Hall, *Eliz. Soc.* 79.

given to Clement Cotterell who held the office of groom-porter[1]. A.D. 1603 —1689.

Under this head may also be noticed the manufacture of gold and silver thread, which was viewed with much suspicion, as it tended to exhaust the treasure of the kingdom. — One method of regulation was tried after another; the claims of the Goldsmiths' Company were set aside, and the trade was conferred on patentees who undertook to import bullion for the purpose; subsequently, under Bacon's advice it was, like the manufacture of saltpetre, taken into the king's hands to be exercised only by his agents[2]. *Gold and silver thread.*

From all this it is clear that the granting of a patent for exclusive trade was not objected to by Parliament when a good political reason could be alleged, and the same holds of the attempts (2) to improve the quality of wares. The necessity of some regulation or institution for this purpose was admitted again and again in parliament, and under all governments. The Act of 1624 specially exempts "corporations companies and fellowships of any art, trade, occupation or mistery"; in that very year the Cutlers' Company was incorporated by statute[3] and the worsted weavers of Norwich[4] obtained similar privileges under the Commonwealth. Early in the time of Charles II. the Irish parliament established the office of aulnager as a first step to introducing a drapery trade[5]: the regulation of trade was eagerly undertaken at the very time when the victory of the opponents of monopolies was most complete. (3) It is unnecessary to prove that there was no objection to granting a patent to anyone who introduced a new trade or a real improvement in an old one; the fifth section of the Act of 1624 specially provides for such grants for periods of twenty-one years. *The quality of wares.* *Inventions.*

215. Different methods might be adopted for obtaining these objects however; and under different circumstances one method or another might prove preferable. (i) In some instances the business was taken directly into the royal hands, —this was the case with saltpetre under Elizabeth, with gold thread under James, and with tobacco under Charles in *Methods of control.* *Royal management.*

---

[1] Rymer, *Foedera*, XVII. 236. [2] Gardiner, IV. 18. [3] 21 James I. c. 31.
[4] Scobell, II. 146, 269, 393. [5] 17 and 18 Charles II. c. 15.

Ireland.   The precise limits of the royal prerogative in this matter were the subject of much difficulty; tin in Cornwall came from royal lands, and in regard to goods that came from new colonies there was a similar claim[1]; the clearest definition of what the Crown might restrain to itself, really comes out in the argument of Pollexfen as to what it might grant to a subject, in connection with the East India Trade[2].   But the Commons do not appear to have been much inclined to raise this point directly, either under Elizabeth or James, or to have questioned the royal wisdom in assuming the immediate responsibility for certain trades that admittedly required some sort of regulation.

*Offices
erected.*
(ii)   Another expedient was the erecting of an office to control some business.   The aulnager is the immemorial instance of this method of regulation, and King Charles I. fell back on this ancient precedent in erecting an office for Exchanges.   The reasons for doing so appear to have been precisely similar to those which had influenced Edward I. in organising a similar institution.   It was alleged that the merchants selected heavy coins when they had to make payments abroad, and that the coin of England was being gradually deteriorated.   It does not appear that the king made any effort, such as Malynes would have advised, to control the rates of exchange, but merely aimed at preventing abuses in connection with the currency.   It is worth while to note that the need of some regulations of the kind was strongly felt under the Commonwealth[3].

Companies,
(iii)   The formation of a company to carry on some trade, with full powers of self-regulation, was a favourite expedient. It had long tradition in its favour, for the craft-gilds of mediæval England were institutions of this kind.   At the same time there had been frequent difficulties, when these bodies were not kept under proper control, and these troubles reappeared in the seventeenth century[4].   Their powers might
*how
authorised.*
emanate (a) from the Crown, (b) from Parliament, or (c) from

---

[1] Rymer, *Foedera*, xviii. 72 for tobacco.

[2] *Discourse of Trade, Coyn* &c., p. 70.   [3] Ruding, i. 407.

[4] There is an interesting discussion of the precise legal status of these corporations, and the ordinances which they could (and could not) legally make, in W. Sheppard's *Of Corporations, Fraternities, and Guilds* (1659), § 8, pp. 81—108.

some municipality; and in either case there might be diffi- culties though of rather different types. The difficulties about trades which were authorised by the Crown, and were independent of their neighbours, have been noted above and it is unnecessary to add very much about the matter here[1]; those of the statutory trades became more obvious in the eighteenth century from their want of adaptability, but the jealousy of municipal corporations is a special feature of the times. During the time of Cromwell much was said of grievances which arose in connection with the town of New- *Newcastle.* castle. It possessed very special privileges under a charter granted by Queen Elizabeth in 1601, and these had been specially preserved in the Act of 1624. With these powers the old companies had all come to the front again, and they were brought into bitter hostility with the neighbouring town of Shields. The chief assertor of the common law rights, in opposition to special privileges, was a brewer named Ralph Gardner, who certainly underwent great personal sacrifices in the cause, and brought startling allegations against the Newcastle men for the way they exercised their powers[2]. His opponents were too strong for him, however, and neither the Long Parliament nor the Protector gave him the redress he hoped for.

The granting of patents to corporations was an expedient *Companies and Cor-* of which Charles I., acting on the advice of Noy[3], availed *porations of*

---

[1] § 108 in Vol. I. p. 312.

[2] He asserts that the action of the burgesses from 1642 to 1644 "caused coals to be four pound a chaldron, and salt four pound the weigh, the poor inhabitants forced to flie the country, others to quarter all armies upon free quarter; heavy taxes to them all, both English, Scots, and Garrisons; plundered of all they had; land lying waste; coal-pits drowned; salt-works broken down; hay and corn burnt; town pulled down; mens wives carried away by the unsatiable Scots and abused; all being occasioned by that corporations disaffection; and yet to tyrannize as is hereafter mentioned." *England's Grievance Discovered.* Address to the Reader. The reply of the Corporation, who were represented in London by Mr S. Hartlib, has been printed from a ms. of Alderman Hornby's on *Conservatorship of Tyne* in Richardson, *Reprints of Rare Tracts,* III. p. 35. Many of Gardner's accusations are met by a simple denial of the alleged facts; in regard to the conservancy of the river, the most serious question, they had acted on the advice of the authorities of the Trinity House, p. 62. They claim to retain special privileges on political grounds however, as their town was a defence against the Scots. One of their corporations, the Hostmen, paid £8000 a year to the public treasury and might well expect their privileges to be protected, pp. 43, 44.

[3] Dowell, I. 244.

himself very freely. It seems probable however that these
new corporations were of a different character economically,
from those which Parliament had had in view when the Act
of 1624 was passed. The old companies had consisted of
— men who worked independently, though they worked by
rule; they were analogous to a regulated company for trade.
—The new companies appear to have consisted of men who
carried on all their dealings together, and were analogous to
a joint-stock company. They seem to have been capitalist
affairs, and may perhaps be taken as an early instance of the
introduction of the joint-stock principle into industry. Of
course such a corporation had a monopoly in the strictest
sense of the word, just as much as any individual inventor
to whom a patent might be granted for a limited time.
Charles found in this a convenient expedient for rendering
industry subservient to the fiscal interests of the Crown, and
obtaining, indirectly, the revenue which might have come
from an excise. The grievance in his time was thus a
political one; but in the reigns of Elizabeth and James the
consideration of revenue appears to have been quite subordinate, and the real grievances, of which so much was
heard, were economic rather than political.

*Economic
evils of such
Patents.*
216. The economic evil was of course felt in the form of
enhanced price or worse quality; in fact, as we should say, it
was due to the absence of competition. The whole trade
had got into one man's hands and he could do as he liked;
he had an exclusive right to sell and was a monopolist. But
such monopoly grows up almost insensibly in many cases
where attempts are made to organise a trade. The regulation of any industry is very difficult, unless all those who are
exercising it are drawn under the control of the authority
constituted for this purpose; in mediæval times the gild of
each craft was empowered to control all the men exercising
that calling within the bounds of the town; the *Zunftzwang*
was essential to their successful working; in modern times
Trades Unions endeavour, by vigorous moral suasion, to obtain
a similar position; and so the royal efforts to improve any
industry and regulate it better could be most conveniently
carried through, when the sole right to produce some article

was placed in the hands of an individual or company. But such an exclusive right to sell was a *monopoly*: and the exclusive right to produce might easily become an exclusive right to sell. The men who had a new method of making some kinds of glass were first protected against foreign competition, and then secured an exclusive right for all kinds of glass against other producers at home[1]; the possessor of such a right was practically uncontrolled in the price he asked, and was in a position in which he might make large gains at the expense of the public; while his exclusive claim might also interfere most seriously with the trade of other men, who were already exercising that calling, and who were by the special rights conferred on one man deprived of their livelihood.

As a matter of fact, it was soon found that in many cases the grievance far exceeded the public good which accrued from the royal patents conferring exclusive rights on certain traders; and it was the aim of the Commons under Elizabeth and James, not to prevent the king from regulating industry and trade, but to lay down conditions which should prevent serious grievance from arising, and under which any aggrieved party could obtain legal satisfaction. The *Declaration of Right* appears to have gone further; but the Commons under Elizabeth and James only sought to control the manner in which a recognised prerogative was exercised[2]. The constitutional dispute in these reigns as to monopolies therefore reduces itself to a series of questions as to the amount of grievance which was created under any particular grant, and the public purpose, if any, it subserved.

The report of the debate in Elizabeth's time brings this out clearly. The member for Warwick defined a monopoly as "the restraint of anything public in a city to a private use," and termed the man who enjoyed such a monopoly, the "whirlpool of the prince's profit[3]." The chief grievances were at the hands of the agents or substitutes of the men who held the royal letters patent. Mr Martin spoke of the

Marginal notes:

A.D. 1603 —1689.

Growth of Monopoly,

and consequent grievances,

as stated in Parliament.

---

[1] Gardiner, *History*, IV. 9.
[2] See Mr Moore's Speech, D'Ewes' *Journals*, 654.   [3] *Ib.* 644.

burden of "monstrous and unconscionable substitutes to the
monopolitans of starch, tin, fish, cloth, oil, vinegar, salt, and I
know not what, nay what not? The principallest commodities both of my town and country are ingrossed into
the hand of these blood-suckers of the commonwealth[1]."
On the other hand there was little complaint in regard to
the monopoly of playing-cards, at the mention of which Sir
Walter Raleigh blushed[2]; while there was a storm of indignation at the suggestion that if they did not bestir themselves, bread would be in the list of monopolised articles before
they met again[3]. So far as the patent for tin was concerned
it was maintained by Raleigh that he had so conducted the
business as to give full employment and good wages to all
the miners who liked to apply for work, however the price of
tin varied, and that the monopoly was therefore a real benefit
to the producers generally, and not for his private advantage.

*New
Trades.*
The grievance caused by the monopoly might be felt
either by other traders or by the consumers. In the case of
a new trade, whether newly invented or newly introduced,
rival traders had suffered no wrong, and were not entitled to
complain; this principle was exemplified in 1620, when the
monopoly for salt was adjudged void because the alleged
invention was not new[4]. Hence, as noted above, in the Act
of 1624 which abolished monopolies, special exemption was
made for patents for new industries for twenty-one years,
and patents for new processes for fourteen years[5]; even in
the heat of their indignation against monopolies the Commons did not condemn such grants as these, for they were
not a grievance; while the public advantage through the
introduction of new trades was so great that they certainly
deserved encouragement. Similarly with regard to consumers, to have the necessaries of life enhanced in price was
a real grievance, but a monopoly which affected luxuries like
playing-cards need not be taken very seriously.

*Confusion
caused in
trade by
these grants
even when
most defen-
sible.*
The indirect grievances which might arise from the
granting of a patent were brought into clear light by the
terrible disorder which arose in consequence of the patent

[1] Simon D'Ewes, *A Complete Journal of the Houses of the Lords and Commons*,
646.   [2] *Ib.* 645.   [3] *Ib.* 648.

[4] *Parl. Hist.* I. 1205.   [5] 21 James I. c. 3.

granted to Sir William Cockayne. The English did not excel in the dressing and dyeing of cloth, and a large part of the products of English looms was exported by the Merchant Adventurers, who obtained licences for this purpose[1], to be finished in Holland. To this the clothworkers and dyers of London took exception, and Sir William Cockayne obtained a patent for the sole right of dyeing and dressing cloth. He was not able, however, to carry on the trade satisfactorily; the Dutch retaliated by prohibiting the importation of English cloth undressed and undyed; and thus the staple trade of the country was thrown into confusion[2]. The whole business of the weavers was very seriously affected[3], and the ancient company of Merchant Adventurers had their privileges temporarily recalled. Such were the serious effects of granting an ill-advised patent for the improvement of one department of our staple industry[4].

The story of another trade, silk-dyeing, brings out the *Silk-dyeing.* practical difficulties which were felt in connection with these efforts to regulate the quality of goods. The main abuse in silk-dyeing arose through the addition of gum in the dyeing process; this increased the weight of the silk, but interfered with its quality; in 1606 King James issued a proclamation against this practice and imposed heavy fines, but with no good result; and in 1632 King Charles incorporated the silkmen to have supervision over one another; as however the company "upheld abuses" instead of correcting them, he revoked the charter, and gave the responsibility over them to the London Company of Dyers, who were empowered to seize all silks improperly dyed; this company was however content to exact quarterly payments and connived at the frauds they were expected to prevent. In 1639, accordingly, Charles finding that no search was sufficient to detect the mischief, erected an office, and insisted that all persons in London should bring their silks to be viewed and registered,

---

[1] Spedding, *Letters and Life of Bacon*, v. 169. [2] *Ib.* 259.

[3] It was alleged that the dislocation led to the development of weaving at Frankfort. Battie, *Merchant's Remonstrance*, 3.

[4] Similar confusion occurred in 1629 and 1630 when the merchants both English and foreign lent their support to the protest of the House of Commons, and let their trade cease, rather than pay customs when levied without parliamentary authority. Gardiner, *History*, VII. 83, 168.

A.D. 1603
—1689.

both before the process of dyeing and after. This scheme, it was said, had worked well, and Charles II. was petitioned to take similar order[1].

Patents as expedients for raising a revenue.

217. The discussion of patents and monopolies under Charles assumes a new character, inasmuch as he admittedly used his powers as an expedient for getting money. This comes out very clearly in a most interesting letter from Strafford[2] in regard to the Irish revenue; he suggests that the king should take the business of importing salt into his own hands, and that he would thus get a payment like the French *gabelle*; by similar arrangements for malt he hoped to pave the way for an excise, like those in Holland; and he was sanguine enough to hope that he could get parliamentary authority for these arrangements, while he thought it would be rash to try to effect them without. In England Charles pursued a similar course during his personal government; the various reasons mentioned above were alleged in favour of granting many patents, and in some cases these reasons were sound so far as they went; but there was in addition an underlying motive, which it is not easy to prove in the case of Elizabeth or James, since Charles granted the patents with the distinct view of thereby obtaining revenue.

How far plausible.

Charles and his advisers probably held that, since the government must be carried on, reasons of state justified him in taking every available means of raising funds. But without discussing this issue, it is certainly true that some of these demands by the Crown were more plausible than others.

Salt.

Salt was an article which was largely imported; it was, from the point of view of contemporaries, undoubtedly desirable to introduce the manufacture into England, rather than to continue to depend on foreigners for a necessary; patents were granted for salt-works, and for the manufacture by a new process. So far all seemed well; it was certainly plausible too to urge that a payment should be made by the manufacturers of salt to reimburse the Crown for the loss in customs when this article was no longer imported[3]. Similarly in the very high-handed proceedings, from which the Vintners' Company suffered[4], it was possible to urge in excuse that taverns

---

[1] *Reasons for renewing the Office of Silk Dyeing,* Brit. Mus. 816 m. 12 (96).
[2] *Letters,* I. 193.   [3] (Gardiner, *History,* VIII. 285.   [4] (Gardiner, VIII. 286.

were a growing evil and that wine was an imported luxury A.D. 1603 —1689. the excessive use of which might be fitly restrained by causing the price to be enhanced: King James's patent for ale-houses was defended on sumptuary grounds. But in the Vintners' case, even if this allegation was plausible, there was no serious justification for the way in which they were treated.

In those instances, when the reason for granting a patent was to improve the quality of a manufacture which was already practised in the country, there was if possible less excuse for the Crown to claim a share of the profit of the improved production. This was what occurred in the case of soap however[1]. The intricate dispute between the paten- *Soap.* tees and the independent soap-boilers, the prohibition of fish oil, the solemn washing in public by two laundresses and the adjudication on the merits of the soaps they used, as well as the subsequent incorporation of the independent boilers, are excellently described by Professor Gardiner[2]. But this ela- borate farce could hardly have deceived anyone, and least of all its authors; the real motive was to procure a revenue.

In this Charles was extraordinarily successful; he cal- *Revenue raised and* culated to obtain £20,000 a year from soap alone[3]; but *consequent* he created an extraordinary amount of discontent. Mono- *discontent.* polies for articles of common consumption were those in regard to which the Parliament of Elizabeth had shown itself most jealous; and these were the very things which it was most tempting to touch for revenue purposes, as they might be made to yield a sum that was really worth having[4].

[1] A mass of information on the subject will be found in *A Short and true relation concerning the soap busines* (1641), Brit. Mus. E 156 (6).

[2] Gardiner, VIII. 71.　　　　[3] *Ib.* 75.

[4] It may be doubted if there was much money to be obtained from the man who brought out new inventions; it is not clear that the sanguine speculators were able to pay the sums they promised for exclusive rights; Sir William Cock- ayne's patent was unprofitable, and it is hardly conceivable that any large number of the schemes now floated really answered. Engines for cutting timber, for draining marshes, and transporting horses were patented in 1629 (*Foedera*, XIX. 40) as well as a medicine for the rot in sheep; in 1630 the king secured one-third of the profits accruing from a new invention for extracting gold and silver from copper, tin and lead; David Ramsay patented nine inventions in 1631, including one for making boats, ships and barges go against a strong wind and tide; another gentleman, Thomas Grent, patented a windmeter, a fish call or looking-glass for fishes, a water bow and a hydraulic cabinet for putting people to sleep. *Ib.* XIX. 239, 371. It may be doubted whether there was much money either for the paten- tee or for Charles in these inventions.

At the Council at York he was obliged to declare many of
the patents void; but enough remained to call forth an
indignant declamation from Colepepper in the Long Parliament. "I have but one grievance more to offer unto you, but
this one compriseth many; it is a nest of wasps, or a swarm
of vermin, which have overcrept the land, I mean the
monopolisers and pollers of the people. These, like the frogs
of Egypt, have got possession of our dwellings, and we have
scarce a room free from them; they sip in our cup, they dip
in our dish, they sit by our fire; we find them in the dye-vat,
wash-bowl, and powdering tub; they share with the butler
in his box, they have marked and sealed us from head to foot.
Mr Speaker, they will not bate us a pin; we may not buy
our own clothes without their brokage. These are the
leeches that have sucked the commonwealth so hard, that it
is almost become hectical. And some of these are ashamed
of their right names; they have a vizard to hide the brand
made by that good law in the last Parliament of King James:
they shelter themselves under the name of a corporation;
they make bye-laws, which serve their turn to squeeze us,
and fill their purses; unface them and they will prove as bad
cards as any in the pack. These are not petty chapmen,
but wholesale men[1]."

*The Com-
monwealth
and the
excise.*

Under the Commonwealth and Charles II. the granting
of patents and formation of exclusive corporations did not
cease; but the reasons for which they were given commended
themselves to public opinion as good and sound. As an
excise had been introduced, there was no longer the same
motive for trying to tap this fund of revenue by indirect
means. But the old motives for improving trade or planting
some new trade still held good. After Cromwell's breach
with Spain and ineffectual attempt to destroy her command
of American silver and gold, the trade in Norwich goods,

*Norwich
weavers.*

which had been exported in large quantities to Spain, was
much interrupted and the manufacturers were greatly distressed[2]; Parliament was forced to try and do something to
mitigate the evil, and a new corporation of weavers for this
district was the result. Similar bodies were erected by

---

[1] *Parl. Hist.* II. 656.   [2] Carte, *Ormonde*, II. 342.

Charles II. for carpet-weaving at Kidderminster[1] and for the silk-throwers[2]; but these were done without any fiscal object; and though they might be condemned by modern economists they do not seem to have provoked much hostile criticism, and they certainly had no constitutional significance.

A.D. 1603 —1689. Carpet-weaving.

218. There are two subjects of considerable interest to which some allusion may be made here; they are at least cognate to industrial regulation in the wide sense in which it was understood in the days of the municipal craft gilds. These had been the organisations by which order was maintained, as masters were responsible for the good conduct of the apprentices and journeymen who lived in their houses. From whatever cause we find, especially in the early part of the seventeenth century, considerable difficulty from the alleged increase of drunkenness[3]; it is almost the typical complaint of the time, as the number of tramps and vagrants had been the striking feature of the sixteenth century.

Craft gilds and police regulation.

Drunkenness in the 17th century.

In large towns there were an excessive number of taverns, where wine was drunk; and in the reign of Charles II. we hear of the increasing consumption of French brandy, as a habit which was both deleterious and unpatriotic[4]. But the chief outcry seems to have been in regard to ale-houses; there had been, as the records of manorial courts show, immemorial efforts to control the breweresses; but ale-conners and ale-tasters were chiefly interested in securing ale of the proper quality and strength as laid down in the Assize. Parochial officers were not efficient agents in putting down tippling; the constables were inclined to connive at it, or visit a house 'under colour of search' in the hope of getting beer from the company[5]; while the penalties were so excessive in the first statute on the subject[6] that they could not be enforced. The Act[7] in the first year of James was intended to restrain inordinate haunting and tippling in inns

Taverns.

Ale-houses.

Stringent Act in 1604.

---

[1] 22 and 23 Charles II. c. 8. [2] 14 Charles II. c. 15.

[3] Hall, *Elizabethan Society*, 76. Camden definitely dates the introduction of this vice from the Netherlands in 1581. *Elizabeth*, p. 263.

[4] *Grand Concern* in *Harleian Miscellany*, VIII. 559. The substance of this and the following paragraphs appeared in the *Contemporary Review*, Nov. 1886.

[5] Lupton, *London and the Countrey carbonadoed*, in *Harl. Misc.* IX. 330.

[6] The Act of Edward VI. (5 and 6 Ed. VI. c. 25) gave power to the justices to suppress unnecessary tippling-houses, but it was chiefly directed against disorder, not against excessive drinking. [7] 1 James I. c. 9.

and ale-houses; it declares "the true use of ale-houses" to be for the relief of wayfarers and not for the "entertainment of lewd and idle people." There was to be a penalty of ten shillings for permitting "unlawful drinking," and all drinking was unlawful except by *bona fide* travellers, by the guests of travellers, and by artisans and labourers during their dinner-hour. The licensed ale-house was only to be open to residents in the locality for one hour in the day, for the consumption of liquor on the premises. An additional measure was passed in 1607[1], and these acts were made perpetual in

1624. the last parliament of James[2]. The fines on unlicensed ale-houses were so high that offenders could not pay them, nor "bear their own charges of conveying them to gaol"; so that constables were "much discouraged" from presenting them[3].

1628. Accordingly the penalties were somewhat relaxed under Charles I., but the evil seems to have gone on increasing. The Brewers' Company in 1647 were much aggrieved about the laxity of the magistrates in neglecting to put down "unlicensed ale-houses, which are the only receptacles of drunkards." They hoped that a consideration of the heinousness of the brutish sin of drunkenness would "move the hearts of the pious magistracy of these times to have a more vigilant eye over these irregular unlicensed private houses," and to show a just appreciation of the merit of the Company of Brewers. But the evil does not seem to have abated, for in

1659. the year preceding the Restoration a French Protestant wrote from London, "there is, within this city, and in all the towns of England which I have passed through, so prodigious a number of houses where they sell a certain drink called ale, that I think a good half of the inhabitants may be denominated ale-house keepers....But what is most deplorable, where the gentlemen sit, and spend much of their time drinking of a muddy kind of beverage, and tobacco, which has so universally besotted the nation, and at which I hear they have consumed many noble estates....And that nothing may be wanting to the height of luxury and impiety of this abomination, they have translated the organs out of the churches[4] to set them up in taverns, chanting their dithyrambics and bestial

---

[1] 4 James I. c. 5.　　　　[2] 21 James I. c. 7.
[3] 3 Charles I. c. 4.　　　[4] Thursday, May 9, 1644. Scobell, *Acts*, i. 70.

acchanalias to the time of those instruments which were A.D. 1603 —1689.
wont to assist them in the celebration of God's praises, and
egulate the voices of the worst singers in the world, which
re the English in their churches at present[1]." This lan-
uage might seem to be mere exaggeration, but it receives
onsiderable confirmation from other sources. The Newcastle
nagistrates asserted that out of 200 inhabited houses in—
Shields no fewer than 140 were ale-houses[2]; and the vice *Shields in* 1653.
ertainly seems to have affected many classes of society.
Vorden describes the habits of the squireens[3], while Puritan
ninisters made the "great pains they had taken in preach-
ng" an excuse for smoking and drinking in the vestry[4].

The changes which were made in the taxation of the *The Excise.*
ountry under the Commonwealth gave government new
tatus for dealing with the matter. The imposition of an
xcise brought the whole trade directly under the supervision —
f revenue officials[5]; there were heavy penalties, for fiscal
easons, on unlicensed houses; and the loss of a licence was a
evere punishment to hold over the head of an ale-house
keeper. The Commissioners for Excise thus came indirectly
o be concerned in putting down the worst classes of houses;
nd by a curious arrangement, the Commissioners of Customs
were empowered to deal in a summary manner with the
nost frequent offenders. These were the watermen on the
Thames and the carmen and porters at the quays, and such
persons were liable to be arrested without warrant and dealt
with summarily for drunkenness or disorderly conduct[6].

219. If we find it hard to sympathise with the minute *The growth of London,*
egulation of industry, we are even more inclined to be
urprised at the measures for restraining the growth of
London[7]. Much indeed is said in the present day about the
nanner in which the agricultural population flocks to the
owns, but it has not been recently suggested that we should

---

[1] *A character of England,* in *Harleian Miscellany,* x. 193.
[2] *Conservatorship of Tyne* in Richardson's *Reprints of Rare Tracts,* III. p. 46.
[3] See below, p. 183, n. 5.   [4] Scrivener, *Treatise against Drunkenness,* 83.
[5] 14 Aug. 1649, c. 50. Scobell, II. 72.   [6] 1654, c. 38. Scobell, II. 320.
[7] Sir Thomas Roe asked, "Whether, indeed, London doth not monopolise all rade? In my opinion it is no good state of a body to have a fat head and lean nembers." *Harl. Misc.* IV. 436. But some provincial towns like Manchester, Leeds and Halifax were growing too. (Inderwick, 93.)

try and check the tendency by prohibiting the expansion of
the great city.   At the same time, there were many reasons,
political, municipal, sanitary and economic why the rapidly
increasing growth of London[1] was viewed with suspicion, and
attempts were made to check it under one government after
another from the reign of Elizabeth to the time of Charles II.

*Political
reasons.*
  a. The political importance of London was very great,
and the influence it exerted in the constitutional struggles of
the seventeenth century was decisive.   It did much both
with men and money to contribute to the victory of the
Parliamentary forces; but there was some danger that the
crowds of citizens and other inhabitants would be able to
interfere with the freedom of Parliamentary debates, and to
put an undue pressure upon the members.   The incidents
connected with the women's petition in 1643 seem to show
that there was a dread of external pressure under the Commonwealth[2], as well as under Charles I.   Dislike of these
crowds was after all something different from jealousy of the
true political influence of the City; the proclamations, which
were intended to check the growth of the suburbs, were not
really inimical to the interest of the old corporation, and
seem in several instances to have had its approval.   It is
difficult to see that jealousy of the wealth and power of the
City of London, as a real political influence, had anything to
do with these measures, though no political party could view
with perfect equanimity the presence of large numbers of
human beings, who were under no effective control.

*Municipal
and
industrial
regulation*

*of the
suburbs.*
  b. The difficulties in regard to the municipal government of London, with which the Metropolitan Board of
Works and the London County Council have successively
attempted to deal, were beginning to show themselves in the
sixteenth century.   Suburbs were springing up outside the
limits of City authority.   Spitalfields was beginning to be
occupied by weavers, and the Whitechapel district was filling
up; while houses were being also constructed in S. Giles's.
But all these districts lay outside the area of the City and of
its corporations.   In Henry VIII.'s time, attempts had been

[1] Creighton, *Epidemics*, 470.
[2] *Parl. Hist.* III. 161; see also the apprentices.   *Ib.* 717, 887.

made to increase the powers of the citizens for purposes of industrial regulation[1]; and this was undoubtedly one element in favour of trying to restrict the growth of the town.   In 1632 the Mayor and Aldermen petitioned the Council in regard to the growth of suburbs; but the suggestion of the Council that the ungoverned area should be divided between the cities of London and Westminster, fell to the ground[2]. King Charles subsequently erected a new corporation for the industrial regulation of these suburbs[3]; but this experiment was viewed with much suspicion by the Londoners, and this new body had in all probability a very brief existence.

A.D. 1608 —1689.

1636.

c.   The exceedingly insanitary condition of London was evidenced by the special outbreaks of Plague, as well as by the ordinary death-rate.   In 1593 it raged in a very alarming fashion, and Bartholomew Fair was not held as usual[4]; the excitement which these successive visitations occasioned gave rise to a useful institution; as the first steps were taken for compiling statistics of deaths by the weekly bills of mortality[5].   There is ample evidence that the whole City was in a most unhealthy state; the water-supply was poisonous in the extreme[6]; the houses were overcrowded; and there were frequent encroachments on the remaining open spaces.   There were also many elements of risk from the manner in which houses were built, especially from the number of wood buildings; and a large number of the proclamations and acts which deal with the subject, and limit or regulate the building in London and its suburbs, were concerned with the question in these sanitary aspects. The Act of 1593 may be quoted as summarising the evils which had been observed even at that time : " For the reform-

Insanitary condition

and risk from fire.

---

[1] 14 and 15 H. VIII. c. 2.   [2] Gardiner, *Hist.* VIII. 288.

[3] Rymer, xx. 173. "Upon the earnest and frequent complaints of our loving subjects the inhabitants of the places as well within the City of London exempt from the freedom thereof, as without our said city and within three miles of the same of the great grievances by them sustained, through the intrusion of aliens and foreigners into those parts, and by the ungoverned exercise of trade there."

[4] Rymer, xvi. 213. On the whole subject see Creighton, *Epidemics*, cc. VI. x. and XII.   [5] Macpherson, *Annals*, II. 231.

[6] Thames water formed the chief supply and was laid on to houses in 1594, but the first great improvement began in 1605, when an Act was passed for bringing in a stream of running water to the northern parts of the City of London (3 J. I. c. 18), and the New River Company was formed. Clutterbuck, *Hertfordshire*, II. 5.

ing of the great mischiefs and inconveniences that daily grow
and increase by reason of the pestering of houses with diverse
families, harbouring of inmates, and converting of great
houses into several tenements or dwellings, and erecting of
new buildings within the cities of London and Westminster
and other places neare thereunto adjoining, whereby great
infection of sickness and dearths of victuals and fuel hath
grown and increased[1]," it ordains that no new buildings
shall be erected within either city or within three miles of
them unless for 'inhabitants of the better sort,' that houses
shall not be broken up into tenements, and that no commons
shall be enclosed. The last provision had reference rather
to the practice of archery than to the healthfulness of open
1618. spaces. Similar reasons were alleged in subsequent proclamations[2], though under James some stress was laid on the
unsightliness of the "noisome pestes of bulkes, stale-sheds,
cants, jutties wherewith our streets are in all places so much
cumbered and amazed that it taketh away the benefit of
air, sweetness and decency of the same[3]," and special regard
was had to appearances in laying out a new district like
Lincoln's Inn Fields[4], under the advice of Inigo Jones. In
the time of Charles I., there were very precise directions as
to the character of all new buildings erected; every whole
story was to be ten feet high, and the walls of three story
houses were to be two bricks thick[5]. A similar measure was
passed in 1656[6]; a fine of one year's rent was imposed on all
houses, with less than five acres of ground, which had been
erected since 1620 in the City of London or within ten miles
of it; and a fine of £100 to the state, £20 per month to the
poor, was imposed on all houses erected after 1657 on new
foundations. Any house rebuilt was to be of brick or stone,
and without jetting or butting out[7]. The limitation and
regulation of building in the City, in sanitary interests, and
for the sake of security, was kept steadily in view from the
time of Elizabeth to the Restoration.

[1] 35 Eliz. c. 6.   [2] *Foedera*, xvii. 107.
[3] *Ib.* 143.   [4] *Ib.* 119.   [5] *Ib.* xix. 179.
[6] Compare petition of Brickmakers in 1652. Inderwick, 85, quoting *State Papers*, Vol. xxiii. March, 1652.
[7] Scobell's *Acts*, ii. 484. 1656, c. 24.

d. There were also difficulties about providing supplies for the inhabitants of this great city, and economic reasons for deprecating its further growth. The water-supply has been already alluded to; but there was also a very real difficulty in procuring fuel. The scarcity of wood was being felt more and more all over the country, and the Londoners had been gradually forced to take to burning coal, not only in bakeries and workshops, but for domestic fires. As a result a very great trade sprang up with the Tyne, since Newcastle was by far the most important coal-field then open. It was asserted early in the eighteenth century that "the Colliery trade brings up a greater number of Seamen, than all our navigation elsewhere[1]"; most of these vessels coasted between the Tyne and the Thames. This trade formed a favourite source of revenue, and the charge of re-erecting public buildings after the Great Fire was defrayed by an additional custom on coals[2].

The disaster of the Great Fire showed that the measures we have discussed had been introduced too late to render the City at all secure; but advantage was taken of the opportunity thus offered to try and remedy the old defects. Not to the full extent indeed; order and proportion were but little regarded, and the beautiful plan devised by Sir Christopher Wren was set aside and the streets rebuilt on the old lines[3]. But an honest effort was made by the Long Parliament of the Restoration to see that the houses of different classes should all be fairly substantial, and that the worst evils in the old city should be avoided. It was also thought necessary to revert to the old practice of legislating against excessive demands on the part of labourers. When there was such a sudden necessity for new buildings the operatives might have secured very exceptional rates of pay; and there was still enough of the old feeling on this subject to induce Parliament to pass a measure against possible extortion on their part, as well as against unreasonable charges by those who supplied building materials[4].

---

[1] C. Povey, *A discovery of indirect practices in the coal trade* (1700), p. 43.
[2] 18 and 19 C. II. c. 8, § 34.   [3] Loftie, *History of London*, I. 373.
[4] 18 and 19 C. II. c. 8.

A.D. 1603
—1689.
*Mainten-
ance of old
policy with
regard to
the im-
portation
of manu-
factured
goods.*

220. The general policy with regard to the encourage-ment of industry, which was maintained during this century, has been so fully described in treating of earlier periods that it is unnecessary to do more than add a few illustrations.

a. There was still a divided feeling against importing goods which we could produce or manufacture for ourselves. The importation of foreign lace and embroidery[1], and of wool-cards[2], was specially objected to, as successful efforts had been made to prosecute these manufactures; and the hatters received the same sort of protection[3] that had been accorded to the cappers in bygone days. But an excellent example occurs in connection with another trade.

Salt-works had been promoted in England under Charles I., as the fishing interests were very insufficiently supplied with foreign salt, especially in 1628 and 1629. It therefore became a matter of great importance to develop the native *Salt-pans
at Shields.* production; salt-pans were erected in the neighbourhood of Shields, and a corporation was formed. Their chief competi-tors appear to have been the Scotch manufacturers, who were charged with a higher imposition than the English makers, but on more favourable terms than the foreigners[4]. The men of Shields argued that "coals, labour and diet, being above one-half cheaper in Scotland (especially during the troubles and heavy taxes in England) a much heavier imposition on their salt than on our own was necessary[5]." In 1647 Parliament accepted this view and removed the excise on English salt, leaving the imposition on Scotch salt as before[6]; but the makers still found that "the English salt could not keep market with the Scottish"; and in 1649 the imposition on Scottish salt was raised to the same figure as that on other foreign salt; but almost at the same time an excise was laid on English salt, at the request of the impor-ters of Scottish salt[7]. Under Cromwell Scotland was united to England for commercial purposes, and the salt-pans at Shields were demolished. The tract from which this infor-

[1] 14 C. II. c. 13. This trade provided employment for very many families and children.   [2] 14 C. II. c. 19.   [3] Scobell, *Acts*, II. 88, 5 Sept. 1649.
[4] Ordinance of Parliament, 9 Jan. 1644. Scobell, I. 60.
[5] *Narrative concerning Salt-works of the North*, in Richardson, *Reprints*, III. p. 13.   [6] 11 June, 1647.   [7] *Narrative, Reprints*, III. 16.

mation comes is an appeal to Charles II. to give the salters better encouragement by insisting on the use of English salt in the fishing trades; it urges on general grounds, that it is the "wisdom of a kingdom or nation to prevent the importation of any manufacture from abroad which might be a detriment to their own at home, for if the coin of the nation be carried out to pay for foreign manufactures and our own people left unemployed, then in case a war happen with our potent neighbours, the people are incapacitated to pay taxes for the support of the same." It is obvious that this economic reasoning was generally accepted as sound, but in the particular case there was some difficulty in seeing how far Scotland was to be treated as a foreign country.

b. Illustrations may also be found of measures which *Securing raw materials.* were designed to prevent the export of unmanufactured materials. The most frequent cases are connected with the woollen trades. Pains were taken to develop the production of alum when it was discovered in 1609[1]. In 1660 an act was passed against exporting wool, woolfells, woolflocks, fuller's earth, or any kind of scouring earth[2]; and in 1662 one against exporting raw hides[3]. The attempt to encourage the import of wool may also be noted in this connection[4].

c. It is in this period that we find the most curious *Promoting consumption.* illustration of the policy of encouraging the consumption of English manufactures. An act was passed in 1666 for bury- *Burying in woollen.* ing in woollen only, under a penalty of £5[5]; and in 1678 machinery was organised for seeing that this act was properly enforced[6]. Parish registers of the time afford ample evidence of these burials in coffins lined with woollen cloth and in woollen shrouds. The later act gives a fuller statement of the aims of these measures. They were intended to lessen the importation of linen from beyond the seas (and so to prevent money from going abroad), to encourage the woollen manufacture (by promoting consumption), and to prevent a reckless consumption of linen fibre (so as to assist the paper manufacturers). With the development of a native linen manufacture, many of the reasons for the measure

[1] Seyer, *Bristol*, II. 263. [2] 12 C. II. c. 32, and 14 C. II. c. 18. [3] 14 C. II. c. 7.
[4] Inderwick, *The Interregnum*, 79. [5] 18 and 19 C. II. c. 4. [6] 30 C. II. c. 3.

A.D. 1608 —1689. passed away, and the policy of the acts was severely criti-cised by Davenant[1].

Immigra-tion of aliens en-couraged, d. In all these respects the authorities in the seventeenth century continued to follow the traditional English methods of encouraging industry; but the great epochs of progress had been marked by the incursion of one wave of foreign immigrants after another, and the example of Holland[2] rendered statesmen specially anxious to attract foreign arti-sans. Edward III. and Elizabeth had alike encouraged the immigration of skilled workmen from abroad; and though sub-sequent events had amply justified the wisdom of the course they had taken. it had been somewhat unpopular at the time[3].

but viewed with jealousy. There had been a constant effort to confine alien mer-chants to their proper functions, and to prevent them from interfering with the internal trade[4]; and this was one element in the jealousy of aliens which found expression again and again during the seventeenth century. There had also been a constant desire on the part of native workmen to obtain supervision over the foreigners who settled beside them and *Suburbs.* practised similar callings[5]; and this feeling comes out pro-minently in connection with the desire of the City to exercise control over the aliens in the suburbs[6], and to prevent the expansion of these ungoverned districts. Englishmen were *Scots.* by no means anxious to encourage the naturalisation of Scotchmen among them in the early years of James I.[7], and *Jews.* Cromwell's action in re-introducing Jews into the country met with a good deal of hostile criticism[8]. The feeling found expression on more than one occasion in parliament. In 1647 a petition from divers well affected young men and apprentices of the city of London in favour of the king, called attention to the intrusion of "foreigners into suburbs and places adjacent to the city, whereby your petitioners are *Naturali-sation of aliens.* much discouraged in their service, the freemen of the city prejudiced" &c.[9] But the chief discussion took place in

---

[1] *East India Trade,* in *Works,* I. 99.

[2] Fortrey, *England's Interest* in *Select Tracts,* 226.

[3] See above, Vol. I. pp. 284 n., 312, II. 47.   [4] See above, Vol. I. 351.

[5] See above, Vol. I. § 313.   [6] 14 and 15 H. VIII. c. 2.

[7] Mr Fuller, *Parl. Hist.* I. 1082.   [8] See p. 353 below.

[9] *Parl. Hist.* III. 684.

1672 when a bill was introduced for the general naturalisation of protestant aliens. One member was ready to encourage foreign artisans, but was not anxious to see foreign
merchants and shopkeepers here, and another foresaw difficulty about admitting foreign artisans to our corporations[1].
The bill appears to have been dropped, though alien merchants, whether denizens or not, received a considerable boon
in the same year, as the duties they paid on the exportation
of English products and manufactures were reduced to the
rates paid by English subjects[2].

The troubles of the Huguenots under Louis XIV., which *Incursion of Huguenots*
culminated in the revocation of the Edict of Nantes, roused
a very generous feeling on their behalf; and native artisans
who were jealous of their intrusion had little opportunity of
making an effective opposition. In 1681, Charles II. made
an edict granting the refugees letters of naturalisation and
trading privileges, and authorised a charitable collection on
their behalf[3]. They were to be admitted, with their tools
and merchandise, custom free. A similar course was adopted
by James II. in 1685, when a very large number of the
refugees from Normandy and Brittany settled in Spitalfields,
Long Acre, Soho, and the other London suburbs. Nearly a
third of the whole came to those districts, and the remaining
two-thirds were distributed at Canterbury, Sandwich, Norwich, Southampton, Glastonbury, Winchelsea, Dover and
Wandsworth; a small colony migrated as far as Edinburgh[4].
Despite the hearty welcome they received, they were not
admitted to full citizenship until the reign of Queen Anne[5].

The influence of these incomers on industry was very *and their trades.*

---

[1] *Parl. Hist.* IV. 577. [2] 25 C. II. c. 6.

[3] Weiss, *History of French Protestant Refugees*, 211. Povey refers to this as a
proof of the generosity of the public when their sympathies were roused, "We
have no reason to call in question the bounteous liberality of so many hundreds,
if not thousands, of well-disposed people, who gave to the Brief of the French
Protestants 5, 15, 20, 30, 40, 50 and some an 100 *l.* and few of any repute less than
5, 10, 15 or 20*s.* By which means a very large sum of money was raised; for the
second brief brought in between 40 and 50,000*l.*, and the last 25,000*l.*, there being
five briefs on that occasion." Povey, *Unhappiness of England as to its trade*, 58.

[4] Some attempts were made at cultivating mulberries on Moultrie's Hill
(S. James' Square), Mackay, *Barony of Broughton*, 57.

[5] Weiss, 230. There was also a settlement of French and Flemish woollen
weavers near Bristol. Rudder, *Gloucestershire*, 601.

considerable[1]; it affected, not only the silk and linen trades,
but such manufactures as those of paper, clocks, glass, locks
and surgical instruments[2].   The settlement in Spitalfields
long preserved its special character, and the inhabitants were
marked by tastes and interests in which the English workman
scarcely shared[3].

V. AGRICULTURE.

*Enclosing
for pasture
farming.*
221.   It has been explained above that in the sixteenth
century, two distinct kinds of change are included under the
term enclosing.   On the one hand the enclosing might be
undertaken for the sake of increasing sheep farming and at
the expense of tillage, or on the other hand it might be
carried out as a means of improving tillage.   So far as such
a movement can be definitely dated it may be said that
enclosing for the sake of sheep farming almost entirely
ceased with the reign of Elizabeth[4].   When enclosing was
advocated, and it was advocated in the seventeenth century,
the design in view was the improvement of tillage, not its
disuse.   Before going into the particular grounds on which
this statement rests it may be worth while to call attention
to certain general considerations which seem to confirm it.
During the preceding century, grazing had been restricted;
in the seventeenth, efforts were made to promote it with
regard to cattle; the very statute, which gives the fresh
1664.   opportunity for the export of corn, is strictly protective
against the importation of fat cattle, as it had been found by
experience that the English cattle breeders were suffering
from foreign competition[5]; and a few years later the cattle
farmers of Ireland[6] were prohibited from continuing a trade
which was proving very profitable.   Nor is it only in regard

---

[1] Weiss, 252.   [2] Colston, *Incorporated Trades*, p. 15.
[3] *Report* 3, &c. 1840, xxiii. 57.
[4] Contrast however the account (1609) of the country in Symond's *Sermon* (Gen.
xii. 3), Anderson, i. 197. See above, p. 53. Blith (*English Improver*, p. 4)
regards the grazier who never grew corn as behind the times. Coke in 1620
speaks from his own experience of the "Depopulatar who turns all out of doors
and keeps none but a shepherd and his dog" as one that never prospers. *Parl.
Hist.* i. 1198.
[5] 15 Charles II. c. 7, § 13.   [6] 18 and 19 Charles II. c. 2.

to cattle farming that we find this anxiety; the chief agricul- A.D. 1608
tural writer in the middle of the century urged that the —1689.
fears which had been entertained in regard to the increase of
sheep farming were quite illusory. Dymock points out that
since England now manufactured its own wool, an increased
supply of this raw material, and of flax, would give far more
opportunity for employment, and consequently would render
possible a larger population than could be maintained by
additional tillage[1]; while the desirability of keeping more
sheep is pressed by Silvanus Taylor as one of the reasons for
enclosing forests and chases[2]. The old scare about sheep
farming was at an end, though the memory of it was not forgotten, and all admitted that it had been an evil as carried
out in the old days[3].

Enclosure as a method of agricultural improvement was *Enclosing*
a very different matter; and one after another of the agricul- *as a step*
in agricul-
tural writers insist upon it. As usual they hold up the *tural im-*
provement.
example of Flanders and Brabant, and the excellent methods
employed there[4]. But even without the introduction of any
new crops much might be gained. "Enclosure with a good *Tillage.*
tall hedgerow, preserves the land warm, and defends and
shelters it from those nipping winds, that generally nip and
destroy much of the corn, pulse, or whatsoever grows on the
open field or champion grounds, and preserves it also from
those drying and scorching winds more frequent in hot
and dry springs, much damaging the champion lands; it
much preserves that fertility and riches the land is either
subject unto, or that is by the diligent care and cost of the
husbandman added. It furnisheth the owners thereof with

---

[1] *Samuel Hartlib's Legacy*, 55. Samuel Hartlib is sometimes credited with
being the author of this work, as for example by Thorold Rogers, *Agriculture and
Prices*. But his own Prefaces as well as the Memoir by Dircks make it clear that
this is a mistake. Hartlib constituted himself into a sort of Society of Arts and
had a large correspondence with specialists in different departments. Of his own
acquaintance with the subject of husbandry he observes:—"I cannot say much of
mine own experience in this matter, yet Providence having directed me by the
improvement of several relations with the experience and observations of others,
I find myself obliged to become a conduit pipe thereof towards the Publick."
(Dircks, *Biographical Memoirs of Hartlib*, p. 63.) Dircks attributes this tract to
Cressy Dymock, p. 69.   [2] S. Taylor, *Common Good* (1652), 32.
  [3] See especially Blith, *English Improver*, p. 33, 37.
  [4] *Samuel Hartlib's Legacy*, p. 54.

a great burthen of corn, pulse, or whatever is sown thereon. Also when it is laid open for meadow or pasture, it yields much more of grass than the open field land, and the hedges being well planted with trees, affords shelter and shadow for the cattle, both in summer and winter, which else would destroy more with their feet than they eat with their mouths, and might lose more of their fat and flesh in one hot day than they gain in three cool days[1]."

Still more definite opinions on the gain to agriculture, from breaking up the common fields, are expressed by Taylor[2]. If common fields already in tillage were enclosed, "I desire it may be considered if these benefits would not follow; as first whether it would not be more profitable if enclosed, and that every man had all his own ground at his own disposing to make choyce of these grounds most fit for corn, then to employ with less labour, less cost, and much more increase; for oftentimes it is seen, that the common fields are very much impoverished by continual ploughing, especially in light, sandy, and gravelly grounds, or in any other like ground where the soil is but shallow....Besides such light ground in wet years doth produce tares, and other weeds, very destructive to the corn; all which would be avoyded, if the husbandman could make choyce of his ground to such uses as his experience shall find it most fit for." The

argument in regard to the enclosing of common waste, the possible hardship and the probable gain, can be more satisfactorily dealt with in connection with the arrangements that were made for the poor.

222. It is exceedingly difficult to estimate the progress that was made in agriculture during this time; several important treatises were published on the subject, by Gervase Markham, Platt, Hartlib, and Worlidge, which contain many recommendations for horticulture, and there is every reason to believe that under their guidance a great improvement

took place in gardening[3]. Serious efforts were made under

---

[1] Worlidge, *Systema Agriculturae* (1687), 10.

[2] *Common Good*, 13.

[3] Worlidge, 164. Compare also *Adam armed;* an essay presented by the Gardeners' Company which was chartered in 1606.

James I. to introduce the cultivation of mulberry trees, so A.D. 1603 —1689. that we might be able to provide the raw material for the silk manufacture[1]. Root crops appear to have been intro- Roots. duced to some extent as a course of husbandry. Weston refers to them[2], and Arthur Young had occasion to criticise the manner of growing turnips which had become traditional at the date of his tours; but on the other hand it does not appear that much practical result followed from the recommendation of clover[3], sainfoin and lucerne as means of cleaning the Grasses. fields; the cultivation of these grasses seems to have been one of the distinctive improvements of the eighteenth century.

The critics of seventeenth century agriculture did not Tenant Improvements, dwell on improvements that would require a great deal of capital, but on changes in the course of husbandry and in the implements employed, which would be advantageous to the tenant and would positively improve, or at least would prevent the exhaustion of the land. It was therefore to the tenant they looked, rather than to the landlord, for improvements[4]. The possibility of the small freeholder making any improvements hardly appears to be raised. The picture which Norden[5] gives of him is not a flattering one; it may

---

[1] *Hartlib's Legacy*, p. 72.

[2] *Discourse of Husbandrie used in Brabant* (1652), p. 25. Also Worlidge, p. 46.

[3] Weston, *Discourse of Husbandrie*, 11, *Hartlib's Legacy*, 1.

[4] At the same time some of the operations would strain his resources. Markham, *Farewell*, 4; Plat, *Jewel House*, 46.

[5] *Surveyor's Dialogue*, p. 16, also the following passage. *Lord.* "As far as I can perceive, an observing and painful husband liveth, fareth, and thriveth, as well upon his Farme of rack rent, as many do that are called freeholders or that have leases of great value for small rent. *Surveyor.* There is some reason for it, which every man either seeth not, or seeing it doth not consider it, or considering it, hath no will or power to reforme it. Some freeholders, and the Lessees of great things of small rent, bring up their children too nicely, and must needs, forsooth, gentleize them; and the eldest son of a meane man must be a young master, he must not labour, nor lay hand on the plough, (take heed of his disgrace) he shall have enough to maintain him like, and in the society of gentlemen, not like a drudge. And when this young gentleman comes to his land (long he thinks) he hath no leisure to labour for Hawking or Hunting or Bowling or Ordinaries or some vaine or lascivious or wanton course or other, leaving ploughe and seede and harvest, and sale to some ordinary hireling, who may do what he list, if the poore wife be as carelesse at home, as the husband is abroad; and at his elbow he hath perchance some vaine persons, that dissuade from covetousness and from too much frugalite and that he needes not to care for getting more, he hath no rent to paye, but some to receive, which will maintaine him; and when he is gone, all is gone; spending is easier than getting. And thus by little and little roweth himself and

not be altogether fair; but it certainly serves to leave the
impression that the tenant, who was bound to find means to
pay his rent, was more diligent in his business, and less careless in his expenditure, than the man who had some acres he
*and want
of security.* called his own. It was said however that tenants were
unwilling to improve, because if they did the landlords were
likely to raise their rents to the full value of the improvement. In this difficulty Dymock again got a suggestion from
the Low Countries. "According to the usual custom in
Flaunders, a Law may be made of letting and hiring Leases
upon improvement; where the manner is: that the Farmer
covenanteth on his part to improve the land to such or such
a greater rent, by an orderly and excellent management of
husbandry as well as building. The Landlord on the other
side covenanteth on his part, at the expiration of the said
Lease to give so many years purchase of the Improvement
(according to the agreement) which is for three or four years
or some time more, or, to give out of it such a parcel or
moity of ground. As if land formerly going for 6s. an acre
be upon Improvement worth 10s. or 13s. 4d. an acre, the
Landlord is to give 4s. or 5s. upon every acre, more or less
according to the agreement[1]." Whether from want of security
or from want of energy, the tenants do not seem to have
made any very great improvements; it was not till the
eighteenth century, when the capitalist landlords took the
matter up, that the suggestions of the seventeenth century

the hope of his posterite under water in the calme weather. Whereas, he, that
hath a rent to pay is not idle, neither in head nor hand; he considers the rent day
will come, and in true labour and diligence provides for it, and by his honest
endeavours and dutiful regard, gets to pay rent to his Lord. * * I inferre not yet
by this, sir, that because they sometimes thrive well that live upon rack rents,
therefore you landlords should impose the greater rent or fine; that were to do
evil that good might come of it, nay rather to do evil that evil may followe; for if
there be not a measure in burdens the back of the strongest Elephant may be
broken. And the best and most careful and most laborious and most industrious
husband may be overcharged with the rent of his land." *Surveyor's Dialogue*,
80—81.

So much is sometimes said about the difficulty of accounting for the disappear-
ance of the Freeholders during the seventeenth century that this statement made
at the beginning of the period is at least worthy of notice.

[1] *Hartlib's Legacie, Preface*; Taylor, p. 15, regards 3s. 4d. per acre as a typical
rent and unenclosed downs as worth 1s. 8d., p. 36.

writers began to be put in practice to any considerable A.D. 1603 —1689. extent.

Another improvement, which was not borrowed from the *Manures.* Dutch, was the use of various substances for improving the land. Markham refers to the use of marl as it had been understood from very early ages; and Dymock gives a long list of suitable manures which were available in many parts of England, but which were unknown in Flanders[1]; such as chalk, lime, snagg-root, Cornish sea-sand[2], ashes, salt, fish, and even woollen rags. The judicious application of these various fertilisers was an art that seemed to be but little understood, and there are a whole series of writers who dwell upon the advantages which may accrue from the proper use of marl and lime[3].

Indeed it appears that, during this century, farming must *Character of the seasons,* have been a somewhat speculative business. There were one or two years of excessive dearth, notably 1661—62[4], when those who had managed to save their crops would realise unusual prices, but the century was curiously remarkable for the way in which the seasons ran in successive periods of longer and shorter duration, of good years and of bad years. Good years meant but little remuneration for the farmer, as prices were low; bad years might bring in a profit, or might ruin him altogether. No similar run of seasons has been traced by Professor Thorold Rogers in the three centuries and a half which preceded it; and the eighteenth century presented a remarkable succession of fairly good harvests, followed by a long period of great irregularity. In the seventeenth century only, "the good[5] and bad seasons lie in groups of more or less extent. The fact was recognised in a rough way by the agriculturists of the time." The business of the farmers was accordingly a highly speculative one; *and uncertainty in farming.* it might be profitable, or it might be the reverse. On the whole however the price of corn ranged high as compared with other articles of produce, and arable farming was prosecuted with increased energy, while the measures that were

---

[1] *Hartlib's Legacy*, p. 43. [2] 7 James I. c. 18.
[3] Blith, *Husbandry*, 60; Plat, *Jewel House*, 21; Markham, *Farewell*, 32.
[4] *Thorold Rogers, Agriculture and Prices*, v. 213. [5] *Ib.* 173.

taken after the Restoration tended to the encouragement of
the agricultural interest. Just as the increased pasture
farming of the fifteenth and sixteenth centuries directly
tended towards a diminution of employment, and consequent
depopulation in rural districts, so the gradual change which
ensued, when this tendency was checked and arable farming
was prosecuted with more and more success while domestic
industries were developed more and more, must have tended
to diminish the numbers of the unemployed, even if the
rates of remuneration were not particularly liberal.

*Rise of
Rents*
An incidental proof of the prosperity of agriculture is to
be found in the gradual increase of rents, on which Professor
Thorold Rogers lays considerable stress[1]. This rise was not
like the enhancement of the sixteenth century, which seems
to have been due to the increased value of unimproved land
for grazing purposes; but it followed in consequence of actual
improvements, especially, as Best notes[2], of enclosing pasture.
It appears that the tenants sometimes had reason to fear that
their rents would be increased in consequence of improvements made by themselves and at their own expense. But
without discussing the question as to how far the landlords
were harsh in exacting increased payments from leaseholders[3], or large fines on renewals[4], we may note that the
land had increased in value, so that there was actual com-
*through
com-
petition.*
petition for it. Norden[5] had seen and observed among the
tenants, "a kind of madness as I may call it, but in the best
sense it is a kind of ambitious or rather avaricious emulation,
wherein they strive one to outstrip another in giving most;

---

[1] *Agriculture and Prices,* v. 803. Contrast however Glanville's assertion
that rents could hardly be collected, and the price of land had fallen in 1620 from
20 to 14 or even 12 years purchase. *Parl. Hist.* I. 1188, 1194.

[2] "The lands in the pasture weere (att my father's first cominge) letten to our
owne tenants and others, for 2s. a lande; afterwards for 2s. 6d. a lande, and lastly
for 3s. a lande; but nowe, being inclosed they will let for thrice as much." *Rural
Economy in Yorkshire* in 1641 (Surtees Society), 129.

[3] There seems to have been some encroachment by lords upon the tenants,
who paid fines to the crown to have their ancient customs (Hunter, *Doncaster,*
I. 158, 7 James I. c. 21). I should gather from Norden that the chief tenants'
grievance was when the Lord insisted on forfeiture on insufficient grounds (*Surveyor,* p. 60). According to Thorold Rogers similar harsh treatment was extended
to freeholders under the Statute of Frauds, 29 Charles II. c. 3. *Agriculture and
Prices,* v. 87.

[4] Harrison, *Description* in Holinshed, I. 318.   *Surveyor's Dialogue,* 9.

as when myself have had business of this nature, namely of A.D. 1603 —1689.
letting, setting, or selling of land for years or lives, being, or
neere being determined, in farmes or other like, whereby the
lord hath bin at liberty to dispose thereof at his will, for
best advantage by choice of a new tenant. Proclamation to
that effect hath bin made in open court, where I have seen
and it is daily in use, that one will outbid another, as at an
outcry in London, in so much as I have wondered at their
emulation, and could not have asked what they have raised
it unto themselves. And should any that is in authority in
this case (who in duty is not to hinder the lord, or the lord
himself) exhibit such hot spirits to clime as high for the
lord's advantage as the ladder of their own will, and supposed ability will reach? This is not as one swallow in a
summer, but they are many and everywhere winter and
summer, and yet are other men accused and condemned for
them and their faults if these will be a fault in itselfe; but I
should think it greater madness for a lord wilfully to refuse
what is so voluntarily offered and so willingly given. Now
who is the cause of raysing rents and fines?"

223. Another proof, that arable farming was progressing *The drain-ing of the Fens.*
during this period, may be drawn from the character of the
change which was undertaken, when attempts were made to
carry out drainage works. Under James I. a corporation was
established with considerable powers to carry on the attempt—
which had been begun under Elizabeth; but they only succeeded in rescuing a certain amount of land for pasturage,
and the banks which they made were not always well
designed; they confined the rivers too much, so that when
the waters were high they were only too likely to overflow
the banks if they did not burst them[1]. The fens are a large
stretch of country through which some half dozen rivers find
their way to the Wash; and as the land lies very low these
rivers were always apt to overflow the country. The scheme
of draining which eventually succeeded appears to have been
devised by a Dutchman named Vermuïden[2]. He pointed out *Ver-muïden.*

[1] Vermuïden, *Discourse touching the Draining of the Fens*, p. 11. Dugdale, *History of Embanking*, 391.

[2] Wells, *Bedford Level*, I. 195. Previous attempts recited and object stated in Act of 29 May, 1649. Scobell, II. p. 33.

that it would be a great expense to make sufficient banks
along the course of each of those six rivers and that the
current was not sufficient at all seasons of the year to prevent
the tide from silting up their mouths. He therefore proposed to bring the water from these rivers into two or three
newly formed channels which should carry the river water
across the flat country and which should have body of water
enough to keep their channels open. Parliament gave
him considerable encouragement, and a large number of
labourers from the Low Countries were imported to carry
out the works. There was a regular settlement of them at
Thorney Abbey in Cambridgeshire, but their relations with
*The Fen-
men and
the Dutch.* the fenmen were by no means friendly; these had been
accustomed to live on the products of the waste, and when
the lands were drained, they would be deserted by the water-
fowl and the various products on which the fenmen depended
for a living. The interests of agriculture eventually prevailed however, and the land has been completely rescued so
as to provide one of the finest corn-growing districts in
England.

*Hatfield
Chase.* The draining of Hatfield Chase, which was also undertaken
by Vermuïden, was attended with even greater difficulties.
The scheme, which was originally planned, involved turning
all the waters of the Don into the northern channel of that
river; the southern part of the Chase was improved, but the
northern part suffered severely for many years, till the so-
called Dutch river was cut. As the whole of the property
was vested in the Crown it did not appear at first sight that
*Commoners
and Parti-
cipants.* there would be such legal obstacles as in the Cambridgeshire
fens. But this proved a great mistake; the settlers on the
recovered lands, many of whom were Dutch, were constantly
attacked by the commoners; and from 1626 to 1719 there
were constant struggles, sometimes carried on by legal
means and sometimes by violence. The foreign settlers suffered severely in 1642, when the Lincolnshire committee of
defence took the desperate measure of flooding the country
in order to check the advance of royal troops[1]. When Par-

---

[1] Hunter, *Doncaster*, I. 166. This work contains an excellent history of these
proceedings.

liament triumphed the cause of the commoners was taken
up by John Lilburn[1], and their persistence might have met
with success if it had not been for the intervention of
Nathaniel Reading; he vigorously defended the rights of
those who had obtained shares in the recovered lands. "He
provided horses and arms and necessaries with twenty hired
men with twenty pounds a year each and their diet, with a
chirurgeon in ordinary and upon particular occasions he
hired many more; and after thirty-one set battles wherein
several of his men were killed and diverse others wounded
and lamed,...he subdued these monsters to your obedience
and quieted the Crown and the participants in their allotments, repaired the church, settled another minister;
restored the congregation, and thereby made the said levels
and parts adjacent, quiet, safe and flourishing[2]." The historian of the district takes a less favourable view of the
proceedings. "The work had been, as we have seen, the
cause of infinite natural and moral evils and it may be
questioned whether there was an equivalent advantage in
the conversion into arable land of fifty or sixty thousand
acres of singular, and in some points of view, beautiful country. To the original adventurers the profit was none. In a
few years there was scarcely a foreign name remaining in
the proprietorship." But the work of improving was pushed
steadily on, not only in the low grounds on the east coast,
but on Crown lands in other parts of the country. There
were considerable enclosures of Malvern Chase[3] in 1632,
and on Sedgemoor a few years later[4].

Some proposals were made at this time to carry out other
improvements, for which the example of the Dutch furnished
the usual precedent. England is well supplied with rivers,
but these rivers were not well utilised for purposes of internal communication[5]. Yarranton was a writer who specially advocated this improvement; he urged that the rivers
would be specially convenient for the carriage of a bulky
commodity like corn. He suggested that great granaries

---

[1] Lilburn, *Case of the Tenants of the Manor of Epworth.* Compare also *State Papers Domestic,* cccxc. 89.　　[2] Hunter, *Doncaster,* I. 168.
[3] Nash, *Worcestershire,* p. lxxix.　　[4] *Gentleman's Magazine,* lxv. 300.
[5] Cromwell's Commission, 1650. Inderwick, 74.

should be built by the London Companies near Oxford, and that the navigation of the Cherwell and Thames might be improved so as to render the conveyance of corn from them very easy[1]. He would have erected similar granaries at Stratford on Avon[2], from which the towns in the Severn valley might be supplied. There were also attempts to utilise the Wye in a similar fashion[3]. Charles II. was interested in these proposals, and in the more elaborate designs for connecting the different river systems by means of canals; but communications have generally been improved in order to meet the requirements of an existing trade, and not to call one into being. It was so in this case, and nearly a century elapsed before the use of canals in this country became general.

The Export of Corn.

224. In the reign of Queen Elizabeth public opinion was still divided about the advisability of allowing the export of corn, but it had become much more definite by the time of Charles II. 'Forasmuch," says the preamble of an act for the encouragement of trade[4], "as the encouragement of tillage ought to be in an especial manner regarded and endeavoured; and the surest and effectuallest means of promoting any trade, occupation or mistery, being by rendering it profitable to the users thereof and great quantitie of land within this kingdom for the present lying in a manner waste, and yielding little, which might thereby be improved to considerable profit and advantage (if sufficient encouragement were given for the laying out of cost and labour on the same) and thereby much more corn produced, greater numbers of people, horses and cattle employed, and other lands also rendered more valuable." The encouragement given was two-fold; on the one hand, corn might be exported if the price was below 48s. the quarter, but when it reached this price it might be imported subject to a duty of five shillings the quarter.

Internal Trade.

Nor was there any remaining hesitation in regard to the internal trade, for it was enacted that when corn did not exceed 48s. the bushel, "then it shall be lawful for all and every person and persons (not forestalling nor

---

[1] Yarranton, *England's Improvement*, 180.   [2] *Ib.* 163.

[3] Act for making navigable the Wye passed June 26, 1651, not printed by Scobell though mentioned by him.   [4] 15 Charles II. c. 7.

selling the same in the same market within three months after the buying thereof) to buy in open market and to buy up, and keep in his or their granaries or houses, and to sell again such corn or grain of the kinds aforesaid, as without fraud or covin, shall have been bought at or under the prices before expressed without incurring any penalty, any law statute or usage to the contrary notwithstanding." The importance of this statute can be most clearly realised by comparing it with the practice in preceding reigns and under the Commonwealth[1], or the opinions enunciated by such a well informed man as Harrison in Elizabeth's time. He had denounced middlemen for doing the very thing which they are here explicitly allowed to do; and the object of the whole measure was to keep the price of corn fairly high, so that the farmers might be encouraged in carrying on their tillage.

If there is a contrast with sixteenth century opinion, *The nation's great fund was in land.* there is a still more curious antagonism with our prevailing ideas; it is difficult for us to imagine that any statesman would boldly and officially advocate a measure on the ground that it would raise rentals. A parliament of landlords might have been expected to feel some shame at legislating so palpably in their own interest; but it would hardly have struck them in the same way. Much of our revenue comes from an excise, or from the income tax, which were alike unknown in the earlier part of the seventeenth century; at that date, land was the great fund from which taxation was paid. If rents were high, then there was an abundant source from which revenue could be drawn; if rents were low, even if trade prospered, it made comparatively little difference to the sources of taxation. All through the seventeenth century a rise of rents is treated, not as an especial boon to the landlord class, but as a gain to the public at large, since the *fund* from which revenue was drawn was amply supplied. Only when we remember this, does the language of the statutes or of contemporary writers about high rents[2] become intelligible to

---

[1] The Bedfordshire Sessions Records (1650—1660) are full of charges against men for engrossing corn or buying standing crops. Compare also the complaints in Sir John Cooke's *Unum necessarium* (1648). [2] See below, p. 238.

us. If they had been a parliament of landlords simply and solely legislating in their own private interest, they would hardly have paraded the fact in such a barefaced fashion.

*Rural em-
ployment.* 225. Such were the changes which were occurring in agriculture: it would be a matter of great interest if we could tell how they affected the position of the agricultural labourer. One is inclined to suppose that just as the increase of grazing had diminished rural employment and ruined the small farmer, while it deprived the labourer of the chance of earning his living, so the increase of arable farming would enable him to improve his position. We should expect that the labourer in husbandry would be better off at the Revolution than he had been when James I. ascended the throne.

*Domestic
manufac-
tures.* Besides this, there can be little doubt that domestic manufactures were extending more and more; serious efforts were made to teach the art of spinning; the growth of flax and hemp was encouraged; and by these means the family earnings must have been rendered larger, and the position more stable. But the whole subject is beset with many difficulties; it is so hard to get a clear picture of social conditions which were very different from ours, and the evidence from rates of money wages is difficult to interpret. The servants who were hired for a year or more, were probably accustomed to live in the employer's establishment. Their wages would in all probability not be intended to suffice for a family[1]. The day labourer on the other hand was probably a neighbour and a householder; he would have more or less land to work with the help of his family, and the payments he received do not give conclusive evidence as to his income, still less can we interpret them so accurately as to construct out of them a standard of comfort.

*Labourers'
Meat, 1641.* We have however excellent first hand evidence as to the

[1] These considerations seem to me to weaken the force of one argument in regard to irregularity of employment in the fifteenth century (vol. i. p. 348). But the general conclusion that employment was irregular in the fifteenth century seems to me sufficiently established. Professor Rogers remarks "that the custom of hiring labour by the day is more general during the fifteenth and sixteenth centuries than it was in the thirteenth and fourteenth, mainly because the practice of cultivating land was abandoned by the great landowners and wealthy corporations, and the labour which they hired was occasional and casual." (*Agriculture and Prices*, iv. 493.)

manner in which the labourer was fed when he had rations A.D. 1603
—1689. as part payment. Henry Best, writing in 1641, describes the provision that was made for his labourers; it was, as he notes, unusually good, but as he curtailed the usual wages on account of the special diet, it at least serves as a rough indication of the comforts which the labourer might secure. "Thatchers have (in most places) 6*d.* a day and theire meate, in summer time and in the shortest dayes of winter 4*d.* a day and theire meate; yett wee neaver use to give them above 4*d.* a day and their meat, in summer because their meal is not as in other places; for they are to have three meals a day, viz. their breakfast abt eight of the clocke, or betwixt eight and nine, theire dinner about twelve, and theire supper about seaven or when they leave worke, and at each meale fower services, viz. butter, milk, cheese, and either eggs, pyes or bacons and sometimes porridge instead of milke; if they meate themselves they are usually 10*d.* a day[1]." It is instructive to notice that the winter wages were lower than the summer wages, and this is in itself an indication that the thatcher was not paid at a starvation rate. This was in Yorkshire before the Civil War; there had been a decided rise of wages in Best's memory; but the payments he mentions do not differ very noticeably from those in other counties, as quoted by Professor Rogers.

The opinion that the labourer's position was improving *Pauperism* even before the Civil War, is confirmed as we shall see pre- *and* sently by what we know of the condition of the poor; pauperism does not appear to have been such a pressing evil in the greater part of the seventeenth century, as it had been in the sixteenth and became once more after the Revolution. Perhaps additional confirmation may be drawn from the *Alehouses.* complaints which are so frequent about labourers frequenting alehouses. One statute after another and one pamphlet[2] after another dwells on the increase of tippling; and if we may judge by modern experience, the labourer is less likely to spend money freely at the public house if his wages are not above a starvation rate.

[1] *Rural Economy in Yorkshire*, 138.
[2] Taylor, *Common Good*, 51; see above, p. 169.

C. II. 13

*Rise of
wages
slowly fol-
lowed the
rise of
prices.*

At the same time these general considerations must be checked by the evidence of figures; even if quotations of wages give inadequate data for determining the labourer's standard of comfort, they show us at all events a very important element in his well-being. During the reign of Elizabeth and till the Civil War, prices were rising steadily; the labourer found everything he had to buy dearer, and his money wages rose but slowly. Even if employment was more regular, we must remember that the rate of reward did not rise so fast as the price of corn and other necessaries.

*Effects of
War.*

Money wages had been increasing slowly till the time of the Civil War, when according to Prof. Rogers they rose very decidedly[1]. This was only to be expected, as there was not only a great demand for men to recruit the armies, but stores of all sorts would be required. The demand for men was great, and an ordinance was passed by Parliament for encouraging apprentices to enlist[2]; the husbandman was sorely tempted to leave his land, and go for a soldier on one side or the other[3]; and the labourer, in so far as he had less interest in his tillage, would be more willing to go with the army[4]. A rise of wages at such a time was most natural; but it is also to be noticed that the rise thus secured, was on the whole retained, when peace was restored.

The wages

226. The facts thus indicated present no great difficulty;

---

[1] "The county magistrates under the Commonwealth were more generous than they were under the Monarchy, for the wages of labour are raised from fifty to a hundred per cent." Rogers, v. 98. This opinion appears to rest upon a single instance (in Essex), and it is at least worth while to compare the high Essex rate of 1651 with the Devonshire rate of 1654 (Hamilton, *Quarter Sessions*, 163). The rates in the Western county are very much lower than those in the Eastern; they show only a small advance on the assessment of 1594, and wages in the building trades had not risen at all.   [2] *Parl. Hist.* II. 10.

[3] Chill zell my cart and eke my plow, And get a zword if ich know how, For ich mean to be right; * * * * Ich had zix oxen tother day, And them the Roundheads vetcht away, A mischief be their speed. And chad zix horses left me whole, And them the Cabbelleero's stole: Cheevoor men be agreed. *The Western Husbandman's Lamentation*, Brit. Mus. 669, f. 10 (19).

[4] "The Government of that Time [1647] having been assisted in the Civil Wars by great numbers of the Wool-workmen (who liked much better to rob and plunder for Half-a-Crown a Day, than toil at a melancholy Work for Sixpence a Day) to encourage and reward them, I say and to weaken the Gentry, they made this Prohibition" [forbidding the export of wool]. *Reasons for a limited exportation of Wool*, 1677, quoted by Smith, *Chronicon Rusticum*, I. 257.

it was only by slow degrees that money wages rose so as to be answerable to the rise of prices, but when thus raised, with a simultaneous drain on population, the new rates were on the whole maintained. But the evidence appears to condemn the Act of 1563 as a failure, so far as the assessment of wages was concerned; the machinery it created had not sufficed to raise wages according to the scarcity of the times. These clauses appear to have been practically a dead letter from the first, and wages to have been adjusted much as they are in times when competition is the avowed means of settling prices. Henry Best's[1] account of the hirings is very instructive.

A.D. 1603 —1689. clauses of the Act of 1563

remained a dead letter.

"Wee give usually to a foreman five markes per annum, and perhapps 2s. or halfe a crowne to a godspenny, if hee bee such an one as can sowe, mowe, stacke pease, goe well with fower horse, and hayth beene used to markettinge and the like; for nowe of late wee imploy and trust our foreman with the sowinge of all our seede. Wee give usually 50s. or fower marke to another, and perhapps 2s. or 2s. 6d. for a godspenny, providinge hee bee such an one as can sowe, mowe, goe well with a draught, and bee a good ploweman, and him allsoe wee imploy as a seedesman in haver seede time, when wee come to sowe olde ardure, and nowe and then sende him to markettes with the foreman. Wee give usually seaven nobles to a third man, that is a goode mower, and a goode fower horse-man, and one that can goe heppenly with a waine, and lye on a loade of corne handsomely. Wee give usually 35s. or 36s. to a fowerth man, if the reporte goe on him for a good ploweman, and that wee perceive him to bee of a good competent strength for carryinge of poakes, forkinge of a waine, or the like. Wee give usually to a spaught for holdinge of the oxe plough fower nobles or perhapps 30s. per annum, if hee bee such an one as have beene trained and beene brought up att the plough, and bee a wigger and heppen youth for loadinge of a waine, and goinge with a draught. Wee give usually 20s. to a good stubble boy for drivinge of the oxe plough, and that can (in time of neede) carry a mette or three bushell pease out of the barne into the garner. Wee have usually two mayd-servants, and wee weare wont that wee coulde hyre them for 18s. per annum,

Best's servants and experience of hiring.

[1] *Rural Economy in Yorkshire* (Surtees Society), p. 132.

and 12*d*. or 1*s*. 6*d*. for a godspenny, but nowe of late wee cannot hyre a good lusty mayd servant under 24*s*. wage, and sometimes 28*s*., and 18*d*. or 2*s*. for a godspenny. Christopher Pearson had (the first yeare hee dwelt heare) 3*l*. 5*s*. wages per annum, and 5*s*. to a godspenny: hee had the next yeare 4*l*. wage and 12*d*. to a godspenny, and hee was both a good seedesman, and a very good mower, and did sowe all our seede both the yeares. Henry Wise had the first yeare that hee tooke wage 36*s*.; hee had the next yeare 50*s*. and 4*s*. to a godspenny; and the third yeare hee had fower markes and 2*s*. to a godspenny, and was one that coulde both sowe and mowe indifferent well. Henry Pinder was not full sixteene yeares of age when hee came to dwell heare first, and hee had 24*s*., and the next yeare after hee had five nobles and 12*d*. to a godspenny, for goinge with the oxeplough, and beinge an heppen ladde for loadinge of a waine, and goinge with a draught. Thomas Smyth had (the first yeare hee dwelt heare) 20*s*. for drivinge the oxeplough, and the next yeare fower nobles and 6*d*. to a godspenny, and was to have a payre of olde breeches. Priscilla Browne had (the first yeare shee dwelt heare) 18*s*. wage and 12*d*. to a godspenny, the next yeare 24*s*., the third yeare 28*s*. and 2*s*. to a godspenny, and might have had the fowerth yeare 38*s*. and 12*d*. to a godspenny. Wee had (att this time in our owne handes) all the lands belonging to the demaines, all the lands belonginge to the West hall, all the lands belonginge to the West house farme, and the Fower oxegange which apperteine to John Bonwickes howse; wee kept constantly five plowes goinge, and milked fowerteene kyne, whearefore wee had allwayes fower men, two boyes to goe with the oxeplough, and two good
Clothes. lusty mayde-servants. Some servants will (at theire hyringe) condition to have an olde suite, a payre of breeches, an olde hatte, or a payre of shoes; and mayde servants to have an apron, smocke, or both, but it is but sometimes and with some servants that such things are desired. In hyringe of a servant yow are first to make sure that hee bee sette att liberty; after that to inquire of him wheare hee was borne, in what services hee hath beene, with what labour hee hath beene most exercised, and wheather hee can doe such and such thinges;

and after that to goe to his master, or some neighbour of his that yow are acquainted with, and tell them that yow are aboute to hyre such a servant, and soe knowe of them wheather hee bee true and trustie, if hee bee a gentle and quiett fellowe, wheather hee bee addicted to company-keepinge or noe, and lastly to knowe what wages hee had the yeare afore, but if hee have any of the forenamed ill properties, the best way will bee to forbeare hyringe of him. In hyringe of mayde servants yow are to make choice of such as are good milkers, and to have a care of such as are of a sluggish and sleepie disposition, for dainger of fire; and neaver to hyre such as are too neare theire friends, for *occasion* is sayd *to make a theefe;* and, beinge hyred, yow are not to committe over much to theire trust, but to see into all thinges your selfe, and to keepe as much as yow can under locke and key. When yow are aboute to hyre a servant, yow are to call them aside and to talke privately with them concerninge theire wage, if the servants stande in the churche-yard, they usually call them aside, and walke to the backe side of the church, and theire treate of theire wage; and soe soone as yow have hyred them, yow are to call to them for theire ticketts, and thereby shall yow bee secured from all future dainger; their ticketts cost them 2*d.* a peece, and some masters will give them that 2*d.* againe, but that is in the masters choise, unlesse they condition soe before the servant bee hyred. Some servants will condition to have soe many sheepe wintered and sommered with theire maisters, and looke howe many sheepe there is, wee account that equall to soe many eighteene pences. Aboute a fortnight or tenne dayes afore Martynmasse, the cheife constable of every division sendeth abroad his precepts to all pettie constables, willinge them to give notice to all masters and servants within theire severall constableries howe that hee intendeth to sitte att such a place on such a day, commandinge everie of them to bringe in a bill of the names of all the masters and servants within theire severall constableries. There are usually two, and sometimes three, sittinges or statute-dayes for every division, whereof the first is a weeke or more afore Martynmasse, and the next three or fower dayes after that; for hee perhapps sendeth one warrant to soe many townes to

A.D. 1603 —1689.

Maid servants.

Statute.

meete him att such a place on such a day, and another to
other townes to meete him againe att another place, or perhapps att the same place on such a day; and the townes that
are first called, are the most priviledged; for masters that
wante servants, and servants that wante masters, have the
benefitte of the next sittinge to provide for themselves;
whereas those townes that are not called till the latter
sittinge have but one day to provide themselves in, for the
servants in these townes cannot bee hyred till the townes bee
called, that theire masters, or some for them, bee there to sette
Constables. them at liberty; the first thinge that the cheife constable doth
is to call the constables of everie towne, and to take in the
bills, and then to call the masters by theire names, in order as
they are sette in the bills, and to aske them if they will sette
such and such a servant att liberty; if the master will, then
hee maketh the servant his tickett, and the servant giveth
him 2d. for his paines; if the master will not sette him att
liberty, then the cheife constable is to lette them knowe what
wages the statute will allowe, and to sette downe a reasonable
and indifferent wage betwixt them, and hee is to have one
penny of the master for every servant that stayeth two yeares
in a place, or is not sette att liberty, and this the pettie constables are to doe for him, viz.; to sende in bills of the names
of all such servants as stay with theire olde masters, and to
gather the money, and sende it him. Our sittinges weare
both att Kirkburne this yeare; the cheife constable sate att
Mr Whipps, and the servants stoode in the church-yard,
there is allwayes a sittinge att Killam the morrow after All
Saint day, and usually another at Sledgmour, two or three
dayes after. A master cannot turne away his servant, nor a
Warning. servant goe from his master, without a quarters warninge;
servants will usually give theire olde masters a day, some
two dayes, and some will stay three dayes with theire olde
masters, and goe away on the fowerth day after Martynmasse.
They stay usually two or three dayes with theire friends,
and then aboute the fifth or sixth day after Martynmasse
will they come to theire newe masters; they will depart from
theire olde services, any day in the weeke, but theire desire
(hereaboutes) is to goe to theire newe masters eyther on a

Tewsday, or on a Thursday; for on a Sunday they will A.D. 1603
—1689.
seldome remoove, and as for Munday, they account it ominous,
for they say

> *Munday flitte,*
> *Neaver sitte:*

but as for the other dayes in the weeke they make no greate
matter. I heard a servant asked what hee coulde doe, whoe
made this answeare,

> *I can sowe,*
> *I can mowe,*
> *And I can stacke,*
> *And I can doe,*
> *My master too,*
> *When my master turnes his backe.*

They will say to a mayde, when they hire her, that if shee
have but beene used to washinge, milkinge, brewinge, and
bakinge, they make no question but shee can sweepe the howse
and wash the dishes. When servants goe to the sittinge,
they putte on theire best apparrell, that theire masters may
see them well cladde; they gette theire breakefasts, and soe
goe to the sittinge immediately, yett the townes are seldome
called before tenne or eleaven of the clocke, yett they will
stay till it bee allmost darke, afore they come hoame, and
then have they theire dinners; and if they bee hyred, they
are not to goe to the latter sittinge."

From this it appears that the clauses about leaving service were strictly attended to, but the wages seem to have *Justices'*
been a mere matter of agreement[1], though the statute is *Assess-*
just alluded to. During the seventeenth century the justices *ments.*
did sometimes assess wages[2], but only occasionally. It does

[1] The Warwickshire magistrates in 1684 proclaimed severe fines against those
who did not adhere to the assessed rates (Rogers, vi. 700); and in the North
Riding several persons were "presented" for refusing to work at the assessed
wages (*Quarter Sessions Records*, i. 114, 141, 202, 220, in *North Riding Records
Society Publications*), but the constables seem to have discontinued the attempt,
as the last instance I have noticed is in 1614, and it does not appear that any
penalty was inflicted; compare on this point *ib.* i. 141, ii. 53. Under Charles I.
in 1631 an order was issued insisting that the statute of labourers for retaining of
servants and ordering of wages betwixt the servant and the master be not deluded
by private contracts before they come to the statutes. *Orders and Directions*,
Eden, i. 156. Brit. Mus. 1027, i. 16 (9).

[2] Rogers (*Agriculture and Prices*, v. 618, vi. 685) gives eleven cases; other
published lists are Devonshire, 1594, 1654 and 1712 (Hamilton, *Quarter Sessions*,
pp. 12, 165, 273); Bucks. 1688 (*ib.* 249); Hertfordshire, 1631 (Clutterbuck, i.

not seem that the rates were actually enforced under
penalties even when they were publicly declared, and if the
proclamation was omitted, there could apparently be no prosecution[1]. The wages clauses had been inoperative during
the reign of Elizabeth[2], and under the circumstances they
cannot have had much practical effect during the seventeenth
century. In the published records of the West Riding Sessions[3] for 1597 and 1601 there is no mention of setting wages,
or of any disputes arising in connection with wages. Similarly
the Bedford Sessions records[4] which have been preserved from
1650—1660 show that the apprenticeship clauses of the statute
of 1563 were carefully enforced, but are entirely silent in regard
to the assessing of wages or cases arising in connection with
wages. Highway business and prosecutions under the game
laws are plentiful, but there is no instance of any action
which shows that the justices habitually took cognisance of
rates of wages. During this period there were considerable
fluctuations of prices; the Cambridge wheat rents for 1654-5
are at 24s. 9½d. and those for 1658-59 at 52s. 2¼d. Yet
though the price of corn thus doubled in this brief period
the Bedford justices do not seem to have felt called upon to
make any new order or to try to enforce a different rate of
wages. It thus appears that the justices did not assess wages
with any regularity as the statute required them to do, and
that when they did occasionally fix rates, these rates were
not adhered to by employers[5].

VI. The Poor.

227. The problem of pauperism is a recurring one and
it differs much in different ages. In the time of Henry VIII.
and Edward VI. we get an idea that the able-bodied tramp,
who had no employment, was the chief difficulty. In the

p. xxii.); Derbyshire, 1634 and 1648 (Cox, *Derbyshire Annals*, II. 239, 241), and
Lancashire (1725), *Annals of Agriculture*, xxv. 305. See below, p. 359.

[1] Sheppard, *Justice of Peace*, c. xxii. § 7, p. 148.

[2] 1 James I. c. 6, preamble and § 2.

[3] Yorkshire Archaeological Association, Record Series, III.

[4] I am indebted to the courtesy of the Clerk of the Peace for permission to
examine them.

[5] Sir Matthew Hale appears unaware of any legal provision against the starvation rates of pay of which he complains. *Provision for Poor* (1683), p. 18.

seventeenth century we hear less of this evil, except in so far A.D. 1603 as it was directly due to the war. The mischief was specially —1689. noticeable when soldiers were disbanded, and the treatment they received, even if they were maimed or wounded, was most cruel[1]. In the year 1629 Charles I. disbanded his Irish army and they swarmed across the Channel to various ports. Proclamations were issued for forcing them to return to Ireland[2], and passing them from parish to parish to one of 1630. the ports of embarcation. The royal action in this case had evidently given rise to the evil; but it was also exerted to *Rochester.* remedy it, by appointing a commission and issuing elaborate instructions to manorial lords, justices and others, for controlling the swarms of "rogues and beggars" that had been let loose on the land[3].

On the whole however, there seem to have been fewer beggars than in the sixteenth century; as noticed above, depopulation had practically ceased, and the colonies and Ireland afforded space for the surplus population. Still, the weak point in the Elizabethan system had never been remedied, and the difficulty of raising a stock and finding employment for the poor came into prominence from time to *Providing* time. This seems to have been specially noticeable in the *employ-ment after* years succeeding the Civil War, when a good many pam-*the Civil War.* phlets were issued, with proposals for building hospitals and setting the poor at work. *Stanley's Remedy*, the work of a repentant Elizabethan highwayman who desired to confer a benefit on the public he had injured, was printed in 1646; Sir John Cooke,—the lawyer who suffered, in spite of his able defence, for his part in the execution of King Charles,— published his *Unum necessarium* in 1648, in which similar measures are advocated; and Parliament intervened in 1647 by erecting a corporation for employing the poor in London[4]. In 1649 a pamphlet appeared entitled the *Poor Man's Advocate*[5], which suggests that the remains of the crown lands as well as of the episcopal and cathedral revenues should be

---

1 *Greevous Grones*, quoted in Eden, I. 155.   2 Rymer, XIX. 72.
3 *Orders and Directions*, compare Eden, I. 156.
4 16 Dec. 1647. This is not printed by Scobell but merely mentioned. There is a copy in the British Museum [1627, i. 16 (10)].
5 By Peter Chamberlen.

A.D. 1608
—1689.
165⁵.
utilised in this way.   Sir Matthew Hale[1] wrote in the same
vein in 1683; though after the strain of the war was over and
prosperity had revived[2], the arguments about the employment of the poor usually take another form.   They no longer
dwell so much on the existence of sturdy beggars; tracts were
written by men who were eager to promote some branch of
industry and who refer to the employment of the poor as one
Developing new indus- tries. of the incidental advantages it would subserve.   It is in this
spirit that Haines advises that the poor should be employed
in the linen manufacture[3], which was the favourite experiment when workhouses were necessary and were established[4];
or that Goffe[5] and others[6] urge that they might be employed
in connection with fishing; and that Yarranton[7] enunciates
different possibilities for different parts of the country.   It is
not till the close of the century when the combined pressure
of heavy taxes and bad seasons was being severely felt that
the growth of pauperism and the rapid increase of the poor
rates became once more a cause for public alarm.

*Disturb-
ance of
trade in-
creased the
number of
bankrupts,*
The Civil War did of course cause great loss in many
ways; the staple trade of the kingdom was greatly affected[8]
and the propertied classes were hardly hit[9].   These affected
the manufacturers and merchants, aud the mistaken policy
of Cromwell in forcing a quarrel with Spain[10] was fraught

---

[1] *Provision for Poor.*   [2] *World's Mistake* in *Harl. Misc.* I. 288.

[3] *Proposals for building * * a Working Almshouse,* 1677 (*Harl. Misc.* IV. 489).

[4] For example by Firmin in London, Eden, I. 202 note; the account of his
scheme shows that the class of poor for whom employment was sought was not the
same as the able-bodied vagrants whom Stanley had in mind and for whom Harman
provided. *Ib.* 168.

[5] *How to advance the trade of the nation and employ the poor,* in *Harl. Misc.* IV.
385.   Undated but seems to be of the time of James I.

[6] *Grand Concern* in *Harl. Misc.* VIII. 581; I. D. in a *Clear and Evident Way*
(1650), p. 15.   [7] *England's Improvement* (1677), pp. 47, 56.

[8] J. Battie, *Merchant's Remonstrance* (1648), p. 24.

[9] "In respect of the troubles of the times, the meanes of the said Hospitall
hath very much failed for want of charitable benevolences which formerly have
beene given and are now ceased, and very few legacies are now given to Hospitals,
the Rents and Revenues thereunto belonging being also very ill paid; besides the
want of bringing cloth and manufactures to London, which have formerly bin
brought to *Blackwell Hall:* the hallage whereof was a great part of the poore
children's maintenance, which being decayed by these and other meanes, the said
Hospitall hath not been able to take in any children for two yeares past." *True
Report of the Great Costs and Charges of the Foure Hospitals* (1644), 669, f. 10 (2).

[10] *World's Mistake* in *Harl. Miscel.* I. 289.

with long-continued disaster for these classes. The uncertainties of civil and foreign war however gave rise to conditions that tended to the increase of bankruptcy[1], but do not
seem to have done much directly to reduce the labourer to
dependence on the rates. They had hard times in bad years
of course[2]; but while the Sessions Records of Yorkshire in *but did not*
1601 are full of difficulties about the pressure of the rates[3], *directly pauperise*
there is no mention at all of the poor or of any necessity for *labourers.*
relieving them in the Bedfordshire Sessions from 1650 to
1660. The inference seems to be that despite the disturbances
caused by the war, pauperism had on the whole declined; —
and this is borne out by direct evidence. In his excellent
history of the poor in Colchester[4], Morant writes: "Notwith- *Colchester.*
standing these laws [5 El. 14 El.] the poor continued to be
relieved by the voluntary alms of well disposed persons (for
the reception of which a trunk or box was set up in every
church) or else by collections at the church doors, as is still
practiced in many countries, until the 39th and 43rd of Elizabeth, when overseers of the poor were appointed and their
manner of election, office and duty settled and limited by
statute. Which method of relief is still used in this nation."

Under this new law, the maintenance "of the poor of this
town was at first very easy, as appears by the note below[5],
and so it continued for about 40 years. Of which these were
the natural causes: a good trade; difference in the manner of

---

[1] See below, p. 210.

[2] Sir John Cooke writes in 1648 (*Unum necessarium*, p. 5) "There was never
more need to make some provision for the poor than this year; a Labourer will
thrash as much corn in a day as the last year in two; and corn being deare, those
that kept three servants the last yeare, will keep but two the next; those that had
two but one, and those that had one will do the work themselves; and every one
projects for himselfe, to spend as little as may be, but who takes care for the poore,
how shall they be provided for? If a poor man have work all this winter, and get
six pence a day; what will three shillings a weeke do to maintaine himselfe, his
wife and three or foure children? For English families commonly consist of six
or seven." The remedy he suggests is that of preventing or limiting brewing so
that barley may be available for food (p. 28). He discusses the practice in other
countries of authoritatively fixing the price of corn (p. 7), but is curiously silent
about the powers of the Justices to raise wages.

[3] *West Riding Sessions Rolls* (Yorkshire Archaeological Association, Record
Series, III.) pp. 43, 75, 84, 96, 118.   [4] Morant, *Essex*, I. 180.

[5] He quotes the rates at which different parishes were assessed in 1602 and 1610.
S. Mary's paid £19. 0s. 4d. In 1768 it had risen to £280 per ann. in the same parish.

living from what it is now; cheapness of provisions; money
going a great way; the nation not so populous; few or no
luxuries imported, or at least not dispersed among the poor;
not so great a number of alehouses and incentives to vice and
drunkenness; few taxes, and public impositions, which being
infinitely multiplied since, have greatly enhanced the price
of everything. But the unhappy siege brought universal
distress and poverty in this place. However trade and
riches flourished among us again."

The evidence which has been already adduced as to
the condition of the employed is confirmed by the apparent
decrease in the numbers of the unemployed.

228. Such is the history of pauperism in the forms of
which the Elizabethan legislators had chiefly taken account;
but there were some difficulties of another kind, which had
at all events new importance. There were so many people who
had little ostensible occupation, and maintained a miserable
Squatting on the commons. and disreputable existence as squatters on the common wastes.
They had a few sheep or cattle, they managed to get their
fuel, and they would perhaps secure some game. But they
led an idle, ill-conditioned life and their children grew up
to form the same sort of habits.

The existence of this class is dwelt on in the tracts which
Dymock. advocated the enclosure of common wastes[1]. Dymock pro-
pounds these questions on this subject; "whether Commons
do not rather make poore by causing idlenesse, than maintaine them; and such poore who are trained up rather for
the gallows or beggary, than for the Commonwealth's service? How it cometh to pass that there are fewest poor
where there are fewest commons, as in Kent, where there is
scarce six commons in a county of considerable greatness?"
The remedy he suggests is that of enclosing the commons
and allotting a couple of acres or so to each of these families.
Taylor. Taylor is still more explicit; he would have tried to train
these people to engage in spinning and manufacturing rather

[1] It was also argued that the rich men who put large flocks on the commons
for a time, and ate them bare, gained at the expense of other commoners. *Hartlib's
Legacy,* 54. The destruction of commons and need of enclosing in the interest of
the commoners comes out in regard to Herefordshire, 4 James I. c. 11.

than that they (as usually now they do) "should be lazying A.D. 1603
upon a common to attend one cow and a few sheep for we —1689.
seldom see any living on Commons set themselves to a better
employment. And if the father do work sometimes, and so
get bread, yet the children are seldom brought up to anything; but being nursed up in idleness in their youth they
become indisposed for labour, and then begging is their portion, or theevery their trade, so that though Commons be a
help to one, yet its a ruine to many[1]." Worlidge also agreed *Worlidge.*
that the common rights of the Poor do very much injure
them and the Commonweal in general. "For here, by reason
of and under colour of a small advantage on a Common, and
by spending a great part of their time in attendance and
seeking after their cattel; they neglect those parts of Husbandry and Labour, that otherwise would maintain them
well, and educate their children in these poor cottages, as
attenders on their small stocks, and their neighbours' greater,
for a small allowance; which is the occasion that so many
poor cottagers are neare so great wasts and commons.
These open and Champion Counties, by reason of the
multitude of these cottages, are the Producers, Shelterers
and Maintainers of the vast number of Vagrants and Idle
Persons, that are spread throughout the greatest part of
England; and are encouragements to theft, pillage, lechery,
idleness and many other lewd actions, not so usual in places
where every man hath his proper lands inclosed, where every
tenant knows where to find his cattel, and every labourer
knows where to have his day's work[2]." The existence and
importance of this class come out incidentally in the stories
of occasional riots, as in the enclosing of the fens, but it was
of lasting importance partly because it gave rise to far-
reaching legislative changes and partly because it brought
about a state of feeling when the war upon cottages was *The war on*
regarded as a sort of duty[3]. Taylor complains that people *cottages.*

---

[1] Taylor, *Common Good*, 8.

[2] Worlidge, *Systema Agriculturæ*, 13.

[3] This was ordered to be a matter of official enquiry by the Commissioners in
1631. A case came before the Bedfordshire magistrates at the January Sessions
in 1654. Where the man could obtain four acres of ground there was no legal
objection to the erection of a cottage, as he was supposed to have the means of
supporting himself. A. Moore, *Bread for the Poore* (1653), p. 15.

gave way to the building of cottages, "for the ease of your
parish, or out of a base fear of your Lord.   The parish sometimes wants habitation for their poor, and then with consent
of the Lord there is a new erection, and for which there are
very few Lords but contrary to Law do receive rent, so that
he careth not how many are erected.   Again, many times
the Lord gives way to erect without consent, either of free
or copyholder, and if such are prosecuted yet very seldom
redressed[1]."   Nations learn in time, but they are only too
apt to rush into an extreme from the effort to avoid a recognised evil, and the easy-going action of the manorial lords of
the seventeenth century, was followed by a violent corrective,
when deliberate and cruel efforts were made to remove them
and diminish the numbers.

*The Act of
Settlement.*
229.   The chief legislative measure of this period was
the famous Act of Settlement in 1662.   The poor were most
unequally distributed throughout England, and the burden
of maintaining them and difficulty of employing them

*Great pres-
sure at
Sheffield
in 1615.*
pressed very severely in certain places.   In 1615 Sheffield
appears to have been in a frightful state[2]; how the trade of
the town managed to grow, despite the burden caused by a
pauper population which was something like a third of the
whole, is difficult to guess.   In some places relief could be

*Effects of
laxity*
counted upon, and "wilful people finding that they having
children, have some hopes to have relief from the parish
wherein they dwell, and being able to labour and thereby to
relieve themselves and their families, do nevertheless run
away out of their parishes, and leave their families upon
the parish[3]."   On the other hand a pamphlet of the same

---

[1] *Common Good*, 38.

[2] "By a survaie of the towne of Sheffeld made the second daye of Januarie 1615
by twenty foure of the most sufficient inhabitants there, it appearethe that there
are in the towne of Sheffelde 2207 people; of which there are 725 which are not
able to live without the charity of their neighbours.   These are all begging poore.
100 householders which relieve others.   These (though the best sorte) are but
poore artificers; among them there is not one which can keepe a teame on his own
land, and not above tenn who have grounds of their own that will keepe a cow.
160 householders not able to relieve others.   These are such (though they beg not)
as are not able to abide the storme of one fortnights sickness but would be thereby
driven to beggary.   1222 children and servants of the said householders; the
greatest part of which are such as live of small wages, and are constrained to work
sore to provide them necessaries."   Hunter, *Hallamshire*, 148.

[3] 7 James I. c. 4, § 7.

reign complains that in other districts the poor were shame- A.D. 1603 —1689. *and neglect.*
fully neglected. "Though the number of the poore do dailie
encrease, there hathe beene no collection for them, no not
these seven yeares[1], in many parishes of this land, especiallie
in countrie towns, but many of those parishes turneth forth
their Poore, yea, and their lustie labourers that will not
worke, or for any misdemeanor want worke, * * so that the
country is pittifully pestered with them[2]." As mentioned
above Charles I. appointed a commission in 1631[3] with the
view of bringing pressure upon the Justices and other local
authorities to do their duties; he seems to have thought
that the existing measures were fairly satisfactory if only
they could be enforced.

The remedy, which was attempted for these evils, was
that of defining the local responsibility more clearly, so that *Local re-* *sponsibility defined.*
it might be possible to say what place was responsible for
the maintenance of any particular persons. "The necessity,
number and continual increase of the poor," says the Act[4],
"not only within the cities of London and Westminster, with
the Liberties of each of them, but also through the whole
kingdom of England and Dominion of Wales, is very great
and exceeding burdensome, being occasioned by reason of
some defects in the law concerning the settling of the Poor[5],
and for want of a due provision of the Regulations of Relief
and Employment in such parishes and places where they are
legally settled, which doth enforce many to turn incorrigible
rogues, and others to perish for want": it adds, "that by
reason of some defects in the law, poor people are not
restrained from going from one parish to another, and therefore do endeavour to settle themselves in those parishes
where there is the best stock, the largest commons or wastes
to build cottages, and the most woods for them to burn and
destroy[6], and when they have consumed it, then to another

---

[1] Eden (I. 144) states that no rates were levied in some parishes for 20, 30 or 40 years after 1601.　　　　[2] *Greevous Grones*, by M. S.; Eden, I. 155.
[3] *Orders and Directions*, 6 Charles I., Jan. 5; Brit. Mus. 1027, i. 16 (9). Compare Eden I. 156.　　　　[4] 13 and 14 Charles II. c. 12.
[5] On the Law of Settlement under the Commonwealth, see Inderwick, *Interregnum*, 91.
[6] The importance of wood as the chief source of fuel comes out in these discussions. One of the severest attacks of a socialistic kind on the privileges of

A.D. 1608
—1689.
parish, and at last become rogues and vagabonds, to the
great discouragement of parishes to provide stocks whereby
it is liable to be devoured by strangers." According to the
preamble the statute was aimed at this vagrant class, and
gave powers to remove a new comer within forty days, if
there was a danger of his becoming chargeable to a parish,
to the place where he had last been legally settled. But
like so many pieces of social regulation it had most unfore-
seen effects, and a measure which had been intended to fix
local responsibility and check vagrancy came in the succeeding century to have a most disastrous effect on the English
artisan[1]. It interfered with the employment of the industrious, and it chained the unemployed to districts where
no work could be obtained.

*The alter-
native lay
in national
regulation.*
    It was perhaps wise to try and strengthen local responsi-
bility and use the local authorities, whether in parishes or in
townships[2]; but much of the evil was due to national action,
and many difficulties would have been removed if it could have
been dealt with by national regulation that worked similarly
in all places[3]. Possibly such a system might have been characterised by undue laxity, but all the expense of proving settlements and of removing paupers would have been saved.

*Prisoners
for debt.*
    230.   A second class who attracted attention during this
period, and who were constantly spoken of as objects of
charity, were poor men imprisoned for debt. The statutes of
Henry VIII. and Elizabeth[4] had treated the bankrupt as a
criminal, who through carelessness or fraud cheated honest
men of their dues; he was liable to imprisonment by the
Lord Chancellor, and by Commissioners appointed by the

manorial, was a claim on the part of commoners to have their share in all wood
grown on the commons. *Declaration from the poor oppressed people of England*
(1649) [Brit. Mus. 1027, i. 16 (3)]. Even in London people were hardly reconciled
to the use of coal for domestic fires. It had been prohibited in 1306; Stowe, *Annals*,
1652, p. 1502. Locke, who suffered from asthma, was unable to reside in the city in
1679. (*Reports, &c.* 1871, xviii. 828.) The 'fine-nosed city dames' complained, "Oh
Husband wee shall never be well wee nor our children while we live in the smell
of this Cities Seacoale smoke." *Artificial Fire* (1644), Brit. Mus. 669, f. 10 (11).

    [1] Adam Smith, *Wealth of Nations*, pp. 57—59, 191.

    [2] In the large parishes in the north of England the parish was regarded as too
large a unit for administering the poor law.

    [3] See below, p. 385, on Massie; also a proposal in 1652, *State papers addressed
to O. Cromwell*, 89.   [4] See above, p. 92.

Chancellor. The first parliament of James I. took a similar A.D. 1603 —1689.
view of the case, and rendered the machinery for realizing
the bankrupt's assets and making payments to his creditors
more stringent than before. The practices of bankrupts *Fraudulent bank-ruptcy,*
were said to be so secret and so subtle that they could
hardly be found out or brought to light[1], and the Commissioners for Bankruptcy had enlarged powers for imprison-
ing offenders, especially if they were endeavouring to evade
full inquiry into their possessions. But while the law was
becoming stricter, there are signs of a change in public
opinion; it was obvious that in some cases the bankrupt *and un-fortunate*
might be an object of commiseration; while it was also clear *debtors*
that the unlimited incarceration of the debtor did not tend
in any way whatever to re-imburse the creditor. The case
is strongly put in a *Declaration and Appeal*[2] which was *in the Fleet.*
drawn up in 1645 and signed by a hundred debtors confined
in the Fleet. They were the spokesmen of a considerable
class, as they estimated that there were 8000 debtors thus
confined throughout England and Wales, and they urged
that as they were neither villains nor slaves the treatment
to which they were subjected was unconstitutional; and the
highhandedness of Sir John Lenthall was a special subject of
complaint[3].

No public action appears to have been taken in the *Repeated measures of relief.*
matter however till September 1649[4], when an act was passed
for discharging from imprisonment poor prisoners unable to
satisfy their creditors; an additional act for the further relief
of poor prisoners was passed in December 1649. Prisoners,
who had no possessions worth more than £5 and their
clothes and tools, were to take an oath to this effect before
the justices; and after due notice was served on the creditors,
so as to allow of their taking objection on sufficient grounds,
the prisoners were to be discharged[5]. Further facilities

---

[1] 1 James I. c. 15.   [2] Brit. Mus. 669, f. 10.

[3] Both debtors and creditors complained of his management of the Upper
Bench and a Committee was appointed to investigate the charges in 1653. Whitelock, *Memorials*, 555.

[4] In 1648 when prices were high the sufferings of the prisoners were notorious.
Cooke, *Unum necessarium*, 42.

[5] Scobell, *Acts*, 1649, cc. 56, 65, Vol. I. 47, 99.

were given in April 1650; and additional measures were
passed in April 1652, October 1653[1] and in 1656. As in
other matters the Restoration Parliament adopted the
measures passed under the Commonwealth, and acts on
behalf of Insolvent Debtors were passed in 1671[2] and 1678[3].

*Politic
bankrupts.*
It must not be supposed however that the prisoners were
always the victims of relentless creditors. In some cases
they were 'politic bankrupts[4]' who remained in prison by
preference, as a means of evading the just claims that might
be made on them. The committee appointed in 1653
ordered the debtors in the Upper Bench to "show cause why
their estates should not be sequestered for payment of their
just debts[5]"; and a clause in an act of 1661 facilitates proceedings against "many persons" who "out of ill intent to
delay their creditors from recovering their just debts, continue prisoners in the Fleet[6]."

*The un-
happy
times.*
These measures have been mentioned in some detail as
the constant attention given to the subject seems to show
that bankruptcy was very frequent. The times were so
unsettled that they must have been very disastrous for
many traders, and the great increase in the numbers of
insolvent debtors need not be a matter for surprise. Little
is said in the statutes about the causes of bankruptcy,
though the Act of 1671 specifies the late unhappy times and
the sad and dreadful fire as the causes of much misfortune[7].

VII. Finance.

*Treasure
procured by*
231. As the whole economic policy of the country was
regulated during this period with reference to the maintenance and increase of national power, a great deal of attention
was, as a matter of course, directed to the maintenance and
increase of the national treasure. This object was kept
prominently in view during the whole century; there was,

[1] Scobell, *Acts*, ii. 265.
[2] 22 and 23 C. II. c. 20.
[3] 30 C. II. c. 4.
[4] Dekker, *Seven Deadly Sins* (1606), p. 1.
[5] Whitelock, *Memorials*, 555.
[6] 13 Charles II. st. ii. c. 2, § 4.
[7] 22 and 23 Charles II. c. 20.

however, a great change effected in the means adopted for securing this result. A.D. 1603 —1689.

The older scheme of policy has been already described above[1]; it was chiefly aimed at retaining our store of bullion, and preventing leakage. In its simpler form as practised in many reigns this method for securing treasure was embodied in laws for preventing the export of bullion; in the more elaborate form in which it was pressed upon the government it would have insisted on regulating the rates of exchange, so as to prevent bullion from passing to and fro in the ordinary course of commercial transactions, except at specified rates. This was the *bullionist* policy, which aimed at increasing treasure by laws which directly regulated the transmission of the precious metals. This system was very effectively carried out in Spain, and vigorously urged by Malynes in this country in tracts already quoted. *amassing bullion*

But such regulations with regard to the transport of bullion greatly hampered the transmission of commodities; this was especially the case in the East India Trade. The advocates of that trade succeeded in convincing the public that it did lead to the introduction of bullion on the whole and in the long run, although it involved the export of a certain amount of bullion in the first instance: in fact it appeared that it was possible to secure a supply of treasure by carrying on a trade which induced a steady flow of bullion into the country, despite some initial loss. Put more generally, the newer school held that the important thing was to attend to the flow of bullion in the course of trade and not to concentrate all the energy in preventing leakage. In other words, they advised that there should be "free trade" so far as the export of bullion was concerned, because they held that it was possible so to regulate the course of trade in commodities that a balance should be due on commercial transactions and that a stream of bullion must inevitably flow into the country. This scheme may be described as mercantilist in distinction to the bullionist measures already described; the bullionist regulations were said to hamper the trade in commodities unnecessarily, and in the case of *to the disadvantage of trade*

[1] Vol. I. p. 354, II. pp. 16, 128.

14—2

A.D. 1603
—1689.

the East Indies they would have rendered trade impossible if strictly enforced. Those who wished to develop this commerce argued that by direct legislation about trade in com-

or by the balance of trade.

modities, the flow of bullion could be regulated, indirectly but none the less certainly through the *balance of trade.*

Mun 1664.

Sir Thomas Mun's exposition of this view in his *England's Treasure by Foreign Trade* has obtained a world-wide fame through the mention of this tract in the *Wealth of Nations.* The decline of bullionist Spain, and the rise of Holland with the help of an East India trade, seemed to give practical illustrations of the superiority of the new scheme for securing treasure. The advantages of the two methods for maintaining a supply of bullion had been most carefully examined by

1669.

the Council of Trade. They noted the great difficulty in enforcing laws against the exportation of bullion; and compared the condition of Spain with that of Tuscany, Genoa and the Netherlands,—places in which there were no restrictions on export; the experience of Venice was almost crucial, as that city had tried a bullionist policy and had given it up. To carry on the highly profitable trade with the East Indies, and to enjoy the full advantage of trade with Norway and the Levant, an export of bullion was necessary; and they therefore concluded "that time and experience instruct, and the present state of traffic throughout the world require, that, for the increase of the stock of money in these your Majesty's kingdoms, some way of liberty for the exportation, at least of foreign coin and bullion, should be found out and put in execution[1]." Parliament gave effect to this advice in the statute of 1663: full liberty was granted to traders to carry out foreign coin and bullion, after entering the amounts at the custom house but without paying any duty, in the hope of keeping and increasing the coin of England. It had been found by experience that bullion was " carried in greatest abundance, as to a common market to such places as give free licence for exporting the same[2]."

---

[1] *Advice of His Majesty's Council concerning the Exportation of Gold and Silver concluded* 11th *December* 1660. (*Political Economy Club, Tracts on Money,* edited by Macculloch, p. 153.)

[2] 15 Charles II. c. 7, § 9.

From this time onwards, the doctrine of the balance of A.D. 1603
—1689.
trade dominated in all commercial legislation; the calcula- *Importance*
tion of the balance of trades, as a whole, and of the balance *of this*
obtained by particular trades, came to be regarded as a *doctrine.*
matter of great importance; it was the only possible means
of seeing how far the current expedients for the introduction
of treasure were working well, or needed to be re-cast; while
the particular balance in each trade was supposed to show
which branch of commercial intercourse was beneficial and
which was 'hurtful'[1], the general balance served to show
how much of the precious metals the king might hoard in
any given years without withdrawing money from circulation; but the faculty as well as the opportunity was required if treasure was to be amassed, and the Stuarts did
not excel in that particular virtue.

232. The accumulation of bullion was viewed with in- *The*
terest, not only as the means of amassing treasure, but with *currency.*
the view of meeting many grave difficulties connected with
the coinage; some of these had arisen from the greater
currency which was now given to gold; and some from the
deficiency of coinage[2], which was generally alleged to be due
to the melting of silver to sell for gold coin. This would
occur if the nominal value of silver was too high. A contemporary writer[3] complained that this was the case; silver
was all melted or transported, so that it was exceedingly
difficult to get silver for gold coins in London; and the silver *Deficiency*
which remained current was said to be very light. Similarly *of silver.*
a member of the Privy Council in a remarkable speech
pointed to the defect in the double standard as the main
cause of the evil, and recommended that "the proportion of

[1] See above, p. 127.
[2] See below, § 245, p. 254. In 1620 there was a very interesting debate on the scarcity of money which was then supposed to be due to a recent decline of the cloth trade, and decrease of exports to Spain. *Parl. Hist.* I. 1194.
[3] Rice Vaughan, *Discourse of Coin and Coinage* (1675), in *Political Economy Club, Select Tracts*, p. 42. This contains interesting criticism of various proposals for altering the currency; the author seems to incline to solve some of the diffi-
culties by issuing silver of about the size and weight of the silver actually current, as he thought these light coins stood in about the right proportion to gold, p. 46, and that this was better than to alter the gold. Another proposal discussed is for abolishing coinage except as a guarantee of quality, and making all payments by weight, p. 108.

gold and silver to each other be wrought to that parity
by the advice of artists, that neither be too rich for the
other[1]."

*Suggested
alterations*
    Two methods of altering the currency were suggested;
one was a plan in 1640 for increasing the proportion of alloy
in the coin which was to be used for paying the Scottish army.
The more specious proposal, to give a higher nomenclature
to a smaller piece of silver, was brought forward more than
once; in either case there would have been a temporary gain
to the Crown, but obtained at the expense of a permanent
loss of revenue. As the privy councillor pointed out, the
impolitic.   Crown had by successive alterations, lost two-thirds of its
revenue from estates since the time of Edward III[2] Neither
of these proposals for altering the currency were carried out
however; and there was no serious effort at amendment till
after the close of this period, when the re-coinage was under-
*General
incon-
venience.*
    taken in 1696. Lowndes thus describes the inconvenience
which was then felt from the debased state of the current
money,—"Great contentions do daily arise amongst the
King's subjects, in fairs, markets, shops and other places
throughout the kingdom, about the passing or refusing of
the same, to the disturbance of the public peace; many bargains, doings and dealings are totally prevented and laid
aside, which lessens trade in general; persons before they
conclude in any bargains are necessitated first to settle the
price or value of the very money they are to receive for their
goods; and if it be in guineas at a high rate, or in clipt or
bad moneys, they set the price of their goods accordingly,
which I think has been one great cause of raising the price
not only of merchandises, but even of edibles, and other
necessaries for the sustenance of the common people, to
their great grievance. The receipt and collection of the
public taxes, revenues and debts (as well as of private men's

---

[1] *Political Economy Club, Select Tracts on Money,* edited by Macculloch, p.
131. The speech was published in 1641, as a speech made by Sir Thos. Roe in
the previous year, but in 1651 it was attributed to Sir Robert Cotton and supposed
to have been made in 1626. *Ib.* 123.

[2] In 1344 five groats weighed one ounce, whereas the Stuarts only received an
ounce of silver for every five shillings due to them. *Political Economy Club,
Select Tracts on Money,* Macculloch, 128.

incomes), are extremely retarded[1]." Altogether things were A.D. 1603 —1689. Gold and Silver standards.
in a bad way; and though the re-coinage of silver, which was
then the standard of value and basis of exchange with other
countries, had many good results, the old evils soon began
to re-appear; the proportion between gold and silver was
unaltered, and from its convenience, gold had practically
become the standard coin for large payments. An attempt
was made to rectify the evil in 1717 under Sir Isaac
Newton's advice[2], when the guinea was "enhanced" or
raised in nominal value from twenty to twenty-one shillings;
this proved an insufficient corrective, however; and there
was difficulty about keeping silver coins in circulation till
1816[3], when gold was adopted as the standard[4] and silver
was reduced to a mere subsidiary coin.

233. The fall in the value of silver had seriously re- Sources of Revenue.
duced the revenue of the Crown; according to ancient usage
the King had been able to live of his own, and had recourse
to Parliament in emergencies. The chief problem of the
seventeenth century financiers was to find a source of revenue
which should supply a regular income, that might adequately
correspond to the increased responsibilities of government in
these more modern times. The first attempt to do this was
in the Great Contract, proposed to the Parliament in 1610;
by this James proposed to relinquish all the occasional
payments from feudal tenures, in return for a regular income
of £200,000 to be derived from parliamentary supplies[5].

As this bargain broke down, James was a considerable Constitutional struggle.
sufferer; Charles I., to whom Tunnage and Poundage
were not voted for life, was left in a position of direct
dependence on parliamentary grants, and he did not conceal his resentment. During both of these reigns every
effort was made to secure supplies from extra-parliamentary

---

[1] Lowndes, *Essay for Amendment of the Silver Coins (Select Tracts)*, 233.
[2] *Representation* in *Select Tracts*, 270.   [3] Macculloch, *Select Tracts*, p. 264.
[4] This was pretty much what Lowndes had proposed, except that there was a
slight depreciation of the standard of gold coin, while he had wished to keep it at
the old rate—the guinea of twenty shillings; his scheme was probably bimetallic,
however, as he meant to retain silver as a standard as well as gold. The reasoning
by which he supported his proposal was by no means sound, and was vigorously
assailed by Locke.   [5] *Parl. Hist.* i. 1134.

sources; while the Commons, who were eagerly anxious to assert their position and exercise a real control over the foreign as well as the domestic policy of the realm, were always on the alert to thwart these attempts. The main interest of the whole matter is constitutional rather than economic,—indeed it lies far deeper than any questions of the forms of the constitution, or the precedents that could be alleged on either side. The issue lay between, the personal sovereignty of a King, claiming to rule as God's minister who was bound to do his best for the people committed to his charge, as in the sight of God, and the sovereignty of the people, claiming to be supreme in the management of their own affairs. Popular sovereignty obtained a substantial success, and personal sovereignty was condemned by the logic of events; and under these circumstances the constitutional questions come to be mere legal curiosities. The opinion of the most recent investigators appears to be that the Crown was exceedingly well advised in the various attempts to obtain an extra-parliamentary income.

Impositions on foreign   The expedient which James attempted was that of levying impositions on foreign commerce; a considerable revenue was obtained from tobacco, but the imposition of five shillings per hundredweight on currants was resisted by a Turkey merchant named Bates. The important trial which ensued resulted in the success of the Crown[1]; and fortified by this decision, the authorities issued a new Book of Rates; in this, however, so far as we can judge, there was no very heavy increase of the dues to be paid, and the increase of revenue which accrued was small. Considerable anxiety was expressed about any attempts to obtain a *and internal trade.* revenue by exactions from internal trade[2]: the king was forced to forego the impositions on alehouses and on coals; they rested on an entirely different footing, as they had nothing to do with foreign commerce, and the national pride was peculiarly tetchy on the subject of an excise. Freedom from inquisitorial taxes on internal trade, which were common on the continent, seemed to be one of the great liberties

[1] See the argument fully analysed in H. Hall, *Customs Revenue*, I. 152.
[2] Dowell, *Taxation*, I. 216.

which Englishmen prized, and which they continued to enjoy A.D. 1608 till the time of the Civil Wars and the Commonwealth. —1689.

Though the prerogative of the Crown with respect to the *Direct taxation.* rates of duties on foreign imports was established, it had not proved easy to raise much money from this source; and King James I. and his advisers turned their attention to the possibility of obtaining revenue by means of direct taxation. The most successful expedient was a tariff of honours which was apparently directly imitated from the great French financier Sully. £1,095 was charged to persons who were otherwise suitable for a baronetcy, £10,000 for a barony; a viscount paid £15,000 and an earl £20,000[1]. It was not the only instance in which James followed the example of this minister.

234. King Charles was more hardly pressed than his father; and his necessities called forth much ingenuity of invention. The granting of patents to corporations was *Patents.* carried out on a large scale; it was thus possible to put an indirect tax on articles of common consumption[2], and to bring in a considerable income from internal trade. But Noy's great masterpiece was in the drafting of the writs for Shipmoney[3]. The Commons had complete control over the *Shipmoney.* levy of direct taxation under the ordinary forms; and they held the purse strings carefully; they made no grant to Charles on the basis of tenths and fifteenths, and this mode of levying taxes came to an end; but they granted a considerable number of subsidies, on the system framed under the Tudors. During the period of personal government this source of revenue ceased; and an attempt was made to levy money from the maritime towns by writ, on the plea that the realm was endangered by the Barbary pirates who pursued our ships and captured them even in the Channel[4], and

[1] Dowell, *Taxation,* I. 245. [2] *Ib.* 244, see above, p. 166.

[3] Special care was also taken with the assessment for this tax, and it was admittedly fair. Davenant, *Ways and Means* in *Works,* Vol. I. 37.

[4] The destruction of Baltimore, a corporate town in County Cork, in 1631, made a deep impression, "All of them English most of them Cornish, suddenly surprised in the silence of the night." Fitz Geffrey, *Compassion towards Captives,* 46. Some instances of plucky resistance and escape from Algiers' pirates will be found in *A relation of a ship of Bristol,* 1622 [Camb. Univ. Lib. Bb. 11. 39]. H. Robinson urged that a blockade of Constantinople with forty ships would force the Grand Turk to give redress. *Libertas* (1642), p. 8.

A.D. 1608 —1689. that it was necessary to provide " for the defence of the kingdom and safeguard of the sea." There was no persistent opposition to this claim, by means of which £100,000 was obtained; in the following year, £200,000 was levied by similar writs from inland as well as maritime towns[1]; an extra judicial opinion supported Charles in his action, and when the matter was tried, through the refusal of John Hampden to pay his quota, the Chief Justice with a majority of the Bench concurred in supporting the royal action[1].

1640. When the troubles in Scotland forced Charles' hand, it was of course possible for Parliament to pass a declaration on the subject and to alter the law for the future; and they at once availed themselves of their opportunity. The struggle became embittered, and the Civil War ensued; Charles had great difficulty in procuring any supplies, and his armies were maintained by the personal generosity of his supporters, and occasionally by mere pillage[3]; indeed there was no other expedient for obtaining money that demands our attention, so far as the royalist cause was concerned.

Parliamentary resources. 235. The case of the Parliamentary party was entirely different; they succeeded in organising a system of taxation, which was called into being to meet the exigencies of the time, but which was regularly organised as a permanent revenue system at the time of the Restoration. The strength of the Parliamentary party lay in London and the Eastern Counties; but the adhesion of the navy, which had been created by shipmoney, gave them the command of the coasts and added very considerably to their strength; for one thing *Customs.* it brought the customs revenues within their grasp[4]; and this they manipulated with great success. The great increase of the customs revenue during the Civil War and

---

[1] Dowell, *Taxation*, I. 234, 263. Sir John Coke urged the necessity of maintaining the sovereignty of the seas, against France, Spain and the Netherlands. Gardiner, VII. 357.   [2] Gardiner, VIII. 279.

[3] A portion of the parliamentary army in 1647 lived at free quarters. *Parl. Hist.* III. 805, 813.

[4] "The late king having the command of the Inlands and the Parliament of most of the seaports, they had no better way than to put an excise on goods, whereby their enemies, making use of the said goods, paid the excise, and so the Parliamentary Army." *Trades Destruction in England's Ruin, or Excise Decryed*, by W. C., 1659, p. 5 [Brit. Mus. 518, h. 1 (2,)].

under the Commonwealth could hardly be entirely due to an A.D. 1603 increase of trade, but is partly explained by the increase of —1689. 'impositions' which must have been as heavy a grievance as when they were levied by the King. In 1610 the customs revenue had been £136,000; in 1642 it was double; in 1645, £277,000; in 1650, £350,000: so that their command of the sea enabled Parliament to secure very substantial aid[1].

Their method of direct taxation was borrowed from the *Direct* Tudor subsidy, but it was adapted to the exigencies of the *taxation;* *monthly as-* times. It was collected monthly instead of yearly, and the *sessments.* occupiers were responsible for the actual payments, so that absentee owners, who were fighting on the royalist side might not escape[2]. Each month a sum was voted, and the — proportion was assigned to each district; while an official assessment was made according to the actual value of a man's possessions, and not taken on the easy terms at which subsidy men had been rated.

They also levied taxes on internal trade, after the example of the Dutch; Pym braved the popular indignation which neither Elizabeth, James nor Charles had been prepared to face, and in 1643 introduced the excise, on ale, beer, cider and *The* other beverages: in 1644 flesh, victuals, salt, starch, textile *Excise.* goods and all sorts of commodities were charged with this duty. As might have been expected it was not only very profitable but very unpopular, and it was only "established at the point of the sword[3]." In 1649 the government were able to strike out some of the articles of common consumption, and the populace became more reconciled to the tax, which was regularly incorporated into the fiscal system of the country at the Restoration.

The pressure of this taxation was very severe, and royalist *Financial* writers found apparent satisfaction in enumerating the heavy *difficulties* *at the Re-* exactions to which the people had been subjected. One *storation.*

---

[1] H. Hall, *Customs*, I. 184. The customs revenue continued to increase despite the constant complaints of decaying trade, and amounted to £600,000 in 1659. It is possible to reconcile this conflicting evidence when we remember that there was frequent outcry about the large importation of French goods. This would afford revenue from customs, even though it interfered with native industry.

[2] Dowell, *Taxation*, II. 5.

[3] *Ib.* II. 11.

writer collects a list of the sums that had been levied from London alone[1]. Such taxation, coupled with the social disorganisation caused by the war, and the uncertainty about property and titles after it was over, were by no means conducive to the prosperity of the nation; but the expenses had been defrayed by taxes and not by borrowing, and no permanent burden was left, like that which weighed on the energies of the nation after the great wars with France. The country recovered with singular rapidity, and the years immediately preceding 1653 were times of great prosperity[2]. But Cromwell's foreign policy as Protector had most disastrous results on our staple trade, while no corresponding advantage was gained over our rivals[3]. The Navigation Act was fostering our shipping but did not benefit industry, there was distress in different parts of the country in the years succeeding the protectorate. The evil was prolonged by a succession of bad harvests[4], and for one or two years wheat rose to famine prices. Under these circumstances it was only natural that many men should take a somewhat pessimist view of the position and prospects of the country[5]; and the task of setting the finances of the realm on a sound basis was no easy one. There can be no greater testimony to the practical common sense of the Parliamentary party in a sudden emergency than was afforded by the Restoration Parliament, since they adopted the expedients which had been specially devised in order to meet temporary exigencies for the raising of permanent revenue.

Restoration settlement of Revenue.

236. A scheme for settling a permanent revenue on the Crown, similar to the Great Contract, was introduced and carried through immediately after the Restoration; the king was to enjoy a revenue of £1,200,000. The difficulty of

---

[1] *London's Account, or a Calculation of the Arbytrary and Tyrannical Exactions &c. during the four years of this Unnatural Warre*, 1647. [Trinity College Library, v. 1. 56 (16).] [2] *World's Mistake (Harl. Miscel.)* i. 288.

[3] See above, p. 168. The Dutch developed a cloth manufacture, Manley, *Usury*, p. 16, and the consumption of French goods increased enormously.

[4] Thorold Rogers, *History of Agriculture*, v. 212—216.

[5] Roger Coke, *Discourse of Trade*, part i. (1670); Fortrey, *England's Interest* (1673) in *Select Collection of Tracts on Commerce* (Macculloch), 231: *Britannia Languens* (1680), *Ib.* 314. On the other side, *England's Great Happiness, a dialogue between Content and Complaint* (1677), *Ib.* 251.

effecting an arrangement was in some ways greater than it A.D. 1608 —1689. had been in 1610, for the Crown was then in possession of the feudal prerogatives, which had been abolished during the time of the Commonwealth, and could never be revived; it had also suffered by the sale of the royal domains; and the king was now stripped so bare both of prerogatives and possessions that he had nothing to offer from his side. It was fortunate for Charles that the Restoration Parliament was so enthusiastically royalist; in lieu of the feudal claims and the rights of pre-emption and purveyance, they made a grant of £100,000; in fairness this should have been raised from the estates which had been subject to the extinguished obligations, or from lands generally, but neither proposal was feasible; experience had modified the strong prejudice *Excise.* against an excise[1], and a grant was made to Charles and his successors of the *hereditary excise* on home-made beer and liquors, on the new drinks such as tea and coffee, and on imported beer and cider[2]. A temporary excise for the king's life was also granted at the same rate[3]; and the two together amounted to about the charge which had been levied under the Commonwealth[4].

The Restoration Parliament also completely re-organised the customs revenue by passing the Great Statute which included a Book of Rates at which merchandise was charged; *The Book* *of Rates.* tonnage on French or Gascony wine was to be £4. 10s., and poundage was an *ad valorem* duty of five per cent. The duties on cloth were levied by the weight, and both the old drapery and the newer sorts, which had been introduced during and since the reign of Elizabeth, were thus taxed[5].

These two main sources of revenue did not, however, *Hearth* *money.* supply the annual sum that was required, and the Commons feeling that nothing conduces "more to the peace and prosperity of a nation * * than that the public revenue thereof may be in some measure proportioned to the public charges and expenses," levied hearth money[6] which was unpopular, but productive[7]. The Post Office, which had been organised by a

---

[1] *Considerations touching the Excise* (1664), p. 1.
[2] 12 Charles II. c. 24.　　　[3] *Ib.* c. 23.
[4] Dowell, *Taxation*, II. 13, 25.　　　[5] *Ib.* 18.
[6] 14 Charles II. c. 10.　　[7] Davenant, *Ways and Means*, in *Works*, Vol. I. 22.

A.D. 1608
—1689.
patent from Charles I.[1] became a source of revenue under the Commonwealth[2] and was farmed out at the Restoration for £21,500; the monopoly was strictly reserved and no one but the Post Master General was to carry letters for hire[3].

Special demands.

These sums were intended to supply the ordinary revenue of the Crown; for the French and Dutch wars and other emergencies special votes were taken; in 1663, subsidies were granted by Parliament and also by the clergy separately in convocation; but after that year the direct taxation was voted on the model of the Commonwealth assessments, and the tax was levied simultaneously on the property of clergy and laity[4]. Poll taxes were taken on three occasions[5], and an additional excise was levied for nine years from 1671. But the most interesting of these special votes was the alteration of the tariffs for trade with France, which was made, not for the sake of revenue but as a hostile and retaliatory measure. Trade with France suffered a serious check in 1667 when Colbert prohibited the introduction of foreign manufactures into France; the House of Commons retaliated by putting on additional duties in 1668 and 1670 and for a brief period the importation of the chief products and manufactures of France was forbidden altogether.

Gold-smiths.

237. In connection with the collection of these taxes, Charles II. derived considerable assistance from the goldsmiths, as Cromwell had done before him; the practice had been growing among the public of depositing their money with the goldsmiths[6], who lent it out to merchants and others who desired temporary advances. Before long the king became a large and regular customer, as these loans enabled him to obtain immediate use of the supplies which Parliament voted. The bankers made advances to the king on the assignment of taxes voted but not collected[7], and they

---

[1] Rymer, *Foedera*, xix. 649.

[2] It was farmed for £14,000 in 1659. *Commons Journals*, vii. 627?

[3] 12 Charles II. c. 35, § 6.

[4] Dowell, *Taxation*, ii. 32.

[5] *Ib.* 31.

[6] On the shock to credit caused by Charles I. appropriating Spanish bullion in the Tower, see Gardiner, *History*, ix. 170.

[7] McLeod, *Theory and Practice of Banking*, i. 437.

thus enabled him to tide over the period between the grant and the actual collection of the payments.

The bankers paid 6 per cent. to the public on deposits left with them and expected to receive 8 per cent from the Crown: in 1672, however, there was a sudden and violent *The stop of the Exchequer.* interruption to this business, as Charles suddenly stopped the repayments out of the Exchequer of the moneys advanced by the bankers, and thus appropriated £1,328,526 to his own use. It belonged to various depositors, who numbered altogether about 10,000; after an interval of five years, interest at the rate of six per cent. was paid from 1677 to 1683. The depositors entered on long and intricate legal proceedings in order to secure the repayment of the debt with arrears of interest at 6 per cent., and at length an act was 1701. passed decreeing[1] that they should have interest at the rate of 3 per cent. till payment was made of half the debt. Finally the debt was taken over by the South Sea Company; it was never repaid, but is included in the National Debt.

The whole incident is of considerable interest as it throws a good deal of light on the nature and extent of the gold- *Nature of their business,* smiths' business. This wealthy and important body were sub- jected to special taxation in 1670[2], when fifteen shillings per £100 was levied from bankers on all money lent to the king at more than six per cent.[3]: they must have enjoyed a high reputation for probity or they would not have been trusted with such large sums by the public. Their business really consisted in dealing in masses of coinage, and they were commonly supposed to take advantage of the irregularities in the current coins and the variations in the standards to reap what advantage they could. They were frequently charged with culling out the heavy coin, and with exporting bullion[4] when the rates of exchange rendered such transactions profitable: at this distance of time it is impossible to say what ground there may have been for these complaints, but it is of course obvious that the goldsmiths had the opportunity of acquiring gain by such methods if they chose.

---

[1] 12 and 13 William III. c. 12, § 24.   [2] Dowell, *Taxation,* II. 33.
[3] An ingenious method of lowering the interest on money.
[4] Thomas Violet, *Advancement* (1651), and *An Appeal to Caesar* (1660).

A.D. 1603
—1689.
and
gradual
develop-
ment of
credit.

The goldsmiths discharged a most useful function by placing capital in the hands of merchants who were able to use it profitably, and there are signs of increased familiarity with bills and other forms of credit. The Long Parliament agreed to accept Weavers' Hall Bills and Goldsmiths' Hall Bills as well as ready money, in payment for the Bishops' lands which were being bought but slowly[1], and the 'Land Debentures[2]' they issued were intended to liquidate the arrears of pay due to the army; but they appear to have been negotiable. There was no great development of public credit, as loans on assignment of taxes had been in use for long; but there are frequent complaints about reckless trading on credit[3], and there can be little doubt that this involved the more general use of paper in commercial transactions.

238. While the business of banking was thus developing, there were some interesting attempts to devise means for insuring against fire. The successive steps that were taken are detailed by a contemporary, " I find this design was first set on foot immediately after His Majesty's Restoration by several persons of quality, and eminent citizens of London, and Proposals about it then printed by them. But tho the Project and Authors of it were then recommended to the Common Council of London by His Majesty's letters, yet it was not admitted by them, for the very same reason for which those Gentlemen now are not to be countenanced in it; viz. because they thought it impossible for Private Persons to manage, and unreasonable that they and not the City should reap the Profits of such an undertaking. Hereupon this Design, like some Rivers that sink into the Ground, and break not out again, but at a considerable distance, was no more heard of till the year 1670, when it was afresh propounded to the city by Mr De Laun, tho not prosecuted by them. However in the Mayorality of Sir W. Hooker it was briskly revived by Mr Newbold the Merchant,

The Fire of London.

---

[1] 28 Aug. 1649, Scobell's *Acts*, II. 86.

[2] Prendergast, *Cromwellian Settlement*, 196.

[3] The complaint is frequent from the very beginning of the century. Dekker, *Seven Deadly Sins*, The Politic Bankrupt; Sir W. Raleigh's *Observations* in *Political Economy Club, Select Tracts*, p. 18.

who proposed the carrying it on by a Joint Stock to be A.D. 1608 —1689. raised among the Inhabitants and Proprietors of the Houses to be insured. This he communicated to the Lord Mayor, and divers other eminent Citizens. From some of these like *Rival Fire Insurance Scheme.* an Eves-dropper, this Observator caught it; it being then generally discussed and approved of and resolved to be put in practice. * * Mr Newbold therefore waiting for a more favourable conjunction found it not till the Majorality of Sir Robert Clayton to whom on New Year's Day Anno 7⅘ he presented the Model of it, and sometime after printed it under the title '*London's Improvement and the Builders' Security*[1].' Sir Robert Clayton approved of the matter, only advised that instead of a joint stock it should be managed by the Chamber of London[2]." Within a short time three fire insurances were started; one was managed by a committee of the Common Council, and was opened in December 1681; "but this would not take[3]." The Fire Office at the Back side of the Royal Exchange began business a month earlier, and three years later a Friendly Society was started for doing similar business but on a different principle. The respective advantages of these various offices, the rates they charged[4], and the security they offered, were the object of a good deal of discussion[5], in which the respective advantages of municipal action and of private enterprise were freely canvassed.

During the Mayoralty of Sir William Hooker there were *Life Insurance.* also tentative efforts at organising Life Insurance. A certain Mr Wagstaffe laid his scheme before the City authorities, who thought so highly of the project that they appointed a select committee to carry it into effect. Subscribers of £20 each, or of multiples of £20, were to be associated according to their ages; each subscriber was to have an annuity at the rate of 6 per cent., and as some of the subscribers died off, the

---

[1] Brit. Mus. 816, m. 10 (64).

[2] *A second letter to Mr M. T.* by L. R., Brit. Mus. 816, m. 10 (80).

[3] Stow, *Survey*, Vol. I. bk i. 240.

[4] These may be seen in the collection on Insurance in the British Museum [816, m. 10 (71 and 73)].

[5] *A letter to a Gentleman in the country* by *N. B.* is attributed by Dr Bauer to Barbon. He preferred the Fire Office to the Friendly Society and called forth a defence of the latter from H. S. [Brit. Mus. 816, m. 10 (74, 75)].

survivors would obtain proportionally increased annuities. "This extraordinary gain being not only lawful but very advantageous, there can be no other way proposed whereby, in laying out so small a sum as Twenty pounds there can be produced so great an Encrease, as by Survivourship will most certainly accrue to many persons and especially to the Longest Liver of this Rank[1]." Despite the tempting prospect, however, this scheme seems to have shared the fate of the City Fire Insurance project and come to nothing.

The reasons for preferring public management would probably be clearer if we knew more of the history of the private adventure offices that seem to have sprung up at this time. But the following extract from a petition regarding Dorothy Petty is at least instructive. It was said "that the said Dorothy (who is the Daughter of a Divine of the Church of England now Deceased) did set up an Insurance Office on Births, Marriages and Services, in order thereby to serve the Public and get an honest Livelyhood for herself. The said Dorothy had such Success in her Undertaking that more Claims were paid, and more Stamps used for Certificates and Policies in her Office than in all other the like Offices in London besides; which good Fortune was chiefly owing to the Fairness and Justice of her Proceedings in the said Business. For all the Money paid into the Office was entered in one Book, and all the Money paid out upon Claims, was set down in another Book, and all People had Liberty to peruse both, so that there could not possibly be the least Fraud in the management thereof[2]." The profits of such private offices appear to have been very considerable, if we may trust the estimate of Charles Povey, who complained that owing to a "cross incident" he was obliged to sell his undertaking of the Sun Fire Office on very low terms. Had he remained in possession it would have brought him in £600 or £800 per annum[3]. This was in 1709, and early in

---

[1] *Proposals for Subscriptions of Money*, 1674, p. 2 [Brit. Mus. 518, h. 1 (15)].

[2] *The Case of Dorothy Petty in relation to the Union Society at the White Lion by Temple Bar whereof she is Director.* [Brit. Mus. 816, m. 10 (82).]

[3] *English Inquisition* (1718), p. 37. He was condemned for infringing the Post Office monopoly by setting up a "Half Penny Carriage for conveying letters to and fro within the main Pile of Buildings in London." William Dockwra who

which has continued to flourish ever since.

VIII. Economic Doctrine.

239. Frequent references have been made in the pre- *Pamphlets* ceding pages to the very rich pamphlet literature of the *as record-* *ing inform-* seventeenth century: the economic tracts of the time offer *ation and* *as ex-* an almost unlimited field for drawing descriptive information *pounding* *economic* as to the condition of the country, the progress of its industry *doctrine.* and commerce, and the difficulties which had to be faced from time to time. It is worth while to survey these writings from another point of view, and see how far they show greater clearness of thought in dealing with economic problems.

There was some years ago a good deal of discussion as to whether Political Economy is more properly a science or an art, that is whether it is primarily engaged in the scientific investigation of the principles according to which the production and distribution of wealth is carried on, or whether its main object is to make practical suggestions for increasing the production and improving the distribution of wealth. It is important to bear in mind that seventeenth century writers *Practical* *object of* approached the subject entirely from this latter standpoint; *writings.* by far the larger number of tracts are written by men who were advocating some particular proposal, and who adduce reasons in favour of the scheme they had in view. Even when this is not the case, their labour, whether in criticising the proposals of others or in gathering facts, was distinctly and consciously regarded as affording subsidiary helps to the great work of governing the country wisely. The various discussions on coins and money were called forth by a desire to give wise advice in regard to the difficult question of recoinage. The whole subject is approached in its practical aspects by Petty, Locke, and Child, as well as by writers of less note. In so far as contemporary writers discussed *Utopias.*

organised a penny post in London in the reign of Charles II. suffered in the same way.

[1] *Proposals set forth by the Company of London Insurers* (from the Sun Fire Office, April 10, 1710). [*Brit. Mus.* 816, m. 10 (83).]

economic affairs in another spirit, they treated them artisti-
cally in *Utopias*, and *Arcadias* and *Oceanas*, rather than
with any pretence to scientific accuracy. Readers who
thoroughly appreciate the admirable common sense which
these men wrote on many intricate matters will yet miss the
clearness of thought and precision of reasoning, which only
became possible after the more purely scientific studies of
Excellent the followers of Adam Smith. This was indeed inevitable;
treatment till the phenomena of wealth were deliberately isolated from
of special other social phenomena, it was not possible to treat them
Points. with precision. The seventeenth century economists were so
eager about the end they had in view, that they did not concentrate attention sufficiently on the means for attaining it.
Their writings are full of acute remark, and many of them
deal with particular topics in a masterly fashion; but there
is a curious disproportion in the space they assign to these
special points; and they seem to have had no clear conception
of the scope of the subject, or of the divisions into which,
according to our habits of thought, it naturally falls. Hence
there is an appearance of confusion in the writings of the
acutest authors of the period, even when they may be rightly
credited with having anticipated Adam Smith on very many
points.

Careless   The fundamental defect comes out most clearly when we
treatment notice that they pay so little attention to the definition of
of the wealth. They take it in a rough and ready fashion, and
nature of enumerate various kinds of wealth[1] which subserve natural
Wealth. or artificial requirements. There is one striking exception,
for Nicholas Barbon[2] does attempt to analyse the nature of
wealth, and to state the relation of value to price. He calls
attention to the elements of 'Use' and 'Difficulty' in value;
he is perfectly clear that there can be no fixed value for anything, and he has some interesting remarks on the connection
between cost of production ("artificers' price") and market
price.

[1] Compare Fortrey's division of 'store,' *England's Interest* in *Political Economy
Club Select Tracts*, 217.

[2] Dr Stephan Bauer in an excellent monograph has established Barbon's claim
to the authorship of several tracts that were not commonly attributed to him, and
has thus brought out his importance as an economist. Conrad's *Jahrbücher für
Nationalökonomie*, XXI. 561.

" The Value of all Wares arise from their Use; Things of no use, have their Value, as the *English* Phrase is, *They are* *good for nothing.*

" The Use of Things, are to supply the Wants and Necessities of Man: There are Two General Wants that Mankind is born with; the Wants of the Body, and the Wants of the Mind; To supply these two Necessities, all things under the Sun become useful, and therefore have a Value.

" Wares, useful to supply the Wants of the Body, are all things necessary to support Life, such are in Common Estimation; all those Goods which are useful to supply the Three General Necessities of Man, Food, Clothes and Lodging; But if strictly Examined, nothing is absolutely necessary to support Life, but Food; for a great Part of Mankind go Naked, and lye in Huts and Caves; so that there are but few things that are absolutely necessary to supply the Wants of the Body.

" Wares, that have their Value from supplying the Wants of the Mind, are all such things that can satisfie Desire; Desire implies Want: It is the Appetite of the Soul, and is as natural to the Soul, as Hunger to the Body.

" The Wants of the Mind are infinite, Man naturally *Wants.* Aspires, and as his Mind is elevated, his Senses grow more refined, and more capable of Delight; his Desires are inlarged, and his Wants increase with his Wishes, which is for every thing that is rare, can gratifie his Senses, adorn his Body, and promote the Ease, Pleasure, and Pomp of Life.

"Amongst the great Variety of things to satisfie the Wants of the Mind, those that adorn Man's Body, and advance the Pomp of Life, have the most general Use, and in all Ages, and amongst all sorts of Mankind, have been of Value.

"The first Effects that the Fruit of the Tree of Knowledge wrought upon the Parents of Mankind, was to make them cloath themselves, and it has made the most Visible Distinction of his Race, from the rest of the Creation: It is that by which his Posterity may write Man, for no Creatures adorn the Body but Man: Beside, the decking of the Body, doth not onely distinguish Man from Beast, but is the Mark of Difference and Superiority betwixt Man and Man.

"There was never any part of Mankind so wild and barbarous, but they had Difference and Degree of Men amongst them, and invented some things to show that Distinction.

"Those that Cloathed with Skins, wore the Skins of those Beasts that are most difficultly taken; thus *Hercules* wore a Lyons Skin; and the Ermins and Sable, are still Badges of Honour. The Degree of Quality amongst the *Affricans*, is known by the waste Cloth, and amongst those that go naked, by adorning their Bodies with Colours, most rare amongst them, as the Red was the Colour most in esteem amongst the Ancient *Britains*.

"And the most Ancient and best of Histories, the Bible, shews, That amongst the Civilized People of the World, Earrings, Bracelets, Hoods and Vails, with Changeable Suits of Apparel, were then worn: And the same Ornaments for the Body are still, and ever since have been Worn, only differing in Shapes and Fashions, according to the Custom of the Country.

Difficulty. "The Shapes of Habits are much in use, to denote the Qualities of several men; but things rare and difficult to be obtained, are General Badges of Honour: From this Use, Pearls, Diamonds, and Precious Stones, have their Value: Things Rare are proper Ensigns of Honour, because it is Honourable to acquire Things Difficult.

Price, "The Price of Wares is the present Value; and ariseth by Computing the occasions or use for them, with the Quantity to serve that Occasion; for the Value of things depending on the use of them, the *Over-pluss* of those Wares, which are more than can be used, become worth nothing; So that Plenty, in respect of the occasion, makes things cheap; and Scarcity, dear.

"There is no fixt Price or Value of any thing for the Wares of *Trades*; The Animals, and Vegetables of the Earth, depend on the Influence of Heaven, which sometimes causes Murrains, Dearth, Famine, and sometimes Years of great Plenty; therefore, the Value of things must accordingly Alter. Besides, the Use of most things being to supply the Wants of the Mind, and not the Necessitys of the Body; and those Wants, most of them proceeding from imagination, the Mind Changeth; the things grow out of Use, and so lose their Value.

"There are two ways by which the value of things are a *as roughly estimated,* little guessed at; by the Price of the Merchant, and the Price of the Artificer: The Price that the Merchant sets upon his Wares, is by reckoning Prime Cost, Charges and Interest.

"The Price of the Artificer, is by reckoning the Cost of the Materials, with the time of working them; The Price of Time is according to the Value of the Art, and the Skill of the Artist. Some Artificers Reckon Twelve, others Fifteen, and some Twenty, and Thirty Shillings per Week.

"Interest is the Rule that the Merchant Trades by; And Time, the Artificer, By which they cast up Profit, and Loss; for if the Price of their Wares, so alter either by Plenty, or by Change of the Use, that they do not pay the Merchant Interest, nor the Artificer for his Time, they both reckon they lose by their Trade.

"But the Market is the best Judge of Value; for by the *but only determined* Concourse of Buyers and Sellers, the Quantity of Wares, and *in the* the Occasion for them are Best known: Things are just *market.* worth so much, as they can be sold for, according to the Old Rule, *Valet Quantum Vendi potest*[1]."

This is a great advance on current opinion, for it was still customary to treat valuableness as an intrinsic quality belonging to certain things[2], and there was an immense gain in putting forward thus plainly that value does not reside in things, but arises from their relations to changing human needs.

So long as the older conception of wealth lasted it was *Wealth and fair* impossible to get entirely rid of an opinion about exchange *Exchange.* which exercised a very real influence on practical matters. It may be stated thus—If each article had an intrinsic value, then, in every fair exchange, each man obtained an equivalent; but if one man by successive exchanges amasses gain,

---

[1] N. Barbon, *Discourse of Trade*, 18.
[2] Petty, *Treatise.* p. 70. "The proportions between corn and silver signifie only an artificial value, not a natural, because the comparison is between a thing naturally useful, and a thing in itself unnecessary."

A.D. 1603
—1689.
then it appeared that he must be giving less than an equivalent, and that he was gaining through another man's loss.
This notion seems to lie at the root of the wide-spread prejudice against merchants and brokers[1]; in a fair exchange, it
might be said, neither party would gain, because by definition each would get the equivalent of what he had; and if value
is a quality of objects this position seems impregnable. If
you exchange a pound of tea for a pound of tobacco, and a
pound of tobacco for a pound of lead, and this for a pound of
sugar, and have been able to retain a portion of each article
in the process, it is clear that the balances were unfairly
adjusted. But since that which is very useful to me, may

*Mutual
gain is
possible.*
not necessarily be useful to you, we may by exchanging
each get a commodity that is more useful than the things
with which we parted. People had begun to find out that as
a matter of fact the exchange of goods was mutually advantageous[2], before a better analysis of the nature of value
taught them to see how the double gain was possible.

One further indication that the scope of the subject was
still very uncertain lies in the fact that Political Economy
had not yet attained the dignity of a name[3]; it was but a

*Not an in-
dependent
science but
a branch of
state-craft.*
branch of the art of governing, of state-craft; one practical
expedient had been tried after another for increasing the
power of the nation in this or that direction or as one occasion or another called forth some special effort; the general
result of this long experience had been embodied in the legislation of Elizabeth, and was consciously adopted as the best
method for increasing the power of the country. The writers

*Compara-
tive study.*
of the seventeenth century were much engaged in comparing
our experience with that of other cities and countries, and in
thus establishing maxims of more general application, based
on a consideration of the actual progress or decay of different

---

[1] This is familiar all through the middle ages; it held its ground for a long
time, especially in regard to dealers in corn, p. 497.

[2] *England's Great Happiness*, p. 262 in *Political Economy Club Select Tracts*
(Macculloch).

[3] Petty comes near it, "As wiser physicians tamper not excessively with their
patients, rather observing and complying with the motions of nature then con-
tradicting it with vehement administrations of their own; so in Politics and
Economics the same must be used." *Treatise*, 41.

communities. It is therefore convenient to include in the A.D. 1603 —1689. present survey some tracts which contain reflections on the working of measures already described, though they were actually published after the Revolution.

240. All the writers on political philosophy during this period recognised the importance of wealth as a means of obtaining national power. Bodin's *Commonweale*[1], which *Bodin*. was the acknowledged authority on state-craft at the beginning of the century, treats the subject in a superficial fashion, as it only discusses the means by which monarchs might increase their revenue, and does not examine the conditions that affect the sources from which revenue is ultimately drawn. The management of their domains, the tribute of dependence and the spoil of war, together with benevolences, are spoken of as the main sources of income: so far as trade was recognised as a source of gain, it was to be rendered profitable by the successful speculations of the monarch, and very little account was made of the income from rates and taxes. All this is suggestive of the fiscal arrangements of an Angevin king or the cameralistic science of German Dukes[2]: it was quite inadequate for a country in which trade had made such progress as it had in England at the accession of James. In our country it was obvious that we had to rely on trade for those kinds of wealth which were most requisite politically; foreign commerce brought us treasure; and it had come to be of fresh importance in many countries, since the invention of gunpowder and consequent revolution in military operations. Until trade became necessary to provide weapons of war, it was always thought prejudicial to the growth of Empire[3].

The brief chapter in Hobbes' *Leviathan* on the nutrition *Hobbes*. and procreation of states marks an important advance beyond Bodin. The nutrition of the commonwealth consists in plenty of materials conducing to life, in the preparation and conveyance of them, and it depends on the natural plenty afforded by sea and land; and also on the labour and

---

[1] As the English translation of the *De Republica* was entitled. Cf. bk v. c. ii.

[2] Roscher, *Geschichte der Nat. Oek.* i. 219; Seeley, *Life of Stein*, i. 48, 148.

[3] Barbon, *Discourse of Trade*, Preface.

industry of men[1]. In a few pregnant sentences he indicates
the sources from which the prosperity of a people must be
drawn; he is not merely concerned with the income of the
prince, but with the wealth of the community from which
that income must ultimately be drawn, and thus he indicates
the main scope of the art which later writers treated in
greater detail[2]. The productive power of nature received
undue attention from the Physiocrats, while the Mercantilists
also recognised the productive power of labour, and set themselves to develop it.

*Revenue
and Re-
sources.*
        Two brief treatises which were published soon after the
Restoration may be specially mentioned, as they serve to
illustrate how writers who started with the practical problem
of raising a revenue were forced to direct their attention to
the best means of developing the resources of the country
*Fortrey,
1663.*
from agriculture, industry and trade. Fortrey points out
that natural fertility and population are the two main conditions of prosperity, and shows how France has prospered by
its natural riches, and Holland by the industry of its people.
"Two things therefore appear to be chiefly necessary to
make a nation great and powerful, which is to be rich[3] and
prosperous," and England, since it excels in both ways, might
confidently expect "to become the most great and flourishing
of all others." Far more important, as a contribution to
economic doctrine, is Sir William Petty's *Treatise of Taxes
and Contributions*[4], and the practical interest is also strong,
as it was compiled with special reference to the affairs of
Petty,1662.
Ireland, where Petty held an official position. He begins by
enumerating the charges which ought to be borne by the
public, and discusses some savings that might be effected in
particular departments, and also examines "how the causes of
the unquiet bearing of taxes may be lessened." He discusses

[1] Hobbes' Works (Molesworth's edition), III. 232.
[2] Compare for example Barbon on the "native staples" of different countries,
Discourse of Trade, 4.
[3] "Rich" here refers to store of commodities, and not to the accumulation of
treasure, as is obvious from the context. *England's Interest and Improvement* in
Political Economy Club Select Tracts, 218. This reprint is from the edition of
1673, but it was originally published in 1663.
[4] The references are to the edition of 1662. It was reprinted in 1667, 1679 and
1685, also with the title *A Discourse of Taxes* in 1689.

the rival merits and demerits of every possible manner of rais- A.D. 1603
ing revenue with much acuteness, and with occasional humour. —1689.
"A lottery is a tax upon unfortunate self-conceited fools; * * *
now because the world abounds with this kind of fools, it is
not fit that every man that will, may cheat every man that
would be cheated; but it is rather ordained, that the
sovereign should have the guardianship of these fools, or
that some favourite should beg the sovereign's right of taking
advantage of such men's folly[1]." But though it is primarily
a treatise on revenue, it is not by any means confined to the
art of taxation, but deals with the causes that affect the
funds from which each kind of revenue is drawn[2]; his general
view is most easily summarised in his own sentence, "Labour
is the father and active principle of wealth, as lands are the
mother[3]."

In Locke's treatise on *Civil Government* the economic Locke.
side of the life of the community comes in for incidental
notice in the chapter on property; he lays great stress on
the importance of labour as the chief factor in increasing
wealth. "He who appropriates land to himself by his
labour does not lessen but increase the common stock of
mankind, for the provisions serving to the support of human
life, produced by one acre of enclosed and cultivated land,
are to speak much within compass, ten times more than
those which are yielded by an acre of land of an equal rich-
ness lying waste in common. And therefore he that encloses
land, and has a greater plenty of the conveniences of life
from ten acres than he could have from an hundred left to
nature may truly be said to give ninety acres to mankind."
"Of the products of the earth useful to the life of man, nine
tenths are the effects of labour, nay if we will rightly
estimate things as they come to our use and cast up the
several expenses about them, what in them is purely owing
to nature and what to labour, we shall find that in most of
them ninety-nine hundredths are wholly to be put on the
account of labour." "This shows how much numbers of men
are to be preferred to largeness of dominions, and that the

---

[1] *Treatise*, p. 45.   [2] See below, p. 418.   [3] *Treatise*, p. 49.

increase of hands[1] and the right of employing them is the great art of government, and that prince who shall be so wise and godlike, as by established laws of liberty to secure protection and encouragement to the honest industry of mankind against the oppression of power and narrowness of party, will quickly be too hard for his neighbours[2]."

Material require-ments of state.

Here we have a perfectly clear doctrine as to the means of producing wealth: but general principles of this kind, though perfectly understood and implied in the legislation of the seventeenth century, took the statesman but a small way in the art of building up the power of the realm: he had to consider what forms of wealth were most important for national purposes, and therefore he was led to scheme for the increase of treasure, and the development of shipping. These were points to which special attention was directed, but not because anyone supposed that money was the only kind of wealth[3], or that ships were the only kind of wealth; they were quite clear as to the general character of the means by which useful things of all sorts were to be obtained, and it was not necessary to say much about them; but it was their business to devise expedients for procuring wealth in those particular forms, in which it was most available for the defence of the realm[4].

So far for the production of wealth, as considered by

[1] I have ventured to correct the reading "lands." The sentence does not occur in the editions of 1690, 1694, or 1698. It first appears in the collected edition of the works, which was not revised by Locke but came out after his death.

[2] *Civil Government*, §§ 37, 40, 42. Locke's treatise is of still greater interest from the extraordinary indirect effect which it exercised on Political Economy at a later time. It is a most decided expression of the rights of the individual both politically and socially, to be governed according to his own ideas of what is right, and to be secured in the free control of his own property. This treatise had an extraordinary effect in popularising the doctrines which were implicitly assumed by the English *laissez faire* economists. Locke also gave a hint which was developed by the French Physiocrats (see below, p. 436); the extraordinary fertility of his mind is shown when the relation of each of these schools to his work is understood.　　　　[3] See below, pp. 251, 484.

[4] Barbon altogether discarded the obtaining of treasure as an advantage that accrued from trade. "This shows the way of determining those controversies about which sorts of goods are most beneficial to the Government by their making or importing: the sole difference is from the number of hands employed in making them. Hence the Importation of Raw Silk is more profitable to the Government than Gold or Silver." But he thinks that gunpowder and ships are kinds of wealth which are politically desirable. *Discourse*, 39.

writers on the philosophy of the State: there is one curious *A.D. 1608 —1689.* treatise which devotes a good deal of attention to the subject *Harring- ton.* of the distribution of wealth, from the same point of view. Harrington in his *Oceana* traces a connection between the distribution of wealth, and the distribution of power within any country. Political power is necessarily based on wealth; if one man have the greater part of the wealth, especially of the land of the country in his hands, it is natural that the form of government should be monarchical, and so of government by a few or by many, according as the balance of wealth determines. Where this rule is not observed he felt that the government was not firmly based, and that a poor monarch exercised an unnatural and therefore a violent tyranny. In the same way he held that the relations between a mother country and the colonies were determined by the balance of wealth between the two. His treatise was suggested by considering the changes[1] of property and power which had occurred since the time of Henry VII. The rise of a monied class in the latter part of this period, with the rivalry between the landed and monied interest which ensued, is an interesting illustration of his principle. In accordance with republican doctrines, to which he was strongly attached, it followed that a wide distribution of wealth was a necessary condition for good popular government[2], so that the possessions of the many might overbalance those of the few. There has been frequent occasion to point out how political changes brought about alterations in economic conditions, and this doctrine of Harrington's calls attention to one of the ways in which the economic condition of a country affects the stability of its political institutions.

241. In order to argue satisfactorily on the probable *Criterion of pros- perity.* effects of proposals for increasing the prosperity of the country, it was necessary to have some tests of progress or decay. The generally accepted criteria occur in one pamphlet after another; if the rents of land were high, if employment was plentiful, if bullion was flowing in, then things were going well with the country; but it is a little

---

[1] Toland's Life, prefixed to Harrington's *Works* (1737), p. xvii.
[2] Harrington's *Works* (1737), 73.

difficult to see how these tests were taken. What lay on
the surface was that all classes were flourishing, and that
revenue could be raised without much difficulty; and it is not
clear that the public at that time looked at the matter in
any other light. The raising of revenue was the ulterior
object; and just as the "increase of the customs" figures
along with the "obtaining of treasure" as a prime object in
the encouragement of trade, so the facility for raising the
revenue, in the public interest, was consciously present when
they spoke of other advantages which accrued from the improvement of the land.

Rents.   (a) In regard to this last point it is only necessary to
recapitulate what has been noted above[1]. To take an additional instance Fortrey in his tract on *England's Interest
and Improvement* advocates the enclosure of commons as a
real improvement, because landlords favour it and find it
increases the value of their land[2]: the statutes against the
importation of Irish cattle and allowing the export of corn,
were avowedly intended to make farming more profitable, so
that there might be a fund available for paying assessments.
The principle that high rents were a sign of national prosperity was so generally accepted and avowed that it is
unnecessary to do more than quote Locke's statement.
"An infallible sign of your decay of wealth, is the falling of
rents, and the raising of them would be worth the nation's
care, for in that and not in the falling of interest lies the true
advantage of the landed man and with him of the public[3]."

*Employ-
ment and*   (b) Employment was of importance, as it gave opportunity for calling out the energies of the people and setting
them to work and trade[4]. Much is said in the seventeenth
century about the importance of a large population, but the
subject was no longer treated as it had been in the sixteenth

---

[1] See p. 191 above.

[2] "The land of the common fields, almost in all places of this nation, with all
the advantages that belong to them will not let for one third part so much as the
same land would do, enclosed and always several." *England's Interest* in *Select
Tracts*, 228.   [3] *Considerations of the lowering of interest, Works*, IV. 69.

[4] "There is but one infallible symptom to know when trading Nations thrive
and grow rich; that is, when the Inhabitants grow more populous, when they enlarge and new build their Cities and Towns, and when they increase their Ships
and Naval Strength." Barbon, *Discourse concerning Coining*, 51.

from a military, but from an industrial point of view. The A.D. 1608 —1689.
increase of population was approved as a first condition for
the increase of industry, and of wealth by industry. Petty
regrets that Ireland was "under-peopled in the whole[1],"
and Fortrey and other writers advocate measures for attracting as many people as possible to immigrate to England[2].

With respect to employment, it was apparently assumed *large Con-*
very generally that "demand for commodities is a demand *sumption.*
for labour"; more than one writer criticises the policy of
sumptuary laws, and argues that "high living" is advantageous to the nation so long as it takes the form of using
luxuries manufactured at home[3]. "Take away all our super-
necessary trades, and we shall have no more than tankard
bearers and plowmen, and our city of London will in short
time be like an Irish hut." The French trade introduced
new tastes and "set us all agog, and having increased among
us many considerable trades, witness the vast multitudes of
Broad and Narrow Silk weavers, Makers of points and white
and black laces, Hats, Fans, Looking-glasses and other
glasses as I'm told the best in the world, Paper, Fringes and
gilded leather." Barbon recognises a difference between productive and unproductive consumption[4], but another writer
is more extreme and seems to hold that all demand alike. "I
had rather get a thousand pound by lace and fringes than nine
hundred by the best broad cloth that ever I yet saw[5]." The

---

[1] *Treatise of Taxes and Contributions*, Preface.

[2] *England's Interest and Improvement*, in *Select Tracts*, 219.

[3] *Ib.* p. 235. Barbon is almost as paradoxical in his opinion on this subject as
Mandeville in the *Falle of the Bees*. "The two extremes to this Vertue, are Prodigality and Covetousness. Prodigality is a vice, that is Prejudicial to the Man but
not to Trade. It is living a pace and spending that in a year that should last all
his Life: Covetousness is a Vice, prejudicial both to Man and Trade." *Trade*, 62.

[4] "The question which nation thrives most is determined by observing which
imports most of such sort of Goods that must increase or lessen the Labour and
Industry of the people," and this could not be "discerned by the value of the
Goods in the Custom House." *Discourse concerning Coining*, 50.

[5] *England's Great Happiness or a Dialogue between Content and Complaint*
(1677), in *Political Economy Club Select Tracts*, 260, 262. This author writes with
very little implied reference to national "power," and with a strong appreciation
of the advantages of "plenty"; he has no jealousy of other nations but regards
dealings with them as exactly analogous to dealings between individuals in a
nation. "I'll suppose John Nokes to be a butcher, Dick Styles an Exchange man,
yourself a lawyer, will you buy no meat or ribbands or your wife a fine Indian

increase of population was advocated, not merely as a means of increasing the industrial efficiency of the country, but because the increased consumption of food would create an additional demand for products from the soil and thus raise the value of lands[1]. Opening up a vent for products and promoting consumption, appeared the most obvious way to increase opportunities of employment and thus give scope for industrial power.

Balance in Bullion as a criterion of employment.

(c) The management of commerce so as to bring in a balance in bullion was of course a cardinal point with these writers[2]: but it began to attract attention in a new way, not merely as a means of obtaining treasure for the prince[3], but as an index of the industrial condition of the country and the state of employment. If foreign industry and agriculture were employed, and home products and manufactures were neglected, the prosperity of the nation would be undermined: where people were buying commodities from abroad and paying for them in bullion, it showed that certain classes at home were not employed as they might have been: if we brought goods from abroad and sent other goods to pay for them, the producers of the exports were employed as truly, as if the results of their labour were used at home; but if we bought these things from abroad with bullion, we

gown or fan because they will not treat with you for indentures, which they have no need of? I suppose no, but if ye get money enough of others, you care not if you give it away in specie for these things. I think 'tis the same case." P. 261.

[1] *Britannia Languens* (1680), in *Select Tracts*, 852.

[2] Even the sanguine author of *England's Great Happiness*, who ridiculed the idea that the trade with France was a losing one because we exported so much specie there, appears to hold that the total trade of the country with other countries ought to show a balance to be obtained in money: but he seems to have thought that if we developed our industry we were sure to get a market somewhere and need not trouble about the balance on particular trades. "That honest way that finds most employment and gets most money is sure the best for any nation, and this fine manufacture joined to our shipping will perhaps make us the most potent the sun shines on." P. 262. Sir William Petty with some hesitation prefers commerce that carries with it "the condition of having foreign money in specie, and not canvas in barter, between which two ways the world generally agrees there is a difference." *Treatise*, p. 69.

[3] Barbon, who attaches very little importance to treasure, rejects the doctrine. "This opinion," he says, "is grounded upon this Supposition, That Gold and Silver are the only Riches." (*Discourse concerning Coining*, p. 86.)

A.D. 1603
—1689.

were exporting the means of employing our own poor; thus the export of treasure was an index of the subverting of industry and employment at home, on the current assumption as to the relation of demand and employment.

It is of course true that we cannot trade unless we send something from this country to foreigners, and that trade could not continue if the country had nothing to export; but the argument was that it might go on exporting bullion for a long while, and that all the time it procured commodities by so doing, native industry must be in a depressed condition; and that if this continued long enough the extinction of native industry and ruin of the nation must follow. *Consumptive importing trade.*

"On the other side our Importations must as necessarily be increased, both by the decay of our own former Manufactures at home, and by our modern gawd'ry and affectation of foreign Goods[1]; and as our Trade from Port to Port hath become more impracticable to any advantage, the Exporters of our remaining Manufactures and other home-Commodities, must either come back empty, or else must freight themselves homewards with such consumptive foreign Commodities, as for Gawdry, Novelty, Cheapness, or Lyquorishness, will dazle, tempt and bewitch our People to buy them; in which course of Trade our Merchants may gain considerable proportions of our remaining Treasures as long as there is any in the Nation. *Britannia Languens, 1680.*

"Nay, rather than sit idle, they will, and do freight themselves outwards with meer Ballast and Bills of Exchange (by which the Importation of foreign Bullion or money is prevented:) or if Bills of Exchange cannot reasonably be had (as they usually cannot to those Countries where we are overballanced in Trade) then they export Mony and Bullion, and buy and import Consumptive Goods which are spent at home; which kind of Trade deserves rather to be called Foreign Pedling, than Merchandise.

"It may partly be remembred here, how much the beneficial part of our Trade may be prejudiced by the loss of 100000 of our Manufactures, and what odds the same loss

[1] "That trade is certainly best for the kingdome by which gaine ariseth from what is exported and losse by what is imported." Battie, *Merchants Remonstrance* (1648), p. 27.

may produce in our Importations, since if they get but 6*l.*
per Ann. a piece, it must sink the former gain by Trade no
less than 600000*l.* per Ann.

"And on the other side, that if a Million of Families or
Persons in a Nation, do one with the other consume to the
value of 20*s.* a piece more, yearly in foreign Manufactures,
Drinks, &c. than before, this must increase our Importations
to the value of a Million per Ann. which I observe here to
shew how imperceptibly an over-ballance of Importation may
creep upon a Nation; and that the Reader may with the less
difficulty conjecture at the late and present balance of Trade
in England.

"It must also much assist this Importing Trade, if the
Merchants shall export Mony, or Bullion; especially in such
a Nation as England, where a Trade from Port to Port is not
ordinarily practicable to any advantage: for in that Case the
Goods Imported being spent at home, the Treasure Exported
must be lost to the Nation; and as long as the English
Merchant can have Bullion or Mony to Export, and can have
a vent for his Importations at home, his private gain will
never oblige him to complain of the want of Exportable
home-Manufactures, or the Clogs upon Trade, especially in
England, where our Merchants have such a Monopoly of
their Importations on the rest of the People.

"This Consumptive Importing Trade must be of very fatal
Consequence in its Nature; for first, whilest the National
Stock is greater, it will exhaust the Treasure almost insensibly; but as the Treasure grows less and less, it will
work more palpably and grievously, because it will consume
more and more of that little which remains.

"And as the National Treasure comes to be more and
more diminished, the People must generally have less and
less, which must cause the price of all home-Commodities,
and consequently Land-Rents to fall continually, the home
Manufactures must be choaked and stifled by Importations,
so that both the Farmers and Manufacturers must fling up;
the values of their Stocks must be contracted, and will be
eaten out by Rent, Wages and other standing charges before
they are aware; men cannot provide against misfortunes

which have unseen Causes; and as home-trade grows worse A.D. 1608
and worse, Industry it self must be tired and foiled, to the $^{-1689.}$
great amazement, as well as affliction of the People[1]."

This passage I have quoted at length because it is most
important to understand the exact bearing of the doctrine of
the balance of trade in its later form. This writer had no
over-estimate of the importance of treasure as the only kind
of wealth, he was fully alive to the fact that industry was the
true source of prosperity, but he objected to the export of
bullion, because he held that it indicated the subversion of
our native industry, since it meant that we did not obtain
markets abroad, while we opened our own to foreign nations.

There are many matters to which exception may fairly
be taken in his argument[2]: as prices fell, owing to the

---

[1] *Britannia Languens* in *Select Tracts*, 372—374.

[2] On the difficulty of calculating see Barbon, *Discourse on Coining*, p. 86.
"Some men lay so great a stress about the enquiring into this Balance, that they
are of Opinion, *That a Trading Nation may be ruin'd and undone, if there been't Care
taken, by Laws, to regulate the Balance.* And yet there is nothing so difficult, as
to find out the Balance of Trade in any Nation; or to know whether there ever
was, or can be such a thing as the making up the Balance of Trade betwixt one
Nation and another; or to prove, if it could be found out, that there is any thing
got or lost by the Balance.

"For a Nation, as a Nation, never Trades; 'tis only the Inhabitants and Subjects
of each Nation that Trade: And there are no set days or times for making up of
a general Accompt, every Merchant makes up his own private Accompt; and that's
not done at any set time, one Merchant makes it up one week, and another in
another week; so that there can be no set time when to begin that Balance.

"Therefore those that rely so much upon finding out the Balance of Trade, do
it by taking the Computation from the Trade of several years of one Nation with
another, and think it may be done by examining the Accompt of the Custom-House
Books, and us'd to give for Instance the French Trade; because the Revenue that
arose from those Duties on French Wines, and other Commodities that were imported, were so much greater than the Duties on those Goods that were sent into
France, and therefore us'd to cry out very much against the French Trade: Tho',
perhaps, if that were throughly consider'd, the French Trade was as profitable
to the Nation as any other Foreign Trade; which might be made to appear, if
it were proper for this Debate.

"But to make up the Balance of Trade by the Custom-House Books, is a very
uncertain way of reckoning: For all Foreign Goods that are imported, pay a
greater Duty than the Native Goods exported. 'Tis the Interest of all Trading
Nations to lay easy Customs (if any) upon their Native Commodities, that they
may be sent cheap to Foreign Markets, and thereby encourage both the making
and exporting of them: And to lay high Duties upon Foreign Wares, that they
might be dear, and so not lessen by their cheapness the consumption of the Native
Commodities: So that there can be no Computation of the Balance of Trade from
the difference of the Sum of Money that's paid at the Custom-House for the
Foreign Goods imported, and the Native exported.

16—2

export of bullion, merchants would find it was less profitable to import goods from abroad, and the exhaustion of treasure would be most unlikely to continue: and the movements of bullion are affected by so many other matters, that the balance could never be an accurate index of the increase or decrease of employment; but the matter of importance is, that many of the writers who used it in this way, and condemned one trade as hurtful or consumptive, or approved another as giving a vent for our commodities, were clear on the main point that the development of native industry was the real secret of continual national prosperity.

Need of more accurate data.

242. Allusion has been made above to Roger Coke and other authors who took a pessimist view of the condition of English agriculture and industry at this time, and wrote at some length on the subject: but these various treatises appear very inconclusive, as the writers possessed so very

"But suppose there should be an Allowance made, in casting up the Accompt, for the greatness of the Duties that the Foreign Goods pay more than the Native, yet that can be no advantage in the discovering the Balance of Trade; because they cannot discover by the Custom-House Books, what the Native Goods are exported are sold for: For the Balance of the Trade must arise from the Value of the Goods that are sold, and not from the Quantity that are exported or imported. And that's known only to the Merchant that sells the Goods, and 'tis not for his Interest to acquaint others with it, and thereby discover the Profits of his Trade: So that there can be no finding out the Balance of Trade by the Custom-House Books.

"Some are of the opinion, that the way to find out the Balance of Trade, is by the Foreign Exchange. And they reckon that if the Exchange run high upon a Nation, 'tis a sign that there are more Foreign Goods imported, than there are of the Native exported; and therefore there are Bills of Exchange drawn to answer the Effects, and make up the difference in the Value of what the Native Goods were sold for less than the Foreign. This seems to be the nearest way of guessing of the Balance of the Trade of a Nation; but this is altogether as uncertain.

"For Exchanges rise and fall every week, and at some particular times in the year run high against a Nation, and at other times run as high on the contrary. As against a Vintage, a great Mart, or some Publick Sale, the Exchange may run higher to Bourdeaux, Francfort, or Holland, upon an East-India Sale: And at other times the Exchange may have run to the same places as much on the contrary; for no Exchange can constantly run high against a Nation; for then the Merchants that trade to that Country, must always lose by their Trade: For if the Goods that they export, don't yield them as much profit as the Goods they import, they must lose by the Return. And it cannot be suppos'd that Merchants will always Trade to a Country, where they must always lose by Trading; therefore there can be no account of the Balance of Trade by Foreign Exchange.

"As to the rise of the Exchange betwixt Holland and England, that's not to be reckon'd as a Rule, because of the extraordinary charge of the War at this time."

ittle accurate information. Sir William Petty while sketch- A.D. 1608
ng out a more excellent way of study was met by the objec- —1689.
tion " that these computations are very hard if not impossible *Petty,1*662.
to make; to which I answer only this that they are so,
specially if none will trouble their hands or heads to make
them, or give authority for so doing. But withal I say that
until this be done, Trade will be too conjectural a work for
any man to employ his thoughts about; for it will be the
same wisdom, in order to win with fair dice, to spend much
time in considering how to hold them, how much to shake
them, and how hard to throw them, and on what angles they
should hit the side of the tables, as to consider how to
advance the trade of this nation; when at present particular
men get from their neighbours (not from the Earth and Sea)
rather by hit than wit, and by the false opinions of others
rather than their own judgment[1]." The ordinary writers
argue entirely from calculations of the very vaguest sort,
and the prognostications of rapid decay often rested on the
nerest hearsay. "It is a hard matter," one writer confesses,
'to put a just estimate on these yearly losses, for the present
I shall leave it to be computed by our melancholic English
tradesmen[2]." But after all it was idle to spend time in
explaining the cause of the decay, if there was no real decline
it all; and the great necessity of the time was the accumulation of accurate information. This was fully recognised by
some Fellows of the Royal Society, who set themselves to
collect as accurate statistics as possible. The first example
was the work of Captain John Graunt, who analysed the in- *Graunt,*
formation which was available in regard to London: the fre- 1662.
quent complaints of the undue growth of London, and the fears
as to the decay of the city through the drain of the war and
the ravages of the plague, made it desirable that the real condition of the city should be properly investigated, and Graunt

---

[1] Petty, *Treatise*, 34. He notes as one of the causes which aggravate public
changes "Ignorance of the numbers, wealth and trade of the people, causing a
needless repetition of the charge and trouble of new additional levies in order to
amend mistakes." P. 4.

[2] *Britannia Languens*, 405. See also Sir Josiah Child's *New Discourse of
Trades*, Preface.

claimed that it was a branch of "natural history" which
might fitly engage the attention of the philosophers who met
at Gresham College.   His remarks on the study of statistics
are so apposite that it is worth while to quote them.

"Whereas the Art of Governing, and the true Politicks, is
how to preserve the Subject in Peace and Plenty; that men
study only that part of it which teacheth how to supplant
and over-reach one another, and how, not by fair out-running,
but by tripping up each other's heels, to win the Prize.

"Now, the Foundation or Elements of this honest harmless
policy is to understand the Land, and the hands of the Territory, to be governed according to all their intrinsick and
accidental differences : As for example ; It were good to know
the Geometrical Content, Figure, and Situation of all the
Lands of a Kingdom, especially according to its most natural,
permanent, and conspicuous Bounds.   It were good to know
how much Hay an Acre of every sort of Meadow will bear;
how many Cattel the same weight of each sort of Hay will
feed and fatten; what quantity of Grain and other Commodities the same Acre will bear in one, three, or seven years,
communibus Annis; unto what use each soil is most proper.
All which particulars I call the intrinsick value : for there is
also another value meerly accidental, or extrinsick, consisting
of the Causes why a parcel of Land, lying near a good Market,
may be worth double to another parcel, though but of the
same intrinsick goodness ; which answers the Queries, why
Lands in the North of England are worth but sixteen years
purchase, and those of the West above eight and twenty.   It
is no less necessary to know how many People there be of
each Sex, State, Age, Religion, Trade, Rank, or Degree, &c.
by the knowledge whereof, Trade and Government may be
made more certain and regular; for, if men knew the People,
as aforesaid, they might know the consumption they would
make, so as Trade might not be hoped for where it is impossible.   As for instance, I have heard much complaint, that
Trade is not set in some of the South-western and North-
western Parts of Ireland, there being so many excellent Harbours for that purpose ; whereas in several of those places I
have also heard, that there are few other Inhabitants, but

such as live *ex sponte creatis*, and are unfit Subjects of Trade, A.D. 1603 as neither employing others, nor working themselves[1]."

The conclusions at which he arrived are very curious; *The Plague.* some have reference to the increase of certain diseases, and the comparative decline of others; and many of his remarks are suggestive in a sanitary and medical aspect: his main results are summarised in the dedication where he calls on Lord Truro to "consider how few starve of the many that beg, that the irreligious proposals of some to multiply people by polygamy is withal irrational and useless, that the troublesome seclusions in the plague time are not a remedy to be purchased at vast inconveniences[2]; that the greatest plagues of the city are equally and quickly repaired from the country[3]; that the wasting of males by wars and colonies do not prejudice the due proportion between them and females; that the opinion of plagues accompanying the entry of kings is false and seditious; that London the metropolis of England is perhaps a head too big for the body and possibly too strong; that this head grows three times as fast as the body unto which it belongs, that is, it doubles the people in a third part of the time[4]."

Another Fellow of the Royal Society[5], Sir William Petty, *Petty in Ireland.* carried on similar investigations in regard to the state of Ireland where he was officially engaged: on economic grounds he strongly advocated everything that should "tend to the transmuting of one people into the other, and the thorough union of interests upon natural and lasting principles," since he held "that if both kingdoms now two, were put in one, and under one legislative power and parliament, the members whereof should be in the same proportion that the power and wealth of each nation are, there would be no danger such a parliament should do anything to the prejudice of the English interest in Ireland; nor could the Irish ever complain of partiality when they shall be freely and proportionally repre-

---

[1] Graunt, *Natural and Political Observations*, 98.

[2] Since the infection was in the air, not due to contagion, p. 50.

[3] At the rate of about 6000 per annum, p. 59.

[4] Graunt, *Natural and Political Observations*, Dedication.

[5] The opinion that Sir William Petty wrote Graunt's book under an assumed name is carefully discussed and rejected by Macculloch, *Literature of Political Economy* 271.

sented in all legislatures[1]." Petty was fond of exercising his
powers of prevision on the basis of his definite information:
he formulated a law as to the rate of the progress of London,
and held it would reach 5,359,000 of inhabitants in 1800 and
could not increase much beyond that number[2], as from the
area of the country and rate of increase of the rural population it would be impossible to supply them with food. Less
ambitious and therefore more interesting is his *Political*
Progress in England. *Arithmetic*[3]: he examines the common complaint of the
country's decay and the rapid progress of Holland and France,
and while admitting that there were mischiefs of many kinds,
which he attributed to deep-seated popular prejudices, he yet
was confident that as a matter of fact England had increased
in wealth and power during the preceding forty years; he
also urged that the impediments to further progress could be
removed; while France appeared to be under physical disabilities, and could not become a maritime power which was
capable of holding its own against England or Holland, from
the insufficiency of the harbours on the Channel, and the difficulty of training a sufficient body of efficient seamen. In this
as in many other cases he shows more acuteness in stating
and analysing the facts than he does judgment in arguing
from them.

The Currency.   243.   Next to the question as to the general condition of
the country, the most pressing practical problem was raised
by the state of the currency; and this gave occasion to the
promulgation of many crude theories about money and coin.
Cost of Production of Precious Metals. It would be unprofitable to attempt to examine them in detail,
but the fundamental difficulty was due to the backward con-
dition of economic science generally; there had been no sufficient analysis of the cost of production of any commodity, nor
examination of the manner in which the cost of producing any
commodity affects the price of that commodity. Under these
circumstances we cannot be surprised that the writers of that
time, with the notable exception of Sir William Petty[4], appear

[1] *Political Anatomy of Ireland* (1691), 29, 31.
[2] *An Essay concerning the multiplication of Mankind*, 1689, p. 20.
[3] *Several Essays in Political Arithmetic* (1699), p. 141.
[4] Possibly also of Barbon (*Discourse of Trade*, p. 25). He denies that the
precious metals have an intrinsic value, but as noted above, he neglects the im-

ntirely at sea as to the conditions which determine the
)f the precious metals relatively to one another.

ə distinction between the "extrinsic" value of the coin
was given it by the royal authority, and the "in-
" value of the metallic commodity of which it was
was of course clear; and it was also clear that foreign
ges took place according to the "intrinsic" value as a
·dity, and not with reference to the extrinsic denomina-
f the coins[1]: the great difficulty was to explain the
ons in the "intrinsic" value of silver in different

A.D. 1603
—1689.

*Extrinsic
and In-
trinsic
Value.*

of cost of production as a factor in determining the price of commodities;
allude to it in connection with silver mines. Sir William Petty's *Treatise
and Contributions* puts this matter with great clearness: he held that a
corn exchanged for an ounce of silver because the same amount of work
led to produce one as to produce the other: the differences of skill and
d be equalised, over a period of years "the nett proceed of the silver is
of the whole nett proceed of the corn, and like parts of one the price of
ı of the other." With this sound but crudely stated doctrine of cost of
ın as determining the value of commodities, he is able to proceed to
ıe value of the precious metals. "And this also is the way of pitching
proportion, between the values of Gold and Silver, which many times is
y popular errour, sometimes more, sometimes less, diffused in the world;
ror (by the way) is the cause of our having been pestred with too much
stofore, and wanting it now.
ı, I say to be the foundation of equalizing and ballancing of values; yet in
·structures and practices hereupon, I confess there is much variety, and
; of which hereafter.
World measures things by Gold and Silver, but principally the latter; for
y not be two measures, and consequently the better of many must be the
all; that is, by fine Silver of a certain weight: but now if it be hard to
the weight and fineness of silver, as by the different reports of the ablest
ərs I have known it to be; and if silver granted to be of the same fineness
ht, rise and fall in its price, and be more worth at one place then another,
· for being farther from the Mines, but for other accidents, and may be
rth at present, then a moneth or other small time hence; and if it differ
oportion unto the several things valued by it, in several ages upon the
and diminution thereof, we shall endeavour to examine some other natural
ls and Measures, without derogating from the excellent use of these.
Silver and Gold we call by several names, as in England by pounds,
, and pence, all which may be called and understood by either of the
ʒut that which I would say upon this matter is, that all things ought to
l by two natural Denominations, which is Land and Labour; that is, we
say, a Ship or Garment is worth such a measure of Land, with such
measure of Labour; forasmuch as both Ships and Garments were the
s of Lands and mens Labours thereupon: This being true, we should be
nd out a natural Par between Land and Labour, so as we might express
ı by either of them alone as well or better then by both, and reduce one
ıther as easily and certainly as we reduce pence into pounds." P. 25.
ndes, *Essay* in *Select Tracts*, 187.

A.D. 1603
—1689.
countries; till this was accomplished, the practical difficulties connected with the double standard were involved in hopeless confusion. Silver was the only money, and gold was "a commodity next like to money[1]," but no account of the "intrinsic" value of these precious metals as commodities could be given except that they had a conventional value in each
Convention.
nation. It was an age when original conventions and social contracts played a great part in all political reasoning, and hence it was natural to assert that the precious metals had only a value from the convention of mankind. It seemed to follow from this that what was done by agreement could be altered by agreement, and that the current convention in any country might be altered so as to attract a larger quantity of
Raising money.
the precious metals into that land. "Raising money," so as to make it pass for more wares, was "an art which States have used to rob one another of their money, by setting on higher prices upon it; so that some States being induced, by an unjust device, to draw to themselves the money of their
Vaughan, 1678?
neighbours and others, by a necessity to keep their own. All these parts of the world, for some few hundreds of years, have done nothing but vye one upon another, who shall raise their money highest[2]." The Low Countries indeed never raised their money but "when the people by custom and general use have raised the money beforehand[3]," and there were many people who urged it would be possible by an international convention to agree on a fixed standard of money; but it was not hard to demonstrate that there would be great difficulties in forming or maintaining such an agreement. Vaughan's account of the distribution of silver from Spain through Europe and the East, which goes to show that such a convention would be impracticable, assumes that it is by setting a higher price on it[4] that nations draw silver from Spain[5]. The arguments, against proceeding farther with this "art" of drawing money to ourselves, consist chiefly of demon-

---

[1] Sir William Petty's *Quantulumcumque*, Query 17, in *Select Tracts*, 163.
[2] Vaughan, *Coin and Coinage* in *Select Tracts*, 24.　　　[3] *Ib.*, 89.
[4] Vaughan, *Coin and Coinage* (1675), in *Select Tracts*, 88.
[5] Locke himself uses language that is not altogether dissimilar. The intrinsic value of silver, he says, is "that estimate which common consent has placed on it." *Further Considerations, Works*, IV. 139.

trations of the loss to the prince, and other creditors through A.D. 1603
—1689.uch enhancement.

Considering the charge which is commonly repeated *Money and*
*Wealth.*about these writers, that they thought money was the only true wealth, and the attempts of modern authors to expose their fallacy and prove that other things than gold and silver are useful and are properly described as wealth, it is curious to find that they considered the value of these metals to be the result of mere caprice or convention. "Gold and Silver," says Locke, "being little useful to the life of man in proportion to food, raiment and carriage has its value only from the consort of men": "gold, silver and diamonds are things that fancy and agreement hath put the value on, more than real use, and the necessary support of life[1]." In similar fashion Graunt argues that the art of making gold would benefit neither the world nor the artist[2]. So long as men had no clear ideas of the conditions on which the value of silver as a commodity really depends, a strong opinion as to the practical importance of amassing treasure for political purposes, was apparently quite consistent with a too depreciatory estimate of the "usefulness" of the precious metals.

244.   While there was so much uncertainty about the *The rate of*
*interest.*conditions which affected the value of silver as a commodity, we need not be surprised that there was also some confusion as to the conditions which affected payments for the use of money, or the rate of interest.   As a maximum rate was settled by law, it appeared that authority could settle what should be paid for the use of money, and there were many demands that the rate of interest should be authoritatively *authorita-*
tively
*limited*lowered.   Sir Thomas Culpepper may be said to have devoted his life to the task[3]; he succeeded in getting parliament to reduce the legal rate from 10 to 8 per cent. in 1624; subsequently he saw the rate reduced to six per cent. in 1652, and his endeavours were continued by his son[4] and also by Sir

[1] *Civil Government*, §§ 46—50.   *Works*, IV. p. 364.

[2] *Natural and Political Observations*, 97.

[3] His *Tract against Usury* was first published in 1621 [Brit. Mus. 1029, b. 1 (1)]; it was re-issued in 1668 by his son whose preface to his own *Discourse showing advantages of abatement of Usury* (1668) contains an excellent résumé of the struggle.

[4] *Discourse showing the many advantages* (1668), and *Necessity of abating Usury* (1670), by Sir T. Culpeper, Jr., Knt.

J. Child[1]. The six per cent. rate was maintained by the
Restoration Parliament, though some men tried to exact the
rate which had been legal in the time of Charles I.[2] The
precise influence on trade, of authoritatively restricting the
rate, is difficult to estimate without a very full knowledge of
the commercial conditions of the times. But it was certainly
impossible to force the legal rate below what we should call
the market rate. Sir Josiah Child appeared to think that
the State could decree as low a rate as three or four per cent.,
and showed that these rates[8] were current in Holland. But
other writers saw that this was a mistake; Thomas Manley
asserted that " low interest is, both in nature and time, subsequent to riches, and he that says low Usury begets riches
takes the effect for the cause, the child for the mother, and
puts the cart before the horse[4]." There is of course a reciprocal action; riches renders low interest possible, and low
interest tends in many ways to the increase of riches; but in
any case State action must follow and not precede a change
in the market rate. Locke helped to clear the air by insisting that the attempt to fix a maximum rate was illusory,
since the want of money is that which regulates its price,
and people will pay more if they really need an advance. He
admitted that if all men "consented" to low interest and money
could be borrowed at a lower market rate it would benefit
traders; but he regarded the proposal to fix legal interest at
four per cent. as an attempt to drive the rate down below the
market rate. This would be hard on those who conformed
to the law, it would tempt many to break it, and it would
seriously hamper trade, as people would prefer to hoard their
capital rather than have the risk of lending on such terms[5].
There is no doubt that substantial men could borrow at less
than the permitted maximum; it was commonly said that
the East India Company could borrow at three per cent., but

---

[1] *Brief Observations concerning Trade* (1668), p. 7.
[2] 12 Charles II. c. 13.   [8] *New Discourse*, p. 7.
[4] *Usury at six per cent. examined* (1669), p. 7. Compare also *Interest of money
mistaken, or a Treatise proving that the Abatement of Interest is the Effect and not
the Cause of the Riches of a Nation, and that Six per Cent. is a proportionable Interest
to the present condition of this Kingdom* (1668), p. 13.
[5] *Considerations of the lowering of Interest, Works,* IV. 7, 69.

on the other hand, in special circumstances, money had not A.D. 1608
—1689.
Petty.
been forthcoming at six per cent. Sir William Petty treated
the matter still more fully, as he not only protested against
fixing a legal maximum, but analysed the conditions which
determined the rate of interest with some success; interest
on the best security could not exceed the rent which would
come from a similar sum invested in land; but where there
was no good security, "a kind of ensurance must be enter-
woven with the simple national interest[1]."

[While one writer had so much insight into the causes
which determined the ordinary rate of interest, the old difficulties about the morality of usury had come to be regarded *Usury.*
as the qualms of specially tender consciences[2], and Sir William
Petty could not see why "usury should be scrupled," when a
loan caused or might cause any inconvenience. At the same
time he was to some extent in sympathy with the mediaeval
view, as he did not feel that there was any justification for
taking interest in the case of money which was lent on full
security to be repaid on demand; to his mind the ground for
some charge being made lay in the *damnum emergens*, or *peri-
culum sortis*; while the rate per annum was determined with
reference to the rent of land. He wrote with much severity of
many English prejudices, as became a man of the world who
had lived much abroad, but it is curious to find how much
he sympathised with a mediaeval sentiment which Cromwell
had cast aside. "As for the Jews," he says, "they may well *Jews.*
bear something extraordinary, because they seldom eat and
drink with Christians, hold it no disparagement to live
frugally and even sordidly among themselves, by which way
alone they become able to undersell any other traders, to
elude the Excise, which bears but according to men's expenses, as also other duties by dealing so much in Bills of
Exchange, Jewels and Money, and by practising of several
frauds with more impunity than others; but by their being
at home everywhere, and yet nowhere, they become responsible almost for nothing[3]."

[1] Petty, *Quantulumcumque*, Query 32, in *Select Tracts*, 167; *Treatise*, 29.
[2] See above, § 189.
[3] *Treatise*, p. 64. There are some curious suggestions on the desirability of

While we have here a link with the past, there is a
a contemporary treatise an incidental anticipation of a n
doctrine. In enumerating the tests of prosperity, no m
was made of any criterion which was directly applica
the capital of the country. After the industrial revo
when machinery was largely used and capital entered
obviously into production than before, the increase of c
appeared to be the great means of rapidly developing in

*High
profits and
prosperity.* and commerce, and much attention was given to the 1
profit as a sign of prosperity, since it indicated the efl
inducement to add to capital. Locke did not follow o
matter so far; but while other writers were insisting c
advantages of a low rate of interest, from the facilities i
to merchants to enlarge their business with borrowed c
he pointed out that a high rate was quite compatible 1
flourishing condition of trade. " High interest," he sa;
thought by some a prejudice to trade : but if we look
we shall find that England never throve so well, no
there ever brought into England so great an incre
wealth as in Queen Elizabeth's and King James I. and
Charles I. time, when money was at ten and eight per
I will not say high interest was the cause of it.
rather think that our thriving trade was the cause o:
interest, everyone craving money to employ in a pro
commerce. But this I think I may reasonably infer fr
that lowering of interest is not a sure way to improve
our trade or wealth[1]."

*The circu-
lating
medium.* 245. While English merchants were complaining
disadvantages to which they were exposed from the
terms on which foreigners obtained the use of capital,
was also a great deal of grumbling about the insufficie
our coinage to carry on the trade of the country. Tha
coins were scarce was of course the case, owing to the g
corruption of the circulating medium; and the pri
question as to whether larger issues of money were 1

subjecting the newly returned Jews to a strict discipline in *England's Want*
p. 40. [Camb. Univ. Lib. R. 10, 10 (16).] Compare also T. Violet, *Petition
the Jewes* (1661), and the petition in Stow, *Survey*, II. 243.
 [1] Locke, *Considerations of the lowering of Interest, Works*, IV. 66.

could not be answered, unless there was some understanding of the quantity of coin that was required to drive the internal trade of the country. Sir William Petty set himself to investigate this subject, and came to the conclusion that the amount of bullion which was coined into money, ought to be quite sufficient to do all the work that was really required[1]. He pointed out that the nation might have an undue *Forms of credit.* quantity of its wealth lying idle in the form of coin, just as a merchant might; and that it was possible to have too much money; while he also showed that the erection of a bank was the best way to increase the circulation, if the currency was really insufficient[2]. This view had been elaborated by a merchant named Francis Cradocke, who in 1660 addressed Charles II. on the advantages which would accrue from starting a bank; he believed the profit would be so large, that it would be possible to dispense with all customs and taxes[3]. Though no immediate action was taken on the lines they suggest, this and similar tracts[4] were yet of the first importance and helped to form public opinion, so that it was ripe for the great financial scheme which was floated after the Revolution—the foundation of the Bank of England.

The ideas of this age in banking bore fruit in the erection of the Bank, which afforded means for prosecuting the great French wars; its ideas on the hurtfulness of certain trades were abundantly exemplified in the legislation of the next century with regard to trade with France. A survey of the literature of the seventeenth century is of no slight assistance in throwing light on the events of the eighteenth.

[1] *Political Arithmetic*, Chapter IX. 270.
[2] *Quantulumcunque*, Query 26, in *Select Tracts*, 165.
[3] *An expedient for taking away all impositions* (1660), 7.
[4] R. Murray in his *Proposal for the advancement of Trade* (1676), 4, advocates the establishment of magazines, where traders might deposit surplus stock &c., and receive advances on the value of the goods deposited so as to carry on their business.

VIII. THE STRUGGLE WITH FRANCE.

I. THE FALL OF THE MERCANTILE SYSTEM.

A.D. 1689 —1846. Rivalry with France,

246. FOR a second time in her history England entered on a great struggle with France; not that as in the time o Edward III. and Henry V. English statesmen proposed t themselves to conquer the country; but they were led t interfere again and again either to prevent France from obtaining a supremacy in Europe, or to check the expansion of French power in America and the East. So long as thi

and the success of the mercantile system.

national rivalry lasted[1], the mercantile system continued i its essential elements; in the Orders in Council, as in th Methuen Treaty, the object in view was that of regulating trade so as to increase the national power, and so as to giv no support to the power of our great rival. With the fall c Napoleon, this sense of rivalry for power was lulled to rest fo a time; and when the special political basis on which th actual enactments rested was thus withdrawn, the whol fabric fell to pieces.

When all the blunders of theory and of practice on th part of the politicians and economists of the sixteenth an seventeenth centuries have been fully exposed,—and thei blunders were many,—the fact still remains that the mer cantile system justified itself in the only possible court c appeal,—by the logic of events; the power of England was s maintained that Wellington won the battle of Waterloo an

---

[1] The jealousy comes out again and again in the debates on the American Wa The Duke of Bolton spoke of "Our natural enemies, the several branches of tl House of Bourbon." *Parl. Hist.* xix. 819, 931, 968.

Napoleon went to S. Helena. It is of course easy to say that if A.D. 1689
a different economic system had been adopted, England might $^{-1846.}$
have triumphed more easily: but the speculation as to what
would have happened if something else had not happened is
the most futile of all forms of prediction. We know what
did happen. In the time of Louis XIV., William III. organised what seemed a desperate resistance against French
aggression, and managed to hold his own with the help of
many allies. In the time of Napoleon, England bore the
brunt of the struggle alone, and crushed the military power
opposed to her. The maintenance of power by means of
trade had been the aim of a long line of politicians, and they
had their reward. It may point the contrast if we remember
that the resources of England had failed to enable Edward
III. or Henry VI. to retain what had been conquered; but
the resources of England did suffice to carry the struggle
with France to a successful issue, when George III. was
King.

But the strain of each of these struggles was desperate; *The strain*
in the fifteenth century, as we have examined it, there were *the French*
signs of ruin on every side,—the coasts undefended, agricul- *wars,*
ture declining, the towns stagnating; a similar period of
difficulty and apparent disaster fell on England when the
special conditions produced by the long wars came to an end,
and attention could be turned to domestic affairs. The agricultural interest saw ruin staring them in the face, while the
artisan classes were suffering terribly from overwork and insufficient pay—a blight had fallen upon the whole land.

There are many interesting analogies between these two
periods, and it is suggestive to note how the strain of the
wars operated in each case. In the fifteenth century England *in the*
was far less homogeneous than at the later date; one *fifteenth*
town might be totally ruined while others suffered but little:
one manor might be cleared and enclosed for sheep, while
other villages became more populous, as the cloth manufacture was practised with increased success. But in the nine- *and in the*
teenth century the nation was far more homogeneous: a great *nineteenth*
system had been built up, and the strain affected all parts of *century.*
the nation—not indeed equally—but alike, while the burden

of the debts then contracted still weighs upon our tr
day.   When the strain of the Hundred Years' War '
moved, there was no obstacle to recovery, but the d
ment of our industry in the present day is still hampe
the taxes which pay interest on our national debt, a
that portion of the burden is removed we can hardly '
to have entirely got over the effects of the last strugg
France[1].

The Mer-
cantilists
and the
Industrial
Interest

247.   The policy which had been put in the foref
the mercantilists, especially after the Revolution, was
developing the industry of the country in every wa
could.   The landed interest they protected from the
of neighbours—like the Irish cattle breeders—whil
tried to equalise the uncertainties of the profit obta
different seasons by the corn laws; still it may be sa
the industry of the country was fostered with speci
The wealth of the country and the sources of taxati
been hitherto chiefly found in the land, and during t
half of the eighteenth century a similar condition cor
to prevail.   But in the latter half a change was see
great era of industrial invention began to make its
and the power of production in different trades was
lated a hundredfold, first by the utilisation of water
and later by the introduction of steam.   Owing to

which over-
balanced
the landed
interest,

causes the industry of the country advanced by lea
bounds, and began to 'overbalance' the landed inte
wealth and eventually in political power, when the
1832 at length enfranchised the great factory towns,
repeal of the Corn Laws gave English capitalists the
tage of a cheaper food supply.

and out-
grew the
old regula-
tions.

By this great advance English industry outgr
various regulations and conditions which had been ir
for its encouragement and support.   All the regulati

---

[1] The keen manner in which our statesmen watched France comes
and over again.   Compare e.g. Burke's speech on Economical Reform, F
xxi. 9.   "Let the nations make war upon each other (since we must n
not with a low and vulgar malignity, but by a competition of virtues.   I
only way by which both parties can gain by war.   The French have im
let us, through them, imitate ourselves; ourselves in our better and hap
If public frugality, under whatever men, or in whatever mode of gove
national strength, it is a strength which our enemies are in possession of b

apprenticeship had been intended for a condition of manufac- A.D. 1689
ture where the skill of the individual workman was the chief ―1846.
element in turning out a valuable product.   With the introduction of machinery it came to be of less relative importance, and new forms of skill were required.   The conditions,
which had been necessary for securing the training of new
generations of workmen, merely hampered the factory owner
in developing his business, while they no longer served any
appreciable purpose so far as the character of the output was
concerned.   The introduction of machinery brought about a 1563.
collapse of the industrial system of Elizabeth.

This change had all sorts of indirect effects on other sides
of English life; domestic manufactures were forced to give *Decay of*
domestic
way to factory industry, and the population of the rural dis- *manufac-*
tricts, instead of being spinners and weavers who were also *tures and*
agriculturists, were left with only one line of employment.
Agricultural employment could not furnish as good a livelihood as had been formerly obtained from the double source
of family income.   Concurrently with these industrial changes *Agricul-*
there were great alterations in the business of the British *tural Revo-*
lution.
farmer.   Under these new conditions the yeomen farmers
could not make their holdings pay, when worked on the traditional methods, especially during a period of bad seasons;
the labourers' wages were not adequate to maintain them
properly in rural employments, so that they had to obtain
supplementary aid from the rates, or they were tempted to
devote themselves exclusively to industrial pursuits.   Thus
the industrial revolution served to accelerate an agricultural
revolution.   When every effort was made to work the land on
more profitable principles, and pasture was ploughed up on
every side, when small farms gave place to larger holdings,
and wages were paid on a scale which forced the able-bodied
labourer to rely on the rates, the Elizabethan rural system
had broken down, and the character of the poor relief was 1795.
entirely changed.

Similarly, when the American colonies threw off their *American*
Indepen-
connection with the mother country, the whole character of *dence and*
our shipping trade was necessarily changed; the laws which *the Naviga-*
tion Acts.
had been formulated for the encouragement of shipping, were,

under changed conditions, no longer applicable, and another great branch of the mercantile system had to be recast. The efforts which were made to arrest these changes and to reconstruct new economic regulations were only fitful and half-hearted, for a general feeling was being diffused that the attempt to regulate these affairs, so as to really promote the power of the country, was futile and even hurtful. The grave practical difficulties attending endeavours to regulate trade, and the real practical mischief they caused were deeply impressed
on the public mind by the writings of Adam Smith. As the old regulations of various sorts proved impracticable, men became more inclined to let the whole attempt drop, rather than to devise new regulations consonant to the changed conditions of the age.

Decay of the Mercantile System.
It thus came about that, when the great political motive —the jealousy of the power of France—ceased to operate actively, the mercantile system, which had seemed so firmly established in the time of Adam Smith, was already decayed in every limb. The reaction which followed on the strain of the long struggle proved its death-blow, and the attempt to maintain the corn laws was the final effort of the old economic policy of the country; for though the navigation laws were not formally abolished till a later date, they had comparatively little practical importance at any time in the present century.

Adam Smith treated Economics
248. While the old political aim at which the economists[1] of the two preceding centuries had consciously striven —the increase of national power—was removed, much of the wisdom which had been formulated with reference to the pursuit of this special object, remained; it was the good fortune of Adam Smith to recast the old wisdom and adapt it to the new conditions. With him the Wealth of Nations came to be the object of study, not as heretofore the pursuit
without direct reference to foreign or of those special forms of wealth which contributed most effectively to the maintenance of the power of England. The old study became wider in character; it was not to be merely an

---

[1] Dudley North in *Discourses upon Trade* (1691) and Malachy Postlethwayt in *Great Britain's True System* show much less of this jealousy of rivals than most writers. See below, pp. 420, 581 n.

investigation as to the means of so developing the resources A.D. 1689
—1846. of England as to increase her power, but as to the increasing the mass of the necessaries and comforts of life in any forms, whatever the special position or requirement of a country might be. The study of economics could thus be pursued without reference to external political relationships; and in the same way, questions of internal politics could be laid aside. The balancing of the monied interest against the *domestic politics.* landed, or the merchant against the manufacturer seemed to be futile, when the question of power was no longer kept in the forefront; the increase of the riches of each added to the aggregate wealth of all. From this point of view it was possible to investigate the causes of the increase or decrease of the wealth of every nation, without reference either to the political environment of any one, or to the distribution of political power within its borders. In taking this more general character, Political Economy ceased to be mainly a branch of practical statecraft, and came rather to be a science which set itself to investigate a certain group of phenomena, those of wealth, whether personal wealth, or the aggregate of personal wealth which is sometimes called national.

249. The phenomena of wealth, when thus studied, were *Political* analysed and described and defined with far greater accuracy *Economy* than had ever been the case before; but when we view Political Economy, not as a science but as a doctrine affecting events, we must take account of the manner in which it was influenced by the changed sentiments of the times. As the more accurate knowledge came to be applied, there were new conditions which controlled or modified the direction in which it was employed. The strong sentiment of national *less na-* ambition and national jealousy was less effective in the eco- *tional, but more* nomic sphere, and its place was taken by a narrower and by a wider enthusiasm. On one hand we have an intense indi- *individual-istic* vidualism, the belief that to give the greatest play to the energies of each citizen is to leave him free to increase his personal wealth, and therefore is the one certain method to increase national wealth. The old opposition which had been traced between private lucre and public weal was denied; private lucre seemed to be the one effective power for in-

A.D. 1689
—1846.

1825.

creasing the public wealth.   This intense individualistic sentiment led to the breaking down of all the apprenticeship laws and eventually of the combination laws. The sentiment of Parliament, from the beginning of the century, was strongly against any rules which prevented a man from pursuing his calling in the way he found most profitable to himself, for it was currently believed that this must necessarily prove most profitable to the nation in the long run. The House of Commons economists applied their principles relentlessly: it was a grave misfortune that so much influence was exercised by *doctrinaires* " who, with the entire superciliousness of the followers of a still young theory, spoke with contempt of the glorious reign of Elizabeth as of the time when nothing was yet known of the infallible doctrine of the new era[1]."

On the other hand, when a larger sentiment does operate, it is one that is equally strange to the mercantilist period. National ambition might lead to attempts to injure other nations; but as the national rivalry declined, the current *and cosmo-* sentiment became much more cosmopolitan and humani-*politan.* tarian.   There was less desire to injure others as if that brought an indirect benefit to ourselves; and Englishmen began to interest themselves in the social condition of distant peoples, even when they were black.

Thus it was that under new political, social and moral conditions,—when the industrial revolution had combined with great agricultural changes, and the revolt of the colonies had interfered so much with our shipping, when there was a great growth in knowledge as to the causes of national wealth, and of new sentiments to influence the direction in which it was applied,—that the mercantile system broke *Divisions.* down. The story of its gradual decline and final collapse may be most clearly told by dividing it into stages and taking, first, the period from 1689 to 1776, when the American States declared their independence, and when Adam Smith published the *Wealth of Nations;* secondly, from 1776 to 1815, when the Battle of Waterloo brought the struggle with France to an end; and thirdly, from 1815 to 1846, when we can examine the effects of the exhaustion caused by the war.

[1] Brentano, *Gilds*, 128.

PART I. 1689—1776.

II. COMMERCE.

250. The results of the negociations in which English A.D. 1689 —1776. statesmen were engaged in the early part of the eighteenth *Interna-* century illustrate clearly the character of the commercial *tional re-* motives, which were dominant at the time and about which *lations.* so much has already been said. There were, of course, all sorts of intricate interests at stake in the agreements made between different nations; at times the question of commercial intercourse was comparatively unimportant; but there was one occasion, early in the century, when it came into prominence. Portugal had been successfully drawn into the great alliance against France by the promise of naval and military assistance and protection from England and Holland[1]; though this friendship had political and military importance, it proved specially welcome to Englishmen as it gave an opportunity for reopening a market which had been partially closed. During the preceding twenty years, the Portuguese, in the hope of fostering a native manufacture, had prohibited all importation of English cloth[2]. Mr Methuen was sent as a *Methuen* special ambassador and intimated that it would be very *Treaty,* acceptable to the Queen of England "if the woollen cloths, *1703.* and the rest of the woollen manufactures of Britain, might be admitted into Portugal, the prohibition of them being *Cloth ex-* taken off[3]. He was able to carry this point; on the other *ported in* *return for*

---

[1] Chalmers, *Treaties*, II. 296 (16 May 1703).

[2] *British Merchant*, III. 82. This Portuguese manufacture appears to have been due to the energy of an Irishman in 1680 who took a band of artisans over with him and established the trade. It is very curious that this migration from Ireland should have taken place before the prohibitions which are so commonly spoken of and while the general movement appears to have been that of a migration to Ireland. Bischoff, *Woollen Manufactures*, I. 83.

[3] Chalmers, *Collection of Treaties*, II. 304 (27 Dec. 1703). In his adverse criticism of this treaty, Adam Smith (*Wealth of Nations*, IV. 6, p. 224) does not take sufficient account of the circumstances under which the agreement was made. Englishmen who were bargaining for liberty to trade at all, could hardly hope to obtain exclusive or preferential privileges at a single stroke. According to the statement in the *British Merchant* (III. 89) the cloth manufacture in Portugal was entirely ruined when the market was opened to British goods. The subsequent

hand, he conceded to the Portuguese that their wines should always be admitted into England at two-thirds of the duty paid on French wines. This treaty had some curious minor results; through its operation the culture of the vine was somewhat extended in Portugal[1]; and the wines thus introduced into England supplanted Burgundy[2] on the tables of

Port Wine and
those who adapted their consumption to the supposed advantage of the realm. The man who drank his bottle of port could feel that he was dealing with people who were large customers for English cloth, and indirectly facilitating the employment of the poor at home. The extent to which Portugal took off our manufactures and thus encouraged industry in this country appeared to be measured by the vast

Bullion.
amount of Brazilian bullion which was annually imported from Portugal. This was estimated at £50,000 per week; and though Adam Smith shows good reason for regarding this as an exaggeration[3], there can be no doubt that the amount of bullion which flowed into England through this trade was very large. We cannot wonder that, according to the ideas of the time, Methuen's achievement was rated very highly[4]: he had opened up a large foreign demand for our goods and had thus stimulated the employment of labour at home; while much of the returns from Portugal came to us in the form which was most necessary for restoring the currency and most convenient for carrying on the great European War.

The Peace of Utrecht.
251. When the first act of the long struggle was over and the peace of Utrecht was concluded with France, an earnest effort was made to open up commercial relations with that country. The treaty of peace was accompanied by a commercial treaty of which the 8th and 9th articles guaran-

The Commercial Clauses.
teed freedom of commerce between the two countries; French goods were to be received according to the tariff of 1664, or

revival of the manufacture by the Marquis of Pombal rendered the arrangement nugatory so far as English manufacturing interests were concerned; see below, p. 511. Leone Levi, *History of British Commerce*, 81.

[1] The Portuguese appear to have been very anxious to maintain their special advantage over France. *Parl. Hist.* VI. 792.

[2] Stanhope, *Queen Anne*, 112.   [3] *Wealth of Nations*, IV. 6, p. 228.

[4] Compare Smith's *Chronicon*, II. 51 note.

on the same terms as the most favoured nation[1]. A bill was drafted[2] to give effect to this agreement and make the necessary alterations in the tariffs, which then imposed more than fifty per cent. on French imports[3] above what was taken on the goods of other countries. But the proposal roused a storm of indignation; the government endeavoured to be loyal to their agreement, and tried to secure the suspension of the duties on French wines for two months, in the hope that there would be difficulty in re-imposing them; but though they commanded a majority in the House of Commons, the motion was rejected. A very interesting struggle followed, as both the government and their opponents endeavoured to win the day by convincing public opinion. Daniel Defoe[4] was employed to carry on the *Mercator* which *The* was published thrice a week and which was devoted to *Mercator.* demonstrating the beneficial character of the French trade. "As he had," to quote his opponents' complaint, "a knack of writing very plausibly, and they who employed him and furnished him with materials, had the command of all public

---

[1] Koch and Schoell, I. 214. Macpherson, III. 34.

[2] This and other documents are printed at length in the *British Merchant*, Vol. I. 130.

[3] Adam Smith summarises the matter thus in the third edition, "Higher duties are imposed upon the wines of France than upon those of Portugal or indeed of any other country. By what is called the impost 1692, a duty of five and twenty per cent. of the rate or value, was laid upon all French goods; while the goods of other nations were, the greater part of them, subjected to much lighter duties, seldom exceeding five per cent. The wine, brandy, salt, and vinegar of France, were indeed excepted; these commodities being subjected to other heavy duties, either by other laws, or by particular clauses of the same law. In 1696, a second duty of twenty-five per cent., the first not having been thought a sufficient discouragement, was imposed upon all French goods, except brandy; together with a new duty of five and twenty pounds upon the tun of French wine, and another of fifteen pounds upon the tun of French vinegar. French goods have never been omitted in any of those general subsidies or duties of five per cent. which have been imposed upon all, or the greater part, of the goods enumerated in the book of rates. If we count the one-third and two-third subsidies as making a complete subsidy between them, there have been five of these general subsidies; so that before the commencement of the present (1783) war, seventy-five per cent. may be considered as the lowest duty to which the greater part of the goods of the growth, produce, or manufacture of France were liable. But upon the greater part of goods, these duties are equivalent to a prohibition. The French in their turn, have, I believe, treated our goods and manufactures just as hardly." *Wealth of Nations*, IV. 3, Pt. 1, p. 192.

[4] Smith's *Chronicon*, II. 105.

papers in the custom house, he had it in his power to
great deal of mischief, especially amongst such as were
skilled in trade, and at the same time very fond of Fr
wines, which it was then a great crime to be against[1]."

opponents of France however started an opposition p

The British Merchant. named the *British Merchant* which came out twice a w
several leading merchants were among its contributors
they were practically successful, for the Methuen Treaty
maintained, and no effect was given to the comme
clauses of the treaty with France. Trade between the
countries was carried on under scarcely altered condition
more than eighty years after the signing of the Met
Treaty.

The form in which the Methuen Treaty was drawn
a very strong position to those who were opposed to ope

Arguments which prevailed. up commercial relations with France. If we admitted Fr
wines on as favourable terms as Portuguese, we shoul
fringe the Methuen Treaty, and the Portuguese would
be at liberty to retaliate by prohibiting our woollen g
The loss of this market would affect the manufacturers
were engaged in producing cloth, and the landlords, w
rents improved when the price of wool kept up and pa
farming was profitable. The authors of the *British Mer*
were anxious to convince our legislators " that the prese
our looms and the rents of Great Britain was of gr
consequence to the nation than gratifying our palates
French wine[2]." It would be tedious to attempt to f
these controversialists through the mazes of their argum
it may suffice to say that the authors of the *British Mer*
were successful in securing the practical measures
desired; and their principles continued to dominate ove
minds of legislators and students alike till the time of *A*

The general and the particular balance. Smith. The older mercantilists like Mun who were an
to see masses of bullion flowing into the country to fo
treasure, would have been satisfied if the *general* ba
was in favour of England; but the more modern s
who took the balance of bullion as an index to

[1] *British Merchant,* I. x.   [2] *Ib.* ix.

stimulus which any trade gave our industry, wished to see A.D. 1689
that the balance with each particular country was in our −1776.
favour. They eagerly discriminated the more and less bene- *Hurtful*
ficial and the hurtful trades; and they held that according *trades.*
to these lists the trade with Portugal was a most beneficial
trade which it would be well to develop[1], and the trade
with France was condemned as positively injurious. Elaborate calculations were made which estimated the detrimental effect of trade with France on our country at more
than £70,000 a year. And the ideas which are embodied in
the *British Merchant* held their own during the greater part
of the eighteenth century; there were men who saw that the
balance of trade did not really give a satisfactory criterion of
the condition of industry[2]; but the belief that it did (and no
mere Midas-doctrine of wealth) was the formative principle
in the great system of commercial regulation against which
Adam Smith led the attack.

252. When we pass from the consideration of European *The East*
commerce to a survey of distinct trades, we see that the most *India Company*
important commercial transactions of the time were those
carried on by the East India Company, which enjoyed a
monopoly from the Crown of the maritime trade between
England and the East. It had soon become a joint-stock
Company in form as well as in fact[3]; and the peculiarities of
its constitution brought it into constant collision with other
English merchants and complicated its relations with its own
servants. During the period on which we are now entering
this great Company bore the brunt of the struggle with
France, and entered into important relations with the native
powers, so as to increase enormously the political influence of
England. But in so far as it is necessary to deal with these
matters it will be more convenient to treat of them in connection with English settlements abroad than in relation to

[1] See the *General Maxims* in the *British Merchant*, I. 22, and the subsequent
discussion of special trades.
[2] See above, § 241, p. 240.
[3] Originally each separate venture was conducted on a separate 'fund' for
which members of the Company subscribed in the proportions they liked, but there
was never any private trading by members on their own account. See above, pp.
26, 124.

English trade.   The settlements were the results of th trade, and contributed immensely to its expansion; but th territorial and political problems which the Company had face were not directly connected with its trading interest[1].

as a commercial monopoly.
Modern critics have been inclined to assume that Engli trade with the East Indies would have developed mor rapidly if the Company had never acquired territory and h confined itself to maritime trade, and it has also been urge that it would have been wiser to allow each trader to condu his business independently rather than to organise the whol business in a single Company.

Interlopers and
The right of the interlopers to trade, despite the chart from the Crown, had been declared at the Revolution[2]; bu it does not appear that their experiments were successfu The difficulties which the English experienced, in obtainin a footing at first, in securing the favour of the Gre Mogul[3], and in holding their own against the French an Dutch, seemed to show that a number of independent trade would have had very little chance of doing any business all.   If territorial settlement and diplomatic relations wi

Political complications.
native powers were inevitable, then the formation of corporation to conduct both the commercial and politic business would also appear to have been necessary; and th

---

[1] In 1689 the Court of Directors wrote as follows "the increase of our reve is the subject of our care, as much as our trade:—'tis that must maintain force, when twenty accidents may interrupt our trade;—'tis that must make n nation in India;—without that, we are but as a great number of Interlopers, und by His Majesty's Royal Charter, fit only to trade where no body of power thi it their interest to prevent us;—and upon this account it is, that the wise Dut in all their general advices which we have seen, write ten paragraphs concern their government, their civil and military policy, warfare, and the increase of th revenue, for one paragraph they write concerning trade." (Bruce, III. 78.)

At the same time it appears that the Dutch subordinated their interests settlers to the promotion of trade and were much less carried away by politi ambitions than either the Portuguese or English. (Raynal, I. 178.) Indeed failure of the Dutch to maintain the advantage they secured by ousting Portuguese was largely due to the fact that they did so little to develop resources of the Spice Islands as plantations and endeavoured to make their pr by keeping a strict monopoly and selling at high prices. (*Ib.* 254.)

[2] Not explicitly but by implication in the Declaration of Right.

[3] Sir Thomas Roe who was sent as an ambassador to Jehangir obtaine promise of liberty to trade and establish factories at Surat, Bengal and Sinde any part of the Great Mogul's dominions. Mill, *History of British India,* I. On the successful negociations a century later, see Mill, III. 23.

view is confirmed by the action which was taken by the interlopers. Their attempts at legitimate trade appear to have been chiefly directed to points where Englishmen had acquired a footing through the action of the Company; and from the time of the Revolution onwards, the chief inter- lopers found it advisable to form a new association among themselves. The intense irritation which the Company felt against interlopers becomes intelligible when we see that their legitimate trade was dependent on privileges secured by the Company; it appears excusable when we realise that a great deal of their trade was mere piracy, and that the Company suffered severely in their relations with the native princes because of outrages committed by Englishmen for whom they were in no sense responsible. The worst offenders were the adventurers from New York and Rhode Island, who deliberately and publicly fitted out ships for piracy in the Indian seas, with the connivance of the local authorities[1]. But there was no security that interlopers would not engage in these profitable but discreditable voyages. Thus in 1695 one of the interlopers, who had failed to make a profit on his cargo, seized some native ships, including one belonging to Abdul Gophor, a leading merchant at Surat, and one belong- ing to the Mogul, which was carrying pilgrims to Mecca. As the natives could not distinguish between one English ship and another, the Company were held responsible for these outrages, and very serious complications ensued[2].

The power which the Company had of dealing with these *The Company's Judicial Powers.* abuses was directly derived from the Crown. On the accession of William III., the English merchants had regarded him with considerable suspicion, as they feared he might subordinate their interests to those of the Dutch East India Company[3]; but William's necessities, in connection with his continental wars, rendered him not unwilling to grant privileges to English merchants who were able to assist the Government. The Company had been empowered to execute martial law, and to exercise Admiralty jurisdiction at Bombay[4], and 1684. under these powers they carried out very severe sentences

---

[1] Weeden, *New England*, 344. [2] Bruce, III. 187 sq.
[3] *Ib.* 5. [4] *Ib.* II. 497.

A.D. 1689
—1776.

upon their competitors in trade[1]. Still the Company cou
not but feel that their position was somewhat insecure; a
the chief object of their policy at home was to procure
confirmation of their privileges, not merely by Charter t
by Act of Parliament. In this however they were foil
and the Company had to be contented with receiving t
additional Charters in 1693[2]; by the latter of these th
monopoly was granted for twenty-one years; the consti
tion of the Company was carefully defined, and it was p
vided that the dividends must be paid in money onl
There was also a provision that the Company should expo
each season £150,000 worth of English manufactures[6].

New
Charters.

Rivalry of
Darien
Company
and

The Directors did not however lose heart, and the succ
of the Scotch (East India) Company in obtaining Parliame
tary powers[6] (it was the only success which the ill-fated Dari
Company did obtain) encouraged them to hope that they wou
meet with similar favour[7]. Although their resources we
somewhat crippled, they spent large sums in corruptir

[1] One case " was rendered famous by the altercation which in 1666 it produ
between the two houses of parliament. Thomas Skinner, a merchant, fitted o
vessel in 1657. The agents of the Company seized his ship and merchandis
India, and the island of Barella, off Sumatra, which he had bought of the kin
Jambi. They even denied him a passage home; and he was obliged to tr
overland to Europe." The Lords took up Skinner's cause, but the Company w
not acknowledge their jurisdiction and appealed to the Commons who sent Skin
to the Tower. He obtained no redress, though the Lords had awarded him £5
Mill, I. 71.   [2] Bruce, III. 133, 134.

[3] This was one of the points in which the East India Company differed f
the Dutch which paid its dividends partly in produce. Another point lay in
constitution of the Dutch Company in "Chambers" which appears to have g
more elasticity to the management and which certainly enabled the Compan
exert a more complete influence in Holland, than our Company ever succeede
doing in the English Parliament (Bruce, III. 135). The constitution is descr
in detail by Raynal (I. 249). Its peculiarities were due to the fact that
Company was formed by fusion of several Companies (*Ib.* 169).

[4] This was a stroke of policy which had been entirely neglected by the Po
guese. The effort to garrison their foreign possessions drained the mother cou
of its population and industrial resources, while the trade gave no stimulu
Portuguese agriculture or manufactures; it was the object of William to i
that the Company should give a vent for English products and not merely s
as a means of enriching the official class. (Raynal, I. 153).

[5] Norfolk camlets and certain West of England serges were expressly m
factured for this trade. See below, p. 636, note 4.

[6] *Acts of Parliaments of Scotland*, IX. 377 (June 26, 1695).   [7] Bruce, III. 1

[8] This was not a new thing; the Long Parliament had a bad reputatio
regard to bribery. Gardiner, *Civil War*, III. 317.

public men. The House of Commons ordered an inquiry into this matter, and found that in 1693 the amount expended had reached £90,000 of which it is said that £10,000 were traced to the king[1]. The feeling of the House of Commons was thoroughly hostile to the existing Company, which they regarded as utterly corrupt. They passed a resolution "that it was the right of all Englishmen to trade to the East Indies or any part of the world unless prohibited by Act of Parliament[2]"; and in a subsequent session they inflicted a very serious blow on the existing London Company by passing an Act, which enabled the interlopers to float a new or General, as distinguished from the London, Company[3]. The Company so formed was a regulated Company, and each of the members was able to trade on his own account; but two days afterwards a number of them, who desired to do so, were empowered to trade together on a joint stock.

A.D. 1689 —1776.

of the General Company. 1698.

For these rights the interlopers, who floated the new Company, were forced to pay exorbitantly. They advanced £2,000,000 to the Government at 8 per cent.[4], on the understanding that they should have an exclusive right to trade after 1701. This new Company was from the first hampered by want of capital. They had difficulty in getting their calls paid, and no ready money[5] was available until the Govern-

Difficulties of the new company.

---

[1] Mill, *India*, i. 98. [2] *Parl. Hist.* v. 828.

[3] 9 W. III. c. 44, § 52. The general society was entitled to the advantages given by an Act of Parliament for advancing a sum not exceeding £2,000,000 for the service of the Crown.

[4] Bruce, iii. 252—5. This offer was preferred to that of the old or London Company who were willing to provide £700,000 at 4 per cent. but the exigencies of the European war made Parliament prefer the larger and more expensive loan.

[5] The success which attended the banking operations of the Bank of England had a very detrimental effect on the plans of other promoters who seemed to think that they could carry on a mercantile business in distant lands by means of credit and without a sufficient capital. The schemes for the Land Bank and the South Sea Company were all affected by this misunderstanding as to the nature of credit and the extent to which it could be utilised to save the employment of capital. Even in the East India Company the same defect was noticeable; so much money was employed for political purposes at home and abroad that they were constantly hampered for want of capital to carry on the trade. An attempt was made to remedy this by 7 Geo. I. c. 5, § 32, which authorised the Company to borrow to the amount of the sums due to them from the public. This also explains the extraordinary difference between the profits of the English and of the Dutch Company. The latter divided 25 per cent. from 1732—36 when the English could only pay 7 per cent. (Mill, iii. 35). Of course the money sunk in diplomatic and

A.D. 1689
—1776.
ment interest was paid. The London Company did i₁
utmost to maintain its advantages during the three yea
that remained to it, and it also subscribed to the ne

Action of the old company. Company, so that it might be able to carry on its operatio
as an independent trader within that body, when its ov
exclusive rights had come to an end. The position whi
was thus created by the rivalry of the two Companies bo
in the East and in England was soon found to be qui
intolerable, and after lengthy negociations Lord Godolph
was empowered by Act of Parliament[1] to arbitrate betwee
them; as a result of an arduous investigation, the Unite

The United Company. Company of Merchants of England trading to the East Indie
was established in 1708. By this means the exclusive right
of the Company were guaranteed not merely by the Crow
but by Act of Parliament till 1726, and by a later Act ti
1733[2]. It may be said that the view of policy for which th
Directors of the London Company had contended was no₁
endorsed by Parliament; so far as the principle of a join
stock was concerned, the experience[3] of the English Compan₁
the members of which at one time opposed, told in its favou
Parliament had also accepted the principle of giving a corpo
ration of traders exclusive rights as against other Englis
subjects; in 1718 they sustained the objection to interlope
so far as to empower the Company to punish their competi
tors when trading under foreign commissions[4].

The contest renewed in 1730. 253. In 1730, three years before the expiry of the Unite
Company's privileges, the struggle was renewed. It was no'

---

judicial expenses at home and abroad was unremunerative. The capital of t₁
Dutch Company was only £565,286 (Raynal, I. 259) while that of the Engl₁
Company at the same period was over £3,000,000 (Mill, III. 18, 359). The extr
ordinary luck of the Dutch in capturing Portuguese vessels and supplanting th₁
in foreign states enabled them to obtain a footing with this very small capit₁
while they confined their political ambitions abroad, and owing to their constitut₁
secured a large interest in the Councils of State at home.

[1] 6 Anne, c. 17.   [2] 10 Anne, c. 23.

[3] A second charter dated 5 Sept. 1698 (quoted 6 Anne, c. 17) empowers t
majority of the members of the newly created Company to trade as a joint stoc
This joint stock branch of the General Company was technically the Engl₁
Company referred to in the text. Bruce, III. 257.

[4] 5 Geo. II. c. 21. A proclamation to this effect had been issued by the Cro₁
in 1716. Mill, III. 18. These powers were further enforced and extended by 7 G₁
I. c. 21; 9 Geo. I. c. 26.

admitted by the opponents of the Company that it was A.D. 1689
—1776. necessary in the interests of trade to maintain considerable establishments abroad. Under the existing régime the expenses of these establishments were defrayed out of the gross profits of the joint stock Company. The new proposal was *Mainten-* that these charges might be met by the interest paid by the *ance of the Factories.* Government, together with customs on the trade; and it was argued that if the factories were maintained in this fashion, it would be possible to dispense with the joint stock and throw the trade open to the public. This scheme was supported by petitions from merchants in London, Bristol and Liverpool. Public opinion, which exaggerated the gains to be derived from the East India trade, was strongly in favour of the new project; and the Company could only secure the renewal of their exclusive privileges till 1766, by consenting that the rate of interest paid by the Government should be reduced to 4 per cent., and by contributing a fine of £200,000 for the renewal of their privileges[1]. In 1744, however, they gave *Privileges* additional assistance to the Government, during the war of *continued* the Austrian Succession, by lending them £1,000,000 at 3 *1744.* per cent.; and they thereby obtained an extension of their exclusive privileges till 1780[2]. Before that time arrived, the magnitude of the interests involved, and the discreditable rumours which were afloat, had roused a storm of indignation. The House of Commons appointed a committee of *Regulation* inquiry in 1766, and the Company was reconstructed in 1773. *Act 1773.*

During this period the possessions of the Company had undergone startling vicissitudes; they had been almost *The French* destroyed by the French, but their fortunes were restored by *and* the skill and energy of Clive, and the English influence had *Clive.* at last triumphed in all the three Presidencies. Clive's greatest achievements had been effected in open disregard of the instructions of the Directors; and his whole career illustrates the extreme difficulty under which the Company laboured, from its relation to servants who were so far distant *Officials* as to be exempt from all practical control. He believed that the Company would be better served if their officials enjoyed a better status and more freedom from routine. The system

---

[1] Mill, III. 84. 　　　　　　 [2] 17 Geo. II. c. 17.

A.D. 1669
—1776.
on which they were paid was very unsatisfactory; the
salaries were small, and they were obliged to maintain them
selves by engaging in the internal trade of the country (
and private trade. their own account. The Company reserved the trade b
tween the Indies and Europe as a strict monopoly for itse
but allowed its servants to engage for their own advantag
in trade between different parts of the Indies. This priva
trade led to many imbroglios with the natives, as in certai
cases where the goods of the Company were passed free (
custom by the authorities in Bengal, their agents endeavoure
and not without success, to pass their private speculations :
the same time[1]. Private trade was looked on with disfavou
because many officers were apt to give their best attention t
their own ventures and to neglect the affairs of the Compan
they served. One of the reforms which Clive endeavoure
to carry through in 1765 was the establishment of a monopol
of salt, betel-nut and tobacco; this monopoly was intende
to be carried on for the benefit of the superior servants of th
Company[2]. The Directors were strongly opposed to th
private trade society and it was abolished in 1768[3].

Indeed it may be said that while the chief troubles of tl
Company in earlier times were due to the interlopers, tho
which occurred during a great part of the eighteenth centu
Official fortunes and big dividends. arose from the conduct of their servants. They often acquir
large fortunes[4]; and their successes stimulated the imagi
tion of the proprietors, who recklessly insisted on securi
large dividends, and embarrassed the Company by dividi
sums which had not been earned, and which, as the Direct
knew, exceeded what the Company was able to pay.

Not only were there difficulties in regard to the person
conduct of officials, but the management of the Compan
The Direc-tors and their agents frequently differ own affairs gave rise to differences of opinion between t
Directorate and the Company's agents in India. There w
one point in regard to which they were in constant confli
It was necessary for the presidential governments to ha

---

[1] Mill, III. 25, 230.   [2] *Ib.* 289.   [3] *Ib.* 310.
[4] Clive is reported to have said that the temptations held out to adventu
in that part of the globe, were such as flesh and blood could not withstand. *P
Hist.* XXI. 446.

considerable treasure in bullion to meet emergencies, and A.D. 1689 —1776. they were therefore inclined to limit the amount of their 'investment' in goods for transmission to England. The *about the investment and* profit on the trading, and the dividends, depended on the goods sent to England; it was therefore to the interest of the Directors and shareholders that the investment should be large. Here was one cause of trouble; another arose when, as occasionally happened, the Council of a Presidency tried to replenish their local treasury by opening it to receive 'remittances'; they would encourage the Company's servants *remittances.* to pay cash into the treasury, which might then be remitted by means of bills to England and the value paid to the representatives of the servants there. But there was danger, at all events, that the Council would issue more bills than the Court of Directors at home were able to meet[1], and this was another cause of dispute.

Not only were there difficulties of management, from the practical independence of the servants and from the difficulty of maintaining two treasuries so as to meet the necessary payments, but the trading business itself was exceedingly *Nature of the Trade and* complicated. Fine muslins and silks were among the largest imports. In the process of buying goods the European agent was five removes distant from the workman. Each of these intermediaries obtained his commission; the complicated machinery of trade gave rise on the one hand to great oppression of the labourer, while on the other it afforded frequent opportunities for malversation and fraud. The officials of the Company were organised in four different *Organisation and* classes. They entered as writers, after five years' service they became factors, three years later junior merchants and after three years senior merchants. The high official positions were given to senior merchants[2] and promotion was almost entirely by seniority. The patronage which the Directors were able to exercise was a very valuable power, and was of more importance to many of them than the wealth which accrued from their ownership of shares in the Company. Under these circumstances there can be little wonder that Clive, at the beginning of his second adminis-

[1] Mill, III. 312.　　　　[2] *Ib.* 16.

tration, should report that the whole administration was corrupt[1] and that the Directors should complain of the "deplorable state to which our affairs were on the point of being reduced, from the corruption and rapacity of our servants, and the universal depravity of manners throughout the settlement. The general relaxation of all discipline and obedience, both military and civil, was tending to a dissolution of all government. We must add that we think the vast fortunes acquired in the inland trade had been obtained by series of the most tyrannic and oppressive conduct that ever was known in any age or country[2]."

As the result of the storm of indignation which these disclosures aroused, and which was partly promoted by retired servants and by interested proprietors who were discontented with their position, a Parliamentary inquiry was undertaken and an Act regulating the Company was passed in 1769. It is evidently drafted on the assumption that the Company had control of enormous riches, whereas the large dividends which had been recently paid had brought them to the verge of bankruptcy[3]. It was now determined that the Company should pay annually into the Exchequer a sum of £400,000, that they should export £380,000 worth of British merchandise and that their outstanding debts should not be allowed to exceed the amount of the sums due to them from the Government. On the one hand provision was made for reducing the payment, if the dividend fell off, and on the other, for increase of their loans to Government if they had a surplus. But almost immediately after the Act was passed, the public became aware of the real position of the Company and there was the strongest excitement against the Directors for having, as it was supposed, frittered

---

[1] Both the Portuguese and the Dutch had to contend with similar difficulties in regard to their officials. The utter demoralisation of the Portuguese who settled in India, was perhaps the chief reason of the destruction of their power (Raynal, I. 141.) On the Dutch see Raynal, I. 266.

[2] Mill, III. 279. It was one of the great achievements of Lord Cornwallis that he raised the tone of the Indian service in such a remarkable manner. Chesney Indian Polity, 23.

[3] The French Company, organised by Colbert in 1664, was equally unskilful its trade; in 1684 they lost half their capital, and they were still in an embarrassed condition in 1722. Malleson, History of the French in India, pp. 27, 57.

away the exaggerated resources at their command. There A.D. 1689 were two opposite suggestions for remedying a condition of —1776. affairs which all regarded as discreditable. The scheme of the Directors was to exercise a more complete control over *The Direc-* their servants by sending out supervisors, who never arrived[1], *tors and the Officials.* and by promoting a Bill for increasing their powers, which the House of Commons would not pass[2]. The opposing scheme was that of giving the English Government a more complete control over the Company both at home and abroad[3]. The Ministry proposed a series of changes which aroused the alarm of Directors and they protested that "notwithstanding the Company were thus deprived of their franchise in the choice of their servants, by an unparalleled strain of injustice and oppression, they were compelled to pay such salaries as Ministers might think fit to direct, to persons in whose appointment, approbation, or removal, the Company were to have no share[4]." The opposition was taken up by the City of London, but it had no results, and the new order was constituted[5].

The effect of these new measures as they influenced the administration in India will be considered below; but so far as the internal constitution of the Company was concerned, the principal change was that of raising the voting qualifica- *The Pro-* tion of a shareholder from £500 to £1000. A large number *prietors and their* of the smaller proprietors were thus disfranchised, to their *dividends.* great indignation[6]; but it was apparently supposed that the Directors would be less tempted than before to try and meet their wishes by paying extravagant dividends. Their demands were undoubtedly due to the extraordinary over-estimate of the riches which the Company handled, and the efforts of the Directors to keep down the dividend rendered them very unpopular with the proprietors, who were besides able in 1767 to force them into courses which they knew to

---

[1] Mill, III. 340.   [2] Ib. 343, 345.

[3] The probable purity and value of direct government control must not be judged by present standards. See the debate on Contractors in *Parl. Hist.* XXI. 423.

[4] Mill, III. 349. The case of Lord Pigot and Tanjore illustrates these difficulties, *Parl. Hist.* XX. 864.

[5] 13 Geo. III. c. 63, 64.   [6] Mill, III. 349.

A.D. 1689
—1776.
be imprudent. Through all the changes and difficulties the East India Company still retained its old character and remained as it had been in fact, if not in form, from the very first a joint stock Company.

The Afri-can Company.
254. In a preceding section the African Company was put alongside of the East India Company since they were the two principal trades conducted by joint stock. The history of the two differs greatly, however, and chiefly on this account,—whereas the East India Company had always been an object of the greatest suspicion, since its trade appeared to enrich particular merchants, while it seemed to do little or nothing for the prosperity of the country as a whole: on the other hand the African trade and the Company which worked it were always the objects of special patronage and care. While the East India Company appeared to draw away our silver and to introduce rivals to some of our native
appeared specially advanta-geous.
manufactures, the African trade brought gold to England and enabled us to supply labour for the development of the sugar plantations[1]. It was thus generally recognised as a beneficial trade, while the East India trade was always suspected of being hurtful. When allowance is made for this great difference, however, one finds a certain parallelism in the history of the two Companies. The African Company which existed at the time of the Revolution was the fift exclusive Company, which had been formed with the view of prosecuting that trade; it had been founded under royal au

---

[1] The colonists complained that the monopoly of the Company increased the price of negroes. "Heretofore we might send to Guiney for Negroes when wanted them, and they stood us about seven Pound a Head. The Account short and plain. For they cost about the value of forty shillings a Head Guiney; and their freight was five pound, for every one that was brought ali and could go over the ship side. But now we are shut out of this Trade, and Company is put upon us, from whom we must have our Negroes, and no other w A Company of London Merchants have got a Patent, excluding all others, furnish the Plantations with Negroes; some great Men being joyned with the with whom we were not able to contend. * * And now we buy Negroes at the p of an engrossed commodity; the common rate of a good Negro on shipboard be twenty pound. And we are forced to scramble for them in so shameful a mann that one of the great Burdens of our Lives is the going to buy Negroes. But must have them; we cannot be without them and the best men in those count must in their own Persons submit to the Indignity." *Groans of the Plantat* (*Barbados*) 1689, p. 5. The Guinea negroes worked better than those from o parts of Africa. *Alarm Bell* (1759) p. 8 [Brit. Mus. T. 18° (4)].

noble patronage in 1672. But like its predecessors this A.D. 1689
—1776. Company had a constant struggle with interlopers; the *Inter-* Declaration of Right put an end to its exclusive privileges *lopers.* along with those of other chartered Companies, except in so far as they were confirmed by Act of Parliament. As the interlopers had no expense in maintaining forts and factories, they were able to outbid and undersell the Company, and in 1698 Parliament was forced to interfere. The Act then passed, definitely declared the trade open, but insisted that the traders should pay a 10 per cent. duty to the Company, which might enable them to maintain the necessary fortifications and establishments[1]. The Company continued their *Factories.* joint stock trade, but failed in their attempts to secure a monopoly[2]; while the interlopers were equally unsuccessful in obtaining admission to the Company[3]. But the affairs of the Company did not prosper; the duties paid by the interlopers did not cover the expenses of the maintenance of the forts. In 1711 the Company were forced to get a special Act to enable them to make an arrangement with their creditors, and were obliged to make a call of 5 per cent. on the shareholders in 1722. Like the East India Company the African Com- *Want of* pany were weighted, because they had wasted much of their *Capital.* capital or sunk it in forms which were not directly remunerative; and in 1727 they attempted to cut down their nominal capital[4] so that each proprietor of a nominal £800 should be credited with only £100 of actual capital[5].

As however the nation was determined to support the Company and maintain trading settlements in Africa, Parliament granted them £10,000 a year annually from 1730 onwards[6]. Even this liberal aid proved insufficient; and affairs became so desperate, that Parliament interfered[7], and passed a measure[8] in 1750, which wound up the joint stock African

---

[1] 9 W. III. c. 26.   [2] Macpherson, II. 702 and III. 17.   [3] *Ib.* III. 9.

[4] The want of success which attended the operations of the African Company is reflected in the price of their stock, which was selling at £4. 10s. per £100 share in 1711 when the East India Company shares were at £124. 10s., the Bank shares at £111. 5s., and the South Sea shares at £77. 10s. (Macpherson, III. 22.)

[5] Macpherson, III. 186.

[6] In 1744 £20,000 was granted. Macpherson, III. 154.

[7] See the debate and petitions, *Parl. Hist.* XIV. 564.   [8] 23 George II. c. 31.

A.D. 1689
—1776.
*Company
reconsti-
tuted as a
Regulated
Company.*
Company and incorporated all merchants trading to Africa as
a regulated Company. The fine for admission was fixed at
40*s.*, and the members of the Company[1] in London, Bristol
and Liverpool, chose members of a committee who were to
manage the trade, subject to the approval of the Commissioners for Trade[2]. The public compensated the old Company
for their forts etc. with £112,000; and the new Company
were vested with all their property, were empowered to arm
military forces, to punish offences, and to decide mercantile

*New
Scheme of
Manage-
ment.*
cases[3]. Under this new arrangement the expense of maintaining the forts etc. was borne by the nation, but the public
funds were administered by a committee of merchants; all
British subjects were practically able to join in the trade and
to have a voice in the election of the committee[4]. But the
experience of a few years showed that this method did not
answer better than the old one, so far as the maintenance o

*Cost to the
public.*
the forts was concerned[5]. The total public money which
passed through the hands of the committee between 1750
and 1776 amounted to £343,400; while the fortifications had
become ruined and useless, and the officials of the Company
made use of their position to carry on private trade on much
more favourable terms than could be done by private traders.
The Company had thus existed in three distinct forms
as an exclusive and joint stock Company, and this had failed
several times; secondly as a joint stock Company trading
alongside private traders who paid it duties; thirdly as a
regulated Company; but at no time had it been able to work
at a profit, and in both of its later forms it had been largely
subsidised by Government.

*The
Hudson's
Bay Com-
pany*
255. A few words may be added here about another
joint stock Company which had been formed in 1670 by
Prince Rupert to trade for furs to Hudson's Bay and if
possible to open up a passage to the South Seas. The limits
of the Company are laid down in an unusually vague fashion

---

[1] On the working of this scheme compare *Parl. Hist.* xix. 301.
[2] Macpherson, iii. 280.   [3] *Ib.* 290.   [4] 4 Geo. III. c.
[5] The trade appears to have been very profitable. Hippisley, *Essays on
trade populousness &c. of Africa* (1764), p. iii.
[6] Report of Commissioners of Trade to House of Commons summarised
Macpherson, iii. 603. See the debate in *Parliamentary History*, xix. 1.

rown was apparently unwilling to commit itself to a A.D. 1689
—1776.
opinion as to the latitude in which any of the places
ie Company erected a few forts; but their property
t appear to have been very valuable, and in their
urs to prosecute their trade they were brought into
; collision with the French[1]. The outside traders
longer prohibited from engaging in the trade after
olution; but the Company were recognised by Parlia- *was gener-*
ally regard-
id a tax of 5 per cent. was imposed on them by Par- *ed with*
favour.
in 1693[2]. The trade was favourably regarded as it
us to procure furs[3] by our own exertions, instead of
:pendent for them on Russia; and we purchased them
as of our own manufactures, especially by woollen
There was a proposal to throw the trade entirely
d support the establishment at the public expense,
een done in the case of the African Company[4], but
e of the Company with the Indians appears to have
pecially adapted for regulation, and it was not so
e as to tempt many competitors. Indeed, the whole
as on a comparatively small scale, until the new im-
: emigration which began about 1820 directed atten-
he advantages of some of the territory within its limits.

On the whole it may be said that public opinion, in *Exclusive*
Companies
o these trading companies in the eighteenth century,
striking contrast to public opinion in the seventeenth.
arlier part of the seventeenth century it appeared to
ned that the organisation of trade by persons who
icerned in it was essential, and the only discussion
o the form in which it was to be carried out. In the *might be*
necessary
the Georges, new exclusive companies were not *politically,*
and the real question was as to how far the old ones

ierson, II. 625, 628, 654, 691, III. 27.   [2] *Ib.* II. 652.
i transactions of the Hudson's Bay Company in 1733, one beaver's skin
ndard medium of circulation and was worth one pound of brass kettles,
d a half of gunpowder, five pounds of shot, two of sugar, an ounce and
ermilion. A gallon of brandy was worth four skins and a blanket went
obbs, *Account of the Countries adjoining the Hudson's Bay* (1744), 193.
ierson, III. 159.
ure the pamphlet controversy between Mr Dobbs and Captain Middleton
letails about the trade. Macpherson, III. 234. See also Mr Robson,

should be maintained. In the case of distant trades, wh
forts and armaments were necessary to protect the mercha
the company might have its privileges continued in or
that these forts might be retained without public expe
ture; this was done with the East India Company. On
other hand the company might be maintained as the n
convenient instrument for managing the public funds devo
to the purpose. But so far as purely trading interests w

*but had
been dis-
carded so
far as
well
ordered
trade was
concerned.*

concerned, the very idea of maintaining a "well-order
trade, where the company attempted to secure that its me
bers should deal in goods of sound quality and should
spoil the market by eager competition, had passed av
The evils of the competition of interlopers were notori
and patent, but the companies had not been able to con
their own servants or to justify the retention of their pr
leges. A well-ordered trade meant an exclusive and confi
trade; open trade, with all its faults, meant expanding tra
and Parliament, as representing the English public, deci
in favour of expanding rather than exclusive trade.

*Regulated
Com-
panies.*

Turkey.

The companies, which had been originally regula
companies and which still survived, do not appear to h
been very prosperous. The operations of the Turkey C
pany on its route to Persia were restricted by the competit
of the East India Company on one side, and for a time
least by the Russian Company on the north[1]. The Tur
Company was universally recognised as doing a benefi
business; they sold large quantities of English cloth[2]
imported raw silk, so that on either side their operations c
duced to the maintenance of English trade. Their c
difficulties were due to the commercial competition of Fran

*French
Com-
petition.*

English merchants in Italy were accused of the unpatri
conduct of exchanging French cloth for raw silk and t
opening markets to our greatest rivals in the woollen
dustry. Parliament interfered to support the Company

---

[1] 14 Geo. II. c. 36.   [2] Macpherson, III. 159 and 427.

[3] The advocates of the Company argued that the French trade was stri
monopoly, while there were no real restrictions on English subjects engag
the trade. *Some remarks on a late pamphlet* (1753). [Camb. Univ. Library L
40.] For the whole history of this trade see *Observations on Religion d
Turks* (1771), p. 361.

prohibiting the importation of raw silk[1] from any part of the Levant but those where the Company had their privileges. The evil however continued[2]; some changes were made in the constitution of the Company, chiefly by reducing the fine which was payable on admission to membership[3]. This brief recital indicates one reason for the decline of these companies; it was necessary for them to go to Parliament in order to have the requirements of their trade enforced; they were no longer empowered by the Crown alone, but they derived their authority from Parliament. There was very little advantage in retaining them as mere councillors to advise Parliament about particular trades; there was thus an increasing tendency to regulate trade directly by statute and by tariffs without depending on organised intermediaries.

There were indeed a few cases where new joint stock companies were organised, but the object with which this was done was no longer that of regulating trade, but of obtaining sufficient capital to attempt or to maintain a very risky trade. One such company was the Company of the Royal Fishery of England, which was intended to develop our fisheries; but the entire capital was soon expended; the subscribers of a second stock in 1683 were equally unfortunate[4]. A similar attempt was made in 1750, the special object being to gain the white herring fishery from the Dutch; the cod-fishing was also to be attempted. It was regarded as a political step of the first importance, and had been undertaken in response to an appeal made in the King's speech in 1749. Continual payment and allowances were made to support the operations of the Company, but it never answered the expectations of the promoters, and it called out the scathing criticism of Adam Smith.

Another trade in which the Dutch maintained their supremacy and from which they had ousted the English in

A.D. 1689 —1776.

Preferable modes of regulation.

Joint Stock Companies

for Fishery.

Whale Fishery.

---

[1] 6 Geo. I. c. 14.

[2] Compare the long debate in 1744. *Parl. Hist.* XIII. 895. The bill for opening the trade was seriously affected by jealousy of the Jews, who would have been admitted to the Levant trade if it had passed. Their naturalisation was carried in 1753, after interesting discussions, *Parl. Hist.* XIV. 1365 (26 Geo. II. c. 26), but repealed in the next session (27 Geo. II. c. 1) in consequence of the general outcry raised by the measure. *Parl. Hist.* XV. 91. Compare Tucker's *Letter concerning Naturalisation* (1753). [3] 26 Geo. II. c. 18. [4] Macpherson, II. 584.

the time of James I. was the whale fishery off the
Greenland[1]. A joint stock Company was formed i
and they were subsequently permitted to import 1
duty-free[2]. In the course of a very few years, howe1
ran through their capital of £82,000 and the trade
till the South Sea Company endeavoured to re-open
they prosecuted it without success. From this time
however, the business was left to the enterprise of

*Private
Enterprise
and
Bounties.*
individuals, though Parliament paid large sums 1
view of stimulating that enterprise. In 1733 a b
20 per ton on vessels engaged in the business was
in 1740 it was raised to 30, and in 1749 it was 1
40. This large bounty was successful in stimula
trade, but though it was continued for many years it
serve to make it prosper. In 1755 no less than £55
paid for this purpose, but in 1770 the tonnage emplo
so far declined that the bounties had fallen to
Arthur Young, who wrote in 1768, did not notice a
of decay, and thought the merchants at Hull deserve
commendation for entering into a business so e:
expensive, hazardous, and so often disadvantageous'
alleged justification for this continued expenditure, in
ing English capital to a direction in which it did
profitable employment, was of course political; it 1
posed that we could in this way furnish ourselves wit
oil on easier terms than by buying it from foreign a
successful fishermen, and this had been the underlyin
from the first[5].

*Com-
mercial
Policy.*
257. When we turn to consider the shippin
pursued in regard to trades under direct Parliament
trol, it is not necessary to attempt to follow it out i
for different trades, but it may suffice to disting
various objects which Parliament kept in view.

(a) Besides endeavouring to encourage shipp
seamanship by means of the Navigation Acts, the le

[1] Macpherson, II. 287.   [2] 4 W. and M. c. 17.
[3] 7 and 8 W. III. c. 33.   For an account of the Iceland Trade from I
see Pennant, *Journey from London to the Isle of Wight*, I. 112.
[4] *Northern Tour*, I. 176.
[5] Macpherson, II. 563; III. 179.   25 C. II. c. 7.

'the time paid considerable attention to subsidiary points. A.D. 1689 he greater part of the materials hitherto used in England —1776 r building and fitting ships had come from Scandinavia; *building materials* ut the Tar Company of Sweden took such advantage of *and naval stores.* heir monopoly[1], that English statesmen endeavoured in 1703 o obtain their own supplies; and bounties were offered on he exportation to England from the American plantations f pitch, tar, hemp, turpentine, and masts and spars. The reamble to this statute gives an admirable résumé of the easons for offering such large bounties, and for insisting on reater care in the consumption of foreign trees in the Vorthern American colonies[2]. "Whereas the royal navy, ad the navigation of England, wherein, under God, the realth, safety and strength of this kingdom is so much con- erned, depends on the due supply of stores necessary for the ame, which being now brought in mostly from foreign parts, a foreign shipping, at exorbitant and arbitrary rates, to the reat prejudice and discouragement of the trade and naviga- ion of this kingdom, may be provided in a more certain and eneficial manner from her Majesty's own dominions: and hereas her Majesty's colonies and plantations in America ere at first settled, and are still maintained and protected, t a great expence of the treasure of this kingdom, with a esign to render them as useful as may be to England, and he labour and industry of the people there, profitable to hemselves: and in regard the said colonies and planta- ions, by the vast tracts of land therein, lying near the sea, nd upon navigable rivers, may commodiously afford great quantities of all sorts of naval stores, if due encouragement e given for carrying on so great and advantageous an under- aking, which will like wise tend, not only to the further im- ployment and increase of English shipping and sea men, but lso to the enlarging, in a great measure, the trade and vent of the woollen and other manufactures and commodities of this kingdom, and of other her Majesty's dominions, in

---

[1] Supplies were also obtained from Russia (1721) but the conditions of trade were equally unsatisfactory. *Parl. Hist.* VII. 928.

[2] 3 and 4 Anne, c. 10. Macpherson, II. 724, 726. 8 Anne, c. 10, § 30; 9 Anne, . 17; 12 Anne, c. 9.

exchange for such naval stores, which are now purcha
from foreign countries with money or bullion: and
enabling her Majesty's subjects, in the said colonies a
plantations, to continue to make due and sufficient retu
in the course of their trade."

Ship building.

Bounties were also given to those who built good a
defensible ships, such as three-deckers. Three-deckers of
least four hundred and fifty tons—capable of carrying thir
two guns, were allowed a tenth part of the tunnage a
poundage duties on the first three voyages of each vessel[1].

Seamen.

(*b*) Considerable attention was also given to the positi
of seamen, especially with the view of inducing them to se
in the Royal Navy. A register was opened for the purp
of inscribing the names of 30,000 sailors of different class
they were to receive a retaining fee of £2 per annum on t
understanding that they should always be ready for pub
service when called upon[2]. They were to receive larger sha
of prize-money than unregistered men, and to have bet
chances of promotion to the rank of warrant officers. Th
also were to have rights, as well as their widows and childr

Greenwich Hospital.

to maintenance in Greenwich Hospital, an institution wh
was to be maintained by a sort of compulsory insurance;
per month was to be deducted from the wages of all seam
whether in the mercantile or royal navy, for its maintenan
Considerable changes were made under Queen Anne, wh
the registration of seamen ceased[4]; but there was a success
of statutes for enforcing their payments to the support of
hospital[5]. The residue of the money accruing from the c
fiscation of the Earl of Derwentwater's estates, was used
completing the building[6]. The distant prospect of a pensi
or a home, must have been a poor compensation for the inc

---

[1] 5 and 6 W. and M. c. 24.

[2] On the difficulty of procuring seamen compare *Parl. Hist.* vi. 518. Als
the consequent interference with commerce (1740). *Parl. Hist.* xi. 579, xiv. 5

[3] 7 and 8 William III. c. 21; 8 and 9 William III. c. 23; cf. 31 Geo. II. c. 1

[4] 9 Anne, c. 15, § 70.

[5] 10 Anne, c. 27; 2 Geo. II. c. 7; 18 Geo. II. c. 31.

[6] 8 Geo. II. c. 29. On abuses in connection with Derwentwater property
Pennant, *Journey*, i. 18. For Greenwich Hospital see *Parl. Hist.* xix. 991,
and the long account in xx. 475.

veniences to which seamen in the navy were forced to submit. A.D. 1689
An attempt was made to remedy their grievances in 1758 by —1776.
an Act for "establishing a regular method for the punctual,
frequent and certain payment of their wages; and for
enabling them more easily and readily to remit the same
for the support of their wives and families; and for preventing frauds and abuses attending such payments[1]." But despite
these measures, the Government was frequently in difficulty
about manning the navy, and had recourse to the high-
handed practice of impressing men[2] to serve.

Such were the provisions for men who served in the
Royal Navy, but the Merchant Service was not forgotten.
Attempts were made to give definiteness to the contracts of
Masters and Seamen[3], and a corporation was erected for
the relief of disabled seamen, and of the widows and orphans
of seamen in the Merchant Service[4]. During the time of
Queen Anne special arrangements were made for appren-
ticing pauper boys to a seafaring life[5], and great facilities
were given for the naturalisation of foreign seamen who
should serve for two years on English ships[6].

(c) Public attention was also directed to the dangerous *Light-*
nature of our coasts, and the authorities of Trinity House *houses.*
took in hand the erection of a lighthouse on the Eddystone. *Eddystone*
A London merchant named Winstanley first proved the *1698.*
possibility of the attempt; by unremitting labour he succeeded in erecting the wooden lighthouse in which he eventually perished. The expense, however, of this work far
exceeded the ordinary resources of the corporation, and they
were empowered to levy 1d. per ton on all shipping in order
to carry out this work in 1696. Their lighthouse was
destroyed by a storm in 1703, and resort was had to a similar
expedient for its re-erection[7]. In some cases the work of

---

[1] 31 Geo. II. c. 10.

[2] The impressing of fishermen &c. to serve as mariners only was permitted by
5 Eliz. c. 5, § 41. Charles I. obtained parliamentary powers in 1640 to impress
carpenters, surgeons &c. for his fleet against the Algiers pirates (16 Charles I. c. 26).
On complaints of the system in London in 1777 see *Parl. Hist.* xix. 61; compare
also 237, 1159, and xx. 966.

[3] 2 Geo. II. c. 36.   [4] 20 Geo. II. c. 38.   [5] 2 and 3 Anne, c. 6.

[6] 13 Geo. II. c. 3.   [7] Macpherson, ii. 682; 4 Anne, c. 20; 8 Anne, c. 17.

A.D. 1689
—1776.

Skerries.

Spurn.

erecting lighthouses was undertaken by local bodi
by private persons who were empowered to recei
maintain the light. The first light on the Ske
Holyhead, was put up by Mr William Trench[1]; tl
Spurn at the mouth of the Humber was recons
one of the neighbouring proprietors[2], though subsec
matter was taken over by Trinity House[3]. Light
erected, and landmarks and buoys placed, so as t
navigation to Chester[4]; there were some signs o
ment in the construction of lights, especially i
erected near Ipswich in 1778[5].

Harbours.

A good deal of attention was given to the impr
harbours. Some had been destroyed by the care
sailors, who threw out their ballast on the shore b
water mark, with the result that the harbours got
this practice was prohibited by a statute passed
There was an immense number of acts for impr
ticular ports; as Dover[7], Bridlington[8], Ramsgate
Haven[10], Whitehaven[11], S. Ives[12], Wells[13], Great Y
Glasgow and Port Glasgow[15], Ayr[16], Hull[17], Boston[18]
and for improving the Clyde[20].

It was also found that the charts of the west a
west coast of Britain and Ireland were very imperf
statute was passed in 1741 for surveying them
pletely[21], while attention was also given to navigat
high seas; rewards were frequently offered for
method for discovering longitude at sea[22]; at last
paid to John Harrison[23] for his discovery.

[1] Macpherson, III. 157; 3 Geo. II. c. 36.   [2] 6 Geo.
[3] 12 Geo. III. c. 29.   [4] 16 Geo. III. c. 61.   [5] Macph
[6] 19 Geo. II. c. 22. It had long been a cause of dispute in regi
trade. The colliers had little return cargo to fetch back from Londoi
and so carried much ballast, which they had difficulty in discharging
mischief. *Conservatorship of the River Tyne* in Richardson, *Reprin*
[7] 31 Geo. II. c. 8.   [8] 8 and 9
[9] 22 Geo. II. c. 40. Pennant, *Journey*, I. 114.   [10] 31 Geo.
[11] 2 Geo. III. c. 87.   [12] 7 Geo. III. c. 52.   [13] 9 Geo.
[14] 12 Geo. III. c. 14.   [15] 12 Geo. III. c. 16.   [16] 12 Geo.
[17] 14 Geo. III. c. 56.   [18] 16 Geo. III. c. 23.   [19] 16 Geo.
[20] 10 Geo. III. c. 104.   [21] 14 Geo. II. c. 39.
[22] 12 Anne, ii. c. 15; 26 Geo. II. c. 25; 2 Geo. III. c. 18.
[23] 3 Geo. III. c. 14.

258. It is perhaps not unnatural to turn from these A.D. 1689 —1776. attempts to preserve ships, to give a brief account of the *Marine In-* facilities which were now devised for reimbursing those who *surance.* incurred losses by sea. Loans on bottomry[1] had served the purpose of marine insurance during the Middle Ages; in the fifteenth century the practice of premium insurance became common[2], and there appear to have been a considerable number of people engaged in this occupation in London in 1574, when a patent was issued for giving a certain Richard Candler the sole right to register policies and instruments of insurance[3]. Subsequently a mixed commission of merchants and lawyers was established to deal with cases arising out of this business[4]. But their jurisdiction gave little satisfaction, and the commission was modified soon after the Restoration[5]. Altogether, though fire and life insurance were developing[6], we hear very little of this business till the time of George I.[7], when more than one attempt was made to form a Company to carry on the business with a joint stock. In 1720 two schemes, which were pushed in concert but under the guise of competition, succeeded in procuring sanction from Parliament[8], and the London Assurance Corporation

---

[1] See above, p. 93.

[2] Mr Hendriks (*Contributions to History of Insurance*, 16) shows that premium insurance was in use at Pisa about 1400 and at Barcelona before 1435. The rate from London to Pisa was 12 per cent. or 15 per cent. "according to the risks apprehended either from pirates or other sources." Foreigners could not take advantage of these facilities for insurance in Pisa; an attempt was made to impose a similar restriction in England in the 18th century. *Parl. Hist.* XII. 18. Pelham, *Essay towards deciding the question Whether Britain be permitted * * to insure the Ships of her enemies?* (1758). See also *War in Disguise*, 84. On the Spanish practice see Stevens, *Spanish Rule of Trade* (1702), 319.

[3] Stowe, *Survey*, vol. II. bk v. 242. For a curious dispute in 1572, see Hall, *Elizabethan Age*, 57.   [4] 43 Eliz. c. 12.

[5] 14 C. II. c. 23.   [6] See above, § 238, p. 224.

[7] Insurance business of different sorts was a favourite field for Company promoters at this time. At the Crown Tavern, Smithfield, a subscription book was opened for establishing "an Insurance Office for Horses dying natural deaths, stolen, or disabled"; at the Fountain Tavern there was started "a co-partnership for insuring and increasing Children's fortunes"; at another place in the city subscribers came to put their names and money down for "Plummer and Petty's Insurance from Death by drinking Geneva." * * * Then there were started offices for "Assurances from lying"; for "Insurance from house-breakers"; for "Rum Insurance"; for "Insurance from highwaymen" and numerous others. Martin, *History of Lloyd's*, 89.

[8] *Parl. Hist.* VII. 649.

C. II.   19

A.D. 1689
—1776.
*Royal
Exchange
Assurance
and
London
Assurance.* and Royal Exchange Assurance Corporation were created. These companies are still large and flourishing institutions; in their earlier days they had considerable difficulties, especially through the loss of a fleet of Jamaica ships; the London Assurance was deeply involved, and its shares fell within a month from 160 to 60 and thence to 12[1]. The two undertakings had agreed to pay £300,000 into the exchequer[2], but subsequently, in 1721, half of the sum was remitted. The Act which the companies then obtained[3] gave them the exclusive right of carrying on this business on a joint stock, but did not interfere with the business of private individuals who were engaged in underwriting.

In the early part of the eighteenth century the practice had come into fashion of resorting to coffee-houses for all sorts of intercourse, whether social, political or commercial. Persons engaged in shipping appear to have used a coffee-*Lloyd's Coffee House.* house kept by Mr Edward Lloyd, who was a very energetic man, and published a newspaper chiefly devoted to foreign and commercial news in 1696[4]. It did not last very long, *Lloyd's list.* however; but it was succeeded in 1726 by Lloyd's *List*[5], which contained ship-news, together with the current rates of exchange, the prices of shares, and so forth. The coffee-house, though convenient, was the resort of some doubtful characters; and it was determined by the respectable brokers and underwriters, who frequented Lloyd's, to establish a new resort for themselves. They secured the property in Lloyd's *List*; and after various attempts to get satisfactory premises had failed, they obtained quarters in the Royal Exchange in 1774[6]. The new Lloyd's Coffee-house, which was there established, contained a public room and also a subscribers'-room, and the committee enforced various regulations in regard to the business which was done by the members. In 1779 they

---

[1] M. Postlethwayt, *Universal Dictionary of Trade*, article on *Actions*.
[2] Martin, *Lloyd's*, 99.   [3] 6 Geo. I. c. 18.
[4] Martin, *Lloyd's*, 74. The following announcement which first appeared in No. 61 shows the nature of the publication and the aims of the proprietor:—
"All Gentlemen, Merchants, or others, who are desirous to have this News in a whole Sheet of paper (two leaves instead of one leaf), for to write their own private Concerns in, or other Intelligence for the Country, may be suppli'd with them, done upon very good Paper, for a Penny a Sheet, at Lloyd's Coffee-House in Lombard Street."   [5] Martin, *Lloyd's*, 107.   [6] *Ib.* 120, 145.

drew up a general form of policy which is still adhered to, and which has been taken as the model for marine insurance business all over the world[1]. It is curious to notice that they regarded the business of life-insurance with much suspicion[2], as it seemed to be merely speculative[3] and lent itself to all sorts of nefarious practices. At a meeting of the subscribers, in March, 1774, a resolution was passed of which the preamble states that "shameful practices have been introduced of late years into the business of Underwriting, such as making Speculative Insurances on the lives of persons and of Government securities." It continues that "in the first instance it is endangering the lives of the persons so insured, from the idea of being selected by society for that inhuman purpose, which is being virtually an accessory in a species of slow murder." The subscribers were therefore to refuse to undertake such business and to show "a proper resentment" against any broker who attempted to introduce it[4].

It thus came about that the underwriters, who had been left outside when the two great companies were formed in 1720, had practically formed themselves into a body resembling a regulated company. The forms under which business was done were now definitely established; but the immense increase in the risks of loss which British shipping ran during the great wars[5] rendered it necessary for all ship-owners to protect themselves by insuring and caused a very rapid expansion of the underwriters' business.

A.D. 1669 —1776.

Life Insurance.

---

[1] Martin, *Lloyd's*, 157.

[2] Martin, 117, quoting *London Chronicle* for 1768, also pamphlet entitled *Every Man His Own Broker*. See also the Act regulating Life Insurance, 14 Geo. III. c. 48.

[3] The valuation of Life Annuities had been already put on a scientific basis by De Witt, whose treatise has been reprinted by Mr Hendriks in his excellent monograph, *Contributions to the History of Insurance*, 40, as well as by Halley, *Phil. Trans.* 1693, but they attracted no attention among business men. The Society for Equitable Assurances was the first Company founded on a scientific basis; this was established in 1762, but the promoters failed to procure a charter. E. J. Farren, *Historical Essay on the doctrine of Life Contingencies* (1844), p. 94. The Amicable Society, which was incorporated in 1706, was originally a sort of Tontine. *Ib.* p. 35.   [4] Martin, *Lloyd's*, 157.

[5] Compare debates on Miscarriages of the Navy (1708), *Parl. Hist.* VI. 618, Merchants' Petition (1742), *Ib.* XII. 446, 753, Commercial Losses (Feb. 6, 1778), *Ib.* XIX. 709, also XX. 1144. Also on the alarm caused by Paul Jones and pirates on our coasts, *Ib.* XXI. 486; difficulties with Holland, *Ib.* 968.

A.D. 1689
—1776.
The Navi-
gation Act;

criticism
by Child

and by
Adam
Smith

compared.

259. During the whole of this period the Navigatio
Act was maintained, and maintained with hardly any modif
cation[1]; at the same time there were not wanting voices t
criticise it severely. An admirable résumé of these argu
ments is given by Sir Josiah Child in his *New Discourse* c
Trade, published in 1692. He was a warm supporter of th
Act, though he was perfectly aware that it was directl
favourable to the merchants and shipowners, who were but
limited class, and that the "interest of the greater number
of Englishmen would be "that our native commoditie
and manufactures should be taken from us at the best rate
and foreign commodities sold us at the cheapest," and it wa
obvious that the interest of the ordinary producer and ordi
nary consumer would be promoted by giving perfect freedor
of trade to ships of all nations. He at once admits that "thi
may be true, if the present profit of the generality be barel
and singly considered; but this kingdom being an island, th
defence whereof has always been our shipping and seamen,
seems to me absolutely necessary that profit and power ougl
jointly to be considered, and if so, I think none can deny bu
the Act of Navigation hath and doth occasion building an
employing three times the number of ships and seamen, the
otherwise we should or would do, and that consequently,
our force at sea were so greatly impaired, it would expose i
to the receiving of all kind of injuries and affronts from ot
neighbours, and in conclusion render us a despicable an
miserable people[2]."

Adam Smith repeated both these objections although h
decided in a different sense. He is inclined to write as if th
merchants had over-persuaded the Parliament to regulat
trade in the interest of their own class and to the injury o
the general body of producers and consumers; but the uj
holders of the Navigation policy would always have replie
with Child, that Parliament were considering the ulterio

---

[1] By 3 and 4 Anne, c. 8, the exportation of Irish linen cloth to the Engli
plantations was permitted. This was done in order that the Irish linen tra
might be stimulated. It was also found necessary by the 15 Geo. II. c. 31 to ta
measures to prevent foreign ships from trading to British colonies under colour
certificates improperly obtained.

[2] *New Discourse of Trade*, 114.

effects upon national prosperity, and that they were justified A.D. 1689 —1776. in imposing this expense upon producers and consumers, not for the sake of a few merchants, but from a far-sighted regard *Its effect* to the welfare of the State in the future. Adam Smith's *on employment* conclusion differs from that of Child chiefly because he concentrates his attention on the immediate effects of any measure, as shown by changes in the national income. He says "the riches, and so far as power depends upon riches, the power of every country must always be in proportion to the value of its annual produce, the fund from which all taxes must ultimately be paid." He therefore sets himself to discover which mode of employing capital maintains "the greatest quantity of productive labour and increases the most the annual produce of the land and labour"; he regards capital employed in a distant trade as less advantageous, according to this test, than capital which is employed nearer home and turned over more frequently. He complains that the Navigation Acts and whole colonial policy of England tended to divert trade into less profitable channels[1]. But the upholders of the policy would have refused to judge it by simple reference to the employment of productive labour and the increase in the value of annual produce. They were anxious to promote particular forms of national industry which contributed directly to the power of the nation, even though they may have checked the increase of riches. It is on this account that Child maintains that "no trades deserve so much care to procure and preserve, and encouragement to prosecute, as those that employ the most shipping, although the commodities transported be of small value in themselves; * * * for besides the gain accruing by the goods, the freights, which is in such trades often more than the value of the goods, is all profit to the nation, besides, they bring with *and on power.* them a great access of power (hands as well as money), many ships and seamen being justly the reputed strength and safety of England[2]." We have already seen how much money was devoted to fostering the Greenland trade, and one of the

---

[1] *Wealth of Nations,* pp. 153, 247.
[2] Child, *New Discourse,* Preface.

A.D. 1689
—1776.
reasons for incurring this outlay was that it induced the building and manning of ships of unusually large burden[1].

Adam Smith would not, after all, have contended that the annual income or rate of profit on capital gave a measure as to the relative advantage of different employments that can always be relied on[2], or that the points on which Child insists were unimportant politically. The mercantilists were thus quite justified in attempting to judge of the benefit or hurtfulness of trade by considering its direct bearing on some element of national power: their mistake was in being willing to purchase that element of power at too dear a rate; and it was only after a long experience that the nation realised how much the various regulations hampered trade and thus came to understand what a high price they were paying for attempting to procure these powers. The practical conclusion which Adam Smith supported by illustrations drawn from the experience of the preceding century is unimpeachable, but it was rather by summarising the results of that experience than by pointing out any fallacy in their principles that he succeeded in overthrowing the system which the mercantilists had set up[3].

III. PLANTATIONS.

Ireland after the Revolution. 260. During the period from the Restoration to the Revolution, Ireland had begun to settle down and enjoyed some years of unwonted prosperity. By the Revolution, and the subsequent war, the whole country was once more thrown into a state of chaos. The misfortunes of the time, terrible as they were, are at least instructive; for they serve to bring out very clearly the principles on which Englishmen acted in managing the resources of their various dependencies.

It must not be forgotten that England was engaged in great military struggle with France. Under these circumstances politicians felt that it was a matter of the first importance that the available sources of public revenue should

---

[1] Macpherson, III. 179, and p. 121.

[2] See Prof. Nicholson's note 20 in his edition of the *Wealth of Nations*.

[3] Compare my article on the *Relativity of Economic Doctrine* in *Economic Journal*, March, 1892.

vents not be diminished. The colonies and Ireland *A.D. 1689*
—1776.
nds with no great industrial development[1], and there *Danger of*
seem to be much hardship in insisting that their re- *tapping the*
sources of
should be newly developed on lines which would not *English*
revenue.
existing industries in the mother country. These
ies were being fostered as the chief means of gaining
e, and they thus were either directly or indirectly a
portant source of the Customs Revenue. The colo-
d Ireland on the other hand did not yield a revenue
iament to control. The development of their resources
to be desirable, but not at the expense of the mother
or so as to weaken her power.

he case of Ireland the anxiety on this head was some- *Parlia-*
mentary
ronger; not so much because Parliament were jealous *jealousy of*
Irish, as because they had so little confidence in the *the Crown.*
and were nervously anxious not to increase the royal
Charles I., Charles II. and James II. had all suffered
e distrust of their subjects; and William III., even
he had been invited to come, did not succeed in
g confidence; he bitterly resented the treatment he
l. As Ireland was an independent kingdom, the
House of Commons had no direct control over its
and there was a constant dread lest power which the
xquired in Ireland, should be used without the con-
e of the English Parliament[2] or even against English
t. Twice within the seventeenth century serious
s had been made to develop the resources of Ireland,
rafford, and under Charles II. and James II.; in both
ie result had been that the King had found himself
ssion of power that seemed to menace his English
t. Under these circumstances there was the strongest

---

ny article in *Eng. Hist. Rev.* I. 277, from which the substance of the
paragraph is taken. There had been a manufacture of freize by the
h from very early times (*Rolls of Parl.* II. 372 a), but it seems to have
chiefly for home consumption and very little of it was exported. Petty's
Anatomy of Ireland (1691), 81, 98, 111. It is to be noticed however that
four, 114) mentions an important manufacture of serges at Limerick;
seems to have been a similar manufacture for export in the fourteenth
Fazzio degli Uberti, Il Dittamondo, IV. c. 26, l. 28. About the same time
n of Catalonia were accused of "basely imitating the serges of Ireland,
g the belles of Florence in them to our injury." *Reports*, 1840, XXIII.
[2] *An Answer*, p. 8, 21. [Brit. Mus. 1029, e. 14 (1).]

political reason for dreading any development of the wealth of Ireland that took place at the expense of England, since this really implied an increase of the power of the Crown at the expense of the power of Parliament[1].

Irish parties.

Within Ireland itself, as viewed by contemporary politicians, there were two great classes; those who could be counted upon to assist in building up a social and economic life like that in England, and those who were opposed to the scheme, and who were therefore elements of disorder. Among these elements of disorder were included all those who in the troubles of the preceding half century had been evicted from their possessions on one excuse or another; and as many of them had rallied round James II. and were attached to the faith he professed, they came to be marked as the native Irish, or the Papists, in opposition to the Protestant interest. Political and religious hatreds,—the memories of 1641 and of 1689,—tended to embitter the relations of these two parties; and politicians deliberately set themselves to harry and hunt down the native Irish, so that those who were not exterminated might be absorbed into the Protestant interest. In broad outline, the policy which Parliament tried to pursue was that of promoting the prosperity of the Protestant interest in any direction[2] in which it did not compete with the wealth of the mother country.

The Protestant interest.

The drapery manufacture

These political views give a simple explanation of the policy which was pursued with regard to the recently planted manufacture of drapery in Ireland[3]. During the period from 1665 to 1687 there had been various attempts to create a cloth manufacture in Ireland; this was one of the staple trades of England. Between 1665 and 1677 there had been, as stated

[1] Traces of this feeling were found in 1779 and later; as for example speeches by Lord Shelburne (*Parl. Hist.* xx. 1163), and Fox (*Ib.* x 1297).

[2] The prohibition of tobacco growing so as not to interfere with the established trade of Virginia would have been justified on similar principles, but it may regarded as an exceptional case.

[3] In legislating about the Irish woollen trades the manufacture of freize specially excluded from the duties that were placed on the export of the old new drapery. In any case the native cloth was apparently chiefly made for home consumption and the quantity exported was so small that the new duties might prevent the development of the trade but would only be a slight injury to those who were already engaged in it.

above, a considerable migration of manufacturers from the *A.D. 1689 —1776.* West of England to different towns in Ireland, and measures had been taken for regulating the trade so that the quality of the goods produced might not be inferior to the work of English looms. Immediately after the Revolution, however, *introduced* the drapery manufacture in Ireland seemed to start forward *by migra- tion from* with great rapidity. The West of England clothiers asserted that "during the late rebellion in Ireland many of the poor of that Kingdom fled into the West of England where they were put to work in the woollen manufactures and learned that trade; and since the reduction of Ireland, endeavours are used to set up those manufactures there[1]." The main attraction of Ireland to weavers was the cheapness of living and the cheapness of wool, and these advantages had drawn a considerable number of English-bred workmen to Ireland, so that in 1697 it seemed probable that the Devonshire industry would soon be transplanted to Dublin. There does not appear to have been much excitement in the northern[2] and eastern centres of the clothing trade; but the West of *the West of* England clothiers averred that their long celebrated manu- *England.* factures were decaying while the Irish industry increased; labour was attracted away and Irish wool was intercepted on its way to them. They were stirred, not by a mere anticipation of possible competition, but by actual experience of the migra- tion that had already taken place. What they demanded was that such countervailing duties should be imposed as would serve to neutralise the advantages in Ireland, and to put both countries on equal terms;—so that the migration of industry from one to the other should cease[3]. Of this

[1] *English Commons Journals*, XII. (Tiverton) 63; compare also (Taunton) 37, (Barnstaple) 40, (Ashburnham) 64. Massie, *Observations on Cyder Tax*, p. 2.

[2] They complained at this very date of the export of wool to Scotland. *Com- mons Journals*, XII. 64.

[3] The rate which was actually levied was 20 per cent. on the old drapery and 10 per cent. on the new. This was arrived at after the Irish woollen manufac- turers had been heard on the subject, and though it actually proved to be a pro- hibitory and not merely a countervailing tax it was obviously intended to be merely countervailing. The Commissioners on Trade after going into the matter actually recommended 48 per cent. and explicitly remarked that they proposed this as a mere countervailing duty and not as a heavier tax which "would in effect amount to an absolute prohibition of the exportation of that sort of cloth from Ireland, which we humbly conceive can never be intended by that bill." *Commons Journals*, XII. 439.

particular grievance inflicted upon Ireland it may therefo
be said that it had little or no effect upon the native popul
tion and that the immediate sufferers were the Protesta
interest in Ireland.   There is no sign of jealousy of the
prosperity, in the sense in which there was jealousy of th
possible prosperity of the native Irish when the penal law
were passed; the real motive lay in the desire to prevent th
Protestant interest in Ireland from undermining the succes
of an established English trade[1].

However, even from their own standpoint, it appear
that the measures proved hurtful and failed to secure th
object which the promoters had in view; while they di
irreparable mischief in Ireland in preventing the develo
ment of an industry for which she was admirably adapte
The Irish were deprived of their home market for wool a
exported it in a raw or half-manufactured state to Franc

[1] The action of the Irish woollen manufacturers during this period confi
this view of the case.   They were on the one hand anxious to improve the regr
tions about the quality of cloth, and on the other hand they were anxious
establish themselves in a closer corporation.   According to their account the r
trade had begun to attract some of the native Irish after 1692 and the Dul
weavers were moving the Irish Parliament to confine the trade more strictl
the Protestant interest for the future.   "A Petition of the Protestant Woo
Manufacturers in the City & County of Dublin, as well Freemen as Foreign
in behalf of themselves & the Rest of the Woollen manufacturers of Irela
addressed to the Irish House of Commons in 1698, asserts "that the Papist
the Year 1692, were but very few in the Woollen Manufactory of this Kingd
& for six years last they have gotten the third Part of the said Manufactory
their own Hands, for great Numbers of them have left the Trade & Calling t
were bred to, viz. Brogue Makers, Mealmen, Bakers etc. & have set up
follow the Woollen Trade, without serving any Time, and carry on a greater Tr
than most of the Corporation: That the said Papists for want of Knowledge in
Trade have made much bad Goods, which have gone off by the Lowness of
Rates, and is an absolute Cheat to the Buyer, who cannot always disting
between good and bad Goods, all which have much damnified the Protes
Interest in this Kingdom, and caused a Jealousy in England that our Manufac
will damnify theirs: for Prevention whereof, and for the Preservation of the .
testant Interest in this Nation, the Petitioners humbly propose to the Consid
tion of the House the disabling Papists from following or working in the Woo
Manufactory, except spinning, whereby the others may return to their for
Trades, or take to the Linen Manufactory, and that no Protestant or Pe
whatever, may keep above three Apprentices at once, and they to serve full s
Years Time, whereby the goods will be well made, and bear such a rate as,
sidering the Dearness of the Necessaries we have from England, we shall no
able to afford them cheaper than they."   *Irish Commons Journals* (12 Oct. 1
II. i. 247.

[2] *Causes of Decline* (1744), p. 30.   Caldwell's *Enquiry* in *Debates,* 760—769.

while the workmen who could no longer earn a living in Ireland found their way to foreign countries where they started industries which became more formidable rivals to the English manufactures than the Irish would have been likely to prove. The single competitor was ousted from the field; but while doing this our statesmen unwittingly called into being new rivals in the neighbourhood of our best markets.

But if the policy was mistaken, even with reference to its professed objects, we who look back from the present day can easily see what was pointed out by pamphleteers, at the time, that the scheme of policy was bad, since it was so short-sighted. There were one or two voices which pleaded for the new industry as a strength, not merely to the Protestant interest, but to Ireland and indirectly to England too[1]. They held that the development of this new industry in Dublin, and the encouragement of Englishmen and aliens to flock there, would give a great impetus to the prosperity of the sister isle, and change her into a new source of strength to the realm. If she had more plenty, she could do more to support the united power of the two kingdoms. As manufacturing increased, the price of raw products would go up. The Irish peasantry would have a better market both for wool and for food stuffs; the general increase of plenty, and new intercourse between Protestants and Romanists, might well be expected to give better conditions for the growth of social institutions and for steady political progress. All this was hoped for; all this, so far as we see, might have been; but these beneficial results were frustrated by the measures which checked the development of the drapery trade. The fiscal loss would have been very serious, if the Devonshire manufacturers had been ruined, but the ultimate gain from an Ireland that was in any degree prosperous and contented would have far outweighed it.

also p. 335 below. It was denied however that this occurred on as large a scale as is commonly said; (Macpherson, III. 182); but others alleged that it seriously affected the profit of the grazier in England. *Graziers' Complaint* (1726), 19. He gives a curious estimate of the different expense of production in Ireland and in Lincolnshire.

[1] Arthur Dobbs, *An Essay on the Trade and Improvement of Ireland* (1729) in *Collection of Tracts* (1861), II. 336; *List of Absentees* (1729), *Ib.* II. 279. Also *Collection of Tracts concerning State of Ireland* (1729), p. 45. See below, p. 420, note 1.

The chance of securing such prosperity was sacrificed; and no more English capital found its way to Dublin for the establishment of weaving; but even in the narrowest commercial sense the ultimate loss to England was very great. All those who had attempted to make the most of Irish industries had seen that it could be done most quickly by attracting British industry and capital to settle there. With the reduction of Ireland a new opportunity had opened. English enterprise and industry were beginning to find their way to Ireland once more, not now to dispossess men of their hereditary lands, but to give a better market for the produce of each man's land and labour, and better opportunities of satisfying his wants. Much national benefit might have accrued even if the drapery manufacture had been developed on the restricted lines which the Dublin weavers suggested; but this great opportunity was thrown away for the sake of an immediate pecuniary gain[1], and because the English Parliament deemed it wise to sacrifice the development of Irish resources, for fear they should unduly increase the wealth and power of the Crown.

Linen manufacture. 261. The linen manufacture was an important textile industry which had never been successfully prosecuted in England[2], although various attempts had been made to plant it. No forebodings were aroused by attempts to develop it in Ireland, and there was reason to believe that the country was specially adapted for the growth of flax and for carrying on the spinning and weaving of linen. Incidental notice of

[1] It has been assumed in the foregoing section that contemporaries were right in believing that Ireland had special advantages for carrying on the woollen manufacture; this may be doubted, for the Irish weavers did not succeed in catering even for the home markets. The trade continued to exist but in a depressed condition. The Irish Parliament insisted that the Weavers Companies in Dublin and other towns should exercise a more effective supervision over the manufacture. *Irish Commons Journal*, II. i. p. 482. The weavers of Dublin complained of the ruin of their trade in 1732 (Martin, *Ireland*, 39), and there were frequent petitions describing the distress of the woollen and worsted weavers of Dublin and Cork in 1783, 1787, 1788, 1793 and 1800 (*Ib.* 49). There was considerable progress about 1801 and for a few subsequent years when machinery worked by water power came into vogue; but hand spinning and weaving seem never to have prospered. This was due partly to difficulties in procuring a supply of suitable wool. (Letter to Mr Spring Rice, 3 *Hansard*, XXII. 1257.)

[2] Hale speaks of it as in "some degree used in Lancashire, Leicestershire and some other places." *Discourse touching Provision for Poor* (1683), p. 18.

linen manufacture occurs as early as the fifteenth cen- ry, since Irish linen cloth is mentioned by the author of the *bel of English Policy*. Before the Civil War linen yarn was ported from Ireland to be woven in Manchester[1].

Strafford usually gets the credit of introducing this trade, nce he encouraged it among settlers in the north[2]; but 1635. hatever he did was swept away in the troublous times that ollowed; and for practical purposes the art was introduced gain in the time of Charles II.[3]; the trade appears to have ncreased steadily till the time of the Revolution. Con- emporary statesmen thought they saw their opportunity f benefiting the one country without risk to the other; und a series of efforts were made to develop this trade in Ireland. They recognised that it would be distinctly desirable *Reasons for* hat England should draw her linen supply from a depen- *encourag-* lency rather than pay for it from foreign countries[4], and they *ing it*

---

[1] Roberts, *Treasure of Traffike*, p. 32. The linen manufacture is mentioned in ngland in 1189 (Macpherson, i. 348), and there are several incidental notices of linen avers in various towns. See above, Vol. i. 285. Under King James I. it was ported by the Commission of Trade in 1622 that the Eastland Company had merly brought in flax and hemp in great quantities which afforded employment r many people in dressing and manufacturing it. They complained that the merchants now brought in finished goods instead and that the manufacture had clined (*Foedera*, xvii. 410). Almost immediately after the Restoration an Act s passed for encouraging the home manufacture and discouraging the importation f foreign linen. The introduction of Indian muslins somewhat interfered with s use of linen, and the chief supply, during the Restoration period, appears to ve come from abroad (Macpherson, ii. 540). Immediately after the Restoration great corporation of linen manufacturers was formed which is said to have been ined by stock-jobbers (*Angliae Tutamen*, 24). In any case it is clear that there as no established linen industry in England which was comparable in importance the clothing trade.

[2] See above, § 208, p. 136. On early history see *Reports*, 1840, xxiii. 458, 521.
[3] Macpherson, ii. 559.
[4] Sir W. Temple's *Miscellanea* (1681), p. 114. "The Soil produces Flax indly and well and fine too, answerable to the care used in choice of seed and ercise of Husbandry; and much Land is fit for it here, which is not so for Corn. he Manufacture of it in gathering or beating, is of little toyl or application; and the fitter for the Natives of the Countrey. Besides, no Women are apter to in it well than the Irish, who labouring little in any kind with their hands, have their fingers more supple and soft than other Women of poorer condition among s. And this may certainly be advanced and improved into a great Manufacture f Linnen, so as to beat down the trade both of France and Holland, and draw uch of the Money which goes from England to those parts upon this occasion, into the hands of His Majesties Subjects of Ireland, without crossing any interest f Trade in England. For besides what has been said of Flax and Spinning, the

hoped that the foreign Protestants who were leaving France
might be attracted to settle in Ireland and carry on their
calling there. "Whereas there are great Sums of Money and
Bullion yearely exported out of this Kingdome for the purchasing of Hemp Flax and Linen and the Productions thereof
which might in great measure be prevented by being supplied from Ireland if such proper Encouragement were given
as might invite Forreigne Protestants into that Kingdome
to settle[1]."

Attempts to encourage the linen trade had gone on *pari
passu* with the repression of the drapery trade. The English
Parliament relaxed the Navigation Act in its favour by
allowing the exportation of Irish linen to the English plantations, on the ground that the Irish Protestant interest in
Ireland was promoted by giving the greatest encouragement
*and steps
taken with
this object.* to the linen manufactures of that kingdom[2]. The Irish
Parliament, which passed the 'countervailing' duties on cloth,
gave great attention to the possible development of this
trade[3]; fines levied for infractions of the laws about wool
were devoted to stimulating the Irish linen manufacture[4].
Under these encouragements, the linen trade attained considerable proportions[5]; but it did not spread over the whole
island[6]. It began to show signs of declining in the reign of
George III.; though additional bounties were given in 1769[7],
Ireland did not share in the encouragement which was given
to English and Scotch manufacturers in that year; new
duties had been laid[8] on foreign linens, and the proceeds were
constituted into a fund for encouraging the growth of hemp
and flax in Great Britain[9]. Spinning-schools had been established in many parts of Ireland in 1708; and a Frenchman

Soil and Climate are proper for whitening, both by the frequency of Brooks, and
also of Winds in the Countrey."

[1] 7 and 8 W. III. c. 39.   In 1709, 500 families of poor Palatines were sent to
Ireland to carry on husbandry and the linen manufacture. *State Papers, Treasury,*
1708—14, CXIX. 1; also 1714—19, CLXXXVII. 25.

[2] 3 and 4 Anne, c. 8.   On Dupin and his corporation see Molyneux' Letter to
Locke in Locke's *Works*, IX. 389, also pp. 436, 448.

[3] *Irish Commons Journals,* II. i. 287.   [4] 10 and 11 W. III. c. 10, § 2.

[5] As is shown by the Foundation of the Linen Hall in Dublin in 1728. Lecky,
II. 321.

[6] *Essay on the Ancient and Modern State of Ireland.* Dublin, 1760, p. 63.

[7] 10 Geo. III. c. 38.   [8] 7 Geo. III. c. 58.   [9] 10 Geo. III. c. 40.

ned Crommelin secured a patent, though with some A.D. 1689
ficulty, for starting the trade in other districts[1]; but he —1776.
uld not obtain enough capital to make much headway.

Such was the general scheme of policy; Ireland was pre- *But this*
nted on the one hand from having any advantage over Eng- *policy was not really*
nd in the drapery manufacture, but it was proposed to give *pursued.*
ll scope to the natural advantages of Ireland, combined with
e cheapness of living, for developing a linen manufacture.
his scheme was never fairly carried out[2], with the direct
sult that the Protestant interest in Ireland was sacrificed;
he duties on the drapery goods were, as has been seen,
actically prohibitive though supposed to be countervail-
g. But there was another principle which operated to the
rious detriment of Ireland. The whole mercantile system *Difficulties*
as designed to promote English power and English ship- *about ship-ping.*
ing; and as a consequence there was no attempt made to
ut Ireland on an equal footing with England, so far as ship-
ing was concerned. It was merely idle to profess to develop
n industry, while there were grave hindrances to the sale
f the product. On the other hand the colonial policy of
ngland implied that each distant member should strengthen
he head, and not at all that these members should mutually
rengthen each other. On this principle Ireland was
ebarred from the colonial trade; it was by a clause in an
nglish act[3] about the export of wool that the final blow 1699.
as struck at the drapery trade. Some of the hindrances to
xport affected the linen as well as the drapery trade, and
here can be no doubt that there were English statesmen *Fears of*
ho regarded it with some jealousy. They feared that if we *English Clothiers.*
id not take our returns from the Low Countries in linen,
hey would close their ports against English woollen cloth;
nd thus, while the Irish clothing trade was extinguished, the
rish linen trade was also offered as a sacrifice to the staple
ndustry of this country[4]. The Irish also had to contend *Scotch*
with the competition of Scotland, which after the Union in *Competition.*

[1] *State Papers, Treasury*, 1702—7, LXXXIII. 104; XC. 28, 261.
[2] For testimonies, however, to prosperity of Ireland, Macpherson, III. 228, 289, 318, 350.
[3] 10 and 11 W. III. c. 10.
[4] (Rockingham), *Parl. Hist.* XX. 640; (North), *Ib.* 1275.

1707 began to share in the same commercial liberties &
England enjoyed: this was specially clear in the jealousy (
Glasgow merchants in 1778[1].

*General
condition
of the
country.*

262. Excluded from commerce and prevented from makin
the most of the resources of their own country, the Protestar
population of Ireland could find but little profit in supplyin
the home market. At the time of the Revolution, the rac
conflict had broken out more terribly than ever befor
and the progress which had been made during the Restora
tion period came suddenly to an end. As in 1641, so i
1689, the action of the Celtic population gave an excuse fo
the terrible retaliation which followed. The Cromwellia
settlement had been deliberately undertaken with the vie
of crushing out the Celtic proprietors; and James II, wh

*Attack on
the Pro-
testant
interest.*

saw in the Celtic population the means of bringing Irelan
once more under the Roman obedience, entered on a seri
of measures for dispossessing men who had held their lan
by Parliamentary title for eight and thirty years, and f
returning the estates to the representatives of their form
owners. Mr Lecky has shown that, from the point of tho
who regarded James as their lawful king and the upholde
of William as guilty of treason, there was little in the conf
catory legislation of 1689 for which ample precedent cou
not be found[2]; but it was a deliberate attempt, on the pa
of James and his supporters, to destroy the Protesta
interest, and thereby to detach Ireland from England; wh

[1] *Parl. Hist.* xix. 1117. Compare the whole debate and specially Burke's lett
to Bristol Merchants, *Ib.* 1100. "Trade is not a limited thing; as if the obj
of mutual demand and consumption could not stretch beyond the bounds of
jealousies. God has given the earth to the children of men, and he has
doubtedly, in giving it to them, given them what is abundantly sufficient for
their exigencies; not a scanty, but a most liberal provision for them all. :
author of our nature has written it strongly in that nature, and has promulga
the same law in his written word, that man shall eat his bread by his labour; ʉ
I am persuaded, that no man, and no combination of men, for their own idea
their particular profit, can, without great impiety, undertake to say, that he s
not do so; that they have no sort of right, either to prevent the labour, or to w
hold the bread. Ireland having received no compensation, directly or indirec
for any restraints on their trade, ought not, in justice or common honesty, to
made subject to such restraints. I do not mean to impeach the right of
parliament of Great Britain to make laws for the trade of Ireland. I only sp
of what laws it is right for parliament to make."

[2] Lecky, ii. 186.

it failed at the Boyne and Limerick, the Protestants *A.D. 1689 —1776.* were determined to establish themselves more firmly than ever. They realised, of course, that wealth was a source of *The Penal Laws.* power. They deliberately set themselves to secure the whole power of the country, by enacting the penal laws which rendered the Romanist proprietors the prey of every unscrupulous member of their own families or of other informers; they put a premium on the conduct of those who deserted their hereditary faith; and these measures were deliberately designed to destroy any remaining influential families of the proscribed religion. In the latter part of the reign there were other disturbing causes; the jealousy of the English Parliament forced William to resume the grants he had *Resumption of Lands.* made to his Dutch generals. By these successive measures the whole fabric of society was reduced to utter chaos, and a most pitiable description of its condition is given in the address of the Irish House of Commons to the Crown in 1703. their Journals[1].

In the beginning of the eighteenth century the Protestant *Protestant Dissenters.* interest was still further weakened by having its divisions exposed through the enforcement of laws against Protestant Dissenters. The Test Act was extended to Ireland in 1704 and the Schism Act in 1714[2]; but there were other ways in which the maintenance of the Established Church acted prejudicially on Irish welfare. While tithes were exacted on *Tithes.* cultivated land, pasturage was free, and there was as a consequence a distinct discouragement to agriculture and an inducement to use land for cattle-breeding and grazing[3]. The amount of cereals produced was extraordinarily small[4], and the Celtic population were even then reduced to subsisting on the potatoes which they grew on their miserable holdings. The 'sculoag' race disappeared before difficulties, similar to

[1] *Irish Commons Journals* (20 Oct. 1703), ii. pt. 1, 342.

[2] 12 Anne, ii. c. 7; repealed 5 Geo. I. c. 4.

[3] The frequent agrarian crimes which took place in the first decade of the eighteenth century appear to have been a protest against the graziers. There was no loss of life but the persistent houghing and slaughtering of cattle whose carcases were left about and used as food by the cottiers. But although they were the only people who profited by it, it was organized on an extraordinary scale, and the ring-leaders appear to have been men of wealth and position. Lecky, ii. 351.

[4] On other discouragements to agriculture, see below, p. 523.

C. II. 20

A.D. 1689
—1776.
those which were to destroy the English yeomanry in later years; and the soil was left, to be used by cattle-farmers on the one hand and by cottiers on the other. The worst of the evils, which had been anticipated in England in the time of the Tudor enclosures and which had been already checked in Ireland by the laws against the exporting of cattle under *Absentees.* Charles II., re-appeared in the eighteenth century. There were no great households to give a market for small produce, as many of the landowners were absentees. Some of them resided in Dublin; and their expenditure was not of a kind that was calculated to increase the material prosperity of the country; living was cheap, and those who had an income *Extrava-* lived extravagantly. In many ways this extravagance was *gance.* hardly to be deprecated, as the standard of artistic taste[2] and the literary interest in Dublin was far ahead of that in London or at any rate of any other English town than London. But the indulgence of these cultivated tastes did not directly re-act on material prosperity, and the amount spent by the Irish gentry on claret, and on keeping carriages, was out of all proportion to their income. This last extra-vagance may perhaps be connected with one of the redeem-ing features in the economic condition of Ireland; according to the testimony of Arthur Young, the roads were generally speaking far better than those in England[2]. Many of the absentees, however, were ordinarily resident in England, and the continual drain which was required to remit their rents to England acted as an oppressive tax.

This evil was not counterbalanced by the importation of the mass of bullion, which was annually required to aid the government of the country in securing the docility of the *Bribery* Irish Parliament. There was perhaps no stronger argument *and Cor-* in favour of the administration of India in the eighteenth *ruption.* century by a joint-stock company than that which was fur-nished by the appalling corruption of the government of Ireland; bribery was a recognised instrument of statecraft in England, but in Ireland it was used more shamelessly still.

[1] Lecky, ii. 323.
[2] Tyerman's *Life of Whitfield*, i. 147; Arthur Young, *Tour in Ireland* (1780), ii. 150. On the road-making at Letterkenny, see Pocock's *Tour*, p. 53.

The great peculations of such patriots as Hutchinson[1] were imitated by the minor officials; in the story of the chartered schools of Ireland[2] we find a disgraceful record of the expedients to which government could resort in the effort to stamp out the ancient faith. *A.D. 1689 —1776.*

Almost the first sign of a better state of things is seen in the formation of the Dublin Society; this was founded in 1731 by Samuel Madden, and consisted of a number of gentlemen who devoted themselves personally to acquiring information on agricultural and industrial subjects, and who, both by issuing papers and offering prizes, did much to improve the arts of every kind. After a few years the society obtained a grant of £500 a year from the Civil List and a charter[3]. The existence of such a society, at a time when no similar institution existed in Britain, shows that there were a considerable number of public-spirited and energetic gentlemen, who were willing to put themselves to much trouble and expense in order to benefit their country; among those who worked manfully for benefiting Ireland, as he had done for civilising the native races of the American continent, there was none who was more judicious or more far-seeing than George Berkeley, Bishop of Cloyne. *The Dublin Society.*

On the whole, however, the condition of the population was most miserable; there was already a constant stream of emigration to foreign lands. As has been noted above many artisans found their way to the Continent[4], others crossed the Atlantic to the American plantations, and large numbers were drafted as recruits into foreign service[5]. The condition of the people was only one symptom of the misery of the country, for there had been a scandalous waste of the resources of the island. In the time of Strafford the forests of Ireland furnished a magnificent supply of wood and fuel, but they had been recklessly depleted until the country was left comparatively bare. There is no department of land management in which the rapacity of a single owner may *Emigration.* *Destruction of Forests.*

---

[1] The author of the *Commercial Restraints of Ireland*. See the introduction by Carroll to the edition of 1882, p. xiv.
[2] Lecky, II. 200.
[3] *Ib.* 302.
[4] § 260, p. 299.
[5] Lecky, II. 397.

A.D. 1689
—1776.
more rapidly use up the natural products of previou
centuries more wastefully; in a country where native co
cannot be easily obtained, the destruction of the ordinar
supply of fuel was a most serious matter[1].

*Political
ambitions
of English
in India*

263. The English had showed themselves successf
imitators of the Dutch in their commercial relations wit
India, but they did little to build up a political power unt
the French had led the way and roused their jealousy. "Th
restless action that had made the France of the seventeen
and eighteeenth centuries the fomenter of disturbances i
Europe soon found in India a wide field for its display, whil
*stimulated
by the
French.*
the ambition, that had urged her most famous monarch t
dream of universal dominion in the West, began before ver
long to form plans for the obtainment of a French Empire i
the East. He was a French statesman who first dared to a
pire to subordinate the vast Empire of the Mogul to an Eur
pean will. He was a French statesman who first conceived tl
idea of conquering India by the aid of Indians—of armin
drilling, and training natives after the fashion of Europee
soldiers, thus forming the germ of that Sepoy Army whi
has since become so famous. They were French soldie
who first demonstrated on the field of battle the superiori
of a handful of disciplined Europeans to the uncontroll
hordes of Asia[2]," and the condition of India in the ear
eighteenth century gave great opportunities for the taler
which the French displayed. It was by imitating the
measures that the English were able to hold their own, a
their ultimate success was chiefly due to the extraordina
supineness of the French government in leaving the abl
generals unsupported, and to the mutual jealousies of the
generals themselves.

1707.

When Aurungzebe died in 1707 the Mogul Empire cou
no longer be held together, and the Nawabs and Subahdars
various districts soon attained a practical independence; t
Nawabs of Oude and Bengal with Behar and Orissa we
practically independent; so were the Subahdar or Nizam
the Deccan and the Nawab of the Carnatic; while the Hind
for a time succeeded in asserting themselves under Siv

---

[1] Lecky, II. 328.   [2] Malleson, *French in India*, I. 1.

and the Mahrattas[1]. Each of the states, thus practically A.D. 1689
—1776. independent, opened a field for intrigue; and there were special temptations when a vacancy in the throne gave rise to a disputed succession. By taking advantage of these opportunities, and by supporting his candidate with a small but effective army, Dupleix succeeded in forming exceedingly *Dupleix.* strong political connections throughout the Deccan and Carnatic and over a great part of the rest of India.

The most important of the privileges, which the English *English* obtained from the Mogul government, was secured after *privileges from the* tedious negotiation in 1717[2]. The president of the factory *Mogul.* at Calcutta was permitted to sign *dustucks*, which exempted the Company's goods from the duties and taxes of the native government. The permission thus obtained led to frequent quarrels with the Viceroy of Bengal; but it was the main advantage on which the English relied for successfully prosecuting their trade[3].

The European struggle between England and France was reflected in the battles which took place in India between the French and English and the puppets whom they respectively supported. The genius of Clive first saved the *Clive.* English cause from ruin by his success at Arcot. Somewhat later he obtained a still greater success in Bengal. The Nawab had broken up the factory at Calcutta, and a hundred and 1756. twenty-three Englishmen had perished miserably in the Black Hole. Clive, with an army of three thousand one hundred men, of whom only about nine hundred were English, came to the rescue, and defeated fifty thousand natives[4] at Plassy in 1757. The immediate result of this victory was that the English became a considerable political power; though for some years they acted as the officials of the Nawab. During Clive's second administration, the English obtained from the Emperor a grant of Bengal,

---

[1] Chesney, *Indian Polity*, 2.   [2] Mill, iii. 23.

[3] Each of the rival powers placed their faith in the contest on some exclusive privilege. The Dutch carefully guarded their harbours at the Cape of Good Hope; the French had a similar point at which ships might break their long voyage, at the Mauritius. Similarly the English prized above everything else the freedom from custom which they had been able to secure.

[4] Mill, iii. 133.

A.D. 1689
—1776.

Behar, and Orissa; and in 1772, the English assumed th.
entire government of this district. Two years after Plassy
Coote had to face an European army, when he defeated th.
French under the leadership of the brilliant, but most unfor
1760. tunate Irishman, Lally. The battle of Wandewash brough
the struggle between the French and the English to a clos
so far as India was concerned. The mere fact of the conflict
apart from its issue, had the extraordinary result of forcing
the East Indian Company to engage in defensive and offen·
sive operations on such a scale that they had been transformed
into a great territorial power. The first recognition of the

*Recon-
struction of
Company.*

new character, which the Company had now obtained, occurred
in 1773 when the constitution of the Company was altered[1]
By the Act of 1773 the Presidency of Bengal was placed
in a position of ill-defined superiority over the other Pre

*Relations
of the Pre-
sidencies.*

sidencies. The Presidents and Councils of Bombay and
Madras maintained their own position, so far as interna
administration was concerned; but for the purpose of makin
war or carrying on negotiations, they were only to act witl
the approval of the Governor-General and Council of Benga
unless they had received orders direct from England, or ther
were circumstances of imminent danger. This complicate
scheme proved most disastrous to the English interest
during the Mahratta war, which broke out in 1775[2]. I
Bengal itself the President and large Council, in which ther
were frequent changes, was replaced by a Governor-Genera
and Council of four, who were to hold office for five years·

*Military
Powers
and Ju-
dicial
Adminis-
tration.*

Hitherto the Company had only engaged in military opera
tions under cover of a clause in their charter which permitte
them to defend their settlements; but the new Act recog
nised the necessities of the situation, and it also establishe
a Supreme Court of Judicature. But the attempt to appl
the principles of English Common Law to settle Easter
cases was disastrous, so far as the natives were concerned[4]

[1] Chesney, *Indian Polity*, 12.   [2] Chesney, 16; Mill, III. 430, 433.
[3] Chesney, 12.
[4] "The defect in the institution seemed to be this; that no rule was laid down
either in the act or the charter, by which the Court was to judge. No description
of offenders, or species of delinquency, were properly ascertained, according to th
nature of the place or to the prevalent mode of abuse. Provision was made fo

and no immediate success attended the efforts which were
made to check the misdeeds of the Company's servants,
though the high officials were now relieved from the necessity of obtaining a living by irregular means, as their salaries
were calculated on a liberal basis[1]. Such was the first effort
at establishing an English Government in a country which
had been conquered by the operations of English traders.
The trial of Warren Hastings, who was the first Governor
under the new system, called public attention to the real
nature of the situation, and served to show that much remained to be done before it could be said that a satisfactory system of administration had been established.

264. In the West Indies also, political conditions fur- *Rivalry in the West Indies* nished the underlying reasons for much of the commercial
regulation. Jamaica, Barbados and the West India Islands
had been of comparatively little value until sugar-planting
was introduced; but even before that time, and for long afterwards, the trade of these colonies was viewed with particular
favour, as they furnished products which could not otherwise
be procured, without buying them from foreigners. The
French appear to have been more successful as planters than
the English. They had been established by Cardinal Riche- *between French and* lieu in 1638; and though there was less room for political *English.*
intrigue than in a great country like Hindoostan, there was
much commercial rivalry between the planters of the two
nations. In 1689 the French settlers on S. Christopher's
massacred the residents on the English portion of the island;
but it was at length secured to this country at the Peace of
Utrecht. The French and English planters were rivals for
the lucrative trade with Spanish Central America, which the

---

the administration of justice in the remotest part of Hindostan, as if it were a
province in Great Britain. Your Committee have long had the constitution and
conduct of this Court before them, and they have as yet been able to discover very
few instances (not one that appears to them of leading importance) of relief given
to the natives against the corruptions or oppressions of British subjects in power.
So far as your Committee have been able to discover, the Court has been generally
terrible to the natives, and has distracted the government of the Company, without
substantially reforming any one of its abuses." Burke in Ninth Report of Select
Committee, 1783. *Reports.* East Indies, VI. (1783), p. 48.

[1] Mill, III. 351.

Spaniards prohibited[1]. They also competed for the trad
with British North America[2]; and the heavy duties tha
were imposed on the importation of West Indian produc<
other than that of the English islands[3], was the cause of th
jealousy which the northern colonies cherished against th
southern ones.

*Mexican
Trade.*
The illicit trade with Mexico[4] was valued because i
enabled the colonists to procure quantities of silver[5] wit
which they paid for European goods[6]. It was with the vie¬
of securing this trade that the expedient was tried, in 176<
of establishing in Jamaica four free ports, into which foreig
vessels were allowed to import the produce of foreign colc
nies[7]. Unfortunately however, the English officials kept
list of the names of those who imported bullion; the Spanisl
government succeeded in obtaining a copy of this list an<
severely punished some trades for the illegal exportation
For the second time this trade was interrupted by the actio
of English officials; the difficulty was now due to mei
neglect; on a previous occasion[9] it had been injure

---

[1] On the history of this dispute seé Coxe's *Walpole*, i. 556. Mr Keene, ti
English representative at Madrid, thus summarised the matters in dispute. "Up<
the whole the state of our dispute seems to be, that the commanders of our vess
always think they are unjustly taken, if they are not taken in *actual* illicit cor
merce, even though the proofs of their having loaded in that manner be found ,
board of them; and the Spaniards on the other hand presume, that they have
right of seizing, not only the ships that are continually trading in their ports, t
likewise of examining and visiting them on the high seas, in order to search {
proofs of fraud, which they may have committed; and till a medium be found <
between these two notions, the government will always be embarrassed with co
plaints, and we shall be continually negotiating in this country for redress, witho
ever being able to procure it." *Ib.* p. 561.

[2] The West Indian colonies furnished rum, which was the chief article
trade between the colonists and the Indians. *Parl. Hist.* viii. 994.

[3] 6 Geo. II. c. 13.

[4] The English claimed a right to cut logwood at Campeachy, but the Spania
repudiated it. *Parl. Hist.* viii. 684.

[5] F. Hall, *Importance of the British Plantations* (London, 1731), p. 41.

[6] The colonies had some difficulty in finding suitable returns for their purcha
from England; hence the advantage from cultivating new products. On the int
duction of rice into Carolina by Woodward (about the year 1702) see F. H.
Importance of British Plantations, p. 18.

[7] Foreign manufactures, and produce of British Colonies which served as {
raw material for British manufactures, were not included in this permission. 6 G
III. c. 49.

[8] Edwards, *History of the West Indies* (1801), i. 295.   [9] *Ib.* i. 294.

by the sudden vigilance of those who treated Spaniards A.D. 1689
—1776.
engaged in this trade as offenders against the Navigation
Laws.

There was plenty of inducement for the Northern Co- *Trade with*
Northern
lonies to drive an active trade with the West Indian Islands, *Colonies.*
as they were favourably situated for the export of fish and
lumber, which was hardly worth sending on the long voyage
across the Atlantic[1]. The Northerners were also able to procure a supply of Spanish silver[2], which certainly facilitated
their trade with the mother country. It was of course desirable for them to have as large a market as possible, but the
English islands found that they suffered by the successful
competition of French planters. That English colonists
should trade with French planters, rather than with their own
kindred, was apparently inconsistent with the principles of
statecraft; and the trade of the French colonies was destroyed
by the additional duties which were levied in 1733[3]. The
author of a very able pamphlet[4], which was published
thirty years later, argued with great force that this measure
was an entire mistake, from the point of view of statecraft;
he admitted that any colonial trade which interfered with the
interest and manufactures of Great Britain should be totally
prohibited, but he urged that discouragements to the Northern
Colonies re-acted disastrously on the market for British goods;
he maintained that the effects of the act had been disastrous
to the North, and to the mother country alike; and that it
had conferred no corresponding benefit upon the South.

265. There was another trade which connected the *The Slave*
Trade.
West Indian Islands, not only with the Spanish mainland
and with some of the English plantations on the mainland,
but with Africa as well. The African slave trade appears to
have been encouraged, if not devised, from motives of philanthropy. The American natives were physically unfit for
hard toil on the plantations[5], and Bartholomew de las Casas

---

[1] *An Essay on the Trade of the Northern Colonies* (Philadelphia and London,
1764), p. 3 seq. [*Brit. Mus.* 108, k. 50].

[2] *Weeden, New England*, 208.   [3] 6 Geo. II. c. 13.

[4] *Essay on the Trade of the Northern Colonies*, p. 19.

[5] *Edwards*, II. 45. This did not give them immunity from slavery, however.
"The traders on the Mosquito shore were accustomed to sell their goods at very

A.D. 1689
—1776.

urged that Africans were so constituted that they could work hard in this tropical climate without serious injury[1]. In the northern colonies, where white labourers were able to exert themselves fully, there was no advantage in the employment of negro labour; though there were direct voyages from the African coast to Newport[2] and other ports on the mainland the more usual practice appears to have been to ship the slaves to the West Indian Islands from Africa, and thence as they were needed, to Spanish America and the Virginian plantations.

The Assiento.

The ordinary Englishman of the eighteenth century simply regarded the slave trade as a great branch of the carrying trade which gave employment to English shipping the Assiento[3] Treaties were a bargain with the Spanish

high prices and long credit, to the Mosquito Indians, and the mode of payment set on foot by the British settlers, was to hunt the other surrounding tribes of Indians, and seize them by stratagem or force, from whence they were delivered to the British traders as slaves, at certain prices, in discharge of their debts, and were by them conveyed as articles of commerce to the English and French settlements in the West Indies. The person among others, concerned in this shameful traffic had been the superintendant himself, whose employment was ostensibly to protect the Indians, from whence, as the House will easily perceive all kinds of jealousy, distraction, and distrust had prevailed: several of the Indians and particularly the king, complained to my friend of the distracted state of the natives, from this species of commerce." *Parl. Hist.* XIX. 62.

[1] Robertson, *America*, I. 318.   [2] Bancroft, II. 550.

[3] English jealousy was roused by the treaty of 1701, which gave the French Company of Guinea the exclusive right for ten years. The Company was allowed to furnish annually 4800 slaves and in time of war 3000, on payment of 100 livres tournois each for the first 4000, the remainder to be free. For this they advance 600.000 livres to the King to be paid back during the last two years of the Treaty. The Company had the right to export goods or metals to the value of the slaves imported. The Kings of France and Spain each had a share of ¼ in the Treaty, and as the King of France did not find it convenient to pay his share of the capital 1,000,000 livres, the Company was to advance it to him at 8 per cent.

In Art. 12 of the Treaty between Spain and England in 1713, Spain gave to England and the English Co. the Assiento to the exclusion of Spanish subjects and all others for thirty years dating from 1713 on the same conditions on which the French had formerly held it. In addition the Company holding the Assiento were given a suitable piece of land on the Rio de la Plata to deposit there the negroes till sold. Specifically the rights were:

i. Leave to import 4800 negroes annually at 100 livres duty per head, on condition that 600,000 livres were paid to the King of Spain, to be repaid to the Company during the last ten years of the Treaty.

ii. During the first twenty-five years the Company might import as many up to the specified number, as it thought fit.

iii. They could employ English or Spanish vessels as they thought fit.

government, by which England secured the sole right of im- A.D. 1689
porting slaves into the Spanish colonies; and there appears —1776.
to have been an entire want of any humanitarian feeling on
the subject. The New England colonists were quite as callous[1],
and carried on the trade without scruple; there was some uneasiness in the southern plantations, for the enormous number
of slaves was regarded as constituting a grave political danger.
But from the point of view of English merchants, this was a
lesser evil than the development of such an industrial popu- *Fear of*
lation in the plantations, as would interfere with the sale of *industrial rivalry.*
English products. "Were it possible for white men to
answer the end of the negroes in planting, must we not drain
our own country of husbandmen, mechanics and manufacturers too? Might not the latter be the cause of our colonies
interfering with the manufactures of these kingdoms, as the
Palatines attempted in Pennsylvania? In such case, indeed,
we might have just reason to dread the prosperity of our
colonies; but while we can supply them abundantly with
negroes, we need be under no such apprehensions; their
labour will confine the plantations to planting only[2]." Besides *The*
this, the African trade took off a considerable amount of *African market.*
English manufactures, and the returns were largely furnished
by slaves: both as regards manufactures and shipping, the
slave trade appeared most beneficial to the mother country[3],

iv. They were allowed vessels of 400 tons to export goods from America
to England.

v. The Kings of Spain and England were each to have ¼ of the profits.

The English put the liberty accorded to them to great abuse by means of
tenders to supply their ships and got much of the Spanish American trade into their
hands. The arrangement expired with the outbreak of war in 1739, but was
renewed in 1748 at Aix la Chapelle for four years, to make up for the years of
which the Company had lost the benefit. There is no mention of the Assiento in
the Treaty of Paris (1763). Koch and Shoell, *Histoire Abrégée des Traités de
Paix*, I. 214, 315.

[1] A contrary view is expressed by Bancroft, II. 552; but see Weeden, *Economic
and Social History of New England*, I. 108, 148, 451, 834. Also Wakefield, *England
and America*, II. 25.

[2] *The African Trade, the great pillar of the British plantation trade* (1745), p.
14. Postlethwayt, who is said to have been the writer, assumes that self-sufficiency
was a necessary condition without which the plantations could not secure political
independence. "Negro labour will keep them in due subserviency to the interest
of their mother country; for while our plantations depend only on planting by
negroes * * * our colonies can never become independent of these kingdoms.'

[3] There was some anxiety as to the drain on the population of Africa, for fear

and there are numerous official expressions of the high opinion which Englishmen entertained of its value[1].

*Slavery
and
Baptism.*

The only symptoms of humanitarian feeling in England were shown, by a curious irony, in dicta which tended to confirm the rights of the slave-holder when popular opinion did not altogether endorse them. There was a general impression in South Carolina that a Christian could not be retained as a slave—that the rite of Baptism at once conferred freedom[2]. This opinion tended to check any efforts for the instruction and conversion of the slaves. Bishop Gibson, of London, was too good a canonist to countenance it for a moment, and the opinions of the Solicitor and Attorney-General as to the unaltered right of property in Christian slaves were eagerly welcomed by George Berkeley and those who had the welfare of the blacks at heart[3].

*Extent of
the import
trade.*

That the negroes were terribly degraded cannot for a moment be doubted; dragged as they were from different African tribes with no common language or common custom they had no traditions or interests of their own. The horrors of the middle passage caused a frightful amount of mortality and must have left most serious results even in the cases of those who survived. The total number of those who were thus exported from Africa has been very variously estimated but a writer who was professedly correcting exaggeration and giving what appeared an unusually low estimate, put it at an annual average of twenty thousand from 1680 to 1786. The trade had attained its "highest pitch of prosperity" shortly before the commencement of the American war. Of the hundred and ninety English ships engaged in this trade in 1771 a hundred and seven sailed from Liverpool[5], fifty

---

the sources of supplying the slave markets should be exhausted. Hippisley discusses the conditions of Africa and pronounces these fears illusory. *Essays &c.* p.

[1] Bancroft, II. 557, 559.

[2] This had not served to prevent the 'spiriting away' of Englishmen born the plantations. See Eggleston, in *Century Magazine* (October, 1884), N.S. VI. 8

[3] Bancroft, II. 553.

[4] Bancroft calculates the average loss of life in this way at 12½ per cent. those exported from Africa, II. 550.

[5] In 1804 Liverpool possessed six-sevenths of the whole trade. Young, *W. India Common Place Book*, p. 9.

eight from London, twenty-three from Bristol, and four from A.D. 1689 —1776. Lancaster; the total export in a year of great activity was about fifty thousand[1]. The dimensions of the trade, and the importance attached to it, are a sufficient illustration of the manner in which English merchants were ready to push their commerce at the time; but there is a curious irony in *Its economic effects.* noticing that subsequent events raised a doubt as to whether the trade had after all proved beneficial. The labour which was supplied by English ships to rival plantations enabled, as it was said, the foreign planters to develop more rapidly than they could otherwise have done; it was held that by carrying on this traffic England had after all only succeeded in raising up competitors with whom we found it hard to cope.

There is, as might be expected, a great conflict of evidence as to the manner of treatment which the slaves received. *Treatment of the slaves.* The most favourable statement in regard to the planters generally appears to be that the race as a whole distinctly improved under the care of their masters[2], physically, intellectually and morally, and the most serious evil in the condition of the West Indian slaves was imposed by a British Act of Parliament and in the interest of the British creditors of the planters[3]. In accordance with this Act the home of the negro who had lived for years on an estate might be suddenly broken up, he himself sold to the continent, and his wife and children scattered. This was a matter of frequent occurrence, and could not be excused as an exceptional outrage, as might be argued in cases of severe flogging. Those who held that on the whole the position of the slaves would not be improved by suddenly giving them freedom and ruining their masters, argued for such an alteration in their legal condition that they should be astricted to the soil, and only sold as part of the estate, and this alteration of the

---

[1] Edwards, II. 65. A statement of the trade for several years occurs in *Parl. Hist.* XIX. 302; it appears to place the numbers somewhat lower. A very much higher estimate is given by Raynal, who is said by some authorities to have under-rated the numbers. Bancroft (II. 555), however, considers him to have erred on the side of excess; this tends to confirm the estimate given by Edwards.

[2] Against this must be set the insurrection of the slaves in 1760 (Macpherson, III. 327). Compare the attempts to incite to insurrection in southern colonies during the American war of Independence. Burke, *Parl. Hist.* XIX. 698.

[3] 5 Geo. II. c. 7.

law was effected by a Bill introduced by Mr Edwards in 1797 [1].

Missionary efforts.

266.   The islands appeared to offer facilities for trying to discharge those duties in regard to the moral and spiritual welfare of the coloured races, which Englishmen were so ready to neglect.   Something had been done by Parliament in 1649, and a missionary corporation had been founded *Boyle.* after the Restoration by Boyle [2].   But a special interest attaches to a scheme which was the darling project of George *Berkeley.* Berkeley.   His idea was that the first step to be taken was to found a college, where clergy might be trained to minister among the English planters and to act as missionaries to the slaves and the Indians.   It would offer opportunities for the instruction of the children of the planters and eventually *College in the Bermudas.* of the Indians as well.   Both climate and productions seemed to point out that the Bermudas were more favourably situated for such an undertaking than Barbados, on which a somewhat similar college was founded under General Codrington's will, in 1710 [3].   Berkeley succeeded in obtaining his charter and a promise of £20,000 from the government but this money was never paid, and Berkeley was forced to make a start with what he could obtain from the liberality of his friends or spare from his own resources.   He crossed the Atlantic to Rhode Island, where he waited to be in readiness when the Ministerial promise should be fulfilled; but he waited in vain, and after a few years he relinquished his project and returned to work in Ireland.

Change in public feeling.

His scheme would have had more chance of success if it had been floated earlier.   During the Restoration period there had been an interest in all matters connected with the Colonies, as the long list of new plantations shows.   At the Revolution, European interests became more absorbing, and though there was some slight revival of the old enthusiasm under Queen Anne, it did not last long, and gave place under the Georges to a spirit of dread lest the Colonies should sap the strength of the mother country.   This carelessness, to

[1] 37 Geo. III. c. 119; Edwards, II. 184 n.; *Parl. Hist.* XXXIII. 831.
[2] Macpherson, II. 489; Anderson's *Colonial Church*, II. 209, 495.
[3] See *A Proposal* etc., *Berkeley's Works*, III. 219.

call it no more, about the well-being of the English settlers, A.D. 1689 —1776. deepened into almost absolute indifference regarding the coloured races who were their dependents or their neigh- bours.

267. With these ineffective efforts on the part of the *French Missions in North America.* English must be contrasted the energy of the Jesuit mission- aries on the North American Continent. The first Frenchmen who made their way into Canada were inspired by simple religious enthusiasm. The Franciscans were first in the *Franciscans.* field, and Le Caron penetrated to Lake Huron in 1615. The Jesuits followed before many years had elapsed, and founded *Jesuits.* villages and churches, and entered into the most friendly re- lations with the native races. In 1660 they had forced their way as far as Lake Superior and had established connections with the Indians of Ohio; by this means they worked on- wards among the Sioux Indians and established themselves in the Mississippi Valley; and explorers sailed down this river in 1673. From the south shores of the S. Lawrence they were constantly attacked by the Mohawks and hostile tribes; but in the wake of the Missions, French commerce *French trade and settlements.* was established and French forts were reared. Year by year the same devotion, as that which was shown by the first preachers, distinguished their successors; and not a few were examples of a glorious heroism when they suffered as martyrs all the horrors that Indian cruelty could devise[1]. The English colonists fully appreciated the advantage which accrued to the French from the success of the missionaries in civilising the Indians, and held the Jesuits in special oppro- brium. In 1670, Roger Williams, the celebrated Indepen- *English hostility* dent minister, complained that " the French and Romish Jesuits, the firebrands of the world, for their godbelly sake, are kindling at our back in this country their hellish fires with all the natives of this country[2]." In 1687 the Governor of New York, in an official report to the Lords, pointed out that the Five Nations were a bulwark against the French, and that he suffered no Christians to converse with them[3] without

[1] Marshall, *Christian Missions*, III. 289 et seq.
[2] *Massachusetts Historical Collections*, 1st series, I. 283.
[3] *Documents relating to the Colonial History of the State of New York*, III.

A.D. 1689
—1776.
his license. Some of them had been converted and gone t
Canada, but he determined to check the stream. The
methods of advance adopted by the two nations were differ
ent : and the French were far more successful in penetrating
into the heart of the country and establishing friendly rela
and demoralis- ing influ- ence on natives. tions with the natives[1]. The English suspicions of the
Jesuits and their emissaries were excusable, but there could
be no justification for the demoralising traffic in alcoho
which they carried on. The Bishop of Quebec had pro
hibited the trade in alcoholic liquors; but the English and
Dutch, who were not subject to his censures, forced this
trade wherever they could[2].

268. At the time of the Revolution the French had a
enormous range of influence, but their numbers were very
few. The English, on the other hand, formed a range o
prosperous settlements stretching along the shore. The
The atti- tude of the English policy of James II. had been as unpopular in the new England
as in the old, and the colonists hastened to re-assume the char-
tered privileges of which they had been temporarily deprived
They had been habituated to self-government. Parliamen
was not inclined to interfere in their internal affairs excep
as they affected English industry and commerce. In each o
the successive struggles which reflected in America the grea
contests that England and France were waging elsewhere
the English advanced and the French influence decline
until, at last, it totally disappeared. It is noticeable that bot
towards the natives and the French. in India and America the French were far more successful i
establishing friendly relations with the natives, but the Eng
lish eventually succeeded in making their hold upon the

393. The Governor continues "The French Fathers have converted many of these
[Mohawks, Senecas, Cayngas, Oneidas, and Onondagas] to the Christian Faith
and doe their utmost to draw them to Canada to which place there are already si
or seven hundred retired, and more like to doe, to the great prejudice of thi
Government, if not prevented; I have done my endeavours and have gone so fa
in it that I have prevailed with the Indians to consent to come back from Canad
on condition that I procure for them a piece of land * * 40 miles above Alban
and there furnish them with priests." The people of Albany supported this pro
posal, but the scheme was allowed to drop.

[1] Compare the account of the work of Sebastian Rasles. Bancroft, II. 471—474

[2] Marshall, III. 245; Brasseur de Bourbourg, t. I. pp. 139, 140; Henrion, II. 2d
partie, 609.

country good by conquering both the natives and the French. A.D. 1689
—1776. This, in part, explains the bitterness of the English denunciation of the French for employing Indians to do their fighting; but the English had never scrupled to use similar aid when they found it both possible and convenient[1].

At the time of the Peace of Utrecht, England had considerably reduced the sphere of French influence, and a much-enlarged but badly-defined territory was assured to her by the Treaty. The Mississippi still remained to France; but the whole of Hudson's Bay and its borders were granted to England; so was Newfoundland, though certain fishing rights were reserved to France, as well as Acadia (Nova Scotia); but these various territories were so badly defined as to give occasion for endless disputes. Louisiana, as the English understood it, was a colony at the mouth of the Mississippi, while the French held that it included the whole of the valley to the Alleghanies. Acadia might be regarded as including New Brunswick, or it might not; and the territory of the Five Nations, over which England had established a sort of protectorate, was equally undefined. There was, therefore, plenty of occasion for further disputes[2]. Both on the north and on the west the French took their stand upon the rights of discovery, and the regions that had been assigned to the first settlers by charter. In the case of Canada, this included the valley of the S. Lawrence, with the tributary streams which flowed into it from New York and Vermont[3]. To this region the Dutch had never laid claim, and the English could not receive from the Dutch what they had never possessed. But by making arrangements with the chiefs of the Five Nations, the English were able to erect a solitary fort in the S. Lawrence valley at Oswego[4]; they then urged that this territory was part of the protectorate which had been conceded to them under the Treaty of Utrecht. The whole of the valuable fur-trade, however, remained in the hands of the French, who further secured it by re-erecting a fort at Niagara.

The territorial arrangements under the Treaty of Utrecht

were badly defined.

The French claim the great river basins.

---

[1] Compare speeches by Earl Gower (*Parl. Hist.* XIX. 508), Wilkes (567), Luttrell (579), Burke (694), and Pownall (702).

[2] Bancroft, II. 392.   [3] *Ib.* 475.   [4] *Ib.* 477.

A.D. 1689
—1776.
*The Mis-
sissippi.*
In the West the position of the French was precisely
similar; working upwards from the Mississippi, they claimed
the whole of the valleys of the Alleghany and the Tennessee;
they had entered into negociations with the Delaware
Indians, with the view of detaching them from the English
interest, so that the French had thus extended their influence
to the very borders of Pennsylvania. This enormous region
had been definitely included in the charter which Louis
XIV. had granted to Crozat in 1712[1], who had devoted himself to fruitless prospecting for the precious metals; in 1716
his trading rights were assigned to the Mississippi Company,
which had been instituted by John Law. But the French
have never shown themselves adepts in colonisation; and
Law's great scheme for planting this enormous valley was
conducted most extravagantly. In 1720, when the Company
collapsed and the outlying settlements were deprived of support at home, troubles with the Indians ensued; the natives
were not unjustly suspicious of the schemes of the French
soldiers, and a number of them were murdered in 1729 by
the Natchez, on whom a terrible vengeance was subsequently
wreaked by the French; the greater number were annihilated[2], and the chief, with four hundred other prisoners, was

*Steady
extension
of French
influence.*
sold into slavery. On the whole, however, the French traders
and settlers, guided by an absolute ruler in Paris, were able
to take advantage of all the opportunities which offered for
advancing their interests; while the line of English colonies,
with separate governments and distinct interests, could make
no united resistance to the advance of their great rivals.

Ohio.
They were most obviously unsuccessful in their efforts in
the West; Halifax with the Board of Trade advocated the
establishment of a colony in Ohio in 1749, but the English
were foiled in their efforts by the activity of the French[3]. In

Braddock.
1755 matters came to a crisis; General Braddock was sent
from England with instructions to carry on a defensive war
and establish the rights of England over the territories
which she claimed under the Treaty of Utrecht. This
involved the destruction of French forts at Niagara, and the
cession or evacuation of territory south of the S. Lawrence,

---

[1] Bancroft, ii. 482.   [2] *Ib.* 495.   [3] *Ib.* iii. 115.

ll as the destruction of the forts as far as Wabash[1]. A.D. 1689
ock marched out with his British regiments and Ame- —1776.
troops; they were moving on Fort Duquesne which
d to be in a desperate position; but the English
were unaccustomed to deal with Indians or to fight in
st. The men entirely lost nerve; although led with
ate valour by Braddock and his officers, the expedition
in utter and disgraceful disaster. Fort Cumberland 1755.
acuated and £100,000 worth of stores destroyed[2]; the
effects of the expedition were found in the greatly
ed reputation of Colonel Washington, and in the loss
prestige which British regiments had hitherto enjoyed
the colonists.

the northern frontier, in Acadia, events were proceed- *Acadia*
ich left a deeper stain on the British name. A popu-
of natives, French in sympathy and Romanist in
n, had been living under nominal British rule for forty
When English colonists began to move up among
it was determined that their submission to the English
hould be a reality, and an oath of allegiance was forced
them; this they resisted on the ground that they
not commit themselves to be called upon to serve
t France. Their refusal was treated as treason, and
maintenance of their faith rendered them recusants.
cuse was thus found for deporting the whole popula- *denotated*.
No element of cruelty was wanting in the treatment
ceived; by a most unworthy stratagem the men were
med from their houses to a convention at which they
eized and sent, without possessions of any sort, to the
olonies. Their wives and children shared the same
id the population, to the number of 7000, was scat-
mong the English settlements; their goods were con-
l, and their homes were destroyed. "We did," said
d Burke, "in my opinion, most inhumanly, and upon
es, that in the eye of an honest man were not worth
ing, root out this poor, innocent, deserving people,
our utter inability to govern, or to reconcile, gave us

---

[1] Bancroft, III. 115.   [2] *Ib.* 125.

A.D. 1689
—1776.

*English
advance.*

no sort of right to extirpate[1]." Some success had attended another military expedition which took place in the same year as Braddock's discomfiture at Fort Duquesne. The colonists had been successful in clearing the French from the west of New York, and in strengthening the British position at Oswego; and thus the English, partly by fraud, and partly by force, were advancing towards the north and beginning to contemplate an attempt at the conquest of Canada.

*French
victories.*

The first attack, however, came from the side of the French, who, with the assistance of a large force of Indians, forced the English to surrender Fort William Henry in 1757. All Montcalm's efforts to control the savages and to make them spare the English soldiers, to whom the honours of war had been secured, were unavailing; the Indians were much embittered by the recent events in Acadia; they had obtained rum from the English, and in the morning, after their revel, they massacred some twenty or thirty of them, while many were made prisoners. It thus resulted that France had driven back the English from the Mississippi and had destroyed their only settlement in the valley of the S. Lawrence[2].

The Conquest of Canada

When, however, Pitt assumed the reins of government he set himself to organise a scheme for the complete conquest of Canada. He invited the colonies of New England and New York to raise an army of twenty thousand men; England would provide the arms and ammunition, while the colonists should find pay and clothing. A similar army was organised in Pennsylvania and the South, to go against the French in the Mississippi Valley. But the victory was not so much due to the vigour of the army as to the exhausted state of Canada, which made Montcalm's situation most

*when left to
its unaided
resources.*

critical. The British fleet rendered it impossible for him to obtain assistance from France; for more than one season the crops had failed in Canada, so that his troops were badly provisioned and the country was in danger of famine. It was under these circumstances that Wolfe's great movement was crowned with success, and that he won the victory

---

[1] Bancroft, III. 136.   [2] *Ib.* 174.

led to the surrender of Quebec. The victory which A.D. 1689
—1776.
een so dearly won was secured by the Treaty of Paris.
: English had already established themselves along the
and in Michigan, they had completely annihilated the
a influence on their northern frontier.

e immediate effect of the destruction of the French *Effect of*
in America was to leave the colonists free from appre- *colonial sentiment*
ns on their own account, and therefore less willing to *towards England.*
any sacrifice on behalf of the mother country, and in
tion to France. They seemed to have no more con-
1 the matter. This had been obvious to independent
ers for many years before. Kalm expressed his opinion
18 in terms which are worth quoting. "I have been
y Englishmen, and not only by such as were born in
ca, but even by such as came from Europe, that the
h colonies in North America, in the space of thirty or
ears, would be able to form a state by themselves,
ly independent on Old England. But as the whole
y which lies along the sea-shore is unguarded, and
: land side is harassed by the French, in times of war
dangerous neighbours are sufficient to prevent the
tion of the colonies with their mother country from
quite broken off[1]." The French in North America were
lief influence which urged the colonies to submit to
iglish crown. There had been many causes of irrita-
p to this time; but in the new condition of the conti-
the colonies were unwilling to put up with interference
would not have caused so much resentment before.

9. It must also be noticed that during the course of *Self-depen-*
uggle with France, the colonies had begun to realise *dence of Colonists*
own power. The disasters under Braddock and others
jured British prestige, and the effort to oppose a com- *and closer*
e had drawn the colonists into closer connection. The *connection of Colonies.*
ndent character of the government of each colony had
great cause of weakness[2]; and James II., as Duke of
had pursued a wise object when he tried to unite them
one rule. He was by no means well-advised, however,

m, *Travels into North America*, I. 265.
opare in regard to Carolina, Macpherson, III. 141, and Georgia, *Ib.* 185.

A.D. 1689
—1776.
Their rela-
tions to the
Crown,

and de-
mands for
revenue

from Bar-
bados

and
Jamaica.

Adminis-
trative
difficulties.

in the means which he took, and the colonists bitterly resented his scheme of suppressing their ancient privileges and
establishing a military despotism[1]. After the Revolution,
the colonists were able to assert their ancient privileges.
William III. found a series of settlements, in each of which
were different elements of population, and each of which had
a somewhat different system of government and proprietary
rights; while the relation of the Crown to all of them was
uncertain. But the attempt was constantly made to use the
power of the prerogative to control their governments and to
obtain a payment of regular revenue to the Crown. These
efforts were more successful with regard to the islands than
in the continental colonies. In 1663, King Charles succeeded
in obtaining a regular impost from Barbados for himself
and his heirs for ever, the value of which was calculated at
£6,000 or £8,000 in 1684. This money continued to be paid,
though the government had not erected the public buildings
and forts for which it was supposed to be granted[2]. In
Jamaica, the conflict had lasted much longer, as the assembly
there refused to submit to the payment of a revenue similar
to that contributed by Barbados; but in 1728 the Jamaica
assembly granted a "standing irrevocable revenue" of £8,000
per annum[3]; as the contributions from the sugar colonies
were so large, we can easily understand that their interests
were favoured by the home Government in the dispute with
the northern colonies.

Successive attempts were made under Anne and George I
to obtain a revenue from the continental colonies; but the
mode of administration adopted in England was most incon-
venient. The Board of Commissioners for Trade and Plantations had no access to the deliberations of the Cabinet, and
no means of enforcing its decisions. There were frequent
quarrels about the grants for the maintenance of government
officials. Though Parliament was interested in regulating
the commerce of the country, it took little part in the constant differences between those who represented the Crown
in the colonies and the British subjects there[4]. These various

[1] Bancroft, II. 155.   [2] Edwards' Hist. of West Indies. I. 335.   [3] Ib. 226.
[4] Bancroft, III. 13.

elements of discontent rendered it exceedingly difficult to A.D. 1689 —1776. unite the colonies under the British crown; and the effort of Halifax to get powers from Parliament to strengthen the royal prerogative, and thus to override the special privileges of each colony, was foiled by the vigour of the colonists[1].

Side. by side with these difficulties about taxation, there *Colonial defence.* had been other controversies about military forces. One of the earliest schemes of the Board of Trade and Plantations, which was formed in 1696, had been to appoint a captain general of all the forces of the militia[2]. The scheme was revived again in 1721; the captain was to be attended by two councillors from each plantation, and a hope was cherished that the colonies would then be willing to contribute a sufficient revenue. But the first serious attempt at giving effect to this scheme occurred in 1756, when the Earl of Loudon was appointed commander-in-chief. As it was ruled that the Mutiny Act[3] did not apply to the American colonies, there was no constitutional objection in England to raising troops and quartering them on the Americans without their consent, whatever the practical difficulties might be[4].

All parties were agreed on the necessity of a closer union *Schemes for closer union.* between the colonies[5]. The one question in dispute was whether it should be a federal union among the various colonies and therefore based on a democratic principle, as had been proposed by Franklin in 1754[6], or whether to adopt a monarchical plan, in which the representatives of the different colonies might form an administrative council for the governor[7]. This was proposed by Halifax; but a mode of administration which had been condemned in the old world was not destined to succeed in the new. Pitt, when organising the conquest of Canada, had shown complete reliance on the willingness of the colonists to do their part, independently

---

[1] Bancroft, iii. 33. [2] *Ib.* 150.
[3] *Ib.* 152. [4] *Parl. Hist.* xvi. 605.
[5] One difficulty which kept them apart was due to the differences of the currency in different colonies. Little metallic money was in circulation, paper money was issued by each colony separately. *Proposals for uniting the English Colonies in America* (1757), p. 18 [Brit. Mus. 102, d. 33]. Compare Bancroft, ii. 529, also 286; iii. 34. Weeden, *Social and Economic Hist.*, 38, 203, 324, 474, 797.
[6] *Short Hints* in *Works* (1840), iii. 26. [7] Bancroft, iii. 109.

A.D. 1689
—1776.
and in their own way[1]. The success which attended th
operations in which the colonists took part, as compared wit.
the failure of the British arms, did much to pave the way fo
union among the colonists themselves and to diminish th
prestige of their distant head.

*The right
of Parlia-
ment to
impose
taxes.*
During the whole of this time the right of the Englis
Parliament to impose taxes had hardly ever been questioned[1]
but when a serious attempt was made to carry out the ob
noxious Stamp Act in the colonies, the question of the obli
gation to obey the laws, made by a body in which they wer
not represented, at once came to be discussed by the colonist
From the point of view of Whig principles, as embodied i
Locke's Political Philosophy, there could be but one answer
They were not bound to obey a statute to which they ha
never given their consent; and a Parliament in which the
were unrepresented[2] appeared to have no right to tax then
Had their revolt been against the prerogative of the Crowr
they might have received much more sympathy in Englanc
As it was, the pride both of Parliament[4] and of the King wa
hurt; and the efforts of some far-seeing ministers to allay th
irritation were unavailing. Nor was it so hard to unite th
colonies in a federation, both for military and legislative pur
poses, as it would have been at the time of the Revolutior
Their common action in opposition to France had drawr
them more closely together, and their independence of Eng
land was declared and successfully maintained[5].

*Economic
policy of
England
towards
these
colonies.*
270. The policy which Parliament pursued with regar
to American industry, furnishes additional illustrations of th
principles, on which they had persistently acted and whicl
had been already fully explained in regard to Ireland. I
was, of course, obvious to those who desired to strengther
the British navy and increase the number of British seamen

---

[1] Bancroft, III. 192.   [2] Lord Lyttelton, *Parl. Hist.* XIX. 493.
[3] On the difficulty of being heard, even by petition, compare the debate o
a Rhode Island petition. *Parl. Hist.* VIII. 1261.
[4] Among many Englishmen there was no serious desire to conquer. "War o
punctilio, not of profit," Col. Barré (*Parl. Hist.* XIX. 468), Savile (*Ib.* 471)
"False dignity and a mere feather," Luttrell (*Ib.* 579).
[5] Governor Pownall's warnings (1769) as to the resistance which might b
expected from the colonists were amply justified by the result. *Parl. His*
XVI. 498.

that the colonies should be excluded from the carrying trade. Thus even when permission was given to export West Indian sugar direct from the English islands to foreign countries, American ships were excluded from taking part in the trade[1]. In 1724 the Board of Plantations supported the Thames ship-carpenters in their complaint that their trade was declining through the increase of ship-building in New England[2]. Here it is explicitly said that workmen were emigrating; and there seemed to be a danger that this most important trade for the maintenance of our navy would be transplanted to the New England colonies. Mr Joshua Gee was most earnest in his advocacy of the policy of prohibiting colonial manufactures. He would have allowed the colonists to raise the raw materials of silk and flax and to work them for their own domestic use, but not to manufacture them for the market. There was, of course, a special jealousy against any attempts to compete with England in the woollen manufacture; and it became a matter of American patriotism to wear the somewhat coarse cloth which could be manufactured from native wool rather than to buy it from England[3]. In 1699 Parliament prohibited the export of woollen manufactures from one colony to another[4]. But there was equal jealousy in regard to the manufacture of other products with which America was well supplied. The manufacture of hats was a flourishing trade[5], but it was rigorously put down; and both iron-masters and the owners of fuel united in discouraging the iron trade in the plantations[6]. This became the subject of the deliberation of a Committee of the House of Commons in 1751[7]. The Committee reported in favour of allowing the manufacture of pig-iron for exportation to England; but

[1] Bancroft, II. 522.

[2] Chalmers, *Revolt of American Colonies*, II. 33. On the rise and progress of this industry, see Weeden, *Social and Economic History of New England*, 252, 366, 574.

[3] Bancroft, III. 478, 566. *Importance of British Plantations in America* (1731), p. 75 [Brit. Mus. 1029, e. 15]. *State Papers, Treasury* 1708—1714, p. 530.

[4] Bancroft, II. 284.

[5] 5 Geo. II. c. 22. *Importance of British Plantations* (1731), p. 80. In 1729 a hat could be bought in Rhode Island for 13s. 6d. that would have cost 30s. in London. *Reflections on Importation of Bar Iron* (1757), p. 13. But compare Weeden, 309.   [6] Bancroft, II. 521.   [7] *Ib.* III. 42.

would have forbidden the manufacture of nails or steel; they even considered whether existing slitting mills should be abolished. The whole discussion is instructive; the iron manufacturers[1] desired to get bar-iron cheap from the colonies, but to secure the subsequent processes of the trade for the support of English hands. They were "men of middling fortunes," but were numerous; the iron-masters who owned the forges were large capitalists, and they were opposed to the colonies competing in their trade; and the proprietors of woods objected to the intended development of mining and smelting in the plantations as likely to affect the value of woods in England; they were joined by the tanners who were interested in procuring the bark of the wood used for smelting. The underlying assumption always is the necessity of keeping up English manufactures as they existed in order to maintain the wealth and power of the nation. Despite this jealousy of Colonial manufactures, there was every desire to encourage native products; the protection which was accorded to the tobacco in Virginia has been already described; and there was a constant encouragement given to the export of naval stores which enabled us to dispense with the aid of Sweden[2]. On similar grounds the planters of Carolina pleaded that they should be allowed to transport rice direct to Spain and Portugal[3], and that it should cease to be an enumerated commodity[4], and this was permitted in 1730[5]; direct encouragement was also given to plant indigo[6] in Carolina, and coffee in Jamaica[7].

Raw Products.

English policy contrasted

271. The whole of the English policy with regard to our dependencies has been very severely criticised. Two

---

[1] *The case of Importation of Bar Iron from our Colonies* (1756) [Brit. Mus. 1029, e. 15]. An answer appeared entitled *Reflections on the Importation of Bar Iron* (1757) [Brit. Mus. 8229, i. 1].

[2] Bancroft, II. 287; Gee, *Trade*, 146. 3 and 4 Anne, c. 10, 8 Anne, c. 13, 9 Anne, c. 17, and 12 Anne, c. 9; also Macpherson, III. 49 and 50, 2 Geo. II. c. 35.

[3] *Reasons humbly offered for permitting Rice* &c. [Brit. Mus. 356, m. 2 (37)].

[4] Enumerated commodities were those enumerated in 12 Charles II. c. 18 and other acts, such as Sugar, Tobacco, Cotton-wool, Indigo and other dyes; they might not be shipped to any place not in the English dominions.

[5] 3 Geo. II. c. 28.

[6] 21 Geo. II. c. 30.   [7] 5 Geo. II. c. 24.

things, however, ought to be distinguished,—the aims of the *A.D. 1689 —1776.* statesmen and the practical measures they adopted for carrying them out.

It certainly appears that the aims of the English states- *with Dutch* men were wiser than those of the Dutch whom they persistently copied, inasmuch as they established a commercial empire on a firmer basis. The Dutch had inherited an exceedingly profitable trade They tried to secure the monopoly, by guarding the Cape of Good Hope as a station at which none but their own ships might break the long voyage. They tried to keep a rich monopoly; but it was not necessary for them to develop new connections or take much pains in pushing the trade. They were content, too, to gain by the profits of importing and of carrying; while all this strengthened their shipping it had little or no effect in encouraging their industry. But English statesmen always *in its permanent results.* had a keen eye to the increase of our manufactures; they believed that the permanent increase of commerce depended on the increase of the things we had to sell; and they tried to push their trade in such directions as might furnish us with materials on easier terms, or enable us to obtain new markets for our goods. It was chiefly owing to this difference of aim that the English were able to leave their old rivals entirely behind, and to establish a commercial empire on a firm basis.

The French, under Colbert's influence, had set themselves *Contrast with France as regards shipping.* to encourage manufactures most heartily, but they never succeeded in raising their marine to be so important as that of England or Holland. Their shipping was outnumbered at every point by the vessels of England[1] and their generals both in India and Canada were left with but little support from the resources of the mother country. Their leaders conducted a spirited struggle and they showed real genius in the policy they pursued, but they were left without the material means of carrying out their schemes or resisting the English attacks.

The Mercantile System, then, as carried out in England, *Economic success of Mercantile System.* was not without marked elements of success. The statesmen

---

[1] *Present State of Revenues and Forces of France* (1740), pp. 15, 19, 31.

desired to develop shipping and industry; and under their
policy the mercantile marine increased, so as to rule the
waves, and England became the workshop of the world. The
foundations of her supremacy in commerce and in manufactures were laid by the men who deliberately set themselves
to cultivate these two sides of national life, and they succeeded in their aims.

*Political
experi-
ments,*
On the other hand it may be said that the greater part of
the eighteenth century shows us a series of experiments
which Englishmen made in governing their dependencies,
and that each of those experiments was very imperfectly successful. India was handed over, with what controversy and
misgivings we know, to an exclusive company; and the result
was such that Parliament had to interfere to overhaul their
affairs and to recast their constitution. Ireland and the
plantations were administered chiefly by the Crown, but in
the former there was constant corruption; and the colonists
had much reason to complain of the action of royal officials.
The interference of Parliament was hardly more judicious;
they brought about the worst wrongs of the West India
slaves, and they forced on the quarrel with the American
*adminis-
trative
blunders,*
colonies. On the whole it was in these North American
colonies that the administration was least unsatisfactory; for
the fear of Parliament prevented the Crown from straining
its prerogative in an arbitrary fashion, and thus gave greater
opportunity for the development of self-government. The
pressure of a common foe brought these different colonies to
realise their common interests and to act together; but the
effective system of government, that was thus developed,
would no longer lend itself to the aims which British statesmen cherished. Difficulties of administration in every instance interfered with the success of the mercantile scheme
of policy. It is also to be noticed that many of the measures
failed to have the expected effect or brought about greater
mischiefs than those they redressed. The world-wide commerce was so complicated that regulations which were passed
for one branch had most unlooked-for results on other trades.
*and errors
of detail.*
This has been abundantly illustrated with regard to that
West Indian trade which was so greatly favoured. But it

came to be seen that, even when regulation is necessary, it is a necessary evil; traders were hampered in many ways, and the dishonest dealer was often able to secure an enormous gain. This becomes especially clear in connection with the measures for encouraging industry. While on the one hand the mercantilists were successful in attracting capital into those directions which contributed to the power of England, their detailed regulations were so mischievous and their means of administration so bad that the great system which they had built up was at least cumbrous, if not obviously noxious.

IV. INDUSTRY.

272. The methods which were adopted during this period *Protection of native industry* for stimulating industry were similar to those which have been already described. It has been shown in preceding sections that the Navigation policy, though originating at an early date in this country, was developed in opposition to the Dutch, who pursued a similar scheme for maintaining their own shipping. In the same sort of way it may be said, that though the protection of native industry had been adhered to from the time of the Yorkists or earlier, the scheme became much more systematic in antagonism to the French, who under the influence of Colbert[1], had organised a thorough- *stimulated under French influence.* going policy of encouraging manufactures. This French scheme had, indeed, been very successful; but owing to religious and political difficulties, the main body of the artisans, who were Protestants, were driven from France; and thus England became the home of much of the industrial skill which the French had developed. It is hardly possible to overrate the importance of the new impulse that was thus given to English industry. In tracing the history of this department of economic life, we may discuss first of all the

[1] For Colbert's industrial policy see P. Clément, *Histoire de Colbert*, I. 287. Col .t's *Political Testament* was translated by Glanville in 1695.

A.D. 1689
—1776.
general line of policy that was pursued, and next the attempts which were made to plant and develop new industries.

Industrial progress
There were various political events that made the earlier part of the eighteenth century a time of rapid progress in British manufactures. The industrial development of Scotland had been suddenly checked at the close of the thirteenth century, and its isolated position and constitutional disorders had prevented it from advancing as rapidly as the southern kingdom had done during the intervening period. By the *in Scotland* Act of Union in 1707 Scotland was suddenly admitted to participate in the widely extended commerce of England[1]. This did not prove an advantage in all respects, but it led to a very marked development in others, and a considerable sum of money was devoted to encouraging her manufactures. The linen manufacture had long been prosecuted in the northern kingdom[2], but under the stimulus which it received from the opening of new markets and with the assistance of French refugees it soon attained much greater proportions[3].

and through new inventions.
The whole of the period from the Revolution onwards had been one of great progress in arts and manufactures, though it was not till the latter part of the eighteenth century that the invention of one machine after another went on so rapidly as to revolutionise the whole character of our industrial system. When this occurred it was found that the measures which had, up till that time, served as supports to strengthen our industry, began to prove fetters that restrained its growth.

Industrial policy.
273. The chief points in the policy of encouraging manufactures were; first, the providing of materials; second, the prohibition of the importation of finished goods into our markets; thirdly, the encouragement of the consumption of our manufactures both at home and abroad; fourthly, the retention of skilled workmen and the introduction of new forms of skill. There are many illustrations of the manner in which these objects were pursued during this period.

[1] The Navigation Act had interrupted the exportation of Scotch manufactures to the colonies, by way of Holland. Access to the plantations was much desired by Scotch traders in 1685. Philopoliticus, *Memorials*, pp. 101, 105.

[2] Bremner, *The Industries of Scotland*, 214.

[3] *Interest of Scotland considered* (1733). The author insisted on the desirability of attracting foreign artisans (p. xxix) and noted that in many burghs the weavers were still called Brabanders, p. 81.

effort was of course made to procure a sufficient A.D. 1689
raw wool and even of woollen yarn for our weavers. —1776.
ʏ which was systematically adopted from the time of (a) Raw
ɪonwealth was precisely the reverse of the measures *materials.*
ɪe taken in regard to corn. In 1648 the exporta-
ol was prohibited[1], in the hopes of thereby keeping
price to the manufacturers; and this line of policy
ed after the Restoration[2]. In the middle of Charles
there was a vigorous pamphlet controversy, between
who defended this policy and those who advocated
o the ancient policy of allowing the export of wool,
a duty[3]. It was not possible to put any premium *Wool.*
wing of wool, as that might have interfered with
ɘ supply of corn; but every effort was made to
rportation from taking place clandestinely[4]; and in
duties were removed from woollen yarn imported
nd, as it was thought that this might be "of use to
facturers of Great Britain[5]." Arrangements were
, with a view to the production of English cloth, for
dyes free of duty[6]; and there were attempts to en-
he cultivation of madder which was largely used
ɪrpose[7].

1647; Scobell, *Acts*, ɪ. 138; Smith, *Chronicon*, 182.   ² 12 C. II. c. 32.
's Interest by Trade Asserted, by W. C.[arter] (1669 and 1671), advo-
ɔy of prohibiting export. In 1677 his reasoning was criticised in an
ɑct entitled *Reasons for a Limited Exportation of Wool* (1677). Thomas
Discourse showing that the Exportation of Wool is Destructive (1677),
osite side, and Carter, who was himself a clothier, returned to the
veral pamphlets. These and several other pamphlets about the
ɪfacture are in one volume in the British Museum [712 g. 16].
was particularly strong on this point, and had an elaborate project
g wool so that it might be secured for the English manufacturer.
ccount of a scheme for preventing the Exportation of Wool (1741). A
ɑl was made by A. Sympson, *A short method to prevent the running*
ɪ).
ɯsier's Complaint (1726), p. 17, complains of the import of Irish wool
ʏ free at that date. 12 G. II. c. 21. The provisions of this Act only
hipments from certain specified ports in Ireland to specified ports in
ɪh like the ports of shipment appointed by Edward III.'s statute of
ɪn 1753 trade was permitted from all ports. 26 Geo. II. c. 11.
. c. 15, §§ 10, 11, and a series of statutes up to 27 Geo. II. c. 18. The
ɘd if the dyes were re-exported.
II. c. 12 and 5 Geo. III. c. 18. With the same object of securing the
ɪɯfacture of cloth to the English artisan a duty was levied by the
on all white woollen cloths exported.

A.D. 1689
—1776.
Silk.
Even greater pains were taken to procure a supply of raw silk, as the manufacturers of such goods were entirely dependent on foreign produce, whereas the native wool of England had been one of the chief reasons for the development of the clothing trade. In 1750 the free importation of raw silk grown in the British colonies was permitted[1]; facilities were given for importing raw silk grown in Persia[2], and the duties on .China silk were reduced[3]; and in 1765 there was a further reduction of the duties[4]. Another protective measure was passed in the same year; it prohibited the importation of foreign silks entirely[5], and thus gave effect to the views of the journeymen silk-weavers in Spitalfields, who assembled in crowds and marched with drums and colours by different routes to Westminster while Parliament was sitting[6]. They protested that they were without employment; and it was believed that the provincial weavers were ready to join with them in a violent outbreak. They did wreck the shops of some of the principal dealers in foreign silks, and procured promises from them that they would countermand the orders they had already given for further supplies.

Iron.   Attention was also directed to the requirements of our hardware trades. Iron smelting was still done with wood, and schemes were mooted for the encouragement of planting. They never received legislative sanction, however, but they serve to show the objects of those who were anxious to promote the importation of American pig-iron[7], as mentioned above. The

Copper.   copper manufacture of the kingdom had reached a high state of prosperity in 1713[8], and as the smelting was entirely done by means of coal, there was no difficulty about fuel[9]. When copper ore was discovered in America, the legislature pursued the usual policy and 'enumerated' it, as a commodity which must be shipped to England[10].

---

[1] 23 Geo. II. c. 20.   [2] 23 Geo. II. c. 34.   [3] 23 Geo. II. c. 9.
[4] 5 Geo. III. c. 29.   [5] 5 Geo. III. c. 48.
[6] *Annual Register*, 1765, p. 41. For other riots see *Reports &c.* 1840, xxiii. 199.
[7] Macpherson, iii. 114, quoting W. Wood.   [8] 12 Anne, st. ii. c. 18.
[9] W. Wood, *State of Copper Manufacture*, quoted by Macpherson, iii. 116. This was the hardware manufacturer who made the celebrated halfpence. A contemporary of the same name was Secretary to the Customs and wrote a *Survey of Trade*.
[10] 8 Geo. I. c. 18, § 22.

274. So many instances have already been given of the prohibition of foreign manufactured goods that it is hardly necessary to cite additional examples. There were, however, one or two cases of special interest. The English manufacturers joined in the outcry against the commercial treaty with France, which had been framed at the time of the Peace of Utrecht, but was never carried out[1]. In some cases measures of this kind were merely temporary, as the prohibition of Flemish lace[2] was intended, not so much as an encouragement to a native manufacture, but rather as a retaliatory measure which might force the people of Flanders to open their market to our cloth[3]. The legislature was in greater difficulty about the East India trade; this supplied not only silks, but muslins and painted calicoes, which were dangerous rivals to the newly-introduced linen industry. It was therefore enacted that these goods should be locked up in warehouses appointed by the Commissioners of the Customs till they could be re-exported, so that none of them should be thrown upon the home market[4]. These two branches of the textile trade, as being of recent introduction and depending on materials which Britain did not furnish in large quantities, were thought to require special assistance of this kind[5].

The policy of encouraging consumption has been already discussed and criticised as the least defensible of the expedients to which these statesmen had recourse. It is of course true that the consumer who pays for any article replaces the capital of the man who made it, and that rapid consumption induces the rapid turning over of capital; but it is also true that the destruction of useful objects is an evil; that if goods did not wear out so rapidly, it would be possible for the consumer to afford other kinds of enjoyment rather than merely replace his old comforts. But there is no saving at all in encouraging the use of substantial goods, in cases where flimsy things serve as well and substantial

Marginal notes:
A.D. 1689 —1776.
(b) Prohibition of finished goods.
Lace.
Muslins.
(c) Encouraging consumption of native manufactures.
Replacement of Capital.

---

[1] Macpherson, III. 84. [2] 5 Anne, c. 17.
[3] 11 and 12 W. III. c. 11; Macpherson, II. 709. [4] 11 and 12 W. III. c. 10.
[5] Arthur Young in *Farmer's Letters*, p. 17, condemns the pains taken to develop such manufactures. J. Massie writes with great discrimination on the kinds of manufacture to be encouraged, and the importance of native materials, *Representation*, 20; *Plan*, p. 10; *Reasons against duties on wrought silks*, p. 4.

wares are no better, since this brings about a misuse and therefore a waste of national resources[1]. In this matter of consumption the Mercantilists appear to have forgotten the distinction they so constantly drew. Rapid consumption and reproduction served for the private lucre of particular manufacturers, but it did not obviously benefit the nation as a whole[2]. The policy, mistaken as it appears to have been, was followed with much persistence. Sometimes reliance

Sumptuary Laws. was placed on sumptuary laws; the most curious of these was passed in 1698[3], and lays down minute regulations in regard to buttons. These had been the subject of legislation under Charles II.[4]; in the time of Queen Anne[5], button holes were also taken into consideration; and the substitution of serge for silk in covering buttons and working button holes gave rise to a stirring debate in 1738[6]. There was similar legislation in 1745, when a penalty of five pounds was imposed on those who should wear French cambrics or lawn; a similar fine was imposed on those who sold it[7]. Anderson[8] expresses doubt as to whether it was seriously intended to try to enforce such a measure; but it is in full accord with the policy which was habitually pursued of giving as much encouragement to the native linen manufacture as could be done without interfering with the supremacy of the cloth trade; and the facts, that it was amended after three years' time, and that the Commons refused to repeal it even when its futility was demonstrated[9], seem to show that the legis-

[1] The American determination to encourage the consumption of coarse native, rather than fine English cloth, was of a different character, economically; as the American cloth appears to have been less fashionable but not less durable.

[2] A curious illustration occurs in 1697, when a petition of two manufacturers of Prunellos was presented; it set forth that the House intended to encourage the woollen manufacture by insisting that all judges, magistrates and students of the law should wear gowns made of the woollen manufacture, and that this would be the ruin of the petitioners and their employés if it was passed. They also urged that it would do little good to the clothiers, as Hair and Silk (the materials for Prunellos) were returns obtained by exporting cloth. *Commons Journals,* XII. 87.

[3] 10 and 11 W. III. c. 2.   [4] 13 and 14 C. II. c. 13.

[5] 8 Anne, c. 6. For employing the manufacturers by encouraging the consumption of raw silk and mohair yarn.

[6] *Parl. Hist.* x. 787.   [7] 18 Geo. II. c. 36 reinforced by 21 Geo. II. c. 26.

[8] Macpherson, III. 245.

[9] Sir J. Barnard's Speech (1753), *Parl. Hist.* xv. 163.

lators were perfectly in earnest. Another measure applied A.D. 1689
specifically to Great Britain and the American colonies. It —1776.
was ordered that every vessel built in this country or America
should be furnished at her first sailing with a complete set of
new sails[1], made of sail-cloth manufactured in Great Britain. *Sails.*
A penalty of £50 was imposed on the master who did not
comply with this order, and sailmakers were obliged to stamp
every sail with their names so as to prevent the fraudulent
substitution[2] of foreign for British sail-cloth. The clothiers
of course advocated measures for increasing still farther the
home demand for cloth[3].

So far for encouraging home consumption. The export *Bounties on*
trade was sometimes stimulated by offering bounties; thus *export.*
in 1722[4] three shillings was granted on the exportation of
every pound weight of silks, four shillings for silk mixed with
gold or silver, one shilling on silk stockings, and so forth. A
more general measure of a similar kind was passed a few
years later, when the duties, which had formerly been levied
on the exportation of all sorts of British manufactures, were
removed. A few commodities only were excepted, such as
wool-cards, white cloths and such other goods as were
requisite for certain processes of manufacture[5].

275. If from these matters of policy we turn to a con- *Encourage-*
sideration of particular trades nothing is more striking than *ment to the*
clothing
the inter-connection between different sides of economic life. *trade.*
For the sake of the woollen manufacture it was desirable that
wool should be cheap, and there was a prohibition of the
export of wool from the Restoration onwards. Through this
policy, wool sank to a very low price, and it was generally *Low price*
believed that there was a great deal of clandestine export. *of wool.*
The landowners were the chief sufferers, and it was argued
by several people that there would be an advantage in return-

---

[1] 9 Geo. II. c. 37; 19 Geo. II. c. 27.

[2] These frauds had apparently been common and called forth more than one
Act. 9 Geo. II. c. 37 and 13 Geo. II. c. 28.

[3] See especially *A brief deduction of the origin &c. of the British Woollen
Manufacture* (1727), p. 51. It gives an admirable description of the local distribution of the trade, of its history with the names of Flemish settlers, and of the
development of foreign competition.

[4] 8 Geo. I. c. 15.   [5] Dowell, II. 94.

22—2

ing to the older policy and allowing the export of wool, subject to a duty which would give a preference to the native manufacturers[1]. In the conflicting statements of opinion which were put forward in different interests it is exceedingly difficult to arrive at any satisfactory light on many points of detail. Defoe, in the *Mercator*, adopted and diffused the opinion that English wool was so good that our manufacturers need not fear the competition of any other nation, and that the dread of French manufactures was illusory. On the other hand the landowners suffered from the low price of wool; and it is not clear that the woollen manufactures, with all the encouragement they received, made any very con-

Markets available.
siderable progress[2]. The Portuguese market had been secured by the Methuen Treaty, and trade with the plantations offered the best markets on which Englishmen could rely; though a good deal of cloth was taken off by the Turkey and East India Companies, the returns which they brought were supposed to interfere with the home market for cloth. The market for English cloth in Flanders could only be kept open by importing linen goods from thence, and England could barely hold her own against new continental rivals[3].

Iron manufacture.
While the woollen trade was thus slowly improving, the iron manufacture seems to have almost declined[4]; and here again we see the antagonism between industrial and landed

Fuel for smelting.
interests. A series of interesting experiments were made in the time of James I., with the view of substituting the use of coals for wood charcoal in the smelting of iron[5]. Owing partly to the jealousy of other manufacturers, and partly to misfortunes of various sorts, these experiments ended in

[1] Bischoff's *Woollen Manufactures*, I. 73.

[2] *Ib.* I. 92, 105 for figures which show a steady but not rapid increase during the first half of the eighteenth century. There seems to have been rapid growth in the West Riding. See below, p. 450, n. 1.

[3] A good many of these trades appear to have been planted by Englishmen; as early as 1665 Thomas Tilham of Warwickshire with two thousand men emigrated to the Palatinate. Bischoff, I. 72.

[4] It could be spoken of in 1756 as the second manufacture in the kingdom (*Case of the Importation*, p. 9), but the admission of bar iron from America was regarded as necessary for its maintenance and development. British Museum. 1029, e. 15.

[5] D. Dudley, *Mettallum Martis*, 5. See also the act in favour of Jeremy Buck. 2 April, 1651. Scobell, II. 153.

; and though there were one or two insignificant
)ts, no great success attended them till 1760, when
ck erected blast furnaces at the Carron works and was
o work entirely with coal. From this time onwards *Woods.*
m trade was no longer hampered by the difficulty of
ing fuel; but, till this era, the dearness of wood had
the trade to decline[1]. There had been legislation for
intenance of woods in England from the time of Henry

When permission was given to import pig-iron from *Importa-*
ca, this Tudor Act was repealed, and landowners were *tion of*
Pig-iron.
ted to grub up their coppices and use the ground for
purposes or for pasture[2]; as mentioned above, this
an excitement among the tanners.

e necessity of importing pig-iron from abroad, while
uantities of the ore existed in this country, is one of
st proofs of the declining condition of the iron-trade.
ilar cause had almost extinguished the iron-manufac- *Smelting in*
Ireland,
i Ireland. So long as the extensive forests were avail-
Ireland, smelting was carried on successfully, especially
i Earl of Cork[4] near Tallow, in Munster; and it even
remunerative to import ore from Furness in Cumber-
ind smelt it on the Ulster coast[5]. The rebellion of
iroved fatal to these industries; but they were revived
ime success under Sir William Petty; and permission
ren to import bar-iron into England duty-free in 1696[6].
ave a great impulse to the trade; and there was also a
import of Irish timber into England. The rapid con- *and de-*
struction of
on of the woods was favoured by politicians as tending *woods.*
p the country in a more settled condition; and the
es which were eventually taken were quite ineffective
ist the destruction of fuel. This reckless wasting
ional resources soon brought its own penalty. Iron-

the introduction of the slitting machine from Sweden by Foley a fiddler,
enor, 120 n.
Ian. VIII. c. 17. Frequent cases of prosecutions under this act occur in
rdshire Quarter Sessions Records in the xvirth century.
ivenor, 79.
ky, II. 330; see also Smith's *Kerry*, 95; Boate, *Natural History*, p. 71;
son, III. 73.
ivenor, 61. The native ore in Mayo was too soft, and required Lancashire
i mixed with it. Pococke, *Tour*, 81.   [6] 7 and 8 W. III. c. 10.

A.D. 1689
—1776. smelting rapidly declined, and by the beginning of the reign of George I. was practically extinct.

Taken together, the history of these two important trades seems to show that the old-established English industries were making comparatively little progress, while it also brings out the close inter-connection between different sides of *Difficulties* economic life. The mischief of the attempt to regulate *of Regula-* industry was chiefly due to the indirect harm that was done *tion.* to other callings by measures that were meant to promote one particular trade. On the other hand, it is curious to notice that, in at least one great industry, the politicians of the Revolution period allowed private lucre to have free play at the expense of permanent national welfare; their want of care for forests brought about the destruction of iron-smelting in Ireland, and the trade was only saved in Great Britain by the discovery which enabled them to utilise a new kind of fuel, and one with which England was richly supplied.

Coal trade 276. The history of coal-mining during this period is *from* chiefly that of the Newcastle district, though mining had *Newcastle* been successfully carried on in Yorkshire[1] and Scotland from time immemorial. There was a great export trade, and the consumption of coal in houses is spoken of by Petty as a new thing in London[2], and the supply was brought by coasting *to London.* vessels from Newcastle. These vessels were owned partly by Newcastle merchants and partly by those of Lynn[3] and Yarmouth[4]; but the vessels were greatly exposed to storm. Defoe tells a story of more than two hundred sail of vessels, mostly colliers, with a thousand lives, which were lost in one storm off the Norfolk coast[5]. The vessels were also in danger of attack from pirates[6]. We hear of other difficulties, many *Host Men.* of them were due to the action of the host men of Newcastle[7]; this fraternity had been incorporated by Queen

---

[1] The Halifax coalfield is mentioned in the Wakefield Court Rolls in 1308. For many references to Yorkshire mining, see Mr Lister's article in *Old Yorkshire.* ii. series, edited by Wheater (1885), p. 269. On the arrangements made for the purchase and supply of coal in Dublin, see Gross, *Gild Merchant*, I. 137, II. 66 f.

[2] Petty, *Political Arithmetic*, p. 99; Macpherson, II. 580. See above, p. 207, n. 6.

[3] Compare Defoe, *Tour*, I. 76.   [4] *Ib.* I. 66.   [5] *Ib.* I. 71.

[6] *Commons Journal*, x. 2, Dec. 1690; Brand, *Newcastle*, II. 300.

[7] For complaints in 1604, see *Report Hist. MSS. Comm.*, VI. Ap. 311.

Elizabeth, for the loading and disposing of pit coals upon the A.D. 1689
—1776. Tyne[1]. The exclusive privileges[2] of these host men were a matter of frequent complaint; while, on the other hand, the host men urged that the action of the Government in pressing keel-men for the fleet caused a serious interruption to the trade[3]. All these obstacles must have tended to keep up the price of coal in London; the complaints on this head are of frequent recurrence[4]; a considerable number of petitions being presented in 1738[5], and during the frost in 1740 the House of Commons addressed the Crown in favour of enforcing the law about regulating the price of coals[6].

In spite of all these troubles, however, the use of coal *Capital in coal mining.* became more and more general; as the century advanced, we find phenomena similar to those in other industries where the powers of exclusive corporations were on the wane and capital was being largely introduced. The charter of the host men had not been renewed after 1679, but their powers as an influential body of traders were only gradually broken. Gray asserts that as early as 1649[7] some "south gentlemen *Pumping machinery 1649.* have, upon great hope of benefit, come into this country to hazard their monies in coal-pits. Master Beaumont, a gentleman of great ingenuity and rare parts, adventured into our mines with his £30,000; who brought with him many rare engines not known then in these parts, as the art to bore with iron rods, to try the deepness and thickness of the coal, rare engines to draw water out of the pits, waggons with one horse to carry down coals from the pits to the stathes to the river. Within few years, he consumed all his money and rode home upon his light horse." Early in the seventeenth century, Lindsay, an ancestor of the Earls of Balcarres, obtained a patent for an engine for pumping water out of mines[8], but Brand does not note any important invention till 1753. 1753, when a Mr Meinzies devised a machine for raising the

---

[1] Brand, II. 271.   [2] *Ib.* 301.   [3] *Ib.* 300.
[4] C. Povey attributed the evil to the desperate competition among dealers and consequent fraud and oppression. *Unhappiness*, 28; *State Papers, Treasury,* 1708—1714, cxli. 2.
[5] Brand, II. 306.   [6] *Parl. Hist.* XI. 435.
[7] Gray, *Chorographia*, 25.
[8] Arnott, *Hist. of Edinburgh*, 67.

A.D. 1689
—1776.
coal by balancing it against a bucket of water[1]. Fire-engines were apparently in use at the time it was introduced[2], as the water which had been used to make the bucket sink was subsequently pumped up from the mines[3] and an improved pump is mentioned in 1778[4].

As in other trades, we hear of disputes between the miners and their employers, especially in famine years like *Miners in Scotland.* 1740[5]; also in 1768[6]. The miners in Scotland seem to have been in particularly unhappy case as they were astricted by law for life to the estate where they were employed; it was therefore enacted that for the future those who were apprenticed to the trade should be free when they had served their time, and that there should be a gradual enfranchisement, over a period varying from three to ten years, so as to avoid any sudden shock to the trade[7]. Other troubles arose; there were difficulties through the oppressions of which the *Coal-heavers.* Thames coal-heavers complained, and the combinations into which they entered to resist them[8]. These complaints are all of the type we may expect to find in an expanding trade, which was being reorganised on a capitalist basis. By the time when steam was really applied to industrial machinery, there was forthcoming a large supply of fuel to take the place of the devastated woods. It was in the reign of Elizabeth that the scarcity of fuel was beginning to be felt as a serious inconvenience[9], but it was not till the time of George III. that the new source of supply was efficiently worked or rendered generally applicable in the industrial arts.

Introduction of new materials. 277. On the whole it appears that the decided increase of English industry during this period was less due to the development of the old established trades, than to progress in the comparatively *Cotton.* new ones. Of these, the most important seems to

---

[1] On the whole subject see *Treatise upon Coal Mines*, 1769 [British Museum, 117 n. 28], p. 100.

[2] They were used for pumping water from tin and copper mines in 1741 (14 Geo. II. c. 41).

[3] Brand, II. 308.   [4] Macpherson, III. 484 and Brand, II. 310 n.

[5] Brand, II. 307, 309.   [6] Macpherson, III. 420.

[7] *Ib.* III. 575; 15 Geo. III. c. 28.   [8] *Ib.* III. 480, 500.

[9] Harrison, *Description of England*, p. 91; Gray, *Chorographia*, p. 26.

have been the cotton manufacture. This had, in all probability, A.D. 1689
—1776. been introduced early in Elizabeth's reign, and it had settled in Manchester and Bolton. Most of the cottons heard of before that time were really a kind of woollen cloth[1]. But in 1641 there is an undoubted mention of the cotton manufacture in the modern sense, as Lewis Roberts describes the Manchester men who bought the cotton wool of Cyprus and Smyrna from London and sold quantities of fustians, vermilions and dimities[2]. Linen yarn was used as the warp in this manufacture. There was, in consequence, a considerable rivalry between the linen and the cotton manufacturers; the former accused the latter of enhancing the price of yarn[3]. The export of cotton goods, as of woollen, appears on the whole to have gone on increasing during the first half of the eighteenth century[4]. But the very rapid progress of the trade began with the *New Inventions.* series of inventions, the first of which was the flying shuttle; *Flying shuttle, 1760.* this was adapted to cotton-weaving about 1760. There was a still more important advance in 1769, when Arkwright patented his spinning roller. A very similar machine had *Arkwright's inventions.* been invented thirty years before by Mr Wyatt, and his spinning-engine was in work at Northampton and elsewhere; but in its details, his machine was far inferior to Arkwright's, who brought out his own invention at Nottingham. Arkwright's successive inventions, with that of Hargreaves, revolutionised the trade. The artisans were, of course, afraid that their employment would suffer, and there were riots in which many machines were broken; and which drove the inventors from Lancashire to Nottingham. Arkwright was also boycotted by the manufacturers, who refused to use the yarn he spun; it was not till after £12,000 had been sunk in the business, and five years had elapsed since the granting of the patent, that Arkwright and his partners began to make a

---

[1] Defoe, among others, appears to have been misled by the name. He spoke of the cotton manufacture as earlier than the woollen. Defoe's *Tour*, III. 246. So too the name fustians could not have originally denoted cotton goods, since it occurs in the 11 H. VII. c. 27.

[2] *Treasures of Traffike*, 32, 33. One of the advantages urged in favour of the Turkey Company was that it provided materials for this manufacture.

[3] Baines, *Hist. of Cotton Manufacture*, 108.

[4] Baines, 110. The export for 1701 seems to have been exceptionally large.

profit[1]. Arkwright's frame spun a thread which was firm enough to serve for the warp; and as Hargreaves' jenny could work an exceedingly fine thread, it was possible to manufacture goods of much finer quality than had hitherto been made in England. Curiously enough, however, this improvement brought the inventors within the scope of an Act which had been passed in 1736[2], and which prohibited the use of pure cotton goods in England on the assumption that the pure cottons came from India, and that in British manufacture the warp consisted of linen threads. It was only in 1774 that an Act was passed which enabled Arkwright to sell the products of his invention[3].

The precise claims of various inventors, both in regard to spinning and carding machinery, are much in dispute; but it was in 1775 that Arkwright patented a series of machines[4] which carried out the various processes more simply than had previously been the case. At all events they made an extraordinary saving in the expenditure of muscular power.

Water-power. Water was the agent which was commonly employed to drive them; from that date it may be said that the factory system commenced, and with it began the long and unequal struggle between domestic handicrafts and machine industry which involved so much suffering, but the result of which was never in doubt.

Framework knitting. While these new inventions were being rendered generally available, serious evils were already observable in the industry in which machines had been first applied. The contest of the capitalist, with the labourer and the system of legislation which was intended to protect him, became patent. The stocking frame had been invented in the time of Queen Elizabeth. Before the time of the Civil War, however, the business was successfully prosecuted by several persons in Nottinghamshire, and even before that time a Company had been formed without apparently any authority, by the London Frame-work Knitters[5]. Their chief point appears to have

[1] Baines, 165. [2] 9 Geo. II. c. 4. [3] 14 Geo. III. c. 72.
[4] Baines, 182.
[5] One man who objected to their regulations tried to migrate with his frames to Amsterdam, but he had no success. Felkin, 61

hat they desired to limit the number of apprentices. A.D. 1689
rere chartered by Cromwell, and again by Charles II.; —1776.
e trade appears to have steadily increased till 1710,
bhe pressure of the wars was severely felt, and the *Overstock-*
rmen drew attention to the persistent neglect of the *ing with*
appren-
ion about apprentices. The journeymen and some of *tices.*
sters endeavoured to enforce this rule in London, but
t success. The machines of one recalcitrant master
Nicholson were broken; and he, as well as two others,
ed to Nottingham. When at a later time the London
ny attempted to enforce the rule against the Notting-
asters, they had no success. As a result there was a
migration of the trade to Leicester and Nottingham;
he Company proceeded to frame a series of bye-laws *The*
were approved by the Chancellor. One of these regu- *Company's*
Bye-laws.
roused much opposition among the provincial masters,
ay appealed to the House of Commons against the new
rs¹; the Select Committee² reported against the Com-
nd the evils it had endeavoured to check became more
are serious. In the decade before the Parliamentary
a, the work in provincial districts appears to have been
done by apprentices bound by their parishes, who
much misused. There was little or no employment for
rmen, and the quality of the output appears to have
ly declined. The decision of the House of Commons *Laissez*
uch interest, however, as it was a very decided step in *Faire.*
ection of setting aside the control of industry a quarter
ntury before Adam Smith wrote, and when the case
rcising that control appears to have been particularly

. The chief development of the arts, however, was *Immigra-*
tion of
due to the introduction of new materials, nor to suc- *Foreign*
inventing during this period, but to the immigration *Artisans.*
ign artisans. In the present day machinery has done
ing to put different races on a level. The inherited

Company deemed that outsiders who bought frames and hired them out
did not themselves deal in the product, exercised an injurious influence
ade.
in, 81.

A.D. 1689
—1776.

skill of the craftsman does not enable him to compete with the machine, and there are some signs of a decentralisation of industry from the districts where it has been long estab-lished and migration to any other region where people are

Great economic import-ance.

competent to tend machines[1]. But in the eighteenth century, labour was the chief factor in the production of wealth, and the introduction of a new trade was effected by introducing labourers who understood the work; whilst superiority in any trade could be maintained, as it was believed, by pre-venting the migration of skilled workmen[2]. This has been already illustrated in regard to the policy that was pursued towards Ireland and the plantations; there seemed to be every reason to believe that the skilled artisans, who were ousted from France, might be induced to prosecute their callings in Great Britain and Ireland, and thus enrich the

Various employ-ments.

nation. There was hardly any line in which we did not benefit by their knowledge of the arts; but the gain was most noticeable in the silk manufacture[3], and the linen manufacture, as in calico printing, paper-making, pottery and other arts. It is also said that there was not only a great increase of manual skill, but that the French weavers and their descendants were men of unusual taste and refinement[4].

On the whole, then, Parliament was prepared to follow the policy which had been adopted at the Norman Conquest by Edward III. and Elizabeth, and to welcome the introduc-

Jealousy of Aliens.

tion of foreign artisans[5]. At the same time it is also true that the jealousy of aliens was not extinct, and shortly after

---

[1] Compare Prince Kropotkin's article in the *Nineteenth Century*, April, 1888. On the other hand it is to be noted that only highly trained workmen can be trusted to use very delicate machinery and that in some departments of work the artisan's skill has the same sort of importance as of old.

[2] Compare the *South Sea Kidnapper*, by J. B. (1730), for Spanish attempts to entice away our artisans. See below, p. 361.

[3] It is not quite clear how the Revocation of the Edict of Nantes affected different centres of French industry. Lyons was the great silk district, and the manufacturers were united in a close corporation under Colbert. From this cor-poration Huguenots were entirely excluded, so that it is difficult to see how the Revocation of the Edict affected this industry in this district. Charmetant on *Les anciennes Corporations de la Soierie à Lyons* in *La Réforme Sociale et le Centenaire de la Révolution* (1890), p. 448.

[4] *Report of Commissioners on Handloom Weavers*, 1840, XXIII. 56.

[5] Some of them arrived in a state of great destitution, e.g. the Lutherans from the Palatinate in 1709. *Hist. MSS. Commission*, VIII. Ap. 1. 47.

ion, when trade was much depressed, the feeling of A.D. 1689
workmen against aliens was particularly strong. It ―1776.
id that aliens would undersell the native workmen,
ey would only swell the ranks of the unemployed, that
o had money would wish to migrate here, and that
·ho conducted a successful business here would return
y their fortunes in their own lands[1]. These fears
to have been exaggerated or groundless; though many
vorkmen were poor and objects of charity, there were
ne wealthy families, and a very considerable sum was[2]
t into the country, while the refugees showed no desire
rt the land of their adoption.

ıre seemed to be special reasons for welcoming the *Linen*
ıanufacturers here, as the materials could be produced *manu-*
facture in
y parts of the country. The manufacture had been *Scotland.*
for a long while, but had never attained any import-
ıd there was but little effort to attract the workers to
d, as there seemed to be many reasons why they should
ıeir way in the comparatively undeveloped regions of
and Scotland. The Scotch Parliament imitated their
ın neighbours, and set themselves to encourage the
y stimulating consumption. An Act for *Burying in*
nen was passed in 1686, while, a few years later, they
wn rules for the uniform working and measuring of
loth[3]. A large portion of the money which the Act of
assigned for encouraging the industrial arts in Scot-
as devoted to the linen-trade; there were premiums
growth of lint, support was given to schools where
ıg was taught, prizes were given to housewives for the
ecimens of linen, and considerable pains were taken to
ı models of improved looms[4]. In 1727 the Scottish *Cambric*
weaving.
ɔf Trustees for Manufactures invited Nicholas D'Assa-
ong with ten experienced weavers of cambric and their
ı to settle in this country. They settled in a suburb
ıburgh, on the road to Leith, and the site of the little

!. *Hist.* vi. 780.
les, *Huguenots in England and Ireland*, 263; Macpherson, ii. 617.
ınner, *Industries of Scotland*, 215.
ınner, 217. On the progress of the art compare *Interest of Scotland* (1733),
0, 178.

colony is commemorated by the name Picardy Place. In 1753 Parliament voted £3,000 a year for nine years to propagate this trade in the Highlands; and such success attended these efforts that in 1800 the Board thought it unnecessary to open a spinning school in Caithness as the art was so generally understood, and there were so many opportunities for learning it[1]. The similar, but somewhat chequered success which attended the linen trade of the Protestant interest in Ireland has been already noted. England appears to have been less energetic in this department than either of the sister kingdoms; but in 1764 a Joint Stock Company with a capital of £100,000 was formed to carry on the manufacture of fine

British Linen Company.

cambrics[2]. A company with a similar capital had been chartered at Edinburgh in 1746 under the name of the British Linen Company; their principal mode of operation was by advancing ready money to the manufacturers, and they thus came to devote themselves to ordinary banking business outside the limits of the special trade they had intended to subserve at first. Under these various encouragements the Scotch linen trade developed rapidly; and, whereas the average annual production from 1728 to 1732 was only three and a half millions of yards, it had reached just double the amount in 1750[3].

Silk.

Another textile trade which was introduced by the Huguenots was the weaving of lustrings and alamode silks. The Royal Lustring Company did not prosper, despite the fostering care that was bestowed upon it[4]; their failure was ascribed as usual to smuggling, but was more probably due to changes of fashion. In 1719 the silk manufacture received an additional impetus by the invention of a machine for silk-throwing, which was erected at Derby by Sir Thomas Lombe, and worked by water power[5].

Calico printing.

The art of calico-printing was another industry in which the Huguenots excelled, and it appears to have been carried on by them in this country about the year 1690, when a small

---

[1] Bremner, 219.   [2] 4 Geo. III. c. 37.

[3] Macpherson, III. 289.

[4] 8 and 9 W. III. c. 36; 9 and 10 W. III. c. 43; *State Papers, Treasury,* 1708 —1714, pp. 274, 315, 327.

[5] 5 Geo. II. c. 8.

ground was established at Richmond in Surrey[1]. The pro- A.D. 1689
—1776. hibition[2] of Indian prints had been enacted in the interest of the English woollen and silk manufacturers, but it told in favour of English calico printing. In the time of Anne an excise was imposed on printed goods[3]. The wares produced in England by printing of white goods imported from India suited the public taste so well, that the jealousy of the woollen manufacturers revived. It appears that there was a violent outbreak especially at Colchester. Defoe gives us a *Riots at Colchester.* curious picture of the conflicting interests at stake. The rioters appear to have mobbed and insulted the women who wore these fabrics, and they even threw aqua fortis over their clothes and into their carriages. If Defoe's[4] statement is to be relied on, we cannot wonder that the taste for these goods developed so rapidly, as they only cost an eighth part of the price of the woollen fabrics they supplanted. He appears, however, to have sympathised with the weavers, as also did Parliament; for in 1720 an Act was passed[5] which prohibited the use of dyed calicoes, whether printed at home or abroad. The trade suffered a severe blow; but was continued in the printing of linens, and later of cotton with a linen warp.

There were several other lines of industry which were *Stone ware.* much benefited under the influence of foreign artisans. Thus the stoneware of Staffordshire was greatly improved by a new method of glazing earthenware which was introduced from Holland by two brothers named Elers. They failed to preserve the secrets of their art, despite the most curious precautions, and the trade continued to make decided progress even before the Wedgewood era[6]. So too with another manufacture. Paper mills had existed here and there in the country since the time of Henry VII.[7], but great improvements appear to have been introduced at this time by the French[8].

---

[1] Baines, 259.　　　　　　　　　　[2] 11 and 12 W. III. c. 10.
[3] 10 Anne, c. 19; 12 Anne, Stat. ii. c. 9.
[4] Lee, *Daniel Defoe*, II. 136, 144. Cf. also his *Plan for English Commerce*, 296.
[5] 7 Geo. I. c. 7, amended 9 Geo. II. c. 4.　　[6] Jewitt, *Ceramic Art*, 76, 83.
[7] Timbs, *Historic Ninepins*, 185. The mill at Fen Ditton existed in 1562. Ames, *Typographical Antiquities*, I. 201.
[8] Macpherson, II. 647. *Abridgements of Specifications relating to Printing*, 82, 1686, Jan. 9, No. 249.

A.D. 1689
—1776.
*Trade or-
ganisa-
tions.*
279. It has been noticed above that the dominant commercial policy in the eighteenth century was to encourage
all who could engage in a trade, rather than to form exclusive trading companies. There was a similar movement
in regard to industry; the fashion for creating exclusive
companies had passed away, though in some few cases the
existing companies were utilised to maintain the standard
of goods, as in the Bricklayers' Company of London[1]. But
on the whole the scheme which found favour was that of
Premiums. offering premiums either in the way of bounties or through
the agency of some special society. The old corporations
continued to exist, and in some towns they had an active
life during the greater part of the century; but, on the
whole, it appears that they were falling into disrepute; and
Companies. the books of some of the companies, both in Coventry and
Hull, show that few apprentices were entered in the latter
half of the century, and that there was but little regularity
in their ordinary proceedings. They were ceasing to be of
practical importance. Where they continued to exist they
were looked on with disfavour[2], and the author of the *Interest
of Scotland* is especially severe upon them[3]. From the

[1] The appeal of the Stationers' Company against interlopers in 1710 (Stowe,
Survey, II. 225) led to the first copyright act (8 Anne, c. 19). On the ineffective-
ness of the printers' monopoly in maintaining the character of production see
Erskine's speech on the University Monopolies of Almanacks *Parl. Hist.* XX. 609.

[2] *Reflexions upon Naturalisation, Corporations and Companies* by a Country
Gentleman, 1753, British Museum.

[3] Lindsay, *Interest of Scotland*, p. 51. "This well deserves the Consideration of
the Royal Boroughs, who grone under a heavy Burden of paying a sixth Part of
all the Land-tax for the seclusive Privilege of Trade, and yet by the indiscreet
Exercise of these Monopolies and seclusive Privileges of their Tradesmen, Trading
is forc'd from amongst them. How many Towns, once wealthy and flourishing,
are by this become mere Deserts, as if they groned under the Oppression of
Tyranny, like those ancient ruinous Cities under the Dominion of the Turk and
See of *Rome?* So that this heavy Burden lies now upon a few, and these not well
able to bear it. They know, from Experience, the unfree Trade, as it is, and ever
will be managed, can yield them but small Relief; but if the Trade and the
Freedom of handicraft Imployments was laid open, as the *African* Trade was, the
Royal Boroughs would reap as great Benefit by the one, as the Nation in general
gains by the other. Many of those unfree Traders, who are now dispersed thro'
the Country, would come and reside in Burghs, where they could carry on their
Business to greater Advantage; the best Tradesmen, the most ingenious Artificers,
Mechanicks, and Manufacturers would, in like Manner, settle in the great Towns;
and the small Burghs of Barony and Regality, where they now live, would, in this

umbers which still survive in the northern kingdom we
hould suppose that they were specially powerful there, but
ldam Smith regarded their actual rules as less mischievous
han those of similar institutions in the south[1]. On the
hole the tendency of the times was against such bodies.
t may perhaps be said that the one or two exceptional cases
rve to test the rule[2]. The use of logwood, instead of *The London Dyers.*
oad, in producing certain dyes was unsatisfactory, and

vmt, become Nurseries for Persons of narrow Fortunes, and those who begin to
de, to stock the Royal Boroughs with wealthy Inhabitants, their Proportion
'the Land-tax would then prove an easy Burden to them; when, as we are of
a Country, under the Dominion of one Prince, and governed by the same Laws,
wy Person should be intitled to the same Privileges, Freedoms and Immunities,
you this sole Condition, Residence, and Subjection to the Rules, Customs,
rvices, and Duties of the Burgh in common with the other Inhabitants."

The various classes of burghs (Gross, *Gild Merchant*, I. 200) existed side by
le in Scotland till 1856; we find them at the capital of the country. Under a
arter of David I. the Abbot of Holyrood erected the burgh of *Regality* of Canon-
te in 1128 (Mackay, *History of Canongate*, 1), while Edinburgh was a *Royal*
rgh. There were also burghs of *Barony*, where the burgesses had no part in the
ction of baillies. The merchants of Royal Burghs had exclusive privileges for
reign trade (*Memorials for Government of Royal Burghs*, 1685 by Φιλοπολιτεῖος,
18), and the craftsmen seem to have been free to ply their craft anywhere
roughout the realm. The respective rights and functions of the *Gilda Mer-
toria* (Guildry) and Town Council, which are problems for the student of English
micipal history in the thirteenth century, gave rise to questions of practical im-
rtance, and to litigation in Edinburgh in the present century. The relations of
a Guildry and the Town Council were adjudicated on by Lord Cringlety in 1820
'alston, *Guildry of Edinburgh*, 71). The relation of the Guildry with the crafts
ncorporated trades) also gave rise to litigation; the right of members of the
uildry to import and sell jewellery was successfully maintained by my grand-
ther Alexander Cunningham, when it had been attacked by the Goldsmiths
803); on the other hand the Guildry were said to encroach on the rights of the
ammermen when they repaired watches (1793). Shaw, *Digest*, I. 214.

In Scotland till 1846 (9 and 10 Vict. c. 17) there were real craft gilds maintaining the old relations with the municipalities. Instances of attempts on the
rt of these incorporated trades to assert their ancient and exclusive privileges
we not infrequent; e.g. lorimers (1829); the Canongate hammermen (1807);
ere was a very difficult point as to the right of men who were not free of tho
avers to set up looms and weave cotton cloth (1778, 1804, 1829). *Ib.* I. 215.

Lindsay (*op. cit.*) also contrasts the trade restrictions in Scottish towns with the
mparative freedom in London. In his time it appears that a man who was free
one company (say the Fletchers) might practise any other trade, and be e.g. a
wer. But he appears to have been mistaken in supposing that this was due to
the one act of the Common Council. See above, p. 47 n.

[1] *Wealth of Nations*, Bk. I. ch. xii. p. 50.

[2] Povey's proposal to introduce a complete system of regulating labour and
ices as if it were a new and unheard-of thing, seems to show that the attempts
organise industry were practically in abeyance in 1701. *Unhappiness*, 32 f.

Parliament gave the Dyers' Company the right of search within a considerable area round the metropolis[1]. There was another case in which two new corporations were erected;

Plate workers. the silversmiths and plate workers of Birmingham and Sheffield suffered greatly in the exercise of their trade for want of assayers "to assay and touch their wrought plate," and an Act was passed by which guardians of the standard of wrought plate were incorporated in each town, to secure the quality of these wares[2]. A corporation of workers in glass was also created in 1773[3].

On the other hand associations of a general kind, for increasing technical skill of any and every sort, were worked *Society of Arts.* with great activity; the most important of these was the Society of Arts, which was founded in London in 1754[4]; a similar society had been formed in Dublin somewhat earlier, and the Scottish Board of Manufacturers administered public funds in Scotland with the same objects The policy of trying to induce enterprise and skill on the one hand, and of punishing fraud on the other, is much more generally applicable and provides greater facilities for expansion than any scheme which places the regulation of the trade and the methods of working in the hands of a limited body; that policy may serve to maintain the standard of workmanship which has been already reached, but it does not give such room for enterprise as the eighteenth century method. The *Reasons for the decay of the Com-panies.* Elizabethan statute was supposed to secure that each work-man had learned his business thoroughly, but the new method of state aid gave scope for improvements, and especially for the introduction of machinery, in cases where the old companies might have preferred to retain their traditional methods. These companies, which were generally speaking on a municipal basis, had in many cases been hostile to the introduction of alien workmen, and the general feeling that the naturalisation of aliens would prove beneficial to the country must have led politicians to look with disfavour

---

[1] 13 Geo. I. c. 24.   [2] 13 Geo. III. c. 52.
[3] 13 Geo. III. c. 38.
[4] Macpherson, III. 303. In the preceding year an Act had been passed by which the British Museum was founded (26 Geo. II. c. 22) for the reception of the Sloane, Harleian and Cottonian collections.

on the bodies which tried to thwart it. There were several A.D. 1689 —1776. strong expressions of opinion in regard to the mischief they wrought during the earlier part of the eighteenth century. In particular, Lord Molesworth[1] urged that the backward condition of many of the old towns was due to the unwise regulations which were framed by the trade corporations.

While special regulation by particular companies was *The Statute of Apprentices.* falling into abeyance, there was difficulty in maintaining the general rules which were embodied in the Elizabethan code for insuring the skill of workmen and the fair character of goods offered for sale. At the close of Marlborough's wars, it was found that there were many soldiers who had not completed their apprenticeship before leaving to serve their country, and who were prevented by the trade corporations, or under the statute of Elizabeth, from obtaining employment. An exemption was made in their favour[2]; but there were other directions in which the law of apprenticeship could not be rigidly enforced. It was, therefore, set aside in regard to dyers in Essex and Middlesex and the counties round London[3].

280. The decreasing attention to regulation becomes *The Assize of Bread.* most obvious in connection with the assize of bread. When we recall the records of the manorial courts and remember how presentments for breach of assize were of frequent occurrence, it is surprising to find how completely the habit of setting the assize was disused. The terms in which it was prescribed were no longer intelligible, and in 1709[4] a measure was passed which was more adapted to the times. In particular it arranged that the price of bread should vary with the price of corn, and not, as in former days, that the weight of the bread should be always changing. There was a further regulation in 1757, at a time of very great scarcity, when all sorts of other cereals are mentioned besides wheat, and prices of bread, of oatmeal, rye and pea-flour are promulgated[5]. This statute, however, only affected places where

---

[1] *Franco-Gallia* (1721), Preface. [2] 12 Anne, c. 13.
[3] 17 Geo. III. c. 83. [4] 8 Anne, c. 18.
[5] 31 Geo. II. c. 29. On the working of this Act compare the Report, *Parl. Hist.* xvii. 555.

the assize was set; as there were many where this practice had been discontinued and the magistrates were at no pains to revive it, another statute had to be passed a few years later for regulating prices in places where the assize was not set[1]. The wisdom of the magistrates who did not attempt to carry out this mode of regulation was certainly confirmed by the experience of the London magistrates.

Difficulties in London. During the great scarcity of 1757 they cut the price of bread as fine as possible and made it follow every symptom of the diminished price of corn[2]. In some cases, even, they set it in anticipation of a further decline. The consequence was that the greatest uncertainty prevailed among those who had stocks of corn and flour; and as a consequence the corn-factors and meal-merchants actually were at the expense of withdrawing their stocks for sale elsewhere. In fact if the assize was set too high, the bakers had an unnecessary profit; if it were set too low, the factors did not bring corn and flour to the town; in either case there was a distinct disadvantage. The only countervailing advantage was that the public were somewhat reassured by this authoritative declaration that the price they were paying was not altogether unreasonable, and were less likely to join in riots[3] against corn-factors and bakers.

Failure of the system of regula-tion. It is obvious that in regard to this important part of national economy,—the distribution of the food supply at fair prices to the public,—competition was answering better than the old method of organisation could do, whether because of the increase of internal communication[4], or because of the rise of a class of wealthy farmers who could hold considerable stocks of corn[5]. The large producers and dealers were now forming, as a matter of private speculation, store-houses and granaries such as Yarranton[6] and other seventeenth century writers had proposed to build at public expense. It was now obvious that under state-management such magazines[7] would be more expensive than they were when constantly attended to by private owners. In this case, at least, private interest

[1] 3 Geo. III. c. 11.
[2] See Smith, *Three Tracts on the Corn Trade*, 28.
[3] 11 Geo. II. c. 22.   [4] See below, § 286, p. 874.
[5] Smith, *Three Tracts on the Corn Trade*, 12. See also below, p. 364.
[6] Yarranton, *England's Improvement*, p. 114.   [7] Smith, *Tracts*, 14.

was on the whole working for the public benefit, and attempts A.D. 1689 —1776. to interfere directly for the public good either enabled the capitalist to reap a large gain without performing any corresponding services, or forced him to hold back his stock and thus increase a public scarcity.

While this oldest scheme for regulating prices was thus *The Assize of Cloth and the Aulnager.* falling into abeyance, there were other complications in regard to the trades for which the assize of cloth had been originally devised. The establishment of an aulnager in Ireland[1], and the desire of weavers there for the better regulation of their trade, serve to show that public opinion endorsed these methods of maintaining quality at the end of the seventeenth century; the Irish Parliament continued to rely on this policy in 1705, and laid down elaborate regulations which they enjoined the corporations of weavers to enforce[2]. But in England, where the manufacture of cloth *Trademarks.* was so large and so various, the system of trade-marks had completely established itself.

The chief evils to which public attention was called, were *Embezzlement and Fraud.* connected with the earlier processes of manufacture; there were many complaints against workmen who embezzled materials, or unduly delayed their work, or broke contracts[3], or were guilty of other frauds, both in the various branches of the textile trades[4] and among shoemakers[5].

It was almost impossible for the clothiers and employers *Supervision of workmen.* to supervise men each working in his own home. In 1727 the Justices were empowered to appoint inspectors who should have the power to inspect all the premises in Wiltshire, Gloucestershire and Somersetshire, where the dry branch of the cloth manufacture was carried on[6], and a similar measure was passed for Yorkshire in 1765[7]. In this, as in many similar measures, Justices of the Peace, who were themselves clothiers, were prohibited from taking a part in these appointments; but the measures did not prove effective, and it was alleged that the clothiers suffered severely from the *Combination of clothiers.* fraud and negligence of the working manufacturers, though

---

[1] *Irish Statutes*, 17 and 18 Charles II. c. 15, § 9.

[2] *Irish Commons Journals*, II. i. 481.   [3] 6 Geo. III. c. 25.

[4] 1 Anne, stat. ii. c. 18; 22 Geo. II. c. 27; 17 Geo. III. c. 56.

[5] 9 Geo. I. c. 27.   [6] 18 Geo. I. c. 23.   [7] 5 Geo. III. c. 51.

A.D. 1689
—1776.

it was rarely worth their while to prosecute a poor man even when he was grossly to blame[1]. Thus masters were allowed to combine for the prosecution of fraud in connection with trade, and in this way a right of combination was conceded to the masters[2], which had been and continued to be denied

1777.

to the men. This measure was passed at the very time when the first important changes were being made through the invention of machinery; there had been riots in Somersetshire[3] against the owners of machines. But attempts were also made to insure fairness on the part of the employers,

Truck.

both by measures against truck[4] and by giving new powers for dealing with masters who acted extortionately towards their apprentices, as well as by imposing penalties where uncertain weights were used in giving out materials[5].

Mischievous effects of Bounties.

Another form of fraud arose out of the special mode of encouraging industry which had become popular during the eighteenth century. Crimes became more frequent, as the offering of bounties had given a direct encouragement to fraudulent attempts to obtain the bounties, without performing the conditions on which they were offered. Frauds of this kind appear to have been very frequent in the linen trade[6] and also in the herring trade. It may be paralleled by the conduct of those burgesses who had in old days coloured the goods of outsiders, and thus joined with them in obtaining a gain at the expense of their town. In the same way there were constant frauds upon the revenue, by passing foreign goods as of home manufacture[7], or by endeavouring in other ways to obtain bounties fraudulently. These, along with the increase of smuggling, were evils which sprang directly out of attempts at the national encouragement of industry. It is impossible to estimate the pecuniary loss which occurred[8], and the demoralisation which was due to these premiums on

[1] All through the eighteenth century, the term manufacturer is applied, as in Johnson's *Dictionary*, to the working craftsman, not to the capitalist, who is generally spoken of as a clothier. [Temple's] *Considerations on Taxes*, p. 2, is an early (1755) instance of the modern sense of the word.

[2] 17 Geo. III. c. 11; 24 Geo. III. c. 3.   [3] Macpherson, III. 592.

[4] 22 Geo. II. c. 27; 1 Anne, stat. ii. c. 18.   [5] 13 Geo. I. c. 28.

[6] 18 Geo. II. cc. 24, 25.   [7] Linen, 18 Geo. II. c. 24; sail-cloth, 9 Geo. II. c. 27.

[8] The smuggling of wool to the continent during the period when the export was absolutely prohibited attained enormous proportions. Bischoff, I. 241.

the law and on dishonesty brought about a serious *A.D. 1689 —1776.*
of the ordinary respect for the law.

The assize of bread had fallen into disuse, and there *The assessment of wages in-operative.*
son to believe that the practice of regulating wages
lance with the plenty and scarcity of the time was
y in vogue during the seventeenth century. There
ccasion of bad harvests and the labourers must have
severely[1]. The price for the four years ending in
s 55/6 a quarter, or more than double what it had
the four years ending with 1691. As the coinage in
er period was much debased and had been restored
, this difference of nominal prices is all the more
ble; but though there was great complaint at various
the want of employment, whether through foreign
tion as in the silk trade, or the overstocking with
ces, or through commercial disasters as in the cotton
it little remark appears to have been made about the
wages. The high prices of corn were maintained till
ien there was a considerable drop; and from 1715 to
m 1729 to 1739, and from 1741 to 1751 the price of
itinued exceedingly low[2]. During these seasons of
he labourer was in all probability well off[3], and no
tion was made in the machinery for regulating wages
'[4]. This measure, however, recognises that the prac- *Enabling Statute.*
assessing labourers' wages had fallen into disuse in
aces, at all events as a regular part of the justices'
for the statute empowered interested parties to
that the justices should state a price; and it was
ling rather than an enacting measure.
795 the practice of assessing wages had not only fallen
ise, but had dropped out of mind. In that year the
ire assessment of wages for 1725 was published as an *Exceptional case.*
l curiosity[5], and it excited surprise "that any magis-

, *History of Prices*, I. 30.   [3] Smith, p. 101.
r Young frequently calls attention to the increase of tea-drinking, and
r was again replacing rye. *Farmers' Letters*, 197 and 283. Smith, *Three*
. Another writer treats the use of butter as a new luxury among cot-
ssay on *Tea, Sugar, White Bread and Butter* (1777) [Brit. Mus. 8275,
See below, pp. 387, 493 n. 3.   [4] 19 Geo. II. c. 19.
Hibbert informs me that a new assessment was made in Shropshire in

trates in the present century would venture on so bold a measure." The assessment enters into great detail as to the wages of servants hired by the year, by the day and week, and by piece-work. The rates named are supposed to be maximum rates, and there is a recommendation that somewhat lower rates should be adopted in the northern parts of the county. The document contains a clear summary of the labour laws of the period, denounces the conduct of "artificers, workmen and labourers that conspire together concerning their work and wages," and notes that the person who gives more than the appointed wages shall forfeit five pounds and be imprisoned ten days[1].

Riots.

There are, indeed, many evidences of dissatisfaction on the part of labourers and artisans, which took the forms of attacks on bakers or corn-factors[2], or riots against machines[3]; but in several cases the rate of wages was one element in a dispute. Thus, the journeymen tailors[4] of London in 1720, like their predecessors three centuries before, were forming combinations and trying to diminish the length of their hours and increase the rates of pay. This was met by a measure which defined the hours strictly, and the pay also, though power was reserved to the local authorities to revise these statutable rates when necessary. There must have been a similar movement on a more widely extended scale among the woollen weavers. They were entering into combinations to frame by-laws and regulate prices and wages, and the legislature interfered[5] on more than one occasion to prohibit their conduct. In these cases it is obvious that they were aspiring at organising a system for regulating the whole trade. The state professed to regulate wages and hours so far as it could be advantageously done, and if this had been really done, these laws would not have been oppressive. When the legislative regulation of hours and wages was entirely discontinued, the combination laws still survived to

Combinations among tailors

and woollen weavers.

1732, and was repeated in full in 1733, 1734, 1735, 1738, and 1739. From 1709 to 1732, the Justices regularly ordered the old rates of wages should continue. Several other cases are alluded to by Mr Hewins, *English Trade and Finance*, pp. vii, 83, 160.

[1] *Annals of Agriculture*, xxv. 305.   [2] *Annual Register*, 1766, p. 127.
[3] Spitalfield Weavers, Lecky, iii. 136.   [4] 7 Geo. I. c. 13.
[5] 12 Geo. I. c. 34; 22 Geo. II. c. 27.

prevent the artisans from joining together to drive more A.D. 1689 —1776.
favourable bargains with their masters[1]; indeed they were
einforced with greater stringency in 1800[2].

But probably the most serious grievances of the artisans *The Poor Law and*
n the eighteenth century were connected with the Elizabe-
han method of relieving the poor. Parliament had created
great pension fund for the worn-out workmen, and the
ettlement Acts of Charles II. had defined the terms of resi-
ence which gave a man a right to claim his retiring allow-
nce in any particular place. The jealousy which was felt in
any districts of the incursion of strangers, who might become
hargeable to the parish, was a serious obstacle which pre-
ented artisans from leaving congested districts and taking
dvantage of higher rates of wages, which might have been
btained in other places. The grievances have been well
escribed in the *Wealth of Nations*[3], and the system did
nterfere with the fluidity of labour. At the same time it
aust be remembered that the problem, which thus presented
taelf, is still unsolved. There is the greatest difficulty in
giving the security of a pension or of maintenance in old *the fluidity of labour.*
age, without tying the labourer to the service of a particular
employer or to some special area, and in so far as this is
done, the fluidity of labour is sacrificed in the hope of securing
the comfort of the labourer in his declining years.

So far as internal migration is concerned, the measures
which discouraged it were not directly aimed at this object.
But there was a very deliberate intention to discourage the *Dis-couragement of Emigration.*
emigration of skilled artisans to foreign countries or to our
colonies. The history of the improvements in English
industry, through the incursion of aliens, as well as the story
of the plantation of the cloth manufacture in continental
lands, seems to show that the danger was a real one, if it was
desired to maintain the relative superiority of England in
any branch of manufacture. Instances have already been
given which illustrate this policy in regard to the colonies; a
very stringent measure was passed in 1718 of a perfectly

---

[1] See below, § 367, p. 608, and § 377, p. 644.   [2] 40 Geo. III. c. 106.
[3] Bk. I. c. x. p. 57. He shows the illusory character of the relief granted by
the system of Certificates. 8 and 9 W. III. c. 30. See also Massie, *Plan*, 96.

general character, as it prohibited artisans from going across the sea at all and insisted that those who had done so should promptly return[1].

V. AGRICULTURE.

282. During the period under consideration there was a considerable expansion of commerce and a marked increase in industry; but by far the most remarkable changes were *Applica-tion of Capital* those connected with the management of the land. These may be summed up by saying that the era of capitalist farming had begun, that the old traditional methods of agriculture were being displaced by men who were bent on improving the production of the soil. It has been pointed out in a preceding chapter that there are traces of the employment of capital in the cloth manufacture in the fifteenth century, and that the division between employers and employed then began to show itself. In the intervening period the formation of capital had been most rapid, and great mercantile enterprises had been floated and developed by means of joint-stock companies; but large funds of wealth were not applied to the improvement of the soil till the eighteenth century. *to the soil* The return of such an employment of capital is always slow and always uncertain; it was perhaps the greatest sign of the increased wealth of England, that so many men were able to devote large sums to costly experiments and gradual improvements. The man with small savings would be more likely to employ it in some remunerative branch of trade *by wealthy men.* where he had the prospect of a more rapid return. Hence we need not be surprised to find that the great revolution in English agriculture took place from above, and that it was first attempted and carried through under the influence of men of wealth. In carrying out these improvements they had to contend, not only with the difficulties which were due to deficiency of knowledge since scientific agriculture did not exist, but with the time-honoured prejudices of those who had

---

[1] 5 Geo. I. c. 27. See above, p. 348, and below, p. 608.

, traditional methods and who were constitutionally A.D. 1689
, any change.   —1776.

ing is more striking than the contrast between the *Modern*
.ch intelligent contemporaries took of these changes *judgments on the*
which is commonly expressed at the present day. *landed gentry.*
resent day we hear of the greed of the wealthy mer-
who bought out the yeomanry to acquire political
r of the selfishness of the landed classes in taking
which should increase their rents. So far as the *Alleged*
iggestion goes, it is sufficient to point out, as Professor *political motive for*
Rogers has done[1], that it was impossible for a land- *buying out free-*
acquire political influence through his tenants, till *holders.*
first Reform Bill, as none but freeholders had votes.
riting in 1766 was apparently quite unaware of this
endency to buy out freeholders. In discussing the
enclosures, and in support of his assertion that
s did not tend to the diminution of the population,
inter alia " there is scarce any county in which the
of freeholders does not turn out upon an election
h more considerable than formerly[2]." The second *The raising*
i gives another illustration of the principle, which *of rents.*
ming clearer during the eighteenth century, that in
ies private interest accords with public gain. Rents
sed; in some cases Arthur Young recommends a
increase of rent as a method of forcing the tenantry
less slovenly methods of cultivation[3]. But on the
e raising of rents followed as a consequence of genuine
e in the management of land on the part of the
It is difficult to conceive what Arthur Young's *Arthur*
would have been, if he had known how posterity *Young's admiration*

sturies *of Work and Wages,* 478.
y on the Nature and Method of the Enclosure of Common Fields, p.
ce the surveyor advises the buying up small freeholds to round off
to render enclosure possible; but his advice appears to have been
nomic grounds, and it is not clear that it was much acted on. *Duty*
1727), Articles xiii., xiv.
m *Tour,* II. 84. " If it be demanded, how such ill courses are to be
nswer, raise their rents. First with moderation, and if that does not
industry, double them. But if you would have a vigorous culture go
row 15 or 20 of these farms into one, as fast as the present occupiers

A.D. 1689
—1776.
for enter-
prising
land-
owners.
would brand the men whose endeavours he watched with
such interest and admiration. To him they were the greatest
of patriots, for whom no praise could be too high. They were
"spirited cultivators" who managed their land in such a
fashion as to deserve "every acknowledgment which a lover
of his country can give." He is full of enthusiasm for their
experimental farms, new patterns of agricultural implements,
and new plans for laying out farm buildings; as well as for
the care which they bestowed on the smallest points of land
management. Perhaps we may feel that the judgment of a
contemporary, who mixed with these men and discussed their
successes and failures, was formed on better grounds than
that of those who decry the landlords at a distance of more
than a century and gratuitously attribute to them the meanest
motives.

The progress was initiated by wealthy landlords; but in
order to carry out their schemes effectively it was necessary
that there should be enterprising farmers too. And those
who were improving estates preferred to throw the farms
together, so as to substitute farms of three hundred acres
and upwards for farms of one hundred acres and under.
With the possible exception of poultry farming there was no
department of agriculture in which small farms proved more
advantageous to the public[1]. As the usual calculation appears to have been that at least five pounds an acre was the
requisite capital in order to work the land, the large farmers
were men who could start in life with fifteen hundred or two
thousand pounds; and thus we find signs of a middle class in
the country, who were capitalists and employers of labour,
but who did not themselves own land, and did not engage in
the actual work of the farm with their own hands. These
men had an advantage over the small farmers, inasmuch as
they were able to hold their stocks of corn for a longer period,
and get the advantage of a rise of price, whereas the poorest
of the small farmers were forced to realise at once, and were
compelled to dispose of their whole harvest by Christmas at
latest[2]. They were also able to afford better seed, better

[1] [Arbuthnot] *An Inquiry into the connection between the present price of Provisions and the size of Farms* (1773), p. 21.   [2] Smith, *Three Tracts*, p. 12.

implements, and to work the land on better principles, and A.D. 1689
hence they were able to pay a larger rent than the small —1776.
farmers who stuck to the old-fashioned methods.

283. Arthur Young has given us an inimitable picture *Arthur Young's*
of England during the period of transition. He was a man *Tours.*
of very varied tastes and interests, who had engaged in farming on a small scale. His observations, when making a
business journey into Wales through the south of England, excited so much interest among agriculturists, that he
planned a northern tour, with the express object of gathering information on the state of rural England; he took considerable pains to render his enquiry as complete as possible.
He advertised in the newspapers which circulated within the *His method*
area of his projected tour, and some of his correspondents *of enquiry*
were able to supply him with accurate statistical information; in other cases he had to rely on what he could gather
in conversation with illiterate farmers, who were suspicious of
his motives in prying into their affairs. "My business was so
very unusual that some art was requisite to gain intelligence
from many farmers, etc. who were startled at the first attack.
I found that even a profusion of expense was often necessary
to gain the ends I had in view: I was forced to make more
than one honest farmer half-drunk, before I could get sober,
unprejudiced intelligence[1]." The contrast between his own
habits of accurate observation and the slovenliness of many
of the farmers is very striking. He asserts that he had the *and quali-*
qualifications for his work which came from practical ac- *fications for the*
quaintance with agriculture; but he adds "what is of much *task.*
more consequence towards gaining real experience, I have
always kept, from the first day I began, a minute register of
my business; insomuch that upon my Suffolk farm I minuted
above three thousand experiments; in every article of culture,
expenses, and produce, including among a great variety of
other articles an accurate comparison of the old and new
husbandry in the production of most vegetables. But in this I
would by no means be thought to arrogate any other than that
plodding merit to which any one of the most common genius
can attain, if he thinks proper to take the trouble[2]." His

[1] *Northern Tour*, i. xiii.　　　　　[2] *Ib.* i. ix.

book abounds with figures in which he was at pains to reduce
the curious and complicated local measures to a common
standard, for the convenience of his readers it is true, but to
the loss of those who are curious in metric systems.

*Survival of
primitive
methods.*
There are, however, many passages in his writings which
describe the survival of primitive practices[1]. Thus at Boyn-
ton, in Yorkshire, he found remains of extensive culture[2].
He was informed by Sir Digby Legard that the farmer on
*Extensive
culture.*
the wolds of the East Riding "every year has been accustomed to plough up a fresh part of his sheep walk, to take a
crop or two, and then let it lie fifteen or twenty years till the
natural grass has again formed a kind of turf, but it will
sometimes be forty years before the land is completely sodded
over. This ruinous practice is but too common; and where
it has long prevailed, the farmer seldom has a three-fold
increase[3]."

*Two-field
and three-
field
systems.*
There were other cases where the two-field or three-field
system was still in vogue, thus in the neighbourhood of
Ecclesfield, in Hallamshire, the usual course was as follows:
first fallow, second barley, third clover, and fourth wheat.
This is obviously the two-field system, with the introduction
of clover in place of every second fallowing. His comment is
a sweeping condemnation of the early middle ages, "This is
very bad husbandry." At Beverley[4] there was a similar
modification of the two-field system, with the use of peas
in place of clover. He notes the three-field system, first
fallow, second wheat, third oats, but does not criticise it[5].

*Plough
teams.*
What however roused his strongest condemnation was the
extravagance of the ploughing[6]. Near Woburn "they use
four or five horses at length in their ploughs, and yet do no
more than an acre a day. The reader will not forget, the
soil being sandy, the requisite team is certainly nearer

---

[1] These are genuine survivals; the primitive character of English Agriculture
in the xviith century is shown from the accounts of the arrangements which were
transplanted to New England; see the accounts of common field cultivation, common fencing, herding etc., in Weeden, *New England*, 58. But these might be
some extent revivals, as well as survivals, since the special conditions of the new
country would require special developments.

[2] *Northern Tour*, ii. 7.　　　　　[3] *Ib.* ii. 14.
[4] *Ib.* ii. 1.　　　　　　　　　　[5] *Ib.* i. 126.
[6] *Southern Tour*, 298, 300.

single jackass than five horses. This miserable management A.D. 1689 —1776.
cannot be too much condemned[1]." At Offley, near Hitchin,
"they never plough without four horses and two men, and do
but an acre a day; this terrible custom, which is such a bane
to the profits of husbandry, cannot be too much condemned;
for the whole expense (on comparison with the common
custom) of tillage might be saved by the farmer if he would
adopt the rational method of tilling with a pair of horses, and
one man to hold the plough and drive at the same time[2]."
He was however by no means a reckless innovator; he was
much interested in weighing the relative merits of oxen and
horses for ploughing and draught[3], and was inclined to question the wisdom of dispensing with oxen[4].

The raising of peas and beans formed part of the tradi- *Peas and Beans.*
tional agriculture: near Woburn "they give but one tilth for
beans alone, sow them broadcast, never hoe them, but turn
in sheep[5] to feed off the weeds and reckon three quarters a
middling crop" from four bushels sown. "This is an exe-
crable custom, and ought to be exploded by all landlords of
the country." In fact the prevailing evil of the old hus- *Weeds.*
bandry was the mass of weeds which sometimes appear to
have got the better of the crop altogether. Thorough ploughing and fallowing did much to clear the land; but it appears
that some of the earlier attempts at improvement were most
unsatisfactory. Thus the introduction of turnips in the East
Riding of Yorkshire seems to have been positively mischievous though "the soil is good turnip land, but," as he *Turnips.*
continues, "their culture is so wretchedly defective, that I
may, without the imputation of a paradox, assert, they had
better have let it alone. Very few of them hoe at all, and
those who do, execute it in so slovenly a way, that neither
the crop nor the land are the least the better for it. With
such management, turnips are by no means beneficial in a
course of crops, as they leave the soil so foul that a fallow
rather than another crop ought to succeed. The great benefit

[1] *Northern Tour*, I. 41. [2] *Ib.* 22.
[3] *Ib.* I. 169, II. 70, and *Southern Tour*, 151, 203, 212.
[4] *Northern Tour*, I. 146. He argues for oxen in the *Farmers' Letters*, 166.
[5] *Northern Tour*, I. 40, 41. Compare the Scotch practice (1735), as described in Alexander's *Notes of Northern Rural Life* (1877). Brit. Mus. 12314, ee. 3.

of turnips is not the mere value of the crop, but the cleaning the land so well as to enable the farmer to cultivate the artificial grasses with profit......The farmers of this country ought therefore to neglect turnips totally, or cultivate them in the clean husband-like manner that is practised in many parts of England, of thoroughly pulverizing the land and hoeing them twice or thrice, or as often as necessary, to keep them distinct from each other, and perfectly free from weeds. Turnips would then be found an excellent preparation for barley or oats, and for the artificial grasses sown with them[1]."

Pasture and Common Fields. Mistakes also occurred in laying down pasture when the land was enclosed and convertible husbandry was introduced. Arthur Young was of course a determined opponent of the common-field husbandry[2]. Indeed, so long as it lasted, the other improvements which he strenuously advocated could not be attempted; but he was an unsparing critic of the expensive method by which this improvement was carried out[3]; the legal charges were exorbitant, and the subsequent expense

Expense of Enclosing. of fencing[4] was very heavy[5]. He was also well aware that enclosing would not by itself work magic, but that there must be careful management of the land when newly laid out, or the profit would entirely disappear. One error of judgment, which he specially condemns, was the conduct of

---

[1] *Northern Tour*, I. 217, 218.   [2] *Ib.* I. 64; II. 74.

[3] The various steps which had to be taken are fully described by Homer, *Essay on the method of ascertaining specific shares* (1766), 42—109.

[4] *Northern Tour*, 23.

[5] *Ib.* I. 223. "The attorney delivers his bill to the commissioners, who pay him and themselves without producing any account, and in what manner they please. Is it therefore any wonder, that the expenses previous to the actual inclosing the ground are very frequently (unless where the township is very small) from £1800 to £2000, all which is levied and expended by the commissioners absolutely, and without control? To this extravagant expense add, that attending the inclosure itself, the making the ditches; the posts and railing; buying and setting the quickwood, etc. this, added to the former expense, must surely run away with the greater part of the profits expected from the inclosure. But what must we think of the indolence of the proprietors who will thus unnecessarily neglect the great improvement of their estates to advance the private interests of the commissioners, etc. For a proof of this enormous power, see the following extract from an Act, which gives an *absolute* and *unlimited* power to the commissioners to raise *whatsoever sums* they please and to assess them in the *proportions* and *in such manner* as they think proper."

·ho sowed their pastures with common clover, which A.D. 1689
n worn out and left the soil bare. —1776.

descriptions enable us to understand the nature of *Root crops*
inges that were taking place. Root crops had been *common.*
ced during the seventeenth century, but in many
hey were badly managed; and in some districts the
i and butchers actually preferred an inferior to a good
' turnips[1]. In such cases the slovenly habits, which
erised the growth of cereals, also affected the green
iat had been much more recently introduced. There
owever some districts where they were little known
ght have been tried with advantage; on the whole,
r, what was needed was the better working of the
so as to keep it clear from weeds. In regard to
iatters, agricultural science was fairly advanced, but
tural practice lagged behind.

the other hand, little progress had been made any- *Seeds and*
with the cultivation of seeds and the extension of *Rye Grass.*
ind rye grass. Arthur Young is particularly careful
i what success attended attempts to cultivate these
and improve pastures[2], and he gets quite enthusiastic
ie accurate results which were recorded at various
iental farms. He was interested in the increased
iion of potatoes, carrots, cabbages, or anything else;
i growing of artificial grasses was the department in
igricultural science, as distinguished from agricultural
i, made most progress during this century[3]. The great
le of the so-called new husbandry was to introduce
tivation of roots and seeds in such a fashion as to
nent corn-growing. There was no desire to substitute
ig else for corn-growing, as pasture-farming had been
ited for arable cultivation in the fifteenth and six-
centuries. The point maintained throughout was, *Fallowing*
careful attention was given to the qualities of the *superseded.*
d energy was expended on the working of the land,
:oot and grass crops might be introduced so as to
unnecessary the fallow shift every second or third

[1] *Northern Tour.* I. 107.   [2] *Ib.* I. 32, 105.
[3] Thorold Rogers, *Six Centuries*, 468.

year. Thus, what he commonly recommends, is a course of turnips, wheat, clover and barley, an arrangement which may be said to be a development of alternate cropping and fallowing. He preferred, however, that the land should be two years under clover, which thus gave a five course husbandry.

Enclosing advantageous

Such improvements in the working and management of land generally though not necessarily involved the enclosing of common fields. As one of the great mischiefs, which eighteenth century improvers wished to remove, was the prevalence of weeds, a single lazy farmer who allowed his strips in the common field to be covered with thistles and let these thistles seed, would do an infinity of mischief to all neighbours. The case of farmer Riccart, near Audley End, brought this home forcibly to Arthur Young[1]. While the one indolent man was able to do much mischief, a man of enterprise was greatly hampered; for if he worked along with his neighbours in open fields, he might be obliged to follow a traditional course of husbandry against his better judgment. In some cases it seemed more practicable to try and modify the common practice on the open fields, than to break up the land into several holdings and set aside

but costly

combined cultivation altogether. Enclosing was so expensive that there were some landlords who set themselves to improve the common cultivation, rather than to break up the old fields and lay out new farms. This policy was even embodied in an enabling Act of Parliament[2], which provided that the commoners might meet and arrange for the adoption of a new rotation of common cultivation; and this Act would apparently have given effect to the policy which Arthur

and not essential to good farming.

Young approved. He knew that enclosing was no panacea, that it was often carried out with reckless extravagance, and that there might be good farming without it. In so far as enclosing was urged, during this period, it was partly in the interest of providing additional coppices and timber[3], as well as for the sake of agriculture itself[4]. An examination of

---

[1] *Southern Tour*, 386. [2] 13 Geo. III. c. 81.
[3] 29 Geo. II. c. 36; 10 Geo. III. c. 42.
[4] John Laurence rector of Bishops Wearmouth wrote decidedly in favour of the change in his *New System of Agriculture* (1726), p. 45; so too Edward Las-

ute Book, and Private Acts, shows us that enclosing
gressing but slowly during this period, and that the
id change took place at the end of the last century
beginning of this.

During the greater part of this period a very re- *The en-*
e policy was in force with regard to the export and *couraye-ment of*
of corn. In 1689 a bounty was given on the export *corn grow-ing*
e price ranged below 48s.[1]; this was continued, with
ons in the four famine years,—1698, 1709, 1740,
The result of this measure was very remarkable;
is time onwards corn was treated as a commodity to
n for export. This policy was exclusively English, *for expor-tation.*
ad been pursued at least occasionally in this country
e agricultural depression of the fifteenth century[2]. The
hich followed was twofold; first, the landed interest
far relieved from loss by low prices, in the case of a
l harvest, that there was a distinct encouragement to
apital in the land; and secondly, by encouraging such
e production of corn there was some security that
supply of the people would not be deficient. By en- *Effect on*
g the growth of corn, as a commodity for export in *regular food supply.*

---

y of a *Steward to his Lord* (1727), p. 37, and John Mortimer, *Art of*
, l. 2 (1721); and the anonymous authors of the *Great Improvement of*
hat are enclosed (1732), and an *Old Almanack* (1735). A vigorous tract
a in reply by John Cowper, *An Essay proving that inclosing Commons is
the interest of the nation* (1732). The difference turned chiefly on the
effects on the population. Cowper (pp. 3, 7, 8) argues that there would
icultural employment, and that the by employments of spinning and
ring wool would also decline, as well as all the subsidiary village trades,
rights, smiths, &c. These writers feared that enclosing meant sheep
it had done under the Tudors; but the price of wool ranged so low that
surely have been a mistake; the process had gone too far. *Graziers*
(1726), 13.
ntroversy broke out again in the reign of George III. Henry
say, p. 35) looked with complacency on the movement of the popula-
the villages. "There is a natural transition of the inhabitants of
here the labour of agriculture is lessened, into places of trade, where our
riority, so long as it lasts, will furnish sources of perpetual employment.
he hands, thus directed from Agriculture to Manufacture, are not in that
re useful to the public, than in their former, is an enquiry which might
prosecuted with some entertainment to the Reader." An opponent of
published an *Enquiry into the reasons for and against inclosing* (1767), to
nington responded in his *Reflections on inclosing* (1769).
lliam and Mary, Stat. I. c. 12.   [2] Smith, *Three Tracts*, 73.
          [3] Vol. I. p. 364.

favourable seasons, an inducement was indirectly given to grow enough for home consumption in unfavourable years.

A great interest attaches to this masterly stroke of policy, since it appears to have occasioned the great advance in agricultural improvement which took place while *Success of this policy* it was maintained. In the famine year of 1757 there was an outcry against the measure, and during the period of its suspension, the wisdom of the law was thoroughly discussed and completely confirmed. There were those indeed who believed that the object might be attained, if the bounties were gradually diminished, by imposing duties on export when corn was dear and leaving it free when the price was low[1]; but when the famine was over, Parliament once more adopted the old policy of granting bounties on export when corn was cheap.

This appears to have been the one part of the scheme known as the Mercantile System which was original to *which was special to England.* England[2]. The French had fostered industry, and the Dutch shipping. The English took a line which promoted the development of agriculture; they thereby were able to supply a commodity for occasional export[3], and thus to employ their shipping, and also to provide food at a moderate rate and thus to encourage industry. In the eighteenth century this measure was proving itself the corner stone of English pros-*Character of Corn Laws.* perity. In the nineteenth century the Corn Laws have been looked on, and had become, a restriction to our food supply; in the eighteenth century they were the security for its abundance. So far as private lucre influenced the pioneers of agricultural improvement, they were attracted by the gain which would accrue from the regular market for corn, rather than by an anticipated increase of rents. The improvement was due to the application of capital to the land, and the capitalist looked for his return, not from rent, but from the sale of the product. It was of course by increased rental that the landlords got a return on their capital, but an increased rent thus obtained was the reward of enterprise, and not the mere result of the possession of a monopoly.

[1] C. Smith, *Three Tracts*, 80.   [2] Faber, *Agrarschutz*, p. 2.
[3] N. Forster, *Enquiry into the Causes of the present high price of Provisions* (1767), p. 70. Dr Johnson, *Considerations*, in *Works*, v. 321.

It has been already pointed out that Parliament regarded A.D. 1689 increase of rent as one mark of national prosperity, and —1776. source for possible taxation. At the Revolution, it was *Rents.* mmon feeling that a fall of rents was a national calamity, that an increase of rent implied a national gain. Various 'ria of national prosperity had been adopted at different 's, such as the balance of trade or high profits. Each of e indicates prosperity in some branch of national life, it is difficult to say how far it was legitimate to lay stress ny one as symptomatic of general prosperity.

285. There are various points of subsidiary importance *Other* he management of land which may be noted here. Direct *products.* uragement was given to the growth of certain products, i as madder[1], which were useful in connection with the *Madder.* ile trades. Tassels or teasels, which were used in the *Teasels.* l manufacture, were grown in considerable quantities in kshire, where cloth dressing was carried on[2]. To us it is resting to find that the common wastes were still treated resources of great value, and that the reckless destruc- of them called forth various measures. This was some- es due to the operations of iron-workers; and in some s to the action of tramps and squatters[3]. While coal *Common* still expensive, the waste lands furnished the chief *Wastes* ply of fuel; but as coal came into more common use this *and fuel.* e of policy ceased to be important. There was one rict in Kent, which supplied kindling for the large faggots ommon use for fires; but as Defoe remarks "since the rns in London are come to make coal-fires in their upper ns that trade declines; and though that article would n to be trifling in itself, it is not immaterial to observe it an alteration it makes in the value of those woods in it, and how many more of them than usual are yearly bbed up, and the land made fit for the plough[4]."

A good deal of improvement also took place in the way *Draining and Banking.*

A. Young, *Farmer's Letters*, 227. See especially Pennant, *Journey*, I. 96.
Arthur Young, *Northern Tour*, I. 191. The want of tassels in Scotland is an of by the author of *The Interest of Scotland*, p. 109, as one reason why the len trade was so backward there.
[1] 28 Geo. II. c. 19, § 8.   [4] Defoe's *Tour*, I. 138.

A.D. 1689
—1776.

of draining[1], and rescuing the land from river floods, and even from the sea[2]. Some of the land thus saved was found to be admirable grazing ground[3]. An enormous number of Scottish cattle, which Defoe estimates at 40,000 a year, were brought to S. Faith's, near Norwich; they were pastured on the great marshes near Yarmouth, and turnip-fed during winter on drier ground[4].

286. There was one change which specially characterised the eighteenth century, and which was partly the effect of these improvements; while it also gave facilities for carrying

Improved roads.

them further. When Arthur Young was travelling, there was occasion for constant reference to the villainous character of particular parts of the highways[5]. At this very time, however, Henry Homer was able to congratulate his countrymen on the immense improvement that had been made during the preceding half century. He describes the state of the roads and difficulties of internal communication as one of the chief reasons for the backward state of the country in the

Homer.

time of Queen Anne. "The trade of the kingdom languished under these Impediments. Few People cared to encounter the Difficulties, which attended the Conveyance of Goods from the Places where they were manufactured, to the Markets, where they were to be disposed of. And those, who undertook this Business, were only enabled to carry it on in the Wintry-Season on Horseback, or, if in Carriages, by winding Deviations from the regular Tracks, which the open country afforded them an Opportunity of making. Thus the very same Cause, which was injurious to Trade, laid waste also a considerable Part of our Lands. The natural Produce of the Country was with Difficulty circulated to supply the Necessities of those Counties and trading Towns, which wanted, and to dispose of the Superfluity of others, which abounded. Except in a few Summer-Months, it was an almost impracticable Attempt to carry very considerable

---

[1] Young, *Northern Tour*, II. 227, 323.   [2] Defoe's *Tour*, I. 5.

[3] In some cases great danger ensued from the breaking of the banks on the Essex coast, and they had to be most carefully watched. Pennant, *Journey*, I. 39.

[4] Defoe's *Tour*, I. 53, 63.

[5] A mass of evidence as to the state of the roads in the xviiith century will be found in W. C. Sydney, *England in* xviiith *century*, II. 1—48.

ntities of it to remote Places.   Hence the Consumption
e Growth of Grain as well as of the inexhaustible Stores
uel, which Nature has lavished upon particular Parts of
Island was limited to the Neighbourhood of those Places
h produced them ; and made them, comparatively speak-
of little value to what they would have been, had the
icipation of them been more enlarged.

To the Operation of the same cause must also be at- *Importance*
ted, in great Measure, the slow Progress which was *for agriculture.*
erly made in the Improvement of Agriculture.   Dis-
aged by the Expence of procuring Manure, and the un-
in Returns, which arose from such confined Markets, the
ner wanted both Spirit and Ability to exert himself in
Cultivation of his Lands.   On this Account Undertakings
usbandry were then generally small, calculated rather to
Means of Subsistence to particular Families, than a
ce of Wealth to the Publick.   Almost every Estate was
mbered with a great Quantity of Buildings, to adapt
n to the convenience of the Occupiers.   The clear Emolu-
t resulting from them both to the Proprietors and
ants was far more inconsiderable than what has accrued
the more extended Plan, upon. which that Branch of
iness is now conducted.

'The great Obstruction to the Reformation, which has *Difficulties
to be faced.*
accomplished, was founded upon a Principle adopted by
tlemen of Property in the Country, which Experience
since proved to be as erroneous as it was selfish ; *viz.*,
it would be injurious to their Tenants to render the
kets in their Neighbourhood more accessible to distant
ners, and consequently a Diminution of their Estates.   It
it for ever to be recorded to the Honour of the present
tury, that it was the first, which produced publick Spirit
igh to renounce that Prejudice, and by this Circumstance
to have given as it were a new Birth to the Genius of
Island.   It is owing to the Alteration, which has taken
e in consequence thereof, that we are now released from
ding the cautious Steps of our Forefathers, and that our
Carriages travel with almost winged Expedition between
ry Town of Consequence in the Kingdom and the Metro-

polis. By this, as well as the yet more valuable Project of increasing inland Navigation, a Facility of Communication is soon likely to be established from every Part of the Island to the sea, and from the several Places in it to each other. Trade is no longer fettered by the Embarrasments, which unavoidably attended our former Situation. Dispatch, which is the very Life and Soul of Business, becomes daily more attainable by the free Circulation opening in every Channel, which is adapted to it. Merchandise and Manufactures find a ready Conveyance to the Markets. The natural Blessings of the Island are shared by the Inhabitants with a more equal Hand. The Constitution itself acquires Firmness by the Stability and Increase both of Trade and Wealth, which are the Nerves and Sinews of it.

Effects of improvement on Land

"In Consequence of all this, the Demand for the Produce of the Lands is increased; the Lands themselves advance proportionately both in their annual Value, and in the Number of Years-purchase for which they are sold, according to such Value. Nor does there appear to have arisen even any local Injury to particular Estates by this Change of Circumstances; though, if there did, they ought to submit to it from the greater Advantage resulting to the Publick; but they are yet more valuable as their Situation is nearer to the trading Towns, and as the Number of Inhabitants in such Towns is enlarged by the Increase of Trade.

and on Internal Trade.

"There never was a more astonishing Revolution accomplished in the internal System of any Country than has been within the Compass of a few years in that of England. The Carriage of Grain, Coals, Merchandize, etc. is in general conducted with little more than half the Number of Horses with which it formerly was. Journies of Business are performed with more than double Expedition. Improvements in Agriculture keep pace with those of Trade. Everything wears the Face of Dispatch; every Article of our Produce becomes more valuable; and the Hinge, which has guided all these Movements, and upon which they turn, is the Reformation which has been made in our Publick Roads[1]."

[1] Homer. *An Enquiry into the Means of Preserving the Publick Roads* (1767), 4 seq.

ere is ample evidence to confirm this account of the
ement. It may be inferred from the increasing prac-
keeping carriages; hackney carriages were brought
from London to ply between Cambridge and Stour-
Fair[1]; and it could hardly have been worth while to
these vehicles for a few days, if the roads had been
here of a very defective character. It is not always
judge how far the internal trade implied good roads
ffic. Corn was taken in bags on horses, though wag-
ere also used[2], and bulky goods were conveyed as far
ible by water[3]; but it appears that live geese were
t from the Fens to the London market in large two-
parts, arranged with four stages, which took them a
d miles to market in two days and a night[4]; and it is
t to understand how such quantities of Scotch cattle
be driven to the Norfolk and Suffolk marshes unless
ras fairly good going.

s not impossible however to reconcile this view as to
neral character of the roads with the complaints which
Young makes of particular highways[5]. There was no
nity of practice throughout the country; till the time of
and Mary the maintenance of the roads had been for
st part a matter of private benevolence, and during
teenth and sixteenth centuries they appear to have
d. In the time of Philip and Mary parish surveyors[6]
istituted whose business it was to enforce the necessary
from each parish. The justices had power to punish
lect of surveyors and to assess the parishes, but the
nery was too cumbersome to be very effective. The
e duty,' which could be required from the parishioners,
rfunctorily performed since there was not sufficient
nce between the calls on large and small farmers and
e and small householders. It seemed that the most
le system would be that "every Person ought to con-

Marginal notes:
A.D. 1689
—1776.
Carriages.

Arthur Young's complaint.

1556.

Negligence of local authorities.

---

oe, I. 97.   [2] Ib. 229; Arthur Young, *Farmer's Letters*, 190.
nchester goods were brought to Stourbridge Fair in horse packs; similar
re taken from Essex to London in waggons. Defoe's *Tour*, I. 94, 118.
54.   [5] *Southern Tour*, 88.
d 3 Philip and Mary, c. 8. The Bedfordshire Quarter Sessions Records
60 have frequent complaints of parishes not appointing surveyors.

tribute to the Repair of Roads in Proportion to the Use they make of, or the Convenience which they receive from them[1]." With the view of carrying out this principle on the

Turnpikes. main lines of through traffic, turnpikes were erected and tolls[2] levied on certain highways under the authority of special Acts; pains were also taken against injuring the roads by very heavy weights or badly constructed waggons[3]. When the wheels were so arranged as to follow one another in the same track, vehicles were freed from half the usual tolls[4]; but the provisions only extended to the highways for

Parish Roads. which special Acts had been procured. The parish roads were not equally well cared for, and under these circumstances we can well understand that there should have been a great variety in the condition of the different roads; and that some should have been left in a very dangerous condition, while others were fairly good. It was in 1741 that a general measure was passed, which rendered it possible to bring all the highways of the kingdom into the same sort of repair as had been obtained by the various bodies of commissioners for turnpike roads.

While these improvements in land carriage were progressing a great deal of attention was also directed to providing new facilities for carriage by water. This was partly

Water Communi-cation. done by opening up the rivers for navigation. In 1740 a scheme, which had been started in Charles II.'s time, was revived, and an attempt was made to render the Medway navigable, chiefly with the view of conveying the timber of the Wealds of Kent and Sussex for the use of the Royal Navy[5]. In other cases canals were cut to connect different river basins; thus in 1768 the idea was revived of connecting the Forth and Clyde[6]; this was carried out, though not on the ambitious scale originally intended, as that would have allowed ships of war to pass from sea to sea. In these matters the eighteenth century, with its largely increased capital, was carrying out the projects which had been mooted

---

[1] Homer, *Enquiry into the Publick Roads*, p. 18.
[2] Arthur Young, *Southern Tour*, 187, 161.
[3] 1 Geo. II. c. 11; 5 Geo. I. c. 12; 14 Geo. II. c. 42.
[4] 5 Geo. III. c. 38.   [5] Defoe, *Tour*, I. 204.
[6] Campbell, *Political Survey of Great Britain*, I. 285.

a century before. Charles II. had been struck by the success A.D. 1689
—1776.
of the Dutch. He had also planned to connect the Severn
and the Thames by Lechlade[1]. The greatest of those undertakings was a scheme first discussed in 1765, for connecting
Bristol, Liverpool and Hull by means of the Severn and
Trent. A great impetus had been given to all such enterprise by the success of Brindley in carrying out the Duke *Bridge-*
of Bridgewater's scheme in 1758[2]. The Duke was the pos- *water Canal.*
sessor of immense beds of coal at Worsley, which could not
be remuneratively worked on account of the cost of carriage
to Manchester; though only seven miles in length, this canal
involved grave engineering difficulties; part of it was tun-
nelled through solid rock, and there was also an aqueduct two
hundred yards long and forty feet high over the river Irwell.
This first success inspired the Duke and his engineer to make
the beginning of that network of canals which was soon
spread over England so as to connect the various river basins
with one another.

VI. THE POOR.

287. During the whole of this period a great deal of *Pauperism*
attention was given to the subject of pauperism. At the *at the Revo-lution.*
time of the Revolution, the charge which arose from the
provision for the poor was excessively heavy. Gregory King
calculated that the total population was five million, five
hundred thousand; and apparently about a fourth of the total
population was more or less dependent on parochial relief[3].
In 1685 the total poor rates for England were estimated at *Poor Rates.*
over £665,000; this sum was, according to Davenant, about as
much as was needed for the maintenance of government and
for our protection in time of peace[4]. In the succeeding years,
with bad seasons, heavy war expenses and interrupted commerce, pauperism increased with frightful rapidity, and several
of the ablest men in the kingdom devised schemes for relieving
the burden and setting the poor to work. One of these was

---

[1] Phillips, *Inland Navigation,* 210.   [2] *Ib.* 88.
[3] Davenant, *Balance of Trade,* in *Works,* II. 184.   [4] *Ib.* I. 38.

A.D. 1689
—1776.
*Setting the
poor on
work.*

*The
Bristol
Work-
house.*

*Reasons
for its
failure.*

brought before Parliament in 1698 and is highly commended by Davenant[1], another was drafted by Locke[2] who was one of the commissioners of the Board of Trade, another by one of the Worcester justices, Mr Apletre[3], and another by Mr Dunning of Devonshire[4]. Locke brought a Bill into Parliament in 1705, but no general Act was passed: though an important experiment was tried in Bristol[5], and the different parishes in the city were incorporated and proceeded to erect a workhouse for employing their poor. One of the weak points of the Elizabethan legislation had been that no sufficient means were provided for raising capital and offering employment, and the various proposals alluded to above were all designed to remedy this defect. The Bristol scheme appears to have been carried through by Mr Cary, who was then a well-known writer on commercial subjects; within a very few years the example, which had been set at Bristol, was followed at Exeter, Hereford, Colchester, Hull, Shaftesbury, Lynn, Sudbury, Gloucester, Plymouth, and Norwich[6]. The Bristol experiment was not however a pecuniary success; and in 1714 the corporation found themselves in great difficulties, as they had entirely lost the fund with which they had started. As a matter of fact it was by no means an easy matter to conduct this business so as to be at all remunerative[7]. In 1758 the experience of fifty years, as to the management of workhouses and the trades which could be carried on in them, was summed up in a treatise by Mr W. Bailey[8] of the Society of Arts.

The cry as to the importance of providing employment for the poor was taken up by that ingenious projector, Sir Humphry Mackworth, whose scheme was welcomed in the House of Commons. His Bill for establishing a factory in every parish was passed by the Commons, but it called forth

---

[1] Davenant, II. 207.   [2] Eden, I. 244.   [3] Ib. 239.   [4] Ib. 248.

[5] John Cary, *An Account of the Proceedings of the Corporation of Bristol* (1700). The children could not spin woollen yarn so as to pay for their own keep until they learned to spin it specially fine, p. 13.

[6] Eden, I. 257.

[7] Pennant writing in 1787 speaks with much enthusiasm of the large house of industry in the Isle of Wight and enumerates the employments. *Journey*, II. 156.

[8] *Treatise on better employment of Poor* (1758).

attack from Defoe, whose *Giving Alms no Charity* A.D. 1689
;reat impression, and the measure was allowed to —1776.
Defoe.
> Lords. But a much humbler scheme of a similar
>rought into operation in 1723[1]; it empowered a *Work-*
> union of parishes, to erect houses for the lodging *houses.*
ying of the poor. The workhouses, which were
:r these acts, were at first managed by contractors;
overseers were empowered to refuse relief to those
  not enter the houses, there was a great check
wing expenditure on the poor. Partly perhaps
.is Act, and partly through the general prosperity
e excitement in regard to the growth of pauperism
have been allayed for nearly twenty years.
neral alarm which had been created, however, was *Anxiety*
mischief; as it caused the ratepayers to act on the *about keep-*
ing the
nd do everything in their power to keep down the *rates down.*
>ry means were taken to prevent any one, who was
ecome chargeable to the parish, from obtaining a
; and very heavy legal expenses were incurred in
> there was a dispute between different parishes
>nus of maintaining some particular person. But
:st means of preventing the parish responsibility
ising, was by diminishing the accommodation for
upers. There was throughout the country an open
t cottages[2]. The results of this deliberate policy
ig rural overcrowding were very serious, and the
: caused very great. Permission to marry was as
itrolled by the parish authorities as it had been
  mediaeval villans.
There is a curious agreement among the writers, *Alleged*
part in the eighteenth century controversies on *cause of*
pauperism.
as to the cause of the evil they deplored; it was
due, as they believed, to mere idleness. Locke[3] *Locke.*
  opinion, that a large proportion of paupers, be-
regular tramps, were merely lazy, and that the
c. 7.

, *Farmer's Letters*, 288. On the complaints of the carelessness of
lowing cottages, see above, p. 205.
[3] *Board of Trade* (1697), in *Account of Society for the promotion of*
indsey, p. 108. [Brit. Mus. 103, l. 56.] Compare Eden, I. 244.

A.D. 1689
—1776.

*Defoe's
criticism of
schemes for
providing
employ-
ment.*
complaint of want of work was a mere pretence. But the
high prices of the dear years had not inoculated the English
with the frugality which the Dutch displayed. Defoe is
perhaps the writer who lays most stress on the faults of the
poor; he was apparently of opinion that there was plenty of
employment at all times. He argued that the real want was
men, not money to employ them, and he pointed to the difficulty of obtaining recruits as proof positive that there was no
lack of employment, for those who wished it. From this of
course it followed that all schemes for employing the poor were
unnecessary, and that in so far as they interfered with the
ordinary trade of the country, they would do an injury to
the industrious[1].

On his assumption, that idleness was the only cause of
pauperism (apart from sickness and old age), it was obvious
that additional opportunities of employment would have little
effect on those who were unwilling to work at all. "I make
no difficulty," he says, "to promise on a short summons to
produce above a thousand families in England, within my
particular knowledge, who go in rags and their children
wanting bread, whose fathers can earn their fifteen to twenty-
five shillings a week but will not work, who may have work
enough but are too idle to seek after it, and hardly vouchsafe
to earn anything but bare subsistence and spending money
for themselves[2]." It may perhaps be said that the hard tone
which popular opinion associates with the dismal science first
shows itself at this period, when philanthropic measures were
denounced on economic grounds, as either useless or baneful,

[1] "Suppose now a workhouse for the employment of poor children sets them to
spinning of worsted. For every skein of worsted these poor children spin, there
must be a skein the less spun by some poor person or family that spun it before;
suppose the manufacture of making bays to be erected in Bishopsgate Street,
unless the makers of these bays can find out at the same time a trade or consumption for more bays than were made before, for every piece of bays so made in
London, there must be a piece the less made at Colchester."
"If these worthy gentlemen, who show themselves so forward to relieve and
employ the poor, will find out some new trade, some new market, where the goods
they make shall be sold, where none of the same sort were sold before, if they
will send them to any place where they shall not interfere with the rest of that
manufacture, or with some other made in England; then indeed they will do
something worthy of themselves, and they may employ the poor to the same
glorious advantage as Queen Elizabeth did." Defoe, *Giving Alms no charity*, in
Works, II. 434.   [2] Defoe, *Giving Alms no charity*, II. 448.

and when the frugality of Dutch craftsmen and French *A.D. 1689* *—1776.* peasants was held up as an example to Englishmen. It took its rise in protesting against the observed effects of indis-riminate State charity.

289. Towards the close of the reign of George II. and *High price* early in the time of George III. there were periods when the *of pro-* *visions.* igh price of provisions, and the frequent disturbances in different parts of the country, directed general attention to the condition of the poor. As in the earlier time, popular opinion ran in the direction of increased employment[1], but it also turned to expedients for keeping down the price of pro-visions[2]. Politicians inveighed against engrossers or those who exported corn according to their fancy; but this outcry only served to call out the conclusive arguments in favour of the existing policy to which allusion has already been made. Arthur Young and other writers[3] were inclined to repeat the *Arthur* *Young.* catchwords, old as they even then were, about the improvi-dence of the poor, and to insist that a high price of provisions acted as a stimulus and forced labourers to work more regu-larly, instead of idling half the week. He believed that the Elizabethan provision for the maintenance of the poor was thoroughly demoralising, and he thought that if the unde-serving could not count on maintenance as a certainty, men would "bestir themselves while in health and youth to practise a life of sober industriousness, that they might be entitled (when misfortunes came that were past their power to remedy) to protection and maintenance from others[4]." Parish relief had taken away all motive for saving and he "never yet knew one instance of any poor man's working diligently, while young and in health, to escape coming to the parish when ill or old[5]." In much the same spirit a com-mittee of the House of Commons reported against out-door relief[6], and urged the general establishment of workhouses.

[1] Eden, *History of the Poor*, I. 311.

[2] See the petitions from the City of London and burgesses of Devizes. *Parl. Hist.* XVI. 394.

[3] Compare Temple, *Vindication of Commerce* (1758), p. 13. Also *Essay on Trade and Commerce* (1770), p. 15. "The manufacturing population do not labour above four days a week unless provisions happen to be very dear." See below, PP. 366, 474, 599.   [4] A. Young, *Farmer's Letters*, 293.   [5] *Ib.* 281.

[6] "That the present method of giving money out of the parochial rates to

A.D. 1689
—1776.

A much more discriminating view of the causes of pauperism is taken by a writer whose errors on matters of fact do not seriously affect the acuteness of his reasoning.

Massie.

Joseph Massie was a student who had a large and accurate acquaintance with economic literature, but he was too much inclined to view the events of his own day in the light of past occurrences. He was aware that enclosing had meant rural depopulation in the sixteenth century and he too hastily assumed that the enclosing which had been proceeding in the eighteenth century was attended with similar results[1]; but the conditions of the time were entirely changed. Despite the reiterated allegation[2], it is impossible to believe that

Enclosing. enclosing in the eighteenth century implied either more pasture farming or less employment for labour. The prohibition of export kept down the price of wool[3], the bounty on exportation gave direct encouragement to corn-growing, the improved agriculture gave more employment to labour than the old[4]. But Massie was perfectly right in maintaining that the new husbandry severed the poor from the land.

The poor severed from the land.

The peasant with his own holding was rooted to the soil, the labourer who worked for wages was dependent upon trade. " The real strength of a country," he says, " doth not consist in the number of men who *live there,* but in those who *defend it ;* and the *source* of that astonishing disparity between the one and the other in England, is *removing multitudes of people from our natural and fixed basis, land, to the artificial fluctuating basis, trade*[5]." He had the highest opinion of the national importance of a peasantry who were rooted to the soil. " To small portions of land, rights of

persons capable of labour, in order to prevent such persons claiming an entire subsistence for themselves and their families from the parishes, is contrary to the spirit and intention of the laws for relief of the poor, is a dangerous power in the hands of parochial officers, a misapplication of the public money, and a great encouragement to idleness and intemperance." *Parl. Hist.* xv. 941.

[1] Wales gives careful statistics of the population in several villages in different parts of the country. *Inquiry into present state of Population* (1781), p. 51.

[2] By the opponents of enclosure.   [3] *The Graziers Complaint,* 15.

[4] A. Young, *Farmer's Letters,* 96. This was only doubtful as he thought in the case of some exceptionally large farms. *Ib.* 107. Compare Tucker, *Elements,* 92.

[5] *A Plan for the Establishment of Charity Houses,* p. 69. Compare John Cowper, *Essay proving that inclosing,* &c. pp. 3, 21. See above, p. 371.

ommoning, and cottages, England is much indebted for the ughty achievements in war which are recorded in the annals f the English nation....The different counties of England ere well peopled, cultivated by their proper inhabitants, d protected from tumults and insults except in time of vil war, oppressions, &c., for it was the true interest of those rdy men to live peaceably, and to guard the country ainst all invaders, because they had their wives and uldren, cottages and land to defend[1]."

While Massie on the one hand advocated the policy of *Criticism of the parochial system of relief.* taining as many people as possible on the land, he was not revented from seeing that some movements of labour were evitable, and on this very ground he took fundamental bjections to the Elizabethan Poor Law. He held that he law of Elizabeth was the chief reason for the growth f pauperism; since by it the poor were confined to their arishes, though the opportunities for employment gradually hanged. He noticed a general course of migration, "from ural parishes to market towns, and from both of them to the apital city; so that great multitudes of people, who were orn in rural parishes are continually acquiring settlements n cities or towns, more especially in those towns where considerable manufactures are carried on; and as trade is not nly of a fluctuating nature, but many towns in England arry on manufacturies of the same kind, and are always gain- ng or losing with respect to each other, although there be an ncrease of manufacturies upon the whole; it must necessarily ollow, that there will be frequent ebbings in the manufac- uries of one or other of our trading towns[2]." "As multi- udes of working people," he continues, "are obliged to travel rom parish to parish, and from county to county, in order to ind employment, proper maintenance or other relief ought to e provided for them, when and where they want it; because here cannot be a better motive for their travelling, than a esire to get an honest livelihood; and therefore they should ave all possible encouragement to persevere in doing what s best for the nation, and for them. Giving every poor erson a right to relief, when and where he or she shall want

[1] Massie, *A Plan for the Establishment of Charity Houses*, p. 63. [2] Ib. 99.

A.D. 1689
—1776.
Criticism
of the Law
of Settle-
ment.
it, would put an end to all law suits, about the settlement of the poor[1]." He also found that the law of settlement was responsible for introducing "a contemptible low cunning among substantial persons, in their dealings with working people, and by common poor; which hath obliged the latter to practise cunning in their own defence, and for this they are called by hard names, although they only follow the example of their betters, and poverty will justify many actions which are disgraces to substantiality[2]." It is hardly necessary to add that a writer who inveighed so strongly against the law of settlement, and advocated a national rather than a parochial provision for the poor, was entirely out of sympathy with the doctrine of Locke and Defoe; he held, not that the laziness of the poor was the cause of their distress, but that the necessities of the poor occasioned by lack of employment were the cause of their vices. "Many people are reduced to that pitiable way of life, by want of employment, sickness or some other accident; and the reluctance, or ill success, with which such unfortunate people do practise begging, is frequently manifested by a poor and emaciated man or woman being found drowned or starved to death; so that though choice, idleness, or drunkenness may be reasons why a number of people are beggars, yet this drowning, and perishing for want, are sad proofs that the general cause is necessity, and if any person thinks those proofs are insufficient, the great numbers of thieves, pickpockets which daily infest this metropolis, will put the matter beyond all doubt; for their not being beggars instead of thieves, is owing to the different effects which necessity produces in different people, according to their turn of mind, time of life, etc., and not to another cause[3].

Causes of
pauperism.

290. While Massie's distinction between the stability of employment of the land as compared with the fluctuating nature of trade, had been generally true up to the eighteenth century, and was partially true in his own time, his argument neglects the fact that the working of land was rapidly becoming a kind of trade. Corn was raised as a commodity for export, not merely to be the food supply of the country. It

Changes
in the
character
of agri-
culture;

[1] *A Plan for the Establishment*, etc., 112.　　[2] *Ib.* 98.　　[3] *Ib.* 50.

is very hard for us to remember that little more than a A.D. 1689
hundred years ago, England was regularly a corn exporting —1776.
country, that the encouragement of corn growing was regarded *Corn*
as an indirect means of increasing our shipping, and that *growing for foreign*
there were writers who argued that Sweden and other coun- *markets.*
tries must always be dependent on our singularly fertile
island for a food supply[1]. In endeavouring to meet this
foreign demand, agriculture was being revolutionised[2], and
the product was a commodity for export not merely provision
for subsistence.

The capital introduced into agriculture was severing the
peasant from the soil, effectually though gradually. The
farmers who had small holdings and were rooted to the soil *Small hold-*
were the men who kept up the old and slovenly methods of *bad farm-*
cultivation. The improving landlord, who preferred to let *ing.*
his land in larger holdings and to substantial men who had
capital to work it effectively, was providing employment for
day labourers; but they were as little rooted to the land as
the craftsmen in the towns[3]. The Acts of Settlement gave
in most cases the chief reason for attachment; and apart from
sentiment, there was little to induce the small farmer to
struggle to retain a holding which he worked on his own
account, instead of accepting the wages which would enable *Day*
him as a day labourer to live in greater comfort. On this *and hus-*
point Arthur Young's testimony is clear. "From all the *bandmen.*
observations I have made, I am convinced that the latter,
when on an equality with the former (little farmer) in respect
of children, is as well fed, as well clothed, and sometimes as

---

[1] Richardson, *Essay on the Causes of the Decline of Foreign Trade*, p. 31, and
the answer in Young, *Farmer's Letters*, 65. On the importance of English corn
for Sweden, cf. *Parl. Hist.* VII. 549.

[2] Massie assumes that a definite quantity of food is required, and that if more
is produced the price will necessarily fall; he thus argues that those who improve
land in one district are really only doing it at the expense of farmers elsewhere
whose business will no longer be so profitable. *Plan for the Establishment of
Charity Houses*, 62.

[3] The agricultural industry was not liable to such violent fluctuations (A.
Young, *Farmer's Letters*, 21) as the manufacturing, especially the manufacture of
goods, the materials for which came from abroad; but the employés of the capitalist
farmer were really "free hands" to quote Sir James Steuart's phrase as distinguished from peasants whose interest bound them to the soil.

well lodged as he would be, was he fixed in one of these little farms; with this difference—that he does not work near so hard. They fare extremely hard—work without intermission like a horse—and practise every lesson of diligence and frugality, without being able to soften their present lot[1]"; and their hopes of saving enough to take a larger holding were seldom realised. Harte's testimony is equally clear; he holds that the little farmer at a rent of thirty or forty pounds a year "works and fares harder and is, in effect, poorer than the day labourer he employs. An husbandman, thus circumstanced, is, beyond dispute, a worthy object of our commiseration and assistance[2]." It may therefore be said that the increase of pauperism would have been checked if Massie's policy had been adopted and the peasantry had remained a fixture on the soil; but this would have been accomplished at the expense of checking the improvement of the English soil and leaving the peasantry at a low standard of comfort.

The low standard of comfort of the small farmers goes some way to explain the re-iterated charges of idleness which are brought against the poor. The farmer class led a hard life; and the weaver or labourer, who earned enough to enjoy similar discomfort, may well have preferred to take out his remaining time in resting, rather than to earn additional wages which would give him little additional comfort that he could appreciate[3]. It may be noted too, that the same low standard of comfort was treated as satisfactory by Arthur Young and the other economists, who praised the frugality of
the small farmers at home and abroad, and complained that the labourer did not work as hard, not that he might enjoy more comfort but that he might lay by and save the pockets of the ratepayers. This was a motive which did not appeal to the mind of the ordinary manufacturer or farm labourer.

Under these circumstances the diffusion of manufactures throughout the country, and the opportunities which they

---

[1] *Farmer's Letters*, 114. See above, p. 359, also 493 below.

[2] *Essays on Husbandry*, 205.

[3] Richardson, *Causes of Decline* (1750), p. 6. "When provisions are cheap they won't work above half the week but sot or idle away half their time." See also pp. 383, 474, 599.

fforded of employment, would not necessarily raise the stan- A.D. 1689
ard of comfort. But there is reason to believe that Arthur $\frac{-1776.}{}$
'oung's generalisations are too sweeping, and that those *Effect of domestic*
istricts where manufacturers were settled were much more *manu-factures,*
rosperous in every way. "As Essex, Suffolk, and Norfolk,"
iys Defoe, "are taken up in manufactures, and famed for
idustry, this county (Cambridgeshire) has no manufacture
; all; nor are the poor, except the husbandmen, noted for
iything so much as sloth, to their scandal be it spoken.
Vhat the reason of it is, I know not[1]." On the other hand
he city and country round Norwich was thickly populated
nd busy, and the weaving trade of the town was supplied
y yarn which was spun in Yorkshire and Westmoreland[2].
.hese avocations would certainly eke out the earnings of the
amily even in cases where the man's employment was
irregular. In the counties where, from whatever cause, spin- *as by employments.*
iing and weaving were unknown, there could have been but
ittle opportunity of supplementing regular wages, though it
was agreed that the new husbandry with its attention to
ietails was beneficial even in this respect[3].

At the same time, while manufactures benefited a district so long as they flourished, "the flux" which Massie had
noted was a very serious evil in many places. Of Braintree *But these were liable to fluctuation.*
and Bocking in Essex, Defoe remarks "these were formerly
very rich and flourishing, occasioned by the great trade for
bays which were manufactured in such quantities in these
two towns as to send weekly to London four, five or six waggons laden with them, but this trade having greatly decreased
in a few years, the inhabitants are in a very miserable condition at present, for by an increase of their poor, their parish
rates are risen so high that in the year 1738 the poor's rate in
Bocking parish was 9/- in the pound, which, together with their
other rates and taxes, rendered it very burdensome to all the
inhabitants[4]." A similar decay is noted at Needham[5], Ipswich[6],
and Lavenham[7] in Suffolk, and Cranbrook in Kent[8]. It may
seem a small point, but it is one of great importance with

---

[1] Defoe, *Tour*, I. 89.   .   [2] *Ib*. 58.
[3] Arthur Young, *Farmer's Letters*, 16.
[4] *Tour*, I. 118.   [5] *Ib*. 40.   [6] *Ib*. 32.
[7] *Ib*. 34.   [8] *Ib*. 192.

A.D. 1689
—1776.

reference to a subsequent period; to note that in whatever way manufactures benefited a neighbourhood, and this is not always clear[1], the entire decay of domestic manufactures proved a ruinous loss.

VII. FINANCE.

291.   The formation of capital, which had caused such changes in industry and agriculture, made itself felt in financial affairs immediately after the Revolution.   It had *Temporary and permanent loans.* frequently been the habit for goldsmiths and bankers to make temporary advances to the government; but it was a new thing to regard the loan as permanent, and for the lender to be satisfied without having some agreement as to the repayment of his principal.   The loans to government which were financed by the Bank of England differed from all that had gone before, inasmuch as those who lent their money to government bargained for the permanent payment of interest and not for a return of their principal.   Government securities thus came to be of the nature of an investment.

It was of course a great convenience to William III. to secure money on such easy terms.   He obtained more *Convenience of the system.* than a million to use; while he did not have to call upon the tax-payers for more than £100,000.   It was convenient to the tax-payers to get off so easily; it was to the interest of capitalists to get such an investment for their money, for so long as the government continued to exist and to be able to pay its way, they were to receive a return with far greater regularity than they could have hoped to do from an investment in land.   No bad seasons could affect

---

[1] It is not impossible that those who were weavers (e.g. in Yorkshire) combined farm labour with their trade, and thus kept themselves in constant employment, summer and winter alike, but the rough work of a farm would not be always possible to men whose hands were needed for delicate textile work. The manufacturers are generally spoken of as a distinct set of men from the labourers. The presence of such manufacturers would of course create a market for produce and there can be little doubt that the wives and children of men employed on the land were able to earn considerable sums by spinning.

returns they received, and no agricultural depression A.D. 1689
ld lessen the value of their property. The national —1776.
.our gave a permanence to the wealth of the capitalist,
secured him regular gains in a manner which had been
:nown to the wealthy men of any previous age.

This was one of the reasons why contemporaries depre- *The Funds*
:d this expedient. If capitalists could get eight per cent. *and enter-*
prise.
a government, they would be less willing to employ their
ley in ordinary enterprise. "The funds," says Davenant,
e so inviting and of such infinite profit, that few now are
ing to let out their money to traders at six per cent. as
aerly; so that all merchants who subsist by credit must
time give over, and they being the greatest part and
iaps the most industrious, any man may judge what
iage this will be to the kingdom[1]." This argument
lects the influence which the funds exercised by stimu-
ng the formation of capital, and there is no reason to
pose that the government would have been able to
row on lower terms. As a matter of fact, from a tenth
a fifth of the National Debt was held by Dutchmen and
er foreigners; and the payment of interest was recognised
eriously affecting the balance of commercial indebtedness
ween the countries[2].

In this way the interests of the monied class came to be *Political*
ociated with the interests of William of Orange and his *influence of*
the Funds.
cessors. Monied men enabled him to obtain large sup-
s without rousing disaffection by heavy taxation; while
monied men found that they were guarded against loss
l that their gains were secured. It was a new fiscal policy
l one that proved convenient both to the borrowers and to
lenders.

The question how far this system was beneficial to the *Effect*
on the
ion is one which it is much harder to discuss. It seems *country,*
improbable that the very facility with which money could
procured tempted governments to incur expense on which
y would not have ventured under other circumstances.

[1] *Essay upon Ways and Means* (2nd Edition, 1695), p. 44.
[2] Hutcheson, *Collection of Treatises relating to the National Debts* (May 14,
7), p. 21.

On the other hand it is quite possible that the security which these investments offered to monied men, may have induced many persons to form hoards and to lend them to government, who would otherwise have felt no inducement to do so. The great motive which inclines men to form capital is a desire of having a fund of wealth, and the promise of the government, when guaranteed by Parliament, gave a security such as those who had previously lent money had never enjoyed. The influence of the opportunity thus offered in giving a new field for the desire of saving is an element which can hardly be calculated. It is true that much wealth was blown away in powder and shot, which might have been more usefully employed in developing the resources of the country or in opening up new trades; but it is also true that the formation of capital went on more rapidly, and that the fears of those who predicted that this new method of finance would drain away the capital of the country and use it up unproductively, were falsified. There was a waste of existing resources, but there was also a greatly increased opportunity for replenishing these resources.

This point appears to have escaped the notice of many of those who, either at the time or in subsequent years, criticised the new method of finance. They held that each generation of citizens was bound to repay, out of taxation, any loans that they themselves had incurred, and that if they did not do so they were laying on posterity a burden which they were bound to bear themselves[1]. The argument seems to assume that posterity did not in any way profit by the political undertakings for which these loans had defrayed the expense, but this introduces another element which is quite incalculable. Political freedom and national glory are things which cannot be assessed in money; it is impossible to say how far the successes in Marlborough's wars conferred a benefit on subsequent generations of Englishmen, that could be assessed in terms of money; so long as any benefit accrues to the nation from the political conditions which were secured at that time, it is impossible to say that subsequent generations cannot be justly called upon to pay for enter-

[1] Jefferson, *Memoirs, Correspondence &c.*, IV. 200.

about which they were not consulted. It does not A.D. 1689 —1776.
that either of the main objections to the new finance *Objections*
mpletely conclusive. It was not necessarily unjust to *to the New Finance.*
posterity in any case where expenditure was inevit-
1 order to preserve the national existence; on the
1and it is not clear that the drain of capital to supply
vernment was not completely overbalanced by the
apid formation of capital which went on under new
ons.

ε new financial expedient adopted by government
tly helped to supply machinery, by means of which
apital was formed; and altogether it may be said that
γu and the Whig statesmen who worked with him *Its apparent*
l an exceedingly powerful instrument of finance. The *success,*
ms which were urged at the time and re-echoed by
day[1] appear to be refuted by the success of England
struggle with France. This mode of raising money is
onsistent with continued national prosperity. At the
ime there may be great difference of opinion as to the
ι of the manner in which this powerful instrument
en used at different times. When taxation is used,
defray the expenses but to pay the interest on
ıl debts, the burden tends to increase; it is a per-
burden which remains, while the advantages which *and the difficulties*
ained in a military struggle may, after all, be only *it involves.*
ary. Since, too, there is a heavy permanent burden
ends to be less room for new and special exertions[2] on
ns of special emergency; and thus while there is
steadiness in the fiscal arrangements the burdens
e increasingly heavy. The question after all must
itself into the practical one whether the object for
the burden was incurred was a worthy one. In con-
g the National Debt of England, we must remember
was incurred for war expenses, that the money was
large extent spent in foreign countries; the defence
is alleged for colonial borrowing in the present day *Was it*
ıot be urged on its behalf, as it did not provide capital *justified?*

bleday, *Financial History*, 46 seq.
renant, *Ways and Means*, 29 and 43, where Spain is noted as a warning.

for carrying on remunerative public works. He would be a
bold man who should maintain that England was necessarily
involved in all the wars in which she took part during the
eighteenth century, and that the national gain of whatever
kind was adequate to the national expenditure. In this as
in other matters the extraordinary advance which was due
to the era of industrial invention makes it difficult for us to
judge fairly. Since the nation has flourished under the
burden it is clear that the change has not as a matter of
fact been ruinous. While on the other hand those who held
that it was rash to incur such burdens[1] cannot be blamed
for not taking account of an enormous development which no
one could foresee.

The policy of borrowing, and the formation of the Bank
of England as the instrument by which national borrowing
was accomplished, were the great features of the finance of the
years immediately succeeding the Revolution. Its detailed
effects may be noted in three different directions as they
affected : (1) Banking and credit, (2) Currency, (3) Taxation.

*The Bank
of England.* 292. The Bank of England was founded with the view
of saving the government from a pressing emergency. The
plan had been submitted to the government by William
Paterson in 1691; but it was not till the spring of 1694 that
it was seriously taken up by Montagu and Michael Godfrey.
They were at their wits' end for money to prosecute the war.
*The Land
Bank.* The scheme of a Land Bank, which was proposed by Chamberlayne and which, if it had been practicable, would have done
much to reconcile the landed gentry to the new government,
had not stood the test of public criticism. That it should
have been even proposed, and seriously considered, showed
that the nature of credit was but dimly understood. But
when this project was dropped, the parliamentary session was

---

[1] Hutcheson wrote most judiciously and with very full information on this
subject. He was much concerned that the debt was continually increasing, and
that both political parties had added to it, and he urged proposals for the immediate payment of the debt as it stood in 1717. He would have advised the
appropriation of a tenth part of all the real estate, and that all the personal estate in
the country should be assigned to the payment of the public debts, in the expectation that there would be such a revival of general prosperity when this burthen
was removed that the landed interest, the trading interest and the monied interest
would none of them really suffer. *Collection*, p. 27, also 22.

already so far advanced that it was almost impossible to <i>A.D.</i> 1689
—1776.
carry through a better scheme. Paterson's plan appealed <i>The monied</i>
not to the landed, but to the monied interest; and the <i>interest.</i>
jealousy of the monied interest was the chief danger which
the project had to face in the House of Lords. The promoters carried their point by a somewhat narrow majority,
but in the city they met with success beyond their hopes[1].
In ten days the whole of the sum of £1,200,000 was subscribed; the Bank received its first Charter and commenced
operations in the Grocers' Hall.

In this, as in so many cases, it appears that a measure,
which was due to a temporary emergency, came to be the
basis of a permanent institution. The Bank consisted of
subscribers who had lent £1,200,000 to Government on the
security that out of the payments of tonnage[2] they should
annually receive eight per cent., or in all £100,000. They
were also permitted to carry on the business of banking in <i>The busi-
ness of the</i>
their corporate capacity, that is to say they were to receive <i>Bank.</i>
money on deposit and to lend it at interest. This business
had been, as we have seen, developed by the goldsmiths;
in 1680[3] the practice was universal with all city men of
keeping their cash at a goldsmith's, so that payments were
habitually made by drawing bills on goldsmiths and their <i>Jealousy of
Gold-</i>
paper circulated freely as a means of discharging debts. <i>smiths.</i>
The business, which had thus been developed, had been
hitherto left in private hands. Many people had urged that
it should be taken over by the state, and a National Bank
formed; few were altogether satisfied with Montagu's proposal to give such an important position to a group of city
men. The goldsmiths were jealous of their new rival, whilst
others detected and not altogether without reason a grave
political danger in erecting a public body which might give <i>and Poli-
ticians.</i>
large supplies to the Crown[4], without the intervention of

---

[1] Macaulay, *History*, iv. 501.

[2] Not the old tunnage paid on wine but the new tonnage levied on ships per
ton. Davenant, *Ways and Means*, p. 60. Hall, *Customs*, i. 9.

[3] *Lives of the Norths*, ii. 174.

[4] § 30 of the Act (5 and 6 William and Mary, c. 20) which prohibits the Bank
from making such advances was inserted to meet this danger. Macaulay, *History*,
iv. 499.

Parliament, and which might exercise a permanent influence over the destinies of the country. Such an influence, for good or for evil, the Bank undoubtedly exercised. The success of the Stuarts would have been ruin to the Bank that had advanced money to their rival, and its credit entirely depended on maintaining the revolutionary settlement[1]. But *Its superior facilities.* when the Bank was established, it entered on a course of vigorous competition with its rivals; none of them had an income in cash approaching to that of the Bank. There was a difference too, in the manner of doing business. Goldsmiths were supposed to lend gold, or paper for which they had gold in their cellars. But the Bank was able to make loans to an amount exceeding the full extent of the deposits it received; as it might issue notes, for which it held no cash in reserve, on the faith of the interest due to it from the government. They were thus able to do a thoroughly sound business on easier terms than the private bankers. Foreign bills were discounted at 6 per cent. and home bills at $4\frac{1}{2}$ per cent.; customers' bills were discounted at 3 per cent. and the Bank announced its readiness to make advances on plate or any of the useful metals at 4 per cent.[2]

Formation and Transfer of Capital. These banking facilities gave increased opportunities for the formation of capital, as the Bank received deposits. But they were still more important from the fact that capital was now transferred on easier terms, into directions where it could be profitably employed. The Bank was willing to lend to landowners or merchants or any one else, who appeared worthy of their confidence, and who was anxious to procure capital in order to carry on a profitable business. Their influence in transferring capital into profitable directions, instead of allowing it to lie idle as men had commonly done a century before, must have been an immense acquisition to men of enterprise in every branch of agriculture or trade.

Crisis at the time of the recoinage. 293. Before long, however, the Bank had to pass through a terrible crisis which appeared likely to shake its stability. For some time past, the coinage, though of standard silver, had been in a most unsatisfactory state; many of the coins had been clipped, and wherever payments had to be made,

---

[1] Addison, *Spectator*, March 8, 1711.   [2] Doubleday, 74.

there was constant quarrelling about every coin that passed. A.D. 1689
So much was the currency worn that the rates of exchange $N^{ec}_{essi}{}^{ty}$
were seriously affected and the remittances to the Low *of the
operation.*
Countries for war expenses could only be negotiated at 20
or 30 per cent.[1], and it was absolutely necessary to rectify
the coinage in order that this heavy addition to the expenses
of the war might cease. Parliament undertook this difficult
operation, after the principles on which they should proceed
had been fully discussed by Locke, Lowndes and other
specialists. The old money ceased to be taken by tale on
1 Dec. 1696[2] and the issue of new money from the mint
went on but slowly. So great was the scarcity of coin that *Scarcity of*
it was difficult for masters to pay their workmen in money[3], *Coin.*
and it seemed as if the country would be forced back into
trading by barter. The difficulty appears to have had some
effect in habituating people to the use of a paper currency[4].
But the rivals of the Bank saw their opportunity; the gold- *Action of*
smiths had been collecting its paper, and on May 4, when *the Goldsmiths.*
the old coinage was withdrawn, they suddenly presented a
quantity of notes for immediate payment. The Bank was
unable to meet its engagements, though it continued for a
time to satisfy the demands which came upon it from
creditors in the course of trade. By making a call upon
proprietors, and by the indulgence of their creditors, they
were enabled to tide over the evil day. The lesson was not
thrown away, as it helped to demonstrate the impossibility of
carrying on extensive credit operations on a fund of wealth,
unless that wealth is in a form in which it can be easily
realised.

This was a principle which men did not find it easy to *Wealth
that can be*
recognise. They saw that the man who had wealth in any *realised.*
shape had credit; but they did not apparently understand
that bills can only be circulated, when there is a certainty
that they can be met on presentation, and that wealth, in
forms which cannot be readily realised, is not a satisfactory

---

[1] Thorold Rogers, *Bank of England*, 43. [2] Ruding, *Annals*, II. 49.

[3] Paying in commodities was prohibited by the various Truck Acts. 1 Anne, ii.
c. 18, § 3; 13 Geo. II. c. 8, § 6.

[4] On the introduction of Exchequer Bills, Macaulay, IV. 698: Hamilton,
National Debt, 122.

A.D. 1689
—1776.

The Land Bank.

Mistakes in the scheme.

Credit and Capital.

basis for a credit circulation[1]. The success of the Bank of England encouraged the Government to float a second and somewhat similar scheme. The project of a Land Bank was revived; William and his ministers counted definitely[2] on the support they could receive from it in the coming campaign, and the scheme was hopefully launched. This rival institution was started just at the time when the Bank of England was suffering from the effects of the re-coinage and the conspiracy of the goldsmiths; but though every effort was made to encourage investors, it was impossible to secure subscribers and the whole scheme dropped ignominiously. The public knew, better than the projectors, that it was impossible to circulate bills on a kind of wealth that could not be realised, and they did not subscribe; but the promoters had besides made extraordinary blunders in calculating the value of landed property. They held that land which a man was entitled to for a hundred years was worth a hundred times the rent, and not something like twenty years' purchase, or twenty times the rent. They thus calculated the land, not at its present value to the purchaser, but at the accumulated value which would accrue by setting aside the rent annually for a century. The prospective savings from land a century hence are not the same as the worth of the land now, but the present worth of the land is the only satisfactory security as a basis for raising credit now. Dr Chamberlayne's project had been approved by the Commons in 1693, and was favoured by the Government in 1696[3].

These misunderstandings as to credit reappear in numberless projects which were floated during the eighteenth century both for commercial and manufacturing purposes. There was apparently great difficulty in understanding that credit is not capital, though it rests upon it, and though it facilitates the transference and use of it. Capital is a fund of material wealth, the forms of credit represent such wealth; and unless wealth can be used to redeem the promises, which are circulating in the form of notes, the credit will be blown

---

[1] The governors of the Bank of Scotland expressed very clear views on this point in 1727. Macleod, II. 208.

[2] Thorold Rogers, *Bank of England*, 57.   [3] Macaulay, IV. 691.

upon and the whole business will collapse. Of numerous instances which might be alleged, the South Sea Company was the most startling; they tried to carry on a great shipping business on the credit of the wealth, which their political concessions enabled them to control; but this was prospective not actual wealth, and they were not able to conduct a profitable business for want of capital.

294.   The new trades which were being opened up, and *The Stock-markets.* the new industrial powers which the credit system seemed to offer, appeared to have turned the heads of many of the men of that day.   Large sums had been made, especially by bankers, and it seemed as if there were no end to the fortunes which might be acquired.   There was, in consequence, an extraordinary violence in the changes of prices.   If a business was doing well, the gains were exaggerated, and many men were eager to rush into it, so that the price which had to be paid for shares was forced up unduly; on the other hand, if a stock fell there seems to have been a regular rush to get rid of it, and the price fell with extraordinary rapidity.   These violent fluctuations must have given extraordinary opportunities to stockbrokers; and one of the reasons why the new finance was condemned was because of the stimulus it gave to this gambling spirit; it seemed to divert men from honest enterprise, and encouraged the wildest speculation[1].   In some *Speculation and gambling.* cases, indeed, government played for this gambling spirit; the great financial expedient, in the year before the Bank of England was floated, was a Lottery; a sum of money was raised on all of which interest was to be paid in the usual way, but every fortieth share was to be entitled in addition to an annuity of a larger or smaller amount lasting for life[2]. This speculative element proved a great attraction, and it may have been the cheapest way of floating the loan, extravagant as the terms appear; but it was severely condemned at the time because of the countenance which Government gave to the gambling spirit.   This spirit showed itself in its *Projects in 1720.* most extravagant fashion in 1720 when an extraordinary

[1] Compare Sir John Barnard's speech during the debate on the Bill to prevent the infamous practice of Stock jobbing. *Parl. Hist.* IX. 54.

[2] 5 William and Mary, c. 7, § 39.

number of wild projects were floated[1]; and the shares of other undertakings were quoted at most extravagant prices[2]. The public were not accurately informed as to the possible profits in various lines of trade. They formed most extravagant estimates of the gain that might accrue from certain political concessions or from new industrial inventions. Of *South Sea Bubble.* these schemes the most celebrated was the South Sea Bubble, which was formed to carry on trade with Spanish America and which hoped to reap large profits both from the slave trade and from whale-fishing. There appeared to be an inexhaustible mine of wealth, and the shares rose rapidly from April 1720 when they stood at £120 till July when they are said to have reached £1020[3]. But, while on the one hand the possible profit had been over-rated, the capital of the Company had been sunk in procuring these concessions and in lending money to government, so that there was no sufficient means of carrying on the trade. When such mistakes

---

[1] There had been many such schemes before. Defoe, writing in 1697, complains of them bitterly. *Essay on Projects,* pp. 11—13.

[2] It may be worth while to insert here a brief account of the most gigantic of these ruinous projects, the South Sea Company. It was partly a trading and partly a financial Company, and as the promoters had secured the assiento contract for supplying Spanish America with slaves, and were also engaged in whale-fishery, they appeared to have great opportunities for profitable commerce. (*Parl. Hist.* VII. 628.) It was, however, as a financial company that they seemed likely to have a fund of wealth which would give them unexampled facilities for using their credit, as the directors were preparing to take over the whole of the National Debt. Under the influence of these large possibilities of gain the public rushed to buy shares which rose rapidly till £100 shares were selling at £890 (*Parl. Hist.* VII. 658) and even higher. Immense sums were made by those who speculated for the rise, while many bona-fide investors who had bought in when the stock was quoted at a high premium were forced to submit to terrible loss. The proprietors who had held on through the rise and the subsequent fall did not, of course, lose so seriously. The attempt to do justice in connection with the affairs of the Company was beset with many difficulties. On the one hand it was desirable to preserve the public engagements unviolated, on the other it was desirable if possible to punish the speculators for the misrepresentations which had gulled the public and if possible to deprive them of their ill-gotten gains. But it was exceedingly difficult to discriminate between the different classes of shareholders who had bought at different dates in any attempt to reimburse them for their losses. The subject is discussed with great care in a series of tracts which were published at the time by Archibald Hutcheson, the Member for Hastings, who criticized the scheme in its earlier stages and kept his head cool during the disaster. The career of the South Sea Company in its financial aspect was at an end; it also failed to find whaling profitable and had many competitors in the slave-trade.

[3] Postlethwayt, *Dictionary,* Art. *Actions.*

were made in commerce, there is no wonder that men entirely A.D. 1689
—1776. miscalculated the possible profits from new inventions, and the list of projects which were floated in 1720 shows an extraordinary willingness on the part of the public to take shares in any scheme however wild[1]. As in more recent times, mining offered a great field for such speculation; there were one or two notorious projectors, like Sir Humphry Mackworth[2], who were for ever producing new schemes. The terrible crisis of 1720[3] did something to secure greater caution, to render the public more chary of being beguiled by every romance and to make them realise the importance of capital as the basis of credit.

295. The development of banking must have been an *The circulating medium.* immense aid in providing a circulating medium for large payments, but it did not do much to facilitate the payment of small sums[4]. There were constant complaints of the export of silver and of mischiefs connected with the other coins. These evils sprang, as it appears, from the same cause; gold, silver and copper were all coined, and the coins in each case were supposed to represent the value of the bullion they contained. The ratio at which silver passed for gold in this country in 1717 was about $15\frac{1}{4}$ to 1; while on the continent the ratio was more nearly $14\frac{1}{2}$ to 1[5]. The result was that it *Export of Coinage.* was always remunerative to export silver to buy gold. There was a similar difficulty with regard to copper. Copper coins were supposed to circulate in accordance with their value as bullion; and there was a great outcry against patentees who obtained the right to coin, because it was said that their money did not contain bullion equivalent to the same amount in silver or gold. This was apparently disproved, so far as the English coinage of copper was concerned, in 1696; but it *Wood's Copper Coinage.* was found impossible to allay the outcry which was raised against the halfpennies coined for Ireland by Mr Wood. He appears to have been a thorough man of business, who carried

---

[1] See the Order of 12th July 1720, and list of Bubbles, *Parl. Hist.* VII. 655.

[2] *Parl. Hist.* VI. 892.

[3] Compare the petitions in *Parl. Hist.* VII. 760.

[4] On currency difficulties in New England and 'country pay' see Weeden, *New England*, 314, 379.

[5] Ruding. II. 67.

A.D. 1689
—1776.

Swift.
.

*Ratio of
Silver and
Gold.*

*Standard
Coin.*

out the terms of his agreement most honourably, but he was not successful in making the coinage uniform; and the lighter halfpennies gave excuse for an agitation of which Dean Swift made himself the spokesman, both from the pulpit and in his celebrated *Drapier's Letters*. It was impossible to allay the discontent; though the halfpence must have been a great convenience, as in some parts of Ireland there was such a scarcity of coinage that wages had to be paid with tallies and cards[1]. The new coins could not be got into circulation; they had to be withdrawn, and Mr Wood was compensated for the loss of his patent[2]. The point on which Swift insisted, was the sentimental one that there ought to be a mint in Ireland[3], and he appears to have greatly exaggerated the possible loss through the deficiency of bullion and Wood's halfpennies. According to Sir Isaac Newton and the other authorities of the Mint, Wood's coins were quite up to the standard of those which had previously circulated in Ireland, and were as good as the copper coinage of England[4].

But after all, the relations of· silver and copper were of much less importance than those of silver and gold. Before the recoinage of silver, when the silver was much clipped and worn, a guinea had gone up to thirty shillings. Even after the recoinage they did not exchange on the terms at which they were respectively rated; and the question began to be seriously discussed which of the two precious metals was the real measure of value and which should be treated as money of account? It was pointed out that silver was, as a matter of fact, the material actually used by the greater number of the inhabitants of the country in measuring the value of a day's labour or of quantities of corn and other necessaries; hence, it was maintained that since silver was the measure of value as a matter of fact it should be retained as the standard, and that gold and copper should be treated as mere substitutes for the standard money[5]. All that was done, however, was to try to improve the character of the gold coin, not to

---

[1] Ruding, II. 68.   [2] Coxe's *Memoirs of Sir R. Walpole*, I. 217.
[3] *Swift's Works*, Vol. XI. 33.   [4] Ruding, II. 70.
[5] Massie, *Observations relating to the Coin*, p. 13.

interfere with the double standard. Gold was to be called in A.D. 1689 —1776. and recoined, and for the future gold was to pass by weight as well as by tale. It has been shewn above that the practice of weighing gold coins continued long after the practice of weighing silver had fallen into disuse[1]; from this time it was revived as a means of doing away with uncertainties which arose from irregularities in the coinage. This occurred in 1774, at the very time when the work of amending the coinage, which had been completed so far as silver was concerned, was extended to gold also[2].

296. The formation of a National Debt introduced a new *Changes in* era in the whole scheme of taxation. The monarchy had been *the import-* supposed to subsist on the Crown lands and feudal incidents, *Taxation.* with recourse to taxation on emergencies. In the Civil War the last remnants of this fiscal policy disappeared and the expenses of government were chiefly borne by direct taxation; but great difficulty was found in devising forms of taxation, and in distributing the burden fairly throughout the country. The expedients which the Commonwealth adopted, left a memory of fiscal oppression which seriously hampered subsequent governments in their attempts to raise money for the ordinary expenses of government; and which rendered it very difficult to provide for emergencies. When the advisers of William III. began borrowing to meet these emergencies, it was necessary that the taxation of the country should *The basis* afford the basis on which the credit of the country rested. *of credit.* There was in consequence a constant dread of any diminution in the available sources of taxation, as it appeared that the whole fabric of national credit would collapse if the revenue began appreciably to contract and did not show signs of expansion as the national responsibilities increased. This was the inner reason of the anxiety to tax the colonies, as may be easily seen by considering the attitude of Grenville, before he was driven to make this attempt. Careful ex- *The* amination of the different sources of revenue was of the *sources of* utmost importance, so as to discriminate those, where the yield could be increased, from others where the limit of profit-

---

[1] Vol. I. p. 300, n. 1.   [2] Ruding, II. 85.

able taxation had been reached[1]. This was necessary, not only to provide for the current expenses of administration, but in order to guard against any risk of national bankruptcy.

Views as to repayment. During this period there was a decided change in the attitude which was taken by statesmen towards these debts. The men of the revolutionary period had regarded borrowing as a merely temporary expedient. In the time of George I., those who were eager to pay off the debt were unheeded by practical politicians, who gave their attention to financial operations by which the annual interest might be reduced; and in the time of George III. the government had become habituated to perpetual indebtedness and was lulled into false security by the existence of a sinking fund[2], so that they rushed recklessly into struggles which added enormously to the burden that had to be permanently borne.

Parliamentary jealousy of the Crown. Another feature which distinguished the finance of the Revolution has been already alluded to, in connection with the repression of the woollen industry in Ireland. The Commons were determined that the King should be constantly dependent on them for supplies. They would not make grants which might enable the most necessary administrative functions to be discharged without constant recourse to Parliament. Thus the customs were granted to the King and Queen, not for life but for a period of four years only[3], an arrangement with which William was by no means satisfied. He had the excise for life, but Charles and James had enjoyed the customs as well; but Bishop Burnet persuaded him to let the House of Commons protect themselves against his successors, though it was at the expense of a slight to himself personally. The same feeling came out as has been already noted in constituting the Bank of England; but it had a real influence on all our fiscal arrangements, and the practice of

---

[1] Davenant, *Ways and Means*, 46.

[2] See below, § 345, p. 545. It had a similar effect at an earlier time (1737). The monied interest held that the Sinking Fund was "a certain way of paying off all our debts" (*Parl. Hist.* x. 96) and opposed Sir John Barnard's schemes for the reduction of interest on public debts to three per cent., and thus relieving taxation (*Ib.* 155).

[3] *Parl. Hist.* v. 561.

making grants for short periods has been usual since the A.D. 1689 —1776.
Revolution.

From this time too, the arrangements for the ordinary expenses of government were organised in a manner which still remains in form, though the scale on which it was devised was far smaller than is necessary at the present day. The whole of the expenses of government in time of peace *Civil List.* were[1] calculated at £1,200,000[2]; of this sum £600,000 was appropriated to the Civil List, which included not only the royal household and pensioners but the judges, ambassadors, and other members of the Civil Service. Before the close of William's reign this was increased by another £100,000[3]; and the hereditary excise and some other branches of revenue were devoted to defraying this sum, though if they yielded a large revenue it was to be at the disposal of Parliament[4]. This was the element of national expense which was practically stable. The naval and military expenditure on a peace footing, was expected to bring the total national expenditure to £1,200,000, but with the frequent wars this sum was constantly exceeded.

297. During the whole of this period there was a great *The incidence of Taxation.* deal of discussion as to the incidence of taxation, partly with reference to the claims of the community who were charged, and partly with reference to the ultimate pressure of the tax, whoever paid it in the first instance.

There was a very general feeling that the taxation of the country fell with unfair pressure on the landowners, and that the monied men practically escaped taxation altogether. Attempts to assess the property of the country, and to tax by *Assessment of Property.* a rate of so much in the pound, were made in the first years after the Revolution; but the assessment was so careless that the amount produced failed to realise the expectations of the Commons; in 1697 they had recourse to the expedient of voting a sum of £494,671, or half a million of money as the

---

[1] Dowell, *History of Taxation,* II. 46.

[2] *Parl. Hist.* v. 193.

[3] 9 and 10 W. III. c. 23.

[4] On the increase of the Civil List, see Wilkes' Speech. It contains a capital résumé of the financial character of different reigns. *Parl. Hist.* xix. 108.

A.D. 1689
—1776.
equivalent of a rate of a shilling in the pound. This was levied according to the assessment of 1692, and just as the tenths and fifteenths had come to be a fixed sum, based on the agreement of 1334, and again the subsidies in Tudor time had come to mean a definite sum of £80,000[1], so the rates upon property came to mean multiples of half a million for every shilling at which the rate was levied. This was locally assessed, and as the original payers of quotas on personal property died, the entire payment came to be assessed on land, and the Property Tax turned out to be a tax on real

Land tax. property only[2]. Even as a tax on real property it was most unfair. Davenant, who examined into the matter with great care, showed that the home counties were assessed much

Pressure in different counties. more heavily than those in the north and west. This had been due at first to the manner in which the Commonwealth had laid the heaviest burden upon the counties on which they could rely. An unsuccessful attempt was made to correct this at the Restoration, when the assessment for ship money had been taken as a model, on account of the known care with which it had been made. Davenant endeavours to show, by appealing to the excise, the poll tax, the hearth rate and the poor rate, that the northern and western counties had improved more rapidly than the home counties in the intervening period, and should therefore pay a larger quota than was charged upon them in the property tax[3]. The property tax was thus doubly unfair, since it fell exclusively upon real property and as land of equal value in different counties bore very dissimilar shares of the burden.

The monied interest. There was in consequence a very decided feeling in many quarters, that it was desirable to lay taxes upon the monied interest, or to find taxes which should touch them. "The ancient subsidies," says Davenant, "did usually consist of a charge by poll, a pound rate upon land, and a pound rate upon money and personal estates, so that all sorts of people did contribute something in the old way of taxing, but such as for their poverty were exempted. The usurers who are the true drones of a commonwealth, living upon the honey

[1] Dowell, I. 197.   [2] *Ib.* II. 53.
[3] Davenant, *Ways and Means*, 66—120.

without any labour, should of all people be brought in to A.D. 1689 —1776. bear their proportion of the common burden. As yet they could never be effectually reached, but they may be fetched in by the wisdom of a Parliament, if the House of Commons would please resolutely to set themselves about it[1]." He goes on to argue that the capital lent out at interest was something like twenty millions, and that if the interest were 5 per cent. a four shilling rate would yield £200,000.

The advisers of William III. adopted some of the expedients which Davenant proposed for reaching other classes. Poll taxes were levied from 1689 to 1698, but the tax was so *Suggestions for reaching them.* unpopular that it had to be dropped[2]; a house tax was supposed to fall on city retail traders[3], and immediately afterwards a license was required from hawkers. The stamp duties were levied in 1694 in imitation of Dutch finance[4]. These were steps in the direction which Davenant advocated; but the attempt to tax the capital in the great joint-stock companies as he suggested, had already been made and discontinued after a year's trial[5]. Such taxes were undoubtedly inexpensive to collect, but as they failed to produce the expected results, great efforts were made to impose indirect taxes which should fall upon all classes in the community. Davenant was a great advocate for an excise; excises would *Excise.* reach "the usurers, lawyers, tradesmen and retailers with all that troop that maintain themselves by our vice and luxury, and who make the easiest and most certain gain and profit in the commonwealth[6]." He would have graduated duties according to the character of the goods, "charging the things of luxury high and the necessaries of life but at a low rate. That kind of revenue must needs be very great where so large a part of the people are every minute paying something towards it; and very easy where every one in a manner taxes himself, making consumption according to his will or

---

[1] *Ways and Means*, 111.
[2] Dowell, II. 48.   [3] *Ib.* 54, and 7 and 8 W. III. c. 18.
[4] *Ib.* 62, and 5 and 6 W. and M. c. 21.
[5] *Ib.* 63, 4 and 5 W. and M. c. 15, §§ 10—12.
[6] He held that they had two-thirds of the wealth of the country while the remaining third, land and foreign trade, bore the main part of the taxes. *Ways and Means*, 122.

ability[1]." He thought that the difficulties of collection were over-rated and that if the tax were levied on bulky articles publicly sold, there would be no necessity for searching private houses[2]. One tax which was levied in accordance with this doctrine was the tax on malt as well as one on leather[3], imposed by William III.[4], also taxes on candles[5] and soap[6], imposed under Anne.

It is perhaps worth while to notice here that the line of argument which Davenant followed was re-echoed by many subsequent writers and was fraught with serious political results when Walpole endeavoured to give effect to it in 1731. His measure, which bore the name of an excise, was after all only a further development of the system of warehousing which had come into vogue in 1700 for foreign silks. He had applied it with success to tea in 1723, so that he had been able to reduce the duty on importation and at the same time to check smuggling[7]. When he tried the same expedient with regard to wine and tobacco, he was met with a storm of opposition from the fact that the bill was termed an excise[8]. It had followed close on the revival of the excise on salt[9], and the wildest passions were roused from a dread that excises were being gradually introduced on all articles of common consumption. Englishmen like Dr Johnson[10] valued a free breakfast table as the badge of national liberty; and Walpole was forced to give way ignominiously[11].

The dislike of an excise was of course due to a dread that the prices of all commodities would be raised and that the course of trade would be seriously affected. Davenant wrote at a period when it was possible to argue that an assize might be set for bread and all other necessary commodities and that, even if the gains of middlemen were kept down by

[1] Ways and Means, 123.　[2] Ib. 131.
[3] Dowell, II. 59 (1697).　[4] 8 and 9 W. III. c. 21.
[5] 8 Anne, c. 9.　[6] Dowell, II. 78 (1712).　[7] Ib. 97.
[8] Parl. Hist. VIII. 1234, 1268; IX. 1. Genuine Thoughts of a Merchant (1733), is a capital pamphlet in support of his proposal. Comparatively low custom duties were to be charged on importation and warehousing, the excise was to be levied when the goods were taken from the warehouse for home consumption. Dowell, II. 98, 103.
[9] Parl. Hist. VIII. 946, 1019, 1040.
[10] Boswell, Life II. 48. See also Excise, in Dictionary.　[11] Dowell, II. 105.

enforcing such regulations, neither the consumer nor producer would suffer; "so that in effect the excise would be answered to the King out of the immoderate and unlawful gain" made by bakers, corn-chandlers, inn-keepers and butchers[1]. But it was becoming obvious even then that this system had had its day and that it was idle to rely upon it. Competition had become so general in all departments of life, that it was possible for Locke[2] to argue that all exactions levied *Locke.* on goods of home production must ultimately fall upon the landlord. Merchants and brokers would raise their prices by the full value of the tax, labourers would obtain higher wages or else come on the parish, and as the farmers would have increased expenses they would necessarily pay a diminished rent. Locke's doctrine on this subject was very generally accepted, and was the basis for all attempts to reform our taxation by substituting direct for indirect taxation. If it be true, as Locke asserted, that all taxation was ultimately borne by the land, why should it not be levied on it in the first instance, and thus leave trade undisturbed? A practical proposal, which at least went in this direction, was strongly advocated by Sir Matthew Decker in the House *Decker.* of Commons[3]. He thought that a tax levied upon houses would be easily collected. The tax was to be graduated; the

---

[1] *Ways and Means,* 126.

[2] *Considerations of the Lowering of Interest* in *Works,* v. 57. Davenant recognised that this was true as a remote consequence but the immediate pressure would fall as he believed on other classes. *Ways and Means,* 153.

[3] In 1739 was written *An Essay on the Causes of the Decline of the Foreign Trade,* which was attributed to Richardson. It is full of excellent criticism on the then existing arrangements for taxation, and it proposes to replace all existing exactions both local and national by a single tax which should fall on every one all round: so far it coincides closely with the plan that was advocated by Sir Matthew Decker, but this new tax was not to be a tax on consumption but a tax that should be levied directly by compelling everyone to take out a license for all sorts of articles of luxury which they might intend to use. The tract was reprinted more than once and appears to have attracted a good deal of attention. It is mentioned here as a curiosity in sumptuary proposals, and as an ingenious attempt to touch the pockets of the consumers directly with the least possible interference with trade, p. 44. Temple (see p. 560 below) and Caldwell (*Debates* 782) attributed it to Decker, but the disregard of Decker's own scheme, and the condemnation of the Navigation Acts which Decker approved, render this most unlikely. Still more interesting is the proposal for substituting direct taxation on land and funded property for the indirect taxes which hampered trade, and which as Locke had argued ultimately fell upon land. *Thoughts on the pernicious consequences of borrowing money* (1759) (Trinity College Library, T. 2. 133).

houses of the poor would be altogether exempt and other houses would pay at rates which would average £10 a house and produce six millions a year. This he argued would allow of applying a million per annum to the reduction of the debt[1].

Financial difficulties at the Union.
298. The pressure of national debt in England was one of the chief difficulties in connection with the Union between England and Scotland. This Union had been long desired, but it was greatly accelerated so far as England was concerned by the events connected with the ill-fated Darien Company. Englishmen recognised that Scotland was in a *The Darien* position to inflict irreparable damage to their commerce[2], *Scheme.* and that the existence of an independent Scottish Parliament was a source of serious danger. The Darien Company had been authorised by the Scotch Parliament to colonize, make fortifications, fit out vessels of war and contract alliances. Their settlement in Darien was to have been a free port, which would have seriously affected the success of the English Navigation policy. They might break through the monopoly of the East India Company; they had secured the parliamentary authorisation for which the English Company were pleading in vain; they opened an office and received subscriptions in London. They were preparing to compete in those trades which Englishmen prized most highly; while they also aroused the Spaniards and strained their relations with Englishmen, both with regard to the West Indian and the African trade. Their schemes for trading with Archangel, and of carrying on the whale fishery, were opposed to the interests of the Russian and Greenland Companies. On every side the leading English trades were threatened; and the embroglios which followed with the Spaniards rendered it impossible for King William to support his northern subjects in their great undertaking. The seeds of failure were thus sown in the expedition from the first; and the Scottish indignation, which was roused by the narrative of the survivors, who returned from Darien, was embittered by the sense of a pecuniary loss which the

---

[1] *Serious considerations on the several High Duties*, London 1744, p. 17. This is undoubtedly Decker's; the seventh (1756) edition bears his name, as well as the title-page of Horsley's reply. (*Serious Considerations examined*, 1744.)

[2] *Parl. Hist.* v. 975.

country could ill afford. The Scotch assumed a menacing A.D. 1689
—1776. attitude; and the English learned that a complete legislative Union of the two countries must be procured at any cost[1].

When the Commissioners met, the English proceeded to deal with this point first of all. The English were deter- *Terms of* mined to have a legislative as distinguished from any form *Union.* of a federal union, and insisted that this matter should be voted on first, before entering on the discussion of any details[2]. But when this was once secured, they appear to have treated the Scotch Commissioners generously on all points of detail. The quota which Scotland was to pay towards a land tax of four shillings in the pound was £48,000 as against £2,000,000 from England[3], while certain duties on malt and coals which were to expire within a brief period were not imposed upon Scotland at all. But besides this, Scotland received a considerable equivalent on account of the debt with which England was burdened. The portion of each class of taxation, whether customs or excise, which was appropriated to the English Debt was taken, and the proportion which they bore to the whole customs and excise in England was calculated out[4]. Similar calculations in regard to the different branches of the Scottish revenue brought out the fact that £398,085. 10s. would be a fair equivalent to be paid to Scotland for incurring her share of the English National Debt by submitting to an incorporating Union. This sum was to be applied to winding up the Darien Company and paying other debts[5], and to making the

---

[1] For an excellent account of the Darien Company see J. H. Burton, *History of Scotland from the Revolution*, Chap. VIII. The Darien Company suffered from the want of experience of its directors, and almost every one of the difficulties which were felt in the more powerful English Companies. As a trading concern the Directors were entirely ignorant of the right commodities for export, as a colony there was no proper government which could restrain the disorderly and buccaneering elements, and the capital was quite insufficient for the projects they had in view. It had been raised with some difficulty in Scotland, and though the capital was all taken up, it was not a bona fide subscription, as some of the share. holders received guarantees from the Company guaranteeing them against actual loss. (*Ib.* I. 297.) The general impression which was abroad, that the tropics were fertile and wealthy, prevented the Directors from sending out the supplies which might have saved the Colonists from utter ruin.

[2] Burton, I. 407.   [3] *Ib.* I. 412.   [4] *Ib.* I. 415.

[5] The amount allotted to this purpose proved insufficient, and the creditors were incorporated as the Royal Bank of Scotland in 1727. The monopoly of the Bank of Scotland was thus broken down. Macleod, II. 204.

A.D. 1689
—1776. necessary changes in the coinage; while the balance formed
the fund already referred to for promoting Scotch fisheries
and manufactures.

The treaty thus arranged was carried through the Scotch
Parliament in spite of the indignant protests of Lord Bel-
haven. There was indeed one trivial circumstance which
caused much friction after the matter was settled[1]. The
*Scotch
farmers of
customs.* Scotch customs were farmed out, and naturally this arrangement came to an end, when the separate Scotch taxation
ceased. The farmers of taxes, knowing that their time was
short, found it most profitable to levy very small duties and
admit large quantities of goods with which the English
markets were eventually flooded. This brought about considerable commercial disturbance for a time, but no special
measures were taken, as there seemed to be no likelihood
that the occurrence would be repeated.

The figures which have been given above may perhaps
serve better than any others that are available to indicate
*Economic
results in
Scotland.* the relative economic importance of the two kingdoms at the
time of their Union. It does not appear that much progress
was made in Scotland during the first half century after the
Union[2]. It is not improbable that Scottish manufactures
suffered by free communication with English towns, and that
the steel manufacturers at Falkirk and the glovers of Perth
were not so prosperous after the Union as they had been
before. The Scotch towns seem to have been more hampered than the English ones in the eighteenth century by
their exclusive corporations; on the other hand the separate
maintenance of Scotch law had saved the northern artisans
from the injurious influence of the Poor-Laws and Act of
Settlement. But though Scotch banking developed rapidly,
it was not easy to replace the great destruction of capital
by the Darien Company, and in all those departments where
capital was required Scotland lagged behind or made at best
but fitful progress. In the middle of the eighteenth century

---

[1] *Parl. Hist.* vi. 579.

[2] *Parl. Hist.* vi. 1216; Burton, ii. 392, 399. For an excellent account of the
condition of Scotland just before the Union see *Proposals and Reasons for constituting a Council of Trade* (1701). [Brit. Mus. 1029, d. 6.]

there must have been a most striking contrast between the A.D. 1689
—1776. agriculture of the two countries; comparatively little had been done to improve the one and the traditional methods of cultivation were almost universal; but somewhat later a race of improvers[1] arose in the northern kingdom like those who had done so much for England before the days of Arthur Young's Tours.

299. From the time of the Union, the fiscal system of the two Kingdoms became the same; and the changes which were introduced were conducted on the same principles; though they were sometimes directed with special regard to England, as in the woollen trade, and sometimes with special regard to Scotland, as in connection with linen. The administration of Walpole, and the long peace which he *Walpole's* succeeded in maintaining, gave an opportunity for recasting *Adminis-tration.* our fiscal system in many important directions. He made serious efforts to reduce the National Debt by means of a *The Cus-* sinking fund; but his great achievement was in connection *toms and* with the customs. As has been said above, he altered the method of collecting, and reduced the duties so as to diminish smuggling. In regard to other branches however, his changes are of more interest, for he modified the whole of the customs in accordance with the most approved principles *the Mer-* of the Mercantile System. The measures mentioned above *System.* for encouraging the production of timber from Nova Scotia[2], for cheapening the materials and encouraging the export of silk manufactures[3], for relieving the whale-fishery and removing the duties on materials entering the country were all due to his administration, while he also repealed the export duties on all the manufactures of Great Britain with some trivial exceptions[4]. His friends could boast that he had so altered the tariff that he had made it the best in the world. Before his time it had been a jumble of incon-sistencies. "I cannot omit taking notice," says Hutcheson *Hutcheson.* in 1717[5], "how inconsistently we act with relation to our

---

[1] Alexander, *Northern Rural Life*, 101—107.　　[2] 8 Geo. I. c. 12.
[3] 8 Geo. I. c. 15.　　　　　　　　　　　　[4] Dowell, II. 94.
[5] *Collection of Treatises*, p. 21. (*Some Considerations relating to the Payment of the Publick Debts.*)

Exportations. We give a bounty for exporting corn, and in that we do wisely, and yet we have laid Duties on the exportation of many other of the products and manufactures of Great Britain; and, which is still worse, some products, which, if exported unmanufactured, pay no duty, but, if manufactured, are subjected to the same, as if it were a service to the Publick to discourage the Manufactures of Great Britain. But that which exceeds all these Follies, and is indeed amazingly monstrous, is, that some Foreign Products, as Silk for instance, if exported unmanufactured, is entitled to a drawback, but if manufactured is subjected to a Duty. It were endless to enumerate all the discouragements which our Trade lies under."

Increase of the Debt. Walpole's experience was final in regard to attempting to impose an excise on any considerable scale. As a consequence statesmen were forced to give up all idea of meeting large war expenses by heavy taxation within the year, and each new war brought a great increase to the National Debt. Walpole had endeavoured to prevent the war with Spain, which had originated in troubles about the pretensions of the Spaniards to limit British trade with central America and search British ships, but he was foiled by Jenkins[1] and his ear. This conflict, together with the war of the Austrian succession, raised our Debt from forty-six millions to seventy-six[2] millions. The Seven Years' War (1756-1763) cost us eighty-two millions and added nearly sixty[3] to our Debt, and statesmen were at their wits' end how to meet the increasing charges. In Walpole's time the revenue was about five millions and three-quarters; twenty years later (1755) it was six millions and three-quarters, and on the eve of the war of Independence it had risen to ten millions[4]. There had on the whole been a time of prosperity which rendered it possible to bear these burdens. But the strides with which the Debt increased were a continual source of anxiety.

Necessity for increased taxation. Henry Fox was well aware of the evil effects of heavy customs on our commerce, but he argued with great force that since money must be had somehow, there was no better

---

[1] Coxe's *Walpole*, I. 578.   [2] Dowell, II. 111.
[3] *Ib.* 131.   [4] *Ib.* 111, 130, 163.

method by which it could be obtained. The hearth money A.D. 1689
—1776. under the Stuarts, the poll-taxes under King William and Walpole's excise created such discontent that no minister could dare to have recourse to them, and an increase of the customs seemed to him the only means that was available[1]. He persuaded the Commons, though not without difficulty, to grant a subsidy of 5 per cent. on the value of goods as already rated[2]. But the chief increase on taxes during this period was by additional exactions on spirits and on beer[3]; *Beer and Spirits.* these measures had the support of Pitt, who had come to regard excises as inevitable, though he was anxious that they should be imposed judiciously and should not render it necessary for Government officials to search private houses. It was on this account that he opposed an excise on cider[4]. *Cider.* Despite his opposition the Act passed; for Grenville, who regarded the financial situation as extremely serious, followed the line taken by Fox and challenged Pitt to suggest any other possible source of revenue. Great disturbances ensued in the cider counties, and the case was so serious that Lord Bute was driven from office and the obnoxious measure was shortly afterwards repealed.

It was at this time that George Grenville endeavoured to give effect to a project which had been under long and careful consideration. He adopted a scheme for a Stamp Act for *American* America, which had been rejected by Walpole many years *Stamp Act.* before[5]. The measure raised a storm of indignation in the

---

[1] *Parl. Hist.* xiv. 164—72.

[2] 21 Geo. II. c. 2.

[3] Dowell, ii. 139.

[4] The excuse for the new cider tax was obviously that it was a mere equivalent for the excises on beer which were levied in other parts of England. Mannie's opposition to it is particularly instructive. He was most anxious to insist on the principle that the prosperity of the whole depends on the welfare of each part. At that very time there was, as he proved, a tendency for the woollen manufactures to migrate from the cider counties to Yorkshire. This migration denuded Devonshire of its population and added enormously to the poor-rates from the necessity of supporting the unemployed. To levy a tax on the cider counties would be to give an additional premium to migration to the north where "greater plenty of firing and cheaper rates of other necessaries of life favour their increase much more than in our southern counties." *Observations on the New Cyder Tax.* Number 4.

[5] Dowell, ii. 150.

colonies, it proved utterly unremunerative[1] and its repeal was effected by Pitt. But though this was a failure, it was not so clear that the imposition of customs, which might be regarded not as a method of raising revenue but as a scheme for regulating trade, was equally open to attack. Grenville had levied such customs at American ports in 1764, and Townshend thought it possible to add to these customs in 1767. He did not live to see the result of his interference, but the duties which he imposed were for the most part taxes on the importation of English manufactured goods. It was thus obvious that they were imposed not as a trade regulation but as a means of revenue. At the instigation of the English manufacturers the greater part of the duties were withdrawn[2]; but the duty on tea, which was allowed to remain and which was of the trivial amount of threepence a pound, was enough to excite the apprehensions of the colonists who were now thoroughly aroused. The destruction of the tea ships in Boston harbour, the resentment of the Home Government and the Declaration of Independence were consequences which had become inevitable. It was thus that the pressure of National Debt forced statesmen to seek for new sources of taxation, at the very time when the reasons which attached the colonies to the mother country had ceased to be so effective as formerly.

VIII.   Economic Doctrine[3].

Unique position of Adam Smith.   300.   When we turn to examine the progress of economic doctrine during the eighteenth century, we find one writer who occupies a unique position; by universal consent Adam Smith stands out as the founder of modern political economy. He so entirely recast it that the ordinary student of economic doctrine is satisfied to trace the progress from his time, just

---

[1] The yield during the six months when it was in force was £4,000, which came in very slowly, and the expense of collecting was £6,857.

[2] Dowell, II. 161, and 10 Geo. III. c. 17.

[3] This chapter has been already published in the *Economic Journal*, 1891.

as the astronomer marks a new departure in the system of a.d. 1699
—1776.
Copernicus, and modern philosophy took a new shape at the
hands of Kant. In each of those cases. however. it is possible
to note anticipations and suggestions in the thoughts of
previous writers: and those, whose curiosity tempts them to
go behind *The Wealth of Nations* on some tentative explora-
tion, are not unlikely to be surprised to find that so many
men of wide knowledge and accurate habits of thought had
already devoted themselves to the study of economic phenomena. It is a literary problem of no little interest to discover how far these various writers led up to *The Wealth of
Nations*, and to discriminate precisely wherein the secret of
Adam Smith's marked superiority really lay. The impression
he made upon his contemporaries, and the unique position
which his book maintains at the present day, prove beyond
dispute that he was incomparably superior to all his predecessors: but it is not easy to account for the difference. We
cannot detect the characteristic feature in his work by comparing him, not always to his advantage, with some previous
writer who wrote brilliantly upon a special point: and we
can only hope to discover it by reviewing the progress of
economic doctrine for many years before he wrote, and thus
attempting to mark the precise nature of the new contribution which enabled him to transform the study so completely.

It is of course clear that circumstances favoured a great *General
conditions*
advance in economic doctrine during the eighteenth century. *favourable
to progress,*
since there was so much progress in industrial, commercial.
and agricultural affairs. The phenomena connected with the
increase of wealth were more obvious, and a keen observer
like Adam Smith, who had frequent intercourse with practical
men, was in an excellent position for reflecting on the causes
of this progress: but before his time, the changes, though decided, had been slow: other observers had noted and described
the more important facts, and traced out the causes that were
at work. A general condition of this kind, though it accounts
for the progress of the study as a whole, does not help to ex- *but these do
not explain*
plain the special eminence of Adam Smith. We shall find a *his special
eminence.*
better guide if we recur to the writers of the revolutionary
period for a starting-point and look at the mere form and

divisions of the subject in the treatises which were published
then, and compare them with *The Wealth of Nations*.

*Davenant
and Petty
deal with
revenue,*
301. Davenant and Petty were writers of extraordinary
acuteness. Their works are full of careful statistics, and of
accurate and ingenious remark. Numberless phrases can be
culled from their works which anticipate the reasonings of
later writers, but the very titles of their chief books show
that their view of the subject is restricted. They deal with
the expenses of government as the one important topic;
Petty's great work is *A Treatise of Taxes and Contributions*,
which was written with special reference to the fiscal administration of Ireland; Davenant compiled *An Essay on Ways
and Means of Supplying the War*. The central thoughts
with both are the expenses of government and the modes of
defraying them; though from this starting-point they proceed
to treat the subject with much judgment and skill, the form
which all the problems take is affected by the point of view
from which they look at them.

*the funds
from which
it was
drawn,*
Since these economists dealt primarily with English
revenue, there were three main funds to be considered; the
increase of treasure which was necessary in order to defray
the expenses of war and thus to render the Government
secure against emergencies; the increase of commerce and of
the customs; and the increase of the wealth of the landed
class who contributed such a large proportion of the revenue
of the country. Bullion gave the means of gathering and
amassing treasure; and if trade were so managed as to afford
an opportunity for accumulating treasure there seemed to be
plain evidence that the Government was in good case; and
the Balance of Trade apparently offered a simple means of
estimating how far this was so. The customs had been an
important source of revenue from the time of Edward III.;
and the resources of the landowners as a fund for possible
taxation had been kept in view since William noted the
assessment of every estate in Domesday book.

*and the
factors
which
maintained
them.*
The economists of the Revolution era also looked below
the funds from which contributions were paid, and tried to
analyze the causes which might keep these funds amply supplied; they were ready to look at the factors which go to the

production of national prosperity—factors which facilitated A.D. 1689 —1776. the cultivation of land, and which worked up the manufactured goods which we exported to other lands. Locke laid stress on labour as the productive cause of value; while Gregory King and others insisted that labour depended for its effect on the fund which employed it, and studied the condition of various ranks of society with special reference to their ability to save capital. Capital, too, was able to utilize and send to market the results obtained through the productive power of nature; and thus attention was not exclusively given to the funds from which taxes were defrayed, but also to the factors by which these funds were maintained.

When economists thus examined the factors which produced national prosperity it became possible for them to *Possibility of comparison.* compare the working of these factors in various countries even though these countries presented many differences. The English method of taxation from the land was repugnant to French subjects, who had, however, no strong objection to an excise, which the English freeholder hated as the worst of tyrannies. Differences of national temperament[1] rendered it difficult to compare the fiscal policy of the two Governments or to discuss the relative advantages of either method; but after all the source, from which revenue was ultimately derived in both cases, was the material wealth of the subjects. In both cases labour, capital, and land were the factors which went to produce it, though they might contribute in different proportions to the prosperity of different lands; and hence the respective advantages and disadvantages of two or more countries could be discussed and compared.

302. During the first sixty years of the eighteenth *Fiscal difficulties.* century the financial condition and the fiscal possibilities of England were still the chief topics to which economic writers addressed themselves, and not without reason. Although there had been, as we see now, a remarkable growth in many directions, there were not a few causes for grave anxiety about the time of the Seven Years' War. The growth of the National Debt and the impossibility of finding new sources of taxation alarmed more than one statesman, and there

[1] Sir James Steuart, *Works*, I. 17.

were not a few economists who took a pessimistic view of the condition of the country. Their writings, however, are of far more interest from the light they throw on passing events, and ;from the statistics they contain, than from any very remarkable advance in economic doctrine. They all start from the old standpoint; their writing was of practical interest and their aim was that of rendering the nation prosperous and powerful as compared with other nations[1].

Postle-
thwayt.   Malachy Postlethwayt[2] was the most celebrated of these writers. Quite in the old manner he compares the commercial and colonial policy of England with that of Holland and of France, and tries to show how the British system might be improved, so as to outdo our rivals. Others were alarmed, not at the prosperity of our ancient rival, but at the pressure of indirect taxation. There were pamphlets without end as to the absolute necessity of living on the national income; and the failure of the Sinking Fund filled economists with the wildest forebodings as to the future of the country and the continued pressure of debt. There were others who were more concerned at the indirect effects of this indebtedness. Large debts meant heavy interest, and heavy interest meant that commerce was hampered by large custom duties. This was the cry of Decker, Richardson, Fauquier[3] and Tucker[4];
Prejudicial and in their enthusiasm for an unfettered commerce they
effects of
customs. were apparently inclined to sweep away all the expedients for directing trade. Indeed one main objection which was urged to their schemes was that they practically involved having free ports, and that this might lead to the cessation of any governmental efforts to guide the direction of capital. But though Richardson and Decker are apparently in favour of free trade, the manner in which they talk about the Balance of Trade goes to show that they were

---

[1] Even Caldwell does not appear to see that the principles of free intercourse which he urges for England and Ireland are of more general application, but treats them as a means of opposing France. He is remarkably clear in pointing out that an accumulation of bullion may injure a country's trade, and in some points he anticipates Wakefield; see below p. 605. *Enquiry* in *Debates*, 750.

[2] *Great Britain's True System* (1757).

[3] *Essay on Ways and Means for Raising Money* (1757).

[4] *Brief Essay on advantages and disadvantages of France and Great Britain* (1753), p. 42. [Temple?] regarded the outcry as mistaken, and thought the habits of the manufacturers, not the taxes, were the cause of injury. *Essay on Trade*, p. 13.

still on the platform of those who were considering the A.D. 1689 —1776. national prosperity as their main object, and chiefly interested in national wealth because it was the source of power.

In order to judge of the condition of any of the funds from which the revenue was drawn, and thus of the expediency of the rules then current for its conduct, it was convenient either to measure these resources as completely as possible, or to take some group of phenomena as typical of the rest. Torrents of schemes issued from the press, *Estimates of the condition of* containing wild guesses as to possible amounts, and wilder *dition of* interpretations of these uncertain data. *The Mercator* and *trade.* the *British Merchant* are full of figures, and Massie's numerous tracts are crammed with calculations; but the methods of statistical study were little appreciated, and few of these writers seem to have made serious efforts to check the accuracy of the figures on which they relied. Petty, of course, stands by himself as a pioneer; his work was of unexampled excellence, but those who imitated his studies were very far from following his example. In some cases those who did not attempt to compute the changes in England as a whole, were satisfied to take one branch of trade as exemplifying all the rest[1]. There was still one department of economic life which had a peculiar interest for Englishmen, and which was treated as of special importance—this was the maintenance of shipping as the means of offence and defence; *Shipping.* and this was regarded as an object of policy towards which the Government were bound to direct the three factors which increased wealth. It was a matter of public importance; and the art of government, as it was conceived in the eighteenth century, consisted in so guiding the private interest of individuals that they might work for the public good. In the sixteenth century moralists had written of private interest as if it were invariably hostile to public advantage. Men were expected to carry on their trade in a public-spirited fashion and not to regard their private lucre; but in the eighteenth century the force of self-interest was

---

[1] Thus Povey, who thought that the coal-trade employed most of English shipping, felt that a decline in this trade was conclusive as to the decay of English commerce. *Unhappiness of England*, 28.

recognized as a power that was rather indifferent than hostile to the public good, so that it seemed as if a very moderate amount of direction might be brought to bear, and thus induce men who were guided by self-interest alone to carry on their business in a manner that accorded with public prosperity[1].

Although it was particularly important to measure the improvement or decay of any of the factors which made for the production of wealth, it was by no means easy to do so. Political arithmeticians could, however, note symptoms which were specially striking; and they could look either at the results of our industry (agricultural and manufacturing) or at the conditions under which it was carried on,—these conditions having reference both to the facilities for procuring *Criteria commonly used.* capital and to the effectiveness of labour. These three points were most easily examined by considering three criteria, first the Balance of Trade, as showing the profitableness of our commercial intercourse with various countries; second, the rate of interest, as showing the facility with which capital might be procured, either for agriculture, manufacture, or commerce; thirdly, the condition of the poor, as showing how far the labourers could maintain themselves and add by their work to the wealth of the country, or how far they were dependent on funds procured by others.

303. These were the main topics of discussion among the economists in the middle of the eighteenth century, in so far as they dealt with anything larger than the *technique* of particular arts or of commercial transactions as a whole. *Change of view in regard to the balance of trade,* There was plenty of writing on these special points, as there had been in the preceding century; but little of it is of first-rate importance with regard to the general progress of economic study. This was gradually penetrating more deeply, however; and the writers of the middle of the eighteenth century were able to neglect subjects which their predecessors at the time of the Revolution had put into the forefront. Since the expenses of government could be defrayed by borrowing, the policy of hoarding treasure was no longer of importance; it simply drops out of sight altogether. Though

---

[1] Sir James Steuart, *Works*, I. 4.

attention was still constantly directed to the Balance of A.D. 1689
Trade, the significance which was attached to it had entirely —1776.
altered. In the seventeenth century, it was supposed to
measure the possible accumulations of treasure; in the
eighteenth it was treated as a criterion of the flourishing
condition of our industry.

There are other matters in regard to which we may *high rents,*
detect a change of view, for we hear far less about the high *and*
rental of land as a matter of congratulation. This was perhaps partly due to a change of fiscal policy; the land-tax had
been assessed permanently, and there was less possibility of
expansion in the revenue derived from this source. But it
was also due to the fact that though the theory of rent was
not generally understood, there was a clearer apprehension of
the truth that the production from the soil was primarily
dependent on the capital employed in improvements, and
that if capital were plentiful, agriculture and all connected
with it would be flourishing too. The time of rural improvement had begun, and capitalists, under the inducement
offered by the bounty on export, were sinking their capital in
land. There was no need for special anxiety about this
source of taxation. Besides this, Walpole had reorganized
another of these funds—the Customs, for he had effected a *the*
revolution in our tariff; he tried to reconstruct it entirely with *Customs.*
a view of promoting our industrial prosperity, and did not
regard it merely as a source of revenue, but chiefly as an instrument for directing industry, or stimulating it. It thus
came about that the three topics which had engrossed attention in the seventeenth century, the balance of trade, high
rents, and the customs, entirely lost their old importance.
Though the old subjects are discussed and many of the old
phrases are retained, there is a marked advance ·in the
thoroughness of economic studies in the middle of the
eighteenth century, as compared even with those of the
revolutionary period and certainly with the writers of still
earlier times.

304. Indeed, while there was the same desire as of old *Historical*
to guide the industry and commerce of the country so as to *studies.*
promote its power, there are general indications that men

were beginning to feel a difficulty in applying any of their tests rigidly, and deciding what would prove beneficial. Some were inclined to collect additional information, to fall back upon the history of some department of industry for a considerable number of years, to note its periods of prosperity or of failure and to try and assign the causes which had affected it in either case. The most remarkable and complete of such

J. Smith. treatises is John Smith's *Chronicon-Rusticum-Commerciale, or Memoirs of Wool*, a book which gives an exceedingly detailed account, based on documentary evidence, of the growth of this staple trade. The policy, which was pursued in one period, is contrasted with the line that was taken at another time, and contemporary literature is drawn on in the fullest possible manner, with the view of indicating the bearings of the change.

Bishop Fleetwood.   These careful historical monographs had a very direct bearing on some of the practical questions of the time. It may be said that all the inconvenience then felt about the coinage was ultimately connected with the difficulty of fixing on the best standard of value. A flood of light was thrown on this subject by the excellent work of Bishop Fleetwood. He had preached a sermon, which had been one of the first utterances that called attention to the deficiencies of our coinage, and the evils of a clipped currency; and the manner in which he discussed the variations of silver as a standard of value showed that he had clearer views on the subject than many of his contemporaries. It was comparatively easy to prove that coins could not be rated very differently from the exchange value of the bullion they contained, but it was not so easy to see what determined the value of the precious metals as bullion. The difficulty was rendered greater since men argued that while other commodities were naturally sought after because they supported human life, or ministered to individual human needs, silver was only prized because mankind had agreed to use it as money. Locke was a mercantilist to the backbone[1], but so far from regarding money as the only kind of wealth he is inclined to deny that it was of the nature of wealth at all, except by mere agree-

---

[1] *Farther Considerations, Works*, v. 152.

ment. Under such circumstances it was plausible to maintain that the same convention which caused it to be wealth,
definitely assigned its value in exchange. No serious attempt
could be made at adopting a single standard for the coinage
and keeping to it, till the fact that the value of silver bullion
varied with regard to the other precious metals and with
regard to commodities of every sort, was fully recognized.
Fleetwood's *Chronicon Preciosum* takes the form of a discussion on a point of casuistry. 'The statutes of a certain
college,' he says, '(to the observation of which, every one is
sworn, when admitted ·fellow) vacating a fellowship if the
fellow has an estate in land of inheritance or a perpetual
pension of £5 per annum, I desire you would be pleased to
give me your answer to the following questions, when I have
first told you that the college was founded between the years
1440 and 1460.' The third question was the important one;
it ran as follows:—' Whether he who is actually possessed of
an estate of £6 per annum as money and things go now, may
safely take that oath, upon presumption that £6 now, is not
worth what £5 was, when that statute was made.' He goes
on to show that gold and silver had both fallen in value with
regard to commodities, but that they had kept about, though
not quite, the same proportion towards one another. The
discussion of the silver coinage is very careful, and there is a
mass of facts in the two chapters in which he proves that
silver had fallen very greatly in value as compared both with
corn and with the rates and wages.

Both of these works give evidence of exhaustive research
and of intelligent criticism. In their own departments they are
hardly rivalled by the extraordinary collection of information
on all matters connected with English industry and commerce, which was originally published in 1764 by Mr Anderson. His *Chronological Deduction* is a monument of painstaking industry, and there is no branch of the subject in
regard to which it does not render invaluable service, but
the work is primarily one of reference; it is a collection
of materials which seems to be almost inexhaustible, and
later students cannot be sufficiently grateful for the painstaking industry of this careful historian; but since the work.

A.D. 1689
—1776. is arranged in the unpretentious form of annals, it does not
pretend to be more than a storehouse of materials; and
though there is some acute criticism, the book is less effective as a whole than might have been the case, if there had
been a serious attempt to string these disjointed fragments
into a connected history.

Massie.   The one man who united a profound knowledge of economic literature, as it had grown up in the two preceding
centuries, with a keen interest in the practical economic difficulties of his time, was Joseph Massie. He had spared no
expense in forming a collection[1] which contained some fifteen
hundred tracts and treatises; and the study of these had
served to make him a discriminating critic. In particular he
had felt that numbers of pamphleteers, who pretended to be
arguing for the good of the public, were really actuated by
some selfish and personal motive. Statements of fact in
many cases required careful examination; and in not a few
instances the writing was so specious, and the motive of
private interest was so plain that it was necessary to discount
much of the argument. To his mind the real need seemed
to be a criterion which would enable us to distinguish the
national from the personal interest. His scheme for attaining this desirable end was thorough and painstaking, as he
believed it might be reached, not by trusting to a single
His scheme criterion, but by an exhaustive examination of the phenomena
of economic of industrial and commercial life so as to establish 'com-
study. mercial knowledge upon fixed principles.' 'There is no other
way,' he says, 'to acquire a satisfactory knowledge of the
state, &c., of the manufactures and trade of this kingdom
than by treating of each branch separately, so that their
increase, decrease, influence, &c., may appear; for every part
must be distinctly known or the whole cannot be well understood[2].' Even with the pains and attention which he had
given to the matter, he had found it impossible to carry on
his researches in the thorough fashion which he deemed
desirable, though he was by no means inclined to pursue a

---

[1] The catalogue, which is a unique storehouse of information regarding economic bibliography, will be found in the British Museum, Lansdowne MSS., 1049.

[2] *A Representation concerning the Knowledge of Commerce*, p. 14.

subject with pedantic curiosity beyond the limits that were needed for bringing out points of lasting importance. 'So that facts, circumstances, and controversies, which either never were nationally interesting in themselves, or have been rendered useless in that respect by length of time, should not be inserted in a general work that is intended to promote commercial knowledge; for there ought to be a keeping of proportion in books as well as in pictures; and the several parts of a subject should be so treated of, that the mind may discover which are the principal objects therein, as the eye is enabled to distinguish the principal figures in an historical picture[1].' But though he was so discriminating, his scheme of studying each branch was extraordinarily thorough; he proposed to divide his historical account of every branch of manufacture into sixteen heads, under one or other of which, fragments of information might be classified, in the hope that the whole account would sooner or later be made sufficiently complete.

The mere fact that Massie regarded such an investigation *The national interest.* as necessary in order to discriminate what was really of national concern, shows that he was by no means satisfied with the rough and ready schemes of national success or decay which were based on some particular set of figures. His whole appeal for investigation is an implied confession that his contemporaries had no satisfactory means of determining where the national interest really lay. His very attitude is a condemnation of the methods of reasoning which satisfied the ordinary writer, or were bandied in the House of Commons. But despite this, he is still on the standpoint of the Mercantile System. He believed that it was possible to attain to a knowledge of principles which should tend to increase the prosperity and power of the country, and that when these principles were detected it was necessary to carry them out, and to take active measures to check the private interest which conflicted with them. His attitude comes out curiously in his criticism of Sir Matthew Decker's scheme of taxation. He shows that the abolition of customs, which might favour trade in some ways, could not be accomplished

---

[1] *A Representation concerning the Knowledge of Commerce*, p. 16.

without repealing all tariffs and thus discarding the instrument by which trade could be directed into channels of
national advantage.   When he had pointed out that this was
implied in the proposal, he felt that he had demolished the
whole thing, for he had the firmest conviction of the necessity
for suppressing private interest and regulating trade for the
national weal.

*Reflection
on Con-
temporary
Evidence.*

305.   Other thinkers tried to frame a satisfactory system
for promoting the power of the country by thinking out
a scheme in which the different factors might work har-
moniously; they relied not so much on new investigation as
on more careful reflection.   It was obvious that the regulations which had been made for encouraging manufactures
and increasing the customs might be detrimental to the rent
of land.   Such for example was the case with the laws which
prohibited the export of wool or encouraged the importation
of pig-iron from America.   Both the welfare of the landed
interest and of the manufacturers were important objects of
policy, but one conflicted with the other.   What favoured
the one might be detrimental to the other; hence it might
frequently be necessary to balance the landed against the
manufacturing interest, and try to give each its due develop-

*Arthur
Young.*

ment.   Arthur Young was constantly complaining, under the
influence of the French Physiocrats, that manufactures were
unduly developed and the agricultural interest too much
neglected.   The right course, as he conceived, would be to
develop agriculture first of all to its fullest extent[1], with an
easy confidence that manufactures and commerce would follow
naturally in its wake.   But whenever we get this idea of a
due proportion between the various parts of the social fabric,
we must have some ideal or form to which we desire to make
our practice conform.   The eighteenth century had a keen
eye to proportion in the structure of buildings, and eagerly
followed the classical type, while adapting it to modern requirements; and in the same way their discussions of the
due proportion between manufactures and agriculture imply
some more or less definite conception of an ideal economic

---

[1] Arthur Young, *Farmers' Letters*, 4.

condition, which should possess in its highest form the ele- A.D. 1689
—1776.
ment of stability.

Sir James Steuart, who wrote in 1764[1], was an author *Sir James Steuart.*
who deliberately devoted himself to working out such an
ideal. He set himself to discover 'a good plan of economy'[2]
by a wide course of observation and reflection. "The speculative person," he says, "who, removed from the practice
extracts the principle of this science from observation and
reflection, should divest himself as far as possible of every
prejudice in favour of established opinions however reasonable when examined relatively to particular nations; he must
do his utmost to become a citizen of the world, comparing
customs, examining minutely institutions which appear alike
when in different countries they are found to produce different
effects; he should examine the cause of such differences with
the utmost diligence and attention; it is from such inquiries
that the true principles are discovered[3]." Not only must he
take account of the present but of the past, and by so doing
he may be able to follow "the regular progress of mankind
from great simplicity to complicated refinement[4]." In this
way he believed that he might obtain a science of which the *His view of the science.*
principles were 'universally true,' and it would then be the
business of the statesman to direct the industry and commerce of any given people in the closest practicable accord
with those principles. "The principal object of this science
is to secure a certain fund of subsistence for all the inhabitants, to obviate every circumstance which may render it
precarious, to provide everything necessary for supplying the
wants of the society, and to employ the inhabitants in such
a manner as naturally to create reciprocal relations and
dependencies between them, so as to make their several
interests lead them to supply one another with their reciprocal wants[5]." It must, however, be confessed that in plunging
into this sea of 'metapolitical' speculation, Sir James Steuart
fails to attain very important results. He did, indeed, make
important contributions to particular doctrines; but his
general art of political economy and his general maxims are

---

[1] *Works*, III. 166, some parts were written as early as 1756, *Ib.* I. 16.
[2] *Ib.* I. 5.　　　[3] *Ib.* I. 4.　　　[4] *Ib.* I. 20.　　　[5] *Ib.* I. 8.

for the most part mere truisms, for which he is himself inclined to apologise; and his imaginary history of the development of human civilisation is but dull reading after all. He had come deeply under the influence of Montesquieu, and the effect of the *Spirit of Laws* is obvious over and over again,—in particular, in the attention he gives to the spirit

The spirit of the people. of a people. "The great art of governing," he says, "is to divest oneself of prejudices and attachments to particular opinions, particular classes, and above all to particular persons, to consult the spirit of the people, to give way to it in appearance, and in so doing to give it a turn capable of inspiring those sentiments which may induce them to relish the change which an alteration of circumstances has rendered necessary[1]." Statesmen were to guide the people by reason and not by artifice, for experience showed that a people "tricked into an imposition, though expedient for their prosperity, will oppose violently at another time a like measure even when essential to their preservation[2]."

In thus guiding the citizens towards the economic ideal, the statesman was called upon to deal with purely self-regarding interests[3]. The principle of competition is abundantly recognized throughout his treatise as usually operative in all commercial transactions. "The best way to govern a society, and to engage everyone to conduct himself according to a plan, is for the statesman to form a system of administra-

Private Interest and tion, the most consistent possible with the interest of every individual, and never to flatter himself that his people will be brought to act in general, and in matters which purely regard the public from any other principle than private interest. This is the utmost length to which I pretend to carry my position. As to what regards the merit and demerit of actions in general, I think it fully as absurd to say, that no action is truly virtuous, as to affirm that none is really vicious.

Public Spirit. "It might perhaps be expected that, in treating of politics, I should have brought in public spirit also, as a principle of action; whereas all I require with respect to this principle is merely a restraint from it, and even this is perhaps too much to be taken for granted. Were public spirit, instead of

----

[1] *Works*, I. 16.   [2] *Ib.* I. 18.   [3] Tucker, *Elements*, 8.

private utility, to become the spring of action in the indi- A.D. 1689 viduals of a well-governed state, I apprehend it would spoil —1776. all. Let me explain myself.

"Public spirit, in my way of treating this subject, is as superfluous in the governed, as it ought to be all-powerful in the statesman: at least, if it is not altogether superfluous, it is fully as much so, as miracles are in a religion once fully established. Both are admirable at setting out, but would shake everything loose, were they to continue to be common and familiar. Were miracles wrought every day the laws of nature would no longer be laws: and were everyone to act for the public and neglect himself the statesman would be bewildered, and the supposition is ridiculous.

"I expect, therefore, that every man is to act for his own interest in what regards the public, and, politically speaking, everyone ought to do so. It is the combination of every private interest which forms the public good, and of this the public, that is the statesmen only, can judge[1]."

The opposition between private interest and public good *The last of* is really reduced to a minimum in such a doctrine as this, *cantilists.* *the Mer-* but Sir James is still definitely within the circle of the Mercantilist's ideas, since he holds so strongly that it is wise for the statesman to direct industry and commerce into the right channels; though he realizes, as few of his predecessors had done, that this is a most difficult and delicate operation.

306. The way was now fully prepared for the genius of *The public* Adam Smith to give a new turn to the old inquiries, and *accept* *prepared to* thus to revolutionize the whole nature of economic doctrine. *Adam* *Smith's* Like all strokes of genius, what he did was extremely simple, *doctrine.* and it was none the less a stroke of genius because the work of preceding writers had so far paved the way that the public were able to appreciate the merits of *The Wealth of Nations* at the moment when it appeared. He was prepared to go one step further than Sir James Steuart. The latter had aimed at, though he did not attain, an ideal scheme of national economy, while Adam Smith held that no such system was necessary. His predecessors had believed that *Its sim-* the statesman must play upon private interests so as to force *plicity.*

---

[1] *Works,* I. 220.

them to conduce to the public good, and the maintenance of national power. In Sir James Steuart this guiding aim becomes a mere abstraction, and the chief point to be considered in adjusting that aim is another abstraction—the spirit of the people. Truly the mercantile system was ready to vanish away. Adam Smith did not attempt to correct any previous system of economy, he was content to insist that all systems were idle, if not positively noxious. Other writers had begun with the requirements of the State, and had worked back to the funds in the possession of the people, from which these requirements could be supplied. Adam Smith approached the subject from the other end. The first object of political economy, as he understood it, was, " to provide a plentiful revenue or subsistence for the people," the second was, "to supply the State or commonwealth, with a revenue sufficient for the public services[1]." He simply discussed the subject of wealth ; its bearing on the condition of

Isolation of Wealth as a subject of study. the State appeared an afterthought. His great achievement lay in isolating the conception of national wealth, while previous writers had treated it in conscious subordination to the idea of national power.

So far as ' political economy considered as a branch of a science of a statesman ' was concerned, it was now possible to regard material wealth as a main object in view ; and if this was the main object in view, then the systems of policy which had preferred one kind of wealth to another, or one kind of trade to another, on political grounds, had simply lost their

Natural Liberty. *raison d'être.* The system of natural liberty was the necessary outcome of the new turn which Adam Smith had given to the old problem. We have already seen, in connexion with Massie and Sir James Steuart, how little his ablest predecessors were satisfied with the expedients then in vogue ; and when Adam Smith propounded the new doctrine that all efforts to direct trade wisely were labour thrown away, the public of his age were ready to give him a hearing and to accept the new principles which followed from concentrating attention not on power, but on the necessaries and conveniences of life.

[1] *Wealth of Nations,* IV. introduction, p. 173.

At no previous time perhaps would it have been possible A.D. 1689 to proclaim this doctrine with any chance of success, but the —1776. circumstances of the day supplied the conditions which his principle assumes. The local obstacles to the fluidity of *Fluidity of* capital were for the most part disappearing. Even in towns *Capital.* like Hull, where the trading corporations had had a little interrupted tenure of power for centuries, their influence was coming to an end, and the incorporated companies for commerce and for industry were no longer so exclusive or no longer so important. Everywhere there was freedom for internal commerce, and thus capital was able to flow into any direction which the rate of profit rendered attractive to the capitalist, and where, as that very rate of profit showed, there was opportunity for developing some neglected side of national wealth. Till this was approximately the case, it would not have been so easy to urge that the system of natural liberty was most consonant with national prosperity.

In regard to other individual factors, there was no such free play; the system of natural liberty was realised in a somewhat one-sided fashion. The English law of entail and the custom of common-field cultivation sufficed in many places to prevent the improvement of the land. The laws of *Less* settlement placed crushing restrictions on the fluidity of *fluidity of* *Labour.* labour, and the laws against combinations put the workers at a terrible disadvantage in competing for better wages. Adam Smith was prompt to denounce these evils, but the British public were not prompt to recognise them. It was not till the progress of the industrial revolution had demonstrated the frightful mischief of a partial adoption of natural liberty —that is to say, the adoption of this principle in regard to one factor of production, while it is wholly disregarded in relation to another—that the conditions of society were rendered more completely accordant to those which Adam Smith's principle assumes.

307. By isolating wealth, and the causes of wealth, as a subject of study, which could be pursued apart from the investigation of other political phenomena, Adam Smith laid *The dis-* the foundation of modern political economy. It was in this *tinguishing feature of* way that he differed from all his predecessors, so far as I have

been able to examine them. There are two different sides
from which we may obtain confirmatory evidence in regard
to this characteristic feature of his work. We may note (i)
the manner in which he treats previous writers, and (ii) the
reception of his book by his contemporaries.

Firstly, the whole force of his criticism both of the Mercantilists and of the Physiocrats depends on the assumption
that they were discussing economic problems in the more
*The posi-
tion of the
Mercanti-
lists*   definite sense in which he himself regarded them. But this
assumption, which is never explicitly stated, was wholly un-
true. The English Mercantilists were considering how the
power of this country might be promoted relatively to that of
other nations. The object of their system was not absolute
progress anywhere but relative superiority to our political
neighbours. Their commercial jealousy followed from political distrust; and Adam Smith appears to admit that from
this point of view their reasoning was right. " The wealth,"
he says, " of neighbouring nations, however, though dangerous
in war and politics is certainly advantageous in trade. In a
state of hostility it may enable our enemies to maintain fleets
and armies superior to our own, but in a state of peace and
commerce, it must likewise enable them to exchange with
us[1], to our mutual advantage." As the Mercantilists were
avowedly writing from a political standpoint they were bound
to consider how to guard against these dangers. Adam
Smith in criticising them persistently refuses to take their
*misrepre-
sented.*   point of view. He assumes that they were trying to devise
means for increasing wealth, or as they would have said,
riches, as an end in itself, while every page of their writing
showed that they were doing nothing of the kind. As a consequence, his vigorous attack misrepresents them strangely.
They had attached political importance to treasure, but it
would be easy to show that they rather underrated than
overrated the importance of gold for commercial purposes
and as an element of riches. And so with all the other
points of their policy; they did not imagine they increased
the riches or wealth of the country by the restrictions on
colonial trade, but they did think that they increased its

[1] *Wealth of Nations*, IV. III. Nicholson's edition, 201.

power, and the events of the eighteenth century went a long way to prove they were right.

Similarly with the Physiocrats; when Quesnay spoke of *His criticism of Quesnay* agriculture as productive, and of all manufacturers and commercial men as sterile, he is not considering the means of procuring the necessaries and conveniences of life; he is pointing to a source from which in the progress of the society, an agricultural state may derive a permanent revenue with the least possible inconvenience to the citizens in their ordinary avocations. He points to an unearned 'increment from land,' though economic science had not so far advanced as to enable him to name it quite definitely. Adam Smith assumes in his criticism that Quesnay is really discussing the *irrelevant.* causes of the increase of national wealth—the necessaries and conveniences of life—as they act in any country, and that he represents the produce of the land as the sole source; but Quesnay's maxims were avowedly devised for an agricultural realm[1], and he explicitly notes that the scheme would be inapplicable to small maritime states which are dependent on commerce[2]. He was not discussing the growth of riches, but the most convenient source of taxation in a special community. But Adam Smith's criticism was not less damaging because it was quite irrelevant.

The misrepresentations of both these systems are glaring, *Were these misrepresentations unconscious?* and of course it can never be possible to decide with certainty how far Adam Smith mistook the purport of these writers and how far he was unfair. But when we take account of the acumen and character of the man, it is as difficult to the historian as it was to contemporaries in Paris to believe that his misrepresentations were unconscious[3]. The story of Adam Smith's relations with Hume[4] shows that he was distinguished neither for frankness nor moral courage; and there is little reason to plead for him as a judicial critic, if an adequate motive can be assigned for the misrepresentation of his predecessors; and the motive is not far to seek. His treatise was thoroughly practical; he may well have believed,

---

[1] Quesnay, *Œuvres*, edition by Oncken, 328.   [2] *Ib.* 338.

[3] See M. Oncken's *Preface* to his edition of Quesnay.

[4] Haldane, *Life of Adam Smith*, 37.

as others had done, that the whole scheme of Government interference, and the whole fiscal policy which rested on it, was bad. Under the circumstances he rightly desired to sweep it away and to have the revenue system altered in accordance with the maxims which he had adopted from M. Moreau de Beaumont[1]. But by attacking the mercantile principles on which our existing system was founded, and by discrediting the Physiocratic principles which had been stated by Locke[2], and had become popular in France[3], he could hope to clear the way for the reforms which he approved, and which were, in some of the most obvious points, effected by

The practical object in view. Pitt. He seems to have had a practical object in view ; the alterations in his third edition show that he was ready to write for the times, and his practical purpose required that he should state his case in a fashion in which it would catch public attention. It was easier to discredit his opponents than to refute them by meeting them on their own ground or by showing that their position was untenable ; and Adam Smith apparently sacrificed the part of a fair-minded critic, though he has certainly achieved the reputation of a great practical politician.

The reception of his book and its influence 308. Secondly, the enthusiastic reception accorded to his work by his contemporaries was chiefly due to the extraordinary simplicity and clearness of his treatment, as well as to the excellence of the style. But this simplicity was secured by the definiteness of his new conception of the object of political economy. It had to do with the necessaries and conveniences of life, material commodities, definite concrete things. There was much clever compilation in the book, but it made no demand for additional enquiry as Massie

---

[1] Adam Smith's celebrated maxims about taxation are improved in form, but in substance they are found in the *Avertissement* to the splendid *Mémoires* which were compiled and printed for the French government in 1768.

[2] *Lowering of Interest, Works*, v. 55, 60. "This by the way, if well considered, might let us see that taxes, however contrived, and out of whose hands soever immediately taken, do, in a country where their great fund is land, for the most part terminate upon land. . . . It is in vain, in a country whose great fund is land, to hope to lay the public charge of the Government on anything else: there at last it will terminate."

[3] They were partly commended to Quesnay by the results of agricultural protection in England. *Œuvres*, 230.

had done, nor was much stress laid on that impalpable abstraction, the spirit of the nation; and the "disagreeable discussion of metaphysical arguments" was avowedly abjured[1]. It was all to be plain sailing for the man of ordinary intelligence; and within a few months of its publication the book had become a considerable power. In 1777 North had *on North* borrowed some suggestions[2] which Adam Smith had incorporated from Moreau de Beaumont; Pitt's French policy *and Pitt.* followed the principles he had laid down, and which he amplified in the edition[3] of 1784; the great minister explicitly referred to the book in introducing his scheme for modifying the pressure of taxation in 1792, and was determined by it in his action on two later occasions[4]. National prosperity and relative superiority were vague and difficult notions, but when the whole discussion was made to turn on wealth, the treatment seemed to be more concrete and definite, and it took hold upon the public mind.

There were of course some economists who never really *Dissenti-* adapted their habits of thought in accordance with Adam *ents and hostile* Smith's principles. Playfair speaks of him with respect, but *critics.* he continued to draw his beautiful diagrams of the Balance of Trade, as if he still thought it furnished a criterion of something. His *Inquiry into the Permanent Causes of the Decline and Fall of Powerful and Wealthy Nations* enumerates all sorts of influences, physical and moral; but fails to reach any very perspicuous conclusions. He admired *The Wealth of Nations*, but it seems to have left him unaffected. There is far more interest in the attitude of the hostile critics and the points which they singled out for attack.

(*a*) Governor Pownall, whose *Letter* was published some *Colonial* few months after *The Wealth of Nations* had been issued, *Trade.* subjected it to very acute criticism. He was prepared to admit that some of the colonial restrictions worked badly, but he defended the principle on which they rested, and which

---

[1] *Wealth of Nations* (ed. Nicholson), 349.
[2] Dowell, *History of Taxation*, II. 169.
[3] See especially the passage inserted in IV. III. "It is in consequence—commerce with the other" (ed. Nicholson, 202); and "By the second—calicoes and muslins," pp. 203—205.
[4] Haldane, *Life of Adam Smith*, 76.

Adam Smith had ignored. He was prepared to relax restrictions that cause a roundabout trade, "always however keeping
in view this object and end namely, that so far as our colonies
have to be considered as an institution, established and
directed to increase the naval force of our marine empire,
and so far as that force derives in any degree from the operations of their commercial powers, so far that monopoly which
engrafts them upon our internal establishment, is indispens-
able and ought never to be departed from or relaxed[1]." In
fact he held that the object of a 'political economy' was not
merely any kind of wealth, but the maintenance of English
power[2].

*Produc-
tion of
wealth.*
        (b) Pownall also criticised Adam Smith's account of the
production of wealth. In this he had apparently followed
Locke. The fertility of this master mind is strangely shown
in the fact that his writings contain the germ of the Physiocratic doctrine of taxation as well as the germ of Smith's
doctrine of the production of wealth and the measure of
value. "Labour," he had said, "puts the difference of value
on everything," or, as he corrects it, "labour makes the far
greater part of the value of things we enjoy[3]," but Adam
Smith uses the principle in its most absolute form. In
Labour.
the first sentence of *The Wealth of Nations*, labour is
spoken of as if it were the sole source of value, and therefore
it is subsequently used as a measure of value. Against all
this Pownall protested; "Labour is not the measure of value
but the mixture of the labour and the objects laboured upon
which produces the composite value. The labour must
remain unproductive, unless it hath some object whereon to

----

[1] *Letter*, 27. This is a remarkable statement as coming from a man who was
the chief spokesman in laying American grievances before Parliament, and was a
recognised authority on the subject. *Parl. Hist.* xvi. 331, 485; xvii. 1199, 1282.

[2] Similarly the clergyman, who had lived in Paris and signs himself T. A.——,
apparently held that the special resources of each country rendered a special
system of economy desirable for each. The principles of Adam Smith were all
very well for a maritime country, but would not serve for an agricultural country
like France. He appears to have failed to grasp Adam Smith's main position, but
his criticism is none the less instructive as showing where *The Wealth of Nations*
struck him as novel. *Dr Smith's System considered*, p. 67. Appended to *Suppression of French Nobility Vindicated* (1792).

[3] *Civil Government, Works*, v. 361, 362.

exert itself[1]." " There is no one commodity," he adds, " that A.D. 1689 —1776.
will measure all others, but that all are to one another in
their reciprocal value alternate measures, and that gold and
silver is only the most common and most general, almost the
universal measure[2]." " Correlative value between commodities must depend upon, and derive from reciprocal higgling
of bargain and sale, and are not measured by labour[3]." In
accordance with this principle he urges that " as there is no
real measure of value so I think there is no fixed natural
rate of value or real price distinct from the market price[4]."

(c) Similar criticisms were urged in a much less friendly *Unpro-ductive Labour.* spirit by Mr Simon Gray in his own name, and under the
somewhat thin disguise of George Purves[5]. He is specially
bitter on Adam Smith's distinction between productive and
unproductive labour. He considered that Adam Smith's
phraseology tended to foment class hatreds, as it seemed to
represent all other classes as paupers who subsisted as mere
drones and at the expense of the manual labourers. He
argues in opposition that all labour is either directly or indirectly productive[6], and that the real question is who are more
and who are less productive? But his chief point is that the
cause of wealth lies not in mere labour, but in effective
demand, a doctrine for which he argues with much acuteness. There are necessary limitations which he does not
sufficiently take into account[7], such as the law of diminishing
return from land, and his optimistic conclusions are illusory;
but none the less is his criticism exceedingly instructive,
especially in the way he develops a doctrine of demand as
determining supply. He gives far more scope to the idea of
reciprocity than is found in most writers of his day.

309. Whatever may be thought of the worth of this con-

---

[1] Pownall, *Letter*, p. 10. .   [2] *Ib.* 13.   [3] *Ib.* 15.   [4] *Ib.* 13.
[5] *All Classes Productive*, 228.   [6] *Ib.* 81.
[7] He does not ignore these limitations however. "With regard to the progress in national wealth, whatever tends, directly or indirectly, to give more employ-ment and better prices to a nation, must tend to enrich that nation, or to promote its progress in the acquisition and accumulation of wealth. Thus, whatever aug-ments or diminishes the demand, will assist or check a nation in this progress. As for the supply, that will always rise with facility to the amount of the demand; except in cases where nature has set limits, universal or local, or meddling states-men have interposed their foolish restraints." *The Pamphleteer*, xvii. 399.

A.D. 1689
—1776.
*Adam
Smith's
precise con-
tribution to
science.*
temporary criticism, it is of the first importance, since it helps us to understand the precise nature of Adam Smith's contribution to science. By isolating wealth as a subject for study he introduced an immense simplification. The investigation of economic phenomena was more definite, and just because he achieved this result his work rendered it possible to ask new questions, and so to make a real advance in every direction of social study. Not till we isolate wealth and examine how it is procured and how it may be used, can we really set about investigating how material goods may be made to subserve the highest ends of human life. National rivalries and national power are but mean things after all; but till the study of wealth was dissociated from these lower aims, it was hardly possible to investigate empirically how we could make the most of the resources of the world as a whole, and how material goods might be best applied for the service of man. It is owing to Adam Smith and the manner in which he severed economics from politics that we can raise and discuss, even if we cannot solve, such problems to-day.

Similarly, we find the clearest testimony to his greatness in the new form which the old enquiries assumed. He severed economic science from politics; he dealt with it as concerned with physical objects and natural laws. To his English predecessors it had been a department of politics or morals; while many of his English successors recognised that in his hands it had become more analogous to physics and delighted to treat it by the methods of mechanical science. Whether consciously or unconsciously, he gave the turn to economic problems which has brought about the development of modern economic theory.

The progress that has been made in this direction amply justifies the line which Adam Smith took in isolating the study of material wealth; but however complete our analysis may be, it is well to remember that we have merely analysed a group of phenomena which we have first isolated as a matter of convenience. We cannot forecast at all unless we go outside economics and take a wider view of human life. For all questions of history in the past, for all questions of duty now, for all ideals of progress in the future we must not

be content to take the phenomena of wealth as if they were A.D. 1689
isolated, but to take them in their relation to Man. For all —1776.
these purposes we must seek to "restore mind to its proper
rank[1]"; and even if there be no general formula which
adequately describes the relations of moral phenomena to
wealth, we may none the less hope to make good progress in
all other sides of social study, if we use as our starting-point
the vantage ground which Adam Smith has given us by isolating the conception of material wealth.

[1] Purves, *All Classes Productive*, 240.

PART II.   1776—1815.

IX. GENERAL SURVEY.

A.D. 1776
—1815.
Rapid
changes in
our com-
mercial and
industrial
system.

310. The period from the Declaration of Independence to the Battle of Waterloo was marked by startling changes on every side of our economic life. The revolt of the most flourishing Colonies brought the existing commercial system to an end, while on the other side of the world the reconstruction of the East India Company gave more stability to our Empire in the East. But the revolution within the country was even more striking than the changes in our relations with other lands; the era of industrial invention had commenced; the application of coal to smelting, and the introduction of the steam engine, gave an extraordinary impetus to both the hardware and textile manufactures. These new developments re-acted on the population; there was a great deal of migration and a very rapid increase, while various influences combined to bring about an agricultural revolution. Under the pressure of bad seasons and the difficulties caused by the migration of industry, the agricultural interest was in great straits; there was need to have recourse to new soil, and to introduce the most economical habits of tillage, in order to procure supplies on which the increasing population could subsist. Just when the struggle for existence was so severe, there was also an increasing burden of taxation; England was engaged in the crowning struggle with France, and drew on its prospective resources with apparent recklessness; while the war greatly obstructed English commerce, and added to the risks which English seamen had to face. On every side there were startling changes; and as these for the most part originated in distinct causes, there is a great difficulty in following out the interaction of these different changes on one another. The revolt of the colonies, the industrial inventions, the years of famine, and the Napoleonic wars were separate and distinct affairs, each one of which had a far-reaching influence, on all sides of

our economic life; it is not easy to assess their relative im- A.D. 1776 —1846. portance or to trace out the precise influence which they exercised, separately and in combination.

There can however be little doubt as to which of these *Primary importance of industrial progress.* changes was destined to be in the long run of greatest economic importance. The introduction of machinery continues slowly but surely to revolutionise industrial life, not only in England but throughout the world. It marks one of the great stages in the growth of human power to overcome nature. Just as the discovery of the New World entirely altered the commerce of Europe both as to its magnitude and its methods, so the application of physical powers on a large scale, to do the work which had hitherto been accomplished by human drudgery, was a new departure, which must take the chief place in the economic history of the world. On these grounds we need have no hesitation in regarding the industrial change as the most fundamental and far-reaching of all the great movements of this time. It originated in England but it was of importance for the whole world.

311. In looking backwards, too, from this distance, we *Growth of towns and political consequences.* may feel that the very rapid progress of industry at a time when agriculture was depressed and commerce was endangered, has left permanent marks on the development of our national life. The growth of the great provincial towns was the direct consequence of the Giant Industry; these again were the centres of agitation for changes in our constitution, both in its parliamentary and municipal aspects. In them too, began that movement for free trade which reversed the policy of centuries both as to agriculture and shipping.

Besides these political effects, there were social changes *Relative depression of labour.* which the new industrial methods accelerated. Labour became less important relatively to capital; and while the gains of some of the owners of capital were sometimes enormous, the labourers were prevented from maintaining the old safeguards, and were forced to a lower level of life. The problems of capital and labour appeared on an unexampled scale, and the pressure of poverty was felt, not merely among those who were unemployed, but also among those who were over-worked. The old social regulations entirely failed to

meet and, in some cases, intensified the mischief. Bad
seasons might have come and gone, as at the end of the
seventeenth century, when, though they caused great suffering, they did not bring about permanent degradation ; but
circumstances had changed. The incidents of the industrial
revolution determined the special form that was taken by the
terrible misery that followed the long war.

*Decay of
domestic
industries
in rural
districts.*
    While the industrial revolution raised new social pro-
blems in the towns it also intensified the prevailing difficulties in rural England.   Factory towns displaced the
domestic manufactures which had given employment to so
many of the inhabitants of country villages.   They had
supplied by-employments which greatly increased the prosperity of many households, and the weaver had been able to
prosecute his calling in the healthier conditions which the
country afforded as contrasted with the towns.   The with-
drawal of these employments meant, either the migration of
population to less wholesome conditions, or serious loss and
a heavy increase to the rates, when they remained after
the work had departed.   But it was after the Peace of 1815
that the depression was generally felt, though it had been
noticed in some districts a few years before[1].

*Effect on
foreign
commerce*
    The strides with which industry advanced entirely changed
the character of the relation in which it stood to commerce.
It appears that the staple articles of commerce in the first
half of the eighteenth century were raw products, coals and
corn, with the possible exception of one manufactured article,
woollen cloth.   It had been the object of the legislature
in Walpole's time so to regulate commerce that industry
might flourish.   With the invention of machinery, industry
began to flourish in England as it did nowhere else in the
world.   We could make as much of goods of every kind as
might be wanted, not only in our own island but throughout
the world ; and commerce became the means of opening up
new markets for our rapidly extending industries.   Formerly,
regulation of commerce had been needed so that new employments might be planted and fostered.   Now industry was so
vigorous that it could hold its own and employ commerce to

[1] See below, p. 480.

distribute our manufactures to distant places. The whole A.D. 1776 —1815. endeavour to produce as largely and as cheaply as possible, so as to command the markets of the world, though not unknown[1] before, took a firmer hold after the industrial revolution. We lost the idea of first supplying ourselves and finding a vent for our surplus, we began to manufacture with a view to the requirements of distant parts of the globe.

The new development of industry was also the source of *and on* our strength in the Napoleonic struggle. England had taken *National Power.* the lead in manufacturing[2] and her trade could not be suppressed. The industrial progress of England opened up national resources which it was possible to mortgage, so as to provide the sinews of war. On the other hand the successive wars re-acted very seriously on English industry, since they introduced great fluctuations into trade of every kind. In some cases there was difficulty in obtaining raw materials, such as Spanish wool[3]; while in others, the market for which our manufacturers catered, in the Peninsula or in America, was suddenly closed. This seems to have been felt alike in the cloth manufacture of the Eastern counties, and in Lancashire[4], though there are similar complaints about the carpet trade at Axminster[5] and nail making at West Bromwich[6]. In times of peace there was a sudden revival; while the Napoleonic wars so injured industry on the continent, as to give an unnatural stimulus to some branches of British trade. In these ways the course of the European struggles brought about some violent fluctuations in English industry, and even agriculture was directly affected by these events; but on the other hand the development of our industry was not an unimportant factor in deciding these great political issues. On every side the industrial revolution appears to have been

---

[1] "Most if not all the manufactures [at Colchester in 1784] are for foreign consumption especially for the Spanish American demand. A few for the Portuguese, but not in considerable quantity; but at Coggeshall they are entirely in that branch." *Annals of Agriculture*, II. 108.

[2] In 1792 there was no cotton manufacture of any importance out of Great Britain, and the export of cotton twist began about 1794. *Reports* 1833, VI. 41.

[3] Bischoff, I. 250.
[4] *Annals of Agriculture*, XX. 184.
[5] *Ib.* XXVIII. 628.
[6] *Ib.* IV. 157.

of fundamental importance at that crisis in English history[1].

312. The foregoing statement may have served to indicate what will prove the most convenient mode of trying
to unravel the complicated phenomena of the period on which
Order of we are entering. We may start with an examination of the
treatment. changes which took place in industry; we may next consider
how these changes re-acted on agriculture and on the condition of the labourers. It will then be possible to discuss the
effects on our commercial relations with other countries and
the changes in our dependencies. In every direction we shall
be able to notice how the changes which were special to each
of these departments co-operated with the effects of the
industrial revolution; and the whole results can be most conveniently reviewed in connection with the finances of the
realm.

There is indeed one department in which it may be
possible to adopt a different treatment, from that which has
been attempted in discussing the preceding periods; from
Political the time of Adam Smith, Political Economy became a formu-
Economy. lated body of doctrine; in it too there has been progress,
since the reflection of subsequent thinkers has given great
clearness to parts of the subject where Adam Smith's treatment was confused, and definiteness to language which was
vague or ambiguous in his pages. But progress in economic
science is not so directly connected with our subject that it
is necessary to follow it minutely in order to understand the
growth of industry and commerce better. Political Economy
has in some degree developed under influences of a purely
intellectual character; its form has been affected, at one time
by physics and at another by biology. Such changes as
these have their proper place in the history of Economic
Science, but our interest in Economic Science lies in its connection with economic phenomena. In the writings both of
Malthus and Ricardo there were newly-observed phenomena
which led them to formulate the doctrines associated with
their names, and in such cases we must include them in our
survey. There are also not a few instances where economic

---

[1] Compare Arkwright's claim about paying the National Debt. Baines, 196.

doctrine has influenced the mind of legislators and thus A.D. 1776
affected the course of affairs; in such cases too, we shall —1815.
require to note the fact. But changes in the form of the
science as a whole, important as they are, may be omitted
from consideration here.

X. Industrial Progress.

313. The remarkable series of inventions with which *Richard*
the name of Arkwright is associated was introduced with *Arkwright and Cotton*
great rapidity; employers in Derby, Leicester, Nottingham, *Spinning.*
Worcester, Stafford, York, Hertford, and Lancaster made use
of his machines, and Arkwright made an enormous fortune,
not only by supplying machinery but by carrying on large
businesses in different counties. But this gives no real idea
of the extraordinary development of the cotton trade; for Arkwright found that his machinery was used by a large number
of Lancashire employers, who formed an association which was
eventually successful in setting Arkwright's patent entirely
aside. His specifications had been drawn with the deliberate
view to conceal the nature of his invention. Baines mentions "as specimens of this studied obscuration that the very
first article in his specification and drawing was a hammer,
not of his own invention and of no use in the cotton manufacture, but merely used to beat hemp; and that the wheels
by which the whole machine was turned were not introduced
at all[1]." No mechanic could construct the machines from
these specifications, and Arkwright's plea that he desired to
prevent foreigners from copying his invention is hardly admissible. Arkwright failed to maintain his patents in the
courts, and his appeal to the popular judgment entitled,
"*The Case of Mr Richard Arkwright*," failed to create the
impression he had desired.

He was however more successful in attaining pecuniary *Samuel*
success than most of the other inventors of the day. Samuel *Crompton.*
Crompton made a considerable step in advance by the inven-

[1] *Cotton Manufacture*, 188.

tion of the mule; in this the spindles are placed on a carriage which as it wheels out four or five feet from the beam, stretches and twists the thread which is wound on to spindles as it returns. Crompton's machine was made for his own use, though the superiority of the yarn he spun with it compelled him, somewhat reluctantly, to make his invention public; but he took out no patent. Ten years after its invention, in 1790, Mr Kelly of Lanark succeeded in applying water-power to turn the mill; thus the machinery for spinning cotton was advanced to a very high state of perfection, and there was every opportunity for a still more rapid development when the invention of Boulton and Watt gave the manufactures a new source of mechanical power.

Water power.

Village factories.

It should not be forgotten however that in the first days of the factory system, horse-power and water-power were generally employed, and there was little or no temptation to attempt to concentrate the workers in towns[1]. Steam engines had been used for long for pumping water from mines; but the first engine which was constructed for a cotton mill was erected at Papplewick in Nottinghamshire, in 1785. The first engines in Manchester and Glasgow were introduced in 1789 and 1792 respectively. In consequence of Watt's invention waterfalls became of less value; and instead of carrying the people to the power, it was found preferable to place the power among the people wherever it was most wanted[2]. The steam engine was not the forerunner of the factory system, but the complicated machinery which was employed in the textile trades called forth the application of this new mechanical power.

Effect of Steam Power.

314.   There is nothing more curious, about the story of these successive inventions, than the personal proclivities of the inventors, and the circumstances which brought them to interest themselves in mechanical arts. Crompton was a weaver, who was anxious to produce a good yarn for his own use and thereby improved spinning machinery; but Dr Edmund Cartwright, who was a Kentish clergyman, knew

Cartwright and the Power. Loom,

[1] *Reports Misc.* 1802.3, v. 246, 257 (Sheppard).
[2] Kennedy, *Rise and Progress of Cotton Trade,* in *Memoirs of Literary and Philosophical Society of Manchester.* Second Series, Vol. III. p. 127.

nothing about the textile trades and had never interested himself in machine construction, until he invented the power-loom. While at Matlock, in 1784, he had had some conversation with spinners there, who were contending that such a vast quantity of yarn was now spun that it would soon be impossible to get hands to weave it. His suggestion that a weaving machine should be invented was apparently treated with scorn; but as he believed that only three movements were required in the process, he set himself to construct a machine with the help of a carpenter and smith. His machine was cumbrous in the extreme, and it required two strong men to keep it going even slowly, but he was proud of his invention and patented it. It then occurred to him to go and see a weaver at work; with the result that he was able to improve on his first rough attempt and to produce a machine which was eventually a commercial success; Dr Cartwright's own attempts to make it remunerative proved a failure[1], and it was not till 1801 that mills were started at Glasgow, where it was worked to advantage[2]. *which was not remunerative at first.*

The failure of Cartwright, who was however consoled by Parliament with £10,000, contrasts with the extraordinary commercial success of Arkwright. One obstacle to the general introduction of the power-loom lay in difficulties connected with the dressing of the warp; but about 1803 Johnson, an employé of Messrs Radcliffe and Ross of Stockport, who devoted great attention to the improvement of their plant, invented a dressing machine; and in this way the main difficulties in regard to power-loom weaving were removed. Mr Horrocks of Stockport was able to introduce some further improvements in 1805 and 1813 with which he could manufacture cotton cloth that has attained a worldwide reputation[3]. *Dressing the warp.*

315. The revolution in the staple trade of the country, the drapery manufacture, was much more gradual, as machinery was substituted for hand labour in one process, and then, after an interval, in another. The manufacture was, as we *The cloth trade.*

---

[1] Cotton weavers continued to be fully employed; indeed owing to the plentiful supply of cotton yarn weavers were attracted from woollen to cotton. *Annals of Agriculture*, XVI. 423.　　[2] Baines, 231.　　[3] *Ib.* 234.

have seen, very widely diffused through different districts; and the introduction of machines for any one particular process, did not take place simultaneously throughout the whole country. In some counties new improvements were adopted which were not introduced in other districts till ten or fifteen years later. The course of the substitution of machinery for hand labour is rendered more obscure, since other changes were taking place which are not obviously correlated with the introduction of mechanical improvements. Allusion has already been made to the violent fluctuations which were due to the successive wars; while the steady migration of industry from the Southern and Eastern Counties to the West Riding of Yorkshire continued[1]. The distress in the parts of the country from which trade was withdrawn was commonly assigned to the introduction of machinery; this was doubtless a concomitant, but it seems impossible to say how far the distress, and consequent riots in Wiltshire and in Suffolk, were due to the inventions, and how far to other circumstances.

i. Many of the machines for the cloth trade were adapted from inventions that had been already introduced into the cotton manufacture; but in one instance the machine was invented by a woollen manufacturer, though it does not appear to have become a practical and commercial success till it was perfected in connection with the cotton trade. Lewis Paul, who constructed a horizontal cylinder for carding wool, and thus applied rotatory motion to this operation, was an inhabitant of Birmingham; he took out a patent in 1748, and his machine was used at Northampton, at Leominster, and subsequently at Wigan[2]. Before the close of the century, machine carding appears to have been in very general use, as well as other machines for preparing the wool before spinning. In 1793, Arthur Young "viewed with great pleasure the machines for unclothing and puffing out wool, if I may use the expression, also for spinning and various other operations[3]." Similarly we hear that in the West Riding, people

---

[1] Laurence (*Duty*, p. 36) notes in 1727 that Sir Walter Calverly by building fulling mills on the Aire, had attracted clothworkers and their families so as to increase the rental of his lands.   [2] Bischoff, I. 313.

[3] *Annals of Agriculture*, XXVII. 310. Many of these were driven by steam.

in general approved of machinery for the preparatory pro- A.D. 1776
cesses, and when wool was given them to weave, took it to —1815.
the "slubbing engine to be scribbled, carded and slubbed[1]."
Mr Howlett, writing from Dunmow in 1790, in enumerating
various recent inventions, mentions mills "for grinding the
wool preparatory to carding, by means of which the master
manufacturer has as much done for $1\frac{1}{2}d.$ as used to be performed for $4\frac{1}{2}d.$[2]" I do not recollect any distinct evidence of
violent opposition to the introduction of these machines.

ii.   When the spinning-jenny was adapted to the require- *Spinning.*
ments of the woollen trade it was regarded with considerable
suspicion, which deepened into violent hostility.   Mr Benjamin Gott, of Leeds, has generally got the credit of introducing these improvements into the woollen manufacture[3],
about 1800 or a little later.   But though he may have
organised the manufacture more successfully than others, or
may have been the first to introduce it into the West Riding,
machine-spinning had been adopted for some years in other
districts.   In 1791 spinning-jennies were in use at Barnstaple and Ottery S. Mary; they had caused some uneasiness
among the spinners, but had had no sensible effect on the
trade[4].   At Kendal there was machine-spinning at the same
date; at first it seemed to hurt the hand-spinning, but the
complaints on this head did not continue[5].   The true character
of the competition was becoming apparent however; for it
was observed at Pucklechurch that the machines were ousting
the inferior spinners, and that there was a demand for finer
threads, so that the spinners, who were paid by the pound,
were obliged to do more work for the same money[6].

There were however other causes at work which tended
to depress the rate of pay for hand-spinning, and therefore to
delay the introduction of machinery.   There was an increasing scarcity of wool, after 1785, when Norfolk fleeces sold for
9s. the pack, and the price rose steadily till in 1795 it reached
the unprecedented figure of 19s. 10d.   Such dearness of the
raw material can only be described as a wool famine, and

[1] *Reports Misc.* 1806, III. p. 992.   [2] *Annals of Agriculture*, xv. p. 262.
[3] Bischoff, I. 315.
[4] *Annals of Agriculture*, xv. 494.   [5] *Ib.* 497.   [6] *Ib.* 585, also x. 580.

after 1798 prices again leaped upwards till 1809, when the pack was sold for 34s.[1] This must have meant diminished employment and therefore lower rates of pay for spinning; and this was a matter of universal complaint, even as early as 1784, when the price was unusually high for a time. Governor Pownall urged in 1788 that wages for spinning must be raised so that the spinners might have enough to live on, or that machines must be introduced and the manufacture 'broken up.' He calculated that a spinner walked thirty-three miles, stepping back and forwards to the machine, in order to earn 2s. 8d.[2] The lack of employment, with starvation wages for spinning, would of course be most noticeable in districts from which the trade was migrating, as for example in the Eastern Counties; they had fallen to 4d. a day as compared with 7d. or 8d. forty years before[3]. On the other hand the developing trade of the West Riding found employment for all available hands in 1791; Halifax masters had to pay spinners at the rate of 1s. 3d. or 1s. 4d.[4] These high rates were partly due to the concurrent demand for labour for cotton spinning[5]; but as a consequence machinery was being constantly erected in Leeds and Bradford, and one manufacturer procured 500 workhouse children from London. The introduction of spinning-jennies in the Eastern Counties would hardly be profitable while hand-spinning was so inexpensive, and the accounts of the riots in 1816 seem to show that the obnoxious machines were still somewhat novel[6].

To whatever cause the starvation rates for spinning in the old centres of the manufacture may have been due, the effects were very serious. Spinning was ceasing[7] to be re-

---

[1] Bischoff, i. 407. [2] Annals of Agriculture, x. 546.
[3] Ib. xv. 261. [4] Ib. xvi. 423.
[5] "The rapid progress of that business [cotton spinning] and the higher wages which it affords, have so far distressed the makers of worsted goods in that county [Lancashire], that they have found themselves obliged to offer their few remaining spinners larger premiums than the state of their trade would allow." [Bouyer,] Account of Society for Promotion of Industry in Lindsey (1789), Brit. Mus. 103. l. 56. [6] Annual Register, 58, Chronicle 67.
[7] In 1793 Arthur Young notes in regard to Huntingdonshire that "women and children may have constant employment in spinning yarn which is put out by the generality of the country shopkeepers; though at present it is but a very indifferent means of employment and they always prefer out of door work when the season comes on." Annals of Agriculture, xxi. 170.

munerative, even as a by-occupation. In 1795, when the Berkshire justices organised the allowance system, Davies was pleading the case of the rural labourers and insisting on the gain to their households from spinning. But the opportunities of obtaining work of this sort were being curtailed, at all events in the old centres of manufacture; the fine spinning, which was so much in demand, was badly paid, while the inferior hands were left idle altogether. The interruption of the wool supply from Germany and Spain[1], and the closing of the ordinary channels for exporting cloth, caused violent fluctuations; and these together with the migration of industry to the West Riding, involved thousands of families in the rural districts of Southern England in great distress. Spinning had been the mainstay of the household, and spinning could no longer be counted on; as a consequence numbers became dependent on parish relief, and the Berkshire justices apparently tried to grant an allowance in lieu of spinning, rather than alter the rates for agricultural labour. In 1786 Arthur Young had noticed that the fluctuations in trade threw workers on the rates[2], so that spinning was regarded as a manufacture which brought "the burthen of enormous poor charges[3]"; this had also been observed at Chippenham and Calne in 1776[4]. But the distress which attracted so much attention in 1795 was more than a mere fluctuation. The wool famine may have made the work less remunerative, and special causes rendered it inevitable that the pressure should be felt more severely in some districts than others; but machines did the work better, and they gradually ousted the immemorial method of domestic work. In Cornwall in 1795[5] the competition of jennies was clearly felt; and in other cases, the improved rates for weaving rendered the women and children independent, and unwilling to "rival a woollen jenny[6]." Bit by bit, and from different

---

[1] *Reports Misc.* 1802—3, v. 266.   [2] *Annals*, v. 420.   [3] *Ib.* 221.

[4] *Ib.* VIII. 66. In this case it may have been connected with specially bad methods of administering the poor rates.

[5] "The earnings by spinning have for the last year been much curtailed, owing to the woolstaplers using spinning engines near their place of residence in preference to sending their wool into the country to be spun by hand." *Annals of Agriculture*, XXVI. 19.   [6] *Ib.* XXVIII. 134.

causes in different districts, domestic spinning died out, and machine spinning in village factories by water-power became more prevalent[1], and before the close of the war, machine spinning had been, generally speaking, ordinarily substituted for the other process.

iii. The principal mechanical improvement in weaving during this period was the introduction of the flying or spring shuttle; by its assistance one weaver could weave broad cloth by himself, and do the work of two men[2]. The result was a considerable rise of the money wages earned by the best weavers, who continued to receive employment, and who were paid by the piece, while the inferior hands were discharged altogether. The price of cloth in 1803 was said to have risen 30 per cent., while weavers' wages had risen 100 per cent. There is ample evidence that the hand-loom weavers looked back on the period of the war as one of exceptional prosperity[3].

The introduction of this appliance must have tended to discourage domestic spinning. The weaver would require more yarn than formerly and would thus be forced to buy materials, if his household supply had sufficed before. There must have been a change of system from the old practice of giving out wool to be carded, spun and woven, to giving out woollen yarn to the weaver. In 1793 the "little grass farmers" near Leeds used to "buy the wool they work and go through the whole process of converting it into cloth, going to market twice a week to sell it[4]," and domestic carding and spinning were profitable at Kendal in 1791[5]. But there was a tendency for the weaver to buy yarn, and his wages were so good for a time that there was less induce-

---

[1] In 1788 there was a total revolution in [cotton?] spinning in Lancashire; "water engines make such fine level threads, spinning by hand engines is entirely abolished." *Annals of Agriculture*, x. 580. Evidence from Gloucestershire in 1802 stated that in consequence of machinery it was necessary to form factories in villages where there were advantages for using water-power. *Reports Misc.* 1802—3, v. pp. 246, 257.

[2] Arthur Young notes at Colchester in 1784, "The manufactory is exceedingly improved by means of a mechanical addition to the loom, which enables one weaver to do the business of two. In wide stuffs they formerly had two hands to a loom, now only one." *Annals of Agriculture*, II. 109.

[3] See the interesting evidence in *Reports*, 1840, XXIII. 417.

[4] *Annals of Agriculture*, XXVII. 309.   [5] *Ib.* xv. 496.

ment for his wife and children to supplement his earnings by spinning. Hence the weavers came to be congregated more and more round the village factories[1] where yarn was obtainable; while the masters found that there were many advantages in having the work done under their own supervision. There was thus a concentration of the trade in the neighbourhood of water-power, and it was withdrawn from the cottages where it had been previously carried on[2]. High rates of pay for the employed were quite consistent with the fact that a large number of weavers were left unemployed, especially if they would not migrate. Undertakers had to pay high wages to get men to work under the conditions in which the trade could be most successfully prosecuted.

The work of weaving could be learned in about a year, and by far the larger number of the weavers, who were concentrated near the water-power in Gloucestershire, had served no apprenticeship. The unemployed and 'legal' weavers not unnaturally demanded that the existing law should be enforced, and that employment should only be given to legally qualified men. They did not protest against the new invention, but they objected to the re-adjustment and concentration of the trade which had come about in connection with the improvement. Their complaints received very full attention from Parliament; but it was not possible, in the public interest, to comply with their demands. There was no evidence that a long apprenticeship was needed, or that the work could be done as well and as cheaply if the old conditions were insisted on. After considering the whole subject, Parliament determined not to re-enforce the Elizabethan law[3],

---

[1] *Reports Misc.* 1806, III. 577.

[2] There is a curious conflict of evidence as to the course of the change. The Select Committee thought (*Reports Misc.* 1806, III. p. 578 f.) that the apprehensions of the domestic weavers were groundless: Cookson's evidence (*Ib.* 1803—4, v. 325) points the other way.

[3] This marks the breakdown of the system of apprenticeship as regards cloth-weaving. No one at this date proposed to re-enforce the old laws regulating the precise length, breadth &c. of different kinds of cloth, though the manufacturers were doubtless liable to penalties for infringing them; such prosecutions were prevented by 43 Geo. III. c. 136, which was continued in successive years till the repeal of most of the laws regulating the woollen manufacture in 1809 by 49 Geo. III. c. 109.

but to suspend it, so as to give free play to the new conditions of trade and to allow clothiers to employ weavers who had not served a regular apprenticeship.

iv. So far as these processes are concerned, the new inventions revolutionised the cloth trade without creating serious disturbance. Improvements in carding were generally welcomed; the substitution of machine for hand-spinning was tided over by the allowance system, and the flying shuttle increased the remuneration of the best weavers. The introduction of machines for dressing and shearing called forth far more opposition. In Gloucestershire[1] indeed this hardly seems to have made much stir; gig mills appear to have been in general use, and the work they did was thoroughly satisfactory as regards quality; but in Wiltshire the attempt to introduce gig mills[2] gave rise to serious riots; and they were the occasion of much disturbance in the West Riding. Mr Benjamin Gott had taken the lead in introducing them, and thus completing the application of machinery to the cloth manufacture in 1805; but the shearmen were bitterly opposed to them, and the infection of the Luddite riots spread to Yorkshire in 1812, when concerted attacks were made on the shearing frames[3]. Stringent measures were taken with the rioters; their appeal to violence prejudiced the public against them, especially as there was no longer any question about the quality of the work turned out.

In the last decade of the century, an unprecedented improvement was effected in the worsted manufacture. The *The worsted trade.* worsted, as distinguished from woollen, is manufactured from wools with long staple; the fibres are straightened out as in the linen or cotton manufacture; while the woollen manufacture, properly so called, is dependent on wools with a short staple, the fibres of which have much tenacity, and which can

---

[1] *Reports Misc.* 1802—3, v. 251, 254.

[2] Gig mills were prohibited by 5 and 6 Edward VI. c. 22, and there was some hesitation about legalising them (43 Geo. III. c. 136, § 2). It is difficult to know how far the new gig mills corresponded to the old ones. Mr Wallington said that the old mills were used for perching and burling and the new ones for rowing and mosing, but that the name was applied differently in different parts of the country. *Reports Misc.* 1802—3, v. 251. For a full description of these different processes see *Reports* 1840, xxiv. 388.

[3] *Annual Register*, Vol. 54, Chronicle, pp. 51, 54, 114.

thus be matted into a thick material like felt. Till the time A.D. 1776
of Edmund Cartwright, wool for the manufacture of worsted —1815.
had been combed by hand; but between the years 1790 and *Cartwright*
1792 Cartwright perfected his second great invention. The *and wool-combing.*
estimate which he gave of the importance of his invention
sounds like an exaggeration, but a brief experience showed
that there was no real over-statement; "a set of machinery
consisting of three machines will require the attendance of
an overlooker and ten children, and will comb a pack, or
240 lbs., in twelve hours. As neither fire nor oil is necessary
for machine combing, the saving of those articles, even the
fire alone, will, in general, pay the wages of the overlooker
and children; so that the actual saving to the manufacturer
is the whole of what the combing costs by the old imperfect
mode of hand combing. Machine combed wool is better, *Extra-*
especially for machine-spinning, by at least 12 per cent., being *ordinary Saving.*
all equally mixed, and the slivers uniform and of any required
length[1]." With all its advantage, however, it did not immediately become remunerative to the inventor, but its success
was sufficient to arouse the antagonism of the hand wool-
combers; especially as machines on a somewhat different
principle were invented in 1793, by Toplis, Wright, and
Hawksley[2]. As nearly fifty thousand men were employed in
this trade in different places, the excitement became con- *Wide-*
siderable in many parts of the kingdom, and when a Bill was *spread opposition*
brought into the House of Commons for suppressing the
machine, upwards of forty petitions were presented in its
favour. The line which the House of Commons had previously taken with regard to the frame-work knitters showed
the scheme of policy which eighteenth century legislators *but no legis-*
favoured. The Bill was thrown out, and the only relief which *lative re-striction.*
was given to the wool-combers was that of relaxing 5 Eli-
zabeth c. 4 in their favour, and allowing them to apply
themselves to any trade in any part of the kingdom[3]. As a
matter of fact the machine only managed to compete in
certain classes of work; the real contest between hand and
machine combing was delayed till some time after the great

[1] Burnley, *Wool and Wool-combing*, 115, 129.
[2] *Ib.* 136. Also by Popple. Bischoff, i. 316.   [3] Bischoff, i. 316.

A.D. 1776
—1815.
strike in 1825. One reason, which undoubtedly weighed with the Commons, was the allegation that the wool-combers were wastrels who would not work more than half their time, and the prospect of being able to rely on getting the work done in a given time was welcomed by the employers[1].

Diminished supply of wool

316. Though the price of wool was low at the beginning of this period[2], there was soon a rapid rise. This may have been partly due to an increased demand on the part of spinners and weavers, who were enabled by the use of machinery to work at cheaper rates, but it may also be traced to the rapid progress of enclosure and the manner in which land was ploughed up for tillage. The bad seasons at the close of the century accelerated this process; but it appears that during the period under review the requirements of the population increased so fast, that England ceased to be a corn-exporting country and came to rely on the import of food. It was of course possible to maintain considerable flocks; but it appeared that, though the weight of wool was increased, when sheep were fed on clover and turnips, the quality produced was inferior to that from sheep *and high price.* fed on the downs and heath[3]. From whatever cause, there was without doubt a decided rise in the price of wool[4], and the manufacturers were alarmed at the increasing difficulty of procuring a supply. This feeling comes out in regard to three points to which allusion may be made here, though it will be necessary to return to each of them below.

Higher price in Ireland.

i. Dear though wool was becoming in England, it was dearer still in Ireland; possibly the repression of the woollen manufactures had been only too complete, and wool-growing, under all the discouragements to which the manufacture was subjected, had ceased to be so profitable as to lead men to prosecute it on a considerable scale[5]; but whatever the reason

---

[1] Bischoff, I. 316. On frauds by weavers before the factory time see *Reports Misc.* 1802—3, v. 257. Also for unfair advantages taken by workmen when prepaid, *Considerations on Taxes as they affect Price of Labour* (1765), p. 17.

[2] Sir John Dalrymple, *Question Considered* (1781). Tucker, *Reflections on Low Price of Coarse Wools.*

[3] N. Forster, *Answer to Sir J. Dalrymple* (1782), p. 27; also Alexander Williams, *Address to the Woollen Manufacturers* (1800), quoted by Bischoff, I. 334.

[4] Bischoff, I. 324 and 405.

[5] Pococke in 1752 calls attention to the specially good quality of wool pro-

may have been, the fact remains that the price of wool ranged much higher in Ireland[1]. In the Act of Union it was proposed that there should be a free interchange of goods between England and Ireland. The manufacturers had hitherto enjoyed a monopoly of the home supply; they believed they had reason to fear that export to Ireland, which had hitherto been prohibited, would force them to pay at a still higher rate. There were some signs of the old jealousy of Irish manufactures; but the opposition was chiefly due to a belief that English wool, if readily transferred to Ireland, would be *Possibilities of clandestine export.* clandestinely exported thence to the continent, and that our rivals in France and the Low Countries would secure a regular supply of English wool, which would enable them to manufacture goods of a class for which Englishmen believed they had exceptional advantages.

The agitation gives us an interesting light on many matters connected with this manufacture. A rise in the price of wool would have affected all branches of the trade, and the outcry came from all parts of the country; the outburst was far less local than in 1697, when it had been concentrated in the West of England, whence artisans were migrating. A hundred and thirteen firms in London petitioned against permitting export to Ireland, and they were *Distribution of manufacture* supported by petitions from[2] Cornwall, Exeter, Totnes, Tiverton, Welshpool, Frome, Bury S. Edmund's, Huddersfield, Tavistock, Painswick, Rochdale, Huntingdon, Norwich, Somersetshire, Sudbury, Halifax, Gloucester, Bury, Preston, Market Harborough, Witney, Wivelscombe, Southwark, Bradford, Cirencester, Colne, Burnley, Banbury, Shrewsbury, Leeds, Wakefield, Haworth, Kendal, Addingham, Kidderminster, Keighley, Skipton, Salisbury. A glance at this list shows how widely the trade was diffused; and it is also evident that the manufactures in Yorkshire were superseding those of the Eastern

---

duced near Galway: *Tour*, p. 108. Much of the Irish wool thus found its way to Cork, p. 118. For licenses for export of wool from Ireland see *Calendar of State Papers, Home Office*, 1760—65, pp. 251, 375, 508, 687.

[1] In England in 1795 wool was 8¼d. per lb. as against 11d. per lb. in Ireland. In 1797 wool in England was 8¾d. as against 9¾d. in Ireland, and in 1799 wool was 8d. per lb. in England as against 1s. 3¼d. in Ireland. Bischoff, I. 324.　　　　　[2] *Ib.* 321.

A.D. 1776
—1815.

Counties and the West of England[1]. Very severe pressure was brought to bear in favour of an amendment moved by Mr Wilberforce " to leave out of the resolution what relates to suffering wool to be exported from this country, but that the Irish should be allowed to work up the wool which they themselves grow[2]"; but Pitt was anxious to carry the complete commercial union of the two countries and argued at length against the amendment, which was lost.

ii. Since the demand for wool was increasing while there was constant encroachment on the area of pasture farms, there was a natural desire to find some other field for wool-

Australian wool-growing.

growing.   This led to attempts to introduce sheep into Australia; the enterprise was one of considerable difficulty for the voyage was so long, that it was by no means easy to carry over the live sheep. The first attempts were utter failures, but shortly after the beginning of this century Australian wool-growing had become a considerable trade,

1808.

and Captain Macarthur made a formal statement of his experience as to sheep farming at the Antipodes.

Merino sheep.

iii. Eager efforts were also made by English agriculturists to improve the breed of sheep, especially by the introduction of merino-sheep from Spain. The price of wool was not high enough however to make these experiments very profitable; and when the peace brought a sudden fall in the prices of produce in 1815, those who had devoted themselves to this line of policy, found that they were in danger of serious loss. They demanded therefore an encouragement, similar to that which they enjoyed with regard to corn. Lord Milton argued that permission to export would raise the price of wool and would thus tempt the landed men to increase the supply of wool[3]. There was in consequence a very decided effort made on behalf of the landed interest to permit the export of English wool[4] on the one hand, and on the

---

[1] Norfolk was still "full of manufacturers" in 1779. *Parl. Hist.* xx. 644.

[2] Bischoff, I. 327.   [3] Bischoff, I. 411.

[4] There had been a similar controversy in 1781 when Sir John Dalrymple urged that exportation should be permitted (*The Question Considered*). This pamphlet called forth answers from Tucker and Forster, and support from Chalmers (*Propriety of allowing Qualified Exportation*, 1782). The Gentlemen of Lincolnshire formally advocated it, while the manufacturers agitated against it. *Short View of Proceedings*, Brit. Mus. B 546 (18) gives a full account of the controversy.

other to put a duty on the importation of foreign wool. A.D. 1776 —1815. Those who were engaged in the woollen manufacture struggled successfully to prevent this new limitation[1].

317. The application of machinery brought about an *Smelting by coal.* enormous increase of production in the textile trades; but the change was still more striking in regard to the iron trade. During the earlier part of the century this trade had been declining, from the difficulty of procuring fuel; with the practical application of coal to smelting, this decline was checked, but there was no very rapid progress till about 1790[2], when steam-engines were introduced to work the blast furnaces. With this more powerful blast they were able to save one-third of the coal hitherto used in smelting. The old blast furnaces had been worked by water, and consider- *Blast furnaces.* able ingenuity had to be exercised in order to get a powerful and uninterrupted blast[3]. The effect of these improvements was unprecedented, and in 1796 the production of pig-iron was nearly double what it had been eight years before. Mr Pitt had proposed in 1796 to tax coal, and pig-iron in 1797, but he was forced to abandon both projects. When the latter was revived by Lord Henry Petty in 1806, the Bill passed the second reading by a narrow majority, but was dropped in committee. The returns which were made, and discussions which took place in connection with these proposals, have put on record an immense amount of information in regard to the manufacture of pig-iron, at the time when these new inventions caused it to advance with the greatest rapidity.

Shortly before these improvements in blast furnaces had been introduced, two very important inventions had been made by Mr Cort, of Gosport; in 1783 he obtained a patent for converting pig-iron into malleable iron with the aid of coal in a common air-furnace by puddling[4]; in the following *Puddling and Rolling.* year he obtained a patent for manufacturing the malleable iron into bars by means of rollers, instead of the forge hammers which had been hitherto in vogue. Like so many of the other

[1] Bischoff, i. 409. [2] Scrivenor, *History of the Iron Trade*, 87.
[3] See the account of the Devon Iron-works, in Sir J. Sinclair's *Statistical Account of Scotland* (1795), xiv. 626.
[4] Roebuck also had claims to this invention, see above, p. 341.

A.D. 1776
—1815.

inventors, Mr Cort derived little personal benefit from inventions which have been of world-wide importance, and the history of this invention is recounted in the petition in which Mr Cort's son pleaded for a grant from the House of Commons in 1812[1]. These last inventions were a great saving of time and labour; but it was the new form of the blast-furnace which had the most remarkable effects on the distribution of

Change in centres of trade.

the iron trade. While it had been dependent on wood, it had flourished in Sussex and the Forest of Dean; when coal came into use it could be located in regions where water-power was available; hence the revival of the South Wales iron-works which had been discontinued long before from want of fuel; the use of coal and water-power gave a new impetus to the works at Cyfartha, and Dowlais[2]. The application of steam, however, rendered the iron-masters independent of water-power, and blast furnaces could be erected wherever the presence of coal and iron rendered it convenient. In Gloucestershire the supply of fuel from the forest was readily replaced with coal; but in other cases, and notably in Sussex, the ancient iron-works ceased to be of importance; while enormous new centres of activity and industry were created in parts of Scotland, Wales and the North of England which had been practically barren before.

Expansion of Coal Trade.

318.   The decrease of other fuel rendered it necessary for the population to have recourse to coal more constantly than before, and the new inventions in connection with the iron-trade created a sudden demand. This acted not merely in the way of increasing the output at the existing fields, though it did this both at Newcastle and in Scotland[3], but the

---

[1] Scrivenor, 119.   [2] *Ib.* 122.

[3] It is not a little curious to find that the prospective expansion of coal-mining, to meet the requirements of the iron-trade was the cause of some little anxiety, in Scotland. It was said that the demand due to blast furnaces would be so great as to raise miners' wages enormously and thus enhance the price of coal used for domestic purposes. The argument seems to assume that colliers were a special class and could not be readily recruited from outside, which was of course, to a great extent true. "Five blast furnaces will require 262 colliers and miners; formerly employed in preparing collieries for work, or in working coals for the domestic consumption of the inhabitants of Scotland. This evil is only beginning to be felt it being certain from the present high price and great demand for cast iron * * that twenty additional blast furnaces will be erected in Scotland within the space of ten years from the present date, requiring a supply of 2,048 colliers

increased facilities for internal carriage rendered the coal A.D. 1776 —1815.
fields of Lancashire and the Midlands much more available than formerly. The South Wales and Cumberland fields were also worked in a way that had been unknown before, and the increase of production in the country generally was enormous. The Commissioners of 1871 estimated it as follows[1].

1660	...	...	2,148,000	tons.
1700	...	...	2,612,000	„
1750	...	...	4,773,828	„
1770	...	...	6,205,400	„
1790	...	...	7,618,728	„
1795	...	...	10,080,300	„

There are some features of very special interest in the history of the coal trade during this period; it was the only industry in which a system of regulation as regards prices, and of astriction as regards labour was retained, or rather was re-introduced. In other industries attempts at regulation entirely broke down during this period; but coal-mining had some special characteristics of its own, chiefly because of the large amount of capital invested in the mines, and the trade was deliberately organised in the Newcastle district with the view of giving a regular and steady return to all the capital invested in this employment throughout the district.

The 'vend' was an agreement among the Newcastle *The Vend.* coal-owners which has curious analogies with the stint[2] of the Merchant Adventurers; it appears to have come into being about the year 1786. The object apparently was to give the owners of mines, which yielded inferior sorts of coal, a chance. The shipowners preferred to load the best sorts of coal; and if there had been no regulation, the whole trade would have been monopolised by a few collieries which yielded the best qualities, and the other owners would be ruined. This result,

and miners. This supply of hands must either be drawn from the collieries now working coal for the consumption of the inhabitants of Scotland,—in which case coal will increase in price above any calculation now possible to be made;— or, erectors of ironworks must be compelled to find hands for their works, by being prohibited * * from employing any colliers now employed at the collieries." *Reports, &c.* 1871, xviii. 847.

[1] *Ib.* 1871, xviii. 852.   [2] See above, p. 120.

A.D. 1776
—1815.
as was argued in 1800, would not really benefit the public[1], since the few high class mines that were left would be able to charge what they liked for coals. It thus came about that the 'vend' was organised; it was an agreement which was officially described in 1830. A committee was formed to represent the different collieries, and "the Proprietors of the best Coals are called upon to name the price at which they intend to sell their Coals for the succeeding twelve months; according to this price, the remaining Proprietors fix their prices; this being accomplished, each Colliery is requested to send in a Statement of the different sorts of Coals they raise, and the powers of the Colliery; that is, the quantity that each particular Colliery could raise at full work; and upon these Statements, the Committee assuming an imaginary basis, fix the relative proportions, as to quantity, between all the Collieries, which proportions are observed, whatever quantity the Markets may demand. The Committees then meet once a month, and according to the probable demand of the ensuing month, they issue so much per 1,000 to the different collieries; that is, if they give me an imaginary basis of 30,000 and my neighbour 20,000, according to the quality of our Coal and our power of raising them in the monthly quantity; if they issue 100 to the 1000, I raise and sell 3000 during the month, and my neighbour 2000; but in fixing the relative quantities, if we take 800,000 chaldrons as the probable demand of the different markets for the year; if the markets should require more, an increased quantity would be given out monthly, so as to raise the annual quantity to meet that demand, were it double the quantity originally assumed[2]."

It was possible to argue that the vend was an arrangement which merely secured a reasonable price, and that while it benefited the producers as a body, it did not entail ultimate loss on the consumers[3]. But the relations which existed between the coal-owners, in some parts of the country, and

Bondagers in Scotland.

---

[1] See the evidence of the Town Clerk of Newcastle, *Reports from Committees of House of Commons, Misc. Subjects,* x. 544.

[2] *Reports* &c. 1830, viii. 6.

[3] Especially as the arrangement only held good in the Newcastle district which was exposed to competition from other fields. *Ib.* 1830, viii. 17.

the labourers were much less defensible. It was important A.D. 1776 —1815.
to the employer to be able to command the regular and constant service of a number of labourers, and customs grew up[1]
by which the miners were just as definitely astricted to particular mines as villans had been to particular estates in
the middle ages. This custom was specially noticeable in
Scotland; an attempt had been made to break it down in
1775[2], but apparently with little success, for farther legislation was necessary in 1799[3]. The bondsmen were born in a
state of subjection, and an attempt was first made to free
them gradually; but many of them failed to take advantage
of the opportunity, while others became deeply indebted to
their masters, and thus sank to a position of absolute dependence[4]. In other cases the system of apprenticeship operated *Appren-ticeship.*
so as to produce similar results. "Here," said the commissioners in Staffordshire, in 1842, "is a slavery in the middle
of England as reprehensible as ever was the slavery in the
West Indies, which justice and humanity alike demand
should no longer be endured[5]."

319. It is exceedingly difficult to find any terms in
which to estimate the effect of the industrial inventions.
There are of course two different aspects in which they can
be viewed, first, the extent of the industrial changes themselves, and secondly, their indirect effects on society.

The extent of the industrial changes can indeed be stated
in various ways. There are at all events approximate estimates of the yards of cloth that were woven, or the tons of
iron that were smelted, which give at least an impression of
the magnitude, and still more of the rapidity of the change.
The tables in the appendix may serve to give a brief résumé
of the change in so far as it can be estimated by figures.

There was however a far more important change through
the introduction of machinery into the textile industries,
since there was not only an increase in the quantity, but an

---

[1] Cosmo Innes considers it was not a vestige of mediaeval serfdom. *Early Scottish History*, 499; May, *Constitutional History*, III. 38.

[2] 15 Geo. III. c. 28.   [3] 39 Geo. III. c. 56.

[4] 39 Geo. III. c. 56, § 5. This measure seems to have proved effective. *Reports &c.* 1844, XVI. 9.

[5] *Ib.* 1842, XV. 54. There was soon a great improvement. *Ib.* 1844, XVI. 56.

A.D. 1776 —1815.

Improved character of machine production.

improvement in the quality of the output. Work could be done under more effective supervision and therefore with greater regularity. The best hand-work might probably be more than equal to machine-work, but machine-work was much more reliable than the work of the ordinary weaver. There has been a tendency to idealise the character and skill of those who prosecuted domestic industries, but we ought not to shut our eyes to the abundant evidence that the weavers were irregular in their manner of working, and that the quality of the goods gave rise to difficulties from time to time. In the factory system there was much more effective supervision, and production took place more regularly. The improvement in the quality was perhaps most obvious in connection with spinning; Crompton's invention was really due to a desire to obtain better yarn for his own loom than he could always procure from spinners in his neighbourhood, and the jennies provided finer and better woollen yarn. It is of course possible that human hands at their best can do work which no mill can approach, and the thread of Indian muslins shows what inherited skill can accomplish with the very simplest implements; but for all that, the introduction of machinery appears to have given a higher average quality than before.

Better quality at the price.

At any rate it gave a better quality at the prices which had been previously paid. Quality and price must always be taken into account together, in considering the condition of any industry; and machine production was cheaper production, so that the English could offer a good and serviceable cloth on lower terms than before. The excellent quality for the money, which their looms turned out, gave them a hold upon the markets of the world. English commerce could not be destroyed by the Berlin Decrees; since English manufactures, by their superiority, were in constant demand even in those countries which they could only reach by roundabout routes. This is one of the points which renders the influence of these industrial improvements incalculable. It was apparently by means of them that we were able to hold our own against Napoleon; who shall say how far we could have done so under other circumstances?

Looked at in this way we can see that the purely eco- A.D. 1776
—1815.
nomic gain from the age of invention was enormous. The *Indisput-*
question how this gain was distributed throughout the nation *able econo-*
opens up a series of most complicated problems; in not a few *mic gain.*
cases there was actual loss and terrible suffering. That is
not a thing to be forgotten, still less to be made light of;
but it need not cause us to ignore the other fact that the
economic gain to the country as a whole was immense, and
this by whatever test we try it. Far more goods were produced for consumers, and there was greater plenty or rather
less scarcity than would otherwise have been the case, while
on the other hand the nation was raised to the highest
pinnacle of power. The industrial changes have given England a far larger population, and have given enormously increased facilities for clothing, feeding and housing them.
However much we may deplore the social evils which have
accompanied these industrial changes, the economic gain is
indisputable; nor does it seem possible for anyone in the
present day to argue seriously that Parliament would have
done well to prohibit the introduction of machinery, as the
wool-combers and others would have urged them to do.

320. The effects of the industrial revolution upon society *Social*
were very startling and in many ways were obviously evil. *effects of*
At the same time we shall find that they were for the most *Industrial*
part due to the simultaneous occurrence of changes, which *Revolution.*
have already been examined as they occurred separately and
on a smaller scale.

(*a*) There was in the first place a migration of industry *Migration*
from certain districts to new centres. This has been already *of employ-*
spoken of in the sixteenth century, and as Defoe observed *ment.*
it, in the earlier part of the eighteenth. Towards the end of
the eighteenth century and the beginning of the nineteenth
it continued with extraordinary rapidity[1]. Not only did the
districts where water-power and coal were available draw
away the trade from the Eastern and Southern Counties, but

---

[1] This concentration occurred in many trades. Pennant (*Journey*, I. 58) notes
potteries in Essex; see also *Annals of Agriculture*, II. 143, for Lowestoft. But
this trade now centres in Staffordshire. So too glovemaking has been concentrated at Worcester. *Annals of Agriculture*, VI. 121.

even in the most prosperous districts there was a migration of employment from villages to towns. Perhaps the most lasting mischiefs due to the industrial revolution lay in the loss of those who no longer found employment, or whose wives or children no longer found employment, in connection with textile trades. The uprooting of established family stocks[1] and substitution of a migratory wage-earning class was a very serious change.

*Employ-
ment of
children.*
(b) Again, we shall have to look at the conditions under which work was carried on, in the new centres. The chief evil was one that was not wholly new, but one that had never been felt in the same degree, as it was by the journey-men calico-printers after 1790[2]. In all the earlier struggles between employers and employed, from the fifteenth century onwards, we hear of overstocking with apprentices. This practice had been specially denounced by those who took up the cause of the frame-work knitters; but in consequence of the introduction of machinery, there was opportunity for em-ploying children to an extent that had never been previously known. By far the larger number of the evils, which rightly roused so much indignation in connection with the factory system, were indirectly due to the scale on which this was practised.

*Real wages
of labour.*
(c) We must further consider the rate of reward. The real wages of labour were very seriously affected during the last decade of the eighteenth century by a long succession of bad seasons. In 1795 distress was widely spread, and the House of Commons were practically unanimous in seeking to find a remedy by modifying the Elizabethan legislation. But there were grave difficulties in the way. At this particular juncture the wages paid to the cotton-weavers were very high, and the rapidly developing industry was attracting labourers from the country[3]; but within a few years the tide

---

[1] Le Play, *Les Ouvriers Européens*, I. 384.

[2] *Reports Misc.* 1806, III. 1127; also 1808—4, v. 889.

[3] *Ib.* 1808, II. 119. Mr Atherton said that the wages of agricultural labourers near Bolton, which were from 3s. to 3s. 6d. a day in 1808, rose at the time when weavers' wages were high; "they rose up from 2s. 4d. a day when wages were so that we [weavers] could get a living; at that time people would not work out-work, if they could get weaving." "The pay of agricultural labour

turned, and the cotton-weavers' wages gradually declined, till A.D. 1776 in 1808[1] they seem to have been little more than a third of the rate paid ten years before. This newly-developed and suddenly-distressed industry was the field on which the battle between the old method of regulating wages and the new system of depending on free competition was fought out.

The first attempt at giving any relief was made soon after the fall of wages had commenced; it aimed at providing a cheap and summary mode of settling disputes; the Arbitration Act of 1800[2] empowered the weavers and their employers to go before Arbitrators in case of any dispute as to wages, and arranged that the rates thus fixed by arbitration should be enforced. It does not appear that this measure served to confer any benefit on the weavers[3]. The reason of this was not far to seek. The rapid development of the trade had attracted a large number of men to engage in it, some of whom were mere speculators with nothing to lose[4]. The markets were overstocked, and the uncertainties of war and effects of the Orders in Council rendered all business very speculative; prices could not be maintained, and the masters again and again lowered wages, but always with disastrous effects. The diminution of wages[5] only tended to increase the

Arbitration.

---

is much higher than it has been, owing to a great many cotton manufactories being erected in this county" (Cumberland in 1795). *Annals of Agriculture,* xxiv. 813.

[1] *Reports,* 1808, ii. 108, 110. It is difficult to calculate precisely as the length of the piece was increased, while the wages decreased and the outgoings were heavier proportionally on the lower wages. For the piece (two weeks' work) in 1797, fifty shillings was paid, and in 1808, only eighteen shillings.

[2] 40 Geo. III. c. 90.   [3] *Reports* &c., 1808, ii. 111.

[4] "It has arisen in this way, that people having very little or no capital, have been induced to begin by the prospects held out to them, perhaps by people in London, and when they have got the goods into the market, they have been obliged to sell them for less than they cost, or without regard to the first cost, and this has injured the regular trade more than anything else. I think * * when the regular manufacturer finds that he cannot sell goods at the price they cost, he is compelled to lower his wages. * * Perhaps three, four, or five [of the new persons] may be insolvent every year in the neighbourhood [of Bolton], and when they come to be examined before their Creditors, it turns out the cause of their Insolvency is, the goods being sold for less than they cost." (Mr Ainsworth's evidence *Reports* &c. 1808, ii. p. 102.) See also the *Report on Manufactures, Commerce &c. in* 1833. "Trade at present requires industry, economy and skill. During the war, profits were made by plunges, by speculation." *Reports,* 1833, vi. 27.

[5] It also affected the home demands prejudicially; with starvation wages,

production, as the weavers worked longer hours in the hopes of making up the old rate of income[1]; and they were forced into deeper and deeper misery. In this case it is to be noticed that the evil was not due to the competition of machinery, for the power-loom had not come into practical operation when the period of disaster began. It was simply due to a ruinous competition among capitalists, which led them to cut down wages in self-defence. As was to be expected the small employers, who were not in a substantial position, were chiefly to blame for cutting prices lower and lower. Many of the masters would have been willing to see

Minimum Wage. some method adopted of fixing a minimum wage for the weavers; and this was the demand of the men themselves. But the temper of the times was against it. There is a great difference of tone between the debate on Mr Whitbread's motion[2], for fixing a minimum wage, in 1795, and that on the similar proposal in 1800[3], or that on Mr Rose's Bill[4] for fixing a minimum for cotton-weavers in 1808. The demands made by the Lancashire operatives were so piteous, however, that they could not be ignored. A Committee of the House of Commons took evidence on the subject[5], and reported very decidedly against the proposal, as impracticable and likely to aggravate the distress[6]. From that time the system of attempting to assess rates of wages was doomed; and the wages clauses of the Act of 1563 were repealed in 1813[7].

The strong opinion which was held in Parliament[8] against attempts to regulate wages by authority, and the reiterated expression of a belief that such a policy would necessarily

labourers could not buy cloth so largely. Brentano, *Anfang und Ende der englischen Kornzölle*, p. 13.

[1] *Reports &c.*, 1808, II. 119.
[2] It was read a second time *nem. con.*, and was sympathetically criticised by Fox, *Parl. Hist.* XXXII. 700.
[3] *Ib.* XXXIV. 1426.
[4] *Parl. Debates*, XI. 425.
[5] *Reports &c.*, 1808, II. 97.
[6] *Ib.* 1809, III. 311.
[7] 53 Geo. III. c. 40; see below, p. 578.
[8] Many of the millowners as well as the hands would have welcomed it. "'Do you know whether the head manufacturers of Bolton are desirous of this minimum?' 'The head manufacturers in general are. Mr Sudell told me he wished it might take place, and he should call a meeting in Blackburn about it; the smaller manufacturers in our town in general have petitioned for it; there are very few who have objected to it'." *Reports Misc.* 1808, II. 119.

aggravate the evil, deserve very full consideration. With A.D. 1776 —1815.
our experience of the effects of the rising standard of comfort among artisans it is difficult to suppose that they were
right, especially at a time when England had a practical
monopoly of the markets of the world for some classes of
goods[1]. But if the strong opinion they held about the evils
of regulation is borne in mind, it may help us to understand
the otherwise inexplicable tyranny of passing additional laws
against combination at this very time. If a fixed minimum
of wages was an evil and tended to aggravate distress even
when it emanated from public authority, the attempts of
private individuals to take the matter into their own hands
and enforce such a regulation by the strength of a combina- *Combina-*
tion was still more to be deprecated. This seemed to be *tions.*
doing a bad thing in the worst way. The year 1800 was a
time of terrible distress, when both Houses debated long on
the dearth of provisions and the best means of remedying
them. The labourers and artisans must have been reduced
to terrible straits, and may well have associated together in
the hope of bettering themselves; but very severe measures
were passed to render all combinations for obtaining advanced
wages or improved conditions of work, illegal. Every effort
was made to suppress trade-unions by imposing penalties on
attending their meetings and by prohibiting contributions to
their funds. The policy of the doctrinaire economists of the
day was embodied[2] in this most mischievous measure.

Since the Elizabethan policy with regard to wages was
being formally and deliberately discarded, it became necessary to try and meet the current and wide-spread distress in *Allow-*
some other fashion, and a fatal step was taken; wages were *ances.*
allowed to remain at starvation rates; but the local authorities supplemented wages out of the poor's rate[4]. In this way

---

[1] Mr Helps, a wholesale dealer, stated in evidence that with a rise of 10 per cent. in the price of cotton goods, "not a piece the less would be sold." *Reports Misc.* 1808, II. 111.

[2] 39 Geo. III. c. 81, 40 Geo. III. c. 106, 41 Geo. III. c. 38.

[3] See below, § 356, p. 578.

[4] The practice of granting 'exhibitions' to supplement wages, though not provided for by the then existing law appears to have been common in the time of
Charles II. Sir M. Hale, *Provision for the Poor*, 6.

A.D. 1776
—1815.

earnings continued to be kept at a very low rate, while the necessaries of life were increasing in price, and large numbers of the population became habitually dependent on the rates and were pauperised. The inherent weakness of the Elizabethan system at length became apparent. That code had assumed that all who desired it could find employment; this had never been wholly true, though, with the gradual progress during the eighteenth century, it may not impossibly have been more nearly true than in previous times. The law had also assumed that those who had employment would be able to live by their wages, and had devised the machinery for securing this result; but the machinery had broken down and the administrators determined to accept the position. They declined to take active steps with the view of reintroducing the old conditions and enabling the labourer to live by his work. Thenceforward he was in many cases unable to maintain himself, and he was tempted to sink gradually into the condition of claiming support at public expense

1795.

whether he worked or no. The Berkshire Justices who made allowances in aid of wages doubtless assumed that the difficulty was merely temporary, and that when better seasons returned they would be able to discard this expedient. They failed to take account of the demoralising effect of out-door relief, and they established a precedent which worked most calamitously, till a drastic measure of poor-law reform was demanded and was passed in 1834.

Outcry against Machinery.

It was not unnatural that the workers, who suffered so severely both from lack of employment, from under-paid employment and from the general dearth, should hastily conclude that the cause of their misfortunes lay in the introduction of machinery and in that alone. There probably was some truth in their view of the situation. Before the close of the war the spinning-wheel was superseded by the self-acting mule, and the women and children in each household were prevented from helping to eke out the family income in the old way. Besides this, quantities of cotton yarn were exported, the spinners were glad to supply any market with the yarn which was so rapidly spun, and weavers on the Continent produced a better article by using British yarn than they had previously been able to do. It seemed as if the very success of the capitalist spinners was ruining the weavers. There were those who argued seriously against the export of English yarn on the ground that the manufacture ought to be completed at home, but Parliament was opposed to any restrictions of the kind, and the lot of the weavers became worse and worse. Hence it appears that *Spinners and Weavers.* while the spinners suffered by the introduction of machinery, the weavers were reduced to great straits before the power-loom was generally introduced, by the competition of foreigners who supplied their own markets with cloth woven from English yarn[1].

(d) In all the conditions of work the arrangements in *Factories and Domestic Shops.* the first factories were exceedingly bad. The lofty rooms and appliances for preventing dust and providing ventilation, which are found in modern mills, were quite unknown, and if the conditions under which work was done then are compared with those which are usual at the present day, it seems as if the first factory-owners were criminally careless in regard to the comfort of the employés. A single case may illustrate the change. Arkwright's mill at Cromford, Derbyshire, was used till it was partially destroyed by fire in 1890, but the proprietors had found it necessary to remove every second floor, and thus double the space provided, in order to fall in with modern requirements on this point. If on the other hand the comparison is made, between the conditions in which weavers worked in their own cottages, and those of the first mills, the case is not so clear. If nineteenth century opinion condemns the old mills, it likewise condemns many of the old cottages. There is every reason to believe that under the old poor-law, when so few new houses were built, there were grave risks of overcrowding; and the numerous cottages which remain in the West Riding of Yorkshire, where the upper floor was specially lighted for the sake of the looms it contained, show that the domestic industry was not carried on in ideal conditions.

(e) The change which was perhaps most painful, to *Strain of work.* those who found employment in connection with machine

---

[1] Radcliffe, W. *New System of Manufacture*, 49 et seq.

spinning and weaving, was the increased strain that was put
upon them. They were now forced to work, not at their own
pace but at the machine's pace; not during their own hours,
but during the hours when the master kept his machines
going. The human beings became subordinate to machines,
and with the ever-increasing improvement and acceleration
of pace there was an increased strain on the faculties and a
sense of restraint and tension. The increasing intensity of
labour is a very serious matter, of which it has not always
been easy to take account; and in so far as the hours of
labour were unduly extended, the loss of freedom which was
due to the dependence of the worker on machinery, was a
terrible evil. But even in this most serious matter there has
been a decided gain, since so much success has attended
efforts to reduce the hours of labour to reasonable limits.

*Regularity
of work.*   (*f*) There is great danger in any attempt to describe
the habits of a class, but there seems to be abundant evidence
that the artisan of a hundred years ago was less regular in
his work and less steady in character than the skilled artisan
of the present day. Those who labour on the land are forced
by the changes of the seasons to carry on the successive
operations of tillage in due course, but the weaver who worked
on his own account, at his own loom, was absolutely his own
master, and not always a wise master. There seem to have
been many who did not set themselves to do regular daily
work, but who idled half the week[1] and worked for long hours
during the rest of the time. The long hours of factory labour
were a real evil; but they probably appeared far less
onerous at the beginning of the century, as they were not
very different from the hours which weavers had voluntarily
adopted, on the days when they worked at all. Not only is
there direct evidence as to the habits of the domestic
weavers from eighteenth century sources, but in some at
least of the cases where domestic industries survive, the men
who live by them still bear the old reputation for irregularity of habits. The first introduction of machinery was

---

[1] Even when the men were industrious the conditions of domestic industry in
the West Riding were such that the men lost about a third of their time. *Annals
of Agriculture,* xxvii. 311. See above, pp. 383, 388, and 599 below.

accompanied with many evils, but in so far as it tended towards regular habits of daily work it has been eventually beneficial. The more it is possible to shorten hours and to improve the conditions of work the better, but the fact that under the régime of machinery the man who is employed has more regular hours is in itself an immense improvement in the condition of the labourer.

When we look at the details of a period of transition we *Evil of any* cannot but be appalled by the misery that occurred. This *period of* *transition.* was true of the Tudor enclosures, it was true too of the beginnings of the factory system; but it is not clear in either case that the change has really been an evil. We could not wish to retrace our steps to a time when there was no machinery. In most of the machine industries, things have already so adjusted themselves, that the remuneration of the worker is greater and the conditions under which he does his work are more wholesome than in the old days. It is not in the trades where machinery is used, but in those where there is little or none, that there is the greatest suffering at present. Those who are constantly working with delicate machines are bound to exercise an amount of care and deftness which was not formerly required, and if we compare the factory hand of the present day with the domestic worker as he really was in the eighteenth century, it is hard to point out any characteristic trait, or any single circumstance in which he has really suffered.

XI. AGRICULTURE.

321. The change in English agriculture during this period was almost as great, though by no means so sudden, as that which was taking place in industry. In all previous times England had, unless in famine years, been able to produce enough corn for the population and had often been able to export a surplus. But before the close of the *Increased* eighteenth century[1] this was no longer the case, and England *demand for* *corn.*

---

[1] Sir Edward West specifies the years from 1766 to 1773 as the time when

had come to be dependent on foreign countries for a portion of the regular food supply. The precise steps in this very important change would be of great interest, but unfortunately they are somewhat obscure. There is ample evidence, however, that the impulse was really due to an increase of population. From 1715 to 1765 the range of prices had been exceedingly low, and there is reason to believe that the ordinary standard of comfort, as well as the numbers, were considerably raised[1]. Nor is there any doubt that population increased with great rapidity during the latter half of *The range of price.* the eighteenth century[2]. This increase of the regular demand affected the range of prices; the average from 1715 to 1762 was about thirty-six shillings, while from 1763 to 1792, it was about forty-eight shillings; and this was the price at which, according to the Act of 1773, importation was allowed to begin[3]. This great rise in the range of prices must have rendered the business of the capitalist farmer specially profitable, and we need not be surprised that the new system of farming continued to supersede the old, but *Progress of enclosing for arable farming.* with increasing rapidity. The outward and visible sign of the introduction of the new system is marked by the progress of enclosure. In the reign of Anne there were 3 private bills for enclosure; in that of George I., 16; under George II. 226; and in the reign of George III., from 1760 —1775, there were 734; from 1776—97, 748; from 1797 —1810, 956; and from 1810—20, 771: besides this, there was a general enclosure Act in 1801[4].

Such averages and figures, however, conceal many matters of which it is desirable to take account. In not a few seasons the price was particularly high on account of dearth. As has *Occasional dearth and* been noted above, the seasons from 1765 to 1774 were specially inclement, and from 1775 onwards they were very irregular; thus in 1779 there was an unusually plentiful crop, while 1782 was a very bad year, which was followed

---

our imports of corn began to exceed our exports. *Price of Corn.* p. 10. Mr Pro-thero notes however that it was not till 1793 that the importation of corn finally turned the balance. *Pioneers of English Farming,* p. 88.

[1] Malthus, *Principles of Political Economy,* 253.
[2] Rickman, *Observations,* p. 9.   [3] Tooke, I. 69.
[4] *Ib.* I. 72; Prothero, 257.

by two others that were distinctly below the average. It A.D. 1776 —1815.
thus appears that the inclemency of the seasons does not
serve to account for the high range of the average prices;
but the irregularity of the seasons had a great effect in
producing sudden fluctuations of price. At Lady-Day 1780,
the price of wheat was thirty-eight and threepence; at
Michaelmas forty-eight shillings; and at Lady-Day 1781,
fifty-six and elevenpence[1].

These violent fluctuations of price would often give the *effects on the capitalist farmers.*
capitalists who could hold large stocks of corn opportunities
of realising enormous profits. On the other hand the small
farmers, whether they worked in common fields or in separate
holdings, who were forced to realise their corn immediately
after harvest, suffered immensely. In 1779 in particular,
prices were so low that many farmers were ruined[2]; in later
seasons, when prices fell, there was another great period of
agricultural distress, which caused very wide-spread ruin;
though in 1793, the capitalists suffered as well as the small
farmers. About the year 1782 a number of country banks
had been formed; this was a sign of the increased facilities
for saving money and for applying capital to land[3]; but in
1792, when prices were low, a considerable proportion of
these country banks appear to have got into difficulties;
there were a large number of failures in that and the following year, so that the whole credit system of the country[4] was
seriously affected; there can be little doubt that when the
large capitalists were so badly hit, the small farmers would
suffer as well.

Some of the other changes of the times were specially *Special difficulties of small farmer.*
burdensome to the small farmer as compared with his
wealthier neighbour. Thus the charges of enclosing fell
far more heavily proportionately on the small farmer, and
so too did the expense of fencing their land when separate
portions were allotted to them. But the greatest grievance
of all was connected with the Speenhamland policy[5] of

---

[1] Tooke, I. 76.　　　　　　　[2] Arthur Young, *Annals of Agr.* xxv. 460.
[3] Tooke, I. 193.　　　　　　　[4] *Ib.* 195.
[5] See below, p. 494. That this policy was practically in operation for some years before is shown by David Davies, *Case of Labourers in Husbandry* (1795), p. 25. See also above, p. 471, note 4.

A.D. 1776
—1815.
*Rates in
aid of
wages.*
granting allowances out of rates in addition to wages. The small holder had to pay the rates; since the labourers were not maintained by the wages paid by their employers, but partly from the rates, it followed that the small holders were taxed for the benefit of the large farmers. As these small occupiers worked their own land and hardly employed any paid labour they received no benefit from the rates[1].

1801.
"Perhaps it may not be an extravagant conjecture to venture, if one were to affirm that if the small farmers should remain under a pressure of poor's rates for ten years to come equal to the pressure which they have experienced during the last ten years, that so useful and respectable a set of men must necessarily be exterminated entirely in many districts of the kingdom, and many respectable fathers and mothers of families would themselves become objects of that charity which they had been ruined to support; their farms would, on the first vacancy, be purchased by neighbouring gentlemen or by opulent farmers; and eventually, by the entire suppression of small occupations, every hope would be taken away from the labouring poor of ever bettering their condition by renting and cultivating a few acres for their own comfort and advantage[2]." It may perhaps thus be said that the pressure of poor-rates was the determining cause which rendered the yeomanry willing to sell, while the high prices of the last years of the war gave them the opportunity of selling advantageously.

Fluctuations from interruptions of commerce
The fluctuations of price became still more extraordinary in the succeeding decade; for since England was now dependent for her ordinary food supply on importation, a war which interfered with the usual course of commerce immediately affected the price to the English consumer. The high prices during the war, seem to have been chiefly due not to increased consumption, though this may have been operative to some extent[3], but to a decrease in the regular supplies through the interruption of commerce. It does not appear

---

[1] *Annals of Agr.* xxxvii. 106, 109. [2] A Country Clergyman, *Ib.* 109.

[3] Our soldiers and sailors were not entirely supplied with food from England, but they were to some extent, and with more expensive victuals than they would have consumed as peasants or artisans. The feeding of prisoners of war is also spoken of as a considerable item. *Annals of Agriculture*, xxxvi. 38.

that the wars of the earlier part of the eighteenth century, A.D. 1776 —1815. when England was not an importing country, had any similar effect upon prices. There were however, at the close of the century, several years of unexampled scarcity. Such were 1795, 1796, 1800, 1801[1]; these were bad seasons to begin with, and the hindrances to importation turned the dearth *and famine* into a famine. Those farmers who had a crop, however, *years.* must have been reaping splendid profits, and there was no wonder that an enormous extension of arable farming took place, while as a matter of course this arable farming was all of the modern type.

When at length the ordinary channels of commerce were *The fall of* re-opened, in 1815, there was an immediate fall in prices, *prices and* and much of the land which had been brought into culti-vation ceased to be remunerative. The area of tillage was somewhat reduced, but the old agricultural methods had been swept away for ever. The sudden change in prices, on the close of the war, appears to have given the finishing stroke to many of the yeomanry, who had successfully held *the* their own during the period of enclosing. Some had been *yeomanry,* tempted to realise during the time of war prices; others had burdened themselves with obligations, which they could not meet when their income was suddenly reduced[2]; and though some of them continued to struggle on, there were no men of a similar class to take their places when the small properties came into the market[3]. During the eighteenth *who were* century the yeomanry had prospered, in so far as they were *not re-* *placed.* able to improve their methods of cultivation. The freeholders were not bought[4] out then, as is so commonly asserted, partly at all events because they did not wish to sell; but in the

[1] Tooke, I. 226.

[2] A full discussion of these influences and of the destruction of this class will be found in the Report of the Committee of 1833. *Reports* &c. 1833, v. questions 1262 (Wiltshire), 1691 (Worcestershire), 3103 (Yorkshire), 4862, 9196, 9269 (Somer-set), 6056 (Cheshire), 6156 (Shropshire), 6957 (Cumberland), 12216 (Nottingham).

[3] Prothero, 83.

[4] Laurence advises stewards to purchase freeholders' lands when they could, but the chief motive was economic, to facilitate the enclosing of common fields, *Duty of Steward*, 36. Cowper (*Essay proving that enclosing commons* &c.) p. 18 criticises him for wishing to take advantage of the 'necessity of the poor free-holders.' "I know no set of men who toil and labour so hard as the smaller farmers and freeholders."

A.D. 1776
—1815.
time of the war prices at the beginning of this century, many of them were willing to sell; and when others in subsequent years were forced to sell, they could hardly find any purchasers except among the neighbouring proprietors, so that their farms were merged in larger estates.

Through these three causes then, first, the increase of population, secondly, the advantages of the capitalist in speculative farming, and thirdly, the high prices due to our dependence on imported supplies, the whole character of English agriculture was changed. There was a considerable increase of arable farming; the common field system of cultivation gave way in numberless districts to the modern methods of tillage, and the English yeomanry were superseded by capitalist farmers and agricultural labourers.

Differentiation of town and country.

322. The invention of machinery and the changes it introduced re-acted with great effect upon rural life. The differentiation between town and country became more complete. The gradual changes by which the towns lost their rural character are probably hopelessly obscured. The *Artisan farming and allotments.* Survey of 1615 shows that Sheffield cutlers, who had a considerable struggle to pay their way, combined the management of some land with the production of whittles[1]. At Pudsey, in the neighbourhood of Leeds, the woollen weavers practised agriculture as a by-employment at the beginning of the present century. They were able to add considerably to their personal comfort and to pay high rents for pasture land[2], though their agriculture was backward in the extreme[3]. The woollen weavers, in all parts of the country, appear to have enjoyed allotments or large gardens; but some of those who were engaged in the more recently introduced

[1] Hunter, *Hallamshire*, 148.   [2] *Annals of Agriculture*, XXVII. 809.

[3] *Ib.* XL. 135. "The land in this part is almost wholly occupied in small plots or farms, by manufacturers, merely for the convenience of keeping a few cows, for milk for their children, apprentices, and inmates, and a horse to job to and from the mills, market, &c.; hence it is, that the business of a farmer has, for a long time, been a subordinate consideration with almost every manufacturer, his views and ideas are narrow and contracted, and are confined to the cloth trade; in this method he jogs on; and such is the force of prejudice, that if anyone does not follow the old course of husbandry, he is frequently laughed at by his neighbours, and very invidiously considered as a visionary and an innovator; and the chief reason which they advance in defence of this old antiquated procedure, is, that their forefathers have practised it."

cotton-industry were aggregated in towns, and suffered from A.D. 1776 the want of healthful relaxation which could be combined —1815. with work at their looms[1]. In many small towns like Kettering[2] the artisans had allotments or pasture rights, and hence it may be said that at the beginning of this century there was a large part of the industrial population[3] which was not yet divorced from rural employments.

It is still harder to trace the steps by which those who *Domestic industry of* were mainly supported by labouring on the land ceased to *agricul-* practise industrial pursuits as by-employments[4]. It does *tural popu-* *lation.* not appear that the ordinary husbandman engaged in weaving though some of them seem to have done so in the Leeds district[5]; but it is quite clear that spinning was very generally practised as a domestic industry and was carried on by the wives and children of husbandmen[6]; spinning was thus a by-employment which gave an additional source of income to families.

The invention of machine-spinning and the enormous *Spinning.* saving which it effected, rendered it impossible for the hand-spinners to compete; so much depends too on procuring a perfectly even thread, that the operation is one in which the greater regularity of machine-work is specially advantageous. Machine-spun yarn was distinctly preferable, and hand-spinning could not hold its own. Since it had merely been a by-employment, the women and children could not follow the work to factories, unless these were established at their very doors; and as agricultural wages were unusually high during the first decade of the century, they had but little temptation to try and compete with machines; there

---

[1] *Annals of Agriculture*, xxxviii. 546.   [2] *Ib.* xxxix. 259, 244 note.

[3] At West Bromwich, the seat of the nail trade, agriculture "is carried on so connectedly with manufactures that it is subservient to them." *Ib.* iv. 157.

[4] D. Davies urges the necessity of finding winter-employments for men and boys; this was in a county where there were no manufactures in 1795. (*Case of Labourers*, p. 78.) The same sort of evil would arise as a new thing in districts from which manufacturing was withdrawn.

[5] "Many persons [at Armley] who have small farms also carry on clothmaking, employing their wives, children and servants; they send them out to work in harvest time." "We have not a farmer who gets his living by farming without trade, in the township." *Reports*, 1806, iii. 602, 607.

[6] Davies, who gives some most interesting family budgets, shows the great importance of spinning. (*Case of Labourers*, 83.)

C. II.   31

was no violent opposition to the change at the critical time. As a consequence this by-employment in rural districts died out, while nothing was substituted for it as a means of augmenting the family income[1].

Weaving not a by-employ-ment.

The introduction of power-weaving did not take place to any great extent till after the close of the war, but its effects on the agricultural population were not so great, since weaving had not been a by-employment of husband-men, but was pursued as a distinct craft[2]. Since it was a distinct craft, the weavers would probably be able to follow the employment to the factory districts; as a matter of fact hand-loom weaving was specially concentrated in those dis-tricts where yarn was spun by power, and the cottages round Halifax with their well-lighted upper storeys were obviously built for the convenience of hand-loom weavers.

Effect of migration on village life.

Local demand reduced.

The migration of the craftsmen from the villages to the towns would chiefly affect the village prosperity by reducing the demand for its produce. The small manufacturing popu-lation created a demand on the spot; and articles could be sold which might not perhaps bear the expense of transport to the towns. It might appear that the villager would gain by the improvement in production and would pay less for his clothes[3]; but the double cost of carriage, of his produce to the town and his purchased cloth to the village, would

---

[1] *Reports*, 1843, xii. 159.

[2] Radcliffe appears to state, *New System of Manufactures*, 59, 60, that this was not the case and draws an ideal picture of the comfort of such a manufacturing husbandman; but he was probably a weaver with an allotment, not a labourer in husbandry. I cannot suppose that this was the usual arrangement, since the manu-facturers and the husbandmen are habitually spoken of as distinct classes, and the irregularity of the work of the manufacturers and their idleness is a constant subject of complaint. If their manufacturing had merely been a by-employment, it could not have been regarded in this light. When in 1795 Arthur Young issued inquiries to friends in different parts of England as to the condition of the labourers, their wages, poor-rates, &c. (*Annals of Agriculture*, xxv. 344) he only inquired into earnings by spinning. The eighteen replies which he received show that spinning was still more or less generally practised and other by-employments for women and children are mentioned (*Ib*. 484), but there is no mention of weaving as a by-employment. Bone lace was recommended as a trade to be taken up when spinning began to fail (*Ib*. xxxvii. 448). This was still common in Devonshire as a by-employment in 1843 (*Reports*, 1843, xii. 32), and button-making was practised in Dorsetshire.

[3] On the change in the habits of farm servants compare *Reports*, 1833, v. questions 6174—7, 10324 f.

diminish his receipts, and might enhance the price which A.D. 1776
he had formerly paid, so that his gain from this source would —1815.
hardly be appreciable. This destruction of local demand was
certainly an important matter, at the time when steam was
superseding water-power. In the first days of the factory
industry, there were many villages situated on a stream
with sufficient force to drive a single mill, and village factories, as we may call them, flourished for some time in
many places. When, however, improved machinery was introduced, they were no longer remunerative and had to be
closed[1].

The migration of spinning and weaving was the most
noticeable change which occurred; it left the husbandmen
and their families entirely dependent upon the soil, but
other influences were just beginning to change the character *Village
of country life. Machinery has been adapted to so many artisans
purposes that the village artisan is no longer required[2]. superseded.*
The capitalist farmer in all probability preferred the better
goods which he bought for less money at a distance, to
the productions of the local artisans; as a consequence there
have come to be fewer by-occupations than before. The
husbandman, who has skill as a thatcher, can no longer find
the opportunity of adding to his income. Professor Thorold *Thorold
Rogers[3] draws a most interesting picture of the condition of Rogers'
testimony.*
a village in his early days, where the revolution in the
textile trades hardly operated at all. "In my native
village" he says, "in Hampshire, I well remember two instances of agricultural labourers who raised themselves
through the machinery of the allowance system to the rank
and fortunes of small yeomen. Both had large families, and
both practised a bye-industry. The village was peculiar
in its social character, for there was not a tenant-farmer in
it, all being freeholders or copyholders. The rector was
opulent and generous, and there were a few persons of some

---

[1] One such mill, originally a paper mill (Nash, *Worcestershire*, II. 232) and subsequently a silk mill, existed at Overbury in Worcestershire. The proprietors were
forced to work almost entirely with apprentices, and the apprentices who had
served their time and could obtain no employment were a serious evil in the village.
[2] J. Cowper, *Essay proving that inclosing Commons is contrary to the interest
of the Nation* (1732), p. 8. [3] *Six Centuries*, 502.

A.D. 1776
—1815.
private means in the parish. But on the whole, the rates
and the allowances came from the resources of occupying
owners, and were, therefore, the contribution of the vestry
from its own resources, the only non-employers being one
or two humble tradesmen, the rector, and a country gentleman, whose house and grounds were not a hundred acres
in extent. There was no poverty in the whole place. Most
of the labourers baked their own bread, brewed their own
beer, kept pigs and poultry, and had half-an-acre or an acre
to till for themselves as part of their hire. But they had
regulated wages, and, when their families were large, allowances. There were not infrequent sales of land in the village
as families came to an end, but rarely in large quantities.
The rector built extensively, parsonage, schools, and finally
church from his own means, and, therefore, employment
was pretty general. The village mason became a considerable yeoman. But the two labourers of whom I am speaking
had their allowances, lived on their fixed wages with the
profits of their bye-labour, one being pig-killer to the village,
and, therefore, always busy from Michaelmas to Lady-day,
at a shilling a pig, and the offal, on which his family subsisted, with the produce of their small curtilage for half the
year. In the end, the allowance, saved scrupulously, and
I presume, made a profound secret was invested in land by
each. The one bought some forty acres of poor soil, on
which he got a comfortable and independent living; the
other some twenty, on which he did still better, for the land

Variety of employ-ment. was some of the best in the village." Mr Prothero writing
of an earlier time enumerates some of these by-employments,
"hitherto[1] the rude implements required for the cultivation
of the soil, or the household utensils needed for the comfort
of daily life, had been made at home. The farmer, his sons,
and his servants, in the long winter evenings carved the
wooden spoons, the platters, and the beechen bowls; plaited
wicker baskets; fitted handles to the tools; cut willow teeth
for rakes and harrows, and hardened them in the fire; fash-
ioned ox-yokes and forks; twisted willows into the traces and
other harness gear. Travelling carpenters visited farmhouses

[1] Prothero, 67.

at rare intervals to perform those parts of work which needed A.D. 1776 their professional skill. The women plaited the straw for —1815. the neck-collars, stitched and stuffed sheepskin bags for the cart-saddle, wove the straw or hempen stirrups and halters, peeled the rushes for and made the candles. The spinning-wheel, the distaff, and the needle were never idle; coarse home-made cloth and linen supplied all wants; every farm-house had its brass brewing kettle......All the domestic in-dustries by which cultivators of the soil increased their incomes, or escaped the necessity of selling their produce, were now supplanted by manufactures." But this change had only proceeded a very little way before 1815.

323. The preceding sections have served to indicate the nature of the reasons which called forth the rapid agri-cultural improvements of this era, and the manner in which the course of affairs was modified by the industrial revo-lution. It is worth while to look a little more closely at *Enclosing* the nature of the changes themselves. The progress of *of* enclosing was very rapid, as may be seen from the figures already given, but it is not easy to say how far the area under tillage was increased. The calculations on the subject do not distinguish between the acres of common field en- *Common* closed and the acres of common waste[1]. The acres of common *Fields and* waste enclosed were of course a real addition to the arable area; but though the acres of common field, when enclosed, were utilised to better purpose and were rendered more pro-ductive, they were not a substantial addition to the area under plough; they might bear better crops, but not more frequent crops of corn, than under the old tillage. This distinction is too often neglected. Politicians sometimes speak as if the whole of the four million acres which were enclosed during the eighteenth century had been drawn from the common wastes of the kingdom and were cultivated, to the loss of the commoners who had pasture rights over them; but of these four million acres, a very considerable quantity must have lain in common field, and the only pasture they afforded was the stubble which remained on the ground

[1] The *General Report on Enclosures*, p. 46, of the Board of Agriculture gives the total acreage enclosed from Queen Anne's time till 1805 at 4,187,056.

between harvest and the next ploughing. Such rights would be worth little; and it is difficult at this distance of time to form any opinion as to the practical value to the small farmer of pasture rights on the commons. It is to be feared that between the drovers who pastured their cattle on unstinted commons and the rich inhabitants who put a large number of beasts on the land, the pasture rights of the poor husbandman were not always very valuable. At any rate it seems quite impossible to assess them now, or to see how far the loss of such rights was a real element in the depression of the yeoman during this period.

Though we cannot pretend to estimate the extent of the evil so frequently alleged, there is no reason to doubt its reality. Enclosure was carried on by means of private bills; these were passed through Parliament without sufficient enquiry, and when many of the inhabitants were quite unaware of the impending change or were at all events powerless to resist it. Very clear light on this subject is given by a debate in the House of Lords in 1781; the Bishop of S. David's[1] objected to the manner in which the claims of the tithe-owner were adjusted when land was enclosed; Lord Thurlow, who was then Chancellor, expressed himself in very strong terms as to the injustice to small proprietors which frequently occurred in connection with such measures[2].

Where the enclosing was carried out with a due regard to the interest of all the occupiers, there was an immense gain from the more economical tillage which could be introduced. This was questioned by the opponents of the change, but it is proved up to the hilt. The enquiries of the Board of Agriculture, which were undertaken in every county in England, are decisive, and an excellent statement of the whole case is given in their *General Report on Enclosures*, which was published in 1808. At the same time the expenses connected with enclosing were enormous. It undoubtedly was a difficult matter to re-allot the lands fairly, so that each of the landholders should have such a piece as was really the equivalent of the scattered strips and patch of meadow and pasture rights which he had previously pos-

[1] *Parl. Hist.* XXII. 47.   [2] *Ib.* 59.

sessed. It was a difficult duty, and one which was generally A.D. 1776 —1815. assigned to strangers, who might be supposed to make an *but costliness of the change.* award unbiased by personal friendship. But it was a frightfully costly change. The parliamentary and law expenses were very heavy, but these were not all. The new farms were permanently separated from one another, and it was necessary to fence them; so that the expense of making the change imposed a very heavy burden on the village, and the shares of the poorer inhabitants for these expenses, or for fencing, involved many of them in debt and led to their ruin.

The enclosure of this period was in a way the continuation of a change which attracted great notice in the Tudor *Contrast between two periods of enclosure.* times, but was entirely different. Under the Tudors pasture farming was increasing at the expense of tillage; in the time of the Napoleonic wars, arable farming had become the more profitable of the two. In the Tudor times the landlord was apt to appropriate the common pasture for his own flock; in the eighteenth century there was probably less enclosing for pasture, as the landlords no longer wanted to obtain pasture, but to make the most of the land for tillage. If the common waste could not be profitably tilled there was no temptation to encroachment. For these reasons it seems probable that encroachment on the common pasture rights of the small farmers was less frequent and less serious than it had been in the sixteenth century.

Enclosures, however, as usually carried out, did have a *Effect on the rural labourers.* very serious result on the condition of the labourers; there were many cases where cottagers had encroached upon commons and the owners had connived at the practice. These men had perhaps been able to keep a cow; but when *A cow's grass.* the common waste and common fields were alike enclosed they had no longer the opportunity of doing so. A commissioner of enclosures, in looking back on the effects of twenty enclosures in which he had taken part, "lamented that he had been accessory to injuring two thousand poor people at the rate of twenty families per parish. Numbers in the practice of feeding on the commons cannot prove their right; and many, indeed most who have allotments have not more than an acre, which being insufficient for the man's cow, both cow and land are usually sold to the opulent farmers[1]."

Arthur Young, who had done so much in advocating enclosure, was greatly distressed to find that the labourers had suffered so severely. He set himself to collect evidence[2] on this special point, and found that out of thirty-seven eastern county parishes which had been enclosed, there were only twelve in which the labourers had not been injured. From the fact that there were twelve, he rightly argues that it was possible to carry out enclosure, and to obtain all the national benefit which it afforded, without perpetrating such injustice on the poor; but he urges that in all future acts of enclosure special care should be taken to insert clauses which would adequately protect the labourer in his accustomed privileges. Of all the changes which were affecting his position at the time this was probably the only one from which the agricultural labourer consciously suffered as a real grievance.

324. During the whole of this period there were great improvements in English agriculture, not so much through the introduction of any special improvement, as by the diffusion throughout the country generally of information regarding experiments which had answered in particular districts. In 1793 a Board of Agriculture was established by Pitt at the instance of Sir John Sinclair; in Arthur Young it found a competent secretary, while it succeeded in pushing on many practical improvements. Its publications contain much information as to the actual state of agriculture in different parts of the kingdom; a general survey, as it may be called, of the agriculture of England was undertaken with the view of promoting enclosures, and the results are embodied in an interesting report. Another institution which was founded in the same year was the Smithfield Club. Scientific tillage had advanced rapidly, but sheep-breeding and cattle-rearing had not been neglected. Mr Bakewell of Leicester appears to have been the pioneer in both directions; but he was specially successful in improving the breed

[1] *Annals,* xxxvi. 516.   [2] *Ib.* 513.

of sheep. Through the middle ages sheep had been chiefly A.D. 1776
bred for the sake of their wool, and cattle for the sake of _{—1815.}
their powers of draught as oxen; it was Bakewell who re-
garded these points as subsidiary and studied the breeding
of sheep and cattle with reference to the food supply[1].

During the period we are considering, the high range of *Farmer*
prices rendered agricultural improvement profitable, and it *George.*
also became fashionable. King George III. devoted himself
enthusiastically to the concerns of his Windsor farm; he
wrote articles which he signed Ralph Robinson, and many
of the nobility in different parts of the country followed
him in this pursuit, and set an example which found
many imitators and which proved exceedingly profitable so
long as the high prices lasted. The Duke of Bedford was
one of the principal improvers; and the sheep-shearings of
Woburn were remarkable gatherings of gentry who were *Woburn.*
interested in encouraging the breeding of sheep. Prizes were
given for this object as well as for the improvement of agricultural implements. There was an even more celebrated
meeting, instituted by Mr Coke of Holkham in Norfolk, *Holkham.*
where the prizes offered included rewards for labourers who
showed special skill in particular departments of farm work[2].

325. During the period of bad seasons and scarcity
there were of course very high prices; and in the good years
which were interspersed, prices fell to a very low level. It
was possible to urge that both results were due to the
changes which had taken place in the Corn Laws in 1773[3].
Arthur Young, who had protested against such a change at *The Corn*
the time[4], on the ground that the price at which export *Laws and Prices.*
was permitted should not be too low, was justified. He held
that, with the increasing demand and increasing difficulties
of production, the farmer in 1770 ought to be able to calculate on a higher price than he could look for in 1689, and
that the legislature should endeavour to keep the price of
corn as steadily as possible at this higher level. Parliament
had attempted instead to make corn cheaper, with disastrous

---

[1] Prothero, 51.   [2] *Annals of Agriculture*, xxxix. 42, 61.
[3] 13 Geo. III. c. 43.
[4] *Expediency of a free Export of Corn*, p. 24; *Political Arithmetic*, p. 40.

A.D. 1776
—1815.

results, to the consumer in bad years, and to the producer in good ones[1]: but the subsequent alterations which took place in the corn laws were of the nature of temporary modifications and did not imply an entire change of system[2]. It was not till the close of the war in 1815 that this legislation took the highly protective form which afterwards gave rise to the agitation for repeal.

The promoters of agricultural improvement had however to face a more delicate question than that of foreign competition. The main line of policy which they advocated was that of enclosing the common fields, but in such enclosures there was great difficulty about making a satisfactory allotment for tithes. The Bishop of S. David's was the spokesman of a large number of clergy who disliked a change by which they were forced to undertake the management of a glebe, instead of obtaining tithes from the occupiers[3]. On the other hand, the agricultural improvers could not but feel that tithe was a form of tax which had a baneful influence upon agriculture. Mr Howlett, the vicar of Great Dunmow, calculated that the tithes in his neighbourhood had increased in value twelve times as much as the rent[4]. While a charge of this sort was a real obstacle to improvement, the recent changes made it more difficult for the clergy to consent to accept an arrangement, by which they agreed for themselves and for their successors, to forego the advantage which might arise from any further increase of cultivation. The benefits which had come to the Universities from the law which assigned to them corn-rents were well known, and it was not obviously politic to accept a change in system. In this way it came about that the tithe-owners were inclined to regard the Board of Agriculture and their supporters with much suspicion, and this was in all probability one of the influences which caused the discontinuance of this department in 1819.

Enclosing and Tithe.

Gains of Tithe-owner.

---

[1] *Annals of Agriculture*, XLI. p. 308.

[2] 31 Geo. III. c. 30; 44 Geo. III. c. 109. There is an interesting discussion of the effect of variations of price in encouraging improvement, and the nature of the policy required, in *Reports, Misc.* 1803—4, v. 479 f., also on the danger of special modifications unless in extreme necessity.

[3] *Parliamentary History*, XXII. 47.   [4] *Annals of Agriculture*, XXXVIII. 132.

The existence of tithe had also a curious effect upon the farmers in making them prefer the policy by which labourers were maintained out of the rates to that of raising their wages. .Tithes are levied on the produce after the rates have been allowed for, but without taking account of the expenses of cultivation, so that the farmer who employed labour would pay a smaller tithe if the rates were high and wages low, than he would have to do on the same crop, if rates were low and wages high. This is another of the minor causes which contributed to render the pauperising policy of allowances popular with the large farmers[1]. *A.D. 1776 —1815. Incidental effect of tithe on the labourers.*

XII. THE POOR.

326. There is a remarkable change in the tone of Poor Law legislation and administration, in the period we are considering, as compared with that which ruled in the earlier part of the century. The vast increase of pauperism in the Restoration and Revolutionary periods had caused a general scare. It found its fiercest expression in Defoe's pamphlet, but it had a marked effect on legislation. Workhouses were sanctioned in many places, and in 1723 a workhouse test was imposed[2], as those who refused to go to the workhouse lost their claim on relief. The lbcal administration was carried on in the same spirit, for every overseer seemed to regard it as his primary duty to keep down the rates at all hazards. Dr Burn's pungent sentences may be quoted as the opinion of a contemporary: "The office of an overseer seems to be understood to be this: to keep an extraordinary look-out to prevent persons coming to inhabit without certificates, and to fly to the justices to remove them; and if a man brings a certificate, then to caution all the inhabitants not to let him a farm of £10 a year, and to take care to keep him out of all parish offices; to warn them, if they will hire servants, to hire them half-yearly,......or if they do hire them *Change of tone regarding the poor.* *Workhouse test.* *Overseers.*

---

[1] *Annals of Agriculture*, xxxviii. 184.   [2] 9 Geo. I. c. 7.

for a year, then to endeavour to pick a quarrel with them before the year's end, and so to get rid of them. To bind out poor children apprentices, no matter to whom, or to what trade, but to take especial care that the master live in another *Parish Ap-* parish[1]." The miserable oppression of parish apprentices *prentices.* called[2] forth, as we have seen, some of the earliest philanthropic legislation ; but at the close of the eighteenth century there was more of this humanitarian feeling in the treatment of the poor, and some of the grievances from which they suffered were removed, with the approval of all schools of *Settle-* social reformers. The Acts of Settlement had always given *ments.* ground for criticism, and we have already seen how severely they were condemned by Massie[3]. Adam Smith's opinion was equally decided, and no one had a word to say in their favour. The tyranny of the overseers had been specially felt by such new-comers in a parish as might become chargeable at some future time ; but in 1795 an act was passed which protected them from interference until they actually became chargeable. This measure did not render it easier to obtain a new settlement, but it enabled labourers to live and work in any parish, so long as they could pay their way and did not come upon the rates; and it protected them from the cruelty of sudden and injudicious removal, if they did by sickness become dependent on parochial relief[4].

The philanthropic feeling, however, went much further than this. The dangers of lavish relief were no longer *Decrease* obvious and had apparently been forgotten. Under the *of Pau-* influence of the workhouse test and the harshness of over- *perism.* seers, the sums expended in poor relief had diminished, from £819,000 in 1698 to about £689,000 in 1750. The cheapness of food and steady development of the country would all tend towards the reduction of pauperism. Under these circumstances we need not be surprised that there was a decided movement in favour of relaxing the stringency of the existing system. The first step in this direction was taken by Gilbert's Act, which was an enabling

---

[1] Burn, *History of Poor Law*, 211.   [2] 18 Geo. III. c. 47; 32 Geo. III. c. 57.
[3] See above, § 289, p. 385.   [4] 35 Geo. III. c. 101.

measure, but as many parishes[1] took advantage of it, it A.D. 1776 —1815.
exerted a wide influence.

The motive for introducing it was probably due to the *Relaxation in 1782.* clauses which effected improvements in the administration of the law, especially by enlarging the areas through the union of several parishes for the erection of workhouses and for other business connected with the relief of the poor. But it also embodied considerable modifications of principle; the character of the workhouses, as understood by the Act of 1723, was changed and they were regarded as places for the maintenance of the impotent poor rather than as places for employing the able-bodied. The able- *Labour made a 'test' in-* bodied were now to be provided with work near their own *stead of a 'means' of* houses by the Guardians; for this they were to be paid at a rate that should suffice for their maintenance. By this *support.* means, the system of outdoor relief for the able-bodied was re-established, though they were forced to qualify for such relief by working. But it appears that this qualifying work was listlessly done and was not infrequently a mere pretence[2].

We have fortunately very clear information as to the standard of comfort[3] which was to be aimed at in relieving *Standard of Comfort.* the poor. The inquiry into the state of the poor, instituted by the Hampshire justices at the Epiphany Quarter Sessions 1795, resulted in an interesting report; it maintains "that animal food and beer are necessary parts of the proper subsistence of labourers to enable them to do justice in their work to themselves, their employers and the community[4]," and that " the labourer should have meat once a day or at any rate three times a week." The report continues,—" to the want of sufficient subsistence on animal food and malt

---

[1] Aschrott, *English Poor Law System*, 21; 22 Geo. III. c. 83.

[2] G. Nicholls, *Poor Law*, ii. 97.

[3] There is much interesting evidence as to the actual standard of living of labourers in different counties in Davies, *Case of Labourers* (1795). See also the estimated budget for a clerk on £50 a year. *Considerations, &c.* by J. W. (1767). Such definite statements give the best data for comparing the condition of the labourer at different dates; the difficulty of interpreting the facts as to rates of wages and prices of food renders it almost impossible to rely on these sources for trustworthy evidence on the comfort actually enjoyed. It is worth while to compare R. Hitchcock's account of *English Army Rations* under Elizabeth (Arber, *English Garner*, ii. 209), or the rations of a villan on *dies precariae*; though both of these may represent something a little better than normal peasant fare. Cf. Vinogradoff, *Villainage*, 284.   [4] *Annals of Agriculture*, xxv. 365, 367.

liquor are to be attributed several pernicious habits, particularly the use of spirits, and, what has of late increased to a very injurious degree, of tea as a substitute[1]—bad indeed for almost all other support—being a vain present attempt to supply to the spirits of the mind what is wanting to the strength of the body; but in its lasting effects, impairing the nerves, and thence equally injuring both the body and the mind, and, though perhaps beginning with elevation certainly ending in depression[2]."

The action of the Berkshire justices in 1795 was a rapid development of the policy, which was legalised by Gilbert's Act 1782, of supplementing from the rates the wages actually earned by able-bodied men. The years immediately preceding, had been marked by a great scarcity, and there was a vast amount of terrible suffering. The debates in the House of Commons, and the Bill introduced by Pitt himself, served to show how much the legislators were alarmed at the general distress[3]. It was specially felt in the districts where cloth-weaving was practised; spinning had been plentiful and well paid at Reading in 1793[4], but it appears to have been very much less remunerative and harder to get in subsequent years, and there doubtless seemed to be good reasons for taking exceptional steps to tide over a period of bad trade which might perhaps be of no long continuance. The Berkshire justices met to consider the situation in the Pelican Inn at Speenhamland and agreed to the following resolutions: "1. That the present state of the poor does require further assistance than has generally been given them. 2. That it is not expedient for the magistrates to grant that assistance by regulating the wages of day labourers according to the directions of the statutes of the 5th Elizabeth and 1st James; but the magistrates very earnestly recommend to the farmers and others throughout the county, to increase the pay of their labourers in proportion to the present price of provisions; and agreeable thereto, the magistrates now present have unanimously resolved that they will in their several divisions, make the

---

[1] Cobbett's opinion on this beverage is worth notice. *Rural Rides*, I. 87. See above, p. 859, n. 3. [2] *Annals of Agriculture*, xxv. 867.
[3] *Parl. Hist.* xxxii. 285, 687. [4] *Annals of Agriculture*, xx. 179.

following calculations and allowances, for the relief of all A.D. 1776 —1815. *Allow-ances.* poor and industrious men, and their families, who, to the satisfaction of the justices of their parish, shall endeavour (as far as they can) for their own support and maintenance; · that is to say, when the gallon loaf of seconds flour, weighing 8 lbs. 11 oz. shall cost 1*s.*, then every poor and industrious man shall have for his own support 3*s.* weekly, either procured by his own, or his family's labour, or an allowance from the poor-rates; and for the support of his wife, and every other of his family, 1*s.* 6*d.* When the gallon loaf shall cost 1*s.* 6*d.*, then every poor and industrious man shall have 4*s.* weekly for his own support, and 1*s.* 10*d.* for the support of every other of his family. And so in proportion, as the price of bread rises or falls, (that is to say) 3*d.* to the man, and 1*d.* to every other of his family, on every 1*d.* which the loaf rises above 1*s.*[1]

This was the beginning of what was known as the allowance system, and the example thus set was widely imitated throughout the country. So that the resolutions by which the justices gave effect to their powers under Gilbert's Act were so generally operative as to be nicknamed the "Speenhamland Act of Parliament."

In the following year the facilities for obtaining out- *Outdoor Relief.* door relief were still further enlarged, as it was held to be expedient to grant temporary relief for limited periods. By the successive relaxations the stringency of the law and still more of the administration, as it had existed in the earlier part of the century, was entirely done away, and at the same time the pauperism of the country increased by leaps and bounds. · The charge of £619,000 in 1750 had risen to more than £4,000,000 in 1803[2]. It must of course be remembered *Increased charge.* that the seasons had been far less favourable, the price of corn higher and the difficulties of trade far greater from 1765 onwards; but when all these influences are taken into account, it is plain enough that the lax administration had given scope for the growth of pauperism.

[1] Pashley, *Pauperism*, 258; compare also the table in *Annals of Agriculture*, xxv. 537.
[2] Aschrott, 16.

A.D. 1776
—1815.
*Gravity of
the crisis.*
327. These changes in the poor-law system appear at first sight to be absolutely condemned by the consequent increase of pauperism; but though we may condemn them when we see their accumulated effects, we may also recognise that the nation was passing through a terrible crisis, and that there was a very grave difficulty in adopting any other expedient. When the agricultural interest was so badly hit as it was in the years succeeding the Country Bank failures, it would have been hard for the farmers to bear the full burden in the first instance and raise wages adequately; the method which was adopted distributed the burden between the owners of the land and the farmers. Nor did this allowance system entirely prevent a rise of wages. The agricultural labourer earned more wages during the period of high prices[1], while his income was also supplemented by allowances when he needed it. The system must have prevented the poorer villagers from feeling at once the full weight of the loss which came on them through the diminution of by-employments; though it is not impossible that the pressure was all the more severe because it was long deferred. When the war prices came to an end, and rents fell and farmers were ruined, wages could not be maintained, and the allowances became an intolerable burden; but as we have seen, even during the period of low prices, the allowance system gave opportunities which enabled thrifty men to rise in the world.

*Variety of
opinion as
to the cause
of distress.*
At the time when the system was first introduced, there was no doubt as to the reality of the distress; but there was great difference of opinion as to its cause, and therefore as to its cure. All parties were indeed agreed on the one point that it was desirable to save the consumption of corn in every *Reduced
consump-
tion of
corn.* possible way. The justices of Sussex prohibited the use of fine meal[2]; the inhabitants of Kensington[3] determined to go without pastry, and there was an increased reliance on potatoes. In 1800 still more pains were taken to prevent any waste of bread flour; in consequence of addresses from the two Houses of Parliament, the King issued a proclamation requiring that the subjects should reduce their consump-

---

[1] Tooke, *Prices*, i. 329, see also above, p. 468, note 3.
[2] *Annals*, xxv. 27.　　　　　　[3] *Ib.* xxv. 524.

tion of bread by one-third and make similar reductions in
their horses' corn[1]. But it is impossible to judge whether reductions of this kind, on the part of those who had large
households, made any considerable difference in the food
supply available for the labouring classes.

(*a*) In the popular opinion the high prices were sup- *Alleged engrossing and*
posed to be due to the action of capitalist farmers and other
monopolists who were holding stocks of corn. This opinion
appears to have been shared by one of the Berkshire justices,
who proved a far-seeing critic of the Speenhamland regulations[2]; but its mistaken and mischievous character was sufficiently refuted by Lord Sheffield in his charge to the Grand
Jury at Lewes in 1795[3]. There must have been many of the
public, however, who were highly incensed at the conduct of
men they believed to be making fortunes out of public distress, and though rick-burning did not feed the hungry, it *Rick-burning.*
was a popular mode of punishing such offenders.

This view had certainly a very strong hold on the public
mind[4]; when the scarcity returned in 1800, there were
renewed and serious riots[5]; and it was even proposed that a
maximum price should be fixed, and that no one should be
allowed to sell at a higher rate. The best known precedents
for such a policy were drawn from the disturbed times of
Edward II. in England and Robespierre in France. Still the
members of parliament for Worcester were induced to pledge
themselves to support this scheme[6], though it was obvious to
all sensible men that there could be no guarantee for a continuous supply of food, if prices were forcibly reduced and
farming became unremunerative. The whole aim of far-
seeing men was to render agriculture so profitable, that more
land might be taken into cultivation and the food supply
increased. Compulsory sale might have given some temporary relief, but would be almost certain to bring about a
chronic dearth.

(*b*) There was a very general feeling in favour of re- *Assess-*

---

[1] *Annals*, xxxvi. 194.   [2] *Ib.* xxv. 636. See below, p. 501.
[3] *Ib.* xxv. 29. The Hampshire Report already quoted also discusses the
matter at some length. *Ib.* 351.   [4] *Ib.* xxxvi. 36.
[5] See Proclamation of Somerset Justices in 1801. *Ib.* xxxvii. p. 133.
[6] *Ib.* xxxvi. 103. 54.

A.D. 1776
—1815.
*ment of
wages*
introducing the practice of assessing wages in accordance
with the price of corn[1], and it seems to have been generally,
if not universally agreed, that this was the fair principle on
which to proceed[2]. There was however a great difference of
opinion as to whether this should be done by authority, or
whether it could be brought about in the ordinary course
of bargaining between employers and employed. Arthur
Young's correspondents were of opinion that the law would

*would in-
volve
serious dif-
ficulty,*
be inoperative. It was urged that the inefficient labourers, if
they had to be paid the full wages appointed by law, would
find no employment at all[3]. Others feared that such a
measure would cut down the earnings of all to the same
level, and thus discourage the more industrious men[4]. Besides this, it was clear that wages were rising, slowly but
surely, and this gave some reason for hoping that they would
reach a level which would serve to maintain the labourer in
comfort, without legislative interference[5]. On the other hand

*but seemed
requisite to*
it was argued that "to expect that the farmers and other
employers of the poor should generously come forward, and of
their own accord vary and increase the wages of their workmen, in exact proportion to their varying and increasing
necessities, is utterly hopeless ; they will no more do it than
they would make good roads without the aid of turnpikes, or
the prescription of statutes enforced by the magistrate, though
both one and the other would be often really and truly their

*Suffolk
Justices*
interest[6]." The Suffolk justices petitioned in favour of a
legislative regulation of wages, and Arthur Young appears
himself to have inclined to approve this policy[7]. There was no
more interesting argument in support of the proposal, how-

*and
Norfolk
Labourers.*
ever, than that of the Norfolk labourers who held a meeting
in Heacham church " in order to take into consideration[8] the
best and most peaceable mode of obtaining a redress of all

---

[1] Davies, *Case of Labourers*, 106; also Pownall, *Considerations on Scarcity*
reprinted from *Cambridge Chronicle*, 1795.

[2] Mr Howlett, whose opinion was worthy of great respect, held that corn did
not form such a predominating element in the labourers' expenditure that wages
should be regulated by it alone. He was however strongly of opinion that it
should be regulated by law on the basis of the food, fuel, and clothing necessary
for a family in each district. *Annals*, xxv. 604, 612.

[3] *Ib.* xxv. 618; xxxvi. 270.   [4] *Ib.* xxv. 502, 626.   [5] *Ib.* 565.
[6] *Ib.* 612.   [7] *Ib.* 640.   [8] *Ib.* 504.

the severe and peculiar hardships under which they have for many years so patiently suffered. The following resolutions were unanimously agreed to :—

"1st. *That the labourer is worthy of his hire,* and that the mode of lessening his distresses, as hath lately been the fashion, by selling him flour under the market price, thereby rendering him an object of a parish rate, is not only an indecent insult on his lowly and humble situation (in itself sufficiently mortifying from his degrading dependence on the caprice of his employer) but a fallacious mode of relief, and every way inadequate to a radical redress of the manifold distresses of his calamitous state.

"2nd. That the price of labour should, at all times, be proportioned to the price of wheat, which should invariably be regulated by the average price of that necessary article of life; and that the price of labour, as specified in the annexed plan, is not only well calculated to make the labourer happy without being injurious to the farmer, but it appears to us the only rational means of securing the permanent happiness of this valuable and useful class of men, and, if adopted in its full extent, will have an immediate and powerful effect in reducing, if it does not entirely annihilate that disgraceful and enormous tax on the public—the POOR RATE.

"Plan of the Price of Labour proportionate to the Price of Wheat.

When wheat shall be

£14 per last, the price of labour shall be 14*d.* per day.

16	.,	„	„	16	„
18				18	
20				20	
22	„			22	
24				2/-	
26				2/2	
28 ·				2/4	
30				2/6	
32				2/8	
34	„	„ .	..	2/10	
36	„	„	„	3/-	

And so on, according to this proportion.

32—2

"3rd. That a petition to Parliament to regulate the price of labour, conformable to the above plan, be immediately adopted; and that the day labourers throughout the county be invited to associate and co-operate in this necessary application to Parliament, as a peaceable, legal, and probable mode of obtaining relief; and in doing this, no time should be lost, as the petition must be presented before the 29th of January 1796.

"4th. That one shilling shall be paid into the hands of the treasurer by every labourer, in order to defray the expenses of advertising, attending on meetings, and paying counsel to support their petition in Parliament.

"5th. That as soon as the sense of the day labourers of this county, or a majority of them, shall be made known to the clerk of the meeting, a general meeting shall be appointed, in some central town, in order to agree upon the best and easiest mode of getting the petition signed; when it will be requested that one labourer, properly instructed, may be deputed to represent two or three contiguous parishes, and to attend the above intended meeting with a list of all the labourers in the parishes he shall represent, and pay their respective subscriptions; and that the labourer, so deputed, shall be allowed two shillings and six pence a day for his time, and two shillings and six pence a day for his expenses.

"6th. That Adam Moore, clerk of the meeting, be directed to have the above resolutions, with the names of the farmers and labourers who have subscribed to and approved them, advertised in one Norwich and one London paper; when it is hoped that the above plan of a petition to Parliament will not only be approved and immediately adopted by the day labourers of this county, but by the day labourers of every county in the kingdom.

"7th. That all letters, post paid, addressed to Adam Moore, labourer, at Heacham, near Lynn, Norfolk, will be duly noticed."

This proposal in Parliament.   On the whole it appears that this measure which was advocated in more than one session by Mr Whitbread[1], was generally considered impracticable, while there appeared to

[1] *Parl. Hist.* xxxii. 700, xxxiv. 1426.

be a danger that it would deprive inefficient men of all A.D. 1775
employment and would depress the earnings of the more —1815.
industrious men.

(c) These reasons, together with the general belief *The chief*
that wages and prices were righting themselves and that *evil of the allowance*
temporary assistance was all that was required, inclined a *system is in*
large number of persons to the policy of allowances in some
form or other; either by supplying flour at special rates, or
by employers giving assistance in kind, or by the money
relief administered by the overseers. The difficulties of the
time were so great that it is not even easy to be wise after
the event, but we may at least feel that there were very
strong reasons against following any other course than that
which was adopted. Its greatest evil was in sapping the
spirit of independence, to which the Heacham meeting bears
testimony; and its demoralising effects became apparent to *its pauper-*
one observer at least before it had been in operation many *ising ten-dency.*
months[1]. "From what will follow, emulation and exertion
will be totally destroyed; a man working extra hours &c.,
not doing it for his own benefit, but that of the parish. This
has been the effect of a plan recommended by our magistrates; which, notwithstanding, I cannot but highly approve,
as founded on liberal principles, and perhaps as little excep-
tionable as anything which could have been adopted.

"The effect of this is, that an industrious fellow, who heretofore has earned his fourteen shillings per week, will now
only earn the price of day labour (nine shillings) nor will I
blame him, for extraordinary exertions should have extraordinary reward; nor can a man be expected to work over-
hours for the relief of the poor-rates. Another effect is, those
who work none, receive as much as those who do; but this
we have remedied, by saying, a man having no debility ought
to earn nine shillings. The profligate part of the women
have destroyed or have no wheels, and say they cannot earn
anything unless supplied by the parish. Our rates are thus
risen to about three times their usual quantum, which makes
the farmers highly dissatisfied   *   *   *   *   *

"To avoid this table, the parish are at this moment in the

[1] *Annals*, xxv. 684.

act of beginning a work-house; but, fortunately for the industrious poor, the bill for the relief of the poor in their own
houses meets that oppression."

328.   The pauperising effect of the new development of
the system became only too obvious[1] before many years were
*Change in
character
of the
labourer.* over.   Arthur Young notes[2] that "many authors have
remarked with surprise the great change which has taken
place in the spirit of the lower classes of the people within
the last twenty years.   There was formerly found an uncon-
querable aversion to depend on the parish, insomuch that
many would struggle through life with large families never
applying for relief.   That spirit is annihilated; applications
of late have been as numerous as the poor; and one great
misfortune attending the charge is, that every sort of industry
flags when once the parochial dependence takes place: it
then becomes a struggle between the pauper and the parish,
the one to do as little and to receive as much as possible, and
the other to pay by no rule but the summons and order of the
justice.   The evils resulting are beyond all calculation; for
the motives to industry and frugality are cut up by the roots
when every poor man knows that if he do not feed himself,
the parish must do it for him: and that he has not the most
distant hope of ever attaining independency, let him be as
industrious and frugal as he may.   To acquire land enough to
build a cottage on is a hopeless aim in 99 parishes out of 100."

*Arthur
Young's in-
vestigation.* But he was not content with deploring the evil.   Investigation as to different parts of the country showed that the
pauperism was much worse in some districts than in others;
and a comparison of different parishes[3] served to bring out
the fact that where the labourers had land of their own to
work, they were much less likely to lose the spirit of independence.   Arthur Young seems to have believed that the
*Allotments
condition-
ally let to
them.* general formation of suitable allotments would enable the
labourers to maintain themselves[4]; the desire of doing so
would render them diligent and independent, while even

[1] *Annals*, xxxvii. 33.   [2] *Ib*. xxxvi. 504.
[3] Compare especially Mr Gourlay's long paper on the Lincolnshire cottages in
the *Annals*, xxxvii. 514.
[4] His remarks coincide in many points with those of Sir James Steuart,
Works, i. p. 111.

the prospect of sooner or later obtaining such a cottage and A.D. 1776
—1813.
allotment, would give the labourer a prospect in life which
would have a beneficial effect. It was however a *sine qua*
non with Arthur Young that these allotments should be
forfeited by men who became dependent on the rates[1], as
he desired to make them the means of encouraging independence and not merely a method of relieving the poor.
Arthur Young was of course aware that many Irish cottiers *Peasant*
and French peasants led a miserable existence, despite the *holdings.*
fact that they had little farms of their own. He was clear that
the labourers' allotments should be of such a size that they
could be really made to answer, and he therefore desired that
the allotments should be rented. After his experience of the
French peasantry he would not dare to trust the English labourer with the fee simple of the land, as he feared that this
would inevitably lead to subdivision. This has not been sufficiently taken into account by those who have quoted his
phrases about the ' magic of property,' and represented him as
approving of a peasant proprietary. He advocated a system
by which the peasantry might have the opportunity of using
land on their own account, but he thought it was unde-
sirable that they should own it. It was by no means easy *Suitable*
to lay down in general terms the size and nature of the *allotments,*
allotment which would be really satisfactory. In the grazing
counties, it was proposed to assign the labourer a garden,
and enough grass for a cow. A poor family which could
keep a cow was better off than if they had five or six
shillings of parish allowance[2]; and Arthur Young's idea of
suitable land seems always to have been such land as would
enable them to keep one cow, or at all events some sort
of stock[3]. Sir John Sinclair discusses how this might be *according*
managed in connection with arable allotments, and in counties *to Sir John*
Sinclair..
where little or no grazing land was available[4], and he lays
down the following principles[5].

"1st. That the cottager shall raise by his own labour
some of the most material articles of subsistence for himself
and his family.

---

[1] *Annals,* xxxvi. 641, and still more strongly xli. p. 214.
[2] *Ib.* xxxvi. 510.   [3] *Ib.* 541.   [4] *Ib.* xxxvii. 232.   [5] *Ib.* 233.

" 2nd. That he shall be enabled to supply the adjoining markets with the smaller agricultural productions; and

" 3rd. That both he and his family shall have it in their power to assist the neighbouring farmers, at all seasons of the year, almost equally as well as if they had no land in their occupation."

The last of these touches on the crucial difficulty. If the labourers' allotments demanded more than "the leisure *Allotments* hour horticulture[1]" it would interfere with the labourers' *and Wages.* employment and consequently with his wages. The problem therefore of providing suitable allotments was of this kind,— that the labourer should have so much land, as would enable him to keep a cow, but not enough to interfere with his ordinary work for an employer. There was a very general feeling, at the beginning of this century, that this problem did not present insuperable difficulties; but it is obviously one which is not capable of solution in general terms by such a formula as " three acres and a cow." A good deal was done in giving such assistance to cottagers, but it may be doubted how far it produced the improvement that Arthur Young had hoped for, as those who received allotments were not thereby excluded from participation in poor relief. On the other hand, there were many economists who were inclined to condemn the arrangement, as they held that such assistance would, like parish allowances, lower the rate of wages; while Malthus and his followers condemned it, as an inadequate solution of the recurring problem presented by the pressure of population. I am inclined to believe that these doctrinaire criticisms[2] prevented the scheme from being so generally tried as might have been desirable. Had it been more generally adopted, the fall of prices in 1815 could surely not have been attended by such distress, and there would have been less excuse for an expedient like the Corn Law of that year.

329. As will be shown below[3], there had been a good deal of doubt as to the movements of population during the first three quarters of the eighteenth century; and it was a general, though mistaken, opinion that population was de-

---

[1] *Annals,* xxxvi. 352. [2] See below, p. 578. [3] § 352, p. 561.

creasing. This impression was probably due to the war upon cottages, which was conducted in so many places, in the supposed interests of the rate-payers; but it was also argued that England could not possibly sustain the continued strain caused by military service, in which so many of the population were killed or maimed. Dr Price[1] had given *Apparent decrease of population.* expression to this view; but more careful statistical calculations[2] demonstrated that it was a complete mistake. The gaps which were occasioned by the wars were constantly filled up, and the population increased slowly but steadily; but in the period which we are now considering, the fact of the increase of population was no longer in dispute. The opinion still lingered that it was always a matter of congratulation, in itself and apart from other considerations; but the general tone changed rapidly after the publication of Malthus' *Essay.* Instead of examining the causes of the increase of popu- *Malthus' Essay.* lation, either with a dispassionate scientific interest like Sir James Steuart, or with a practical political interest, men began to fix their attention on the checks to population. They had learned from Malthus that population might be trusted to increase, without any special stimulus, if the preventive and positive checks were removed; and in considering the changes during the period, it is most convenient to discuss them with this modern terminology.

(*a*) The supply of food had enormously increased be- *Increased food supply.* cause it became profitable to take more land into cultivation and to cultivate it on better methods. This was of course due to the development of industry which, as Sir James Steuart[3] had pointed out, acted as a direct incentive to increased agricultural production. Our manufactures were sought for in all parts of the world. In spite of the new facilities for manufacturing there was on the whole much employment for labour; the rapid growth of our trade called forth an army of consumers, whose demand for native products made higher farming profitable, while the increased food supply rendered their permanent maintenance possible.

[1] Price, *Essay on Population of England and Wales,* 29.
[2] Howlett, *Examination of Dr Price's Essay on Population of England and Wales,* 13, 131. There had been a decline in the Eastern Counties and the Fens. See below, p. 700.   [3] See below, p. 560.

A.D. 1776
—1815.
*Large
earnings by
children.*
    (*b*) The development of industry also tended to remove one of the preventive checks to the growth of population. The inability to provide for children had doubtless had the effect of deferring the period of marriage among the labourers, even though it had never been the controlling principle which Malthus thought it ought to be. In all probability it had been operative in a somewhat indirect fashion, from the inability of obtaining house-room, rather than from any conscious grasp of a principle of parental duty. But in those districts where the labour of children was sought after, and where their earnings, even in very early years, constituted a large part of the family income there was no strong practical reason for deferring the period of marriage.

*Mode of
granting
relief, and
increase of
pauperism.*
    (*c*) If this was the effect of the new opportunities for employment, it was also the tendency of the method in which the poor-law was administered. Allowances were granted in proportion to the necessary maintenance of the family, and there was an additional allowance with each child. This was the Speenhamland principle; and though the practice throughout England was by no means uniform, it seems to have been the usual arrangement. It is abundantly evident that it tended to diminish the preventive check. Under these circumstances there need be no surprise that population increased with very great rapidity. It is sufficiently obvious too, that pauperism was advancing by leaps and bounds. The broken spirit of the labourer and his increased dependence on parish support was communicated to his children, and the numbers who were unable to support themselves but were dependent on the contributions of others increased every year. The following figures may be taken as summarising the growth of pauperism: the average charge for the years 1748, 49, 50 had been £689,971; in 1783—5 it had increased almost threefold, and in 1812 nearly ten times, as the total was £6,656,105[1].

*Malthus
and Arthur
Young.*
    These deplorable facts attracted the attention both of Malthus and of Arthur Young. They were on the whole in agreement, though their suggestions for dealing with the difficulty were very different. Malthus would have abso-

---

[1] *Reports*, &c. 1821, IV. 277.

lutely abolished the relief of the poor by the state; as he A.D. 1776
proposed that children born after a certain date should be —1815.
excluded by statute from any claim for relief. In this way
he believed that pauperism would be gradually extinguished,
and that self-reliance and better conceptions of parental responsibility would be formed, if the pressure of circumstances
were brought to bear. Arthur Young, on the other hand,
believed that his independence of spirit would be fostered
by giving the labourer more interests and responsibilities in
life, and allowing him to have, under proper safeguards, the
use of suitable land together with a cow. To Arthur Young,
Malthus' scheme seemed drastic[1] and impracticable; while
Malthus contended that Arthur Young's suggestions gave
no immunity[2] from the recurrence of the danger. It was
obvious that in so far as the spirit of independence was
not cultivated by giving the labourer land, his enlarged
resources would only tend towards the increase of population
in the same way as the parish allowances had done. It is
of course clear that Malthus' argument was sound: the mere
fact that Arthur Young insisted on so many safeguards in
connection with his proposal, shows that he did not regard
it as a complete panacea. On the other hand Malthus had
no practical suggestion to make with the view of cultivating
the spirit on which he laid such stress. He had more sympathy with Arthur Young's proposals than might appear[3],
but he argued that they were no complete remedy. His
followers interpreted him however as if he had condemned
benevolent action as such; they feared that improvements
in the labourers' condition would be inevitably followed by
an increase of population, and they desisted from the schemes
on which Arthur Young had relied for improving, not merely
the condition, but the character of the labourer[4].

XIII. SHIPPING AND COMMERCE.

330. The industrial revolution and the agricultural *Rapid ex-*
pansion of
changes had each an important influence on the expansion *commerce*

---

[1] *Annals*, XLI. 221.　　[2] *Essay*, III. 353.　　[3] *Ib.* 365.　　[4] *Annals*, XLI. 230.

A.D. 1776
—1815.
of commerce.   The improvements in our manufactures gave an impetus to our export trade, as the superiority of British goods was becoming apparent.   On the other hand the fact that we were more and more dependent on the produce of foreign countries for our supplies of food developed a corresponding import trade anew.   The inter-connection between commerce and the other sides of our industrial life was closer than before.   Under these conditions the growth of English *despite frequent inter- ruption.* commerce was very rapid; owing to the political complications of the time it was frequently interrupted, but even these told in its favour on the whole.   When commerce was disorganised corn was dear, especially when harvests were short; and there was little employment for those who made cloth for export.   The food of our people and the employment of our people were becoming dependent on commercial prosperity, and though it was a period of rapid commercial growth, it was also a time of great commercial vicissitudes.

It will therefore be convenient to trace the effects of the political complications in interrupting commerce, while we also bear in mind that in so far as commerce was not interrupted, it was expanding rapidly.   Indeed it was during this *Maritime Supre- macy. 1760.* period that England began to reap the fruits of that maritime supremacy which she had fostered so carefully.   Her superiority on the sea had enabled England to maintain her footing both in America and India, and to destroy the French power alike in West and East.   During this long struggle her mercantile marine provided the sinews of war from sources which Napoleon failed to reach.   During the American war too a fatal blow was inflicted on Holland as a commercial power, and England came to inherit the colonial possessions of both her former rivals; while she also obtained access to territory like the Brazils, which had been previously closed to her shipping.   It was a life and death struggle; but English shipping and English industry had rendered her powerful enough to struggle with success.

Disturbing causes. It may be convenient then to take each of the three wars in turn and to note the interruptions to trade which were directly or indirectly due to each as well as the incidental stimulus which was occasionally given.   We may therefore consider in turn the periods (i) from the Declaration of Inde- A.D. 1776 pendence to the Treaty of Versailles (1783); (ii) from the —1815. outbreak of the Revolutionary War (1793) to the Peace of Amiens (1802); and (iii) the Napoleonic Wars from 1803 till the Battle of Waterloo. The financial history of these wars, and the pressure of taxation, must of course be considered below; at present it is desirable to deal with their effects on commerce.

331. (i) 1776–1783. It does not appear that the imme- *War of In-* diate or direct effects of the rupture with the United States *ence.* were very serious. The market for our manufactures there . was closed; but there must have been an increased demand for the equipment of our armies. There was probably some difficulty about naval stores; but so long as supplies could be obtained from Canada and from the Baltic, this could hardly have been serious. On the other hand the indirect effects of *Indirect* the war were most disastrous, as the regulations we had made, *effects on* and tried to enforce, were so severe that one after another of the neutral powers were driven, not always unwillingly, into a position of open hostility. Dr Franklin, and other representatives of the United States, were able to obtain countenance from various states in Europe, and material support from France. The treaty with the United States in 1778 *France.* was only one of various unfriendly acts of which England complained; but we had not been blameless, as our cruisers . had done much damage to French trade. There were angry communications between the governments and reprisals on both sides, and at length Englishmen with heavy hearts[1] drifted into a war which seemed inevitable. The various branches of the House of Bourbon were so closely connected, that this involved a quarrel with Spain.

Holland was ready to follow suit and to open a trade with *Holland.* the United States. Since New Amsterdam had become New York, Holland had been practically excluded from the North American seaboard by the English Law of Navigation; her treaty engagements with England prevented her from acting as openly as France had done; while the fear of offending France, together with the profitable nature of the new trade,

[1] *Parl. Hist.* xix. 920, 928.

A.D. 1776
—1815. rendered her most unwilling to comply with the English demands, and war was declared in 1780.

The rights of neutrals and the first Armed Neutrality.   In the meantime, however, Catharine of Russia had issued a declaration in regard to the rights of neutrals in matters of trade, which laid down the principles she was prepared to defend by armed force. She contended that neutral vessels should freely trade from port to port on the coasts of nations at war, and that all goods belonging to the subjects of belligerent powers (except contraband of war) should be free in neutral ships. It is needless to point out that these principles favoured the United States.

Sweden and Denmark immediately adopted the same policy, and Austria, Portugal and the Two Sicilies also joined the Armed Neutrality[1]. England found that while she was actually opposed, not only by her own colonies, but by France, Spain, and Holland, she was deserted by the rest of Europe, and received no assistance from any of the powers in coercing the American colonies.

Risks of commerce.   On the whole, it appears, that the frightful increase of risk attending all commercial operations was the principal evil of this period, rather than the mere interruption of any one branch of commerce. Some of the rates for insurance for ships appear to have increased from two guineas to £21 per cent.[2] This was the period in which the practice of marine insurance came to be regularly adopted by ship-owners; but the serious loss, thus temporarily sustained, was amply recouped by the addition we received at the expense of the Dutch, to our East Indian possessions, and by the restoration of West Indian islands occupied by Spain[3].

Peace and projected freedom for commerce.   332. When England at length recognised the independence of the United States, and the Treaties of Versailles with the other belligerents were signed, a new era of commercial prosperity seemed about to commence; each of the European powers had suffered in its colonial connections, and French statesmen were prepared to inaugurate an era of complete commercial freedom. The influence of the French school of economists, who so deeply affected the policy of

[1] Koch and Schoell, I. 477, 479.   [2] Leone Levi, *History*, 48.
[3] Koch and Schoell, I. 462.

Russia[1] and the reforms of Prussia, was strongly felt in Paris; A.D. 1776 —1815. when the arrangements for exclusive trading were everywhere broken down, there was an opportunity for giving effect to their ideas, not only within the realm as Turgot attempted, but in regard to international relations as well[2]. England was not prepared for a complete abandonment of the ancient methods, and she rejected the French proposals; but negotiations were opened with a view to encouraging the trade *French trade.* between the two countries, or rather to removing the numerous restrictions. There had been no good opportunity for considering this matter since the supporters of the Methuen Treaty had succeeded in upsetting the commercial clauses of the Treaty of Utrecht. But much had happened since then, 1713. and under the guidance of an enterprising minister the affairs of Portugal were assuming a new aspect. The Marquis of Pombal[3] had done much to improve the condition of the country; he had fostered the wine trade, but he had also endeavoured to revive the industries which English competition had destroyed. There was no longer such enthusiasm about maintaining the special privileges, which had been accorded to the Portuguese[4] at the expense of the trade with France; and after protracted negotiations, Pitt's commercial *Pitt's Commercial Treaty.* treaty with France was signed[5] in 1786. There was a very considerable reduction of tariffs on each side; but the increased facilities for commercial intercourse were not favourably received in either country; each thought that the other

[1] On Catharine of Russia and Mercier de la Rivière, see P. Janet, *Histoire de la science politique*, II. 686.

[2] Guilhaud de Lavergne, *Les économistes français*, p. 357.

[3] Yeats, *Growth and Vicissitudes of Commerce*, 184.

[4] Adam Smith's criticism of the Methuen Treaty was written after the industrial revival in Portugal. The treaty had not provided against it. Bk IV. ch. vi, p. 223.

[5] Dowell, II. 189. This treaty favoured French agriculture—particularly the production of wines, brandy and oil—and also the manufacture of glass, jewellery, French muslins and millinery. Competition forced the cotton, hardware, saddlery and crockery manufacturers to improve their goods, but until they reached the English standard of excellence there was a temporary loss.

The importation into England of silks, and of cotton and woollen materials mixed with silk being still prohibited, the manufacturers neither gained nor lost. It was urged that the treaty was in favour of France, since it ensured a sale for her natural products, and rendered industrial equality possible. Koch and Schoell, I. 461.

had succeeded in making an extraordinary bargain to its own detriment, and this irritation remained unabated till the breaking out of the Revolutionary War in 1793. Despite this state of affairs however, the trade with France expanded very rapidly; the condition of the two countries had greatly changed since the time of Queen Anne; British manufactures had come into fashion in France, whereas at the beginning of the century, French manufactures had been the rage in England.

The United States.

There was rapid commercial development in another direction, for the trade with the United States suffered far less than had been anticipated; in fact, it recommenced after the war, upon a scale which it had never previously attained; and though Pitt failed in his attempt to maintain the greatest freedom of intercourse with the new republic, the effect of the restrictions was not noticeable at home, though it re-acted severely on the prosperity of the West Indian Colonies. One

Cotton.

reason for this increase of trade lay in the successful culture of cotton in the Southern States. It had been introduced from the Bahamas into Georgia and Carolina during the War of Independence. Soon after commercial relations were re-opened, Whitney invented the cotton-gin, which separated the fibre from the seed, and thus prepared it for export. In 1794, one million six hundred thousand pounds[1] were exported; and England derived great advantage from securing a new source from which to obtain the raw material for cotton spinning.

The Revolutionary War.

333. (ii) The war which followed the outbreak of the Revolution in France was much less injurious to English commerce than either the war of Independence or the Napoleonic wars. England endeavoured, with considerable success, to ruin the trade and shipping of France; and her high-handed measures with this object were resented by the United States, as well as by Norway and Sweden, who sought to preserve their rights as neutrals. But English relations with the neutral powers, though strained, were not broken, and her commerce continued. In 1795 France succeeded in mastering Holland, and England engaged in the attempt to

---

[1] Leone Levi, *History*, 83.

destroy both her ancient rivals at once. They were unable, A.D. 1776 —1815. even when united, to do her serious damage[1]; the distant *English* trades with India, Africa and Brazil, and with the United *monopoly of distant* States and the Northern Seas, remained open, though they *trades.* were of course attended with unusual risk. The chief privation was due to the fact that none of these distant trades served, as a French trade might have done, to replenish her supplies of food in the years of dearth; the serious risk of not being self-sufficing in our food supply was clearly felt, though there were possibilities of importation even then, as the United States exported food stuffs[2] to Spain and Portugal.

Though the Treaty of Amiens restored to the Dutch 1802. most of the colonial possessions they had lost, they never recovered the effects of this war, in which they were crushed by the hostility of their larger neighbours. The greatness of *Fall of* Holland, like that of Carthage, had been raised, not on the *Holland.* stable basis of land, but on the fluctuating basis of trade[3]. Her one important manufacture, that of linen, was weighted by the pressure of taxation in competing with other countries, and the increasing use of cotton must surely have affected the demand for the higher-priced fabric. The carrying trade, which had revived during the War of Independence, was fatally injured when Holland was forced to side against England in the Revolutionary War, and the blows she then received were anticipations of the complete destruction of her greatness which ensued, when she was drawn by Napoleon into the Continental system.

334. By the Peace of Amiens the whole trade of the *The Peace* world was suddenly thrown open to England. This was not, *of Amiens* as we have seen[4], an unmixed benefit to all classes; continental linen-weavers were supplied with cotton yarn spun on English machinery, and produced a cotton cloth which found its way to markets that had hitherto been supplied by Eng-

---

[1] Reinhard, *Concise History of British Commerce*, 19, 45.

[2] Yeats, *Recent and Existing Commerce*, 237.

[3] "The manufacturers became merchants, and the merchants became agents and carriers; so that the solid sources of riches gradually disappeared." Playfair, *Inquiry*, 66. The whole account of the decline of Holland is interesting.

[4] See above, p. 472.

land alone[1]; but the value of English exports at once increased from £39,700,000 to £45,100,000[2]. A great portion of this increase was due to enlarged trade with the United States and the Brazils; but consumers at home also profited by the opportunities for the importation of foreign corn. The new stimulus which was thus given to trade, however, was not *and rapid* altogether wholesome. The expansion had been so rapid *expansion.* that merchants strained their credit to engage in vast speculations, and when the war broke out in 1803 the consequences were very serious.

Commerce   These months of peace had also a disastrous effect upon *of the* the commerce of the United States France, like other *United* *States.* European nations, had endeavoured to monopolise the trade of her own colonies; and had not opened her ports to the shipping of other nations. During the Revolutionary War, however, it had been convenient to throw the trade open to neutrals; and in this manner the commerce between the mother country and the West Indies had been carried on principally by ships sailing under the neutral flag of the United States. When peace was declared, the Government of France at once resumed the colonial monopoly and excluded the United States ships from a trade which they had enjoyed during the war[3]. Hence during the brief period of peace, the French and Dutch trade revived, and the shipping of the States, which had increased enormously during the Revolutionary War, suffered a corresponding decline. The outbreak of the Napoleonic War opened a new period of prosperity for the States; though none of their ports lay on the direct route from South America or the West Indies to France and Holland, the trade winds and Gulf Stream[4] served in such a fashion, that there was but little delay in transmitting goods by way of some North American port, so that the stream of trade between France and Holland and their West Indian colonies readily shifted, according to the exigencies of the times.

[1] Radcliffe, p. 49.
[2] Porter, *Progress of the Nation*, Section III. 98 (Edn. 1836).
[3] *War in Disguise*, 1805 [by J. Stephen, Camb. Univ. Lib. Z. 24. 24 (2)] p. 19.
[4] *Ib.* p. 43.

335. (iii) When the war broke out again in 1803, Eng- _{A.D. 1776} land again took advantage of the supremacy of her shipping to push her trade in all directions. She opened new markets by force, prevented the transport of other European goods, and did the carrying trade of the world. It is hardly possible to exaggerate the commanding nature of the commercial and industrial position which England had now attained; but it is worth while to quote an estimate published by a German[1], soon after the war with Napoleon broke out.

"It is a fact of public notoriety, that within the last fifty years almost all the English colonies have been improved, and made to yield more plentiful returns; that their population, and even that of the three united kingdoms in Europe, has been considerably augmented: that their manufactures have acquired a much greater degree of perfection; and of course a more wide spread circulation; by which means their trade and navigation have been increased by nearly one half. It is farther known, that within the last thirty years almost every necessary had been enhanced by one-third part of its former price. It is therefore natural that the English receive at present more money for their manufactured products and for the commodities which they import from both Indies, than they used to do formerly; and that in consequence they are greater gainers by it, and can afford, better than ever, to pay taxes*. In all the well governed states of Europe the expenditure has been rising for the last thirty years, and the revenues have risen in proportion.

"He who doubts the advanced flourishing condition of the British commerce and the wealth of the nation, may easily convince himself of his error, merely by comparing the former and present English custom-house entries, the list of imports and exports, and the amount of the duties which they necessarily occasion: to this ought to be added, that the English are now in possession of the greater part of the commerce of the world, and by these means have it in their power to fix

[1] Reinhard, *Concise History of British Commerce*, translated by J. Savage (1805), p. 43.

* "The exports of British produce and manufactories in 1802, amounted to 48,500,683*l.* sterling in value; the number of our ships to 20,000; the tonnage to 4,000,000; and the total number of our sailors to 152,000."

. 33—2

the standard price of almost every commodity. They have besides this, immediately after the commencement of the present war, captured from the French and Dutch great numbers of ships with rich cargoes, the amount of which is estimated to exceed 14,000,000*l.* sterling.

"Allowing that the other commercial nations who are competitors with the English in trade over all the world, even felt themselves inclined to undersell the English in their prices, it would in the first place be incompatible with their interests; in the second, it is out of their power to supply all nations sufficiently, out of the scantiness of their stores. The English possess quantities immensely larger than they do, and barter them for the produce of their manufactures; which is generally the case in every corner of the globe. There is scarcely a single commodity, a single article either of luxury or convenience, that is not manufactured by the English, with the most consummate skill, and in the highest state of perfection.

" The soil of Britain does not indeed produce a quantity of corn sufficient for the exigencies of its inhabitants; and for this reason it becomes necessary, every year, to remit large sums of money for its purchase to the ports in the Baltic; but then nature has indemnified that country with her rich coal mines, the envy of foreigners, who by this means become, in a certain manner, tributary to England; for the English parliament has' laid a considerable duty on the exportation of coals, which foreign nations are obliged to pay.

" A nation whose active commerce is so preponderating, compared with its passive trade, who is herself the ruler of the most numerous and fertile colonies in all parts of the world: a nation that sends the produce of her industry to every zone; that has so formidable a navy, and so wide spread a navigation; a nation, that by her activity and the genius of her citizens, manufactures its numberless articles of merchandise, infinitely finer, in much superior workmanship, in far more exquisite goodness, than all other nations, without exception; and that is able to sell them infinitely cheaper, owing to her admirable engines, her machines, and her native coal; a nation, whose credit and whose capital is so immense as that of England; surely such a nation must render all foreigners tributary; and her very enemies must help to bear the immense burthen of her debt and the enormous accumulation of her taxes.

" The commerce of France and Holland is at present almost totally suspended by the blockade of most of their ports*. Both countries are totally cut off from their possessions in the East Indies, and are allowed to carry on but a very insignificant trade with their West India colonies. How then can these two powers wage war with the produce of their commercial dealings as England does? England alone has room, notwithstanding the harbours that are shut against her, on the extensive globe, and the vast oceans that surround it.

" The sums which Spain and Portugal are obliged to pay to France for their neutrality, cannot, at any rate, indemnify the latter for the expences of the war, for the obstruction of her commerce, and the loss of her colonies. Add to this, that the credit which France and Holland once had, is now so very, very trifling, as to cripple and paralize every important enterprise in which they may happen to embark.

" What then will be the end of this new war, carried on with so much fury? What are the catastrophes that will at

---

* "Before the revolution France employed in its colonial trade, 180,000 tons of shipping. Between the years 1763 and 1778, the returns in produce from the French colonies, consisting of sugar, coffee, indigo, cocoa, and cotton, amounted to the annual value of about £6,400,000 sterling. Of these one-half was consumed in France, the other half exported to other parts of Europe. In 1788 the tonnage employed in the French colonial trade had been augmented to 696 vessels of the burthen of 204,058 tons. The imports rose in that year to the value of about £7,000,000 sterling.

"From an official paper of the French minister of the interior, we learn, that in the year ending Sept. 1800,

	£. Sterling.
The value of the imports of France was . . .	13,500,000
Of the exports	11,300,000
Balance against France in 1800,	2,200,000
In the year, ending Sept. 1801, the imports were .	17,870,000
Exports, ...	13,716,000
	4,654,000
Value of prizes captured this year from the enemy .	670,000
Balance against France in 1801.	£3,984,000 "

last bring back peace, and appease enraged minds ? No mortal will dare to give a decisive answer to these questions. But the attentive observer of the history of his time is, however, at liberty to take a view of matters of fact, and of the resources of the contending parties, from which he may deduce tolerably accurate conclusions."

The Commerce of neutrals

336. Our advantages could not be entirely monopolised ; the United States traders, who saw their way to a profitable commerce, were willing to run great risks for the sake of the profits to be got by trading between the hostile colonies and our European enemies. It was of course our object, as in the Revolutionary War, to destroy the commerce of France and *with hostile colonies* Holland. In this we were extraordinarily successful. "Not a single merchant ship," as was asserted in 1805, "under a flag inimical to Great Britain, now crosses the equator or traverses the Atlantic Ocean * * with the exception only of a very small portion of the coasting trade of our enemies, not a mercantile sail of any description, now enters or clears from their ports in any part of the globe, but under neutral colours[1]." As a matter of necessity the French colonial trade was again opened to neutrals, and the United States took *and to neutral ports.* full advantage of their opportunity. By calling at an American port and taking out fresh papers, a vessel could carry on a regular trade between France and her colonies without having any reason to elude our privateers. Indeed the cessation of the restrictive policy, which France and Spain had pursued, favoured the rapid development of their colonies[2]; and as the neutral traders had no need of convoys, or special rates of insurance, the sugar of the French colonies could be imported on cheaper terms than that from our own islands, even at the very time when we had a complete supremacy at sea. It was further contended that this trade was not a genuine neutral trade, since, owing to the French navigation laws, the neutrals would never have had the opportunity of engaging in it, but for the war; as a matter of fact it had been held illicit in 1756, and our courts had never departed from the rule which was then laid down[3].

[1] *War in Disguise*, p. 71.   [2] *Ib.* 75.
[3] "The general rule is, that the neutral has a right to carry on, in time of war,

In so far then as trade was a source of profit and power A.D. 1776 —1815. to France, it appeared that though we had destroyed her shipping we had not cut off her trade. It was not only carried on by neutral vessels to her own ports, but it reached her through the neutral markets of Hamburg, Altona, Emden, Copenhagen, Gottenburg and Lisbon. The rivers and canals of Germany and Flanders carried produce and East Indian fabrics in all directions from these centres, so as to affect not only our commerce but our manufactures. "They supplant, or rival the British planter and merchant, throughout the continent of Europe, and in all the ports of the Mediterranean. They supplant even the manufacturers of Manchester, Birmingham, and Yorkshire; for the looms and forges of Germany are put in action by the colonial produce of our enemies, and are rivalling us, by the ample supplies they send under the neutral flag, to every part of the New World[1]." Under these circumstances government determined to attempt, not only to destroy French shipping, but to cut off French trade, by putting a stop to "the frauds of the neutral flags."

The situation involved much difficulty, since the United *Double relation with United States.* States had a very large custom for their produce in France and Spain, and were the carriers for the hostile colonies; to this extent they were unfriendly; but they were also large purchasers of English manufactures, and were therefore customers whom it was not prudent to offend. About one-third of our exports to foreign countries in the years 1805–6–7 were conveyed to the States[2]. There was of course a large balance due to this country, which was paid through bills, and ultimately by the produce exported from the States to our European enemies[3]. This was the condition of affairs at

---

his accustomed trade, to the utmost extent of which that accustomed trade is capable. Very different is the case of a trade which the neutral has never possessed, which he holds by no title of use and habit in times of peace; and which in fact he can obtain in war, by no other title than by the success of one belligerent against the other and at the expense of that very belligerent under whose success he sets up his title; and such I take to be the colonial trade generally speaking." Judgment of Sir William Scott, quoted in *War in Disguise*, 13. [1] *Ib.* 78.

[2] Porter, *Progress*, III. 145. [3] *Ib.* 145.

A.D. 1776
—1815.

the time when the Orders in Council and Berlin Decrees were issued.

The Orders in Council, May 1806.

A very important step was taken by the British Government in 1806, when they endeavoured to strike at the neutral trading, by declaring a blockade along the whole of the Channel from Brest to the Elbe. This was merely declaratory, as the blockade was only enforced at the mouth of the Seine, and in the narrow seas; but it was strongly resented

Berlin Decrees.

by Napoleon, who in the Berlin Decree of November, 1806, represented it as an infraction of the recognised principles of International Law, and claimed the right to use against England the same measure which she had meted out to other traders[1]. He accordingly declared the British Isles in a state of blockade; that all commerce and correspondence with Britain should cease; that all British subjects found in countries occupied by French troops should be prisoners of war; that all merchandise and property of British subjects should be a good and lawful prize; and that all British manufactures or merchandise should be deemed a good prize[2]. England thus drifted into an act of aggression towards neutral states, which forced them, as during the War of Independence, into

Orders in Council, January and November 1807.

a position of hostility. By the Order in Council, issued January 7th, 1807, she declared that neutral vessels were not to trade from port to port on the coasts of France or French allies; and further, on the 11th of November, the order appeared, which insisted that neutrals should only trade with a hostile port after touching at a British port and after paying such customs as the British Government might

Milan Decree.

impose. Napoleon retorted with the Milan Decree, which declared that any vessel which had submitted to the British regulations was thereby denationalized.

[1] England was acting in accordance with the rule of 1798 "not to seize any neutral vessels which should be found carrying on trade directly between the colonies of the enemy and the neutral country to which the vessel belonged, and laden with property of the inhabitants of such neutral country, provided that such neutral vessel should not be supplying, nor should have on the outward voyage supplied, the enemy with any articles of contraband of war, and should not be trading with any blockaded ports" (Leone Levi, 108). Napoleon maintained that the restrictions in regard to blockade only applied to places actually invested, England claimed to interrupt commerce at ports which she had not invested.

[2] Leone Levi, *History*, 112.

As the United States had profited more than any of the A.D. 1776 —1815. other neutrals from carrying on the trade between France and her colonies, her ship-owners suffered more than those of other neutral nations by the Orders in Council and the Berlin Decrees; the provocation, which was given by the acts of both belligerents[1], roused increasing indignation in the *Difficulties with the United States and disorganisation of trade.* United States. The Orders in Council were not issued without considerable opposition, and the United States passed a non-intercourse Act in 1809, and made preparations for open hostilities. The Orders in Council, by straining our relations with the United States, had the most serious results on the condition of the country. When their produce was not shipped to Spain and France, the United States could not deal so largely in our manufactures; the interruption of trade with them threatened a third of our foreign trade, increased the difficulties of our food supply, and cut off a portion of the supply of raw cotton for the Lancashire spinners. As competitors in trade, they had foiled our attempts to isolate France and throw her on her own resources. War in disguise had been carried on under the colour of a neutral flag; but in retaliating for this evil, the English Government brought about a condition of affairs, in which every branch of trade connected with America suffered, and suffered severely.

The direct effect of Napoleon's attempt to exclude our manufactures from Continental markets was not, however, so serious as might have been expected. The attempt to close the ports of the Continent against British manufactures was *Failure of Napoleon's attempt.* an utter failure. Napoleon was forced to grant licenses freely[2]

---

[1] Tucker, *Life of Jefferson*, II. 291.

[2] So too did his agents. "Soon after the commencement of the present war Embden became the depôt of British produce and manufactures intended for the German market, which induced the French commercial agent Chevaliere to remove from Hamburgh to the former place, where he practised all kinds of chicanery to impede or obstruct the passage of British goods to the interior of Germany; being unable to effect this, he advised his government to take possession of Meppen, a neutral town, which they accordingly did, and in consequence produced an actual scarcity of English goods at the succeeding fairs of Franckfort and Leipzig, but on the King of Prussia acknowledging Bonaparte in his new capacity of Emperor, Meppen was evacuated by the French troops and Chevaliere was recalled. During the stay of this disinterested republican at Embden, he contrived to make a handsome sum of money, by granting certificates, stating that British goods were Prussian property, which were seldom obtained under several louis d'ors each. In

A.D. 1776
—1815.
for the importation of English manufactures, and the English
Government connived at the system by which neutral vessels,
under the flags of Oldenburg and other small states, were
provided with forged papers[1]. When the governments were
so lax in enforcing a system, it cannot be surprising that
private individuals showed little respect, and that smuggling
became a matter of constant occurrence[2]. But despite all
these mischiefs, the Government pursued its course, though
assenting, in answer to an appeal from Lord Brougham[3], to a
conditional repeal of the Orders in Council when Napoleon's
Decrees should be withdrawn. Before effect could be given
to this view, however, the patience of the United States had
been exhausted. The supporters of Great Britain were foiled,
war was declared, and the quarrel with all its disastrous consequences was only healed at the Congress of Vienna.

XIV. DEPENDENCIES AND COLONIES.

Reversal of policy of

337. The loss of the North American Colonies was immediately followed by an entire change in the policy which
had hitherto been pursued in regard to the industry and
commerce of Ireland. Till this time, her interests had been
subordinated in every way to those of Great Britain ; but the
vigour of the volunteers forced on a great constitutional
change. Poyning's Law was repealed ; the compliance, which
Irish Parliaments had hitherto shown with English requirements, was to be a thing of the past, and serious attempts
were made to apply measures, for fostering the agriculture
and industry of Ireland, similar to those which had proved so
successful in regard to England.

*subordin-
ating Ire-
land to
English
interests.*

The period when the long-continued English policy was
reversed is a convenient one to choose, for briefly considering
its precise effects, and indicating the nature of the purely
economic grievances from which Ireland had suffered. The

justice to this citizen it must be observed, that for money he refused nothing,
and sold even French passports to British subjects, with which they and their
goods passed unmolested through Hanover, Holland, and even on the French side
of the Rhine." Reinhard, p. 18 n.   [1] Porter, II. 147.
        [2] Marquis of Lansdowne, quoted by Leone Levi, 115.   [3] *Ib.* 117.

A.D. 1776
—1815.

miserable jealousy and discord created by the penal laws, and the disabilities to which the Papists were exposed, were constant causes of discord, which militated against the good order of the country and the development of industry of every sort; but it is difficult to trace the precise economic influence they exercised. On the other hand, we may see that Irish enterprise was distinctly hindered from entering on some profitable fields, by measures which were avowedly taken in the interest of England[1]. On the whole it may be said that Ireland suffered economically, not only from direct restrictions on her industries and trade, but even more from the indirect effects of measures devised with an exclusive regard to the interest of England.

Indirect effects of English protective measures.

Probably nothing did greater harm to Ireland than the system of bounties by which English corn-growing was encouraged. The English farmer found it profitable to grow corn, and with the help of the bounty he was able to export it to Dublin at rates which defied competition in a country where wheat-growing had made but little progress. The very same measure which encouraged the application of capital to the English soil, rendered it utterly unprofitable to invest money in improving the cultivation of Ireland[2]. The graziers had suffered under Charles II.; wool-growing was less profitable than it would have been if the drapery trade had had a fair chance; while tillage was depressed by the English bounties. The backward condition of agriculture, despite the excellence of the soil, made a very deep impression on Arthur Young, and the causes are fully described by Mr Newenham. "The different disadvantages which the agriculture of Ireland laboured under * * had, almost necessarily, the effect of preventing an accumulation of capital among those who, with a view to a livelihood, were principally concerned in that pursuit. The wealthier occupiers of the land were generally engaged in the business of pasture; and the profits thence accruing to them were, for the most part, expended in those articles, which the prevailing practice of excessive hospitality

Bounties on Corn-growing in England.

Irish agriculture.

---

[1] Caldwell's excellent criticism, in the *Enquiry concerning the restrictions laid on the trade of Ireland*, p. 753 (appended to his *Debates*, 1766), shows that England really suffered, as well as Ireland.

[2] For an exceptional case of cultivation for export, see Pococke, *Tour*, p. 54.

required; seldom or never in agricultural projects. Several of the country gentlemen pursued tillage in their respective demesnes with some spirit and some skill, chiefly with the view of supplying the demands of their families, but few of them extended their views to the augmentation of their rentals, by the improvement of the waste and unproductive land they possessed. * * The generality of them in Ireland could not, or at least thought they could not conveniently abridge their annual expenses, in such a manner as to enable them to collect a sufficient capital for carrying into effect extensive plans of improvement; and many of them were probably deterred from adding to the burdens of their encumbered estates by borrowing money for such a purpose. The tillage of Ireland for home supply, for there was not sufficient encouragement held forth to cultivate corn for exportation, was chiefly carried on by those who engaged in it with no other capital than the aid of three or four lusty sons as partners, whose united endeavours were directed, during their short leases, to extract from the land as much as the condition in which they found it would admit of; and whose annual profits, hardly earned, after defraying the trivial expenses of their food and clothing, were very rarely sufficient to qualify them for any agricultural undertaking which seemed likely to be attended with even moderate expense. Hence it happened, that the waste land of Ireland, presenting such an immense source of wealth, was left almost neglected until near the close of the last century[1]." We may here see the greatest of the evils which was brought upon Ireland by absenteeism. In England during the eighteenth century the "art of agriculture progressed by leaps and bounds, and this was due to the fact that during the eighteenth century the great landowners were the most zealous students of agriculture, and the boldest experimenters in new methods of culture[2]." Absentees could take no such interest in their estates; and the existing laws did not ensure such profit to the agriculturist as to render tillage a tempting investment in Ireland. The trivial bounties[3] which were eventually

*Absentee-
ism.*

---

[1] Newenham, *View of the resources of Ireland*, 76.
[2] Thorold Rogers, *Agriculture and Prices*, v. p. vii.   [3] Newenham, 124, 130.

given on export (unaccompanied as they were by any protec- A.D. 1776 —1815.
tion against the constant importation of bounty-favoured
corn from England) did not render tillage profitable; landlords were on the whole opposed to it[1], and the measures,
which tried to force them to adopt it, remained a dead letter[2].
Not till England had begun to lose her position as a European
granary and the necessity for import was coming to be regularly felt, was Ireland put on anything like an equality
with her in regard to the encouragement of corn-growing[3].

The English iron manufacturers, suffering as they soon *Irish-smelting in England* did from dearness of fuel, were glad to have smelting carried
on elsewhere, so long as they had advantages in working up
the material provided for them. Just as at a later date they
secured the admission of bar iron from America[4], so in 1696
and 1697 the duties were removed from bar iron imported
into England from Ireland[5]; this led to a rapid destruction
of the Irish forests; though various measures were taken *and Irish Forests.*
to prevent it, and to promote the planting of trees, they
proved utterly ineffective. Not only so, but the exportation
of timber to England was permitted on very easy terms[6], and
as a result the forests of Ireland were absolutely ruined. As
Ireland had at one time been specially well provided with
the materials for building, fitting, and provisioning ships[7],
this wanton waste prevented her from taking the part she
might have otherwise done in the work of ship-building or in
the shipping trades. While thus debarred from building
ships of her own, she was also prevented from sharing in the
trades which were worked by English companies, like the
East Indian trade, or from a direct trade with the colonies[8];
the first relaxation of this policy only enabled her to procure
rum on easy terms from the West Indies, and this again may
be represented as sacrificing native distilling to a trade in
which much English capital was invested[9].

These incidental disabilities, as they may be called, did

---

[1] Newenham, 127.   [2] 1 Geo. II. c. 10 (Irish); Newenham, 128.
[3] 19 and 20 Geo. III. c. 17 (Irish); Newenham, 142.
[4] See above, § 270, p. 380.   [5] 7 and 8 W. III. c. 10, and 8 and 9 W. III. c. 20.
[6] 2 Anne, c. 2 (Irish); Newenham, 153—4.   [7] *Ib.* 156.   [8] *Ib.* 99.
[9] *Ib.* 100. It also encouraged the Irish to purchase West Indian products from
the French Islands; and to pay for them by victualling French ships. Caldwell,
Enquiry in *Debates*, 771.

A.D. 1776
—1815.
Dis-
courage-
ments of
Industry.
undoubtedly inflict very serious mischief on Ireland. Compared with them, the direct discouragement of her manufactures was probably comparatively trivial. The suppression of the drapery trade was the most glaring instance of attempts to hamper a nascent industry; next to it came the dis-

*Drapery,
and Glass.*
couragement of the glass manufacture[1], for which Ireland was specially adapted, by a prohibition of exportation; this was only removed under a sense of panic in 1779.

*The Linen
Trade.*
The only Irish industry which had steadily increased from the time of the Revolution was the linen manufacture; and that could hardly boast of any special encouragement; though spoken of as a fit subject for fostering care, it had really been exposed to rivalry, even in the home market, from the growing linen trade of Scotland and of Yorkshire. Despite of this, or perhaps as some might say because of this, the Irish linen industry had never stagnated. The figures as given by Mr Newenham are exceedingly instructive[2].

*Protection
for Irish
agriculture
and in-
dustry.*
338.   In 1779 Lord North endeavoured to remove the main commercial disabilities of Ireland, and when the Nationalist movement had been so far successful as to obtain a fuller parliamentary freedom[3], a serious effort was made to imitate the measures that had been successful in England, and to foster Irish agriculture and industry. This was the work of the session of 1783–84.

*Corn
bounties.*
One of the most important acts of this Irish Parliament was an attempt to imitate the policy which had been pursued in England with regard to corn. The circumstances of the two countries were somewhat different; for corn did not constitute the food of the Irish peasant, who subsisted chiefly on potatoes; premiums on the growing of corn were a boon to farming as a trade, but did not directly maintain the food supply of the country. Hence the political bearing of the Irish corn bounties was different from that of the English one, even though many of the economic results may have been similar. The bounties gave no encouragement to provide a surplus of food, and no security that a slight failure of

---

[1] Newenham, 104, 192.

[2] Newenham, Appendix, No. vii. p. 10.

[3] 21 and 22 Geo. III. c. 47 (Irish).

the food supply would not result in famine. According to A.D. 1776
—1815. the new law the Irish farmer could count on getting nearly thirty shillings a barrel for his wheat; a bounty of 3*s.* 4*d.* was given on export when the price was not above 27*s.* ; exportation was prohibited when the price was at or above 30*s.* ; and a duty of 10*s.* was imposed on every barrel of wheat imported when the price was below 30*s.*[1] Irishmen believed that the effect of this measure was immediately perceived in the stimulus given to agriculture. The exports of wheat and barley rose very rapidly from 1785, and though they fell back for a time in the last years of the century, this may be partly accounted for by political disturbances, partly by the character of the seasons which were most unfavourable, and partly by the rapid development of the Dublin breweries, which offered an excellent home market for cereals. The manufacture of *Dublin Porter.* porter in Dublin may be said to date from 1792[2], and its influence should certainly be taken into account; but even when this is done, it is difficult to see that the bounties of 1784 did more than give a temporary stimulus, or that they really induced any considerable improvement in Irish agriculture by the application of additional capital to the land[3].

Much greater success attended the attempts to utilise the *Internal Communications.* natural facilities of Ireland for internal communication by water. These had been taken into account many years before, and early in the reign of George I. some undertakers were empowered to improve the navigation of the Shannon[4]. In the reign of George II. commissioners were appointed to devote the produce of certain taxes to this object ; and somewhat later, they were formed into a Corporation for promoting and carrying on Inland navigation in Ireland[5]. They accomplished but little, however, and it was only in 1784 that the matter was heartily taken up, and the work pushed forward energetically, and perhaps extravagantly. The Grand Canal, which connects Dublin with the Shannon, was completed[6] at

---

[1] 23 and 24 Geo. III. c. 19 (1783—84) (Irish).
[2] Newenham, 227.
[3] See the figures in Newenham, p. 216, and Martin, *Ireland*, 63.
[4] Newenham, 143.
[5] 25 Geo. II. c. 10 (Irish).
[6] Newenham, 202.

A.D. 1776
—1815.

Bounties.

an expenditure of more than a million of money; and the navigation of the rivers Boyne and Barrow was improved.

This appears to have been the one permanent result of the very lavish expenditure in bounties, which took place in 1784 and the following years. Fishing busses were subsidised; so too was the cotton manufacture. There was an undoubted stimulus given to various branches of industry; but the expense to the nation was very great[1], and the necessity of some retrenchment became obvious, while the fraud and peculation, in the assignment and payment of the bounties, appears to have been a matter of notoriety. On this matter Mr Newenham[2], who was opposed to the Union, and Mr Martin[3], who defended it, appear to agree. The question where the fault lay is a subtle one; but the fact must be taken into account in considering how far the economic policy of fostering industry, on which the Irish Parliament entered in 1784, was wise.

*Increase
of Trade.*

It was at all events apparently justified by success, for Irish trade increased with great rapidity. This was undoubtedly due in part to the improved facilities, which were given for trade with France by Pitt's treaty. Though the custom-house books do not seem to show it, there can be little doubt that the French trade had always been considerable; the "running" of wool had been a matter of constant complaint[4], and the claret which was so lavishly consumed in Ireland must have been paid for in goods, even if it did not all pay duty. The decline of the new era of prosperity appears to synchronize with the fresh rupture with France; and the rebellion of 1798, with the subsequent re-conquest of Ireland, sufficiently account for the decline of commerce in the years immediately preceding the Union.

The political agitations of the time, with all the disputes about the reform of the Irish Parliament and the removal of Papist disabilities, do not directly concern us, except in so far as they tended, by rendering property less secure, to

---

[1] Martin, 43. Compare Mr Cavendish's motion for retrenchment in 1784, Newenham, 206. This was an old complaint in regard to other bounties. Caldwell, *Debates on affairs of Ireland*, 133, 303, 521.   [2] Newenham, 206.

[3] Martin, 43.   [4] See above, pp. 298, 335.

prevent the investment of capital in Ireland; but it is worth A.D. 1776 —1815. while to note the economic and commercial difficulties of the situation. They were very great, and a legislative Union appeared to offer the simplest means of cutting those particular knots.

By the new position which Ireland had acquired in 1782 it became necessary to arrange for the commercial relationships on the basis of a treaty between the two kingdoms, and not as hitherto by the regulations which England chose *Commercial relations with England and* to impose on a dependency. In 1784 a committee of the British Privy Council examined the trade between the two countries and framed a report which was regarded in Ireland as admirably impartial[1]. Early in the following year a scheme, based upon it, was submitted to the Irish House of Commons and readily accepted by them; but it was not so satisfactory to the English House of Commons, and the draft which contained their amendments roused a strong feeling of resentment throughout Ireland. But the existence of these conflicting views brought out the necessity of creating some ultimate authority which might settle differences as they arose. The English House of Commons had attempted to reserve the power of final decision for England, and this had been the main ground of dissatisfaction with the revised scheme of commercial intercourse. Two other possible arrangements remained; either a legislative union or the *Legislative Union.* "establishment of a board, constituted of independent commissioners, equally and impartially drawn from both kingdoms[2]." This last suggestion was never carried into effect, and a legislative union seemed to offer the only possible solution of the commercial difficulties[3]. The policy of fostering national industry, on which the Irish Parliament had entered, was already discredited in England; and the demands which were commonly heard in Ireland for the prohibition of British manufactures[4] could not be favourably received in England. Ireland desired to enter on a course of building up her national power, in accordance with the economic view which had ruled before the time of Adam Smith; she claimed to do

[1] Newenham, 253. [2] *Ib.* 255.
[3] Compare Lord Sackville, *Parl. Hist.* xxv. 877. [4] *Ib.* 870; Martin, 19.

this in disregard of England. To this claim England could not be expected to submit, and she tried to set the difficulty at rest by attempting to absorb Ireland in 1800.

The Act of Union in its economic effects.

339. As in the case of other measures of great constitutional importance, it is exceedingly difficult to estimate the precise economic effects of the act of Union. Ireland no longer suffered seriously from the special legislation which had been designed to promote English interests, as had been the case up till 1780; nor did her manufacturers enjoy the extravagant encouragements which they had received in 1784. Her lot was cast in with that of England, and her economic history has been merged with that of the larger country. At the same time it may be noticed that, just because her industrial resources were so little developed, she was only able to obtain a comparatively small share in the extraordinary prosperity which English merchants and manufacturers enjoyed during the war; on the other hand she suffered, as the agricultural interest in England suffered, from the inaction that set in after the peace.

Ireland did hardly share in the growth of the carrying trade

The chief gain which accrued to England during the Revolutionary and Napoleonic Wars was the monopoly which she practically secured of the shipping of the world. The United States was a real competitor; but England obtained a position which she had never secured before. Ireland however had little or no mercantile marine; the profits of the carrying trade, and of the forced trade with distant countries, were not for her. What she could do was to provide for the victualling of ships, as well as to furnish supplies of sailcloth; the Irish salt beef which ships obtained at Cork had a high reputation, but a certain new activity in these trades was almost the only advantage which accrued to Ireland from the great commercial monopoly by which England gained so much.

or increase of manufactures,

So far as articles of export were concerned too, she was not able to supply the goods which were so much sought for abroad, and by means of which England was able to force unwilling nations to purchase her wares. Cloth was needed for the French and Russian armies, and this cloth was procured from English looms; but the Irish woollen trade was quite unimportant. The cotton manufacture, which A.D. 1776
—1815. developed so enormously in England during the war, had been scarcely introduced into Ireland, though much had been spent on it in 1784 and succeeding years. Linen, the one department in which Ireland excelled, was hardly a fabric for which foreign countries looked to England at all. Hardware, in which England did such a large business, had ceased to be an Irish manufacture, and the sister kingdom was practically debarred from all the advantages which came to England during the time of war-prices and commercial monopoly.

On the other hand Ireland felt the disadvantages from *but suffered* which England suffered. A silk manufacture had been *from* *Berlin* galvanized into existence by encouragements similar to those *Decrees.* which the Spitalfields Act[1] gave in England; but the weavers were of course dependent on material brought from abroad; and the Berlin Decrees caused a silk famine in 1809 which reduced them to dire distress[2]. In so far as the war-prices gave a stimulus to agriculture, the peace must have brought a reaction similar to that which, despite the action of the Corn Law of 1815, was so seriously felt in England.

So long as water-power was the chief agent employed in manufacturing, Ireland offered, in some districts, great attractions to capital, and the woollen trade obtained a measure of protection[3]. There was however even a more *The* decided objection among Irish than among English workmen *woollen* *trade.* to the introduction of machinery[4], and the progress was not very rapid; with the more general adoption of steam-power, the advantage which Ireland had possessed was neutralized. The one trade which decidedly prospered was the linen manufacture, and in that the Irish continued to advance. Both the quantities manufactured, and the quality of the goods produced, serve to show that the trade was steadily advancing[5].

It became an article of faith with Irish repealers that there had been a great era of commercial and industrial prosperity in the period between 1784 and the Union, and

[1] See below, § 371, p. 624.   [2] Martin, 87.
[3] Ib. 70.   [4] Ib. 72, 73.   [5] Ib. 75.

that Ireland had retrograded in many ways since that event[1]. Mr Martin's statistics go to show at every point that this charge was unproven, that the unnatural stimulus of 1784 had begun to die out several years before the Union[2], and that there had been steady increase of material prosperity of every kind from that event till the time when he wrote in 1843[3]. The close connection between constitutional and economic change has been again and again asserted in preceding chapters, though there has also been occasion to note that the century of most violent constitutional changes in England was singularly uneventful so far as industrial development is concerned. At times of rapid economic change it is not easy to assess the precise effects of a great alteration in the constitution; and the period since the Union has been one of rapid economic changes. It certainly was unfortunate that the Irish leaders and people should attach themselves so passionately to a policy of national self-sufficiency and protection, at the very time when these ideas were losing their hold on the minds of English statesmen.

340. In India too, there were great constitutional changes during this period; though they resulted from causes, which were quite unlike those that led, first to the legislative independence, and then to the legal absorption of Ireland. In 1773 the political character of the East India Company had been recognised; in 1780, as the result of long and acrimonious discussion, a new constitution was created, in the hope that under this régime the Company would show itself more capable of wisely administering the great empire it had conquered. It was in the course of this discussion, and in the events to which it gave rise, that the English nation first began to realise their responsibilities for the government of India. In 1773 the whole subject was treated as a commercial speculation; the nation was jealous of a company which seemed to derive immense wealth from the government of this distant land, and there was a desire that the nation should share in the profits of that rule. But the first experiment at government, by a body which owed its authority

[1] O'Connell's *Address to the Inhabitants of the Countries subject to the British Crown.* Martin, iv.   [2] *Ib.* 43 et seq.   [3] *Ib.* 57.

to the House of Commons, brought to light the real difficul- A.D. 1776
ties of the task which Englishmen had to face in India. The —1815.
select committees which examined into the condition of the *and the dif-*
ficulty of
Indian government in 1780 and 1781, and above all the *governing*
India.
searching ordeal which the first parliamentary governor had
to undergo, when his administration was impeached by
Burke, diffused an extraordinary knowledge of India, and
had a marvellous effect in influencing the spirit in which the
servants of the company undertook their duties.

The administration which had been created by the act of *Lord*
North's
1773[1] would not work. From the first there was a bitter *India*
Regulation
antagonism between Hastings and Francis, one of the mem- *Act.*
bers of the Council; for a time, the Governor had a majority,
with the help of his own vote; but the position, through
various changes in the composition of the Council, became
more and more intolerable; and there was an open feud
between the Governors and the Directors at home. Thus the
affairs committed to the newly created Governor General
and Council were the constant occasion of bitter personal
feuds.

Still more curious and unexpected was the influence of *The*
Judges.
Judicature created by the act of 1773. The King's Judges
in India arrogated to themselves powers which threw the
whole system of government into confusion; while, by applying the rules of English Law to decide cases in which natives
were concerned, they often inflicted substantial injustice.
The respective spheres of the two supreme authorities had
been inadequately defined, and they soon came into open
conflict[2]. But between them they succeeded in upsetting
the fiction under which English rule had hitherto cloaked
itself; and which had been one of the expedients devised by
Clive[3]. The nominal power of the Nawabs had been retained,
both for fiscal and civil (Dewanny) and for criminal jurisdiction
(Nizamut). At the instigation of the Directors, their Council
threw off this disguise in 1772, so far as the collection of
revenue and civil jurisdiction were concerned, and the Company assumed the office of Dewan[4]; while decisions of the 1776.

---

[1] 18 Geo. III. c. 63; Mill, *History*, III. 348.   [2] *Ib.* IV. 17.
[3] *Ib.* III. 363.   [4] *Ib.* 365.

A.D. 1776
—1815.
Supreme Court, which refused to recognise the authority of a
Nawab as Nizam, destroyed the powers of the agent through
whom criminal jurisdiction was professedly administered[1].
English Responsibility. In this way the English responsibility for government was
declared complete, while the whole machinery of government
was reduced to a deadlock. It was under these circumstances that it became necessary to frame a new constitution
for the government of India, a task which was unsuccessfully
attempted by Fox, and accomplished by Pitt. The essence
of Fox's proposal was that for the future "the Board of
Directors shall be chosen not by the owners of the Company's
stock, but by the House of Commons[2]," and as this was much
disliked both by the Company and the King, it was destined
Pitt's India Bill. to fail. Pitt on the other hand, while leaving the directorate
of the Company its existing functions, erected a Board of
Control, which was a new department of State; the members
were to be chosen by the king, and were charged with the
complete supervision of all the civil and military, but not the
commercial affairs of the Company[3]. The constitution thus
framed was embodied without substantial alteration in 1793,
when the charter of the Company was renewed for twenty
years; but the first step was then taken to break down the
commercial monopoly which the Company had enjoyed, as
they were to allow their ships to be used for private trade to
the extent of 3000 tons annually[4].

Warren Hastings. These changes in the form of government would have
made but little improvement, however, if it had not been for
the manner in which the trial of Warren Hastings reacted on
the traditions of official life in India. He had in many ways
set a great example of what a ruler should be, while the trial
was a complete exposure of the evils of the system which
then existed. James Mill, who was a somewhat unfriendly
critic of one after another of Hastings' acts, could not withhold a tribute to his great qualities; "in point of ability, he

---

[1] Mill, iv. 223.

[2] Ib. 386. The connection of parliamentary influence and Indian corruption
was one of the points on which Burke was wont to insist. Ib. v. 22.

[3] Ib. iv. 395; 24 Geo. III. c. 25. As interpreted by Pitt's declaratory act (28
Geo. III. c. 8) however, the whole business of the Company was practically under
its control. Mill, v. 63.   [4] Ib. vi. 1.

is beyond all question the most eminent of the chief rulers A.D. 1776 —1815. whom the Company have ever employed; nor is there any one of them who would not have succumbed under the difficulties, which if he did not overcome, he at any rate sustained. * * He was the first, or among the first, of the servants of the Company, who attempted to acquire any language of the natives, and who set on foot those liberal enquiries into the literature and institutions of the Hindus, which have led to the satisfactory knowledge of the present day. He had the great art of a ruler, which consists in attaching to the governor those who are governed; his administration assuredly was popular, both with his countrymen and the natives in Bengal[1]."

Native States. In spite of his successful and vigorous policy, or as some might say in consequence of it, difficulties arose which landed us in new conflict with native states, and led to the wars by which our responsibilities were enormously increased. From 1773 onwards the story of British rule in India was a story of steady and persistent aggrandisement. In the North-West Provinces, the Carnatic, and at Poona, our Indian Empire was expanded; at the date of the battle of Waterloo the very fear of French influence in India[2] was extinguished, while the British power was effectively felt over the whole country. His conduct towards the Rohillas, the Princesses of Oude, and the Rajah of Benares, were among the most serious charges against Warren Hastings; and the wars with Mysore and the Mahrattas strained our resources at the beginning of the present century.

Administrative difficulties. Whatever may be the ultimate judgment on the British rule in India, it may certainly be said that at the time when this great expansion of power was proceeding so fast, our countrymen were wholly unfit to make the necessary arrangements for its good administration. They were still strangely ignorant of the habits and ideas of the people over whom they were called to rule. Even their attempts at beneficent legislation were fraught with gravest evil. There is a strange

---

[1] Mill, IV. 368.
[2] Several French adventurers served under Scindia in 1803 and commanded at Assaye. *Ib.* VI. 339 et seq., 365.

A.D. 1776
—1815.
The Per-
manent
Settlement
of Bengal. irony in the story of the permanent settlement of the land
revenue of Bengal, as it was carried through by Lord Cornwallis. He was fully possessed with a view, for which English experience in the eighteenth century gave some plausibility, that great landed proprietors with secure possessions
would be the best agency for developing the resources of the
country. He therefore determined on following out a suggestion which Mr Francis had urged long before[1], and treated
*The
Zemin-
dars.* the Zemindars, who were merely responsible agents for the collection of the land revenue of the government as supreme
proprietor of the soil, as if they were themselves proprietors.
Their obligations to the government were fixed, and the quotas
which the ryots paid to them for their holdings were also
regarded as an unalterable quit rent. As the Zemindars
could not raise these rents, they had no motive for improving
the estates or extending cultivation; and as they had not
the old means of recovering their rents, while they were
forced to meet the demands of government punctually, they
were, as a class, ruined by the very measure which had been
intended to give them security in their possessions[2]. On
the other hand the Zemindars were inclined, in their necessity, to bring any indirect pressure they could to bear on the
ryots; and the lot of the cultivators, whose hereditary rights
had been confiscated to create the Zemindar class, was more
miserable than before. Nor were the results more fortunate
so far as the interests of the public were concerned. The
settlement was permanent, and the government was precluded
from increasing its demands when, with the progress of
society and the increase of wealth which ultimately took
place, it might fairly have done so. This disastrous arrangement, which ruined the Zemindars, increased the oppression
of the ryots, and sacrificed the future increase of revenue,
is a sufficient condemnation of the fiscal policy then pursued.
The annals of the dacoits and other crimes of violence would
furnish an equally severe comment on administrative success
in fulfilling some of the other elementary duties of government.

*Trade to
India
thrown
open.* The era which saw this rapid development of the East
India Company as a political power for the government of

[1] Mill, IV. 4.   [2] Ib. v. 345, 367.

India was fitly marked by another change. When the charter A.D. 1776 —1815. was renewed in 1813, the trade to India was at length thrown open[1]. The commercial monopoly of the Company was reserved so far as China was concerned till 1833; but in regard to the great district which it had conquered, it became a purely political and not a commercial institution at all[2]. The steps by which it had gradually acquired a new character have been already sketched; from this time onwards these new and adventitious duties absorbed all its energies, and it ceased to attempt to organise that trade for the sake of which it had been originally incorporated.

341. While the British rule was thus being organised in *Acquisitions from the Dutch* the land which had been so keenly contested by the French, it was also extended during this period to the islands and colonies which had been occupied by the Dutch. They had already been ousted from the mainland; Clive had straitened their influence in Bengal[3] (1759), and Macartney had captured their settlements in Tanjore[4] (1781). The Revolutionary War afforded an excuse for pressing further and attacking their remaining possessions, and a squadron which *in the East* was fitted out at Madras in 1795, and commanded by Admiral Ranier, did its work most effectively. The settlements in Ceylon, Malacca, Banda, and Amboyna were secured by the English without serious difficulty, though they met with long and effective resistance at Cochin[5]. In the September of the *and at the Cape.* same year the colony of the Cape of Good Hope was taken by Elphinstone; though it was restored at the conclusion of the war, it was retaken once more in 1806, and has remained in English possession ever since.

These acquisitions were of great importance for English trade, on account of the products they supplied and the markets for English manufactures which they opened up. But they also furnished stations which were of great value for the victualling of ships. This was particularly true of the Cape of Good Hope, which had been chiefly valued by the

---

[1] 53 Geo. III. c. 155.

[2] It continued to engage in import trade from India as a means of making remittances.

[3] Mill, III. 204.   [4] *Ib.* IV. 157.   [5] *Ib.* VI. 49.

A.D. 1776
—1815.
Dutch as a place of call on the route to India. It came to
have even greater importance for England when their first
Australia. settlement was made in 1788, at Sydney Cove, Port Jackson,
on the huge island, part of which the Dutch had discovered
and called New Holland.

While the revolutionary wars were convulsing Europe the
first beginnings were being made in developing the resources
of Australasia. In the stirring events of the time they
excited but little public interest; but we, who look back
upon them, cannot but feel that supreme importance attaches
to the work of those who laid the foundations of the material
prosperity of the great English settlements at the Antipodes.
Sheep-
farming. The story of Australian progress is the story of sheep-farming
there, though in the early and struggling days of the colony
but little was done in the way of pasture farming. The
colonists were struggling to grow their own food supplies ;
the land was let in small lots suitable for tillage, and no
serious efforts were made at rearing sheep or cattle. The
first sheep introduced were imported from Calcutta, but the
native breed of Bengal is but a poor specimen ; the fleece is of
a poor colour and bad quality[1]. The first important step
in improving the breed was taken by Captain Waterhouse,
Water-
house and
the Merino
Sheep. who was in command of H.M. ship *Reliance*, and called at
the Cape in 1797, during the first period of British possession, on his way to Australia. He then had the opportunity
of purchasing twenty-nine Spanish merino sheep, and he
bought them partly on his own account, and partly for
friends who were willing to join in the speculation[2]. The
passage from the Cape to Sydney occupied nearly three
months, and about a third of the sheep died on the way.
When they arrived in Australia they were carefully tended,
however, and as Captain Waterhouse distributed them among
several farmers[3], the breed in the colony and the quality of
the wool was improved in an astonishingly short space of time.
New source
for supply
of wool. By this means it was demonstrated that Australia was
admirably fitted for wool-growing, and that there might be a
new and practically unlimited supply of the raw material of
our chief manufactures. As has been noticed above the high

[1] Bonwick, *Romance of the Wool Trade,* 81.   [2] *Ib.* 70.   [3] *Ib.* 71.

price of wool and difficulty of procuring enough to meet the *A.D.* 1776 —1815. increasing demand, were matters of constant complaint among our clothiers, and the prospect of a new source from which it could be obtained might well be welcome. Captain Mac- *Macarthur and sheep-* arthur, who had been engaged in farming in Australia for *farming.* some years, and had a flock of 4,000 sheep[1], was the first man who devoted himself to pushing this new trade; he visited England in 1803 with the double object of raising capital to engage in pasture farming on a large scale, and for getting a grant from government of lands suitable for a sheep farm.

In neither object was he very successful, although he obtained the assistance of one powerful authority in pushing his scheme. Sir Joseph Banks, then President of the Royal Society, had accompanied Cook in his voyage of discovery in 1770, when Botany Bay was first sighted, and he had taken a prominent part in the colonisation of New South Wales in 1787. It was now necessary to set aside part of the system which was then adopted in letting land. Grants had hitherto been made with a view to the prosecution of tillage, and with reference to English territorial ideas. Each of the convicts, *Grants of* as he became free, received a grant of thirty or forty acres, if *Land.* he chose to apply for it, at a quit rent, for the property in the soil was carefully retained by the State[2]. The pasture of Australia, though plentiful, was poor, and Captain Macarthur calculated[3] that three acres were necessary for every sheep, and that a square mile would only suffice for a flock of two hundred. There was a strong feeling against allowing any single individual to monopolise large areas of land in the neighbourhood of the growing town. The difficulty was met by a proposal which was put forward by Sir Joseph Banks. "As you and the gentlemen concerned with you" he wrote[4] "seem determined to persevere in your New South Wales sheep adventure, and as I am aware that its success will be of infinite importance to the manufacturers of England, and that its failure will not happen without much previous advantage to the infant colony, I should be glad to know whether the adventurers would be contented with a grant of a large quantity of land as sheep walks *only*, resumable by

[1] Bonwick, 73.　　[2] *Ib.* 104.　　[3] *Ib.* 75.　　[4] *Ib.* 77.

the Government in any parcels in which it shall be found convenient to grant it as private property, on condition of an equal quantity of land being granted in recompense as sheep walk. The lands to be chosen by your agent in lots of 100,000 acres each, and a new lot granted as soon as the former has been occupied, as far as 1,000,000 acres." This

Squatters. was the system which was eventually adopted, and graziers were in consequence spoken of as squatters[1]. Many held the area for grass alone, and removed elsewhere when the Government notified them that the land was required for other purposes. Captain Macarthur may be described as the first squatter; he obtained a grant of 5,000 acres from Government on the terms just described[2], and settled down on the Nepean River. He had failed in obtaining the use of British capital for his enterprise, but he had done not a little to stir up public interest in England, and he certainly laid the foundation of the wool trade on which the prosperity of Australia has been built up.

Difficulties of tenure. The example which had been set was speedily followed, and the terms of Captain Macarthur's grant laid down the lines of the system under which sheep-farming was gradually developed. The term squatter is associated in England with settling on a common; and in Australia the first plan was to grant common grazing rights over a considerable area to a group of settlers[3], by lease. But this system soon proved too restricted for the rapidly increasing flocks, and letters of occupation were granted to some individuals, so as to allow them to range beyond the prescribed limits (1820)[4]. In 1831 the policy of the colony was so far changed that the out-and-out sale of land was introduced[5]—though mining rights were still reserved[6]; but the prices which were charged were prohibitive, so far as graziers were concerned, and but little

Classes of Land. relief was given to them till 1847, when Orders in Council appeared which divided the waste lands of Australia into three classes, and gave the squatters much greater security

---

[1] Bonwick, 78. See above, § 228, p. 204.   [2] Bonwick, 81.
[3] Governor King's proclamation 1804. Bonwick, 105.   [4] *Ib.* 106.
[5] Partly it would appear through the influence of Mr Wakefield. *Art of Colonisation*, 45.
[6] Bonwick, 107.

of tenure than they had hitherto enjoyed. On the settled *A.D. 1776*
lands, which were available for purchase, the squatter had *—1815.*
only a yearly tenure; on the intermediate lands, he was
allowed an eight years' lease; while on the unsettled lands
he might obtain a lease for fourteen years, at the rent of £10
for every 4000 sheep in his flocks[1]. The very form of these
orders shows how completely English ideas on the subject
had changed, since Macarthur first approached the government on the subject in 1803.

342. While our influence was thus being pushed in the *British*
East and by the East, it had considerably declined in the *power and trade in*
West. What we may notice, however, is that though British *America.*
power had suffered, there was a considerable expansion of
British trade. The United States of America continued to
be excellent customers, till the Orders in Council drove them
into hostility, and the provinces which we retained supplied
most valuable products for our trade.

It was by a curious irony that the only North American *Canada,*
Colonies which we retained were those which had been but
recently conquered from France, and where the French
population and language predominated. If they had a traditional quarrel with England however, they had been brought
into direct conflict with the English settlers in America; and
though the French Canadian population has been somewhat
discontented at times with British rule, there was little
apparent disposition to revolt at the critical moment when
the Americans invaded Canada in 1812. A constitution had
been devised in 1791[2]; the Dominion was divided into the *Upper and Lower.*
two provinces of Lower and Upper Canada, and though
there was no extraordinary growth like that of the United
States, there was steady and uninterrupted progress. The
River S. Lawrence afforded excellent means of carriage, and
the trade in lumber was pursued; while a Montreal Company
was organised which had considerable dealings in furs[3]. The
fisheries off Newfoundland were the most valuable in the *Newfound-land.*
world, and the English sovereignty over this island was

[1] Bonwick, 109. [2] *Parl. Hist.* xxix. 864, 31 Geo. III. c. 31.
[3] On the various conflicting interests see Brymner, *Report on Canadian
Archives* (1886), p. xiv., also below, § 864, p. 601.

secured by the treaty of Versailles (1783) as it had previously
been by those of Ryswick and Utrecht[1]. At the same time
the French preserved an interest in these fisheries. The
barren rocks of S. Pierre and Miquelon were all that remained to them of their great possessions in North America,
but the former had an excellent harbour and it served as a
winter residence for the fishing population. They had also
rights to fish within certain limits[2], off the coast of Newfoundland, and to use the shore during the fishing season,
Difficulties with the French. but not at other times or for other purposes. These rights
had given rise to constant disputes which still continue; the
French claim an exclusive right to fish within the specified
limits, while the English colonists claim a concurrent right
in the French fisheries and an exclusive right in those
beyond their limits. They hold that they are justified in
fishing in any part of their own coast, so long as they do not
interfere with the operations of the French fishermen on the
parts of the coast which they are permitted to frequent.
The question as to what is interference with the French
fishing and what is not is evidently a delicate one; as the
French sailors have had difficulty in settling disputes among
themselves about the various fishing grounds[3], it is obvious
that the attempt to enjoy concurrent rights would be likely
to give rise to quarrels between sailors of different nationalities. The farther point as to the precise purpose for which
the French may use the shore, and their rights to river fishing or fishing for lobsters, appear to be comparatively recent
Treaty of Paris. 1763. complications[4]. They were not in contemplation, and were
not therefore provided for, when His Britannic Majesty and
His Most Christian Majesty flattered themselves they had
finally laid the difficulty to rest in 1763. But though the
definition of the rights left to France has given rise to so
much discussion, the sovereignty on the island, and the
rights which it involved, were secured to England. Thus in
regard to the trade with the northern colonies as a whole,
England suffered comparatively little, if at all, by the success

---

[1] Fitzmaurice, *Life of Shelburne*, III. 165, 319.

[2] These limits were altered by the Treaty of Versailles in the hope of rendering collisions less frequent. Koch and Schoell, I. 459.

[3] Appleton, *Newfoundland Fishery Question*, 14.　　[4] *Ib.* 31.

of the States in securing their independence. Those branches <small>A.D. 1776</small>
of the trade of the northern colonies, which had been most <small>—1815.</small>
highly prized and chiefly fostered by the British government,
remained to England; while the newly formed and independent States, as they prospered, offered a better and better
market for English goods.

343. Indeed the chief sufferers at this time appear to *West*
have been the West Indian Islands; a curious combination *India Islands,*
of circumstances told against them. They had always complained of the successful rivalry of the French sugar islands;
and of the unpatriotic trade with these islands in which the
northern colonists indulged. The United States, since their
Declaration of Independence, made no pretence of sacrificing
their interest in this matter; and during the wars, their
shipping was constantly employed in carrying on French *and the*
trade, which would otherwise have been entirely interrupted. *French sugar*
It appears to have been owing to the exigencies of the West *trade.*
Indian trade, in which English capital was so largely invested, that the outcry against the frauds of the neutral flag
was raised; this led to the Orders in Council and the Berlin
Decrees[1]. It certainly was a matter of complaint, whatever
the cause may have been, that the produce of our islands was
undersold by the French colonies in neutral markets, and
even in our own.

But the West Indian Islands also suffered, because they
were no longer such important depots for trade. They had
been the centre, from which communication had been made *Decline of*
with Spanish America and with the Portuguese territories in *trade with Spanish*
South America. During the Napoleonic War, the English *America.*
merchants succeeded in opening a direct trade with these
districts, and purchasing their products with their own
manufactures. Brazil was one of the most important of the
new markets which was opened to English enterprise during
this period; and though the new trade was most profitable
. to the mother country, it diverted a stream of commerce
which had hitherto been very serviceable to the West Indian *The*
planters. Settled as they were in fertile islands, they were *Planters.*

---

[1] Leone Levi, 111. Compare James Stephen's pamphlet, *War in disguise; or .
the frauds of the Neutral flags,* 20, 67, 107 et seq.

A.D. 1776
—1815.

singularly dependent on trade for the comforts and necessaries of life; they devoted their energies to growing sugar,
and relied "on foreign supply for every article of manufacture,
and for the greater part of their subsistence[1]." A diminution
of the trade, which, whether as legal or clandestine, they had
long enjoyed, was a very serious matter; there had always
been something a little artificial in their prosperity, and it
could not be easily maintained, when the new routes and
conditions of trade interfered with the favoured position it
had hitherto enjoyed.

The Slave Trade.

344. The most serious alteration in the conditions under
which industry was carried on in the West Indian islands
was caused by the success of the anti-slave trade agitation.
The most eager of all the philanthropists who devoted them-

Clarkson.

selves to the abolition of this traffic was Thomas Clarkson;
he had his attention drawn to the topic by the subject
of a Members' Prize in the University of Cambridge, for
which he successfully competed in 1784. Three years later
the subject was discussed in Parliament; there was a great
debate on the subject which lasted for two days in 1791[2].

Wilber-force.

The motion of Mr Wilberforce for abolition in 1798 was lost
by the narrow majority of four[3]; and public opinion had so
far ripened on the subject that the traffic was abolished, as
far as England was concerned, in 1807[4]. Previous attempts
to regulate the trade, so as to put down the worst barbarities
of the middle passage, had been comparatively futile[5]; it
appeared that the efforts of the philanthropists to extinguish
the trade gave it a new stimulus, as the dealers were anxious
to make the most of it while they could.

Effects on the West Indies

The immediate loss to the West Indies was not due to a
disorganisation of the existing system for industry, though
there may have been some difficulty in keeping up the full
head of labour on some estates, but to the cessation of a
trade for which the West Indies had served as a depot. The

---

[1] Hamilton, *Introduction to Merchandise*, 513.

[2] *Parl. Hist.* xxix. 250. See also xxvii. 396.   [3] *Ib.* xxxiii. 1376—1415.

[4] 47 Geo. III. *Session* i. c. 36.   51 Geo. III. c. 23.

[5] By 28 Geo. III. c. 54 the numbers of the cargo were limited to five slaves for
every three tons burden. Under these rules the mortality on the passage was reduced to five per cent. Young, *West India Common Place Book*, p. 10.

American continent had on the whole been supplied from A.D. 1776 —1815. the Islands, and when this traffic came to an end, they were no longer able to make their habitual returns for the commodities supplied them. The emancipation of the slaves and all the difficulties which had arisen in connection with it, was the work of a later year.

As England was by far the most important of the slave *and on other nations.* dealing nations, her declaration against the traffic was of world-wide importance; but she was not a leader in the movement. Joseph II. of Austria had declared against the trade in 1782, and the French Convention of 1794 had abolished it, so far as they were concerned. But the Austrian trade was hardly concerned with Africa at all, and though the French sugar colonies were wealthy and prosperous, their shipping had never been sufficient to furnish the main supply for their own islands. England had enjoyed the assiento and had guided much of her commercial policy with a view to the development of this trade; so that there was a remarkable revolution when the greatest trading nation of the world changed her policy and set herself to suppress the very traffic she had hitherto fostered.

XV. FINANCE AND TAXATION.

345. The strain of these long wars caused a very heavy *Improved finance.* addition to the burden of the taxes; at the same time necessity proved the mother of invention, and great improvements were made in the system of taxation, while financiers attained to a much better understanding of the difficulties and dangers connected with the system of relying on loans. No attempt can be made here to trace the history in detail: it must be sufficient if attention is called to some of the more salient points.

The finance of the period had a somewhat doctrinaire character; there were two works in particular which were avowedly followed by different statesmen. Adam Smith's *The Wealth of Nations.* *Wealth of Nations*, containing as it did a special study of

Dutch finance, was a storehouse from which North borrowed not a few suggestions when obliged to provide funds for the American War. Pitt had studied the same work to even better purpose, and took it as his guide in reconstructing and consolidating our fiscal system. The influence of Price's *Treatise on Reversionary Annuities* was almost equally great, but it was exceedingly mischievous. The project of a Sinking Fund, accumulating by compound interest, so as gradually to extinguish the National Debt however heavy and however much it might increase, was an ingenious chimera; but it served to delude Pitt; and the Chancellors in successive administrations were faithful in continuing this scheme and were reckless in borrowing, since they believed they had invented a self-acting safeguard. Just before the close of the War in 1814, Robert Hamilton investigated the whole subject in masterly fashion and demonstrated the fallacies of the scheme by showing how it had actually worked. Our financiers learned by experience but the nation has had to pay heavily for their lessons[1].

Price's Treatise.

The Sinking Fund.

During the Revolutionary War, Pitt made a serious effort to raise the necessary supplies by taxation within the year. This was in 1798; the funds had fallen to 48, Ireland was in rebellion and there was a mutiny at the Nore; and our credit was so low it was useless to think of borrowing. But he could not levy enough; and the additional indebtedness incurred during these wars was enormous, while the amounts paid off during the brief intervals of peace were comparatively small. The eight years of the American War added £115,000,000 to the Debt, the nine years of the Revolutionary War added £271,000,000[2] and the twelve years of the Napoleonic Wars brought the total incurred in our last struggle with France up to £618,163,157.

Increase of Debt.

During the ten years' peace between the American and Revolutionary Wars, which was on the whole a time of prosperity, the nation only succeeded in paying off £10,000,000. Not only were the amounts obtained enormous, but the terms on which money was borrowed were often

Extravagant Terms.

[1] See below on Economic Doctrine.
[2] Robert Hamilton, *Inquiry concerning National Debt*, p. 66.

extravagant. Instead of borrowing at a high rate of interest, A.D. 1776 in the hope of subsequently financing the debt, they borrowed —1815. at a low rate of interest, and were forced to offer all sorts of extra inducements. Thus in 1782 for every £100 subscribed, the Government allotted a £100 in the three per cents, £50 in the four per cents with an annuity of 17s. 6d. for seventy-eight years[1]. Between 1781 and 1784 the sums borrowed amounted to £43,500,000 while the capital funded reached the total £65,248,000[2]. There was, besides, a considerable but varying amount of unfunded debt, which afforded means *Unfunded* of anticipating revenue not yet paid in. This chiefly took *Debt.* the form of Exchequer and Navy Bills. Exchequer Bills for sums of £100 and upwards were issued under Parliamentary authority to those who were willing to advance their value ; they bore interest at threepence to threepence halfpenny a day, and formed a circulating medium. When they were at length paid in, to defray the taxes, the interest due was allowed to the payer[3]. During the whole of the Napoleonic war[4], there were large issues of Exchequer Bills, in connection with votes of credit passed at the end of the Sessions as a safeguard against emergencies; the additions to the National Debt, often took the form of funding a portion of the floating debt.

346. The increasing debt of course involved an increasing burden of interest which had to be defrayed by additional taxation. The second year of the American War is a date of some importance in fiscal history; as Lord North, who had *Lord North* no genius for finance, was able to avail himself of the suggestions in Adam Smith's *Wealth of Nations*. It is somewhat curious that the direct influence exercised by that work on practical politics was not so much due to the principles it contained, as to the information it afforded about the revenue raised in other countries. Adam Smith had drawn largely on the materials contained in the memoirs which had been compiled for the use of a French Commission[5]. Once more an English minister deliberately endeavoured to *adopts expedients*

[1] 22 Geo. III. c. 8.   [2] Hamilton, 68.   [3] *Ib.* 122.
[4] For example in 1796 and in 1802, also in 1808, and following years. *Ib.* 78. 81.
[5] *Wealth of Nations*, Book v. ch. II. part I. p. 343 et seq.

introduce an expedient borrowed from Holland. A considerable revenue was raised among the Dutch by a tax on servants, and this was adopted in 1777[1], while a tax was levied on sales by auction[2]. In the following year a tax was laid on inhabited houses, which was levied, not by some arbitrary criterion like the windows or the hearths, but at a per centage of the annual value; this also was copied from Holland[3]. In all these cases the yield was disappointing, as such taxes only fell upon the richer classes; and in 1779 North was compelled to levy an impost of five per cent. on the customs and excise, in the hope of securing £300,000. In the measures of the following year, when a considerable sum was raised from beer[4], the criticism of Adam Smith was apparently taken into account; while North also levied a succession duty, similar to that in Holland, which had been described by Adam Smith[5].

Pitt.
When however Pitt became Chancellor of the Exchequer, we find that he relied upon the *Wealth of Nations*, not only for information on untried expedients, but for the principles on which the whole scheme of taxation might be revised. Owing to the gradual additions which had been made to the sums levied, the custom rates were extraordinarily confused; each article imported paid a number of separate taxes which were answered under different headings. The collection and administration of such a complicated system was most wasteful; while the taxes, when taken together, were so high as to interfere seriously with the consumption of the article and to offer a great temptation to the smuggler. Adam Smith had laid stress on these matters, and had advocated
Simplification of the fiscal system.
the policy of simplifying the departments and diminishing the taxes in the hopes of lessening the frauds and of putting down smuggling. The duty on tea was reduced from 119 to 12½ per cent. But such a considerable change appeared to be a very rash step. As Adam Smith had pointed out, what was required was an entire change of system[6], but while Pitt set himself to face the difficulties of carrying this through, he

---

[1] *Wealth of Nations*, p. 362. 17 Geo. III. c. 39.
[2] 17 Geo. III. c. 50.   [3] *Wealth of Nations*, 356.
[4] *Ib.* 376. Dowell, II. 171.   [5] *Wealth of Nations*, 363.
[6] *Ib.* 374, On the pressure of existing taxes, see *Parl. Hist.*, XXI. 398 (Bunbury).

was also determined to have a sufficient margin in case the A.D. 1776 —1815. project did not answer his expectations. He therefore levied additional duties on windows and on houses, by the Commutation Act (1784); and was thus able to make his reduction and to wait for the expected expansion of the revenue without hampering any of the departments of Government. The reform thus initiated established Pitt's reputation as a financier; he also set to work to improve the fiscal administration by grouping a certain number of ex- *Assessed Taxes.* actions on carriages, men-servants, horses, etc. and treating them as *Assessed Taxes*[1] (1785) which fell almost entirely upon the richer classes. In a somewhat similar fashion the complicated customs duties were replaced by a single tax on each article; the method of collection was improved, and the proceeds of the whole were lumped together as a *Consolidated* *Consoli- dated Fund.* *Fund* (1787), instead of being kept under separate accounts. Pitt's success, in carrying through these simplifications and changes, was partly due to the care he took to provide some new form of revenue which might tide him over the period of transition[2].

347. But besides working out Adam Smith's suggestions in regard to the simplifications of the taxes, Pitt evidently accepted his doctrine in regard to the distribution of the burden of taxation. The glaring inequalities[3] of the land *The inci-* tax had been somewhat reduced, and the monied men had *taxation.* been forced to contribute through the inhabited house duty and the assessed taxes. But Pitt was desirous that the poorer classes should be, so far as possible, relieved from the burden. This comes out in the measures which he took when the prosperity of the country enabled him to reduce the Government demands. In 1792 he was able to repeal the tax on women servants[4] in poorer families, the taxes on carts and waggons, the window tax on small houses[5], a

---

[1] Dowell, II. 188.   [2] *Ib.* 190.

[3] See above, § 297, p. 405.

[4] This tax had been proposed in 1785 when the group of assessed taxes was formed; this and a shortlived tax on shops, according to the rent of the shop, were intended to draw from the shopkeeper class. Dowell, II. 189. 25 Geo. III. c. 43 and c. 80.

[5] With less than seven windows. Dowell, II. 194.

portion of the tax on candles and a recently imposed duty on malt[1].

Following the same principles, Pitt showed himself most reluctant to impose any taxes upon necessaries when the Revolutionary War unexpectedly burst upon him; and he devoted himself so far as possible to raising the necessary *Taxes on* supplies by taxes which should fall upon property[2]. The *property.* first of these was an expedient which Adam Smith had recommended, and which North had attempted, of taxing successions[3]. North's tax had been easily evaded as it was *Succession* levied on the receipts given by legatees, but executors con-*Duty.* nived at a fraud on the revenue, and did not insist on having receipts; Pitt taxed the property while still in the hands of the executors. He originally intended to include all col-lateral successions to property of every kind, but while he succeeded in the measure which dealt with personal property (1796), that which concerned real property had to be dropped[4]. Another expedient was adopted which told in the same way and brought pressure to bear directly on the propertied *The Triple* classes[5]. This was the so-called *Triple Assessment*; this *Assess-ment,* was intended to be a tax which should fall widely, and which should yet be so graduated as to press less heavily on the poorer classes than on others[6]. The principle of the assessed taxes was that a man's return as to his establishment for the previous year was the basis of payment in the current year according to a graduated scale "which had the effect of increasing the tax for every subject of duty in the larger establishments[7]." In 1797 Pitt proposed that in the fol-lowing year, the payments should be greatly increased, those whose assessment had been under £25 were to pay a triple amount, those who had paid between £30—£40 were to make quadruple payments, while assessments of £50 and upwards were to increase fivefold. The following year it appeared that a better result could be obtained with less

---

[1] Cf. Pitt's splendid oration Feb. 17, 1792. *Parl. Hist.* xxix. 816.
[2] Dowell, ii. 206.   [3] *Wealth of Nations*, 363.
[4] Dowell, ii. 207.
[5] *Ib.* 214.   [6] *Parl. Hist.* xxxiii. 1047.
[7] Dowell (Second Edition, 1888), ii. 221.

elaborate machinery, by imposing a ten per cent. income tax A.D. 1776
on incomes of £200 and upwards. It was graduated for —1815.
incomes between £60 and £200, and incomes of less than
£60 were free[1]. The income tax was repealed by Addington *and In-*
on the close of the war, but had of course to be re-imposed *come Tax.*
in the following year. A more convenient form of return
was adopted, under five distinct schedules.

This was the principal new departure made under the
strain of the great French wars. Pitt and his successors were
anxious so far as possible to pay the current expenses out of
the year's receipts. In this they never succeeded, but in the
endeavour they were forced to make great additions to the
customs and other duties which fell on the trading classes.

XVI. BANKING AND CURRENCY.

348. The Bank of England had been established as an *The Bank*
instrument for relieving the necessities of government. Its *of England*
privileges had been renewed from time to time, and in the
strain of the Revolutionary War, Pitt was forced to rely on
its aid in a fashion which was entirely unprecedented. In
return for the support it afforded the Government, it had
secured an exclusive privilege as to Banking. No other
company was allowed to carry on the business in the form in
which it was then practised, but the Bank had been unable
to extend its business as rapidly as the increasing industry
and internal commerce of the country demanded. There was
an insufficiency of a circulating medium, while the requirement was supplied by the issues of private bankers who did
a speculative and unsafe business. Merchants were forced to *and Com-*
rely on the assistance of banks in the ordinary operations of *mercial*
trade; but at periods of pressure, especially of pressing de- *Credit.*
mands from the Government, the Bank was obliged to be
very circumspect in its issues to the mercantile community
and it was not always successful in steering a judicious
course. The recurring wars, with intervals of peace, led to

[1] Dowell, II. 215.

large demands from the Government on the one hand, and caused reckless speculation and violent commercial fluctuations on the other; and under such circumstances it cannot be a matter of surprise that the credit system of the country sustained a series of violent shocks and that there was a succession of commercial crises of unprecedented magnitude.

Commercial Activity and Crises.

349.   Periods of good trade are those when commercial credit is likely to be overstrained; and some of the important crises followed immediately on periods of active trade.   There had been much commercial disaster on the Continent during 1763, when the Bank of Amsterdam refused support to a firm named Neufville, and there were numerous failures in Hamburg and Germany.   The effect of these disasters extended to England, but the Bank was able to make such advances as to prevent the results from being fatal to many of the commercial houses here[1].

The Ayr Bank.

In 1772 the Bank was less fortunate.   During the preceding year or two, there had been a great deal of over-trading; but the collapse was occasioned by the fraudulent conduct of a man named Fordyce who was partner of Messrs Neale[2]; he made off with £300,000.   His own bank collapsed and carried many other establishments with it; among these was the newly-founded Ayr Bank, which had been much less successfully managed than its older rivals.   A run began on it, just a week after Fordyce had disappeared; after eight days it had to stop payment.   There was still £800,000 worth of its paper in circulation, and the distress the failure occasioned in Scotland could only be compared with the disaster caused by the Darien scheme[3].

Successful policy of the Directors in 1782.

There was another outburst of commercial prosperity on the cessation of the American War in 1782.   The sudden opening up of markets encouraged reckless speculation, and it is said that the Bank were incautious in their issues and thus fostered the evil[4]; but they had wisdom to retrace their steps in time.   Their gold reserve was reduced to a very low ebb, but they thought it was possible by carefully restricting their issues to tide over the time, till specie should arrive in

---

[1] Macleod, I. 502.   Adam Smith, 131.   [2] Macleod, I. 504 and II. 214.
[3] *Ib.* II. 215.   [4] *Ib.* I. 507.

payment of goods already sent to foreign markets. The A.D. 1776
—1815.
point of safety would be marked by a turn in the exchanges,
and they refused to make a loan even to Government in May
1783. It was not till the following October that the favourable signs appeared and that they felt justified with regard
to their own safety, in extending their issues, by lending to
the Government[1].

Ten years later, with continued peace, there had been a *The Country Banks, and*
great expansion of trading and there were premonitory
symptoms of disaster. The period might perhaps have been
tided over, but for the outbreak of the Revolutionary War.
Almost immediately afterwards a great firm of corn merchants was gazetted, and the results were felt immediately all
over the country. The bankers in Newcastle[2] made a gallant
but ineffective struggle ; a general failure of country banks
occurred throughout England (though the Exeter bank survived), and the panic extended to Glasgow as well. There
was a total destruction of credit, and substantial houses were
in imminent danger of failure[3]. It is not perhaps possible to
say that this disaster could have been prevented, but it has
been generally maintained that the Directors of the Bank of *unneces-*
England acted with undue precipitancy; the suddenness of *sary stringency.*
their refusal to allow the usual accommodation gave a shock
to credit, which would have been much less severe if their
action had been more gradual. Besides this, the extraordinary over-issues of paper in France were causing a flow
of gold to this country ; the exchanges were favourable, and
under these circumstances the Directors, especially after the
experience of 1782, need not have been so uncompromising in
their attitude and so timorous for the safety of the Bank[4].

350. The crisis which followed four years afterwards was
due to very different causes; it did not rise directly from
commercial over-trading, but from the enormous demands of
Government, which made it impossible for the Bank to meet
the ordinary requirements of the commercial community. In
1793 Pitt succeeded in carrying a measure, which had been *Pitt's rela-*
intended to protect the Directors in meeting the convenience *tions with
the Bank.*

[1] Macleod, I. 508.　　[2] *Ib.* 510.　　[3] *Ib.* II. 216.
[4] Sir F. Baring's Evidence before the Bullion Committee. Macleod, I. 510.

of Government, but which really gave the ministers of the day irresponsible control over the government of the Bank. In the original Act which created the Bank, the legislature had been careful to provide against the lending of money to Government without the permission of Parliament; but a practice had grown up of advancing sums, which might amount to £20,000 or £30,000 at a time, in payment of bills of exchange. The Directors however had some doubt as to the legality of the practice; and endeavoured to procure an Act of Indemnity for these transactions in the past, as well as powers to continue them to a limited amount such as £50,000. Pitt succeeded in passing the Bill without any specified limitation, and he was therefore able to draw on the Bank as freely as he chose, trusting to the unwillingness of the Directors to dishonour his bills. In December, 1794, the Directors began to find themselves in a position of great diffi-culty, and made repeated representations to Pitt to reduce his

demands. Their remonstrances were ineffective, and they did not perhaps show as much firmness as might have been desirable in the face of the continued drain of gold. They did however contract their issues to commercial men to such an extent as to cause great complaint in the City, while Pitt continued to press for further advances. He had more than once promised the Directors to make payments which would reduce the advances on Treasury Bills to £500,000, but in June, 1796, the debt amounted to £1,232,649, and he suc-ceeded in obtaining £800,000 in the July and a similar sum in the August of that year[1]. The political outlook was in every way gloomy, and the affairs of the Bank dragged on with increasing difficulty till February 1797, when a crisis

was brought to a head by the failure of the Newcastle banks. The dread of a French invasion had caused the farmers to draw their deposits from the banks. The Bank of England was powerless to support any of the country banks, and though the Directors had reduced their issues very considerably, they were forced to obtain an Order in Council empowering them

to suspend payments in cash. When this step was once taken, the Bank could grant accommodation much more

---

[1] Macleod, I. 523.

freely, and a large number of merchants agreed to accept those inconvertible notes. The Bank succeeded in restoring mercantile credit throughout the country, and in saving the commercial world from further disaster. In this case, as in 1793, the Directors had felt themselves bound to act with great precipitude and had not regulated their issues to commercial men by carefully watching the state of the exchanges as they had so successfully done in 1783. *A.D. 1776 —1815.*

351. The suspension of cash payments made a fundamental difference in the character of the currency of the country. Instead of being based on one of the precious metals, it had really become inconvertible, and its value could only be maintained by judgment in restricting the issues of paper. There were various circumstances which tended to conceal the fact that the notes were actually depreciated; they bore on the face of them that they were convertible, and as they were freely and habitually taken in exchange for goods, there appeared to be no distrust of them in the internal trade. As too, gold had almost ceased to circulate, there were few transactions made in gold; and there was no opportunity of observing that the prices in paper, and the prices in gold, were different. In Ireland where similar measures had been adopted, this was not the case; and the variations of prices in paper and gold in the south of Ireland, as well as the rates of exchange between London and Belfast (where specie payments were usual), and London and Dublin, where paper was current, made it obvious to impartial observers that there had been an overissue of paper, and that this over-issue of paper had precisely the same effects on prices and on the exchanges as the depreciation of the silver currency had had in the time of William III.[1] In England, however, the selling of guineas at more than their nominal value was treated as criminal, and there *Inconvertible Paper Currency.* *Disturbance of prices in Ireland.* *Difficulty of detecting variations in England.*

---

[1] Macleod, II. 9—21. Till 1765 the notes of the Scotch Banks were generally issued with an optional clause providing that they should only be cashed six months after date but that they should bear interest from the time they were presented till the six months expired. This was a limited inconvertibility and while it lasted there was a depreciation of the paper currency and difficulties in regard to the exchanges similar to that which afterwards occurred in Ireland and in England. *Ib.* 206.

A.D. 1776
—1815. was nothing to demonstrate that the notes had ceased to be interchangeable for gold. Ample proof however ought to have been easily derived from the state of the foreign exchanges; but it was possible to argue that their adverse character was due to the large payments for the "British armies upon the Continent; slow returns for exports, quick payments for imports and very large stocks of imported goods now on hand in the country[1]."

These facts concealed the true state of the case from ordinary observers; but when the high prices of the Napoleonic wars induced a period of feverish speculation, the issues of the Bank, as well as of newly-formed country banks, increased so greatly, and the variations in the price of gold and in the exchanges with Hamburg were so striking, that attention was directed to the subject in the House of Commons.

The Bullion Committee. As a result a Bullion Committee was appointed, which examined the whole subject with great care; a very valuable report was issued, which had been drafted by Messrs Horner, Huskisson & Thornton[2]. This document traces the whole of the disturbances to the indirect effects of the change which was brought about by the suspension of cash payments, and the depreciation of the notes that had insensibly ensued. The Bank had advanced freely to customers who were substantial men and desired accommodation. The Directors had believed that it was their duty to do so in order to provide a sufficient circulating medium; they had ceased to attend to the exchanges as the index, which showed the flow of gold and helped them to judge of their own safety; and when they disregarded this guide, they had over-issued to such an extent as to bring about a real depreciation of the circulating medium.

Their Report. For nearly a year this Report was shelved; and when it was at length discussed there was a most curious debate, in which the members of the Committee expounded their principles with great clearness, while their opponents brought forward a mass of curious allegations and mistaken assertions; these served however to carry the day; and Mr Horner was defeated by 151 to 75. The Ministry followed up this success

---

[1] Mr Chambers' evidence, Bullion Committee. Macleod, II. 84.   [2] *Ib.* 48.

by passing a series of resolutions, as to the true nature of *A.D. 1776 —1815.* money and principles of banking, which have long since been condemned, and which were indeed sufficiently criticised at the time.

The soundness of the principles of the Bullion Committee *Delay in Resumption.* was curiously verified at the next commercial crisis, which occurred in 1816; it was, as before, directly connected with speculative trading; as before it brought about the collapse of many country banks; their paper became worthless and suddenly ceased to circulate. Although the Bank had enlarged its own issues to some extent, the paper currency of the country was greatly decreased, and the relation between gold and bank notes so far righted itself that there would have been no practical difficulty in resuming cash payments in 1816, as indeed the Bank was prepared to do[1].

XVII. ECONOMIC DOCTRINE.

352. Adam Smith had successfully recast the whole *Increased interest in Political Economy.* subject of Political Economy, and his treatise practically defined the scope of the science; the new clearness he gave it, and the very popularity which it derived from the excellence of his treatment, helped to make it an attractive study. The period immediately succeeding the publication of the *Wealth of Nations* was chiefly marked by hasty application of the new principles, but there was also real progress in the knowledge of Political Economy. In one department after another considerable advances were made.

There are indeed some cases where Adam Smith did not quite succeed in incorporating the best work of his contemporaries and predecessors in his book. In regard to the doctrine of population there had been very careful study *Population.* before he wrote. Benjamin Franklin was much struck with *Benjamin Franklin.* the rapid increase of the population in America. He saw that the conditions of society there allowed of early marriages. " When families can be easily supported more persons marry,

[1] Macleod, II. 62.

and earlier in life." "Land being thus plenty in America, and so cheap that a labouring man, that understands husbandry, can in a short time save money enough to purchase a piece of new land sufficient for a plantation, whereon he may subsist a family, such are not afraid to marry; for, if they even look far enough forward to consider how their children, when grown up, are to be provided for, they see that more land is to be had at rates equally easy, all circumstances considered. Hence marriages in America are more general, and more generally early than in Europe[1]." In fact Franklin calculated that the white population in the northern colonies was doubling in twenty-five years or even less.

Observations on America.

In contrast with this rapid increase of the white population, Franklin noticed that America had been as fully populated as possible at the time of the advent of Europeans; for the native races were hunters, and the "hunter, of all men, requires the greatest quantity of land from whence to draw his subsistence, the husbandman subsisting on much less, the gardener on still less, and the manufacturer requiring least of all." The white settlers were therefore enabled to multiply in a manner that was impossible to the Indians, when their mode of obtaining food was taken into account. But it was impossible for any people to increase "beyond the means provided for their subsistence." Their power of procuring food set a limit, but nothing else did. "There is, in short, no bound to the prolific nature of plants or animals, but what is made by their crowding and interfering with each other's means of subsistence. Was the face of the earth vacant of other plants, it might be gradually sowed and overspread with one kind only, as for instance with fennel; and were it empty of other inhabitants, it might in a few ages be replenished from one nation only; as for instance with Englishmen." With these clear views he condemns all measures that were taken with the view of acting directly on population, as by encour-

Condemns expedients for promoting increase.

[1] *Observations on the Increase of Mankind.* This treatise was written in 1751 and printed by Mr William Clarke as an appendix to a pamphlet of his own in 1755. *Observations on the late and present conduct of the French*, 42 et seq. In 1760 extracts from it were published in London along with Franklin's *Interest of Great Britain considered with regard to her Colonies.* Franklin's *Works* edited by J. Sparks, II. 311.

aging immigration. "The importation of foreigners into a country, that has as many inhabitants as the present employments and provisions for subsistence will bear, will be in the end no increase of people, unless the new comers have more industry and frugality than the natives, and then they will provide more subsistence, and increase in the country; but they will gradually eat the natives out. Nor is it necessary *Ravages of War.* to bring in foreigners to fill up any occasional vacancy in a country; for such vacancy (if the laws are good) will soon be filled by natural generation. Who can now find the vacancy made in Sweden, France, or other warlike nations, by the plague of heroism, forty years ago; in France, by the expulsion of the Protestants; in England, by the settlement of her colonies; or in Guinea, by one hundred years' exportation of slaves, that has blackened half America? The thinness of inhabitants in Spain is owing to national pride and idleness, and other causes, rather than to the expulsion of the Moors, or to the making of new settlements[1]."

Benjamin Franklin's doctrine is expressed with all the vigour which was due to a clear apprehension of the conditions which rendered the native inhabitants so few, and the other conditions which accounted for the very rapid increase among the whites. Sir James Steuart follows out the same *Sir James Steuart.* sort of view with regard to countries that were more fully taken up with agriculture[2]. If the people of any country required more food than could be easily produced at home, it would be well for them to take to industry. "If the demand for food can be more readily supplied from abroad than from home, it will be the foreign subsistence, which will preserve numbers, produced from industry, not from domestic agriculture; and these numbers will, in their turn, produce an *Reflex effect of industry on agriculture.* advance of it at home, by inspiring a desire in the husbandman to acquire the equivalent which their countrymen give to strangers[3]." In this way he argued that the develop-

---

[1] Franklin's *Works*, II. 318.

[2] Sir James Stenart fought on the side of the Pretender in 1745, and was in consequence compelled to pursue his Economic studies on the Continent. Scott's *Journals*, I. 114.

[3] Sir James Steuart's *Works*, I. 155.

ment of manufacturing indirectly increased the food supply, and therefore the population, by giving additional means of subsistence from abroad or by stimulating the effectual demand of the farmers for those things which manufacturers were able to produce[1]. It is thus by the development of manufactures, even including the introduction of machines which displace labour, that the fund of subsistence is increased and that opportunity is given for the development of population.

Sir James Steuart's treatment of this topic is a good illustration of his method. He desired to find a principle to give sound guidance to statesmen. There was a general impression abroad that there might be too many manufactures in a country, and too small a proportion of its inhabitants engaged in agriculture. He tries to show on the other hand that, as the free hands, or manufacturers, can never be fed but out of the superfluity of the farmers, manufactures enabled the free hands to purchase subsistence ; hence the development of industry called forth additional agriculture, and thus tended to augment the population. Attempts to encourage agriculture directly, without regard to an increasing demand for its product, could only end in the loss of the farmers and landed interest.

He is of course clear that the production from agriculture, —the fund of subsistence at any given time,—sets a limit to the possible population. He recognises the positive checks, as Malthus calls them, quite distinctly ; and shows that, if there is no increase of food, a mere increase of births cannot

---

[1] The influence of commerce and artificial wants in promoting the growth of population is very clearly put by Caldwell, *Enquiry*, in *Debates* 747 (1766), and still earlier by William Temple, a clothier of Trowbridge, in his *Vindication of Commerce and the Arts* (1758), pp. 6, 20, 74. He criticises W. Bell, whose *Dissertation on Populousness* (1756), p. 9, had advocated the development of agriculture as the best expedient for bringing about an increase of population ; this essay, which obtained a Member's Prize at Cambridge, achieved some celebrity, and was translated into German by the Economic Society of Berne (*Kleine Schriften*, 1762). Temple's *Vindication* was published under the pseudonym I. B., M. D.; (Macculloch, *Select Tracts on Commerce*, p. xii.); I feel confident that he was also the author of the anonymous tract *Considerations on Taxes as they are supposed to affect the price of labour in our manufactories*, subsequently enlarged into an *Essay on Trade and Commerce* (1770), the arguments of the *Vindication* are reproduced, and there is a similarity in style and arrangement. This is confirmed by an examination of the amusing autograph MS. notes in Temple's copy of *A View of the internal policy of Great Britain*, 1764 [Brit.

augment the population[1]; but he is also clear that it is not impossible for the statesman to provide for an increase of population. The wise statesman will endeavour "to contrive different employments for the hands of the necessitous, that, by their labour, they may produce an equivalent which may be acceptable to the farmers, in lieu of this superfluity; for these last certainly will not raise it, if they cannot dispose of it, nor will they dispose of it, but for a proper equivalent[2]." It is by the development of industry,—giving employment[3] to free hands—that the population multiplies; and thus multiplication is in modern society the efficient cause of agriculture[4]. The enormous increase of population, which has taken place since his time, is at all events completely consonant with the principle which he laid down. The law of diminishing return is an important factor in the problem, of which both Steuart and Franklin were unaware.

There were, however, various phenomena in English society at that date which seemed inconsistent with this view of the case, and made it appear probable that the English population was positively declining. The war on cottages had produced this result in many districts, and there was no accurate knowledge of the numbers in other localities where towns had increased. Dr Brakenridge[5] and Dr Price took this view, and adduced interesting statistical arguments in

Mus. 1250, a. 44]. Temple also wrote a refutation of part of Smith's *Chronicon Rusticum*, as I gather from Smith's reply. *Case of English Farmer* [Brit. Mus. 104, m. 27]. The *Vindication* (p. 37) ascribes the *Essay on Causes of Decline* to Decker (see above, p. 409 n.), so that there was a conflict of opinion on the authorship of this tract among contemporaries.

[1] "Those who are supposed to be fed with the spontaneous fruits of the earth, cannot, from what has been said, multiply beyond that proportion; at the same time the generative faculty will work its natural effects in augmenting numbers. The consequence will be, that certain individuals must become worse fed, consequently weaker; consequently, if, in that weakly state, nature should withhold a part of her usual plenty, the whole multitude will be affected by it; a disease may take place and sweep off a far greater number than that proportioned to the deficiency of the season. What results from this? That those who have escaped, finding food more plentiful, become vigorous and strong; generation gives life to additional numbers, food preserves it, until they rise up to the former standard.

"Thus the generative faculty resembles a spring loaded with a weight, which always exerts itself in proportion to the diminution of resistance: when food has remained some time without augmentation or diminution, generation will carry numbers as high as possible; if then food come to be diminished, the spring is overpowered; the force of it becomes less than nothing." Steuart, I. 25, 26.

[2] *Works*, I. 35.   [3] *Ib.* 45.   [4] *Ib.* 153.   [5] *Ib.* 125.

support of it; but Mr Howlett showed that their reasoning
was illusory[1]. At the same time, the opinion they adopted of
a serious danger to the country from an insufficient population, was commonly held and found frequent expression; as
in the speeches of Chatham or Shelburne on the anxiety about
defence at home, caused by the loss of men in the American
War[2]. The success achieved by Malthus in investigating the
doctrine of population is most easily measured, when we read
such speeches and feel how impossible it would have been for
responsible statesmen to make them after the *Essay on Population* had once made its mark.

*Malthus'
inductive
argument.*
353.   Almost alone among economists, Malthus had set
himself to establish the principles he expounds by a long inductive argument.   He cites instances from every age, from
every climate and from every soil, to show that there is
everywhere a tendency for population to increase faster than
the means of subsistence increase; and he draws from it the
inevitable conclusion that the anxiety which politicians displayed, to provide conditions for the growth of population as
an element in national power, was quite illusory.   The difficulty was not in the birth-rate, but in the raising of children
to be efficient men and women; a low rate of infant mortality
seemed to him to be on the whole the best guarantee for a
sound and well-nourished population.

*Special
circum-
stances of
the times
when he
wrote.*
The conditions of society, at the time when Malthus wrote,
were such as to render the truth of his principle obvious
when once it was stated.   On the one side there was the
greatest difficulty in procuring additional means of subsistence; the war made it difficult for us to buy more with our
increasing manufactures; and though agriculturists were busy
in ploughing up waste ground and taking in a larger area for
the cultivation of wheat, they were experiencing greater and
*Food
supply
limited.*
greater difficulty in adding to the regular produce.   The
means of subsistence could only be procured with an increasing strain, that we find it hard to understand in days when
the powers of purchasing food are so freely used, and the skill
in producing it has advanced so far beyond anything that
Malthus knew.   In his days, and so far as the outlook could

---

[1] Compare also W. Wales, *Inquiry* (1781), pp. 85, 67.
[2] *Parl. Hist.* xix. 599; xxi. 1086.

be forecast, he was justified in urging that the available A.D. 1776 means of subsistence were being increased but slowly, if $^{-1815}$ at all.

With population it was different. The rapid develop- *Rapid increase* ment of cotton-spinning had called new towns into existence; *of population.* and the newly-expanding industries were, as Sir James Steuart foresaw, stimulating the development of population. Besides this, there was an accidental and unwholesome stimulus given by the arrangements of the poor law. The allowances per head, per child, rendered it a distinctly profitable speculation for the ordinary labourer to marry, and claim parish assistance for his offspring; and there was every reason to fear that the eighteen-penny children would replenish the whole land with hereditary paupers. On every hand it was obvious that population was increasing; and that the numbers which were added were brought into the world without any real attempt to provide, by additional effort, for their subsistence.

The circumstances of the times conspired to render the tendency, which Malthus noted, specially dominant; at his time and under the existing circumstances it was working in the fashion that he describes. He regarded the tendency for *Possibility of moral* population to increase as a physical force which could only be *control re-* effectually controlled by a stronger sense of duty acting under *cognised.* better social conditions. He was a little apt to underrate the contributory circumstances that might tend to modify[1] the recklessness he deplored; but he never forgot that the impulse was one that was susceptible of moral control. He has managed, however, to leave a somewhat different impression of his doctrine, by formulating it as if it were a law of *Doctrine was formu-* physical nature, that population tended to increase faster *lated as if* than the means of subsistence increase. The preventive *it were a law of* checks, which are brought to bear by rational self-control, do *physical* not occupy so prominent a place in his essay as to have suffi- *nature* ciently attracted the attention of his readers. At a time of rapid transition and extreme fluidity, rational foresight has little to go upon, and it could not prove an effective force during the industrial revolution. Hence it follows that

[1] On his controversy with Arthur Young, see above, p. 506.

A.D. 1776
—1815.
Malthus, looking at the circumstances of his own day, formulated the principles of population in terms which give an exaggerated impression of the remorselessness of the tendency for a redundant population to arise. What he said *and re- quires more careful statement.* was fully justified in his day; but circumstances have so far changed since, that the mode of statement he adopted needs to be modified if we would put, in simplest form, the truth about the increase of population as it generally occurs[1]. We may see that there were in his day unwonted obstacles to procuring food by human exertion, whether directed to industry or to tillage; while there were, both in the development of the factories and in the nature of the poor-relief, unusual hindrances to the operation of the preventive checks. It was little wonder that population sprang forward apace, or that the truth of his doctrine was so terribly confirmed, when the death-rate of the factory towns, and the visit of the cholera, demonstrated the potency of the positive checks.

Doctrine of Rent   354. The doctrine of rent was another point in regard to which great advances were made soon after the publication of the *Wealth of Nations*. There is a certain want of clearness in Adam Smith's treatment of rent; partly because he deals with such cases as the rent of mines, the rent of fisheries, and competition rent for land, as if the principles which determined them were similar; and partly because he has, as is so often the case, by the use of a careless phrase shown that he has not completely grasped a subject on which he made many interesting remarks.

of Mines,   He was aware that mines might be worked which were just on the margin and which yielded no rent, but such mines were, in Scotland at least, only worked by the owners[2].

of Arable Land.   It is obviously the case that there might be land which was in a similar condition, and indeed Adam Smith has recognised this explicitly. If the ordinary price is more than sufficient to replace the stock employed in bringing corn to market together with the ordinary profits " the surplus part of it will naturally go to the rent of land. If it is not more, though the commodity may be brought to market, it can afford no rent to the landlord, whether the price is, or

[1] See my *Path towards Knowledge*, p. 25.   [2] Book I. ch. XI. pt. 2, p. 70.

is not, more depends upon the demand[1]." He therefore sees A.D. 1776
—1815. clearly that rent " enters into the composition of the price of commodities in a different way from wages and profit. High *Rent and the Price* or low wages and profit are the causes of high or low price; *of Corn.* high or low rent is the effect of it. It is because high or low wages and profit must be paid, in order to bring a particular commodity to market, that its price is high or low. But it is because its price is high or low, a great deal more, or very little more, or no more, than what is sufficient to pay those wages and profit, that it affords a high rent, or a low rent, or no rent at all."

He was, however, of opinion that, owing to the pressure *The de-mand for food and rent.* of population, food was always in such demand that it could be sold at a price which afforded a rent. He does not state this without guarding it somewhat. "Land," he says, "in almost any situation, produces a greater quantity of food than what is sufficient to maintain all the labour necessary for bringing it to market, * * * and to replace the stock which employed that labour, together with its profits. Something, therefore, always remains for a rent to the land-lord[2]." Wherever corn is habitually and regularly produced it is probable that there is some rent. Adam Smith can hardly have meant to deny, what was certainly familiar to Sir James Steuart and is rarely forgotten by British farmers, that it is possible to grow corn at a loss. What he did not understand, was the physical fact of the law of diminishing return, and the indications it affords as to the point where corn-growing ceases to be remunerative and the calculation of economic rent begins.

Shortly after the *Wealth of Nations* was published, the *James Anderson.* doctrine of rent was stated with great clearness by James Anderson, a man whose name is inseparably connected with agricultural improvement in Scotland, just as that of Arthur Young is associated with rural progress in England. In 1777 there was a violent discussion in Scotland on the question of a proposed corn-law, which should give bounties on exporta- *Political and* tion similar to those which had existed in England since the Revolution. Anderson intervened between the angry disput-

---

[1] Book I. ch. xi. pt. 1, p. 61.   [2] *Ib.* p. 61.

ants, and endeavoured to allay the mutual jealousies of the landed and trading interests, but incidentally in the footnotes he gives an excellent exposition of the doctrine of rent. The course of agricultural improvement, with consequent changes of rental, was running its course in Scotland with great rapidity, and Anderson had almost as good opportunities for examining into competition rents, as Franklin had for noting the growth of population. It is, of course, obvious that, till the era of agricultural improvement, economic rent hardly existed at all; only the surplus corn was taken to market; the farmer prosecuted his business for subsistence and not as a trade; whereas the theory of rent assumes that it is dealing with farms of which the produce

is taken to market. The rentals of the small farmers were probably connected, in their genesis, with quit-rents; and these with the services which were due from the villan on the lord's demesne; they were of the nature of a tax rather than a competition rent. But at the time when the old conditions of life were changing and rents were rising with great rapidity, or to put it in another way, when the new husbandry and economic rents were being substituted for subsistence-husbandry and quit-rents, there were unexampled opportunities for observing the causes to which variations in economic rent were due. This Anderson was able to do, and he states his results with great clearness in language which is worth quoting at some length as the original of his hasty pamphlet[1] is one of the rarest of economic tracts.

"It is not, however, the rent of the land that determines the price of its produce, but it is the price of that produce which determines the rent of the land; although the price of that produce is often highest in those countries where the rent of land is lowest. This seems to be a paradox that deserves to be explained.

"In every country there is a demand for as much grain as is sufficient to maintain all its inhabitants; and as that grain cannot be brought from other countries but at a considerable expence, on some occasions at a most exorbitant charge, it usually happens, that the inhabitants find it most to their

---

[1] James Anderson, *Enquiry into the nature of the Corn Laws* (1777), p. 45 n.

interest to be fed by the produce of their own soil. But the price at which that produce can be afforded by the farmer varies considerably in different circumstances.

" In every country there is a variety of soils, differing considerably from one another in point of fertility. These we shall at present suppose arranged into different classes, which we shall denote by the letters A. B. C. D. E. F. etc., the class A. comprehending the soils of the greatest fertility, and the other letters expressing different classes of soils, gradually decreasing in fertility as you recede from the first. Now, as the expence of cultivating the least fertile soil is as great, or greater than that of the 'most fertile field; it necessarily follows, that if an equal quantity of corn, the produce of each field, can be sold at the same price, the profit on cultivating the most fertile soil must be much greater than that of cultivating the others; and as this continues to decrease as the fertility increases, it must at length happen, that the expense of cultivating some of the inferior classes will equal the value of the whole produce.

" This being premised, let us suppose, that the class F. includes all those fields whose produce in oat-meal, if sold at fourteen shillings per boll, would be just sufficient to pay the expense of cultivating them, without affording any rent at all: that the class E. comprehended those fields, whose produce, if sold at thirteen shillings per boll, would free the charges, without affording any rent; and that in like manner the classes D. C. B. and A. consisted of fields, whose produce, if sold respectively at twelve, eleven, ten, and nine shillings per boll, would exactly pay the charge of culture, without any rent.

" Let us now suppose that all the inhabitants of the country, where such fields are placed, could be sustained by the produce of the first four classes, viz. A. B. C. and D. It is plain, that if the average selling price of oat-meal in that country was twelve shillings per boll, those who possessed the fields D. could just afford to cultivate them, without paying any rent at all; so that if there were no other produce of the fields that could be reared at a smaller expense than corn, the farmer could afford no rent whatever to the proprietor for them. And if so, no rents could be afforded for the fields E. and F.; nor could the utmost avarice of the proprietor in this case extort a rent for them. In these circumstances, however, it is obvious, that the farmer who possessed the fields in the class C. could pay the expense of cultivating them, and also afford to the proprietor a rent equal to one shilling for every boll of their produce; and in like manner the possessors of the fields B. and A. could afford a rent equal to two and three shillings per boll of their produce respectively. Nor would the proprietors of these fields find any difficulty in obtaining these rents; because farmers, finding they could live equally well upon such soils, though paying these rents, as they could do upon the fields D. without any rent at all, would be equally willing to take the one as the other.

"But let us again suppose, that the whole produce of the fields A. B. C. and D. was not sufficient to maintain the whole of the inhabitants. If the average selling price should continue at twelve shillings per boll, as none of the fields E. or F. could admit of being cultivated, the inhabitants would be under the necessity of bringing grain from some other country, to supply their wants. But if it should be found, that grain could not be brought from that other country, at an average, under thirteen shillings per boll, the price in the home-market would rise to that rate; so that the fields E. could then be brought into culture, and those of the class D. could afford a rent to the proprietor equal to what was formerly yielded by C. and so on of others; the rents of every class rising in the same proportion. If these fields were sufficient to maintain the whole of the inhabitants, the price would remain permanently at thirteen shillings; but if there was still a deficiency, and if that could not be made up for less than fourteen shillings per boll, the price would rise in the market to that rate; in which case the field F. might also be brought into culture, and the rents of all the others would rise in proportion.

"To apply this reasoning to the present case, it appears, that the people in the Lothians can be maintained by the produce of the fields A. B. C. D. and E., but the inhabitants of Clydesdale require also the produce of the fields F.; so that the one is under the necessity of giving, at an average, one shilling per boll more for meal than the other.

" Let us now suppose, that the gentlemen of Clydesdale, from an extraordinary exertion of patriotism, and an inordinate desire to encourage manufactures, should resolve to lower the rents, so as to demand nothing from those who possessed the fields E., as well as those of the class F., and should allow the rents of all the others to sink in proportion; would the prices of grain fall in consequence of this? By no means. The inhabitants are still in need of the whole produce of the fields F. as before, and are under the necessity of paying the farmer of these fields such a price as to enable him to cultivate them. He must therefore still receive fourteen shillings per boll as formerly. And as the grain from the fields E. D. C. B. and A. are at least equally good, the occupiers of such of these fields would receive the same price for their produce. The only consequence, then, that would result from this Quixot scheme would be the enriching one class of farmers at the expense of their proprietors, without producing the smallest benefit to the consumers of grain— perhaps the reverse, as the industry of these farmers might be slackened by this measure.

" If, on the other hand, by any political arrangement, the price of oat-meal should be there reduced from fourteen to thirteen shillings per boll, it would necessarily follow, that all the fields of the class F. would be abandoned by the plough, and the rents of the others would fall of course; but with that fall of rent, the quantity of grain produced would be diminished, and the inhabitants would be reduced to the necessity of depending on others for their daily bread. Thus it appears, that the rents are not at all arbitrary, but depend on the market-price of grain; which, in its turn, depends upon the effective demand that is for it, and the fertility of the soil in the district where it is raised; so that lowering of rents alone could never have the effect of rendering grain cheaper. But as fields, which were originally in the lowest classes, may, by good culture, be so far improved, as in time to rank among those of a higher class, if proper measures are pursued to give stability to the markets, and due encouragement to the farmer, it will naturally happen, that the price of grain will gradually fall lower than before, while the rents may also rise. And as this effect can never be produced but in consequence of spirited agriculture, it follows, that the only practicable means of lowering the price of grain to manufacturers, and, at the same time, of improving the revenue of landed gentlemen, is to give stability to the market, and security to the farmer; which would be much promoted by an equitable system of corn-laws.

"A necessary inference that follows from the foregoing reasoning is, that if manufactures flourish in any particular district more than formerly, so as to make the population encrease, there will of course be an encreased demand for provisions. But if agriculture has not been duly encouraged, so as to promote improvements in that art, (I call that only an improvement in agriculture, when any particular field is made to afford more sustenance to man on an average of years, than it did formerly), there will be a necessity of raising the market-price of grain so high, as to pay for the expense of cultivating more barren fields, (suppose those of the class G.) to supply the encreasing demand.

"But if the population should thus increase, and if, instead of giving a higher encouragement to agriculture, or raising the price of grain, the inhabitants, by any political regulation, should contrive to diminish, for a time, the price of grain, while the demand for manufactures continued as before, the profits reaped by the manufacturers would become so disproportionately great, that servants, and others employed in the labours of agriculture would betake themselves to manufactures, unless the farmers gave them as much wages as they could obtain at these other employments. In consequence of this, the fields which were formerly in the class D. would be pushed back to the class E. and so on of others; so that it would be impossible to rear nearly the same quantity of grain as formerly, even if the price continued the same as before, and the manufacturers would be under the necessity of giving a much higher price for their grain, so as to diminish their own profits, and drive off the labourers to agriculture again, before they could be supplied abundantly A.D. 1776 —1815. with food. But if, instead of thus foolishly attempting to work impossibilities a regulation was adopted, by which agriculture should receive a steady support, farmers would gradually render their fields more fertile than formerly, so as to make those of the class F. come in time to pass successively through the classes E. D. and C. etc. perhaps to A.; in consequence of which, the quantity of grain produced, would become fully sufficient to maintain the whole of the inhabitants, and at a smaller expense also. The farmer, therefore, might have equal profit, although he should at the same time pay an advanced rent for his lands, and sell its produce at a lower rate than formerly. In this manner it appears, that by adopting judicious measures, both agriculture and manufactures may be encouraged. Farmers may become more opulent and independent, the price of grain may be made to decrease, and the rents to encrease at the same time."

355. Anderson's statement of the principle of rent is admirable so far as it goes; it deals with the effects due to varieties of soil; but he makes no reference to the diminishing return from land[1]; this was an additional element in the classical doctrine on the subject, as stated by Ricardo. The *Ricardo and* agricultural conditions of this time were so very special, that they brought into clear relief the economic relationships between landlord and tenant in modern England. As the work of agricultural improvement progressed, the fact of the diminishing return from land must have been rendered more obvious; and what few could have noticed at all in 1770, was apprehended by more than one observer during the Revolutionary and Napoleonic Wars; and the doctrine of rent was at once recognised as a true account of the phenomena, when it was stated by Ricardo and published in the forefront of his *Principles* in 1817. It is commonly said of Ricardo, that he was exceedingly abstract in his mode of treating a subject; and if this means that he lays stress on prominent features and ignores minor corrections, it is true, as he himself recognised in correspondence with Malthus; but it is also true

[1] See Professor Gonner's Introduction to his edition of Ricardo's *Principles*, p. liv.

A.D. 1776
·—1815.
the special
circum-
stances of
his time.
that when he wrote of agriculture or anything else, he wrote of it with full and special consideration of the circumstances under which it was carried on in his own day. Ricardo's theory of rent is peculiarly a theory of English agricultural rent in the long war and at the peace; for other times and other places it, of course, needs correction, but it was exceedingly true to life, when it was given to the world.

In the first place there was the single market which governed the price of corn; the war and legislation marked out this realm, as a circle within which the home producer had a monopoly; and as farming had become, throughout the country generally, a trade rather than a means of procuring subsistence, the fundamental condition of competition was present. Apparently, too, there were plenty of speculators who were ready to promise high rents, and to go into farming when land fell vacant, so that the influence of prices in causing high rents might have been a matter of daily experience. Even the social limitations on competition, of which so much is sometimes said, were entirely insignificant; as tenant-farmers only became voters in 1832, a man's political opinions would not directly affect him in competing for a farm. There was, on the one hand, a well-defined and similar market for corn; and on the other, holdings were let by competition.

It is well to remember too that the form of expression used by Ricardo might have been suggested by the actual occurrences of his time. Farming in 1815 was still largely extensive; a fall of prices resulted immediately in certain
land going out of cultivation. If prices rose again it might be predicted with certainty that the same land would be brought back again into cultivation. It was thus perfectly possible to point out the land that was on the margin of cultivation and which paid no rent. Now that land is carefully prepared and drained, and the soil made, the conditions are very different; and the language which applied to a time when most English farming was still extensive, is not exactly suitable to modern conditions when tillage is so highly intensive[1]. In bad times land may fall out of condition, but not immediately out of cultivation.

[1] Prothero, 104.

Ricardo then, highly abstract though his mode of state- A.D. 1776
—1815.
ment was, could not but pay his debt to the features of his
time. He wrote when *laissez faire* was most dominant in the *Laissez*
minds of ordinary men; and he was justified in assuming it *faire.*
as the ordinary condition; he was only concerned with the
broad features of society, and this was of obvious importance.
There was no reason to anticipate any marked change, either
in the condition of society, or the methods of agriculture;
and Ricardo wrote of them in terms that were suitable to his
own times; his language is abstract, but for all that, it is true
to life[1]. His way of viewing things may be one-sided, but he
moved on the very flood tide of a strong wave of sentiment
that affected all sides of industrial phenomena and is only
reflected in his writings. Through his work, the word rent
has come to have a precise economic significance; and we
may be grateful to him for doing so much, even though the
variations of high and low rents in new countries or in recent
times cannot be completely explained without taking account
of factors of which he was unaware.

356. Important contributions were made to the doctrine *The Bul-*
of currency at this time by the investigations of the Bullion *mittee.* *lion Com-*
Committee, as well as by the Earl of Liverpool, whose
Treatise on the Coins of the Realm is still the standard
work on the subject. There was much admirable writing
on many topics by different authors, but Malthus and
Ricardo are the two figures which stand out above all
the rest; and the very differences between them, comparatively slight as they were for practical purposes, are
not unimportant in connection with the history of economic
doctrine. They differed in regard to questions of method;
and the practice of Ricardo in regard to the best manner of
conducting economic investigations has left an indelible im- *Economic*
pression on all subsequent writers. *Method.*

Malthus was strictly inductive in the manner in which he *Malthus.*
proved the principle which is associated with his name. It
was a principle which had a direct bearing on questions of
practical administration; and in all other parts of economic
study Malthus was anxious to keep in close touch with actual

---

[1] West's mode of stating the principle seems much less affected by the special
conditions of his times. *Essay on the application of Capital to Land*, p. 10.

life. He had a keen sense of the importance of attending to minor and modifying conditions, and he had the English love of what is practical. On all these grounds he regarded his friend's writings with some hesitation and regret[1]; as they concentrated attention on certain phenomena, in a way that seemed to give rise to exaggeration, and to secure apparent clearness at the expense of a loss of truth.

Ricardo's method

Ricardo's mode of investigating economic phenomena was doubtless due in great part to his own habit of mind[2]; he spoke of it indeed, modestly enough, as a personal defect. But he took the ground which was necessary if Political Economy was to make real and continuous advance. Even as treated by Adam Smith, the subject of study was very wide and very complicated; the only hope of obtaining precision and clearness was to isolate certain portions of the field, and study them by themselves. It was impossible to name all the various factors aright, or to assign them their due importance in the actual world; even Malthus, with all his care, did not escape at least the appearance of exaggera-

hypotheti-cal and deductive.

tion. Under these circumstances it seemed wisest to proceed hypothetically, to make certain assumptions as to society, and to follow out what would be true on these assumptions[3]. His method was thus properly *deductive*, as he reached his conclusions by arguing from certain assumptions, and by this means he was able to impart great force to his demonstrations and to reach conclusions which were set forth with unusual clearness. In so far as the assumptions with which he started were true in fact, in so far were his conclusions also true as descriptions of dominant tendencies in actual society.

Doctrine of Value.

Of the gain in precision of definition and accuracy of thought which has been secured by Ricardo and his followers there can be no doubt; the whole meaning of value, and of other fundamental notions, has been set in clearer light by their efforts; and no wise man will underrate the advantages which accrue to any study from an accurate terminology[4].

---

[1] *Quarterly Review*, Vol. xxx. 307 (Jan. 1824).

[2] Price, *Political Economy in England*, 67.

[3] Senior, *Four Introductory Lectures*, 62.

[4] There has been an apparent reaction against Ricardo and accuracy of language in recent times (Bagehot, *Economic Studies*, p. 49). Mathematicians are apt to take mathematical symbols as the instruments of their own thinking, and then use any

It is only by such means that we can secure accurate descrip- tions of the phenomena we wish to explain, or precise terms in which to state the nature of the causes at work.

Ricardo's method has, however, been the subject of attack *Opposition to Ricardo.* from two opposite sides. Since it is hypothetical, it serves admirably for purposes of investigation; but when the economist comes forward to state his results, he appears to do so in a tentative fashion. There is a want of force about what he has to say, because it only professes to be true on certain conditions. This was a defect which was strongly felt by Nassau Senior. He had served on more than one of the *Senior.* great Commissions which investigated the condition of the artisans, and he was firmly convinced that they were, as a class, ignorant of the great economic forces which were actually at work, and that they were bringing unnecessary misery on themselves by their vain efforts to oppose the prevailing tendencies by futile expedients for limiting production and so raising wages. To him it seemed necessary that economic doctrines should be stated as truths of actual life[1], not merely as conclusions from hypothetical premises, so that their importance might be brought home to the minds of Englishmen of all classes, as forcibly as possible.

On the other hand it has been more commonly alleged that Ricardo and his followers have erred on the side of dogmatism, and have put forward statements as of universal validity which were only plausible, for a very brief period, and were not actually true even then. This is the sort of exaggeration to which Professor Thorold Rogers[2] and other *Thorold Rogers.* historians have been inclined to take exception, and there is some excuse for this criticism, as Ricardo was never sufficiently careful to state the precise nature of the hypotheses he assumed[3]. For the most part they seemed to be obvious facts, which were very generally true in England at the time. *Importance of stating the hypotheses.* And what was true of Ricardo, has been true of some of his

---

language that seems to serve to express their results. If Economists are to keep in touch with the public, they will do well to make the most accurate use they can of the words which are to ordinary men the habitual instruments of thought.

[1] *Four Introductory Lectures*, 63.

[2] Rogers on Ricardo's theory of Rent. *Economic Interpretation of History*, 161.

[3] Marshall, *Principles of Economics*, 218.

followers. They have assumed "free competition," without being careful to define what they meant by it; indeed, Bagehot seems to have been the first of the Post-Ricardian Economists to recognise that it was even desirable to state clearly the postulates which had been assumed[1]. The deductive arguments of Ricardo, from his assumed premises, were unnecessarily general in form; they gave conclusions, which had a universal validity from the supposed premises, and which appeared to be generalisations as to actual fact when the premises were merely implied and not properly expressed. By neglecting to state their assumptions fully, Ricardo and his followers laid themselves open to the charge of dogmatising, from the dominant conditions of their own day, in regard to economic phenomena in all places and at all times.

Political Economy and Physical Science.
It is here that we may see the precise nature of the difference between Political Economy and those mechanical and physical sciences which it so closely resembles in form. The assumption they make, the existence of gravitation, holds good for all human experience; the assumptions of the economist are for the most part only plausible for very narrow areas and very brief periods, and therefore the principles he teaches only hold good for a very limited range of human experience. Human society and human nature as affected by institutions, have changed so much, that there is hardly any statement that can be made in regard to Englishmen for several centuries, so as to enable us to use the Ricardian method with advantage unless for very brief periods.

Error of Hasty Generalisation
As a matter of fact, however, Ricardo hit upon the only method by which there is a definite security against such dogmatism, though he did not adhere to it strictly. There is always a danger of hasty generalisation, and no writers have sinned more grievously in this respect, than those who from the time of Massie onwards have devoted themselves to the study of Economic History. We may misread the present in the light of the past as he did; or we may be guilty of the grossest anachronism by reading experience derived from the present into accounts of occurrences that are long past. The one safeguard against false generalisation lies in *carefully stating the hypothesis on which*

[1] *Economic Studies*, 21.

we proceed; so long as this is done there is little danger of exaggeration, as we are also stating the limits within which our conclusion is valid. Whenever the hypothesis fails, the conclusion is simply irrelevant. We may assume if we like that all the corn in a certain area is grown for sale and brought to our market; we can then follow out and explain the variations of rent within that area with perfect clearness; but our results will be simply irrelevant to any place or time, when corn is not grown for sale, and not brought to market. The clear statement of the conditions implied in Ricardo's doctrine of rent is also the statement of limits to its relevancy.

A.D. 1776 —1815. *and means of guarding against it.*

Ricardo's method is admirable as an instrument of investigation at any place or time; but it is liable to be misunderstood, unless care is taken to state the premises which are assumed as well as the conclusions derived from them. Carelessness in this matter has brought the Political Economy of Ricardo into disrepute, not merely with historians, but with moralists. It has been spoken of as a selfish science which preaches selfishness; to some extent this charge is due to the line which some economists, from the time of Defoe, have taken on the stimulating effect of need. But it is also due, in part, to the manner in which Ricardo and his followers have made use of the principle of free competition. Had it been more clear that the force of individual self-interest was merely assumed for the convenience of study, that the results attained only held good in so far as this principle was dominant, there would have been less misunderstanding. Economists should have made it clear that self-seeking was not a thing which they advocated, and that they were ready to make any other assumption in regard to human nature, if that nature so changed that some other assumption was more convenient. Had this been clear it would have been obvious that the principles of Political Economy were in no sense inconsistent with efforts to improve human nature. Unfortunately it was not possible for Ricardo and his followers to make this clear to others, because they did not keep it clearly before their own minds. Bastiat did apparently think that, owing to some pre-ordained harmony, the deliberate pursuit

Popular misunderstandings of Ricardo.

Self-interest.

of self-interest was wholly admissible; and all the economists of the early part of this century exaggerated the importance of the force of self-interest they had assumed. They held that it was practically supreme; and were blind to the important demonstration which the newly-formed Trades Unions were giving of the willingness of thousands of men to postpone the pursuit of their own individual interest for the advantage of the class to which they belonged.

Unfortunately the hypothetical character of economic laws was entirely forgotten by many of those who were engaged in the work of legislation; they habitually spoke as if they were in possession of principles which would serve to give direct practical guidance in regard to all the economic problems they had to face. They congratulated themselves on possessing knowledge of which the benighted past had been ignorant, and they cheerfully swept away the system that its wisdom had framed. Lord Mansfield condemned the Statute of Apprentices as "against the natural rights and contrary to the common law rights of the land[1]." The clauses which concerned the assessment of wages were repealed in 1813[2]; Lord Sidmouth[3] only thought it necessary to allude to the 'pernicious consequences' of such a law, as obvious to every one, and it seems to have found no defender. The apprenticeship clauses could not be treated so contemptuously; hundreds of petitions poured from all parts of the country[4] in favour of amending and retaining the system, as Mr Rose proposed; it was even the subject of a committee[5], but in the then temper of Parliament[6] the result was a foregone conclusion, and Sergeant Onslow succeeded in forcing the system of natural liberty upon the country[7].

---

[1] Quoted by Mr Thompson, *Parl. Debates*, XXVII. 881.

[2] 53 Geo. III. c. 40.   [3] *Parl. Debates*, XXV. 595.

[4] And from all sorts of different trades. 300,000 signatures were in favour of the law being maintained and 2000 for its repeal. *Parl. Debates*, XXVII. 574.

[5] The evidence adduced was so strong that the Chairman, Mr Rose, apparently changed his view on the subject. *Parl. Debates*, XXVII. 570.

[6] Chalmers (*Estimates*, p. 36) expresses the current view. "This law, as far as it requires apprenticeships, ought to be repealed; because its tendency is to abridge the liberty of the subject, and to prevent competition among workmen." The true interests of a manufacturing community "can alone be effectually promoted by competition, which hinders the rise of wages among workmen, and promotes at once the goodness and cheapness of the manufacture."

[7] 54 Geo. III. c. 96.

PART III. 1815—1846.

XVIII. PRACTICAL INFLUENCE OF THE NEW IDEAS.

357. The long continued war had rendered inevitable A.D. 1815-
a number of measures which were proposed and defended —1846.
as temporary expedients. Such was the suspension of cash *our econo-*
payments which was continued from time to time; while the *mic policy.*
Corn Law of 1815 was intended to grant relief by breaking
the violence of an anticipated change. But at the close of
the war, it was necessary to recast our policy and to adopt
some scheme which should tend to the permanent well-
being of the country. That some changes were necessary
was obvious; and hence the men who had adopted the new
Political Economy, had an unexampled opportunity of making
their influence felt. The years of European peace mark a
period when the doctrinaires were able to carry their theories
into practice, and to recast the whole of our industrial and
commercial policy in accordance with the views propounded
in the *Wealth of Nations.*

They were accustomed to speak of the defects and *The Mer-*
failures of the Mercantile System, and to demand that its last *cantile
System.*
vestiges should be swept away. In this demand they were
probably right; not however because the Mercantile System
had failed, but because the Mercantile System had so completely succeeded in fostering England's greatness and power
that our industrial life had outgrown its old limits; what
had once been useful supports had come to be unnecessary
limitations. The mercantile policy was no longer conducive
to further development, but it had not been a failure. It
would have been rightly condemned as such if English
resources had remained undeveloped under its sway; but
there was no failure in a scheme under which they developed
so fast.

At the same time the policy on which England was
now entering was a complete reversal of that which had

A.D. 1815
—1846.

been maintained, fitfully at first, and then deliberately for four hundred years. It was a complete reversal of principle and not merely of details; and it differs from all previous

Doctrin-aire Re-action. developments of economic policy, inasmuch as the new views were not a matter of experience; they had been argued out in the study and were now applied in actual life, often in opposition to the wishes and arguments of men who had a practical knowledge of affairs. We may see the direct influence of new ideas, as we can hardly trace it in the growth of the Mercantile System; that seems to have grown up piecemeal and slowly, as our own experience, or the experience of other nations, taught us to adopt one part after another. The implied principles were only recognised by subsequent reflection on expedients that had been found to answer, and it was not till the time of Walpole that they were deliberately applied to the whole of our tariffs. But with the doctrines of Adam Smith it was different, they had been stated as economic principles; and a knot of busy and hard-hearted men set themselves to form our practice in accordance with the system of natural liberty. De Tocqueville[1] has pointed out, that the French Revolution was the work of the Girondists, and if the doctrinaire influence in England was less violent, it was almost as powerful and as impatient of any obstacles that delayed its progress.

The contrast between the old and the new view may be most clearly indicated if we attend to two particular points. One has been already discussed in treating of the special

National Power and National Wealth. characteristic of Adam Smith. The Mercantilists aimed primarily at increasing relative power,—the modern economists thought chiefly of the increase of wealth. So long as relative power was the principal aim, so long was there necessarily a jealousy of other nations and an unwillingness to connive at their prosperity, unless we saw our way to a greater gain than others from mutual trade. We have already seen something of the length to which this jealousy was carried in the *British Merchant;* and it assumes more curious forms in the writings of moralists and literary men like Dr Johnson[2], who seemed to hold that in every bargain

---

[1] De Tocqueville, 269.   [2] Boswell's *Life of Johnson,* vi. 56.

one man gained what another lost and that English traders could only make a profit by conscientiously setting themselves to cheat foreigners. These exaggerations may have lent force to the reaction; according to the new views each of the merchants who traded, and both commercial nations, gained wherever an exchange of products and goods was carried on. From this point of view all intercourse with other nations was advantageous; we would be sure to benefit to some extent; it was unnecessary, and childish even if it were possible, to try to estimate which was the greater gainer. National power is relative to the power of other nations; but all may co-operate to enjoy larger shares of the necessaries and conveniences of life without thereby impoverishing any of their number[1].

[1] This doctrine appears in Dudley North's *Discourses upon Trade* (1691), but it seems to have attracted little attention at the time. "That the whole World as to Trade is but as one Nation or People, and therein Nations are as Persons. That the loss of a Trade with one Nation is not that only, separately considered, but so much of the Trade of the World rescinded and lost, for all is combined together. That there can be no Trade unprofitable to the Public, for if any prove so, men leave it off: and wherever the Traders thrive, the Public, of which they are a part, thrives also. That to force men to deal in any prescribed manner, may profit such as happen to serve them, but the Public gains not, because it is taking from one subject to give another." *Preface* in *Political Economy Club Tracts on Commerce*, p. 513. Adam Smith's statement is of course classical (*Wealth of Nations*, IV. 3, p. 201), "The wealth of neighbouring nations, however, though dangerous in war and politics, is certainly advantageous in trade. In a state of hostility; it may enable our enemies to maintain fleets and armies superior to our own; but in a state of peace and commerce it must likewise enable them to exchange with us to a greater value, and to afford a better market, either for the immediate produce of our own industry, or for whatever is purchased with that produce. As a rich man is likely to be a better customer to the industrious people in his neighbourhood, than a poor, so is likewise a rich nation. A rich man, indeed, who is himself a manufacturer, is a very dangerous neighbour to all those who deal in the same way. All the rest of the neighbourhood, however, by far the greatest number, profit by the good market which his expense affords them. They even profit by his underselling the poorer workmen who deal in the same way with him. The manufacturers of a rich nation, in the same manner, may no doubt be very dangerous rivals to those of their neighbours. This very competition, however, is advantageous to the great body of the people, who profit greatly, besides, by the good market which the great expense of such a nation affords them in every other way. Private people, who want to make a fortune, never think of retiring to the remote and poor provinces of the country, but resort either to the capital, or to some of the great commercial towns. They know, that where little wealth circulates, there is little to be got; but that where a great deal is in motion, some share of it may fall to them. The same maxim which would in this manner direct the common sense of one, or ten, or twenty individuals, should regulate the judgment of one, or ten, or twenty millions, and should make a whole nation regard the

A.D. 1815
—1846.

Effect of our maritime supremacy.

This doctrine was readily promulgated, as circumstances had so far changed that expedients for maintaining our power were but little thought of. We had no European rivals either in the East or the West; our maritime power appeared to be supreme; and the more freedom there was for the expansion of our commerce, the more would it tend to the development of our shipping. Our manufactures too, commanded the markets of the world, and the more these markets were opened the greater would be the stimulus to employment at home. So far as commerce and industry were concerned, the older scheme of policy was left without a position to defend; and the views of the doctrinaires received the support of the commercial and manufacturing interests.

England as a self-suf-ficing country

and trade as affording a vent for our sur-plus.

358. The contrast between the new views and the old may perhaps become clearer if we consider them, not with respect to the relations between trading nations, but with respect to the development of English resources. The old scheme of policy had been based on the land,—the physical resources of Great Britain. It had sought to make the most of them, by encouraging agriculture, and to amplify them by rapid communication with dependencies from which deficiencies might be supplied. Our staple manufacture was based on the product of the flocks; a large part of our trade consisted of the export of our mineral wealth, and for many years our corn had been regularly shipped abroad. The maintenance of population, and of rapid communication with our dependencies, had all been intended as a means of rendering the country completely self-sufficing; trade had been valued chiefly as a means of finding a vent for the surplus which we could not use at home. So long as this conception of trade dominates, there is little temptation to push the export trade in goods of any sort. Men desired to sell what could not be used at home and the whole of

riches of its neighbours, as a probable cause and occasion for itself to acquire riches. A nation that would enrich itself by foreign trade, is certainly most likely to do so, when its neighbours are all rich, industrious and commercial nations. A great nation, surrounded on all sides by wandering savages and poor barbarians, might, no doubt, acquire riches by the cultivation of its own lands, and by its own interior commerce, but not by foreign trade."

the elaborate system of exclusive companies had had its A.D. 1815
—1846. foundation in this idea; but gradually and insensibly we had passed to a new condition in which our prosperity no longer rested on the solid basis of land[1], but was shifted to the fluctuating basis of trade. Our land no longer yielded *New de-* a sufficient food-supply as a constancy; our manufacturers no *pendence on Trade.* longer worked up native products, but relied on obtaining materials from foreign parts. Every side of life was interpenetrated with foreign commerce; and the advocates of the new economy were really urging that we should adapt our legislation frankly and thoroughly to the new conditions, and give the freest possible scope to that trade which had become the most vital of national interests.

It was at this point that the advocates of the new views encountered opposition. The traditional policy had favoured the landed interest; and the corn laws had been intended to *Self-suf-* promote a sufficient food-supply and to maintain a regular *ficiency and the* price. They had failed to do either one or the other. Rapidly *Corn Laws.* as agriculture had improved, it had not overtaken the demands of the population; since there was no longer a surplus of native growth, for which a vent could be found in years of plenty, we had lost the means of controlling the price and keeping it steady. The best prospect of a regular supply at a steady price seemed now to lie in the opening of our ports to corn, drawn from as wide an area as possible. The landed interest failed to recognise that, since we had be- *The* come a corn-importing nation, the argument for agricultural *Landed Interest.* protection had entirely changed its character. Doubtless it would be a source of security if we could have continued to provide plenty of food from sources with which no hostile navy could interfere. But since we had, as a matter of fact, failed to preserve our independence in the matter of food, there was less reason for continuing a policy which had actually ceased to subserve any of the objects for which it was designed. It thus came about that the battle between the new schemes of policy and the old was fought out over the Corn Laws.

359. In attempting to estimate the political forces of

---

[1] Compare Cobden and Locke in my *Politics and Economics*, 107.

A.D. 1815
—1846.
the time, it is once more convenient to look, not at the actual legislation, which was more or less the result of compromise, but at the ideas which determined the direction of the constitutional changes. After the Reform Bill of 1832, the classes *The Reformed Parliament.* who had adopted Adam Smith's principles were dominant in Parliament, and they had the means of giving effect to their wishes in the repeal of the Corn Laws; but the play of the different political and social forces can hardly be understood, unless we look at the ideas which they embodied.

Current Political Doctrine and The current political doctrine of the day was completely congruent with Adam Smith's economic teaching; it assumed that the material well-being of the governed was the one object which government should keep in view; and this harmonised with principles, which had set wealth in the forefront and ignored national power as an independent aim. This view had a bearing on internal as well as external politics; it was reasonable to maintain that each individual knew his own interest best, that in pursuing his own interest, he accumulated most wealth for himself, and that in so far as each individual acted in this fashion the aggregate wealth of all individuals and the total wealth of the nation would in- *Laissez-Faire.* crease. There is thus a practical harmony between the *laissez-faire* principle in economics, and the demand for reformed representation in the House of Commons. This line of thought was followed by men like Bentham and Godwin and James Mill. It gave form to the arguments of political reformers and of the Anti-Corn Law League, and its successes in 1832 and 1846 were its chief achievements in practical politics.

Michael Sadler. There were of course men like Michael Sadler who entirely repudiated the whole of these principles; their conceptions of patriotic duty were entirely different, and they came into conflict at every point with the political and economic reforms. Their position, and their criticism of the successful school, are most instructive; we shall have to revert to it below in regard to particular doctrines. But for the present it may suffice to look more closely at the divisions among those who on the whole accepted an individualist standpoint, and for whom material welfare was the ultimate aim of *A.D. 1815 —1846.* political institutions. '

i. The special position of the Manchester School was *The Manchester School and Production* the view that individual interests did as a matter of fact so work together, that the greatest amount of national wealth was thereby produced. As economists, they were inclined to lay stress on the production of wealth, since this was really the increase of the national total. The distribution of wealth among the different citizens was of importance to private persons, but did not concern the nation as a whole. In this way they retained, and continued to use, much of the language in which earlier economists had denounced the selfish- *and class selfishness.* ness of certain classes,—the selfishness of the landed class in demanding protection, or the selfishness of the working class in combining to demand higher wages. Legislative interference, and special combination, alike appeared to conflict with the free play of individual competition; but it was, as they held, by individual competition that progress was made. Since capital had become the dominant factor alike in agriculture, in industry and trade, their ideal, as interpreted by actual circumstances, implied perfectly free play for capital, *Free Play for Capital.* which was the chief agent in increasing the national wealth. Any laws which affected the investment of capital in land and the application of capital to land, any movement which diminished the profits of capital and the inducements and opportunities of saving was to them a matter of regret.

It is easy to see that their views were really a scheme for taking advantage of existing circumstances, so as to promote the national wealth of England. There is nothing cosmopolitan about their views; though they desired to have free and frequent intercourse with the most distant lands. The whole of the older Radicalism, which represented the evils of the world as due to the iniquities of self-seeking rulers, tended to produce the shallow optimism of those who held that the wealth of the nation, and its greatness, would really flourish if we were in earnest with the principle of *laissez-faire* and allowed free play to individual interest.

ii. The most important dissentient from this view was *William Cobbett.* Cobbett. To him and the large masses who followed his

guidance, it was absurd to talk of the free play of individual interest in the State, so long as the great majority of the people were entirely unrepresented. For him, universal suffrage was the first step to be taken. If all interests were alike represented in Parliament, the material welfare of all would ensue; but as it seemed to him, there were many who were oppressed and who had no power of resistance, while *Productive* others recklessly squandered the national resources. It is *and Unpro-* here that we can trace the effect of Adam Smith's academic *ductive* here that we can trace the effect of Adam Smith's academic *Classes.* distinction between the productive and unproductive members of the community. Cobbett followed him in his denunciations of the costliness of the Established Church, and went beyond him in his dislike of National Debts. The monied men, who had invested in the funds, and the clergy with their increased incomes, appeared to him to be useless and costly classes. Financial reform in its widest sense was the object he hoped to gain by universal suffrage. This would be the means of securing cheap government and cheap religion, and thus of removing the burdens which oppressed the poor. Cobbett's principles were very similar to those of the Man-
Universal chester School, but he held that they could only be realised *Suffrage.* through an universal suffrage so that no interest might be neglected. The Manchester view was satisfied if the most powerful modern interest were free to get its own way.

The divergence between these two interpretations of similar principles became apparent in 1832. The middle classes, including the manufacturers and traders, were admitted to power; the working-classes were excluded, more completely excluded even than they had been before. The
Chartism. political aspirations of the working-classes seemed destined to disappointment, while the monied interest was more powerfully established than ever; by the partial measure of reform, the artisans had lost the fulcrum with which they had attempted to work. The cry for universal suffrage and for cheap government became the rallying-point of the Chartist agitation; and though it seemed to end in failure, it forms the foundation of much of artisan politics in the present day. Since Cobbett diverted much of the artisan intelligence to demand political representation as a means of material re-

dress, there was far less direct agitation in regard to social A.D. 1815 —1846.
grievances than might have been expected[1].

360. Besides these directly political movements, there *Moral influences.*
were moral influences at work which affected public opinion
and gave rise to important organisations and special legislation.

i. Men of many parties were agreed in desiring the *Education.*
spread of education[2]. This had been attended to more or less
in all ages as a pious duty from religious motives[3], but the
movement has received an extraordinary impulse since it was
taken up on secular grounds. The point of contact with the
dominant individualism is fairly obvious; the burning of *Riots and Machine destruction.*
ricks and the breaking of machinery in the Luddite riots
were generally condemned as the ebullitions of ignorant
passion; Cobbett did not attempt to defend them and the
Manchester School loudly denounced the outrages on property. It was said that the rioters failed to understand
where their true interest lay; and that education was the
means which would enable them to act not from short-sighted
passion, but from an enlightened self-interest. The education of the poor thus came to be undertaken on a large scale,
partly as a work of charity, and partly as a work to which the
governing classes applied themselves in mere self-defence.
Godwin had been one of the most effective advocates of the
diffusion of education, from the desire of letting the poor see
where their true interest lay[4]. The earliest efforts of government were deliberately confined to supplementing voluntary

[1] Held, 342, 386.

[2] The *Reports of the Society for bettering the Condition of the Poor* show an
increasing interest in this matter, especially as the Malthusian doctrine took firmer
hold, and the advantages of parochial charities, or cheap foods came to be
questioned. (See a paper read at the Oswestry Society, *Remarks on the Present
State of the Poor*; Brit. Mus. 8277, c. 1 (2), 1826). The formation of the British
School Society (1808) and the National Society (1811) is additional evidence of the
importance attached to it. The immediate effects promised well. "Last August
(1807), being at Rodburgh, in Gloucestershire, I inquired what effect had been
produced upon the inhabitants by the introduction of machinery into the woollen
manufactures of that valley, fearing to receive a very unfavourable report. But I
was informed that the poor manufacturers had lately become much more orderly,
sober, and industrious: and as a proof of the truth of this remark the landlord of
the Inn assured me that he now sold £300 worth less of ale and spirits in a year,
than he had done fourteen years ago. This change in the behaviour and morals of
the people he wholly ascribed to the effect of their education by dissenters." *Of the
Education of the Poor* (1809), p. 39. [Brit. Mus. 288, g. 17].

[3] See below, p. 665.   [4] *Political Justice*, I. 44. *Politics and Economics*, 95.

A.D. 1815
—1846.
*Govern-
ment
Grants.*

agency, and any other course appeared injurious[1].   In 1833
Lord Althorp secured some grants to defray the first cost of
elementary schools; and the great work of adult education
which was carried on in Mechanics' Institutes, though begun
somewhat earlier, received a new impulse at this time.

*Robert
Owen and
Co-opera-
tion.*

ii. Closely connected with this view of education, was
the movement which had its rise in the projects of Robert
Owen, and which has resulted in the growth of numerous Co-
operative Societies.   Robert Owen believed that even under
existing political arrangements there might be such a reorganisation of industry that the enlightened self-interest of
each would really conduce to the benefit of all. "To induce men
to adopt any system or mode of life, though even ever so novel
and contrary to their previous habits and prejudices, we conceive that nothing more is necessary than, with giving them
the means of making the adoption, to convince them that
their happiness, both immediate and future, as well as that
of all whom they held dear, would be essentially promoted
by it[2]." Robert Owen hoped to regenerate social life "through
education and mutual self-respect," and his ideals have been
fitfully cherished by Co-operators, while an appeal to self-
interest has been the basis of their success in proselytising.

*Beginnings
of Trade-
Unionism.*

iii. Far less popular, because far less in accord with
dominant opinion, was the first formation of trade-unions.
The combination of workmen was regarded as immoral, even
after the laws were repealed which treated it as a crime.
There were two sides of their action in which unions were
necessarily inconsistent with thorough-going individualist
principles.   On the one hand they were combinations to
coerce the master into giving more wages or better conditions; individualists vied with one another in arguing that
this could not be done, and that if it could, it would drive
away capital, and be disastrous not only to the country but to
the labourers themselves.   On the other hand, these Unions
inherited something of the tradition of the old Companies, in
so far as they had survived in recent days[3].   There was a
curiously conservative element in their action, and they

---

[1] *Report of Select Committee*, 1818, *Parl. Debates*, xxxviii. 1209.
[2] *Co-operative Magazine*, Jan. 1826, p. 8.
[3] *Trades' Societies and Strikes* (Social Science Association, 1860), pp. 479, 522.

represent the sort of artisan agitation which had taken its A.D. 1815 —1846.
stand at the beginning of the century on the statutory rights *Survival of*
of the labourer, and had insisted that the old law of appren- *gild-com-*
ticeship should be enforced in the woollen manufacture. *pulsion.*
These men were inclined to desire that they should have control over all the men engaged in their own trade in that
place; and thus they were apt to coerce unwilling workmen
to join their union. The artisans who formed unions, for improving their social condition and trying to obtain better
terms from their employers, were not on the same plane of
thought as Cobbett and the Chartists. The political aspirations and the industrial movements existed side by side, but
they were quite distinct; and the Unionists were out of harmony with the public opinion of the day, both in their objects
and their methods.

iv. The last social force which we may name, was not
only out of harmony with, but definitely opposed to, the
dominant school of economic and political thought, to which
it offered very effective opposition. It gave a rallying ground *Humani-*
tarian
on which strangely discordant elements gathered in occasional *Sentiment.*
combination. So vague was the sentiment, so different were
the directions where it made itself felt, that it is difficult to
name it; but it may perhaps be described as humanitarian or
philanthropic. The first signs of organised activity were in
1796, in a time of serious privation, when the *Society for
bettering the Condition of the Poor* was founded by Dr Shute
Barrington, Bishop of Durham, and Sir Thomas Bernard[1].
But English philanthropy showed itself in many directions;
it was a sentiment which was aroused by human misery and
degradation, either at home or abroad; thus it gave rise on
the one hand to protective measures on behalf of certain
classes of the community, and on the other to cosmopolitan
intervention in favour of down-trodden races. This sentiment
was closely connected with the evangelical revival[2] and with *The Evan-*
gelical
religious activity at home and abroad. It was successful, *Revival.*

[1] Holyoake, *Self-help*, p. 20.

[2] The precursors of the evangelical movement did not take this line, but retained the Puritan attitude both in regard to slavery and the reckless treatment of
natives. Whitefield complains when writing in Georgia (1738), "The people were
denied the use both of rum and slaves * * So that in reality to place people there
on such a footing was little better than to tie their legs and bid them walk."
Tyerman, *Whitefield*, I. 141.

with the aid of the landed interest and the unrepresented artisan opinion, in carrying through measures, which the thorough-going representative of the Manchester School would have regarded as useless, and some which he denounced as mischievous. When we look back from this distance of time, and note the changes which public opinion *Socialistic* has undergone,—the so-called socialistic legislation and the *Legis-* *lation.* international sympathy in common social movements,—we cannot but feel that the first expressions of this humanitarian sentiment are of extraordinary interest; they indicate the beginning of that reaction against *laissez-faire* which has already become so powerful and which promises to have still greater influence in the near future.

Chimney- One of the earliest of the protective measures was passed *Sweeps and* in 1788 in regard to chimney-sweepers[1]; but it was not effective, and another had to be introduced in 1834[2]. The condition of pauper apprentices generally had deservedly excited commiseration, and various steps were taken to improve their position[3]; but the most glaring evils in regard to the employment of children were found in the factory districts. The *Factory* first Factory Act which was passed in 1802[4] was intended to *Acts.* protect the boys and girls by regulating their hours of labour, and an attempt was made to secure that they should have opportunities of education. The frequency of amending[5] measures shows, on the one hand, the glaring nature of the evils, and on the other proves the persistence of the philanthropists and the willingness of Parliament to give effect to their proposals, even at a time when the *laissez-faire* influence was particularly successful in removing other restrictions on free competition. The evils in collieries attracted less attention, possibly because they were of less recent growth, but there was similar protective legislation in 1842[6].

Seamen. The measures that were passed for the protection of sailors were directed against evils precisely similar to those

[1] 28 Geo. III. c. 48.　　　　　　[2] 4 and 5 W. IV. c. 35.
[3] 56 Geo. III. c. 139. This appears to have been effective of good; less successful attempts had been made by 32 Geo. III. c. 57; 33 Geo. III. c. 55; 42 Geo. III. c. 46.　　　[4] 42 Geo. III. c. 73.
[5] 59 Geo. III. c. 66; 6 Geo. IV. c. 63; 1 and 2 W. IV. c. 39; 3 and 4 W. IV. c. 103.　　　　　　[6] 5 and 6 Vict. c. 99.

to which Mr Plimsoll afterwards called attention[1]; while A.D. 1815
—1846.
pains were taken to define their proper rations[2], and attempts
were made to secure the humane treatment of Lascar and
other Asiatic sailors during their sojourn in this country[3].
But the continued interest which was shown in improving
the condition of negro slaves, and the diplomatic engagements with other lands into which we entered with the view
of benefiting them, are an interesting evidence of a wider
range of philanthropy than had been observable before.

XIX. COMMERCE.

361. During the thirty years which succeeded the Battle *Disap-*
pointed ex-
of Waterloo there were many oscillations in our commerce; *pectations*
the progress was less startling than those anticipated, who *of commer-*
cial pros-
had seen how much obstruction was due to the war, and *perity.*
remembered the rapid expansion in 1803. For this there
were perhaps two reasons; the moment when the economists
could have carried a free-trade policy in France had passed;
and restrictive tariffs, like those of Colbert, were the order of
the day; her policy was followed by other countries[4]. This
of course interfered seriously with the export of our manufactures. On the other hand, there were many of our customers who had not the means of paying for our goods; the
Baltic ports and the United States were regions from which
food might have been obtained, but for this there was, owing
to the Corn Laws, no market in England; suitable return
cargoes could not be readily secured, and commerce languished in consequence. This was especially the case immediately after the peace; owing to the exhaustion of the continental countries there was no market for the English goods,
with which foreign warehouses were stored; disappointed
speculators were ruined and a lengthy depression of the
textile industries ensued.

There were other restrictions, of which merchants began *The Navi-*
gation Acts.
to feel the pressure, which could be removed without engag-

---

[1] 31 Geo. III. c. 39; 3 and 4 Vict. c. 86.   [2] 30 Geo. III. c. 33.
[3] 54 Geo. III. c. 134.   [4] L. Levi, 149.

ing in negociations with foreign countries or direct struggles with the agricultural interest. The first important step in regard to our navigation and colonial policy was taken by the London Chamber of Commerce, which petitioned Parliament for an investigation into the existing commercial regulations. Starting from Adam Smith's standpoint, they urged that free intercommunication between nations tended to their mutual advantage, as they were able to supply each *The London Merchants' Petition.* other with the commodities for the production of which each one was specially fitted[1]; they declared against any restrictive regulations, which were made for protective and not for revenue purposes[2]. In consequence of these petitions, a committee was appointed by the House of Commons, and their report, which was presented on July 18th, 1820, may be regarded as laying down the principles of trade policy which Parliament has gradually but increasingly adopted. As an immediate result, there were great relaxations of the laws in regard to the employment of English ships. The first change had occurred in 1796, when the rule, that all goods imported from America should be in British ships, was relaxed in favour of the United States[3]; similar indulgence was accorded to Spanish America and the Spanish West Indies in 1822[4].

Huskisson and the Colonial System. The same year was signalised by the reconstruction of our colonial system. Huskisson did not propose to abandon the old policy, but to modify it so as to remove the worst grievances. He was prepared to allow direct trade between the colonies and foreign countries in British ships or the ships of those countries so long as the trade between England and the colonies was absolutely reserved and treated like a

[1] L. Levi, 150.

[2] *Ib.* 153. This petition marks an era in the history of public opinion; at the time of the Declaration of Independence many of those who denied that the mother country was justified in exacting revenue from the colonies, would have admitted her right to impose protective regulations.

[3] *Ib.* 159; 37 Geo. III. c. 97. A similar permission was given to the Portuguese of S. America in 1811. 51 Geo. III. c. 47.

[4] 3 Geo. IV. c. 43. The prohibition of the importation of the raw produce of Asia, Africa or America from any country but the place of its production had of course been aimed at the Dutch and it had already been abandoned in regard to those particular articles where inconvenience was most strongly felt: *e.g.* cochineal and indigo, 13 Geo. I. c. 25; 7 Geo. II. c. 18; Persian products, 14 Geo. II. c. 36.

coasting trade between different English ports. "By this A.D. 1815
—1846.
arrangement, the foundation of our navigation laws will be
preserved, whilst the colonies will enjoy a free trade with
foreign countries, without breaking in upon the great principle of those laws in respect to foreign trade—that the cargo
must be the produce of the country to which the ship
belongs, leaving the national character of the ship to be
determined by the rules which apply in like cases in this
country. The importation of foreign goods into the colonies,
I propose, should be made subject to moderate duties, but
such as may be found sufficient for the fair protection of our
own productions of a like nature[1]."

These measures were soon followed by attempts at making *Commer-*
treaties with other countries, so as to remove the mischievous *cial Trea-*
ties.
effects of their hostile tariffs and protective rules. In 1823
Huskisson carried a measure, by which the King in Council
was empowered to place the shipping of any other country
on an equal footing with our own, when that country was
prepared to grant a similar favour in return[2]. The first-
fruits of this policy were arrangements with Prussia, Denmark, Hamburg, Sweden, and the Hanse towns; before
twenty years had elapsed this liberal system had been
adopted in our intercourse with all the more important
nations of the world. The changes which Huskisson introduced into our tariff were beneficial to the revenue, and
favourable to commerce; but their precise bearing may be
more fitly discussed in connection with industrial policy[3].

362. The final opening up of the trade with the East to *The exclu-*
all British subjects marks the complete abolition of the old *of the East*
order. Its exclusive rights had been a matter of dispute *India Com-*
pany
since the East India Company was first organised; though it
was able to hold its own against rival traders for many years,
it failed to maintain its privileges when they were attacked
in the interests of the British consumer. During the
eighteenth century, tea had become a commodity of common
consumption; the East India Company still retained a monopoly of the trade with China, and appeared to reap an enor- *with China.*
mous profit on this particular article. When the Charter

---

[1] 2 Hansard, XII. 1108.   [2] 4 Geo. IV. c. 77.   [3] See below, § 385, p. 667.

was renewed in 1813, the trade to India became open; and the Company only continued to carry on as much commerce as was necessary, with a view to their remittances to this country. Their import trade into India was practically nil[1]. In 1833, after long and tedious enquiries, the last remnants of the East India Company's commerce were done away; and it continued to exist as a political body for the administration of our Eastern Empire. The re-adjustments which were necessary in order to carry out these changes, and to give the proprietors grave political responsibilities, instead of the profitable field for enterprise which they had desired, were no easy matter; but the precise arrangements which were made belong rather to political than to commercial history; and after the experience of a quarter of a century were finally discarded. There are however two points which demand our attention, since they throw retrospective light on the nature of trade as it had been generally conducted in earlier ages.

The price of tea.　　i. The sales of tea offer one of the last instances of a foreign commodity which was disposed of according to a regulated price. The method of sale had been defined by the Act of 1784, when it was determined that the Company should, four times a year, put up for auction a quantity of tea, which they supposed, would meet the demand. The upset price was to be such as would defray the prime cost, freight, etc. The Company however calculated these various items on a system which gave rise to much complaint. It was held that if they pushed English manufactures in China, they could procure the goods on far cheaper terms, that their charges for freight were excessive, and that their costly establishments were an unnecessary burden. The merchants pointed out, that the price of tea in Hamburg was about half of that paid at the East India auctions in London; but the Company retorted that they made no account of the difference of quality. The whole discussion is a curious re-echo of the complaints in the *Rolls of Parliament* about the price of wine[2]; and of the seventeenth century discussions in regard to the stint of the Merchant Adventurers and their failure to push the sale of English cloth[3].

---

[1] Mill, *History* (Wilson), ix. 332.　　[2] See above, § 99, Vol. i. p. 294.
[3] See above, § 206, p. 120.

ii. All the trade between China and the outside world was carried on through the agency of a corporation of merchants known as the Co-hong, who seem to have exercised the same sort of privileges, which were formerly bestowed on Gilds merchant. They were responsible for one another's debts, an arrangement which enabled some of them to trade recklessly on credit, and caused frequent difficulty[1]; and a Hongist was responsible for the good behaviour of each foreign merchant[2]. An exclusive company like the East India Company was organised on lines which they understood; so long as the powers of this Company lasted, its agents sympathised with the native merchants and the central Chinese Government in the desire to put down smuggling, though many of the local mandarins were largely interested in this traffic. The chief article which was run surreptitiously into China, was Indian opium, and this was sold at points on the coast where it was impossible to find a market for manufactures[3]. Opium had been regularly imported under a duty till 1796, when the importation was prohibited; the systematic smuggling was subsequently developed on a large scale. Most of the opium thus introduced was grown in Malwa and other Rajputana states, whence it was conveyed to Karachi and shipped by Bombay merchants under Portuguese colours to China. The East India Company had endeavoured, for the protection of their own opium monopoly, to put down the growth of the poppy in Rajputana; though the treaties, by which the suppression of the cultivation was secured, could not be enforced, they did succeed in greatly limiting the trade[4]; it was chiefly carried on by the Portuguese at Macao, and by other traders, most if not all of them British, at Lintin, a small island at the mouth of the Canton river[5].

The sudden suppression of the exclusive powers of the Company was followed by confusion of every kind. Lord Napier arrived in Canton in 1834 as the direct representative of the British Crown, but the Chinese government had had no information of the intention to send him, and treated him with contempt. The English merchants, as isolated

---

[1] J. F. Davis, *The Chinese* (1840), 46.   [2] *Ib.* 47, 60.   [3] *Ib.* 49.
[4] Mill (Wilson), *India*, IX. 174, 178.   [5] Davis, p. 49.

individuals, had even greater difficulties about recovering debts than in former days[1], while the Hongists were dissatisfied with the change, and demanded that the English should elect a commercial chief to control the shipping.
Opening of Ports. This was much needed, as some of the British traders were mere buccaneers, who were prepared to indemnify themselves by acts of reprisal on their own account[2]. The illicit trade in opium was now carried on without disguise at Canton; and the enforced surrender of a large quantity of the drug led chiefly, though by no means singly, to the complications known as the Opium War. This was concluded in 1842, by a treaty under which Hong-kong was ceded to England, and trade was opened to British subjects at Shanghai, Canton, Amoy, Ningpo and Foo-chow-foo; while the monopoly of the Hongists, as the agents for foreign trade, was entirely done away.

Steamships. The expansion, which has taken place in our foreign commerce, was not so much due to the breaking down of these old monopolies, as to the improvement in the physical means of communication. Steam power was first of all applied to internal traffic by water on the Forth and Clyde Canal and on a larger scale between New York and Albany[3]; an immense saving in time and in the regularity of service was effected by organising steam communication between London and Gravesend. In its earlier days steam was chiefly used for short voyages, when regularity of intercourse was important,—as for example, between Holyhead and Dublin[4], London or Hull and Hamburg, and across the Channel. It was in fact chiefly used for passengers and mails, and for such goods as were of considerable value, in proportion to their bulk. It was obviously desirable to have means of communication which were not liable to be interrupted by adverse winds and not dependent on the manner in which the tide served. In 1838, however, steamers[5] from Cork and Bristol

[1] Davis, 59.

[2] *Ib.* 57, 60. The Chinese were quite incapable of controlling their own subjects. About 1810 the seas were completely infested by a body of pirates, known as Ladrones, who were latterly commanded by a woman, *Ib.* 34. We can perhaps find a parallel in Europe in the fourteenth and fifteenth century, with the Rovers of the Sea (Vol. i. p. 366), or Victual Brothers. Zimmern, *Hansa Towns*, 126.

[3] Porter, *Progress*, III. 44.   [4] In 1820, Leone Levi, 214.   [5] *Ib.* 214.

succeeded in crossing the Atlantic; but the voyage of the *Enterprise* to Calcutta in 1826 had proved unremunerative. When Mr Porter wrote in 1837 sanguine men anticipated regular steam communication with the States; but the difficulties of obtaining fuel, and of working engines in the tropics, rendered the success of more distant voyages problematical.

Under these circumstances the British Government and the East India Company set themselves to develop a more rapid route of communication with India by the Red Sea. This was one of the schemes which we had inherited from Napoleon. In 1835 steamers were sent regularly from Bombay to Suez, while the English Government despatched vessels to convey letters to and from Alexandria[1]. The detailed facilities for this overland route were carried out by the energy of Lieutenant Waghorn; the dromedary post which had been temporarily organised by Bagdad, Damascus, and Beyrout was superseded. The arrangements which were thus made by the Government and the East India Company did not long retain their original form, but passed into the hands of one of the great steam navigation companies, founded by private enterprise; the Peninsular and Oriental Company carried the mails to Gibraltar in 1837; they established a Calcutta Service in 1842, and took over the Bombay and Suez mails in 1854[2].

363. There was also a very rapid growth in many trades which remained unaffected by the new facilities for communications; this may perhaps be traced to the working out of the new scheme of commercial policy. Instead of subordinating the interests of our colonies and, so far as might be, the interest of the other countries with which we traded, to the supposed prosperity of England, we began to recognise that they would buy from us more largely if we accepted the commodities which they produced and were ready to sell. Just as Walpole had reconstructed our tariff in accordance with the Mercantile System, so Mr Labouchere re-arranged it once more, with the view of giving the greatest freedom for self-development to all our colonies[3].

A.D. 1815 —1846.

The Overland Route.

The P. and O. Company.

The New Tariff and the Colonies.

---

[1] Lindsay, *Merchant Shipping*, IV. 358.   [2] *Ib.* 387, 389.

[3] Leone Levi, 253; 1 and 2 Vict. c. 113.

A.D. 1815
—1846.

With-
drawal of
special
favour to
West
Indies.

African
Slave
Trade.

This new scheme of policy was favourable to all our colonies in some ways, but it was not equally favourable to all. . Those which had been hitherto the subject of special favour were seriously injured when the protection was withdrawn. This was especially the case with the West Indian Islands[1]; on the one hand they received manufactures, timber and fish on easier terms, but they were exposed to the competition of sugar-growers in the East Indies (1836); after a severe fight they failed to retain the protection which Parliament had given them against foreign and slave-grown sugar (1848)[2].

The line which England had taken in regard to the slave trade was seriously felt, not only in the West Indies, but on the African coast. Denmark had been the first of the European powers to discountenance the traffic; and England had succeeded in procuring treaty engagements with the principal Continental nations, for the gradual cessation of the traffic; but the trade was still highly profitable, and its existence in any form was a constant interruption to the commercial intercourse which British merchants were trying to develop with the native population of Africa. The visit of a slaver to any point of the coast encouraged the natives to organise a raid and supply it with a cargo; the disturbances to legitimate trade which followed were most serious. Despite the difficulty, however, the commerce of the West Coast of Africa was steadily improving[3]. The long-continued efforts of Wilberforce and Clarkson were crowned with success, when the traffic was declared illegal in 1807; but sixteen years of agitation were still necessary before Parliament took the line of treating slave-dealing as a form of piracy. Lord Brougham[4] was chiefly instrumental in securing this result; the squadron which was posted on the African Coast was successful in greatly reducing the traffic, till other events rendered it more profitable and gave it a new impetus[5] about a quarter of a century later.

---

[1] On the condition of the trade of these Islands since the abolition of slavery, see Dalton, *Cruise of Bacchante*, I. 116.

[2] Leone Levi, 253.   [3] Porter, II. p. 111.   [4] Levi, 195.

[5] Dalton, *Bacchante*, I. 119; Leone Levi, 421; Cairnes' *Slave Power*, 206.

XX. COLONIES.

364. The attempt to put down the traffic in slaves was A.D. 1815 —1846. due to the horrors which it caused in Africa and in the *The re-* middle passage; but it logically resulted in an agitation *demption of the Slaves.* against the existence of slavery in British possessions which was again headed by Lord Brougham. The British Government paid a sum of twenty millions as compensation to the planters when slavery was abolished in 1834. This was of course not a full compensation, as the value of West Indian slaves was said to be forty-three millions[1]. It might of course appear that the command which the planters had over a resident labouring population would enable them to carry on their operations, without a full compensation for the money they had invested in stocking their estates with hands. But *Loss to the West* as a matter of fact, and when viewed retrospectively, it is *Indian* difficult to say that any compensation would have made up to *Planters.* the planters for losing control over their hands. There undoubtedly are populations who would be stimulated to greater exertions by the sense of freedom; but the West Indian negro, at all events, preferred to be idle and poor[2], rather than to exert himself even for comparatively high wages. The whole management of the estates was disorganised; and though the planters strove vigorously to manage their business on new lines, the struggle was very severe and many of them were ruined in the attempt. When the last element of protection was withdrawn, and they were exposed to the full *Competi-* *tion of* competition of the slave-grown sugar on neighbouring islands, *slave-grown* *Sugar.* their condition became desperate. Slave labour was less expensive than free labour in this particular case, and the sugar growing in Cuba and Brazil received an immense stimulus; as a consequence the traffic from Africa, which we had done

---

[1] The compensation appears to have varied from a quarter to a half of the sworn value of slaves of different classes and ages, *Accounts*, 1887—8, XLVIII. 680.

[2] On a corresponding condition in Ireland compare Ricardo, *Letters*, 138, 139. The pleasure of pure idleness is seldom sufficiently recognised by modern economists in working out their calculus of measurable motives. Marshall, *Present Position*, pp. 22, 29. It was perhaps overrated in the eighteenth century. " Mankind naturally are inclined to ease and indolence; and nothing but absolute

so much to put down, revived anew and eluded the efforts we made to check it. In more recent times, the islands have also suffered from the state-aided production of beetroot sugar on the continent; so that the emancipation of the slaves may be regarded as marking the beginning of the decline of that great sugar industry which was so highly prized in the eighteenth century. It is of course clear that a free trade policy, and the cheap importation of articles of common consumption, may be the best course to pursue in the long run; but it is also clear that an industry, which has been nurtured by protection may be destroyed, when that protection is withdrawn.

The Cape Colony.   The abolition of slavery also affected the Cape Colony where much of the labour was done by Malay and other slaves. The Boers had long resented the interference of the Dutch Government in the management of their land, and they were less inclined to submit to English control; as a consequence there were several migrations, some of which were effected at a very considerable sacrifice, northwards to Natal and the Transvaal. In 1820, English emigrants had settled on Algoa Bay; but the frequent Kaffir wars, and the disaffection of the Dutch, have kept this settlement in a backward state; while the opening of the overland route had somewhat diminished its importance as a trading station. So little were its interests regarded, that when the penal settlements in Australia and Tasmania were discontinued, the Colonial Office saw no objection to subjecting the Cape Colony to a similar contaminating influence[1].

Canada   365. Several important changes took place in connection with Canada during this period, and they are of special interest, as they illustrate various points in the changes from the older trading system to the new condition of commerce. The Northern colonies had never had such favour bestowed upon them as the West Indian colonies; but lumber, one

---

necessity will enforce labour and industry. * * Those who have closely attended to the disposition of a manufacturing populace have always found that to labour less, and not cheaper, has been the consequence of a low price of provisions." *Essay on Trade*, pp. 15, 14.

[1] An African penal settlement was projected before Botany Bay was established. Gonner, *Settlement of Australia* in *Eng. Hist. Review*, III. 627.

of their principal products, had been protected by a A.D. 1815 —1846.
discriminating duty. This pressed very heavily on timber
imported from Memel and the North of Europe[1] and appears
to have had the effect of creating the colonial timber trade[2].
It was however alleged that the effect of these duties was to *and the timber duties.*
render timber dear in this country, to put a premium on the
use of inferior qualities, and to encourage owners to use ships
which had better have been broken up for fuel. There was
consequently a steady attack upon the timber duties, as there
had been on the sugar duties; but as they did not affect an
article of ordinary domestic consumption comparatively little
public interest was aroused on the matter, and Canada continued to enjoy the advantage of this tariff till 1860[3].

Canada, as compared with all other English colonies, *Emigration and*
offered the favourite field for emigration at that time; and
the progress which was being made in developing the resources of the country, is reflected in the story of a new
departure which was taken by the Hudson's Bay Company,
and which gave rise to considerable controversy at the time.
The Hudson's Bay Company had obtained from Charles II. *the Hudson's Bay Company.*
one of those extensive charters which gave them the posses-
sion of a large but ill-defined territory known as Rupert's
Land, as well as exclusive trading rights to all regions to
which they could find access by water or land,—that is to
say, the entire trade of the great North-West was granted to
them in perpetuity[4]. They had however done but little to
develop their resources, as they had little more than a few
trading factories; until a large tract of land on the Red River,
amounting to 116,000 square miles, was assigned by the
Company to Lord Selkirk for the purpose of colonisation in *Lord Selkirk.*
1811[5]. This settlement however lay exactly on the route

[1] During the war the duty on European timber per load 50 cubic feet was
raised from 6s. 8d. to 65s. while the duty on colonial timber was never more than
2s. and that was removed before the close of the war. In 1821 in accordance with
the recommendations of a Parliamentary Committee the rate on European timber
was fixed at 55s. and on colonial at 10s. Porter, III. 122.

[2] According to Porter it had no existence before 1803. *Ib.* 122.

[3] Dowell, II. 336.

[4] R. M. Martin, *Hudson's Bay Territories*, p. 4.

[5] *Report on Canadian Archives*, 1886, by D. Brymner, pp. xvii. and clxxxvii.
Part of this settlement was on territory which was recognised in 1818 as belonging to the United States, as it was south of parallel 49°. As the Hudson's Bay

from the Great Lakes into the interior; it was consequently
on the lines on which the French Fur Company, and subsequently the North-West Fur Company of Montreal, had
carried on a profitable trade in furs; this had extended
beyond the Rocky Mountains, and their agents had penetrated into Columbia[1]. The Hudson's Bay Company took
advantage of this position to claim the trading monopoly
given under their charter; and after some years of "savage
and brutal strife" they succeeded in coming to an agreement,
by which the two Companies arranged to work together "to
the exclusion of all others[2]."

In 1849 a project was mooted which gave new importance
to the whole question; on the one hand, considerable advances
were made by the Russian American Fur Company, to whom
a very extensive territory had been assigned in 1799 by the
Relations with Russia. Emperor Paul. The Hudson's Bay Company bore the brunt
of the difficulty of defending British rights in the North-
West from Russian aggression, and maintained an important
trading outpost on the river Stekine[3]; they subsequently
leased the trade over an area which was undoubtedly Russian
in 1840. The Hudson's Bay Company had thus become the
most important body of English traders on the north-eastern
coast of the Pacific; and when the Government of the day
Van-couver's Island. determined to form a colony on Vancouver's Island, and to
develop its rich agricultural and mineral resources, they not
unnaturally fixed on the old chartered Company as appropriate agents for carrying out the scheme.

This project however aroused a considerable outcry; there
was of course the usual objection to the maintenance of a
The trade of the Company monopoly; on this point however the defenders of the Company were able to give a fairly effective reply, as the English
consumer could procure furs from other sources, and there
was no calculated upset price[4], such as had been complained
of in the East India Company's sales of tea. They were less
successful however in rebutting the accusations which were

Company did not protest against this violation of their chartered rights, their
opponents were able to urge at a subsequent time that the Company placed no
great reliance on the validity of that charter on which they subsequently took their
stand. J. E. Fitzgerald, *Examination of Charter of Hudson's Bay Company*, p. 50.

[1] *Ib.* p. 54.   [2] *Ib.* p. 57.   [3] Martin, 29.   [4] *Ib.* 51.

made against them in regard to their treatment of the <i>A.D. 1815 —1846.</i> native races. It is difficult to sift the charges and counter charges which were bandied in regard to the Company's treatment of the Indians, but it seems clear that no serious <i>and their</i> efforts had been made to exercise any civilising influence <i>treatment of Indians.</i> upon the population till 1820. In 1752 the Company issued an express prohibition against instructing the Indians[1]; and no church existed in any part of their territories till the Church Missionary Society began operations in the district in 1820[2]. The contrast with the conduct of the French in Canada is so striking as to need no comment; if the Company found the Indians dishonest and savage, their condition reflected discredit on the Company itself and gave no excuse for the reckless cruelty with which the natives were treated. Regulations were indeed laid down against supplying the natives with alcohol, but these do not appear to have been enforced[3]. As the Indians acquired a knowledge of the use of firearms, they lost their old skill in primitive modes of hunting; they were thus reduced to absolute dependence on the Company for ammunition, and therefore for the necessaries of subsistence. That they were forced to bargain on most unequal terms is only too likely[4]; but the most serious cruelty occurred when any area became somewhat exhausted, so far as furs were concerned, and the Company found it profitable to close the depot and to leave the wretched inhabitants to their fate[5].

366. The changes, which took place in the development <i>Wakefield and the art of colonisation.</i> of our other colonies, may be directly traced to new ideas on the subject of colonisation, which gradually secured an increasing hold upon the public mind. They did not at first bear the full fruit that was hoped for; partly because the promoters of the new kinds of enterprise had to oppose the traditional policy of the Colonial Office, and partly because their schemes were tried in an imperfect fashion and appear to be condemned by failure. The leading exponent of these new views was Mr E. G. Wakefield, and he succeeded in rallying round him a very remarkable group of men;

[1] Robson, <i>Six Years' Residence in Hudson's Bay</i>, 76.
[2] Fitzgerald, 184.　　[3] <i>Ib.</i> 160.　　[4] <i>Ib.</i> 147.　　[5] <i>Ib.</i> 188.

expression was given to his views by Dr Hinds, the **Dean** of
Carlisle, by Mr Charles Buller, in the House of Commons,
and most important of all by John Stuart Mill in his *Princi-*
ples of Political Economy.

Economic
Basis.
      Mr Wakefield and his coadjutors were theorists; they
arrived at their views on a question of practical political
administration by reasoning based on accepted economic
doctrines. To them economic considerations were of primary
importance in connection with colonisation, though they did
not neglect political and social points as well. In 1830
they established a society for promoting systematic colonisation; from that time onwards they were increasingly
successful in obtaining public attention, even when they
failed in their attempts to direct public action. At the
same time, they introduced important modifications in the
Austral-
asia.
plans that were carried out with regard to New South
Wales and South Australia, Tasmania and New Zealand;
though in every case they were foiled in the effort to give
a fair trial to their scheme in its entirety and thus to
submit their doctrine to a crucial experiment.

Systematic
Colonisa-
tion.
      They held that a serious wrong had been done in the
past, since emigration had been for the most part the mere
deportation of convicts and paupers, instead of the systematic planting of a civilised community. Mr Wakefield
attached great importance to every circumstance that might
induce good citizens to emigrate, and he was anxious that
they should have full political freedom and abundant opportunity for the exercise of their religion[1]. But besides laying
stress on the quality and character of the emigrants, Mr
Wakefield insisted on the importance of attracting capital
to the colonies, and the formation of capital in the colonies.
Sales of
Land.
The first point of his programme, which Government adopted,
was the proposal to discontinue the practice of making free
grants of land; he urged that by selling the unoccupied land
it would be possible to prevent too great diffusion, and to form
a fund which might serve to promote and assist the emigration
of selected labourers[2]; this was carried out with more or less
completeness in New South Wales and Tasmania. But the

------

[1] Wakefield, *Art of Colonisation*, 55.   [2] *Ib.* 44.

political project, for giving the colonists a considerable amount A.D. 1815
—1846. of local self-government, was steadily opposed by the Colonial Office; despite the hearty support of the Duke of Wellington[1], it was not put into execution when settlements were made in South Australia and New Zealand.

The strength of the position taken by Mr Wakefield and his followers lay, not in their arguments about the prospective advantage to the colonies, but in their diagnosis *Evils in England from which colonisation would be a remedy.* of existing evils in England, and of advantages which would accrue to the mother-country from systematic colonisation. Since the time of Malthus, it had become a commonplace to maintain that there was a redundancy of population in the country; but the colonising school maintained that this redundancy was felt in every class of society, and not merely among the poorest[2]. They also urged that England was suffering from a plethora of capital; they argued that the *Plethora of labour and capital.* steady formation of capital, while no new fields for enterprise were available, led in an ordinary way to feverish competition among capitalists at a very narrow margin of profit, and occasionally, by a not unnatural re-action, to outbursts of wild speculation and consequent waste of capital[3]. From their point of view what we needed was additional land. "Neither by improvements of agriculture, *Need for more land.* nor by the importation of food, if these fall short of the power of the people to increase, is the competition of excessive numbers in all classes diminished in the least. By whatever means the field of employment for all classes is enlarged, unless it can be enlarged faster than capital and people can increase, no alteration will take place in profits or wages, or in any sort of remuneration for exertion; there is a larger fund, but a corresponding or greater increase of capital and people, so that competition remains the same, or may even go on becoming more severe. Thus a country may exhibit a rapid growth of wealth and population— such an increase of both as the world has not seen before—

---

[1] Wakefield, *Art of Colonisation*, 48.   [2] *Ib.* 66, 74.

[3] *Ib.* 76. Mr Wakefield's letters are well worthy of perusal, as the observations of a judicious and far-seeing man on the actual condition of and probable changes in England. See especially pp. 64—105.

with direful competition within every class of society, ex-
cepting alone the few in whose hands very large properties
have accumulated. * * * * We trace the competition to
want of room; that is to a deficiency of land in proportion
to capital and people or an excess of capital and people in
proportion to land. * * * If we could sufficiently check the
increase of capital and people, that would be an appropriate
remedy, but we cannot. Can we then sufficiently enlarge
the whole field of employment for British capital and labour,
by means of sending capital and people to cultivate new
land in other parts of the world? If we sent away enough,
the effect here would be the same as if the domestic increase of capital and people were sufficiently checked. But
another effect of great importance would take place. The
emigrants would be producers of food; of more food, if the
colonisation were well managed, than they could consume;
they would be growers of food and raw materials of manufacture for this country; we should buy their surplus food
and raw materials with manufactured goods. Every piece of
our colonisation, therefore, would add to the power of the
whole mass of new countries to supply us with employment
for capital and labour at home. Thus, employment for
capital and labour would be increased in two places and two
ways at the same time; abroad, in the colonies, by the
removal of capital and people to fresh fields of production;
at home, by the extension of markets, or the importation of
food and raw materials[1]."

Reaction of Colonisation on England. There was a strong *prima facie* objection to depleting
England of such elements of industrial prosperity as popu-
lation and capital for the sake of developing distant colonies; but the main strength of Wakefield's argument rests
on the position that the development of new colonies would
re-act on the home country so as to insure still greater prosperity than before. "Colonisation," he insists, "has a tendency to increase employment for capital and labour at
home. * * * The common idea is that emigration of capital
and people diminishes the wealth and population of the
mother-country; it has never done so, it has always increased

[1] Wakefield, *Art of Colonisation*, 91.

both population and wealth at home[1]." "Every fresh im- portation of food by means of exporting more manufactured goods is an enlargement of the field of production; is like an acreable increase of our land; and has a tendency to abolish and prevent injurious competition. This was the best argument for the repeal of our corn laws[2]." Mr Mill re-enforced a similar doctrine. "There needs be no hesitation," he says, "in affirming that colonisation, in the present state of the world, is the very best affair of business, in which the capital of an old and wealthy country can possibly engage[3]." The extraordinary rapidity with which our colonies have developed[4] fully confirms the truth of this observation.

XXI. INDUSTRY.

367. There is abundant evidence that the working *Artisan suffering.* classes suffered very terribly during this period; there may however be much difference of opinion as to the precise causes of that suffering; in any case they were very complex; and it is not a little difficult to disentangle them and set the matter in a clear light. A further complication is due to the fact that the rough and ready explanation, which was popularly accepted at the time, has never been seriously called in question. Many capitalists made large fortunes, while the labourers suffered greatly; it appeared obvious *Alleged oppression by Capitalists.* that the capitalists were gaining at the expense of the workers and by successfully grinding them down. This was the accusation which was commonly uttered on many platforms, which was put on record by Friedrich Engels, and which has come to be accepted as authentic history. It has been necessary to remark, in regard to other epochs, that while the evidence of contemporaries was of first-rate importance as to the nature of the phenomena, contemporary expla-

---

[1] Wakefield, *Art of Colonisation*, 92.   [2] *Ib.* 89.
[3] *Principles of Political Economy*, Bk. v. ch. xi. § 14 (People's ed. p. 586).
[4] Caldecott, *English Colonisation and Empire*, 167.

A.D. 1815
—1846.
nations of the phenomena were rarely deserving of much respect. Doubtless there may have been much greed among capitalists; but this factor is quite inadequate to explain the general distress of the English artisans during this time.

The artisan classes unrepresented.
There were certain political changes which may perhaps have done the artisan but little injury, but which certainly served to render him more helpless than before. The Reform Bill of 1832 not only excluded him from any benefit but positively disfranchised a number of artisans. As freeholders many of the weavers in the neighbourhood of Halifax would probably have votes which the factory operatives did not continue to enjoy; while in some towns like Coventry and Preston those who had held the franchise were absolutely deprived of it[1]. The hoped for measure of reform had been passed, but the artisan population had even less political power under the new order, than under the old.

At the same time considerable changes were made in the position of the labourer in its industrial aspects. In 1824 a select committee of the House of Commons was appointed to consider the whole industrial policy of the day, and they reported in favour of allowing the labourer much more freedom of action than he had ever possessed before[2]. In the first place the statutes against combination were repealed[3]; this was not due to any desire to permit combinations, but it was obvious that the Acts were powerless to prevent them, and the common law of conspiracy was deliberately re-enforced[4] after it had been allowed to drop[5]. There had been serious injustice in retaining this single fragment of the old system of regulation, when the authoritative assessment of wages had fallen into disuse, but the passing of this measure was fraught with the happiest results. When combination became legal, it ceased to be a danger to society; there have never been outbreaks of mob-violence since 1824, such as were found in many districts in 1812, 1816, and other years.

Repeal of the Combination Laws.

Freedom to emigrate.
Other restrictions had been imposed upon the labourer from a desire to retain his services in the country and to prevent the migration of various branches of industry to

---

[1] 3 Hansard, IX. 372, 443.   [2] *Reports, &c.* 1824, V. 589.
[3] 5 Geo. IV. c. 95.   [4] 6 Geo. IV. c. 129.   [5] 5 Geo. IV. c. 95, §§ 2, 3.

foreign lands. The deliberate attempts to prevent the development in Ireland or the colonies of manufactures, which
were likely to compete with our own, have been described
above[1], but with changed times and the increasing reliance
on machinery, there was no longer sufficient reason for maintaining these restrictions[2] on the free flow of labour. And
freedom to emigrate was given to the skilled artisan at the
same time that he obtained freedom to form combinations[3].

While we thus see the reversal of the scheme of national
policy with regard to industry, which had held good for so
long, we may also notice that this period saw the death-blow
given to methods of municipal regulation, which had long
before ceased to be of much practical importance. Even in
towns like Shrewsbury[4] or Hull[5], where some of the com- *Subver-*
panies survived in the eighteenth century, they had but little *sion of the last com-*
influence either for good or for evil on the actual conditions *panies,*
of work and wages of the ordinary labourer; yet the entire
decay of these bodies testified to a very real change in the condition of the workman. In the old days, the apprentice and
the journeyman could hope to rise to a position of independence; but under the new order of things, there was no such
hope for nine men in ten or ninety-nine in a hundred. The
labourer must remain a labourer receiving wages from *and of*
another man and thus dependent upon an employer all his *chances of rising to in-*
life. Just as the application of capital to land and the *depend-ence.*
consequent changes in working it, had destroyed the agri-

---

[1] See above, pp. 295, 329.

[2] Manufacturers assumed that they might send artisans abroad to erect machinery, and passports were given for this purpose; but a case was mentioned
where an engineer in France had been compelled to give a bond for £7000 that he
would not entice workmen abroad. *Reports* &c. 1824, v. 8, 9.

[3] See the report in 3 Hansard, XI. 811. The Committee of 1824 did not feel
competent to make any recommendation on the question as to the wisdom of
allowing the export of machinery. Probably the general feeling in the country at
that time was in favour of the policy of trying to retain our industrial supremacy
by prohibiting the export of machines. It was impossible to maintain an absolute
prohibition however, and a good deal of machinery was exported by license while
still more was smuggled. Patterns and drawings were also sent abroad (*Reports*
&c. 1824, v. 7) and machine making was rapidly developed in Belgium and France.
English machine makers consequently pressed to be allowed to export their wares
and a Parliamentary committee reported in their favour in 1841. *Ib.* 1841,
VII. 277, 285.

[4] Hibbert, *Influence of Gilds*, 106.   [5] Lambert, *Two thousand years*, 190.

C. II.   39

cultural labourer's chance of rising to be an independent
farmer; so the application of capital to industry, the introduction of machinery, and the organisation of factories on a
large scale, destroyed the weaver's chance of becoming, or of
remaining, his own master. How highly the freedom was
prized, how much the tyranny of the factory bell was resented,
how much folk feared the demoralising effects of the factory
as compared with domestic industry we shall see below; but
these things must all be taken into account if we would
rightly understand the intense bitterness of the labourer's
feeling during the period we are now discussing.

*Excuses
for class
jealousy.* 　There was indeed ample excuse for bitter class jealousy;
the rise of rents had been enormous during the war period,
as well as the rise in the value of tithes. The land-owners
and tithe-owners had gained, with comparatively little exertion; and the Corn Laws secured the continuance of that
gain at the expense of the manufacturing population. Some
manufacturers too had risen in the world. Many indeed had
failed and become bankrupt; especially was this the case after
the war. Protective tariffs were established in many lands to
keep out our goods and foster native industry, while the corn
laws prevented other lands from selling us their products, so
that they had no means of buying our goods. The foreign
demand was greatly reduced, while the home demand also had
diminished. The "poverty of the poor was their destruction"; they could not make an effective demand for goods of
any kind since their wages were so low; and it seemed not
unreasonable to plead that higher wages would allow of an
increased home demand and would benefit trade. Trade was
undoubtedly bad, but yet the employers as a class had risen
from a social position in which they had been comparatively
little removed above the manufacturers with whom they
dealt. Some of the labourers, as for example the frame-work
knitters, were absolutely becoming poorer and poorer[1]. But
even, if this had not been the case, human beings are apt to
be jealous of prosperity in which they do not themselves
share. Just as the villans were prompted to revolt in 1381,
by the new prosperity of the labourers and yeoman farmers,

---

[1] Report on Frame-work knitting, 1845, xv. p. 107.

while their own condition was as bad or worse than before, so A.D. 1815 —1846. the artisans at the period of the Reform Bill were indignant at the wealth of their masters, while their condition was more hopeless and less prosperous than before. The violence and the bitterness of those days is surely very excusable, and strained as relations still are between capital and labour, there is a marvellous improvement in the methods by which the contest is now carried on.

368. There is no lack of material for following out the history in great detail. The Parliamentary Commissions, which sat from time to time, supply masses of evidence; but there is a real difficulty in arranging it so as to see the precise bearing of the facts adduced, and it is still harder to survey the entire field in such a fashion as to give their due importance to each of the characteristic features of the time. Perhaps it may be wisest to try to understand the *Aims of the artisans* aims and motives of the different actors in these struggles; *and others.* and then to follow out the results which they attained, as well as the reasons of their various failures.

The working classes in many districts before 1824 were actuated by the ideas of industrial policy which had been finally discarded by Parliament in 1813[1]. The demand was made for an authoritative assessment of wages, and an authoritative limitation of the price of food[2]; and there were large areas of the country in which the labourers attempted by violence to insist on compliance with their demands. One of *Bread* the most notable of these cases was the great riot in the *Riots.* eastern counties, at Littleport, Ely and Bury[3]. This was one of the few cases where attacks were made on machines for spinning; but jennies were broken up in several places[4]. At the same time, the positive plan of the rioters for the alleviation of their distress was one that had been well considered and pronounced impracticable; the action of the rioters, in trying to obtain by violence an unreal remedy for their distress, was one which government could not overlook[5], and

---

[1] Repeal of 5 Eliz. c. 4; 53 Geo. III. c. 40.
[2] *Annual Register*, Vol. 58, Chronicle, p. 67.   [3] *Ib.* Vol. 58, Chronicle, p. 67.
[4] *Ib.* 70, there was also an objection to improved agricultural implements, 67, 74.
[5] *Ib.* Vol. 59, Chronicle, p. 15. On the whole subject compare the Report of the House of Lords Committee. *Ib.* Vol. 54, p. 885.

A.D. 1815
—1846.
which the more enlightened leaders of the people did not
defend. In very many cases, there was evidence of malicious
vengeance, which could not possibly benefit anyone and
which had but little influence in modifying the action of the
Swing. propertied classes. The most mischievous of these endeavours
was the burning of stacks[1], a practice which broke out again
and again in many rural neighbourhoods. The clergy were
perhaps the greatest sufferers, as the stacks apportioned for
tithe were frequently destroyed. The grain was often insured
so that the farmers did not suffer directly; but the general
insecurity and prevalence of rural crime increased the difficulties of the agricultural interests. The manner in which
the rioters took up old-fashioned economic views was illustrated by occurrences at Bristol[2], when the mob interfered
to limit and reduce the price at which potatoes were being
Bread
Riots. sold, and at Bideford where they tried to prevent exportation[3]. The attempt to make food plentiful, by prohibiting
the grower from taking a competition price, was one which
the legislature had long discarded. It was most disastrous
that any of the working classes should try to achieve by
violence, what calmer heads had declared unwise.

The most violent outbreaks however were directed against
The
Luddites. certain kinds of machinery. The Luddite riots[4] of 1812
broke out again in 1816, and were evidently carefully organised and skilfully directed. Leicester and Nottingham, as
the centres of the frame-work knitting district, were the
scenes of these outrages; though there was a considerable
force of military employed, the Luddites eluded their vigilance, and even succeeded in breaking machines in a house
where two soldiers had been carefully posted to protect
them. It is to be specially noticed however that these
particular outbreaks were not directed against a new mechanical contrivance, but simply against machinery which had
been in use, with no material modification, ever since the

---

[1] Wakefield, *Swing unmasked*, p. 28.   [2] *Annual Register*, Vol. 54, p. 55.
[3] *Ib.* 58, Chron. 68.
[4] The name is said to be derived from the conduct of a crazy notoriety known
as Ned Lud who having been much teased by some village boys, pursued one of
them into a cottage; the boy escaped him, and he blindly wreaked his vengeance
on the stocking frame. Pellew, *Life of Lord Sidmouth*, III. p. 80.

trade had come into existence, and to which neither steam nor water power had been applied. The evidence appears to show that the Luddites were engaged in executing popular vengeance on wealthy or hard owners of frames, and it is difficult to see that their action was in any way connected with the great mechanical progress of the time.

On the other hand, the riots in Yorkshire were directed *Gig-Mills.* against a newly introduced machine. The mob in the West Riding was carefully discriminating, and concentrated its attention almost exclusively on those parts of the buildings where shearing frames and gig mills were in operation[1]. As the work done by the machines was cheaper and better, the rioters were unfortunate in trying to secure a position, which Parliament had treated as untenable.

This was the one point in which the opposition to *Conflict* machinery came plainly to the front at this date, though it *with ma-* *chinery.* also found expression some years later, when the competition between hand-combing and machine-combing and the hand-loom and the power-loom was practically fought. It is undoubtedly for the good of mankind, and of each nation, that material goods should be produced with as little drudgery as possible, and that the powers of nature should be brought to bear in every possible way to lighten human labour; but it is also true that the machines were supplanting skilled labour[2], and that the skilled artisan was not able to maintain himself as well, by his work, as he had done before the machine era; the diminution of his resources again reacted on his power of purchasing goods, and the stagnation in the home market tended to prolong the depression and prevent a revival of trade. The general policy, which many of the *Limiting* operatives favoured, would have been that of maintaining the *production* hand-worker in his old position, by strictly limiting the hours of machinery. Much of the agitation for the ten hours factory law was due to a hope on the part of the artisan that machinery would "thereby find its level[3]." By this they

---

[1] *Annual Register*, 54, pp. 39, 51, 114.

[2] The effect of the flying-shuttle was to give additional power and higher wages to the skilled men, and thus to throw the less skilled out of employment; but most of the inventions were substituted for, not subservient to, the old forms of industrial skill.   [3] *Reports, &c.* 1833, xx. pp. 40, 41.

meant that the machine would produce no more in its restricted day than the hand-loom weaver could accomplish in
the hours he might choose to work. Such a scheme of policy
as this could only be recommended in a trade like the cloth
trade, where England appeared to have a practical monopoly.
It was obviously absurd in regard to linen or silk where we
had to face successful competition; but in any case it was
condemned as inimical to material progress. It demanded
the maintenance of the art in its existing condition, and the
forcible restriction of improvements, so that they should not
interfere with the existing condition. It was fatal to progress in those arts in which England had an advantage, and
it would soon have ruined the trades in which England was
only holding her own. The opposition to machinery was a
mistaken policy for the artisans to adopt, whether it was
pursued by the rioters who broke shearing frames or by
others who joined in the demand for shortened hours of adult
labour in factories.

*The Great
Strike of
Wool-
combers.*
369. The immediate result of the repeal of the combination laws appeared to justify the worst forebodings of those
who had been opposed to the measure. The Bradford manufacturers were forced to face a tremendous strike for a rise of
wages, and they met it by trying to procure the immediate
re-enactment of the laws which had been so recently repealed[1]. The strike was organised by a large union among
the hands, which received much support from operatives in
other towns. The Committee were able to pay as much as
£800 or £900[2] a week to the men on strike, and the operatives succeeded to a very large extent in boarding out their
children during the summer months; the men appeared to be
holding well together, while there were some dissensions
among the masters, who had entered on an aggressive policy
and endeavoured to break up the union altogether. The
Leeds wool-combers joined those of Bradford in their strike;
but after standing out for twenty-two weeks, the men were
Its failure. forced to give in on every point, and returned to work at the
wages which they had been receiving five months before; this
according to the contention of the masters was the highest

---

[1] Burnley, *Wool and Wool-combing*, 168.   [2] *Ib.* 169.

rate that the trade would bear. The loss in wages amounted to £40,000, though something like half this sum was received in the form of subscriptions to the union; when the work was taken up again some seventeen hundred men found that their places were occupied and that they could not return to the employment they had lost.

This great strike, which was the first of these conflicts *A Strike for higher wages,* between capital and labour after the Combination Laws were repealed, is of very great interest, but two points may be specially noticed; in the first place it was simply a demand for higher wages. The wool-comber was suffering greatly, but it does not seem that it was possible for the employers to remedy that distress. On the one hand the necessaries of life were dear, and this in so far as it was not due to the character of the seasons, was aggravated by the influence of the Corn Laws; and on the other hand, prices of goods were low and trade was dull[1], there had been unexampled commercial disaster in the United States and there was no room for a rise of wages without ruining the employers. But the men were inclined to take their stand on the old system, and to believe that masters and men could unite to assess reasonable wages, and that the sale of the product would not be seriously affected despite the alteration in price[2]. This would of course only hold good in so far as Englishmen had the monopoly in foreign markets, and could thus command their own price for the quantities they sent abroad, as the Merchant Adventurers professed to do in the sixteenth and seventeenth centuries. The appeal of the defeated woolcombers for reasonable wages is most touching[3]; but once again we see that the men were striving to retain the policy which had been current in earlier days, but which was no longer compatible with the conditions of the times in which they lived.

There is a second point of great importance; though so *not against machinery.* many years had elapsed since Cartwright's wool-combing

---

[1] The commission of 1833 found ample evidence of the decay of the cloth trade and shutting up of mills in the West of England. *Reports,* 1833, xx. 950, 960.

[2] This appears to be the view of the men in 1833. *Ib.* 40, 539. It had been entertained by some merchants in 1806. See above, p. 471.

[3] Burnley, 176, 180.

machine had been invented, it had not as yet been generally introduced; despite the commotion which had attended its first introduction some thirty years before, the wool-combers appear to have believed that the scare was idle, and that machines could not really compete with hand labour, except perhaps in wools of a special sort, the combing of which was badly paid. In 1825 the men still shared this confidence, and the assertion that the masters would introduce machinery was regarded as an empty threat. There can be but little doubt that the events of that year, disastrous alike to masters and men, gave a stimulus to the improvement and introduction of machinery, and before 1845 the trade was completely revolutionised. But in order to understand the course of events it is necessary to bear in mind that this great strike was not directed against the introduction of machinery, but occurred in a trade which was still practically unaffected by the mechanical improvements; the hand-combers were much distressed, but this distress was certainly not due to their labours being supplanted by the introduction of machinery.

Capitalists and free competition.
370. If the position which was taken by these workers was untenable, there was much in the actual condition of society which seemed to condemn the economic principles on which the legislators and the capitalists relied. They believed that under a régime of free competition, there would be the greatest possible production in the world as a whole; and that it also gave a desirable stimulus to the energies of each; they were inclined to hope that this increased activity, and rapid development of material resources, must afford the greatest happiness to the greatest number, even if it appeared
its good side,
to press severely in individual cases. On the whole, they were right; competition had evoked new enterprise and had stimulated more energetic labour; this was obvious in regard to rural, as well as manufacturing industries. In so far as competition had these results it was beneficial in an economic sense, even though the changes which it introduced were accompanied with social difficulties during the period of transition. But the competition of capitalists was not always wholesome, even economically. In so far as it called forth more energy and enterprise it was a public boon, and the

capitalist gained because he had succeeded in serving the public better. But competition might drive men to try to gain, (i) at the expense of other dealers by carrying on a speculative trade; or (ii) at the expense of the public, by producing an inferior quality of goods; or (iii) at the expense of the labourers, by cutting down their remuneration. Individual capitalists might find such competition gainful; but it was ruinous to the trade, injurious to the public, and most disastrous to the hands. The obstacles to free competition prevented us from securing its full benefits till after the repeal of the Corn Laws, but long before that time the evils of reckless competition had been apparent. They were most noticeable in the hosiery trade, to which allusion has already been made, and in which there had been no great mechanical improvement. *A.D. 1815 —1846. and the evils of reckless competition. in the hosiery trade.*

i. The very full report which Mr Muggeridge wrote on the frame-work knitters in 1845 gives ample evidence that the trade had been steadily declining from 1815 to 1841. This was generally attributed to foreign competition, and English manufacturers had so completely failed to hold their own in foreign markets that the commissioner reported that there was no export trade to speak of at the time when he wrote[1]. *Decline of trade due to*

ii. Equally striking is the testimony as to the deterioration of the quality of the goods sold; there was a class of hosiery known as *cut work*, and purchasers were not able to distinguish it readily from sound work. Under these circumstances, the demand for sound work had greatly fallen off; and some steps were necessary in order to give the public confidence in the goods offered for sale. The loss of foreign markets was generally attributed to the introduction of these inferior wares, which had brought the whole English manufacture into discredit. Some would have favoured the prohibition of the cheaper goods, and some recommended the two classes of goods should be distinctly stamped[2]; but both proposals were attended with grave difficulty, though it was obvious that this competition was working injuriously in the interest of the consumer. *deterioration of Quality through competition.*

[1] *Reports*, &c. 1845, xv. p. 79.   [2] *Ib.* 96. Felkin, 473.

A.D. 1815
—1846.
Fall of
Wages.

iii. It was notorious that the distress among the operatives had been great and long continued. There was no
doubt of it at the time of the Luddite riots when Byron
made his celebrated speech in the House of Lords[1]. But
according to the figures which Mr Muggeridge gives, wages
had steadily declined from 1811 to 1842, and had on the
whole fallen about thirty-five per cent.[2] The most unsatisfactory thing in the condition of the workers was that they
hired the frames from employers, whose charges for frame
rent were often very arbitrary and were not made the subject
of agreement beforehand,—an evil which Sir Henry Halford
strove unsuccessfully to remedy in 1846 and 1847[3]. There
was also much loss of time to the workers who did not receive
yarn when they gave back the finished goods at the end of
the week, but had to wait till mid-day on Monday[4]. As the
weavers worked at home, they were able to requisition the
assistance of their wives and children, and the whole family
worked for very long hours and at starvation wages, from
which the frame rents had always to be deducted. The business was easily learned, and owing to the conditions in which
it was carried on, the supply of labour, male and female, was
Spreading practically unlimited. In periods of occasional depression
work. even benevolent masters had believed they were doing the
kindest thing in spreading the work among many families,
so as to give all a little to do, on the principle that a little
work was better than none[5]. There was thus a stint on the
employment of each hand and the irregularity of their work
was in itself a serious evil. Mr Muggeridge rightly regarded
this practice of spreading work as the main cause of all the
distress[6], and appears to favour the granting of allotments[7] as

[1] *Parl. Debates,* xxi. 966.

[2] *Reports,* &c. 1845, xv. p. 51. In 1819 a special appeal to the charity of the
nation was made on their behalf by Robert Hall, but the distress was constantly
recurring, p. 107.   [3] Felkin, 473.

[4] *Reports,* &c. 1845, xv. 117. The long established custom of idling on Saturday
to Monday to which the Factory Commissioners called attention in 1833 was not
so entirely without excuse as they believed, but seems to have been originally due
to this unsatisfactory trade usage. *Ib.* 1833, xx. 534.

[5] *Reports,* &c. 1845, xv. 65.   [6] *Ib.* 142.

[7] *Ib.* 138. This practice proved favourable to hand-loom weavers at Bridport
(*Ib.* 1840, xxiii. 288), but its success depended on the precise form of the scheme
and one of the methods tried at Frome did little good. (*Ib.* 300.)

a means of affording valuable occupation in their leisure time. A.D. 1815 —1846.
But though this expedient was tried, it could not serve to
raise wages; the industrial 'reserve[1]' was so large, that the
capitalists could force the stockingers to accept any terms,
while the charge for frame rents ran remorselessly on. The
stockingers had endeavoured to contest these claims and had *Frame rents.*
raised a case under the Truck Acts, but it was given against
them[2]; altogether the circumstances of the trade were such
that capitalists had the opportunity of acting very oppres-
sively towards the men. As appears to have been generally the case, under such circumstances, the larger masters
maintained on the whole an honourable course, but there
were men with small capital who had great difficulty in
carrying on business at all and who were much less scrupulous. The worst cases appear to have been those of the so-
called independent frames[3] which were owned by outsiders *Independ-ent frames.*
who had no footing in the trade, either as masters or men,
but who regarded frames as a paying investment, and speculated in the business. This state of affairs helps to explain
the peculiar character of the Luddite riots and frame-work
knitters' strikes, as they appear to have been specially
directed against particular masters[4], though they were latterly
supported by concerted action throughout the whole trade.

There was no class of workmen who were more dis- *Distress not due to ma-*
tressed during this period than the frame-work knitters, *chinery*
and their case affords a crucial experiment in regard to *but to*
the causes of the distress which fell so generally on the
working classes. There was no great difference between the
conditions of the trade when the riots broke out in 1778
and in 1812 or 1840; there was no new invention which
revolutionised the trade, though it had not been allowed to
stagnate and minor improvements had been introduced from
time to time, but there was no real attempt to substitute
steam or water power[5] for hand labour. In this case there
could be no pretence that mechanical improvements had
even contributed to the degradation of the worker. It was

---

[1] F. Engels, *Die Lage*, 109.   [2] Felkin, 455.
[3] *Reports*, 1845, xv. 68.   [4] *Ib.* 188.
[5] *Ib.* 88, though some unimportant attempts had been made in Manchester. *Ib.* 103.

A.D. 1815
—1846.
*reckless
competition.*
due to a combination of circumstances which may perhaps be best described as reckless competition.

By way of pointing the contrast, it is worth while to refer to the condition of the Somersetshire cloth manufacture; that too, was a declining trade, as it was tending to migrate to Yorkshire. In it too, there was a considerable lack of employment, and yet wages fell but little. These were phenomena which surprised Mr Austen, the Assistant Commissioner on hand-loom weaving in 1840, and he made special enquiries in the hope of explaining them. He came to the conclusion that the Somersetshire manufacturers *Competi-* were forced to try to maintain their position, by aiming at *tion main-* the best quality of goods[1]; that they competed against one *taining* *quality and* another for excellence of quality rather than cheapness of *wages.* price; and that the large and important houses were forced to pay high wages so as to secure the best possible work. There was a danger however that a man might so far lose his eyesight as to be unfit for the best work, in which case he might be forced to take employment with one of the small masters who made a coarser cloth and had to squeeze their profit from any source in their power. In this industry the large capitalists had been inclined to favour the men in a case where they struck for higher wages[2].

Low paid As a matter of fact the impoverished condition of the *labour pre-* frame-work knitters was so far from being the result of the *vented the* *introduc-* introduction of machinery, that it might be more properly *tion of ma-* described as the chief obstacle which hindered this change. *chinery.* The organisation of a factory with new machinery was a difficult and costly experiment; it was sure to be unpopular[3], even if it was not the object of a violent attack, and the restraint and regularity of factory work was so irksome that there was difficulty in procuring suitable hands[4]. No capitalist was likely to undertake all these risks unless he saw his way to make a considerable profit; when labour was very poorly paid and the expenses of production were exceedingly small, there was no reason to suppose that a

---

[1] *Reports*, &c. 1840, xxiii. 289.   [2] *Ib.* 290.   [3] *Ib.* 147, 175.
[4] Ipswich was reported to be very unfavourable for factories from the unwillingness of the people to submit to order and confinement. *Ib.* 196.

profit could be secured by substituting machinery. It was A.D. 1815
—1846.
said that the application of power to frame-work knitting
was perfectly easy, but that the cheapness of labour rendered it unremunerative; in the same way there was a time
when it appeared[1] probable that there would be such a
decline in the rates paid for hand-loom weaving that the
power-loom would never be brought in.

The weaving trade in some of its branches also offers *Competi-* a contrast to frame-work knitting, because though both were *tion of women's* domestic industries, they were not equally available as occu- *labour.* pations for women and children. Certain classes of goods could of course be woven by women, but they had little em-ployment as weavers in the hemp and flax trades, where the fabrics were very heavy; in this case the weavers appear to have had less fluctuating wages than in the other textile industries[2].

Fully recognising then, the enormous economic gain *Limitation* which has come about through competition, it is useless *of competi-tion by Par-* to ignore the fact that there may be unwise competition; *liament* in so far as the effects of competition were found to be nationally disastrous, Parliament has endeavoured with more or less wisdom to interfere. In so far as the comfort of the artisans was concerned, they showed themselves to be very far-seeing when they determined to organise them- *and Trades* selves, so that the undue competition of capitalists should *Unions.* not drive down wages, but that the comfort of the working man should be as far as possible a fixed quantity, and capitalists be made to "compete with each other's profits[3]."

371. When the political agitation was allayed for the time by the passing of the Reform Bill, public attention was at once directed to the social condition of the people. *The social condition of* The Factory Acts, which had been already passed, showed *the people.* that the unreformed Parliament had not failed to take cog-nisance of the new evils as soon as they appeared, but these

---

[1] *Reports*, &c. 1840, xxiii. 307. This opinion rested on the fact that the art of weaving was easily learned (*Ib.* 375) and that there was in England a large surplus population.

[2] *Ib.* 190. At Cullompton women were excluded from learning the trade by a sort of union rule, and so long as this practice was maintained, the rates of wages for men were successfully kept up. *Ib.* 250.   [3] *Ib.* 1833, xx. 539.

measures had been utterly inadequate and remained a dead letter. But the great increase of the factory system attracted notice on every side; while the allegations as to its bad results both physical and moral were constantly reiterated by competent observers; but it was obviously impossible to attempt a remedy until the charges were thoroughly sifted and an opinion could be formed as to the extent and character of the evils. A commission of enquiry was appointed which was excellently organised and obtained an extraordinary amount of accurate information in a short space of time.

Factory Commission.

The Commission of 1833 specially addressed their enquiries to the alleged degradation of the population as a national evil; and hence the points which demanded attention were, the influence of the Factory System on the children who would grow up to be workers, and on the women who would be the mothers of the next generation. If there was physical and moral taint at these sources the future of the English race was imperilled. The men were anxious to have a measure passed that would limit their hours as well, often in the expectation that the shortening of hours would lead to a rise of wages[1]; and the condition of the women and children appeared to be made use of, as an excuse, by those whose real object was to obtain shorter hours for themselves. But the Commissioners were inclined to treat the complaints of the men as irrelevant to their enquiry; since it was obvious that their condition was to some extent in their own hands[2], while the women and children were not free agents in the same sense; and neither the hours nor the wages of workmen in factories contrasted unfavourably with those of men employed in other industries. In the present day we are inclined to think that the hours of all were far too long, and to rejoice in the steps by which artisans have secured a shorter day. But at that date there was nothing special in the condition of the adult hands which marked them out for particular enquiry.

Inquiry as to condition of Women and Children.

Indeed the alleged mischiefs in regard to factories were

[1] *Reports*, &c. 1833, xx. 39, 51.   [2] See below, p. 627.

different in kind from those of which the frame-work knitters A.D. 1815 had to complain; the misery of the latter was simply and —1846. solely due to extreme poverty; they were in distress because they were so badly paid that, however hard they laboured at *Not a ques-* the work offered them, they were quite unable to make a *tion of wages, but* living; but the wages of the factory hands were fairly good *of condi-* as things went[1]. The mischiefs connected with factories were *tions of work.* due to the conditions under which the work was done; whether the reward of work was high or low, the evils attaching to the manner in which it was carried on were very great; but these differed considerably in various trades. In order to understand them at all clearly, we must take the various textile trades in turn, and consider what were the special disabilities connected with employment in each kind of factory. We shall then be able to judge more clearly how far these were evils which were common to all.

i. With regard to the woollen trade, whether in York- *The* shire or the West of England, there was a practical consensus *woollen trade.* of opinion. Messrs Horner and Woolriche after visiting the Stroud Valley gave exceedingly favourable testimony in regard *Stroud* to the conditions of work in that district[2], and indeed through- *Valley.* out the whole area they had visited, though the trade was declining[3] and several mills had been shut up. They particularly testified to the kindly interest which the employers took in their hands[4]; and though there were many matters in which improvement was possible, they found that the employers were, on the whole, ready to make any improvements, the desirability of which was pointed out; they could find no evidence that seemed to them to justify legislative interference. The employers in Yorkshire were equally sure of *Yorkshire.* their position; the trustees of the White Cloth Hall at Leeds met the Commissioners with a petition for exemption from any proposed legislation, on the ground that there were no abuses in their trade which called for it. Some parts of the work were very dirty, but the Assistant Commissioner appears to have been satisfied, after his enquiries, that these opera-

---

[1] See especially Sir D. Barry's Report on this point. *Reports, &c.* 1833, XXI. p. 31, and especially p. 65; also 1833, XX. 807 and 1008.

[2] *Ib.* 929, 1006.   [3] *Ib.* 951, 960.   [4] *Ib.* 1006.

A.D. 1815
—1846. tions were not deleterious. From his remarks it seems that the one point on which he was thoroughly dissatisfied was the early age at which children went to work in these mills[1]. Had all the factories been as well conducted as those connected with the clothing trade, it seems unlikely that public opinion would have been aroused to the necessity for special factory legislation.

Linen Factories.   ii. Very different was the condition of the linen factories. Owing to the nature of the material it was convenient to spin and weave flax when it was wet, and as a consequence, *Wet spinning.* the workers were subjected to a continual spray, from which special clothing was unable to protect them adequately; while they were also forced to stand in the wet, and their hands were liable to constant sores from never being dry. Long-continued work of this kind was fraught with serious mischief, and the Commissioners felt that every effort should be made to reduce these causes of discomfort[2]. There was *Heckling.* besides a process known as heckling[3], which was almost entirely done by children. The machines used were not large, so that there could be great numbers working in each room; the children had to be on the alert all the time, and to be so quick that the strain on them was very considerable; while a frightful amount of dust was set free in the process and the state of the atmosphere in the rooms was exceedingly bad.

Cotton Mills.   iii. The conditions of cotton spinning were similar in many ways to those of flax, though there was nowhere so much dust as in the heckling rooms, and no web spinning, but the temperature in which the hands worked was often very high.

Silk Mills.   iv. The conditions of the silk manufacture were quite unlike those of other textile trades; it was still carried on in the Eastern Counties and in various parts of England, but its *The Spital- fields Act 1773* history was very peculiar. In 1773 the Spitalfields Act was passed, by which the magistrates were empowered to fix wages in accordance with a list agreed upon by representatives of the masters and the men. In the few cases where the parties disagreed the magistrates were empowered to decide between them, and it is said that they had invariably, with

---

[1] *Reports*, &c. 1833, xx. 602, 604.   [2] *Ib.* 328.   [3] *Ib.* 600.

one solitary exception, pronounced in favour of the men[1]. A.D. 1815 —1846. The English manufacturer was protected against foreign competition, and under these circumstances the system of regulation was maintained with fair success. The trade extended moreover into the neighbouring counties; it found its way to Colchester about the end of the eighteenth century and into Berkshire somewhat earlier[2]; and as the cloth manufacture of Bocking and Braintree, Sudbury and Lavenham, and of Norwich migrated northwards, silk weaving was more generally introduced. When however the prohibition *repealed 1824.* on foreign silks was withdrawn, and the Spitalfields Act was repealed in 1824, the trade seriously declined. It is on the condition of the weavers that we get the fullest information; they seem to have been a highly respectable class of men but they suffered frightfully from irregularity of employment; on the other hand the mills were in a most unsatisfactory condition. The work was chiefly done by girls who were parish apprentices, and there was grave reason for complaint as to the demoralising effect of huddling them together during their years of service, as well as of the reckless manner in which they were cut adrift when they had served their time.

In attempting to estimate the general result, it is well to bear in mind that in 1833 weaving sheds were not a regular department of a mill, and that the mill hands were chiefly engaged in preparing the materials and in spinning, though in some cases the work of cloth dressing had been added. Though *Effects of Standing and Stooping.* there were some differences in the machinery employed, the necessity of standing for long hours and of stooping was similar in most of them; and there is abundant evidence that many children were crippled for life and that young women were seriously injured by their occupations. The worsted spinning at Bradford had a specially evil reputation in this respect[3]. The Commissioners rightly connected it with the very early age at which children went to work, and the long hours during which they were employed, and the medical testimony proved that serious mischief of this kind

---

[1] *Reports,* &c. 1840, xxiii. 201.   [2] *Ib.* 129, 138.
[3] *Ib.* 1833, xx. 608.

C. II.   40

A.D. 1815 —1846.

was common in all the great industrial centres[1]. The Commissioners are careful to note that the physical evils due to the over-fatigue of children were prevalent in the well-managed as well as in the badly-managed mills.

For after all there were mills and mills; and though there was much room for improvement in all of them, the crying evils were much more pronounced in some cases than *The small mills;* in others. In every respect the small mills were very much the worst[2], they were carried on by men who had but comparatively little capital, and who had to compete against the better machinery and better power of their neighbours[3]. These smaller mills had an evil reputation in every way; the *cruelty and* cases where children were severely punished by the workmen they assisted were not so common as was popularly supposed, but it was clearly established that this practice was carried on by some of the slubbers[4], though the evil was abating on the whole[5]. In no case that I remember was the connivance of the masters proved, and in some they endeavoured to prevent it[6]. In fact this piece of tyranny appears to have been chiefly due to a few of the more dissipated workmen. In *immorality.* regard to matters of morality too, the smaller mills had an evil reputation. They were carried on by men of a specially coarse type, who were particularly inclined to tyrannise over a class but slightly beneath them, yet completely in their power[7]; there had been some slight improvement, but in all these matters, the small factories were unfavourably distinguished[8]. In fact it is obvious that the worst abuses occurred, not where the capitalist was so powerful that he could do as he liked, but in cases where the capitalist was struggling for his very existence and was forced to carry on the trade in any way he could.

Long hours and irregularity of work with water-power. Similarly, the small mills were the worst places in regard to length of hours; and in those cases, where it occurred, of very insufficient pay. The old-fashioned mills were dependent on water-power; but in many instances the supply was insufficient and the mill worked with great irregularity.

[1] *Reports*, 1833, xx. 32—35.   [2] *Ib.* 25, 64.
[3] *Ib.* 20, 24; 1840, xxiii. 248.   [4] *Ib.* 1833, xx. 23, 28, 49.
[5] *Ib.* 26.   [6] *Ib.* 28.   [7] *Ib.* 20.
[8] F. Engels, *Lage*, p. 184; *Reports*, 1833, xx. 24, 186, 145.

Under such circumstances the hands were obliged at times to work for long hours when the water was available, in order to make up for a deficiency in their wages, owing to the time when they had been left idle from the want of water-power. This irregularity of employment was only too apt to render the men dissipated, as they were forced to alternate periods of excessive work and entire idleness. They frequently had to work extra hours without extra pay, in order to make up for stoppages; by far the worst cases in connection with the treatment of children were due to instances where they were under the control of men, who were working irregularly and with whom they had to keep pace[1]. The race between steam and water-power was not finally decided in 1833; but water-power was still considered cheaper, though steam was pre- *Steam-power and large mills.* ferred, as without it, the manufacturers could not count on a constant supply of power. It is thus obvious that at the time of the Commission things were already beginning to mend. The little mills and water mills were the worst in every respect, but they were dying out in competition with the large capitalists who worked by steam.

The real nature of the evils which were generally preva- *Discriminating proposal of Commissioners.* lent may perhaps be most clearly gathered from the discriminating proposal which the Commissioners put forward. They objected to a ten hours' day, as this would afford insufficient relief to the children, while it did not appear to be necessary for the sake of the adults; and according to the opinion of many workmen and masters it would reduce the income of the men in a fashion for which the shortened hours would give no commensurate advantage. They proposed instead to try and arrange for shifts, by which the labour of the children might be so organised that they should work for shorter hours than adults. An experiment of this kind had been *Shifts.* tried with great success in the Marshalls' flax mills at Holbeck, near Leeds. It was, however, a difficult arrangement to carry out, and in country villages it was not easy to find a double shift of child labour. The manufacturers disliked a proposal that would hamper them, and the parents were on the whole glad to get an income from the children's labour.

---

[1] *Reports,* &c. 1833, xx. 12, 15, 16.

A.D. 1815
—1846.
*Necessity
and diffi-
culty of le-
gislative in-
terference.*

It was this combined influence that rendered the legisla-tive protection of children necessary, but there were grave difficulties in passing the measure as feeling on the subject ran very high. A select committee of the House of Commons had taken evidence in the preceding session and had heard all the witnesses brought forward by Mr Sadler to prove that legislative interference was necessary. The session had closed however before the evidence, which the employers[1] desired to put in, could be taken; and the sense of this injustice rankled in their minds, while the evidence was in many respects un-

*Public Ex-
citement.*

trustworthy[2]. Still the allegations were so frightful that many people believed that immediate action was necessary at any cost; and the proposal in the following year to have a Commission, had been treated as a mere excuse for delay[3]. In the excited state of public feeling, there was great diffi-culty in carrying a well-considered measure, but the Govern-ment were on the whole successful in giving effect to the recommendations of the Commission. The chief debate was upon the proposal to limit the work of those under eighteen to ten hours. Lord Ashley was defeated on this point as the Government thought it necessary to go farther and limit those under fourteen to eight hours; and from the time of this defeat the Bill became a Government measure to which Lord Ashley gave independent support. And in the main the recommendations of the Commissioners were accepted by

*Factory
Inspectors.*

Parliament[4]. They prohibited the more crying abuses, and they appointed a machinery by which the new law might be administered. Little good had resulted from the power of the Justices to appoint Inspectors under a previous Act. But the Inspectors appointed by the Secretary of State have had a very real influence in the gradual amelioration of the con-dition of factories. ·

372. In attempting to estimate the influence of the factory system upon the population, we are brought face to face with a very grave difficulty,—so far as the spinning trades are concerned, and this was the more important part of

---

[1] 3 Hansard, Vol. xv. p. 391.
[2] See the opinions of Mr Drinkwater and Mr Power, *Reports*, 1833, xx. 491, 602.
[3] 3 Hansard, xvi. 641.   [4] 3 and 4 Will. IV. c. 103.

factory occupation at this date. The influence of the factories A.D. 1815 —1846. had been to create a new class, who lived by an occupation which had been carried on in previous generations, by women and children as a by-employment. The factory operatives *A new class of factory operatives.* were a new class that had come into being in consequence of these mechanical improvements. The industrial revolution, along with other causes which have been already discussed, had destroyed the old state of society where spinning was an adjunct in the domestic economy of a husbandman or a weaver. As has been already pointed out there was a terrible loss in the severance of agriculture and industry, since the husbandman became solely dependent upon the land, while the industrial population were solely dependent upon trade. Each was left with a single string to the bow, and was exposed to irregularity of employment and fluctuation of wages, such as were impossible in the old days; but the destruction of this old life was inevitable, if human beings were to take advantage of the new improvements in the powers of production; evil as it was, it was an inevitable *Loss and gain.* incident of real material progress. If we do well to congratulate ourselves on the introduction of machinery at all, we must recognise that the break up of the old domestic system was imperative. The social loss and the moral loss were undoubted at the time[1]. The economic gain is indisputable; we may perhaps believe that the opportunities for moral wellbeing which material gain affords have been already utilised to such an extent, that we need not regret the loss of the old order, with its narrow interests and homely virtues[2].

It was in connection with the cotton manufacture that *Cotton manufacture and overcrowded towns.* men first began to realise that a new class had been called into being. In Manchester and the towns round about it, there was a vast increase of population, and as early as 1796 Dr Aikin and Dr Perceval called attention to the miserable condition in which they lived. Sir Robert Peel's Bill in 1802 and the Select Committee in 1818, had exclusive reference to the cotton trade; as had the Factory Act which Sir John Hobhouse pressed on the Commons for five years, till at last

---

[1] There is however some reason to believe that the good qualities of this bygone generation have been exaggerated. See above, pp. 383, 386, 474, 589, 599.

[2] Engels, *Lage,* 14.

it was carried in 1830[1]. The cotton manufacture was responsible for the growth of large provincial towns. And the
misery the operatives endured was not only due to the conditions under which they worked, but to the frightful accommodation in which they lived. The sudden flocking of the
population to these towns was the occasion of over-crowding
in its worst forms, and gave the speculative builder a magnifi-
The housing of the poor. cent opportunity for erecting insanitary dwellings. Friedrich
Engels' painstaking description of the housing of the Man-
1844. chester poor is well worth perusal[2]. The evil had then been
of long standing, and yet it was so far new that no administrative machinery had been created which was competent to deal
with it. Not till the cholera appeared and it became obvious
that the condition in which the labourer constantly lived was
a source of public danger in times of pestilence were serious
measures taken to improve industrial dwellings and to remedy
the defective sanitation of our great towns.

The factory operatives and domestic workers. Since the factory operatives were a new class, the only
possible comparison in regard to their well-being is with
other classes at the same date. Enough has been said to
show that it was a time of general depression and of dear
food. The whole of the working classes suffered; and the
standard of comfort of all, whether they were affected by
machinery or not was miserably low. But it is difficult to
fix on any point in which the factory worker was worse off
than other artisans of similar skill[3], while he was better off
than those engaged as weavers in domestic industries. In
1833 the power-loom had not become so universal as to compete very seriously with the hand-loom weavers; yet even at
that date the factory operatives appear to have been in
better case[4]. No evidence was called for about the over-
working of children who assisted their parents at home, but
there is no reason to believe that they fared better than their
companions in the mills. In only one point, and that a most
important one, was it alleged that the condition of the
domestic workers was preferable. Parents could look after
their own children and the elder girls if they worked at

[1] 3 Hansard, Vol. XVII. 85.   [2] Engels, *Lage*, 39—88.
[3] *Reports*, 1833, XX. 307.   [4] *Ib.* 55, 1008.

home, whilst the factories had an evil repute. Careful A.D. 1815 —1846.
parents had to choose between the evil of bringing up their
children to an over-crowded and under-paid trade, and the
risk of placing them in evil surroundings[1]. At the same
time it is probable that these evils diminished, as the smaller
mills were broken up; and Mr Bolling, the member for
Bolton, appears to have regarded the evil as illusory so far as
his constituency was concerned[2].

373. The gradual amelioration of the general condition *Alleged causes of the special evils in Factories.*
of the working classes will demand our attention presently;
but in the meantime, it is worth while to look for a little
at the causes of those exceptional evils to which children
in factories were subject, and which the Act of 1833 did
so much to reduce.

While all parties were agreed in deploring the misery
which existed, there was a great difference of opinion as
to the nature of the evil and therefore as to the true
remedy. Colonel Williams probably expressed the com-
monest opinion both in the House and out of doors when
he said that "this practice of over working children was *Avarice of Masters.*
attributable to the avarice of the masters[3]." Mr Hume on
the other hand, defended the capitalists, and as he had
presided over the Select Committee which reported against *Avarice of Landlords.*
the Combination Laws, his opinion on industrial conditions
was entitled to respect. He held that the distress of the
country was wholly due to the Corn Laws and laid the
blame on the owners of land[4]. Mr Cobbett, who was member
for Oldham and had abundant opportunity of forming a
judgment in his own constituency, exonerated the employers.
He held that the immediate blame lay with the parents *Avarice of Parents.*
but that they should not be too harshly judged, as they
were driven to it by the pressure of taxation which as he
believed was the ultimate reason of their distress[5].

So far as the parents are concerned, it is probably true
that many of the baser sort were very reckless in regard

---

[1] *Reports*, &c. 1833, xx. 532, 538. The bad repute of factories was not im-
probably due to their being the resort of apprenticed children and a shifting population when they were first organised.

[2] 3 Hansard, Vol. xix. 910.   [3] *Ib.* xv. 1160.

[4] *Ib.* 1161.   [5] *Ib.* 1294.

to the treatment of their children, and were not unwilling to sacrifice them in order to profit by their earnings; but there were many who felt the evils most bitterly, and who petitioned for an alteration[1]. At the same time it is difficult *Parents cannot be wholly exonerated.* to exonerate them altogether if, as seems to have been the case, their wages were as good or better than those of other labourers. Mr Power, the Assistant Commissioner, seems to have felt this when he wrote that "children ought to have legislative protection from the conspiracy insensibly formed between the masters and parents to tax them with a degree of toil beyond their strength[2]." It is probable that the opportunity of obtaining the children's earnings was a temptation which few parents could resist, even though they might afterwards deeply regret it when it resulted in the deformity of their children. There is no difficulty in reconciling the two statements, that on the one hand the parents frequently succumbed to this temptation and that on the other they were anxious to have the temptation removed.

Corn laws do not account for special evils. So far as the landlords and the Corn Laws are concerned, little need be said. This was a cause which affected the textile industries, like other industries, as it rendered food dear to all labourers; but it will not serve to account for the special mischiefs of the factory system.

Employers and carelessness about accident. With regard to the masters, it may be said at once that it is impossible to exonerate them from all blame, as many of them had been exceedingly careless about a matter which lay entirely within their control, and to which no allusion has yet been made. The frequency of accidents in the mills, with the injury of life and limb, was a feature which specially shocked the public, and it seems to have been clear that many of the accidents were preventible and need not have occurred if certain machines had been properly fenced[3]. So long as any part of the evils were due to arrangements directly under the masters' control and with which no one else could interfere, it is clear that the blame lay with them or with their agents[4].

---

[1] 3 Hansard, xvi. 642.   [2] *Reports*, 1833, xx. 604.   [3] *Ib.* 76.
[4] The punishments which Lord Ashley proposed to inflict on employers in connection with accidents in their mills were very severe. Parliament appears to

But in regard to the other evils, it is not easy to see how far the employers were free agents and how much they were to blame for the condition of the workers. Many of them, like the parents, were in favour of a legislative restriction of hours[1]. Foreign tariffs were prohibitive and foreign industry was advancing, and as the restrictions on the import of corn hindered the sale of our goods abroad, manufacturers found it difficult to make any profit. It was stated in 1833 that for the seven preceding years, the cotton spinners had hardly been able to carry on the trade at all[2], that the trade was in a most uncertain condition, and that capital was being frightened away to new investments[3]. The philanthropists were inclined to assume that English textile manufactures had such a commanding position, that even if the hours were reduced and the cost of production increased, we could still hold our own. Many of the men were inclined to hope that, when the product was limited, prices would rise and their own wages would improve[4]. But this optimist view had little to support it. The cotton manufacture was springing up, both in the United States and in France; the annual output of these two countries alone was two-thirds that of Britain[5], and there was a real danger of driving away trade and therefore employment altogether. As Lord Althorp said when criticising the original form of the Factory measure in 1833, "Should its effect be (and he feared it was but too reasonable to apprehend it might be) to increase the power of foreigners to compete in the British market, and so to cause the decline of the manufacturing interest of the country * * so far from a measure of humanity it would be one of the greatest acts of cruelty that could be inflicted[6]." Under these circumstances, it is impossible to regard the opponents of the Factory Acts as necessarily callous to human suffering. Some of them at least believed that if the product was reduced, the suffering would be greater, though it would arise in other forms.

Margin notes: A.D. 1815 —1846. *How far were they responsible?* *Narrow margin of profit.*

have supposed that they were so excessive that they would never have been enforced. 3 Hansard, xix. 223.

[1] Ib. xvi. 642; xvii. 87.   [2] Ib. xix. 897.   [3] Reports, &c. 1833, xx. 54, 371.
[4] Ib. 40.   [5] 3 Hansard, xix. 911.   [6] Ib. 221.

On this point indeed there was a pretty general con-sensus of opinion; that opinion has since been proved mis-taken, but it was very general; shortened hours appeared almost certain to tend to the reduction of the output. This was the opinion of many of the working classes, who believed that the reduction of hours would mean higher wages and more employment, and who advocated the Ten Hours' Bill on that account. They assumed that the quantity to be made was a constant thing, whatever the price might be; and that if it was produced by more hands, each working shorter hours, the labourers would gain[1]. This expedient for benefiting the working classes was one in which they seemed to place considerable confidence, and it lies at the basis of much of the early agitation, in which they stood out for higher wages. There were of course a few of them who saw that the reduction of the product would probably mean a reduction in pay, and who preferred their present hours and pay, to shortened hours and less pay[2]. But on the whole the artisans appear to have agreed with the masters as to the immediate effect on the output, though they differed as to the ulterior result for themselves.

There was however some little evidence to suggest that the reduction of the product, which was generally expected, need not necessarily follow from shortened hours. There had been

experiments at New Lanark and elsewhere[3], which showed at all events that the product in textile trades did not vary directly according to the length of hours of labour. Mr Robert Owen had reduced the hours of labour for a time without loss; when they were subsequently lengthened again, there was not a proportional increase in the amount pro-duced[4]. The arguments for and against an Eight Hours' Bill render this a familiar idea in the present day. By im-proved machinery, and increased intensity of labour[5], the product has been increased even though hours have been shortened. The facts have neither justified the forebodings

---

[1] *Reports*, 1833, xx. 40, 51.   [2] *Ib.* 367.   [3] *Ib.* 366.
[4] *Ib.* 194. See also Robert Owen's evidence before Sir Robert Peel's Select Committee in 1816. *Ib.* 1816, iii. 255, 272.
[5] Karl Marx, *Das Kapital*, i. 417.

of the capitalists nor the expectations of the artisans; on the A.D. 1815 whole Lord Ashley and the philanthropists[1], who set their —1846. faces against existing evils and determined to risk unknown ones, have been justified by the result.

374. In spite of the improvement which was made by Factory Acts, the condition of those engaged in the textile trades continued to demand attention. In 1839 a Parliamentary Commission commenced investigating the condition of the hand-loom weavers. The substitution of machine for *The hand-loom* hand labour went on at different times in different depart- *weavers.* ments. Power-spinning was established in cotton, before the machinery began to be applied to woollen-spinning; but during the earlier part of this century the substitution was practically complete, and power spinning was used for all materials[2]. We have already seen the struggle in regard to the dressing of cloth both in the West of England[3] and in Yorkshire[4], and the reason why power was not applied to frame-work knitting[5]. Of other processes combing was still done by hand[6], but it was not till the decade between 1830 and 1840 that the struggle between hand-weaving and power-weaving became a serious matter[7].

The weavers' trade as a whole had been depressed since *Long continued depression.* the close of the war[8], and wages had steadily declined[9], but this depression had followed a somewhat different course in different trades.

i. By general consent the linen weavers were suffering *Linen weavers.* more than any other class of weaver in 1839. Their wages had steadily fallen; they had resorted to strikes over and over again but always without success; several distinct price lists had been issued, as in 1829 and in 1837, but the masters did not adhere to them, and each new list gave greatly reduced figures[10]. This depressed condition was partly due to the competition of Irish immigrants[11], but the trade was also over-crowded by cotton weavers. The power-loom had been very generally introduced, so far as cotton fabrics were

---

[1] 3 Hansard, xix. 890.   [2] *Reports*, 1833, xx. 335.
[3] See above, p. 456.   [4] See above, p. 456.   [5] See above, p. 620.
[6] Carding by hand survived to some extent in 1833. *Reports*, 1833, xx. 336.
[7] See above, p. 454.   [8] *Accounts*, 1839, xlii. 609.
[9] *Ib.* 1840, xxiii. c. 280.   [10] *Reports*, 1840, xxiii. 317.   [11] *Ib.* 315.

concerned[1], and the cotton weavers took refuge in the linen trade; thus before the power-loom had been applied to linen fabrics the artisans were suffering most seriously from an indirectly induced competition[2]. The over-crowding of this trade was the more remarkable as linen weaving was exceedingly heavy work in which women did not compete[3].

Silk weavers.

ii. The condition of the silk weavers is not exactly similar to that of men engaged on other fabrics, as this had always been an exotic trade; from the time of the repeal of the protective legislation in 1824 they had been in great difficulties. Their business was not at all hard to learn, and this manufacture also was over-crowded, as cloth weaving was over-crowded, by men who had drifted into it from a similar calling. When the cloth manufacture migrated[4] from Essex

---

[1] At the same time it appears that the immediate result was an extraordinary impetus to the trade; that very few hand-looms actually stopped work altogether, but that the weavers were forced to put up with less regular employment and at somewhat lower rates. After the great distress in 1837 it became obvious that the cotton weaving by hand was doomed to extinction. *Report*, 1840, xxiv. 650, 658.

[2] *Ib.* xxiii. 335. "There are many causes that have been at work in bringing the hand-loom weavers' wages to this starvation price, and we will beg leave to state our opinion of a few of them. The power-loom is one, and though but little progress has yet been made in working linen goods, yet, by having nearly destroyed the cotton weaving, and greatly injured the stuff and woollen weavers' trade, it has driven many out of those branches into the linen trade, and overstocked the market with hands; and the manufacturers have taken the advantage, and reduced the wages; but we believe it is nothing to their profit. Now, these power-looms contribute nothing to the revenue; on the contrary, they have been the means of throwing great numbers out of employment, and has (sic) brought thousands and tens of thousands to sup the cup of misery even to its very dregs, and, if not speedily checked, will, ere long, bring the whole of the weaving trade to complete ruin. We think at any rate the power-loom ought to pay as much as the hand-loom weaver pays, and then we should have some chance of competing with them. Besides the many indirect taxes that we have to pay to the Government, we have other taxes of a still more grievous nature, and it is said by many writers of far greater amount. These taxes cut like a two-edged sword; it is not only the great amount that we have to pay, but at the same time it greatly injures our trade. This tax is what they call 'protecting duties' to the great landed property men of this country, not only the heavy duty on corn, but on every necessary of life, even to an egg."

[3] *Ib.* 191.

[4] The migration of the cloth manufacture from the eastern counties to Yorkshire received a considerable impetus during the long war. The flying shuttle and mill yarn were used in Yorkshire (*Reports*, 1840, xxiii. 417), and wages there were extraordinarily high (*Ib.* 399), while all machinery appears to have been tabooed in the eastern counties (*Ib.* 147), unless in some newly-introduced trades (*Ib.* 175). The last remnants of the eastern counties' cloth manufacture were the camlets

and Suffolk and Norfolk to Yorkshire[1], the Eastern County *A.D. 1815 —1846.*
weavers took up the silk trade[2]; but even in its best days,
they had to work at lower prices than the weavers in Spitalfields[3]. In this case they had over-crowding of every kind; *Over-*
the competition of women's work, of those who picked up the *crowding.*
trade hastily, of foreign weavers, and of the power-loom.
There was violent resistance to the introduction of the power-
loom in Coventry in 1831[4]; but the trade, as taken up and
improved in Macclesfield[5], completely undersold the efforts of *Power-*
the Spitalfields and Eastern Counties weavers, among whom *looms at Maccles-*
apparently the feeling against machinery was so strong, that *field.*
no one attempted to introduce it. In the southern centres
of the trade this employment gave early instances of the
phenomena of spreading work, and the industrial reserve, *Spreading*
alluded to above[6]. One of the Braintree witnesses describes *work.*
how "a manufacturer would give out work to twelve men,
where seven would have been enough to do it, if warp and
shute had been given to them as fast as they worked it up.
The object of this system evidently was to keep a great
number of hands in the trade always at command, in order
that when there was a great demand for goods, the manufacturer might have it in his power to produce them. * * *
Thus the earnings of the weavers were kept down, though
they were said to be employed. This system also kept a
greater number of hands in the trade and thereby kept up a
greater competition for employment, and prevented a rise of
price when there was an increased demand for goods[7]."

The chief remedies which the weavers themselves pro- *The sug-*
posed were either a more rigid system of apprenticeship by *gested remedies*
which the number of competitors might be kept down, or an *were im-*
authoritative price list, such as they had had, under the Spital- *practicable.*
fields Act; but even under that Act they had not enjoyed

---

which were made for the China market as long as the East India Co. had the
monopoly, but when the trade was thrown open in 1833, the Yorkshireman undersold them in this article also (*Reports*, 1840, xxiii. 142). The West of England
manufacture of serges suffered in a similar fashion (*Ib.* 250).

[1] The East Anglian workers stood out against machinery and were thus driven
out. *Ib.* 147, 148.   [2] *Ib.* 129.   [3] *Ib.* 125.
[4] *Ib.* 1833, xx. 899.   [5] *Ib.* 1840, xxiv. 653.   [6] See above, p. 618.
[7] *Reports*, 1840, xxiii. 126.

constant employment and the system had proved unwork-able[1]. It was absurd to ask for elaborate rules of apprentice-ship, which were not needed for the purpose of training the workmen properly[2]; this was merely intended to be an arbi-trary restriction on the number of competitors[3]. Such an expedient could not possibly help them to stand better against the competition of English machinery or foreign workmen. What the Commissioner said of weavers in general was specially true of the silk weaver,—"His best friends are those who assist him to transfer his labour to other channels of industry[4]."

Cotton weaving. · iii. The cotton trade was the first industry in which power-spinning was introduced; there had been a real diffi-culty in getting weavers in sufficient numbers to work the yarn that was spun, and it was in this trade that the power-loom had been most generally applied at the time of the enquiry. The new mode of weaving had brought about an extraordinary expansion of the trade, and it was said that comparatively few hand-looms had been put out of operation altogether[5]. At the same time part of the work that was done by hand, consisted of goods of a class, for the making of which wages were so low that machinery did not pay[6]. The com-petition of Irish immigrants was also severely felt in the West of Scotland cotton district[7]. Wages were exceedingly low, employment for hand-loom weavers was irregular, and in bad times practically ceased.

Relief Funds. There had been a great deal of distress among the Scottish weavers both in 1819 and 1826. Large relief funds were started, to which the upper classes contributed more largely than they would have done in England, where the Poor Law afforded so much relief[8]. But the most serious distress occurred throughout all the textile trades, after the American panic in 1837; and this exceptional distress had

---

[1] *Reports,* 1840, XXIII. 200.
[2] The trade was not at all hard to learn (*Ib.* 215).
[3] *Ib.* 221.   [4] *Ib.* XXIV. 659.   [5] *Ib.* 650.
[6] Blue and white stripes and checks for the export trade. *Accounts and Papers,* 1839, XLII. 535.
[7] *Reports, &c.* 1840, XXIV. 644. *Accounts and Papers,* 1839, XLII. 533—559.
[8] *Ib.* 523.

been the reason for appointing a Commission to enquire into A.D. 1815 —1846. the condition of hand-loom weavers generally[1].

One change was beginning in the cotton trade which is of interest, as it throws distinct light on the substitution of power-weaving for domestic weaving. In 1840 domestic weaving was ceasing in the cotton trade, as it had almost completely done in the Scottish woollen trade. The custom *Hand-looms in factories.* of that trade was to set up hand-looms on the master's premises, so that the weavers did not carry on their trade at their homes, but in factories[2]. The cotton weavers were not reconciled to this practice even though their earnings were considerably increased by conforming to it[3]. Their chief objection arose from the comparative freedom they enjoyed when working in their own houses; they could to some extent keep their own hours and take their own holidays, whereas if they worked in a factory, they felt that they were the slaves of its bell. The masters preferred to have them working on *Advantages and disadvantages.* the premises, as they could ensure much more regularity in executing orders. Domestic weavers could not in these days be counted upon to be punctual in delivering work at the specified time[4]. Besides this, there was much more danger of the embezzlement of materials when they were put out to the workmen's homes[5]. This was a very serious evil in some cases, as the men tried to conceal the fraud by weaving "thin" and suffered in every respect. In other localities this abuse was practically unknown[6], and it naturally differed to some extent according to the nature of the trade and the value of the materials.

It is always difficult to obtain any reliable information as *Improvement in the tone of factories.* to the general character of a class, but it certainly appears that in 1840 the stigma which attached to the Factory operative was undeserved, and that at all events the domestic weaver could no longer be regarded as an example of honest toil[7]. The Commissioners gathered the impression[8] that the

[1] *Reports*, 1840, XXIII. 642.   [2] *Ib.* 647, 649.
[3] *Ib.* 649. *Accounts and Papers*, 1839, XLII. 520.
[4] *Reports*, 1840, XXIII. 683.
[5] *Accounts*, 1839, XLII. 599. See above, pp. 357, 458 n.
[6] As in Yorkshire, *Reports*, 1840, XXIII. 414; Forfarshire, *Accounts*, 1839, XXXVIII. 401.
[7] As early as 1833 the Glasgow weavers had a very bad reputation. *Reports*, 1833, XX. 299.   [8] *Accounts*, 1839, XLII. 609.

A.D. 1815
—1846.
*Deteriora-
tion of
domestic
weaver.*
older generation of weavers were a fine class of men, though other evidence seems to show that there were black sheep among them; but the trade had been decaying since the great war, and those who had been brought up in it under the new conditions of great irregularity and poor remuneration, were of the type of dissipated men, who alternated periods of very severe work with periods of entire and not always involuntary idleness. That they were thus demoralised was undoubtedly their misfortune rather than their fault, but the fact is worth noting as showing that the industrial revolution was becoming complete, and that the workers, who were not only better off as far as wages went, but better in character, were those who had cast in their lot with the new order of things[1].

iv. Much of what has been said in the preceding section applies to woollen, as well as to cotton weaving; but there are several special points in regard to this ancient industry which demand attention. The power-loom had been generally introduced in the worsted trade which centred at Bradford, but it had only been recently adapted to the woollen trade, for which Leeds was the great market[2]. As the power-loom was introduced the market seems to have expanded; or at any rate there was employment for a large number of hands in attending the looms; but still the
weavers suffered severely, and were entirely displaced, as the new work was done not by men, but by women and girls, who had been employed on this work to some extent before, but who now seemed to be preferred to the exclusion of male weavers[3].

This was one reason for the distress felt in this industry, but there was also a complaint of some standing in regard to wages. From 1801 to 1815 wages had been exceptionally high in the cloth trades in Scotland, as well as in Yorkshire.
The special advantages of that county were attracting to it the employment which had been previously diffused through

---

[1] *Reports*, 1840, xxiv. 681. Robert Owen's experiment at New Lanark was perhaps the first instance of a well-regulated factory population, but it did not stand alone, as we may see from the account of Mr Ashton's mills at Hyde. 682.

[2] *Ib.* xxiii. 431.

[3] *Ib.* 431.

other districts; and though wages had not fallen back below the eighteenth century standard of comfort, the weavers had never reconciled themselves to the loss of the prosperity they had enjoyed during the war[1]. And indeed, though the rates of wages had apparently kept up, the work had become somewhat harder, as heavier cloths[2] were being made. At the time when the Commission sat, the power-loom was being gradually introduced; it was general in the worsted trade at Bradford, but had hardly come into operation in the Leeds district[3]. In Scotland the wages of woollen weavers were higher than those of cotton weavers, especially in the Galashiels district, where they made a class of goods which was in great demand and in the production of which there was little competition[4].

Despite this change it yet seemed that there were two *Very low class weavers could not be superseded,* distinct classes of weavers whose labour would not be affected by the introduction of machinery. There was on the one hand, very low class weaving, for which the pay was so poor that the existing machines could not compete at a profit, but this chiefly affected the cotton weavers[5]. On the other hand, those woollen weavers who did not fear the competition of machinery were the specially skilled men, *nor very highly skilled men.* whose work was supposed to be better than anything machines could turn out; ordinary fabrics could be made by the power-loom if the low rate of weavers' wages had not rendered hand-work cheaper[6]; and this was also true of certain branches in other textile trades[7]. It also appeared probable that machinery could not be made to pay in producing goods of which only a small quantity was required or where the fashion changed quickly[8], as was the case with

---

[1] *Reports*, 1840, XXIII. 399. *Accounts and Papers*, 1839, XLII. 563. The decline of wages was partly to be ascribed to the number of discharged soldiers who took up an easily learned employment and "exchanged the musket for the shuttle." *Ib.* 568.

[2] *Reports*, 1840, XXIII. 397.　　　　[3] *Ib.* 431.

[4] *Accounts and Papers*, 1839, XLII. 570. "As the weavers possess and equitably exercise. the power of preserving a just remuneration for their labour, there is no excess of hands. The masters everywhere expressed themselves desirous not to lower wages, fearing that their profits would likewise fall." See also *Ib.* 555, 556.

[5] *Reports*, 1840, XXIV. 651.　　　　[6] *Accounts*, 1839, XLII. 609.

[7] *Reports*, 1840, XXIV. 658, 660.　　　　[8] *Ib.* 651.

Paisley shawls[1]. As in the spinning mills, so in regard to the manufacture of cloth, the wool trade in all its branches appears to have been on the whole better conducted than the other trades; but the chief distress was in the West of England, whence the migration to Yorkshire was still continuing; in that region there had never been the same jealousy of machinery, and some at least were far-sighted enough to expect that the introduction of the power-loom would invigorate the trade and absorb the old hands completely.

Comparison with the Continent.

375. One of the most interesting parts of the Commissioners' Report contains the results of the inquiry they instituted in regard to the condition of hand-loom weavers on the Continent. Their comfort contrasted strikingly with the misery of the operatives at home. In Austria, in Switzerland, the work was done as had been formerly the case in England, by the peasantry. Weaving was a by-occupation[2]; though wages were low, the people were able to live in comfort, as they had two mainstays to the household. Only in one country did they report a state of affairs that at all corresponded with the condition of the English operatives; this was in Normandy[3]: in this case also, weaving was practised as a sole occupation by those who had no other means

Trade and Land.

of support. The English weavers were dependent on the fluctuating basis of trade instead of the solid basis of land. They were exposed to all the variations of circumstances which might arise from changes in foreign markets or contractions of credit. When times were bad, they suffered far more severely than the continental peasant, who had his holding to rely on, and though they might get far higher wages than he ever dreamed of, they were not able to recoup themselves for losses in bad times. In the progress of society the introduction of more powerful methods of production was

The attractive power of Capital.

inevitable, and cannot be a matter for regret; the attractive power of capital and the higher wages it offered had broken up the old system, and the misery which followed was chiefly due to extraneous causes, for the large millowners never initiated a decline of wages[4].

[1] *Accounts*, 1839, XLII. 543.   [2] *Ib.* 623, 629.

[3] *Ib.* 639; the only Scottish weavers who are specified as having a by-occupation were those of Largs, who did a little fishing. *Ib.* 519.

[4] *Reports*, 1840, XXIV. 661.

Even at the time of the hand-loom weavers' Commission. A.D. 1815 —1846.
the worst was past; the six years of factory inspection had *Signs of improvement in factory towns.*
done not a little to raise the tone among mill workers; the
conditions of life, especially with regard to intellectual improvement, and even in some quarters in regard to sanitation
and the housing of the poor, were better than in rural districts. In the opinion of one at least of the Commissioners,
migration from the country to the towns was but the means
by which the population obtained better opportunities of employment and ultimately better conditions of comfort[1].

376. The very success of the Factory Acts incited Lord
Ashley to proceed with efforts for putting down gross abuses
in the conditions of work. The Commission of 1833 had
given information in regard to various employments, such
as the labour in the potteries and in carpet weaving, which
could not be brought under the provisions of the Factory
Acts. Lord Ashley had been taunted at the end of the
session with a special animus against factory-owners, and in
1840 he proceeded to move that a Commission should be
appointed to investigate the whole subject of the employ- *Collieries and Mines.*
ment of women and children in collieries and mines[2]. When
next session the Commission presented its Report, it revealed a state of affairs that was so disgusting and brutal-
ising[3], that there was a unanimity of opinion in favour of
an immediate measure of redress. This was all the more
important as the evils were increasing with frightful rapidity, and were to some extent an indirect consequence of
the Factory Act of 1833. The education clauses in that *Effect of Education Clauses.*
Act had resulted in the discontinuance in many districts
of the employment of children in factories who were under
thirteen years of age. There was however nothing to prevent
their working in mines from very early years and for
the longest hours; and the British parent, who could no
longer exploit his children by sending them to factories,
forced them to go to work in neighbouring mines[4]. This
is one of the pieces of evidence which goes to show that
the capitalist was not solely to blame in regard to the mal-

---

[1] *Reports*, 1840. xxiv. 677. [2] 3 Hansard, lv. 1260.
[3] *Ib.* 1328. [4] *Reports*, 1840, xxiv. 687.

A.D. 1815
—1846.
treatment of children, but that there was at least a reckless connivance on the part of the parents. This indeed became still more obvious when colliers worked their own children in this way; they had not, generally speaking, the excuse of poverty, as their wages ranged considerably higher than in other callings[1]. The measure which was passed followed *Inspectors of Mines.* on the lines which had proved successful in regard to factories by arranging for the employment of Inspectors, but in other ways the circumstances of the case demanded special treatment. Boys under ten years of age were not to be employed in the pits, and the underground work of women and girls was to cease absolutely within a specified time, which it was hoped might allow for their obtaining employment in other callings[2]. There were also careful provisions with regard to the prevention of accidents; and the period of apprenticeship was defined so as to avoid the recurrence of that practical bondage which was once so common in Scotland[3].

377. The Act of 1833, and the special Inspectors who served under it, abolished the worst abuses which were characteristic of particular employments; but such interference *The general standard of comfort.* could not raise the standard of comfort, or even improve the conditions of work of the labouring classes as a whole. That can only be done permanently by calling forth new energy and self-reliance. There is no use in improving people's conditions unless you also improve them; the great work which has been done for the benefit of the working classes *Self-help.* has not been done for them, but by them. The beginnings of Trades Unions show us their first efforts, and often unwise efforts, to improve their own lot, especially by securing higher pay; while the opening of stores, the side on which the Co-operative movement has chiefly succeeded, has arisen from the desire of operatives to improve their condition by securing better opportunities for purchasing the necessaries of life.

Illegal Combinations and Strikes. The period immediately before the repeal of the Combination Laws seems to have been marked by very bitter

[1] *Reports,* 1840, xxiv. 688.   [2] 5 and 6 Vict. c. 99.
[3] *Reports,* 1844, xvi. 9.

struggles between capital and labour. The men had enjoyed A.D. 1815
—1846. high wages in various trades; and reductions were inevitable, when the depression set in at the close of the war. The masters habitually combined to force on reductions which the men were powerless to resist. One of the earliest of *London Carpenters.* these turn-outs was the great stand made by the London carpenters, when they held their ground for sixteen weeks but got beaten in the end. The men had of course combined to resist; several of them were prosecuted, while two of them spent twelve months in prison[1]. On the other hand, when a case was taken up by the men against a combination by masters, no judgment was pronounced[2], and the matter was allowed to drop. This one-sided injustice created a feeling of intense irritation, and it was generally believed that if both parties were on equal terms there would be far less bitterness[3]. Very similar evidence was given in regard to the Liverpool shipwrights, though their grievances *Liverpool Ship-wrights.* were not so much from the reduction of wages, as from over-stocking with apprentices. In 1817 the men were enabled to get their masters to make a limitation[4] through the intervention of the merchants. Under these circumstances it may be taken for granted that they were not demanding anything very unreasonable, but yet under the existing law their conduct was criminal. On the other hand the master shipwrights very often met[5], and issued notices on trade practices or set rates of wages.

It is unnecessary to multiply instances; the history of the growth of unions is a striking contrast to that of the formation of the fourteenth century gilds. The craft gilds *Formation and aims of Unions.* had emanated from lawful authority, and were empowered to act for the general well-being. The unions were in their early days illegal bodies, or they carried on illegal practices under the cover of the legitimate work of a friendly society. The growth of the system by which they were subject to this gross unfairness has been sketched above; but it greatly embittered the struggles of the time, as the men could not but feel that the more the magistrates "spake of law the

[1] *Reports*, 1824, v. 178.   [2] *Ib.* 178.   [3] *Ib.* 179.
[4] *Ib.* 226.   [5] *Ib.* 234.

more they did unlaw[1]." Not seldom the unions were the direct fruit of an unsuccessful strike. The men, baffled for the time, determined to organise themselves in the hopes, not always fulfilled, of better success another time[2]. In almost all cases, the objects which they set before themselves at this date were a rise of wages; and even in cases, like the Factory Act of 1833, when they demanded better conditions for their children, it seems probable that they hoped for a rise of wages as an indirect result[3]. If a rise of wages had been possible it would doubtless have given scope for an increased demand for goods, and thus reacted favourably on some branches of trade, but a rise of wages did not seem at all possible under the then existing conditions. Fortunes had been made by spinning, in the war period; but there was more chance of losing a fortune than of making one in the years after the war. Everything rested on the unstable basis of trade; and the alterations of the currency, and fluctuations of credit, made themselves felt in all directions; while the men had nothing to fall back upon. Trade was uncertain[4], capital was supposed to be seeking other investments, and there did not seem to *The wages fund doctrine* be any room for increasing the pay of the men. It was a state of society where the doctrine of the wages fund, in its crudest form[5], was actually true for a time. The masters could afford a definite sum for wages and no more, while the general depression lasted; the amount available could only be divided somehow among the numbers applying, and in overcrowded trades all must be underpaid. The error of the economists then living was the not uncommon one of generalising from the circumstances of their own time, as if they were normal for all time.

[1] *English Chronicle*, 1087.   [2] *Reports*, 1833, xx. 539, 606, and *Ib.* 1843, xv. 134.
[3] *Ib.* 1833, xx. 57.   [4] *Ib.* 54, 371.

[5] It appears that there is a wages fund at each particular moment, consisting of all the money available then and there for paying labour; but usually this sum is constantly fluctuating and it is never fixed. In the thirties it appeared to be fixed because the conditions which would have enabled masters to raise wages were rarely if ever realised. Especially was this the case in trades where the cost of production by machinery and by hand was very nearly balanced. If wages were raised then machinery would become unremunerative; in cases where it had not yet been introduced, if prices improved and it became profitable to produce on a larger scale, the introduction of machinery would also occur.

For England, in the twenties and thirties, it seems to *A.D. 1815 −1846.* me that on the whole the doctrine of the wages fund was actually true, and that it was impossible for the men to *appears to have been* combine so as to raise their wages. At all events the *true then.* economists, who were the guides of middle class opinion, were fully convinced that this was the case, and denounced all those who made the attempt as blind leaders who disorganised trade and inflicted severe injuries on their own class. There had been a general hope that the repeal of laws against combination would render organisation less fascinating, but it spread with great rapidity. Strikes occurred in all the leading trades on unprecedented scales. They occurred repeatedly in the Barnsley district[1]; and in 1831 there was a ten months' strike at Messrs Gott's in Leeds[2]; the men occasionally endeavoured to forward their cause by acts of violence, and by destroying work. The *Mistakes* point for which they contended could not be secured in the *of the men.* circumstances of the times, and they contended for it in a fashion which roused public opinion against them. The assistant commissioners were inclined to express themselves strongly on the policy pursued by the workmen delegates, and to regard them as persons who for their own advantage traded on the ignorance of the workmen and lured them to disastrous courses[3].

So far as a definite artisan feeling appears during this *Artisan policy.* period, they demanded various expedients which had been enforced among the old craft gilds; they inherited their traditions at all events and may sometimes have claimed an actual lineal descent[4]. In opposition to the practice of spreading work, so that many men had starvation wages, they tried to secure that those who were employed should receive sufficient wages to live upon. The old Poor Law had militated against this result, and it was a long and weary struggle before success attended their efforts; but by contending for a minimum wage which the ordinary *Minimum Wages.* man should have, while the good workman might receive

---

[1] *Reports*, 1840, xxiii. 316.   [2] *Ib.* 399.   [3] *Ib.* 1838, xx. 48, 51, 53. .
[4] Breutano, p. 102. Mr H. Llewellyn Smith informs me that there is evidence of continuity among the porters and other waterside industries in London.

more[1], they did at length succeed in raising the standard of comfort all along the line.

It was however by no means easy to devise any practicable · expedient for declaring what the minimum or any other rate *Lists.* of wage ought to be.   The men constantly demanded a list, to be agreed on by the masters and men, but as trade got worse the masters failed to observe its terms, or insisted on revising it, and the system offered no security. It had practically failed in the Spitalfields trade before it was discontinued, and there was great difficulty in framing a list which should prove satisfactory for good but slow, and bad but quick work[2].   While the conditions of trade were changing, it was not possible to devise a lasting agreement.   Even in more recent times, when a system of payment by a list has been in use in many trades for years, and the data on which it can be calculated for different trades are fairly recognised, there has been difficulty in maintaining it.

Apprentice-ship. In many trades there was, as has been noted above[3], a demand for more strict observance of the apprenticeship system.   The family of the domestic weaver all learned his trade[4]; and it was alleged that the overcrowding would cease if the trade were protected by a limitation on the numbers who took it up.   This was impracticable, and some at least of the friends of the working classes greatly objected to such proposals; they held that it was necessary to increase the fluidity of labour[5], so that men who were ousted from one trade might be willing to accept work in some other industry if it were available.

None of the objects[6] which formed part of the specially artisan policy and were advocated by their organisations,

---

[1] This principle was long misunderstood by the opponents of unions. One master asserted that there could be no union in his trade—engineering—because of the varieties of skill among the workmen in that branch of industry, so that each man was paid what he was worth. But it was still possible to agitate that the slow but qualified workman should be paid a fair wage, and that others should rise from that standard. The Amalgamated Engineers are a practical demonstration that there can be combination in this trade also. *Reports*, 1824, v. 11.

[2] *Ib.* 1840, xxiii. 438.

[3] See above, p. 455.

[4] *Reports*, 1840, xxiii. 206, 221.   [5] *Ib.* xxiv. 661.

[6] The limitation or taxation of machinery does not require special discussion. *Ib.* xxiii. 335, 423.

commended itself to the judgment of the outside public; A.D. 1815
—1846.
there were however two suggestions to which artisans attached
much importance, and to which effect was given. They *Tariffs and*
pointed out that the tariff, as it then existed, was much *Corn Laws.*
against them, as it fell heavily on certain classes of manufactured goods[1]; and there was an increasing demand for the
removal of the Corn Laws so that the real wages of the
labourer might be raised[2]. The Hand-loom Weavers' Commission did not give rise to direct legislation like the Factory
or the Mines Acts, but it may be said that it rendered the
revision of the tariff in 1842, and the repeal of the Corn Laws
in 1846, inevitable.

Side by side with the agitations which gave rise to *The Co-*
Trades Unions, there were experiments which have paved *operative*
the way for the Co-operative Movement. While the policy *movement*
attempted by the Trades Unions, which has, so far as
skilled artisans are concerned, been ultimately justified by
its success, was condemned by public opinion, the co-operative movement was never under a similar ban. In its ideal
side it was quite congruent with the view that was taken by
the ordinary middle class advocates of the education of the *approved by*
poor; the approval which was given to private efforts for *class*
promoting education[3], and the assistance which Parliament *opinion.*
afforded to initial expenses[4] were largely due to a desire to
help the labourer to "see where his true interests lay." It
was by playing upon enlightened self-interest that Robert *Robert*
Owen carried on his remarkable experiment at New Lanark, *Owen.*
at Orbiston and New Harmony. They attracted extraordinary attention at the time, and many of the visitors who
flocked there appeared to suppose that a panacea had been
discovered for all the evils of the time. It seemed so simple
too to adopt the formula that the free play of immediate self-
interest, or competition, is the source of all sorts of evil,
while the free action of enlightened self-interest would be
productive of harmony. Co-operators have again and again
taken up the view with enthusiasm as a means of regene-

---

[1] *Reports*, 1840, xxiii. 271.
[2] *Ib.* 420. And scope given for an increased sale abroad.
[3] 2 Hansard, xxxviii. 1209.   [4] 3 Hansard, xx. 733.

rating the world, while it is also curiously allied to the
laissez-faire doctrine as it was shaped by Bastiat.

On its material side, co-operation received an impetus
from the difficulty which artisans and labourers found in pro-
The Truck curing supplies at reasonable rates.   The truck system,
System. though susceptible of much abuse, was in many ways con·
venient ; it certainly seemed the simplest method of providing
hands, in some out-of-the-way villages where water-power
had called a factory into being, with the necessaries of life :
it was not easily killed and additional measures were passed
by Parliament in 1817 and 1820[1]. We may well believe that
the operatives would be but little better served when they
were forced to rely on little local shops[2], especially if they
had been forced into debt.   Under these circumstances they
made a bold, but as it has proved a wise experiment, in
Co-opera- combining to do their own marketing.   Flour was the first
tive Flour
Mills. article in which they tried to deal, both at Rochdale and
Leeds ; but their success soon justified an extension of the
business ; despite the half-hearted support of less enthusiastic
members and the bitter opposition of the shopkeepers, the
artisans in many towns have succeeded in organising for
themselves a system by which their marketing can be conducted on the most favourable terms possible.   The great
hardships they suffered from the manner in which they purchased have been effectively remedied[3] by their own efforts.

---

[1] 57 Geo. III. cc. 115, 122; 1 Geo. IV. c. 93.

[2] *Reports*, 1843, XII. 140.   On the first attempts to meet these difficulties see
Reports of the Society for Bettering the Condition of the Poor [Brit. Mus. 288, g.
12] I. 17, also 78, 267; II. 60; III. 60, 104.   The account of the store at Mongewell
was communicated by Bishop Barrington, but it is not clear that he organised it,
as is commonly said. (Holyoake, *Self-help*, 46).   Mrs Barrington and the vicar,
Mr Durell (*Reports of Society*, IV. 84), who were resident in the place are more
likely to have organised a shop in Oxfordshire than a Bishop of Durham would be.

[3] On the whole subject compare Holyoake, *History of Co-operation*.   The great
formation of capital by the co-operative stores is a later and incidental development, and will probably lead to co-operative production on the sound basis of
working for a known and calculable market.   There have been many attempts at
co-operative production for the open market, on the supposition that certain trades
can be reorganised on co-operative principles, so as to undersell those organised by
employers.   It is generally supposed that the enlightened self-interest of the men
will do away with the necessity for much superintendence.   An early instance
occurred in the Dyeing Trade at Manchester in connection with the Dyers' Trade
Union. *Reports*, 1833, xx. 52.

XXII. Agriculture.

378. All the phenomena of the time, when closely examined, pointed to the necessity of a change in our agricultural policy and rendered that change inevitable. Both commerce and industry were depressed; and the one suggestion, which commended itself to specialists and the public alike, was the necessity for removing the heavy tax which fell on the food of the people, and interfered with the demand for our goods from corn-growing countries. The burden was everywhere felt, while it was not easy to see who gained.

*A.D. 1815
—1846.
The Corn
Laws im-
posed a
burden,
while no
one seemed
the better
for them.*

It seemed quite clear that the agricultural labourer derived little advantage from the existing condition of agriculture. He was miserably wretched; in many places he had, as enclosures progressed, lost his stake in the country; while the spinning-jenny and the mule had deprived the rural household of by-occupations. During the war his wages had been high[2], and the loss of the additional sources of income would not be felt; but in the years succeeding the war his money wages fell to very low rates indeed[2]. The administration of the Poor Law had degraded him, and the miserable outrages[3] by which he gave expression to his despair made the public at large aware of his real lot.

*Conflicting
evidence
about the
agri-
cultural
labourer.*

[1] *Reports*, 1813—14, III. In the home counties, despite the introduction of threshing machines their condition was much improved (p. 210), corn had advanced 50 per cent. and wages 100 per cent. In Northumberland labour had doubled and rather more in the preceding quarter of a century (p. 218). In Yorkshire it had gone up from 1*s.* 6*d.* to 2*s.* 6*d.* a day (p. 218); according to Messrs Wakefield and Arthur Young the price of labour had generally speaking doubled in the preceding twenty years (p. 233). The extra labour required for fencing &c. in connection with enclosures may have had something to do with this, as well as the attraction of the high wages paid to weavers (see above, p. 469). In some counties, however, distress was already beginning; in Essex many hands were unemployed and wages had fallen three shillings per week (p. 250); in Berkshire the rise had taken place, but wages had begun to fall again (pp. 266, 267), so too in Wiltshire (p. 254); in this county, as in Hampshire, "they are all upon the poor's rates." The change was said to be due to the fall in price of corn, but it was felt first in those districts from which manufacturing was migrating.

[2] According to the report in 1822, the wages of labour which had been 15*s.* or 16*s.* a week before 1815 had declined to 9*s.* a week. *Reports*, &c. 1822, v. 73. This report contains an excellent estimate of pressure of taxation in terms of labour.

[3] Wakefield, *Swing Unmasked*, p. 6. *England and America*, 1. 44 f.

All this appears to be proved by indubitable evidence, and yet there are conflicting statements which it seems hard to reconcile. If things were very bad in 1821, they had begun to recover during the next decade, as the Parliamentary Committee of 1833 reported that the general condition of the agricultural labourer in full employment was better than at any former period, and that his money wages gave him a greater command over the comforts of life[1]. The reason for this alleged improvement is not clear. The graver distress was presumably in those counties where things were going badly even in 1814 and where spinning had been much diffused; while it is not impossible that the rural population had been so much attracted to the towns from the neighbourhood of the new manufacturing centres in Lancashire and Yorkshire, as to afford better employment for those who were left on the land; the extreme distress and the greatest improvement were in all probability special to particular localities. Besides this the opportunities for by-occupation on the part of the farm-labourer himself had not yet been reduced so much as they were in subsequent years[2].

Rural Employment.

A good deal of interesting evidence is furnished by the Report of the Committee of 1843. Lord Ashley and others, who had taken an active part in reforming abuses connected with the employment of women in factories and mines, were twitted with the retort that landowners had better look at home, and that the conditions of rural labour required investigation as much as anything else. When the Committee sat however it became clear that this was an error, as agricultural labour was not proved prejudicial to health in any way, and young girls were not employed at all. There were however some peculiar cases of contract in different parts of the country which required attention. The worst evils connected with parish apprentices were a thing of the past. It had been the practice of overseers to take the children of parents who had parish allowances, and to assign them by lot to

---

[1] *Reports,* &c. 1833, v. pp. vii, viii.
The statement of the Committee must be discounted to some extent; for it assumes constancy of employment, and it lays little stress on sources of income other than the labourers' wages.

[2] See above, § 322, p. 483.

farmers to whom they were bound till they were twenty-one A.D. 1815 —1846. years of age. In some exceptional cases everything went well, but much more commonly the system worked badly, alike for the apprentice who was bullied, and for the master who exacted unwilling service. There were some remains of the system in Devonshire in 1843[1], but the worst evils had been corrected in 1816[2].

In the neighbourhood of Castle Acre, in Norfolk, a *Gangs.* system of ' ganging ' had grown up within very recent years. The parish of Castle Acre was held by several proprietors who did not attempt to limit the cottages; it thus came to be overcrowded with the surplus population of all the surrounding district. There was no sufficient employment for them in Castle Acre, and in many of the neighbouring parishes the farmers were short-handed, so that it was convenient to organise gangs; these worked in the fields under an overseer who had taken a contract for doing a certain piece of work. The gangs were often composed of children, and the overseer was a sweater; the system was thoroughly bad, but it appears to have been quite exceptional even in Norfolk, and unknown elsewhere[3].

There was also a special custom in Northumberland, *Northum-berland.* where farm labour appears to have been in great demand. The villages were so few and distant that cottages were built on each farm; the labourer was engaged for a year, and was bound to furnish the labour of a woman on the farm as well as his own. The system appears to have been advantageous in many ways to the labourer, but it was said that the houses provided were inferior to cottages which were rented in the usual way. Still there was little substantial grievance in the system, but the name of bondager roused sentimental objections, of which Cobbett made himself the exponent.

Certainly the Northumbrian labourers seem to have been well off as compared with those in the southern counties[4]. But though the evidence is conflicting it seems, on the whole, that the pressure of agricultural distress did not

---

[1] *Reports*, &c. 1843, xii. 43.   [2] 56 Geo. III. c. 139.
[3] *Reports*, &c. 1843, xii. 221.
[4] See especially the very complete labourers' budget. *Ib.* 302.

fall so heavily on the farm-labourers as upon the class above them.

379. For it certainly could not be pretended that the farmer was successful. One parliamentary Committee after another reported on the state of the agricultural interest. In 1821 it was shown that there had been many failures among the farmers of Dorsetshire in the preceding years[1]. The small farmers were not hit so hard, but they and the labourers were forced to make reductions in a standard of comfort which was low enough already.

It seemed, of course, that the whole gain had gone to the landowners and tithe-owners; and these classes had to bear the brunt of unpopularity, both in rural districts, and whenever the advocates of political and economic reform assembled. But many of the landowners were in grave difficulties; there had, of course, been an unprecedented rise
of rent during the war. Rents had increased, as it was said, about seventy per cent. since the war began; and few of the landowners had realised that their gains were merely temporary. They had burdened their land with jointures, or mortgaged it to make real or fancied improvements, and thus when there began to be a difficulty about getting rents paid, there was a general feeling among the landlords, that if there was a fall either of rents or prices, they would be unable to meet the obligation which they had incurred. It
was on these grounds that in 1815 a stringent Corn Law was passed, by which the importation of foreign corn was prohibited so long as the price of wheat did not rise above 80s.[2]. No substantial difference was made by the sliding scale of 1828, which permitted the importation of foreign corn to be warehoused, on the payment of duties if it was sold for consumption at home[3]; and though there had been some relaxation in the famine year of 1823, this strict system of protection was maintained, but with more and more hesitation[4], until 1846[5].

All classes were ready to turn on the tithe-owner. He

---

[1] *Reports*, 1821, IX. 138.   [2] 55 Geo. III. c. 26.   [3] 9 Geo. IV. c. 60.
[4] Sir Robert Peel's sliding-scale in 1842 was quite an inadequate reform.
[5] 9 and 10 Vict. c. 22.

had been at no outlay in improving the land; and the A.D. 1815 —1846.
manner in which his demands were levied rendered the
payment a serious tax on agricultural expansion, and militated against the use of a larger area for tillage. There has
been occasion to note the hostility between the tithe-owners
and the pioneers of agricultural improvement. The actual
payment of tithes gave rise to frequent parochial difficulties,
and all parties were prepared for a compromise on the sub-
ject, when the Tithe Commutation Act[1] was passed in 1836. *Commuta-tion Act.*
The average gross tenth for seven preceding years was
taken, which gave the tithe-owners' property at £6,756,105;
and this was commuted for a permanent charge of £4,035,663.
This appears to have been an exceedingly hard bargain for
the tithe-owners; but it must be remembered that the calculation was made during the period of protection, and
would probably compare not unfavourably with the actual
tithe as it had been paid under more normal conditions of
prices in the eighteenth century. The landlords gained
something like forty per cent. of the patrimony of the
Church; but the tithe-owners have suffered even more by
bargaining themselves out of the further increment, which
has accrued through the introduction of higher farming. At
any rate, it can hardly be said that this re-arrangement of
tithe caused such general relief as to justify the opinion of
those, who would have made the tithe-owner the scape-
goat for all the distress that affected industrial, agricultural
and commercial life.

In fact, the distress among all ranks of the agricultural *The failure of Pro-*
interest was so notorious that it lent an additional argument *tection.*
to Cobden[2] and the leaders of the Anti-Corn Law movement.
As a matter of fact, protection had failed to keep the land
of England in good cultivation; it was working disaster
to the industrial and commercial interests, and to the
consumers at large. The agriculturists were inclined to
reply that they were heavily burdened both for local and
national taxation, and that since they had to bear these

---

[1] 6 and 7 Will. IV. c. 71.

[2] Cobden, who was the son of a farmer, showed particular address in dealing
with this aspect of the subject in rural districts.

A.D. 1815
—1846.
Burden of
Taxation.
burdens it was fair that some consideration should be shown them. The terrible impoverishment caused by the long war had led on the one hand to the creation of an enormous class of fund-holders, whose demands for interest had to be met when due, and on the other to a frightful increase of pauperism. The latter burden especially, lay at the landlord's door; while he was justified in arguing that the factory-owners, who had deprived the rural poor of a by-occupation, had caused the pauperism for which the landed interest had to pay. It was here that the pinching was felt; so that despite the new facilities for commerce and the increase of industrial powers, the whole country appeared to be under a blight.

380. The effect of the Corn Law of 1815 was to render farming a highly speculative business. The normal food production, with the existing methods, was insufficient for the population[1]. In years of scarcity a comparatively small deficit in the crop immediately caused a startling rise in price. Encouraged by these rates, farmers would break Alterations in the
margin of
cultivation. up more ground and take crops on a larger area, but a year or two of lower prices would soon compel them to give up the task of trying to grow wheat except on their better land; the uncultivated area was often left wild, without any attempt at laying down pasture. The most serious of these variations of price occurred just after the conclusion of the war. In January 1816 notwithstanding the pro-Fluctua-
tions of
Price. tective legislation, wheat was selling at 52s. 6d.[2]; owing to a deficient harvest in 1816, not so much in our own country as abroad, the price rose very rapidly, and in June 1817 stood at 117s. Similar startling fluctuations characterised the rest of the period, and rendered the farmer's business a constant speculation, which was on the whole unlucky and in which hundreds were ruined.

Agricul-
tural Pro
tection in
18th
century. It is interesting to contrast this period of protection with the eighteenth century. At that time there had been direct

---

[1] The Committee of 1821 believed that enough wheat was grown for the requirements of the country (Reports, &c. 1821, IX. 9); while that of 1833 recognised that we were dependent on foreign supplies. Ib. 1833, v. 5.

[2] Tooke, II. p. 4.

encouragement given to the landed interest in such a fashion A.D. 1815
that a regular supply of food was obtained for the nation $^{-1846}$
at prices which fluctuated within a comparatively narrow
range. In the nineteenth century the landed interest received little benefit, while the food supply fluctuated, and
there were the wildest vicissitudes of price. The justification of protection, which would have been alleged in
both cases, was similar,—that it was desirable that England
should not be dependent upon foreigners for necessary sustenance. The one measure aimed at keeping the price fairly
steady, if a little high; the other gave a practical monopoly
to the home-grower, with the effect that slight variations
in the crop resulted in famine prices[1].

Arthur Young had preached the harsh doctrine that *Necessity and Invention.*
the raising of rents was productive of good farming, and
the very adversity which fell on the agricultural districts
during these evil years appears to have had a bracing effect.
It gradually became obvious that if English agriculture was
to flourish at all, it could not be by relying on the illusory
benefits of protection, but by adopting improved methods;
the chief improvement which was effected during this period
was the systematic introduction of thorough drainage. This
practice had been locally pursued in Essex since the seven- *Thorough drainage.*
teenth century; but it was made the subject of experiments
by Mr Smith of Deanston. By taking the water off the
land, he improved the quality of the soil and greatly increased the number of days, when it was available for
working. His experiments were first published in 1834;
but so rapidly did they take hold of the public mind that
in 1846, application was successfully made to Parliament
to grant loans to landlords to carry out these improvements[2].

There was also a great increase in knowledge of methods *Agricultural Chemistry.*
of manuring the land, since agricultural chemistry was
coming to be pursued as a branch of science and not treated
as mere rule of thumb. It was found that there were valuable elements in all sorts of refuse, as for example in

[1] Compare the discussion of this subject in the report of the committee of 1821. *Reports*, &c. 1821, IX. 19.
[2] Prothero, *Pioneers*, 97, 98.

C. II. 42

A.D. 1815
—1846.

bones, while the better means of communication rendered it more possible for farmers to avail themselves of fertilisers which were not native to their own district[1].

Ireland.

381.   Since the time of the union of England and Ireland the two kingdoms had been one for economic purposes. Ireland had gained a little from the prosperity of the war times, and now it shared in the succeeding depression.   The conditions of life were exactly those which made her feel the brunt of the trouble most severely.   In England, where there was large capital, the distress did to some extent act as a stimulant to call out more skill and enterprise; in Ireland where farming had not yet become a trade, but was an occupation by which men procured subsistence, the pressure of distress could not force on any improvement; it only rendered labourers more miserable than before.   The wretchedness in England was so great, that there was little inclination to attend to the condition of the Irish; though in 1822 and 1831 when the potato crop was short, there was some public liberality shown on their behalf.   This,

The Potato Famine.

however, was but a premonitory symptom of the frightful disaster of 1845 and 1846, when the state of Ireland was forced upon public attention, by the outbreak of the potato disease; the late crop of potatoes, on which the people depended for food, was entirely lost.   As they had obtained fair prices for other produce, they might have got through the disaster with comparatively little help, and the Government contented itself with purchasing a £100,000 worth of Indian corn, and forming depots where relief was administered.

Insufficient measures of relief.

In the following year, however, the destruction caused by the disease was complete; though both public and private charity were largely exerted, the shameful admission remains that very large numbers died through starvation or from those fevers, which are directly due to insufficient nourishment.   Public works were opened and there was very wide-spread sympathy shown to the Irish sufferers from all parts of the world.

Conditions of tenure.

When attention was thus directed to the condition of Ireland it became obvious that some alterations were de-

[1] Prothero, 99.

sirable in the conditions under which agriculture was carried A.D. 1815 —1846.
on. The methods of cultivation were bad, and there was
no one to set improvements agoing. In 1845 and 1846
Lord Stanley and Lord Lincoln made strenuous efforts to
obtain the appointment of a state Commissioner, whose administration might reduce the worst abuses in Irish rural
affairs; but matters were allowed to drift for the time,
and have passed from the domain of history into the region
of party politics.

XXIII. The Poor.

382. A period, like that of the industrial revolution, of *The work-ing popula-tion* extraordinary and rapid transition was exactly the time
when we might expect that many workers would lose their
old employment, and would be forced into pauperism. We
hear so much of the desperate lot of the labourer, and the
outrages committed by starving Luddites and others, that we
should expect to find that it was necessary for many to come
upon the rates, or even to go into the house; we should be
inclined to suppose that since the labourer's position was so
bad, the condition of the pauper would be even more pitiable.
But up till 1834, the pauper was one of the few people who
flourished. There was a painful contrast between the ill- *and the paupers.* conditioned pauper, who was well-supplied at the expense of
others, and the operative who could hardly make a decent
living at the skilled trade of frame-work knitting. There
was much real misery which was practically untouched;
while a very heavy expense was incurred to maintain useless
and disreputable people in idleness. These were phenomena
which were sufficiently patent, and which had been the subject of a select committee in 1817; but the reformed Parliament set to work to investigate the subject with characteristic energy, and a Royal Commission was appointed in 1832.

The Report of the Commission[1] testifies to the most *Commis-sion of* curious variety in regard to the arrangements for the poor in *1832.*

[1] *Reports, &c.* 1834, xxvii.

42—2

different districts. In some parishes the arrangements were admirable; and these instances, isolated though they were, seemed to prove that there was nothing fundamentally unsound in the principles of the existing law, when it was wisely administered. At Southwell in Nottinghamshire, Sir George Nicholls had given great attention to the management of the workhouse; under his advice out-door relief was refused to the able-bodied, and given but rarely to others. The rates were reduced by this means between 1820 and 1823 from £2,006 to £517, and they remained at the latter figure[1]. Similar experience was adduced from Bingham and Cookham and Hatfield; but on the other hand there were parishes where the pauper appeared to be supreme. At Cholesbury in Buckinghamshire, the poor-rate had risen from £10. 11s. in 1801 to £367 in 1832. Here the whole land was offered to the assembled poor, but they thought it wiser to decline and have it worked for their advantage on the old system[2]; and unfortunately this was only a typical case of what was too common in many parts of England.

There was no end to the ramifications of the mischief in these pauperised parishes; of course workhouses, if they had ever existed, had fallen into decay; and there was a great deal of perfectly safe business to be done in providing for the requirements of the paupers and obtaining payment from the parish. "The owner of cottage property," said Mr Nassau Senior, "found in the parish, a liberal and solvent tenant, and the petty shop-keeper and publican attended the Vestry to vote allowances to his customers and debtors. The rental of a pauperised parish was, like the revenue of the Sultan of Turkey, a prey of which every administrator hoped to get a share[3]." So many people of different social grades profited through the existence of the abuses that it was exceedingly difficult to check them or put them down.

These facts must be borne in mind in order to understand the precise nature of the changes which were advocated by the Royal Commission, and to which, though in a modified form, effect was given by the Poor Law of 1834; they were almost

---

[1] Nicholls, Hist. of Poor Law, II. 240—251.   [3] Aschrott, 32.
[2] Edinburgh Review, Vol. LXXIV. p. 28.

entirely changes in matters of administration; the Commis- A.D. 1815 —1846.
sioners had observed that, where the administration was good
all went well; but that throughout the country generally
the administration was most defective; it was on this point
they concentrated their efforts.

The primary responsibility for all the evil undoubtedly *Overseers.*
lay with the overseers; the tradition of the office appears to
have altered considerably since Sir George Burn wrote his
strong denunciation of the class, as it existed in his day.
At that time their main view had been to keep down the
rates; in the early part of the present century, they seem to
have been, as a class, timorously afraid of incurring unpopularity, by refusing to meet any claims, however unjustifiable.

In a few cases, the overseer did endeavour to do his *Justices.*
duty, and a pauper would occasionally appeal against his
decision to the Justices; experience went to show that the
same sort of weakness characterised the magistrates. They
scarcely ever supported the overseer; but almost always preferred to take the more easy and popular course of making
an order for relief[1]. Under these circumstances, it is hardly

[1] Mr Power reported in regard to Cambridgeshire to the Commissioners of
1833. He says "When pressed on the subject of their management, overseers
invariably excuse themselves by alleging the want of co-operation and protection
from the magistracy in their endeavours to check the demand on the parish funds.
Even the paid officers, both in town and country, justify themselves on these
grounds for sparing the time, trouble, and expense of contesting with the pauper
the question of relief before the individual magistrates, or the bench in petty
sessions. Of the many whom I have seen, one and all are in this story. But the
Commissioners will probably consider that I have found a higher and a better
authority on this subject in Dr Webb, master of Clare Hall, the present vice-
chancellor of the University. He has acted as county magistrate for more than
sixteen years; and being resident a great part of the year at his vicarage in
Littlington, he has personally superintended the relief of the poor in that parish,
as well as in Great Gransden, in Huntingdonshire, where the college have been
obliged to occupy a farm of 700 acres, in consequence of their not being able to
obtain a tenant for the same at any price. He is strongly of opinion that a great
part of the burthen of actual relief to the poor arises from the injudicious interference of magistrates, and the readiness with which they overrule the discretion
of the overseer. He has attempted in both the parishes above-mentioned to
introduce a more strict and circumspect system of relief—with great success in
Littlington, as appears by the descending scale of poor-rates in that parish since
1816; the population at the same time having nearly doubled itself since 1801.
In Gransden, he had found less success, being seldom personally present there,
and acting principally through his bailiff. Also he had had less time by some
years for effecting any steady improvement in that parish. He showed me, how-

fair to say that the Elizabethan system had failed.   What
had happened was that the Elizabethan system had been set
aside, by the action of the very men who were bound in duty
to administer it; it was therefore necessary to overhaul the
whole of the existing methods of administration, so that some
more trustworthy officials might be secured.

*Methods of
Relief.*
　　It is impossible to over-estimate the irreparable mischief
which was done to Englishmen for many generations through
the demoralising influence exercised by some of the administrative methods then in use.   The granting of allowances per
child has been freely stigmatised as a mischievous stimulus
to population; as a matter of fact it was much worse; there
is abundant evidence to show that it acted as a direct incentive to immorality[1].   But the evil of the whole system was most
patent from the various ways in which it conspired to render
the inefficient pauper comfortable, at the expense of the good
workman who really tried to earn his own living.   The allowance system must have had an extraordinary effect in diminishing the rates of wages, and forcing men to depend upon
supplementary payments out of rates; yet, as we have seen,
there were many reasons which rendered it convenient and
favoured its general adoption[2].

*Labour
Rate.*
　　An even worse mischief in some ways, was the labour
rate; by this system a ratepayer was obliged to employ
a certain number of pauper labourers in accordance with

ever, by a reference to the books, that he had made the practice of allowing relief
to married men, when employed by individuals, in respect of their families,
entirely disappear from the late accounts.   The principal impediment to the introduction of a better system, he found in the power of the pauper, when refused
relief by the overseer, to apply to the bench in petty sessions; which nothing but
the advantage of an intimate knowledge of his own parishioners, and of uniting in
himself the functions, not the office, of overseer and magistrate, enabled him, by
perseverance, to overcome.   The following case is a sample of their unwillingness
to take the circumstances or character of the applicant into due consideration.   He
refused relief (Nov. 27th, 1829) to Samuel Spencer, knowing him to have received
a legacy of 400*l*. within two or three years before the application.   The man
applied to the bench in petty sessions, where Dr Webb produced to them an
extract from the will (proved 1826), and the assurance of the executor that he had
paid the pauper money since proving the will, to the amount above-mentioned.
Notwithstanding this, they made an order of relief; and the man (able-bodied) has
been from time to time on the rates ever since." *Extracts from Information
received*, pp. 125, 126.

[1] Aschrott, p. 30.　　　　　　　　　　[2] See above, § 327, p. 496.

his assessment, and to pay them regulated wages without A.D. 1815 —1846.
reference to their work[1]. An employer might thus be forced
to dismiss good hands in order to give employment to inefficient paupers. Such circumstances combined to produce
the extraordinary state of affairs in which they lived at East-
bourne, where the pauper labourer received sixteen shillings
and the independent workman was only paid twelve. No
wonder that two women there should complain of the conduct of their husbands in refusing to better their condition
by becoming paupers[2].

383. The chief expedients on which the Commission of
1832 relied for promoting reform, were twofold. On the one
hand, they advised the appointment of a Poor-Law Commission, which might be a permanent authority in all matters of
administration, and which might use its influence to bring up
the practice of the local administration in every part of the
country to a satisfactory level[3]. On the other hand, they *Outdoor Relief.*
regarded out-door relief as the chief secret of all the mischiefs
that had arisen in connection with the growth of pauperism,
and of the gains of those who were interested in the maintenance of abuses. The first essential for giving necessary
relief, in really severe cases of distress, was the existence of a
well-managed workhouse; if acceptance of relief within the
house were made the test of granting it at all, there was no
danger of fostering the inefficient pauperised class, whose
competition forced down the independent workman to a lower
level of comfort than their own[4].

The Act of 1834, which embodied the recommendations *Poor Law*
of the Commissioners in a less stringent form than they *Commis-sioners.*
would themselves have desired, was passed by large majori-
ties[5]. It created the Poor Law Commissioners for England
and Wales; they were charged with the administration and
control of public relief, and were empowered to make
rules for the management of the poor, the government of
workhouses and the education and apprenticeship of poor
children. Much of their time, during the first years of the *Unions.*
Commission, was taken up with the formation of unions of

---

[1] *Reports*, &c. 1834, xxvii. 108; 2 and 8 Will. IV. c. 96.   [2] Aschrott 31 n.
[3] *Reports*, 1834, xxvii. 167.   [4] *Ib.* 146, 147.   [5] 4 and 5 Will. IV. c. 76.

parishes for the provision of workhouses[1], and with the laying down of orders in regard to the administration of relief. During the commercial depression of 1836, a great strain was put upon the new system, and the Commissioners came in for a full share of that unpopularity, which the officials under the older system had so studiously endeavoured to avoid.

Indeed there seemed to be some doubt as to whether Parliament would renew their powers at the end of the five years for which they had been appointed. But the account of the work they had actually done, which they laid before Parliament, spoke strongly in their favour. Their powers were continued; and in 1847 the whole of the Poor Law arrangements of the country had been reconstructed and reduced to systematic shape. The general order of 1847 is the great code which describes the nature and the working of the new system[2].

Sir I. F. Lewis, Sir J. G. Shaw-Lefevre and Sir George Nicholls were the three Commissioners who accomplished this great work. Their action, of course, was deeply resented by the paupers and those who were interested in the abuses of the old system; but it also found many critics among doctrinaire politicians, who were afraid of the influence of centralised departments, and anxious that those who raised the money for the rates should have a full responsibility for the manner in which it was employed[3].

384. It is most remarkable to find that public attention was still forced to the old, rather than to the new social difficulties, in regard to the whole question of poor relief. *Pauperism in Great Towns.* The insuperable problems of our time seem to be those connected with great cities,—with great masses of men huddled together, where there are none of the middle and upper classes, to attend to the ordinary machinery of government in the widest sense of the word. So far as the Poor Law Commissioners of 1834 are concerned, these difficulties might scarcely have existed. That they did exist and were very real, we know from other sources. Dr Chalmers had

---

[1] By disregarding the county boundaries in their arrangement of parishes for poor-law purposes, the Commissioners took a line, which led at a later date to considerable difficulty. .Aschrott, 46.

[2] Aschrott, 47.   [3] Maculloch, *Principles of Political Economy*, 424.

endeavoured to organise a system of relief in Glasgow, which A.D. 1815
—1846. should be given on grounds of charity, and which should not *Chalmers* have the demoralising effects of the aid that could be claimed *and* *Christian* as a matter of right[1]. He was not apparently aware that the *Charity.* legal relief, which he denounced, had been as a matter of fact, the outgrowth of a system of voluntary and charitable assistance, such as he highly extolled. The changed character of poor relief in modern times is but an instance of the alteration which has taken place in regard to so many duties, as they become common, they also become secularised. It is for the rare and exceptional act of virtue that the highest motives only serve. So long as bridge-building or highway repairs or the providing of education or the granting of freedom to serfs were only occasionally done, they were duties which religious men felt called upon to devote their wealth to from religious motives. In so far as in the progress of society, the convenience and necessity of any of these things are recognised, they are provided as a matter of course and as a necessary charge. The religious and philanthropic individual is left free to find new paths of self-sacrifice by which he may benefit his fellow men, till they learn to imitate his efforts once more and so to benefit themselves.

XXIV. TAXATION.

385. When the war closed in 1815, the taxation of the country had been gradually worked up until it had reached enormous dimensions. The debt stood at £860,000,000, or about £43 per head of the population; and the revenue, which was required to defray the interest on the debt and the necessary expenses of government, amounted to seventy-four millions and a half; a quarter of the sum had sufficed before the war. As a necessary result, taxes had been laid *The pres-* upon everything that was taxable and there was no incident *sure of* *Taxation* of life in which the pressure of taxation was not felt. Sidney Smith's immortal summary can never be surpassed, "The school-boy whips his taxed top; the beardless youth manages

---

[1] *Christian and Civic Economy of large Towns*, II. pp. 225—365; *Political Economy, Works*, XIX. 400.

his taxed horse, with a taxed bridle, on a taxed road; and the dying Englishman pouring his medicine, which has paid seven per cent., into a spoon that has paid fifteen per cent., flings himself back upon his chintz bed, which has paid twenty-two per cent., makes his will on an eight pound stamp, and expires in the arms of an apothecary, who has paid a license of £100 for the privilege of putting him to death. His whole property is then immediately taxed from two to ten per cent. Besides the probate, large fees are demanded for burying him in the chancel. His virtues are handed down to posterity on taxed marble, and he will then be gathered to his fathers to be taxed no more[1]." The

Summary. following summary extracted from Mr Dowell's work gives a convenient view of the nature of the taxation levied in Great Britain in 1815.

I.　*Direct Taxes.*

	£
The land tax	1,196,000
The taxes on houses and establishments . .	6,500,000
Property and income tax.	14,600,000
The tax on succession to property . . .	1,297,000
Property insured	918,000
Property sold at auction	284,000
Coaches, posting and hackney cabs . .	471,608
Tonnage on shipping	171,651
Total	£25,438,259

II.　*Taxes on Articles of Consumption.*

		£	£
Eatables:	Salt	1,616,671	
	Sugar . . .	2,957,403	
	Currants, &c. . .	541,589	5,115,663
Drinks:	Beer, malt, hops .	9,596,346	
	Wine. . . .	1,900,772	
	Spirits . . .	6,700,000	
	Tea	3,591,350	
	Coffee . . .	276,700	22,065,168
Tobacco	. . . . . .		2,025,663

[1] Sidney Smith, *Works,* II. 13. *Edinburgh Review,* XXXIII. (Jan. 1820), p. 77.

Coals, raw materials for manufactures, buildings, ship-building, and other trades . . 6,062,214
Manufactures 4,080,721

III. *Stamp Duties.*

Bills and notes 841,000
Receipts 210,000
Other instruments 1,692,000

Total £67,530,688

Of these items by far the heaviest was the income tax; *Income tax.*
public opinion was determinedly set against it, as well as
on a repeal of the last additions to the Malt Tax. These
were accordingly immediately repealed, though it was necessary to add an excise on soap in order to do without the
revenue they brought in; but no real attempt at reform
was made until Robinson and Huskisson came into office,
when a serious movement was made for freeing our com- *Beginning*
merce, by removing the taxes on raw materials. This was *of Reform;*
done in regard to raw silk, while at the same time the strict *taxation of raw ma-*
monopoly of the home market, which the silk manufactures *terials.*
had hitherto possessed, was withdrawn and foreign silks
might be imported on paying a thirty per cent. duty. Huskisson pursued the same course in regard to other trades; the
duties on copper and zinc and tin were reduced to half the
former amount; the duty on wool was also halved, and at
the same time the very high tariffs on foreign manufactures
of different sorts were reduced. Thus in 1824 and 1825
very considerable reductions as well as simplifications were
made in our tariff, and on principles which relieved the
trader, and so far as might be, the manufacturing interest.

The various Chancellors of the Exchequer were able to *Difficulty*
proceed gradually with the remission of taxation, but in 1836 *of further reform*
the commercial outlook became most threatening. The crisis
of 1837, followed as it was by commercial stagnation, told
seriously on the revenues; the deficit in 1838 was a million
and a half; in 1839 nearly half a million; in 1840, a million
and a half; and in 1841, a million and three-quarters; and
in 1842, more than two millions[1]. Under these circum-

[1] Northcote, *Twenty years*, pp. 6, 12.

stances it was necessary that financial affairs should be thoroughly overhauled, and this was done by Sir Robert Peel in his great budget of 1842. In imitation of the policy of Pitt, he determined to make a temporary provision for the expenses of Government, until the new changes had had time to operate[1]. With this view, he desired to re-impose an income-tax of sevenpence in the pound for a period of five years, so that he might be free to deal in earnest with the reform of the tariff. This was a great task; but it was one for which there had been considerable preparation. The principles on which it should proceed had been worked out in 1830 by Sir Henry Parnell, in his treatise *On Financial Reform* and a select committee of the House of Commons had considered the subject in 1840[2]. Peel hoped to revive our manufacturing interest, by abolishing or reducing the taxes on raw materials and half manufactured goods. For the first two years there was some disappointment and the reduction of import duties continued; in 1845 matters were pressed still further. There was a great simplification of the customs, and four hundred and thirty articles of an unimportant kind, which produced but little or no revenue, were reduced altogether[3]. This wholesale reduction of tariffs, though welcomed by the manufacturers, was not universally approved. Those who relied on commercial treaties as means of opening or of securing foreign

Duties and Customs.

Doubts regarding his policy.

---

[1] Northcote, *Twenty years*, pp. 17, 61.

[2] "The Tariff of the United Kingdom presents neither congruity nor unity of purpose; no general principles seem to have been applied * * *

"The Tariff often aims at incompatible ends; the duties are sometimes meant to be both productive of revenue and for protective objects, which are frequently inconsistent with each other; hence they sometimes operate to the complete exclusion of foreign produce, and in so far no revenue can of course be received; and sometimes, when the duty is inordinately high, the amount of revenue becomes in consequence trifling. They do not make the receipt of revenue the main consideration, but allow that primary object of fiscal regulations to be thwarted by an attempt to protect a great variety of particular interests, at the expense of the revenue, and of the commercial intercourse with other countries.

"Whilst the Tariff has been made subordinate to many small producing interests at home, by the sacrifice of Revenue in order to support these interests, the same principle of preference is largely applied, by the various discriminatory Duties, to the Produce of our Colonies, by which exclusive advantages are given to the Colonial Interests at the expense of the mother country." *Reports*, 1840, v. 101.

[3] Northcote, *Twenty years*, p. 65.

markets were somewhat alarmed, as we removed one by one charges which might have formed the basis of negotiation with other countries. This was especially felt in regard to the removal of those protective tariffs, which our manufactures had hitherto enjoyed; but Sir Robert Peel was a convert to the views which Ricardo had expressed on this subject, and he held that we should not ultimately be losers by pursuing the course of removing all obstacles to free commercial intercourse, so far as we could, without waiting to consider the action which our neighbours might determine to take. *A.D. 1815 —1846.*

386. By far the heaviest of all the burdens on the industry of the country remained unremoved, so long as the Corn Laws were maintained. But the force of circumstances was gradually rendering the repeal inevitable. On the one hand there was all the evidence of the Commission on handloom weavers, which showed that the limitation of the food-supply was the greatest grievance to the operative classes, while it was a principal hindrance to the expansion of commerce. The famine in Ireland had presented us with a ghastly picture of the horrors, which might arise from an insufficient food-supply; when in 1845 the harvest was a failure, and prices rose rapidly, Sir Robert Peel was inclined to open the ports, and allow for a time at least the admission of foreign corn, on a merely nominal duty. But there are some measures which if adopted once, are adopted permanently. Sir James Graham[1], and other members of the Cabinet, saw that the suspension of the Corn Laws would in itself be an admission that the system aggravated the evils of scarcity, and that if this point was conceded, the whole system would have to go. For this, the Cabinet were not prepared; and Sir Robert Peel placed his resignation in the hands of the Queen. As no other Government could be formed however, he returned into office on December 20th, 1845, with the full determination of carrying through the repeal of the Corn Laws. The subject was debated at great length in January and February 1846, and the Government proposals were carried by a majority of ninety- *Increased feeling against the Corn Laws.* *Temporary expedient.* *Repeal.*

[1] Dowell, II. 309.

A.D. 1815
—1846.
seven[1]. There was to be temporary protection, by a sliding-scale which levied four shillings when the price of corn was fifty shillings a quarter, and instead of this comparatively light duty a merely nominal tax of one shilling a quarter was to be levied after February 1st, 1849. Even this nominal duty has been more recently removed.

The whole of the contest in regard to the Corn Laws was, of course, determined by the new character which they had assumed in 1815. It was then that a measure was *Protection had come to benefit a class rather than the nation.* definitely passed to protect the landlords, and to enable them to maintain the burdens which had fallen upon them, or which they had too readily undertaken[2]. From that time onwards, it was possible to represent the Corn Laws as a merely class measure and to treat the whole question, as the advocates of the League habitually did, as that of a tax imposed upon the community in the sole interest of a special class. Who were the landlords and what had they done that they should be thus favoured? And when the question was put in this way, it was obvious that there could be but one answer, and that an arrangement, which pressed so heavily upon the community, must be allowed to cease, even though it did enrich a special class, and one on which the chief burden of taxation ultimately fell. It was as a class question that the matter was chiefly discussed, and it was as a class question that it was finally decided.

The fundamental issue obscured. In all this hubbub of conflicting interests, however, the fundamental issue was almost entirely obscured. Disraeli called attention to it again and again, but he seemed to stand almost alone. If the Corn Laws were defensible, they were defensible as a benefit to the nation as a whole; the underlying aim of the whole system was to call forth a sufficient food-supply for the English population. In this they had succeeded till 1773; but the history of English agriculture since the peace, appeared to show that they were succeeding no longer. In so far as the British agriculturist, with protection, failed to supply the British nation regularly with sufficient food on terms that were not exorbitant, in so far protection was a failure; and according to

[1] 9 and 10 Vict. c. 22.　　　[2] 55 Geo. III. c. 26.

this, the deeper test, which was but little argued at the time, A.D. 1815
the Corn Laws were completely condemned; they had failed —1846.
to provide the nation with a sufficient food-supply of its
own growth.

In ceasing to rely for our food-supply on our own soil, *The at-*
and in deliberately looking to trade as the means whereby *self-suf-*
we might procure corn, we were throwing aside the last *ficing re-*
elements of the policy which had so long dominated in the *linquished.*
counsels of the nation. A home-grown food-supply was a
chief element of power[1], it was at least impossible for an
enemy, however strong their navy might be, to cut off
our supplies. It gave the opportunity for maintaining a
large population, accustomed to out-door exercise and in good
condition for fighting; but these elements of power were
now forgotten, in the desire to have food in as large quantities and at as low rates as possible. We reverted from the
pursuit of power in our economic policy to the pursuit of
plenty[2]; we can but trust that by pursuing plenty, we may
find that we are supplied with the sinews of power when
we come to need them.

The exclusive companies had been thrown open; the *The end of*
Navigation Laws had been entirely recast[3]; they were no *cantile*
longer important and were soon to be repealed altogether[4]; *System.*
the doctrine of the Balance of Trade was forgotten, and no
pains were taken to accumulate treasure; the industry of
the country was no longer fostered by special enactment;
and now the agricultural interest also was to be left to its
own devices. With the repeal of the Corn Laws the last
remaining element of the Mercantile System was swept
away.

[1] Compare Strafford's effort to keep Ireland politically dependent by making
her economically dependent for clothing, and salt to preserve meat, her staple
product. *Letters*, I. 198.

[2] See above, Vol. I. p. 416. The triumph of this policy was commemorated by
the Anti-Corn Law League with a medal, which is figured on the title page, by the
kind permission of the authorities of the British Museum, from the example in
their possession.

[3] 12 Charles II. c. 18 was repealed by 6 Geo. IV. c. 105.

[4] 12 and 13 Vict. c. 29, 17 and 18 Vict. c. 104.

XXV. Currency and Capital.

A.D. 1815
—1846.
*The
Currency.*

387. The gradual lightening of the burden of taxation did not produce such favourable results on the industry and commerce of the country as had been anticipated. So long as the Corn Laws existed, this is sufficiently accounted for; but there were subsidiary reasons of some importance, connected with the condition of the currency and the influence which was exerted on commercial credit.

The year 1816 saw an important step, by which one source of confusion was at last removed. Gold had long been the actual standard of value in England, and by an Act of this year it was recognised as the sole standard; silver was demonetised and was only a legal tender for small payments[1].

*Mono-
metallism.*

The example which England then set in becoming a mono-metallic country with a gold standard has been recently followed by the leading commercial nations of the world. It has resulted in the curious anomalies whereby the variations in the value of the precious metals, which formerly affected transactions within the country, have been transferred to be a constant source of uncertainty in the commercial relations of different countries with one another, according as they are silver-using or gold-using nations[2].

*Resump-
tion of
Cash Pay-
ments.*

The next important change, in connection with the currency, was the resumption of cash payments. This might have been easily effected in 1816, when the Bank was well supplied with gold; but the doctrine, to which Parliament was committed, treated the over-issue of bank-notes as a chimera, and the opportunity was lost. A few years later, in 1818, there were signs of a considerable drain of gold, while at the same time nominal prices ranged high, in consequence, as it was believed, of over-issues of bank-notes. Under these circumstances committees were appointed by the Commons and by the Lords; and both bodies agreed that it was highly desirable to revert, as soon as possible, to a metallic basis, and

---

[1] 56 Geo. III. c. 68.

[2] Boissevain, *Bimetallism*, 24. Molesworth, *Silver and Gold*, 38, 64.

that the notes issued by the Bank should really be con- A.D. 1815
vertible[1]. There was much anxiety in the mercantile world, —1846.
lest nominal prices should fall to a serious extent, and trade
should be greatly injured. During the actual change some
relief was given, by allowing the Bank to pay its notes in
bullion at the Mint, as well as in actual gold coins[2]; and on
the whole this great financial operation was effected with
less difficulty than had been anticipated.

Sir Robert Peel had been the chief agent in carrying *Peel and*
through this change; he appears to have been deeply impressed with the mischiefs, which might accrue to the
country, from an over-issue of Bank-notes and an inflated
currency. When the period arrived for renewing the charter
of the Bank of England, he drafted and carried through a
scheme, which took the power of regulating their own issues
of notes out of the hands of the directors; the amount of
their issues was for the future to be strictly limited, by a
reference to the actual bullion in the possession of the Bank,
so that the actual convertibility would not at all depend on
the judgment of the directors but was guaranteed by a
mechanical arrangement.

The Bank Charter Act[3] was severely criticised at the *the Bank*
time when it passed through Parliament; it was held that *Act of 1844.*
the expedients were unnecessary in order to avoid the evils of
over-issue and inflation, and that they might be hurtful, inasmuch as the Bank would be unable to extend its issues at
times of special commercial distress and would no longer be
able to assuage a panic, as it had done with such conspicuous
success, in 1780. The criticism was supported by all the
weight of accurate knowledge, which Mr Tooke[4] embodied in
his *History of Prices;* it appeared to be completely confirmed, when, in the great commercial depression of prices
in 1847, it became necessary to allow the Bank to exercise
special powers, and to suspend the Act which had been
passed only three years before.

388. The commercial distress which marked the end of
this period was not so much due to any changes connected

[1] *Reports,* &c. 1819, III. 14, 17, 367, 381.   [2] 59 Geo. III. c. 49.
[3] 7 and 8 Vict. c. 32.   [4] Tooke, IV. Pt. III. c. 2.

A.D. 1815
—1846.
*The forma-
tion of
Capital.*

with the medium of exchange as to misapplications of capital. During the nineteenth century, despite frequent depression, there had been frequent intervals when trade had been done at highly profitable rates, and very large sums of money had been made. The returns for legacy duty may be taken as indicating the rapidity with which money had been accumulated. The total sums which became subject to legacy duty at the subjoined dates were as follows[1]:

1814	...	£27,299,806
1819		29,411,662
1824		35,852,824
1829		39,667,277
1834		41,574,628
1844	... ...	46,533,908

*Burden of
Interest on
National
Debt.*

i. So far as the vast sums of money made during the war were loaned to Government, they were of course absolutely expended at once; however necessary that expenditure may have been for political purposes, this money did absolutely nothing to increase the material prosperity of the country. Indeed the necessity of paying the annual interest on this debt, amounting as it did to £32,000,000[2], was the heaviest part of the burden which the nation had to bear, and which depressed agriculture, industry, and commerce. The large opportunities for this kind of investment, which the greatly extended public borrowing had opened up, must have tended to increase the numbers of the class who enjoyed a secured income, apart from all the fluctuations of trade.

*The
monied
men.*

Prices might fall and merchants might be ruined, mills might cease to pay and farmers become bankrupt, labourers might be forced to eke out their wages by allowances, but the fundholder continued to receive his dividends with unabated regularity. It had thus come about that the owner of money could find himself secure from the risks which had attached to every kind of productive property. In old days the greatest security had been with the man who could in the last resort fall back for sustenance on the produce of his land, but he might have to fare badly and live sparingly; under

[1] Wilson, *Capital, Currency and Banking*, x.   [2] Dowell, II. 239.

the new régime, the monied man was untouched by any A.D. 1815 —1846. disaster short of national bankruptcy.

This immunity from common risks has been looked upon *Immunity from ordinary risks.* as an unfair privilege which monied men enjoy, but it is a privilege which has been widely diffused by the action of Insurance Companies. Taking advantage of the large income which accrues to the owner of money, they are able to guarantee their customers against loss from many of the ordinary emergencies of life. The immunity which money can secure need not be the special privilege of the rich but may be shared by other classes as well.

ii. In the years succeeding the war and until 1840, the *Investment in industry* new accumulations of English capital appear to have been chiefly invested in industrial improvements, which were soon brought into active operation[1]. There was constant work going on, in building mills and fitting them with the best machinery. These new factories gave additional, and on the whole, more comfortable opportunities of employment; capital thus invested tended directly and immediately to the increase of national wealth.

A certain amount was indeed loaned to foreign govern- *and foreign loans.* ments. When this was done, there was in all probability a temporary derangement of commercial relationships in actually transmitting the capital abroad; while the money was lost, so far as the increase of English production was concerned; though Englishmen had secured a right to tax the subjects of other countries to a given amount annually.

iii. When the public began to realise the great improve- *The Railway Mania.* ments which might be made in internal communication by means of railways, a regular mania for constructing lines set in. Tramways had been in use from the beginning of the century, and the Stockton and Darlington was opened in 1825; but the year 1836 saw a sudden increase in the number of Acts which were passed for raising capital and laying down lines of rails. In the autumn of 1845, 2,069 miles of railway were opened, with a capital of £64,238,600; while 3,543 miles of railway were in progress, involving capital to the amount of £74,407,520[2]. Of course there was no immediate

---

[1] Wilson, *Capital, Currency,* xiii.   [2] *Ib.* vi.

A.D. 1815
—1846.
*Capital
sunk.*
return on this large amount of capital; it was for the time
being absolutely sunk; the investment of so much capital in
forms that were not immediately productive, had the result
of injuring many branches of industry and depressing commerce. In so far as the money devoted to railway enterprise
was withdrawn from circulation the effects were, for the time
being, disastrous. Capitalists found that their sales diminished; they were unable to replace their stock of materials,
or to continue to pay wages, until their stores of finished
goods were realised; and a general stagnation resulted[1]. As

*General
stagnation.*
Mr Wilson puts it,—" Let us suppose manufacturers in Lancashire paying five millions of pounds in wages; that money
is expended in provisions, clothing, &c. by their work people;
and a very large portion in commodities produced abroad; such
as the sugar, tea, coffee, a great part of the material of their
clothes, &c.; but all these commodities are paid for, by a portion of their labour exported in the form of cotton goods.
But on the other hand, suppose five millions paid for wages
on railways; the same portion goes for the consumption of
imported commodities, tea, sugar, coffee, materials of clothing,
&c.; but no portion whatever of their produce is exported, or
can be so to pay for those commodities. Again, with respect
to the money paid for iron; the demand for this article increases the quantity made, which is all absorbed in these
undertakings, but the largest portion of the price goes to pay
wages, which are again to a great extent expended in articles
of foreign import, while no equivalent of export is produced
against them, so that a large portion of the whole money
expended in railways is actually paid for imported commodities, while no equivalent of exports is produced. Now, this
state of things acts in two ways on the commerce of the
country, next upon the exchanges, and quickly upon the

---

[1] The doctrine that demand for commodities is not demand for labour is often
stated in a form which neglects the necessity for the replacement of capital by the
sale of goods which have been actually produced. Unless capital is replaced by
sale and thus realised, it cannot be transferred to other directions of employment.
The permanent effects of increasing unproductive at the expense of productive
consumption are frequently dwelt on in economic treatises, but the railway mania
illustrates the mischiefs which may temporarily arise from a sudden increase of
productive consumption, and a sudden cessation of the ordinary consumption
whether productive or not.

money market. The extraordinary expenditure at home in- A.D. 1815 creases very much the consumption of all commodities, both —1846. of foreign import and home production, and raises their price, as is the case at this time. The high price of foreign commodities induces to a large importation; the high price and home demand for domestic produce cause a decreased export. The exchanges are thus turned against us, and we must remit money for the payment of that balance created by the use of those foreign commodities consumed in this country by those, no part of whose produce had been exported to represent their consumption. One of the most certain symptoms that can be shown of an undue absorption of capital going forward ·in internal investments, is when we see our imports increasing more rapidly than our exports, or when the former are increasing and the latter are diminishing[1]."

The phenomena thus described continued to manifest *Remarkable* themselves for several years; and their effects were in many *budgets.* ways peculiar; in none more so than in bringing about large payments for customs and excise, so that there were prosperous budgets while trade was, generally speaking, depressed[2]. But at length the results could not be ignored, and the whole case was made the subject of investigation by the Commission on Commercial Depression in 1847[3].

iv. The depression, which was due to the very rapid increase of fixed capital, was new, and was at the time almost as unintelligible as it was unexpected; but it was aggravated *Speculation and* by a repetition of occurrences which were already sufficiently *collapse of* familiar. The possible profits of railway enterprise appeared *credit.* to have no assignable limits, and there was a period of feverish speculation when new and impracticable schemes were daily offered to the public, and shares were eagerly taken up. There had been nothing quite like it since the era of the South Sea Bubble. The public were not without warning at this time, for the *Times* and the *Economist* protested again and again against the increasing mischief. But it was all in vain, and numberless bubble companies were floated by men, who were unscrupulous enough to practise any fraud on

---

[1] Wilson, *Capital, Currency and Banking*, p. xxv.
[2] Northcote, *Twenty Years*, 83.   [3] *Reports*, &c. (1847), VIII. i. ii. iii.

the credulity of would-be investors. The evil had reached considerable dimensions in 1844, when a committee of the House of Commons investigated the law of Joint Stock Companies[1], and laid the basis of a measure for their regulation and registration[2]. Though there has been little difficulty in evading its provisions, and in floating fraudulent schemes which yet complied with its rules, it sufficed to expose many of the worst companies, the shares of which were dealt in at the time it was passed[3].

[1] *Reports*, 1844, VII. 1—457.   [2] 7 and 8 Vict. c. 110.
[3] D. Morier Evans, *Commercial Crisis*, 1847—8, p. 45.

CONCLUSION.

389. WITH the repeal of the Corn Laws the last re- maining element of the Mercantile System was removed, and the history of the growth of English Industry and Commerce in modern times may be said to terminate. There has indeed been an extraordinary development during the era of free trade; but that belongs to what may be called recent history, and it is no part of my present scheme to review the work of living men or pass by anticipation any judgment on the occurrences of the last few years[1]. Measures that were passed some forty or fifty years ago, there is but little difficulty in describing or in criticising; distance of time has succeeded in bringing them into something like their due proportion. We can see that some occurrences were of lasting importance; and that others, which created much excitement at the time, were merely temporary incidents which have sunk at last into their proper insignificance. But no human being can pretend to exercise this necessary discrimination wisely in relating the events of his own time. If mere description, in due proportion, is not easy, it is even harder to attempt to pass a satisfactory judgment. As years go by, the course of events gives a final and irresistible verdict on the wisdom or unwisdom of human conduct, in economic as in other affairs. The part of the historian is but to gather up the evidence, as to the success or the failure of any human endeavours, which is furnished by the subsequent years as they rolled by. But in recent history the consequences have not fully declared themselves; the temporary and the permanent results of any measure cannot be discriminated satisfactorily. We may forecast probable results with more or less

---

[1] For a brief sketch of recent history see my *Politics and Economics*.

and practical politics. success, but that is the work not so much of the historian, as of the practical politician; it seems best for the present to leave it to him.

The pursuit of national power 390. The repeal of the Corn Laws, signalising as it did the close of the long era during which the conception of national power had dominated over our economic life, was not only important in itself, but of special interest as marking a crisis in our history. For years the fabric of national commercial and industrial life had been slowly reared; it had flourished more and more in the fourteenth century, while the old municipal organisation of industry and commerce began to decline; the measures which promoted it in all its various parts had been pursued, with more or less constancy of purpose, from the time of Richard II.; under Elizabeth they were consolidated and systematised into a great code for regulating the industry and commerce of the nation, so as to promote its power.

and of plenty. The nation had prospered so far as political power was concerned and it had overthrown its ancient rival; but now it began to consider that this power had been dearly purchased and to look for other good things as well. Thus we returned to the fourteenth century ideal and to guiding our economic policy by consideration of plenty.

The commercial policy of 14th and of 19th century. The struggle between municipal and national commerce. But yet with a difference; there is no possibility of returning upon the past; the new life on which we have entered has some analogies with the commercial schemes of the third Edward, but it differs. Then the transition was going on, from municipal and intermunicipal, to national commerce; the citizens, with their exclusive privileges and rules for combined trading, were after all working in narrow grooves; they could not adapt themselves to the requirements of a worldwide commerce. Hence it was that the fruits of the age of discovery fell, not to the old cities, but to the new nations. The whole of the old organisation, useful as it had been in its day, glorious as are the monuments which survive in the great municipal buildings of continental towns, passed away, as national commerce, stimulated by national rivalry, came more and more to the front.

National and Inter- In 1846 the regulation of industry and commerce for national purposes and with reference to national power *national commerce.* came to an end in England, just as the regulation of industry for municipal purposes and for the good of the town had ceased long before. It has decayed, because a larger life is gradually taking its place; the factors which chiefly contribute to the production of wealth are no longer bounded by national considerations; England has taken the lead in declaring that the fullest freedom of intercourse and exchange of products is beneficial to the wealth of a nation. International agreements and cosmopolitan intercourse have gone so far that an exclusive national policy has proved itself out of date, just as exclusive municipal policy broke down in the Tudor time.

It is easy to see that the fullest freedom of intercourse *Cosmopolitan character of Modern Industry.* is the scheme which favours commerce; but it is also noticeable that the factors, which are chiefly concerned in the production of wealth, are assuming a cosmopolitan character. Capital is indifferent to the direction in which it is employed, *Capitalists.* so long as it earns a profit[1]. British capital has gone freely abroad to build foreign railroads; and there is no land which is not eager to develop its resources with the aid of money procured in London. And as capital is thus cosmopolitan, so to some extent is labour; capital has transformed continental agriculture and industry, as it transformed them in this country during last century and the beginning of this. Scarcely anywhere are there peasants pursuing some industry as a by-occupation. Everywhere the power of machinery has made itself felt; it has drawn the operatives together to do their whole day's work for wages paid by the employer, and it has thus introduced the same social type into all civilised countries. Everywhere the position *The Proletariat.* of the labourer, severed from agriculture, and dependent on the uncertainties of trade, is similar; and hence there is an international sympathy between the labourers of different races and languages which would have been impossible before the present era[2].

---

[1] The line of argument here indicated has been more fully stated in my *Use and Abuse of Money*, p. 47.

[2] Presidential Address to Section F, *British Association*, 1891.

Cobden expected that free trade and commercial intercourse would render nations so completely dependent on
one another that war would be impossible[1]. That prophecy
*Interna-
tional
Links.* has not been fulfilled; but international links, of which he
failed to take sufficient account, are being forged. The investment of British capital in foreign lands is, for good as
for evil, the pledge of an English interest in maintaining the
security of property in that land. The similar condition of
workmen in all lands calls forth a wide human sympathy,
which promotes frequent intercourse and sometimes finds
practical and material expression. The growth of such international sympathy must do much to check national rivalries, as the municipal rivalries of earlier times fell into the
background with the growth of a national life.

*Interna-
tional or-
ganisation.* Nor are signs of international organisation entirely wanting. There are agreements with regard to postal arrangements
Postal. which are not trivial matters and which affect the frequency
and convenience of international intercourse; and the agitation which we have from time to time with regard to the
Currency. currency, and to the possibility of international agreements
about a monetary system, seem to indicate that international
economic organisation is destined to grow, and that the
days of the supremacy of the nation, as a social organism
for economic purposes, are over for ever.

391. The change which was signalised in actual economic life by the repeal of the Corn Laws is also reflected
in the great contribution to economic literature which was
John Stuart published during that decade. John Stuart Mill's *Prin-*
Mill.
ciples of Political Economy mark an epoch in the progress
of the science; this is indicated in the sub-title where it
is described as a contribution to social philosophy. There
is indeed about economics as treated by Mill a synthetic
character, which plainly was a new departure.

With the great work of Adam Smith, Political Economy
had been divorced from the old object which it had hitherto
had in view. It no longer devised means for promoting
the national power; it was content to narrow its range
and simply to study ways and means without forming a

[1] *Political Writings,* 81, 265.

clear positive conception of the end which they might ultimately subserve. The economist of the early part of this *The school
of Ricardo,*
century was emphatically "a man of means[1]." He was pre- *and mate-*
pared to explain how the greatest possible amount of material *rial wealth.*
wealth might be produced, and to show the principles according to which it was distributed in varying proportions among
the individuals who formed the nation. These writers were
intent upon progress,—on giving the freest possible play to
every individual, so that each individual might be permitted
to contribute to the fullest possible extent to the material
wealth of the community; but after all, this was a narrow
and one-sided view. It is convenient to isolate material
wealth as a subject of study, but it is degrading to treat
it as an object to be pursued for its own sake. In the *Reaction
led by Mill.*
writings of John Stuart Mill a new turn is given to economics; he was not satisfied with discussing mere material
progress. He could contemplate a stationary state with calm-
ness; he could not but dwell with bitterness on the great
misery which accompanied increasing wealth; and he tried
to formulate an ideal of human welfare in his chapter on
the Progress of the Working Classes. In this way, he suc- *Means to
the end of*
ceeded in indicating an end towards which the new material
resources might be directed, and thus restored to economics
that practical side, which it had been in danger of losing
since the time of Ricardo. It is important that we should
have a method for isolating economic phenomena and analysing them as accurately as may be, and this Ricardo has
given us; but it is also desirable that we should be able to
turn our knowledge to account,—to see some end at which it
is worth while to aim, and to choose the means which will
conduce towards it; this we can do better, not merely in-
tuitively and by haphazard, but on reasoned grounds, since
the attempt was first made by Mill.

In taking human welfare as an end, we see that Mill *Human
Welfare.*
is aiming at a larger object than had been contemplated
by the predecessors of Adam Smith. Patriotism has inspired the great acts of heroism; it has played a noble part
in the past; it may have a part to play in the future; but

[1] J. S. Nicholson, *Toxar.*

it is responsible for bitter national animosities and deep national hatreds. Human welfare, as Mill conceived it, was not so limited; it was something that the members of all races might enjoy, and towards which each might contribute; it *A Cosmo-politan ideal* was in fact a cosmopolitan as contrasted with a national ideal.

392. There had of course been much action in which this was the leading motive; the whole of the legislation *partly an-ticipated and acted on by phil-anthropists.* which has been described as philanthropic, the whole of the crusade against slavery, had been instigated by a regard for human welfare. The horrors of the middle passage, the cruelties in factories, the scandals in mines, were a shock to public sentiment, and the philanthropists were determined that such things should not be; but they had on the whole been opposed by the economists. The economists had fore-told the ruin of this trade or that, and had prophesied ulti-mate and serious loss. It was in no small degree the work of John Stuart Mill that this opposition has so greatly ceased, and that economists have so largely devoted them-selves to the conscious and reasoned pursuit of philanthropic objects. It was in connection with the abolition of slavery that the forebodings of the economists were most nearly fulfilled, and it was the greatest of the followers of Mill who demonstrated the weakness of the *Slave Power*.

Effective as exerting a negative control, In tracing the growth of the national sentiment in the days when municipal and inter-municipal organisation were supreme in commerce I have had occasion to point out that it first made itself felt in a negative fashion, by the pro-hibition of such conduct as was inimical to national power. Many years had to elapse before a positive conception of the various elements which constituted national power was formed, and schemes could be devised for fostering and pro-moting it. We need not be surprised if the new con-ception of a larger object—human welfare—towards which our material resources should be directed, has come gradually to light in somewhat similar fashion. Its influence was seen in prohibitions of what was noxious to human life or degrading to human nature; but little effort could be made at first to devise conditions which should positively foster a better type of human being.

Nor has Mill succeeded in portraying with perfect clear- *but how shall we conceive it as a positive ideal?* ness an ideal of human welfare which we may strive to realise. It was only after a strange struggle that he learned to formulate for himself an object which might render his own life worth living[1]; it was not his part to be the prophet who should declare a gospel to his generation; but in the story of his own struggles, and among the group of men who surrounded him, we may distinguish the two different forms which that gospel has taken and is likely to take. Material conditions and personal faculties and character are alike elements in human well-being, and no social reformer is likely altogether to ignore either one or the other; but there will be fundamental differences of opinion among them according as they attach primary importance to the environment on one side, or to man himself on the other.

Since the time of Robert Owen there have been those *Robert Owen.* who seemed to think that improvement in material conditions would in itself produce a regenerated society. But the course of history, as we have traced it, hardly serves to give confirmation to this hope. To alter material surroundings for the better is to remove particular obstacles to social well-being[2]; but improved material surroundings are not the only condition which is necessary in order to produce the desired effect. People do not necessarily become better, mentally, morally or even physically, because they are better off; they have the opportunity of improvement if they choose to take advantage of it, but they may throw the opportunity away. In the story of progress in the past, the efficient agents have not been found in mere physical conditions of any kind, but in personal qualities,—in enterprise and skill, in patient accumulation and wise regulation. Men's aims and ideas have shaped the course for their commercial and industrial development, and have enabled them time after time to pass the limits which physical conditions seemed to lay down. At any epoch when material comfort serves to render men listless and apathetic it does not really favour farther advance; at best it affords an opportunity, that is all.

---

[1] *Autobiography*, 184.　　　[2] See above, Vol. I. § 9, p. 13.

The secret of progress lies, not solely or even chiefly in material conditions, but in that energy or enterprise which makes the most of such opportunities as offer. It is Man who directs material things to suit his requirements; foresight and skill, patience and vigour, wring produce from a barren soil and overcome the most untoward circumstances. The active principle is found not in his environment, but in Man himself; those who would promote material welfare will do so most certainly if they help men to become better themselves; this was the hope which inspired the life-work of Frederic Denison Maurice. Wise thoughts and high ambitions are noble in themselves, but they are also powers which direct human energies in the best way, and turn material objects to the worthiest uses. Whatever makes Man better, is sure to serve sooner or later to improve the conditions in which he lives.

F. D.
Maurice.

We may fully recognise that it is not possible to frame such a definite conception of social welfare as shall give us positive guidance in regard to the line of progress; we cannot see the farthest goal which it is possible for Man to attain, and therefore we cannot demonstrate what is the path that will lead to it most directly. But though we cannot forecast the distant future, we may yet have some little guidance if we do not despise the experience of the past; we may see where to take one step forward, and how to take it wisely. There is need for unselfish endeavours of every kind, but not the same need for all; to remove physical obstacles and to give new opportunities for personal comfort is good, but it is not the best; since those who are enabled to call forth greater wisdom in human ambitions and greater firmness in human purpose are helping to replenish the perennial sources of lasting material progress.

APPENDIX I.

On the Difficulty of Interpreting Historical
Statistics.

It is with some hesitation that I append some statistical
tables; information in a numerical form has an appearance of
accuracy and completeness which is often misleading. For the
present century there is an abundance of information available
on many points connected with population, trade, &c. and this
may be of the greatest possible service; but in regard to earlier
times, the data are often somewhat uncertain, and estimates have
to do duty for actual enumerations. Besides, even when the
figures can be relied on, there is often a danger of misinterpreting
them, and so using them as evidence in a way that they do not
warrant.

i. There is the greatest advantage in possessing an enumeration of similar objects (or amounts) at two different periods; as
this may serve (a) to show us the direction of change, and (b) to
measure the amount of change. This is most obvious with regard
to all questions connected with population. Only actual enumeration, or careful calculation, could serve to disprove the opinion
that English population was decreasing during the eighteenth
century. The taking of a census every ten years serves to show
not only whether population is increasing or not, but how fast it
is increasing.

ii. But figures, however accurate, never tell us the reasons
for any change; they may show the direction and rapidity of the
change, but they do not show what brought it about. For
example, figures show that the sums expended in the relief of the
poor diminished during the earlier part of the eighteenth century;
but the figures do not tell us whether this change was due to
greater strictness of administration, or to improved trade and
better employment. The figures give us the combined effect of
both causes, and do not in themselves help us to discriminate the
action of one from that of the other. As there are always many

influences at work in any social movement, it is not easy to measure the precise effect exerted by any one factor singly.

iii. When we are instituting comparisons between long distant times (or places) and our own circumstances, there may be great elements of confusion (a) from differences in the things measured, (b) from differences in the measure. The quality of a pound of mediaeval beef[1] probably differed considerably from the prime cuts of the present day; and at all events the ox or the sheep was undoubtedly inferior to the modern breeds in size and weight. Again, where we have to compare prices at different periods, the alterations in the standard of the currency have to be allowed for.

iv. These are some of the difficulties which have to be faced when we try to compare things that are fairly definite and precise; but the difficulty is greatly enhanced if we set ourselves to compare the "material comfort" of the labourer in different centuries. To solve the question at all we must know (a) not only what he could get by paying for it, as compared with what the modern labourer can get, but we must take account (b) of cases where the modern labourer has to pay for things which the mediaeval labourer got for nothing, and (c) of things which the modern labourer habitually uses, and which the mediaeval labourer never had at all. That is to say, to estimate the standard of comfort, we must not only know (a) the *purchasing power of wages*, but take account (b) of the increased necessity of purchasing *fuel* in modern times, and (c) of the increased use of *tea, tobacco* and so forth. These last obviously imply a change in the standard of comfort, for the better if they are *additional* luxuries, and for the worse, if they are *substitutes* for things containing more sustenance.

There is a further difficulty; it is now recognised that the question of a labourer's comfort depends, not merely on his own wages, but on the family income[2]; Le Play and his school have put this matter beyond discussion. Before then we can get satisfactory information regarding the standard of comfort we must know what opportunities there are for bye-employment and domestic industry.

These considerations are all necessary to get any statement on

[1] Compare H. Hall, on *Roast Beef of Old England* in *Antiquarian*, 1882.

[2] The family is an element of uncertainty both as to income and expenditure. The difficulties of comparing the price of labour in our land in different centuries, are brought out in a few sentences about the price of labour in different states at the same date. "1st. The necessaries of a family is a vague term. 2dly. A family is vague; it may be four or ten persons. 3dly. A day's work is vague; it may be six hours or sixteen. 4thly. The quantity of labour in a state is uncertain. 5thly. The seasons and weather are various as to heat and cold, which must vary the price of labour. 6thly. The value of money is different, so that in one country an ounce of silver will purchase a sack of wheat, and twenty days' labour; in another but a bushel, and five days' labour. What a perplexity arises hence! But when the price of labour is talked of, and compared between two states, &c., all these ought to be considered." [Temple] *Considerations on Taxes*, p. 42 n.

the subject which shall be worth having; but they are so complicated, that it seems impossible to give each of them their due weight. On this ground Professor Thorold Rogers has taken the bold course of simplifying the problem as much as possible, by leaving these confusing elements on one side[1]. He takes individual earnings as typical of family earnings, and discusses the standard of comfort of the labourer on the simpler issue of the purchasing power of his wages. But the quotations for rates of wages, on which he relies, are often statements of payments made *per day ;* if the standard of comfort is to be estimated by the *free income,* which the labourer had (for clothes, &c.) after purchasing necessary food, it is necessary to know how regularly he was employed. Where we do not know this, we are forced to *assume* it, so as to discuss the problem at all. But *regularity of employment* depends on (1) opportunity of employment, and (2) on willingness to work; and these are uncertain elements which make it very difficult to hazard a reasonable assumption for any period in the past.

There are two periods during which it appears, from comparing the price of food and the rates of wages, that the labourer must have been specially well off, viz. 1401–1499, and 1701–66. But it seems very doubtful whether there was much regularity of employment at either time. The evidence of the decay of towns (Vol. I., p. 402, 450), and increase of sheep-farming (Vol. I., p. 361; see above, p. 51) goes to prove that there were many districts where employment was not to be had at all regularly during the fifteenth century. Again, the constant complaint of laziness in the eighteenth century seems to show that the labourers who had the opportunity of working often preferred to take out their enjoyment in the form of idling. (See above, pp. 381 f., 458.)

It has been the habit of economists from the time of the statute of Elizabeth to think of wages as varying according to the plenty and scarcity of the time; that is, that when food is dear, wages should be high, and that wages may be low when food is cheap. But Temple, if he was the author of the *Essay on Trade and Commerce,* gives expression to an opposite view. "It is the quantity of labour and not the price of it, that is determined by the price of provisions and other necessaries." (p. 40.) According to his observations, when men could easily earn a living, they would not work more than half their time, but when food was dear, they were ready to put in six days a week. This doctrine, which was formulated after experience of a period of comparative plenty, was certainly confirmed during the miserable days which

---

[1] "I assumed that the peasant and the artisan work 300 days in the year. It is quite possible that they did not get so much employment, perhaps that they worked more days, or on certain occasions increased their earnings by bye-employments, by the labour of their wives, their sons, and their daughters. But in calculations such as I am making, provided you take what it may be conceived the workmen could not do without, the comparison is made more obvious if the fewest and simplest factors are taken." *Agriculture and Prices,* v. 618.

succeeded the peace, when the men were accustomed to labour for excessive hours because food was so dear.

Where there are high rates of wages and plenty of employment is to be had, it is clear that the labourers have an opportunity of raising their standard of material comfort. There are too many pessimists who call attention to the strength of human passions, and human folly, and who despair of these opportunities being ever well used. The followers of Malthus are inclined to say that if food is cheap, there will only be a reckless increase of the population ; teetotalers are inclined to insist that high wages too often mean a large drink bill ; and others may urge that high wages only lead to idleness and dissipation. With so many temptations at work, it need be no matter for surprise that during all these centuries of increasing wealth, the labourers' standard of comfort has changed but little for the better ; that while many have risen out of the labouring class, the standard of the class has been hardly altered at all. But at least the experience of the past may help us to understand that no permanent improvement is necessarily brought about by increased opportunities for material well-being, but only by the intellectual and moral changes which enable men to take advantage of the opportunities that offer, be they great or small.

From the foregoing remarks it appears that very little reliance can be placed on conclusions drawn from quotations of prices as to the actual material comfort enjoyed by the labourer at any period. At the same time, as the question is constantly raised, it may not be out of place to give the calculations made by Arthur Young and commended by Tooke, for what they are worth.

A. Prices and Wages in England, 1200 to 1810.—Comparative Statement framed by Arthur Young in 1812, upon the principle of representing the facts of 1810 by the number twenty (20), and the facts of the preceding periods by the proportion (in figures) borne by them to that Number.

1	2	3	4	5	6	7	8	9	10	11	12
Periods.		Food.			Victualling Office. Beef and Pork.	Other Articles.				Wages.	
		Wheat.	Barley and Oats.	Beef, Mutton, Veal, Pork, Bacon, Butter, Cheese.		Wool (*Combing*).	Horses.	Coals at Bethlehem Hospital.	Manufactures at Greenwich Hospital.	Agricultural Labour.	Carpenters and Masons.
100	1200-99	5½	4¾	...	...	...	...	...	...	3½	...
,,	1300-99	6¼	5	...	...	...	...	...	...	4¾	4½
,,	1400-99	3	2¾	...	...	...	...	...	...	5½	5¾
,,	1500-99	6	4¾	...	...	...	...	...	...	5½	4⅓
,,	1600-99	9¼	8¼	...	...	...	...	...	...	8	7
,,	1700-99	9¼	11¼	10¼	...	...	...	...	...	12½	11⅓
66	1701-66	7¾	7¼	7½	7¼	12	15¾	13½	14½	10	...
28	1767-89	11	11	11½	11	15⅓	17¼	14⅓	14	12½	...
14	1790-1803	13	16¼	16½	17	16⅛	19½	15¾	15½	16¾	...
7	1804-10	20	20	20	20	20	20	20	20	20	20
34	1767-1800	12	11½	13¼	12⅓	12	...	14¼	15¾	14	...

Note.—This Table may be read thus:—The price of a given quantity of, say, wheat (col. 3), was represented in 1810 by the number 20; and the price of the same quantity of wheat in coinage, of the same weight and fineness, was, in the period, say 1500—99, represented by the number 6; hence, the price of wheat in 1810, compared with 1500—99, had risen 233 per cent.

The "Manufactures at Greenwich Hospital" (col. 10) include shoes, stockings, hats, and mops.

Arthur Young combined several of the separate elements together, in order to simplify the general view, and the following were the results, viz.:

Combinations obtained from the preceding Table.

Periods.	2 Wheat, Barley, and Oats *united.* (Cols. 3 and 4.)	3 *Wheat* and Beef, &c. *united.* (3 and 5.)	4 *Corn* and Beef, &c. *united.* (3, 4, and 5.)	5 Labour, Corn, and Beef, &c. *united.* (3, 4, 5, and 11.)	6 Labour singly. (11.)
1200–99	5	...	...	...	3½
1300–99	5½	...	...	...	4¾
1400–99	8	...	...	...	5½
1500–99	5	5¼	...	...	5½
1600–99	8¾	8	...	...	8
1700–99	10¼	9¼	...	...	12½
1701–66	7⅓	7½	7½	8¼	10
1767–89	11	11¼	11¼	11½	12½
1790–1803	14⅓	14¾	15⅓	16	16¾
1804–10	20	20	20	20	20
1767–1800	11¾	12¾	12¼	13	14

According to these figures, it is obvious that the periods during which a given quantity of *Labour* would command the largest quantity of *Food*, were the periods 1400–99 and 1701–66. Tooke, *Prices*, VI. 391.

B. THE PROGRESS OF PARTICULAR INDUSTRIES is illustrated by the following figures. The first table shows the rapid progress which took place in the woollen manufactures of the West Riding during the second quarter of the eighteenth century. The second shows the progress of the woollen manufacture in Great Britain, so far as that is indicated by the accounts of the raw material imported, of the quantities of wool grown there is no trustworthy information, and the third gives the quantities of cotton wool imported. The fourth gives the quantities of pig-iron made in Great Britain, since coal-smelting began.

i. *Progress of Woollen Manufacture.* Massie, writing in 1764, says that the exports of woollen manufacture, which under Charles II. and James II. "did not much exceed the yearly value of one million pounds, amounted in 1699 to almost three millions sterling, from which vast sum, with occasional ebbings and flowings our annual exports of Woollen Manufactures have gradually risen to full four millions of late years." *Observations on New Cyder Tax*, p. 1. Detailed statements of the values of woollen manufactures exported for every year from 1697—1781 will be found in *Considerations upon the present state of the Wool*

Trade (1781), p. 83. [Brit. Mus. 1103, a. 3 (10).] These are continued to 1840 in Bischoff, II. Ap. VI. The highest point reached was £7,900,000 in 1833. These tables also give the price of wool for each year, but do not discriminate the qualities for which these varying prices were charged.

No. of Pieces[1] *of Broad Woollen Cloth manufactured in W. Riding*, 1726—1750, extracted from Register books kept in said County[2]:

1726	26,671	1739	43,086½
1727	28,990	1740	41,441
1728	25,223½	1741	46,364
1729	29,643½	1742	44,954
1730	21,579½	1743	45,178½
1731	33,563	1744	54,627½
1732	35,548½	1745	50,458
1733	34,620	1746	56,637
1734	31,123	1747	62,480
1735	31,744½	1748	60,705½
1736	38,899	1749	60,447½
1737	42,256	1750	60,964
1738	42,404		

ii. *Foreign and Colonial Wool imported into England* (the United Kingdom from 1766—1857):

	lbs.		lbs.		lbs.
1766	1,926,000	1800	8,609,000	1840	49,436,000
1771	1,829,000	1810	10,914,000	1850	74,326,000
1780	323,000	1820	9,775,000	1855	99,300,000
1790	2,582,000	1830	32,305,000	1857	127,390,000
1799	2,263,000				

An account of the woollen trade of Yorkshire, by E. Baines in T. Baines, *Yorkshire, Past and Present*, I. 637. Cf. also Bischoff, II. App. II.

iii. *Cotton Wool imported. Returns from Records of Custom House.*

	lbs.
1697	1,976,359
1701	1,985,868
1710	715,008
1720	1,972,805
1730	1,545,472
1741	1,645,081
1751	2,976,610
1764	3,870,392

Baines, *Hist. of the Cotton Manufacture*, 109.

[1] Until 1733 or 1734 there were between 30 and 40 yds. in each piece—since then the length has been gradually increased, and each piece is now (1764) near 70 yards.

[2] Massie, *Observations on the New Cyder Tax* (1764), p. 3.

Cotton wool imported for spinning [1] *into England and Scotland,*
1781—1832.

	lbs.		lbs.		lbs.
1781	3,198,778	1799	43,379,278	1816	93,920,055
1782	11,828,039	1800	56,010,732	1817	124,912,968
1783	9,785,663	1801	56,004,305	1818	177,282,158
1784	11,482,083	1802	60,345,600	1819	149,739,820
1785	18,400,384	1803	53,812,284	1820	144,818,100
1786	19,475,020	1804	61,867,329	1821	123,977,400
1787	23,250,268	1805	59,682,406	1822	135,420,100
1788	20,467,436	1806	58,176,283	1823	191,402,503
1789	32,576,023	1807	74,925,306	1824	149,380,122
1790	31,447,605	1808	43,605,982	1825	228,005,291
1791	28,706,675	1809	92,812,282	1826	170,500,000
1792	34,907,497	1810	132,488,935	1827	264,330,000
1793	19,040,929	1811	91,576,585	1828	222,750,000
1794	24,358,567	1812	63,025,936	1829	218,524,000
1795	26,401,340	1813	50,966,000	1830	259,856,000
1796	32,126,357	1814	60,060,239	1831	280,080,000
1797	23,354,371	1815	99,306,343	1832	277,260,490
1798	31,880,641				

Baines, *Hist. of the Cotton Manufacture* in *Hist. of
the County Palatine and Duchy of Lancaster,*
vol. II. 496.

iv. *Quantity of Pig-iron made in England, Wales, and Scot*
land, 1740—1852.

	Tons		Tons		Tons
1740	17,350	1806	258,206	1839	1,248,781
1788	68,300	1825	581,367	1847	1,999,608
1796	125,079	1830	678,417	1852	2,701,000

Scrivenor, 136 (ed. 1854), 256, 302.

C. THE INCREASE OF THE COMMERCE of the country is shown
by the tables of exports and imports ; these are taken for the
longest period where comparison is possible, as the change from
official to real values, though giving greater accuracy, renders
it less easy to indicate the rate of change. To this is added
Chalmers' table of the increase of shipping. *Estimate,* 234.

i. *Official Value of Exports and Imports.*

Exports.

England
1613 [2]	2,487,435	Misselden, *Circle of Commerce,* 121.
1622	2,320,436	,, ,, ,, 128.
1662	2,022,812	Macpherson, *Annals of Commerce,* II. 707.
1688	4,310,000	Davenant, *Works,* II. 270.
1699	6,788,166	Macpherson, *Annals,* II. 707.
1720	6,910,899	,, . ,, III. 116.
1730	8,548,982	.. , III. 160.
1740	8,197,788	, III. 227.
1750	12,699,081	, III. 283.
1760	14,694,970	,, ,, III. 339.

[1] In spinning this, allowance for loss 1½ oz. per lb. should be made, to estimate
total amount of yarn spun. Baines, II. 502.

[2] In 1570 the official value of Exports and Imports according to a State Paper
in the Cotton Collection is given as £26,665 and £45,356 (Hall, *Customs,* vol. II.
App.). It may be doubted however whether this was not a partial return for the
purpose of a contemporary agitation against foreign competition, i.e. to show that
the "balance of trade" was against England.

England	1783	13,896,415	*Finance Reports*, 1797, II. 22, 86.
	1796	29,196,198	
Gt Britain	1798	27,317,087	
	1800	34,381,617	
	1805	31,064,492	*Accounts and Papers*, 1830, XXVII. 208—11.
	1810	43,568,757	
	1815	58,624,550	
	1820	48,951,587	*Accounts and Papers*, 1833, XLI. 48.
United	1825	56,320,182	
Kingdom	1830	69,691,303	
	1835	91,174,456	*Accounts and Papers*, 1851, XXXI. 170.
	1840	116,479,678	
	1845	150,879,986	
	1850	197,330,265	*Accounts and Papers*, 1852—53, LVII. 198.

Imports.

	1618	2,141,151	Misselden, *Circle of Commerce*, 122.
	1622	2,619,315	,, ,, ,, 129.
	1688	7,120,000	Davenant, *Works*, II. 270.
	1720	6,090,083	Macpherson, *Annals*, III. 116.
England	1730	7,780,019	,, ,, III. 160.
	1740	6,703,778	.. ,, III. 227.
	1750	7,772,089	.. ,, III. 283.
	1760	9,832,802	,, ,, III. 339.
	1788	11,651,281	*Finance Reports*, 1797, II. 22, 86.
	1796	21,024,866	
Gt Britain	1798	25,122,208	
	1800	28,257,781	
	1805	28,561,270	*Accounts and Papers*, 1830, XXVII. 209.
	1810	39,301,612	
	1815	32,987,396	
	1820	32,438,650	*Accounts and Papers*, 1833, XLI. 48.
United	1825	44,208,807	
Kingdom	1830	46,245,241	
	1835	48,911,548	*Accounts and Papers*, 1851, XXXI. 170.
	1840	67,432,964	
	1845	85,281,958	
	1850	100,460,433	*Accounts and Papers*, 1852—53, LVII. 198.

ii. *Increase of Shipping.*

THE EPOCHS.		THE SHIPS CLEARED OUTWARDS.		
		Tons ENGLISH.	Do. FOREIGN.	TOTAL.
The Restoration	1663 1669	95,268	47,634	142,900
The Revolution	1688	190,533	95,267	285,800
The Peace of Ryswick...	1697	144,264	100,524	244,788
The last years of William III.	1700 1701 1702	273,693	43,635	317,328
The Wars of Anne	1709 1712	243,693 326,620	45,625 29,115	289,318 355,735
The first of George I....	1713 1714 1715	421,431	26,573	448,004
The first of George II. .	1726 1727 1728	432,832	23,651	456,483
The peaceful years	1736 1737 1738	476,941	26,627	503,568
The War of	1739 1740 1741	384,191	87,260	471,451
The peaceful years	1749 1750 1751	609,798	51,386	661,184
The War of	1755 1756 1757	451,254	73,456	524,710
The first of George III. ...... WAR:	1760 1761 1762	471,241 508,220 480,444	102,737 117,835 120,126	573,978 626,055 600,570
PEACE:	1763 1764 1765 1766 1767 1768 1769 1770 1771 1772 1773 1774	561,724 583,934 651,402 684,281 645,835 668,786 709,855 703,495 773,390 818,108 771,483 798,240	87,293 74,800 67,855 61,753 63,206 72,734 63,020 57,476 63,532 72,603 54,820 65,273	649,017 658,734 719,257 746,034 709,041 741,520 772,875 760,971 836,922 890,711 826,303 863,513

Increase of Shipping (continued).

THE EPOCHS.		THE SHIPS CLEARED OUTWARDS.		
		Tons ENGLISH.	Do. FOREIGN.	TOTAL.
WAR:	1775	788,226	64,860	848,086
	1776	778,878	72,188	851,066
	1777	736,234	83,468	819,702
	1778	657,238	98,113	755,351
	1779	590,911	139,124	730,035
	1780	619,462	134,515	753,977
	1781	547,953	163,410	711,363
	1782	552,851	208,511	761,362
	1783	795,669	157,969	953,638
PEACE:	1784	846,855	113,064	959,419
	1785	951,855	103,398	1,055,253
	1786	982,132	116,771	1,098,903
	1787	1,104,711	132,243	1,236,954
	1788	1,243,206	121,982	1,365,188
	1789	1,343,800	99,858	1,443,658
	1790	1,260,828	144,132	1,404,960
	1791	1,333,106	178,051	1,511,157
	1792	1,396,003	169,151	1,565,154
WAR:	1793	1,101,326	180,121	1,281,447
	1794	1,247,398	209,679	1,457,077
	1795	1,030,058	370,238	1,400,296
	1796	1,108,258	454,847	1,563,105
	1797	971,596	379,775	1,351,371
	1798	1,163,534	345,132	1,508,666
	1799	1,145,314	390,612	1,535,926
	1800	1,269,329	654,713	1,924,042
	1801	1,190,557	767,816	1,958,373
PEACE:	1802	1,459,689	435,427	1,895,116
WAR:	1803	1,245,560	543,208	1,788,768
	1804	1,248,796	553,267	1,802,063
	1805	1,284,691	572,961	1,857,652
	1806	1,258,903	588,700	1,897,603
	1807	1,190,232	600,840	1,791,072
	1808	1,153,488	272,104	1,425,592
	1809	1,318,508	674,680	1,993,188

D. The PROGRESS OF THE REVENUE and the increased CHARGE
OF THE NATIONAL DEBT are shown in the first diagram : the
figures on which it is based are as follows :

i. *Revenue. England, 1660—1789. Great Britain and
Ireland, 1792—1850.*

1660	£1,200,000	Dowell, *History of Taxation*, II. 17.
1690	1,200,000	„ „ „ II. 44.
1712	3,048,000	
1740	3,997,000	
1756	5,150,000	
1762	6,711,000	*Statistical Journal*, XVIII. 250.
1774	7,187,000	
1784	12,995,000	
1789	15,460,000	
1792	18,900,680	
1795	19,657,998	
1800	33,069,775	
1805	50,848,268	*Reports*, 1828, v. 610—645.
1810	66,704,985	
1815	71,900,005	
1820	58,880,373	
1825	52,065,389	
1830	49,889,995	
1835	45,898,370	*Accounts and Papers*, 1841, XIII. 188.
1840	47,351,563	
1845	51,719,118	*Accounts and Papers*, 1851, XXXI. 166.
1850	52,177,141	

ii. *Annual Charge on the National Debt.*

1688	£39,855	
1702	1,310,942	
1714	3,351,358	
1727	2,217,551	
1739	1,964,025	
1748	3,061,004	Sinclair, *History of the Public Revenue*, Part II. 93.
1755	2,396,717	
1762	4,840,821	
1776	4,476,821	
1784	9,669,435	
1790	9,479,572	
1815	30,458,204	*Reports*, 1828, v. 657.
1820	30,147,801	
1825	29,197,187	
1830	29,118,859	
1835	28,514,610	*Accounts*, 1851, XXXI. 166.
1840	29,381,718	
1845	28,253,872	
1850	28,091,590	

E. The INCREASE OF POPULATION is also shown by a diagram,
and is compared with the annual charge for poor-relief, so far as
it was reported to Parliament. The figures are as follows :

DIAGRAM I. See Appendix I. p. 698.

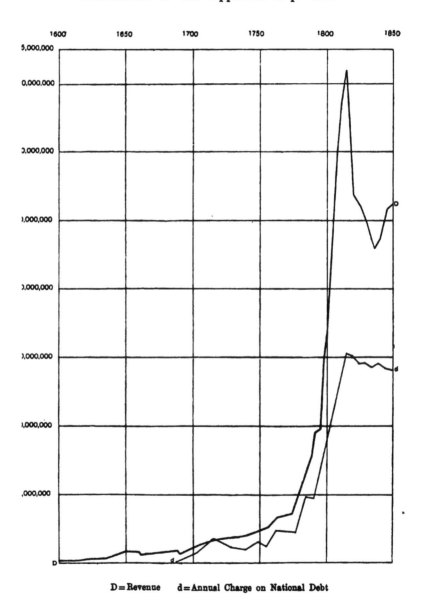

D = Revenue   d = Annual Charge on National Debt

DIAGRAM II. See Appendix I. p. 699.

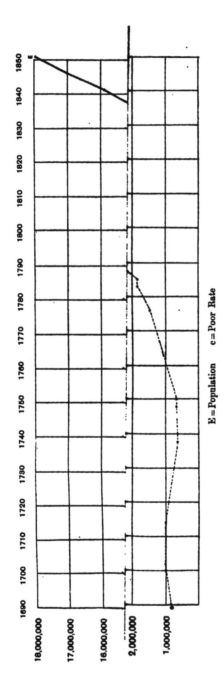

E = Population   e = Poor Rate

APPENDIX II.

Enclosure and Depopulation, 1607.

The following paper, endorsed *A consideration of the cause in question before the Lords touchinge depopulation* and dated 5 July 1607, has been preserved among the Cottonian MSS. at the British Museum (Tit. F. IV. f. 319). It appears to consist of memoranda for consideration by the Council in connection with the Northamptonshire riots. See above, p. 53.

JULY 5, 1607. A CONSIDERATION OF THE CAUSE IN QUESTION BEFORE THE LORDS TOUCHINGE DEPOPULATION.

In redresse of these offences. Inclosurs conuertinge of Arrable. *Depopulation* made the pretended causes of this last tumulte. 2 thinges may falle into consideration

1 Whether the tyme be fitte to gyve remedie, when suche encouragement may mone the people to seeke redresse, by the like outrage, and therfore in Edw: the sixte his tyme the remedie was not pursued untill twoe Yeares after the rebellion of Kette.

2 Whether these pretended be truly inconvenyent and therfore fitt to consider what iust reason may be alleaged for

I *Inclosures* wᶜʰ are

1 Securitie of state from — i fforraigne Invadors whoe cannot see easelie marche spoile and forraye in an enclosed Countrie, as a Champion.

ii Domestike commotions whiche Wilbe prevented when their false pretences (Inclosieurs wᶜʰ they use *ad faciendum populum* ar taken awaye.

2 Increase of welthe and people proued —

i A contrario: the Nurseries of Beggars are Commons as appeareth by ffenns and fforests of Welshe people the enclosed Countries as *Essex Somersett Devon* &c: ffewell wᶜʰ they want in the Champion, is supplied by Inclosures. And laborers, encreased as are their employments by Hodgeinge and ditcheinge.

ii A comparatis: as *Northamptonshire* and *Somersett* the one most Champion, more ground, Litle Waste, the other all enclosed but inferior in *quantitie* and *qual-litie*: Yett by advantage of se-veralitie, and choice of employ-ment exceedinge farre in | People for the Musters of

Profitt or Welthe by the

Horses	North.	20 lances
		80 light horse
	Somersett	60 lances
		250 light horse
ffoote	North.	60 petronells
		600 trayned
	Somerset	600 untrayned
		4000 trayned
		12000 untrayned
Subsidy	North.	976. 1. 4
	Somers	3889.12.10
Fiftene	North.	963. 0. 0
	Somers	1138. 0. 0
Tenthe.cler.	North.	217. 0. 0
	Somers	651. 0. 0

II Leaueinge the Imployment of the ground to discretion of the occupants: see all the howses and Land may be maynteyned in severalle tenantries, Ingroeinge beinge truly the disease and not conuertinge wiche may be iustified for

1 Equallitie, for the Lawe of tillage haveinge Lefte *Essex* and many other Shires to their choice, and therby noe Inconvenience in yᵉ stat found, and that all Arguments alleaged for those Counties will infer as muche for the inland shires of *Northampton Leicester* &c. and because their situation see remote from any porte or nauigable Byver (whearby the charge of carriage farre exceedinge the full worthe of the Corne they well) leaueth to them a disadvantage only: it weare more iuste to gyve the free employeinge of their ground to suche Husbandrie as will reduce them to an equallitie of benefitt wᶜʰ the *Nauigable* shires, (wᶜʰ is by graueinge (to wᶜʰ their soyle is more fitte then other Counties) whearby the rent of suche their Commodities shalbe more

2 ffor the true ballanceinge of our beste commodities, Wolle and Corne (whearin the oueewaight will appear in the Lease) ffor in Henr. the 8. his tyme wolle was the *Todde* vij^d and viij^d. Barlye (the greatest grayne of the Inland shires) vi^d and viij^d the bushell the one is nowe usually xxiiij^d the todde the other xviij^d and xx^d the strike. See Wolle risen above 2 thirdes holdeth almoste a proportion wth all other Commodities treble emproued by the encrease of moneys. And Corne Litle more then doble, is the reason of conuertinge arable to reduce the profites equall to the Husbandman, for keepinge the Land in divided Tenantry, the good individuall is the good generall; for Corne beinge dearer then Clothe or meat comparatively the Husbandman will plowe: since his only ende is profite. If equall or vnder noe reason to constraine him for that Lawe which divideth labor from profite (as the Art of tillage) is that wch causeth the greate difference of the Welbes and abilities of severall shires as the ar oppresed with that *Statute.*

III *Depopulation* w^ch (as all other engrossement) admitteth noe defence doth instlie moue a course of remedie wch muste be for

i A newe Lawe (for the ould is defective) and will hardly support an Information) And to reache to all is moste inst, since by noe reason *Antiquitie* ought to turne mischeffe into conuenyencie, when it weare more fite that he that by Longest offendinge hath done the most preiudice and receyued the beste benefit, should in the punishment vndergoe the greatest Censure. And therfore it weare conuenyent to tye by Statut, all men to hould as their Demeasne not abone the 4th parte of any Mannour, the other 3 to be deuyded into tenements and noe one to exceede 100 Acres. And that noe man in the same parishe should keepe twoe such tenementis in his occupation

or

1 Redresse of what is already done either by

ii By authoritie of Counsaill, as about the 9 of Henr. 7; 22 Henr: 8; and 4 or 5 of Ed: 6 when the offendors weare called uppe, and weare by order enioyned to redifie, halfe as many in every Mannour as they had decayed, and, became bound by recognisance as appeareth in the *Exchequer* in the case of *Andrews of Winwick* and others, from tyme to tyme to mayntayne soe many and soe much Land to them as they were ordered by the Lordes to doe.

or

2 Prevention of that to come. And that may best be to cause throughe the Champion Countries or the whole Kingdome suche a survey to be made by Commission as was 7° of Edw: the first reformed into the Chauncerie and at this daye called the Hundred Rolles expresseinge what Laude is the Lordes Demeasne, and the particular number of all the howsee and quantitie of Laude belonginge to them in euery Parishe in the Kingdome. That done to enioyne in euery Parishe by a newe Lawe that number to be mayntayned: and the *Judges* in their Circuits usually to enquire of all defaults therin. And that upon every decaye or vnpeopleinge of any of those Howses recorded, and noe other wth in the space of one Yeare builded wth in the same Mannour or neare thear vnto wth a like quantitie of ground annexed to it, it shalbe lawful for the Lord Tresorer and Barons of the *Exchequer* to Lease it for 21^ti Yeares only as a Mortmayne, and demise it for that tearme to the King's vse, and retorne it in charge into the *Exchequer.*

By redresseinge the fault of *Depopulation* and Leaseinge encloseinge, and conuertinge arbitrable (sic) as in other shires the poore man shalbe satisfied in His ende; Habitation; and the gentleman not Hindred in his desier: Improvement. But as thear is now a Labour to sute out Dwellinges for as muche stocke of people as the Comon Wealth will beare it muste likewise be fitt, as good husbandes doe withe their groundes to prouide that you doe not over burthen it. But as they doe wth their encrease remoue them to other places: see must the state either by transferinge to the Warres or deducinge of *Colonies* vent the daylie encrease that all will surcharge the State: ffor if in London a place more contagious then the Countrye the number of Cristeninge doth weekely by 40 exceede the buriialls, and that the Countries proportionally doth equall if not outgoe that rate. It cannot be but that in this State, as in a full bodie theare must breake out Yearely tumors and Imposturee as did of late.

LIST OF AUTHORITIES.

The dates are those of the editions actually used. For the convenience of students, reference has been given by preference to reprints and easily accessible editions.

A., T. *Dr Smith's system considered.* Appended to *Suppression of French Nobility vindicated* (1792). 438

Abridgements of Specifications relating to Printing (1617—1857). 351

Accounts of Exports and Imports (Real and Official value). Accounts and Papers, 1830, xxvii. 695

Accounts of Slave Compensation Claims. Accounts, 1837—8, xlviii. 599

Accounts of the Total Amount of the Public Income and Expenditure for the years 1822 to 1850, inclusive: also, Value of Imports into, and Exports from, the United Kingdom, during each of the same years. Accounts and Papers, 1851, xxxi. 695, 698

Accounts of the Total Amount of the Public Income and Expenditure for the years 1822—1852 inclusive: also value of Imports into, and Exports from, the United Kingdom, &c. Accounts and Papers, 1852—3, lvii. 695

Act Concerning Foreigners (1712). 47

Act of Common Council for Regulation of Blackwell-Hall, Leaden-Hall, and the Welch-Hall, and for prevention of Foreign Buying and Selling (1678). 47

Acts of the General Assembly of the Church of Scotland 1638—1842 reprinted under the superintendence of the Church Law Society (1843). 83

Acts of the Parliaments of Scotland (1822). 43, 270

Adam armed: or, an Essay endeavouring to prove the advantages and improvements the Kingdom may receive by the means of a well-ordered and duly ratified Charter for incorporating and regulating the Professors of the Art of Gardening. Brit. Mus. 712 m. 1 (10) (1700?) 182

Advice of His Majesty's Council of Trade, concerning the Exportation of Gold and Silver, in Foreign Coins and Bullion (1660), in *Select Collection of scarce and valuable Tracts on Money* (edited by J. R. McCulloch, 1856). 212

Baines, E. *History of the Cotton Manufacture* in *History of the County Palatine and Duchy of Lancaster* II. (1836). 694

Baines, E. *An Account of the woollen trade of Yorkshire* in T. Baines' *Yorkshire, Past and Present.* 693

Baird, R. *Religion in the United States of America* (1844). 147

Bancroft, G. *History of the United States of America, from the discovery of the Continent* (1876). 108, 148, 314, 315, 316, 317, 320, 321, 322, 323, 324, 326, 327, 328, 329, 330

Barbon, N. *A Discourse of Trade* (1690). 231, 233, 234, 236, 239, 248

Barbon, N. *A Discourse concerning Coining the New Money lighter* (1696). 238, 239, 240, 243

B[arbon], N. *A Letter to a Gentleman in the Country* (1684). 225

Baro, P. *Fower Sermons and two Questions* in Appendix to *A speciall Treatise of God's Providence.* 86

Battie, J. *The Merchants Remonstrance* (1648). 165, 202, 241

Bauer, S. *Nicholas Barbon,* in Conrad's *Jahrbücher für National-ökonomie und Statistik,* N. F. XXI. (1890). 228

Bedfordshire Sessions Records (1650—1660). (Office of the Clerk of the Peace, Bedford.) 191, 341, 377

Bell, W. *A Dissertation on the following subject: What Causes principally contribute to render a nation populous? And what effect has the Populousness of a Nation on its Trade?* (1756). 560

Bell, W. *Von den Quellen und Folgen einer starken Bevölkerung,* in *Kleine Schriften zur Land- und Stadtwirtschaft,* IV. von der ökonomischen Gesellschaft in Bern einzeln herausgegeben. 560

Berkeley, G. *Works* (edited by A. C. Fraser, 1871). 318

Best, H. *Rural Economy in Yorkshire in* 1641 (edited by C. B. Robinson for the Surtees Society, 1857). 186, 193, 195

Bill to explain and amend two several Acts of Common Council (15 April 1606, and 4 July 1712) *concerning Foreigners,* 1712. 45

Bischoff, J. *A Comprehensive History of the Woollen and Worsted Manufactures* (1842). 263, 340, 358, 445, 450, 451, 452, 457, 458, 459, 460, 461, 693

Blanqui, J. *History of Political Economy in Europe* (1880). 13

Blith, W. *The English Improver, or a new Survey of Husbandry* (1649). 180, 181, 185

Blomfield, F. *An Essay towards a topographical History of the County of Norfolk* (1739—1775). 46

Boate, G. *Natural History of Ireland* (1726). 341

Bodin, J. *De Republica* (1586). 233, 237

Bodin, J. *The Six Bookes of a Commonweale* (translated by R. Knolles, 1606). 233

Bodin, J. *Discours sur le rehaussement et diminution des monnoyes* (1578). 68

[Bodin, J.] *Discours sur les causes de l'extrème cherté qui est aujourd'huy en France* (1574), in Cimber (L.) et Danjou (F.), *Archives curieuses de l'histoire de France.* 1re *Série* (1835). 68

Boissevain, G. M. *The Monetary Question* (translated by G. T. Warner, 1891). 672

Bonwick, J. *Romance of the Wool Trade* (1887). 460, 538, 539, 540, 541

Book of Proclamations (Record Office). 53

Boswell, J. *The Life of Samuel Johnson, LL.D.* (1835). 408, 580

Bouron, A. *Guerre au Crédit* (1868). 84

Boys, W. *Collections for an history of Sandwich* (1792). 36

Brand, J. *The History and Antiquities of the Town and County of the Town of Newcastle upon Tyne* (1789). 342, 343, 344

Brasseur de Bourbourg, C. E. *Histoire du Canada, de son eglise et de ses missions* (1852). 320

Bremner, D. *The Industries of Scotland: their rise, progress and present condition* (1868). 334, 349, 350

Brentano, L. *Anfang und Ende der englischen Kornzölle* (1892). 469

Brentano, L. *On the History and development of Gilds, and the origin of Trade-Unions* (1870). 262, 647

Britannia Languens, or a discourse of Trade (1680), in *Select Collection of Tracts on Commerce* (edited by J. R. Macculloch, 1856). 112, 125, 140, 153, 220, 240, 243, 245

Bruce, J. *Annals of the Honorable East India Company* (1810). 268, 269, 270, 271, 272

Brymner, D. *Report on Canadian Archives* (1886). 541, 601

Burgon, J. W. *The Life and Times of Sir Thomas Gresham* (1839). 64

Burn, R. *The History of the Poor Laws: with observations* (1764). 492

Burnet, G. *The History of the Reformation of the Church of England* (edited by N. Pocock, 1865). 45

Burnley, J. *The History of Wool and Wool-combing* (1889). 457, 614, 615

Burton, J. H. *History of Scotland from the Revolution and the extinction of the last Jacobite Insurrection* (1853). 411, 412

C., N. *The great Necessity and Advantage of preserving our own Manufactures* (1697). 131

C., W. *Trades Destruction is Englands Ruine: or Excise decryed* (1659). 218

Caesar, M. P. *A general Discourse against the damnable sect of Usurers* (translated by T. Rogers, 1578). 76

Cairnes, J. E. *The Slave Power: its character, career, and probable designs* (1862). 598, 684

Caldecott, A. *English Colonization and Empire* (1891). 607

Caldwell, Sir James. *An Enquiry how far the Restrictions laid upon the Trade of Ireland by British Acts of Parliament are a benefit or disadvantage to the British Dominions in General, and to England in particular, for whose separate Advantage they were intended* in *Debates relative to the Affairs of Ireland in the years* 1763 and 1764 (1766). 523, 525, 560

Caldwell, Sir James. *Debates relative to the Affairs of Ireland in the years* 1763 *and* 1764 (1766). 298, 409, 420, 523, 528

Calendar of Home Office Papers 1760—1765 (edited by J. Redington, 1878). 459

Calendar of State Papers. Carew 1515—1574 (edited by J. S. Brewer and W. Bullen, 1867). 31, 32

Calendar of State Papers. Domestic 1547—1580 (edited by R. Lemon, 1856). 23, 37, 38, 87

Calendar of State Papers. Domestic 1581—1590 (edited by R. Lemon, 1865). 57

Calendar of State Papers. Domestic 1591—1594 (edited by M. A. E. Green, 1867). 57

Calendar of State Papers. Domestic 1595—1597 (edited by M. A. E. Green, 1869). 53, 57

Calendar of State Papers. Domestic 1603—1610 (edited by M. A. E. Green, 1857). 113

Calendar of State Papers. Domestic 1637—1638 (edited by J. Bruce, 1869). 189

Calendar of State Papers. Ireland 1509—1573 (edited by H. C. Hamilton, 1860). 31, 32, 33

Calendar of State Papers and Manuscripts, Venetian (edited by R. Brown, 1864). 88

Calendar of Treasury Papers. 302, 303, 329, 343, 350

Calvin, J. *Opera,* in *Corpus Reformatorum* (edited by C. G. Bretschneider, &c.). 81

Camden, W. *The History of the Most Renowned Princess Elizabeth* (1688). 26, 28, 31, 32, 56, 154, 169

Campbell, J. *A Political Survey of Britain* (1764). 378

Carlyle, T. *Oliver Cromwell's Letters and Speeches* (1845). 109

Carte, T. *A History of the Life of James, Duke of Ormonde* (1736). 139, 140, 141, 168

Carter, W. *England's Interest by Trade asserted, shewing the necessity and Excellence thereof* (1671). 335

Cary, J. *An Account of the Proceedings of the Corporation of Bristol in execution of the Act of Parliament for the better employing and maintaining the Poor of that City* (1700). 380

Cary, J. *Essay on the state of England* (1695). 154

Case of Dorothy Petty in relation to the Union Society at the White Lion by Temple Bar whereof she is Director. 226

Case of the Importation of Bar Iron from our own Colonies of North America (1756). 330, 340

Chalmers, G. *A Collection of Treaties between Great Britain and other Powers* (1790). 263

Chalmers, G. *An Estimate of the comparative strength of Great Britain* (1810). 578, 694, 700

Chalmers, G. *An Introduction to the History of the Revolt of the American Colonies* (1845). 329

Chalmers, G. *The Propriety of allowing a qualified exportation of Wool discussed historically* (1782). 460

Chalmers, T. *On Political Economy* in *Works* XIX. 665

Chalmers, T. *The Christian and Civic Economy of Large Towns* (1821). 665

Chamberlen, P. *The Poore Man's Advocate* (1649). 201

Character of England (1659) in *Harleian Miscellany* X. (1813). 171

Charmetant, —. *Les anciennes Corporations de la Soierie à Lyon et l'avenir du mouvement corporatif* in *La Réforme sociale et le Centenaire de la Révolution* (1890). 348

Chesney, G. *Indian Polity; a view of the system of administration in India* (1868). 276, 309, 310

Child, Sir J. *A new Discourse of Trade* (1694). 112, 116, 153, 245, 252, 292, 293

Child, Sir J. *Brief Observations concerning Trade and Interest of Money* (1668). 252

Clarke, W. *Observations on the late and present Conduct of the French, with regard to their Encroachments upon the British Colonies in North America* (1755). 558

Clément, P. *Histoire de Colbert et de son administration* (1874). 333

Clode, C. M. *The Early History of the Guild of Merchant Taylors* (1888). 45, 46, 47

Clutterbuck, R. *The History and Antiquities of the County of Hertford* (1821). 173, 199

Cobbett, W. *Rural Rides* (edited by P. Cobbett, 1885). 495

Cobden, R. *Political Writings* (1878). 84, 682

Coke, J. *The debate betweene the Heraldes of Englande and Fraunce* (1550). 49

Coke, R. *A detection of the Court and State of England* (1694). 120

Coke, R. *A Discourse of Trade* (1670). 220

Coke, R. *A Treatise wherein is demonstrated that the Church and State of England are in equal danger with the Trade* (1671). 112

Coke, R. *Reflections upon the East Indy and Royal African Companies* (1695). 125

Colbert, J. B. *The Political Testament of M. Jean Baptist Colbert, Minister and Secretary of State* (translated by W. Glanvill, 1695). 333

Cole MSS. XII. in Brit. Mus. Add. MSS. 5813. 93

Collection of Tracts concerning the Present State of Ireland, with respect to its Riches, Revenue, Trade and Manufactures (1729). 299

Collections of the Massachusetts Historical Society. 147, 319

Colston, J. *The Incorporated Trades of Edinburgh* (1891). 180

Colston, J. *The Guildry of Edinburgh* (1887). 353

Conservatorship of the River of Tyne, in M. A. Richardson's *Reprints of Rare Tracts* III. (1849). 161, 171, 288

Consideration of the cause in question before the Lords touching de-population. Brit. Mus. MSS. Titus F. IV. 319 (1607). 53, 701

Considerations upon the present State of the Wool Trade (1781). 693

Considerations touching the Excise of Native and Foreign Commodities (1664). 221

Cooke, Sir J. *Unum Necessarium: or the Poor Mans Case* (1648). 191, 203, 209

Cooper, T. *Chronicle* (1565). 63

Cooperative Magazine (1826). 588

Cotton MSS. Brit. Mus. Titus F. IV. 259—285. 120

[Cotton, Sir R.] *A Speech touching the Alteration of Coin* (1626) published 1657, in *Select Collection of scarce and valuable Tracts on Money* (edited by J. R. Macculloch, 1856). 214

Cotton, W. *An Elizabethan Guild of the City of Exeter* (1873). 88

Cowper, J. *An Essay, proving that inclosing Commons and Common-field-Lands is contrary to the interest of the Nation* (1732). 371, 384, 479, 484

Cox, J. C. *Three Centuries of Derbyshire Annals, as illustrated by the Records of the Quarter Sessions of the County of Derby, from Queen Elizabeth to Queen Victoria* (1890). 200

Cox, R. *Hibernia Anglicana: or the History of Ireland* (1689). 32, 135, 136, 155

Coxe, W. *Memoirs of the Life and Administration of Sir R. Walpole, Earl of Orford* (1798). 312, 402, 414

Cradocke, F. *An expedient for taking away all impositions and raising a revenue without taxes* (1660). 255

Creighton, C. *A History of Epidemics in Britain* (1891). 172, 173

Cullum, Sir J. *The History and Antiquities of Hawsted* (1813). 52

Culpeper, Jr., Sir T. *The Necessity of Abating Usury re-asserted* (1670). 251

Culpeper, Jr., Sir T. *A Discourse shewing the many advantages which will accrue to this kingdom by the abatement of Usury* (1668). 251

Culpepper, Sir T. *A Tract against Usurie* (1621). 251

Cunningham, W. *Nationalism and Cosmopolitanism in Economics* in *Report of the sixty-first meeting of the British Association for the Advancement of Science* (1891). 681

Cunningham, W. *Politics and Economics* (1885). 583, 587, 679

Cunningham, W. *The Growth of English Industry and Commerce in the Early and Middle Ages* (1890). 14, 16, 21, 25, 37, 40, 47, 66, 70, 74, 106, 161, 178, 211, 301, 371, 403, 594, 671, 685

Cunningham, W. *The Path towards Knowledge* (1891). 564, 686

Cunningham, W. *The Progress of Economic Doctrine in England in the eighteenth century*, in *the Economic Journal* I. (1891). 416

Cunningham, W. *The relativity of Economic Doctrine* in *the Economic Journal* II. (1892). 294

Cunningham, W. *The use and abuse of Money* (1891). 681

D'Ewes, Sir S. *The Journals of all the Parliaments during the reign of Queen Elizabeth* (1682). 158, 163, 164

De Tocqueville, A. *On the state of Society in France before the Revolution of* 1789 (translated by H. Reeve, 1856). 580

De Witt, J. *The True Interest and Political Maxims of the Republick of Holland and West-Friesland* (1702). 112, 114

Digges, Sir D. *The Defence of Trade* (1615). 129

Dircks, H. *A biographical Memoir of Samuel Hartlib* (1865). 181

Discourse consisting of Motives for the Enlargement and Freedome of Trade (1645). 121

Dobbs, A. *An Account of the Countries adjoining to Hudson's Bay* (1744). 281

Dobbs, A. *An Essay on the Trade and Improvement of Ireland* (1729), in *Collection of Tracts and Treatises illustrative of the Natural History, Antiquities and the Political and Social State of Ireland*, II. (1861). 299

Documents relative to the Colonial History of the State of New York; procured in Holland, England and France by J. R. Brodhead (1853). 320

Doubleday, T. *A Financial, Monetary and Statistical History of England, from the Revolution of* 1688 *to the Present Time* (1847). 393, 396

Dowell, S. *A History of Taxation and Taxes in England* (1884). 36, 66, 67, 114, 161, 216, 217, 218, 219, 221, 222, 223, 339, 405, 406, 407, 408, 413, 414, 415, 416, 437, 511, 548, 549, 550, 551, 601, 669, 674, 698

Dowell, S. 2nd Edition (1888). 550, 667

Dowell, S. *A Sketch of the History of Taxes in England* (1876). 65

Dudley, D. *Mettallum Martis: or Iron made with Pit-coale, sea coale, &c.* (1665). 340

Dugdale, W. *The History of Imbanking and Draining of divers Fens and Marshes* (edited by C. N. Cole, 1772). 187

Dunlop, R. *The Plantation of Munster,* 1584—1589, in *English Historical Review* III. (1888). 32

[Dymock, C.] *Hartlib's Legacy* (1651). 55, 58, 181, 183, 184, 185, 204

East-India Company's Answer (1681). 130

Eden, Sir F. M. *The State of the Poor* (1797). 201, 202, 207, 380, 382, 383

Edwards, B. *The History, Civil and Commercial, of the British Colonies in the West Indies* (1801). 312, 313, 317, 318, 326

Eggleston, E. *Social Conditions in the Colonies* in *Century Magazine*, N. S. VI. (1884). 109, 138, 316

Ellis, Sir H. *Original letters illustrative of English History* (1827). 36, 87, 114

Engels, F. *Die Lage der arbeitenden Klasse in England* (1845). 619, 626, 629, 630

England's great Happiness (1677), in *Select Collection of Tracts on Commerce* (edited by J. R. Macculloch, 1856). 220, 232, 239, 240

England's Wants: or, several Proposals probably beneficial for England (1667). 254

English Chronicle. 646

Enquiry into the Reasons for and against Inclosing the Open Fields (1767). 371

Essay on Tea, Sugar, White Bread and Butter, Country Alehouses, Strong Beer and Geneva, and other modern Luxuries (1777). 359

Essay on the Antient and Modern State of Ireland (1760). 302

Essays on the trade of the Northern Colonies of Great Britain in North America (1764). 313

Eton, W. *A survey of the Turkish Empire* (1809). 122

Evans, D. M. *The Commercial Crisis, 1847—1848* (1848). 678

Extracts from the Information received by her Majesty's Commissioners as to the Administration and Operation of the Poor-Laws (1833). 662

Faber, R. *Die Entstehung des Agrarschutzes in England*, in *Abhandlungen aus dem staatswissenschaftlichen Seminar zu Strassburg* v. (1888). 372

Fann Makers' Grievance. 130

Farren, E. J. *Historical Essay on the Rise and Early Progress of the Doctrine of Life-Contingencies in England* (1844). 291

Fauquier, F. *An Essay on Ways and Means for raising Money for the Support of the Present War, without increasing the Public Debts* (1756). 420

Felkin, W. *A history of the Machine-wrought Hosiery and Lace Manufactures* (1867). 346, 347, 617, 618, 619

Fenton, R. *A treatise of usurie* (1611). 76, 81

Ferguson, R. S. and Nanson, W. *Some Municipal Records of the City of Carlisle* (1887). 47

Filmer, Sir R. *Quaestio Quodlibetica* (1653). 76

Fitz-Geffrey, C. *Compassion towards Captives, chiefly towards our Bretheren and Countrymen who are in miserable bondage in Barbarie* (1637). 115, 217

Fitzgerald, J. E. *An Examination of the Charter and Proceedings of the Hudson's Bay Company, with reference to the grant of Vancouver's Island* (1849). 602, 603

Fitzmaurice, Lord E. *Life of William, Earl of Shelburne* (1876). 542

Fleetwood, Bp W. *Chronicon Preciosum* (1745). 425

Forster, N. *An Answer to Sir John Dalrymple's pamphlet upon the exportation of Wool* (1782). 458

Forster, N. *An Enquiry into the Causes of the present high Prices of Provisions* (1767). 372

Fortescue, Sir J. *Works* (1869). 13

Fortrey, S. *England's Interest and Improvement* (1673), in *Select Collection of Tracts on Commerce* (1856). 178, 220, 228, 234, 238, 239

Franklin, B. *Works* (edited by J. Sparks, 1840). 327, 558, 559

Froude, J. A. *A history of England from the fall of Wolsey to the defeat of the Spanish Armada* (1872). 12, 19, 24, 25, 31, 32, 63, 64, 65

Fuller, T. *The History of the University of Cambridge* (edited by Prickett M. and Wright T. 1840). 85

Funk, F. X. *Zins und Wucher* (1868). 87

Gardiner, S. R. *History of England, 1603—1642* (1883). 107, 113, 114, 120, 125, 126, 128, 133, 134, 135, 136, 146, 147, 158, 159, 163, 165, 166, 167, 173, 218, 222

Gardiner, S. R. *The History of the Great Civil War, 1642—1649* (1891). 270

Gardner, R. *England's grievance discovered in relation to the coal trade* (1655). 161

Gee, J. *The trade and navigation of Great Britain* (1767). **330**

Gentleman, T. *England's way to win wealth* (1614). 115

Gentleman's Magazine LXV. (1795). 189

Genuine thoughts of a Merchant (1733). 408

Gibbs, A. E. *The Corporation Records of St Albans* (1890). 48

Godwin, W. *Enquiry concerning Political Justice, and its influence on Morals and Happiness* (1798). 587

Goffe, W. *How to advance the Trade of the Nation, and employ the Poor*, in *Harleian Miscellany* IV. (1809). 202

Gonner, E. C. K. *Settlement of Australia* in *English Historical Review* III. (1888). 600

Gonner, E. C. K. *Introduction to Ricardo's Works* (Bohn Series). 571

Grand Concern of England explained; in several Proposals offered to the Consideration of the Parliament (1673) in *Harleian Miscellany*, VIII. (1811). 169, 202

Grazier's Complaint and Petition for Redress (1726). 299, 335, 371, 384

Graunt, Capt. J. *Natural and Political Observations* (1676). 247, 251

Gray, S. *All Classes Productive of National Wealth* (1817). 439, 441

Gray, S. *The Causes of a Nation's Progress in Wealth*, in the *Pamphleteer* XVII. (1820). 439

Gray, W. *Chorographia* (1649). **343, 344**

Green, E. *On the Poor, and some Attempts to lower the Price of Corn, in Somerset, 1548—1638*, in *Proceedings of the Bath Natural History and Antiquarian Field Club* IV. (1881). 54

Groans of the Plantations: or a True Account of their grievous and extreme sufferings by the heavy Impositions upon Sugar, and other Hardships (1689). 278

Gross, C. *The Gild Merchant, a contribution to British municipal history* (1890). 46, 48, 342, 353

Guilhaud de Lavergne, L. *Les Économistes Français du dix-huitième siècle* (1870). 511

Hagthorpe, J. *England's Exchequer* (1625). 115

Haines, R. *Proposals for building, in every County, a Working-Alms-House or Hospital, as the best Expedient to perfect the Trade and Manufactory of Linen Cloth* (1677), in *Harleian Miscellany* IV. (1809). 202

Hakluyt, R. *Voyages, Navigations, Traffiques and Discoveries of the English Nation* (1600). 24, 30, 31, 144

Haldane, R. B. *Life of Adam Smith* (1887). 435, 437

Hale, Sir M. *A discourse touching Provision for the Poor* (1683). 200, 202, 300, 471

Hales, J. *Briefe Conceipt of English Policye*, in *Harleian Miscellany* IX. (1808). 49, 55, 67, 68, 69, 70, 71, 72, 73

Hall, F. *The Importance of the British Plantations in America to this Kingdom; with the state of their Trade, and Methods for improving it; as also a description of the several Colonies there* (1731). 312, 329

Hall, H. *A History of the Custom Revenue in England* (1885). 216, 219, 395, 694

Hall, H. *Notes on the History of the Crown Lands*, in *The Antiquary* XIII. (1886). 104

Hall, H. *Society in the Elizabethan Age* (1887). 14, 66, 67, 90, 158, 169, 289

Hall, H. *The Roast Beef of Old England* in *The Antiquarian Magazine and Bibliographer* (1882). 688

Halley, E. *An Estimate of the Degrees of the Mortality of Mankind, drawn from curious Tables of the Births and Funerals at the City of Breslaw; with an attempt to ascertain the Price of Annuities upon Lives*, in *Philosophical Transactions* XVII. (1694). 291

Hamilton, R. *An Inquiry concerning the Rise and Progress, the Redemption and Present State, and the Management of the National Debt of Great Britain* (1814). 397, 546, 547

Hamilton, R. *An Introduction to Merchandize* (1797). 544

Hamilton, R. H. A. *Quarter Sessions from Queen Elizabeth to Queen Anne* (1878). 194, 199

Harrington, J. *The Oceana and other works* (edited by J. Toland, 1737). 237

Harris, W. *Hibernica* (1770). 133, 135

Harrison, W. *Description of England*, in Holinshed, *Chronicles* (1807). 13, 14, 35, 54, 65, 66, 91, 92, 186, 344

Harte, W. *Essays on Husbandry* (1770). 388

Hartlib, S. *See* Dymock and Weston.

Hasted, E. *The History and Topographical Survey of the County of Kent* (1782). 37

Haweis, J. O. W. *Sketches of the Reformation and Elizabethan Age* (1844). 82

Held, A. *Zwei Bücher zur socialen Geschichte Englands*, herausgegeben von G. F. Knapp (1881). 587

Hemming, N. *A godlie treatise concerning the lawful use of ritches* (translated by T. Rogers, 1578). 76

Hendriks, F. *Contributions to the History of Insurance and of the theory of Life Contingencies* (1851). 93, 289, 291

Henrion, M. R. A. *Histoire générale des Missions Catholiques* (1847). 320

Henry of Huntingdon. *Historia Anglorum* (edited by T. Arnold in Rolls Series, 1879). 13

Hewins, W. A. S. *English Trade and Finance chiefly in the seventeenth century* (1892). 360

Heyd, W. *Geschichte des Levantehandels im Mittelalter* (1879). 13

Hibbert, F. A. *The Influence and Development of English Gilds* (1891). 45, 46, 47, 48, 609

Hill, G. *An historical account of the Macdonnells of Antrim* (1873). 32

Hippisley, J. *Essays* (1764). 280, 316

Hitchcock, R. *A Politic Plat* (edited by E. Arber, *English Garner* II. 1879). 21, 23, 93, 115

Hitchcock, R. *The English Army Rations in the time of Queen Elizabeth* (1591) in E. Arber's *English Garner* II. (1879). 493

Hobbes, T. *English Works* (edited by Sir W. Molesworth, 1839). 234

Holyoake, G. J. *Self-Help a hundred years ago* (1888). 589, 650

Holyoake, G. J. *The History of Co-operation in England: its Literature and its advocates* (1875—1879). 650

Homer, H. S. *An Inquiry into the means of Preserving and improving the Publick Roads of this Kingdom* (1767). 376, 378

Homer, H. S. *Essay on the Nature and Method of ascertaining the specifick shares of Proprietors upon the inclosure of Common Fields* (1766). 363, 368, 371

Hooker, *History of New England*. See Johnson, E.

Horsley, W. *Serious Considerations on the High Duties examined* (1744). 410

Hotoman, F. *Franco-Gallia* (translated by Lord Molesworth, 1721). 355

Howlett, J. *An Examination of Dr Price's Essay on the Population of England and Wales; and the doctrine of an increased Population in this kingdom, established by facts* (1781). 505

Humboldt, A. *Essai Politique sur le royaume de la Nouvelle Espagne* (1811), in *Voyage de Humboldt et Bonpland* II. 12

Hunter, J. *History of Hallamshire* (edited by A. Gatty, 1869). 206, 480

Hunter, J. *The History and Topography of the Deanery of Doncaster* (1828). 186, 188, 189

Hutcheson, A. *A Collection of Treatises relating to the National Debts and Funds* (1721). 391, 394, 413

Hutchinson, J. H. *The Commercial Restraints of Ireland* (1799), (re-edited by W. G. Carroll, 1882). 307

I., R. *Nova Britannia*. 144, 152

Improvement of Commons that are enclosed, for the Advantage of the Lords of Manors, the Poor, and the Publick (1732). 371

Inderwick, F. A. *The Interregnum* (1891). 107, 118, 119, 171, 174, 177, 189, 207

Innes, C. *Sketches of early Scotch History and Social Progress* (1861). 465

Inquisition upon Enclosures. Lansdowne 1 f. 153 (1517). 52

Interest of Money Mistaken, or a Treatise proving that the Abatement of Interest is the Effect and not the Cause of the Riches of a Nation, and that Six per Cent. is a proportionable Interest to the present condition of this kingdom (1668). 252

Jacob, W. *An Historical Inquiry into the production and consumption of the Precious Metals* (1831). 12

Janet, P. *Histoire de la Science Politique dans ses rapports avec la morale* (1872). 511

Jefferson, T. *Memoirs, Correspondence and Private Papers* (edited by T. J. Randolph, 1829). 392

Jennings, E. *A briefe discovery of the damages that happen to this Realme by disordered and unlawfull diet* (1593). 115

Jewitt, Ll. *The Ceramic Art of Great Britain from pre-historic times down to the present day* (1883). 351

Johnson, E. *A History of New England* (1654). 108

Johnson, S. *Works* (1825). 372

Johnson, S. *A Dictionary of the English Language* (1755). 358, 408

Jones, D. *A Farewel-Sermon* (1692). 76

Journal of Sir Walter Scott (1890). 559

Journals of the House of Commons. 46, 297, 338, 342

Journals of the House of Commons of the Kingdom of Ireland. 136, 137, 142, 222, 298, 300, 302, 305, 357

Journals of the Statistical Society. 698, 699

Kalm, P. *Travels into North America* (translated by J. R. Forster, 1770). 325

Kennedy, J. *Observations on the Rise and Progress of the Cotton Trade in Great Britain,* in *Memoirs of the Literary and Philosophical Society of Manchester. Series* II. iii. (1819). 448

King, C. *The British Merchant; or Commerce Preserv'd* (1721). 263, 265, 266, 267, 421, 580

Knowler, W. *The Earl of Strafforde's Letters and Dispatches* (1739). 136, 166, 671

Koch, C. G. de and Schoell, F. *Histoire Abrégée des Traités de Paix entre les Puissances de l'Europe depuis la Paix de Westphalie* (1837). 265, 266, 315, 510, 511, 542

Kropotkin, P. A. *The breakdown of our Industrial system* in *Nineteenth Century* XXIII. (1888). 348

Lambert, J. M. *Two thousand years of Gild Life* (1891). 45, 47, 48, 609

Lamond, E. *The Date and Authorship of the 'Examination of Com-*

Lupton, D. *London and the Countrey carbonadoed and quartred into severall Characters* (1632) in *Harleian Miscellany*, IX. (1812). 169

Lyon, J. *The History of the Town and Port of Dover* (1814). 94, 113

Macarthur, J. *New South Wales* 1837. 541

Macaulay, T. B. *The History of England from the Accession of James the Second* (1855). 395, 397, 398

Macculloch, J. R. *A Select Collection of scarce and valuable Tracts on Commerce* (1859). 560

Macculloch, J. R. *Note on the Recoinage of 1696—1699*, in *Select Tracts on Money* (1856). 215

Macculloch, J. R. *The Literature of Political Economy* (1845). 247

Macculloch, J. R. *The Principles of Political Economy* (1843). 664

Mackay, J. *History of the Barony of Broughton* (1867). 179

Mackay, J. *History of the Burgh of Canongate, with notices of the Abbey and Palace of Holyrood* (1879). 353

Mackerell, B. *History and Antiquities of the flourishing Corporation of King's Lynn* (1738). 58, 60

Macleod, H. D. *The Theory and Practice of Banking* (1883—1886). 222, 398, 411, 552, 553, 554, 555, 556, 557

Macpherson, D. *Annals of Commerce* (1805). 25, 26, 35, 110, 114, 118, 120, 124, 125, 155, 173, 265, 279, 280, 281, 282, 283, 284, 285, 287, 288, 294, 299, 301, 303, 317, 318, 325, 330, 336, 337, 338, 341, 342, 344, 349, 350, 351, 354, 358, 694, 695

Malleson, G. B. *History of the French in India* (1868). 276, 308

Malthus, T. R. *An Essay on the Principle of Population* (1817). 507, 562

Malthus, T. R. *Principles of Political Economy considered with a view to their practical application* (1820). 476

Malthus, T. R. *Essay on Political Economy* in *Quarterly Review*, XXX. (1824). 574

Malynes, G. de. *A Treatise of the Canker of England's Commonwealth* (1601). 96, 100

Malynes, G. de. *Center of the Circle* (1623). 121, 128

Malynes, G. de. *Consuetudo vel Lex Mercatoria* (1622). 84

Malynes, G. de. *England's view, in the unmasking of two paradoxes* (1603). 121

Malynes, G. de. *The maintenance of Free Trade* (1622). 121

Malynes, G. de. *Saint George for England, allegorically described* (1601). 88

Mandeville, B. de. *The Fable of the Bees* (1714). 239

Manley, T. *A Discourse showing that the Exportation of Wooll is destructive to this kingdom* (1677). 335

Manley, T. *Usury at Six per Cent. examined* (1659). 220, 252

Marchand, C. *Charles I. de Cossé* (1889). 13

Marin-Darbel, G. E. *L'usure, sa définition* (1859). 86

Nicholls, Sir G. *A History of the English Poor Law, in connection with the Legislation and other Circumstances affecting the condition of the People* (1854). 493, 660

Nicholson, J. S. *Toxar* (1890). 683. See Adam Smith.

Nickolls, J. *Original Letters and Papers of State addressed to Oliver Cromwell, concerning the Affairs of Great Britain* (1743). 208

Norden, J. *The Surveyor's Dialogue* (1607). 15, 90, 183, 184, 186

North, D. *Discourses upon Trade; principally directed to the Cases of the Interest Coynage Clipping Increase of Money* (1691), in *Select Collection of Early English Tracts on Commerce* (edited by J. R. Macculloch, 1856). 260, 581

North, R. *The Lives of the Norths* (edited by A. Jessopp, 1890). 395

Northcote, Sir Stafford. *Twenty years of financial policy* (1862). 667, 668, 677

Old Almanack (1735). 371

Oliver, G. *The History and Antiquities of the Town and Minster of Beverley* (1829). 60

Orders and Directions (1630). 199, 201, 207

Original Letters and Papers of State addressed to Oliver Cromwell, concerning the Affairs of Great Britain (1743). See Nickolls, J.

Overall, W. H. and H. C. *Analytical Index to the series of Records known as the Remembrancia* 1579—1664 (1878). 46

Overend, G. H. *Strangers at Dover*, in *the Proceedings of the Huguenot Society of London* III. (1890). 37

Parkes, J. *The governing Charter of the Borough of Warwick* (1827). 93

Parliamentary Debates (edited by Hansard). 39, 470, 578, 588, 618

Parliamentary Debates. New Series (2 Hansard). 593, 649, 667

Parliamentary Debates. Third Series (3 Hansard). 300, 608, 609, 628, 630, 631, 632, 633, 635, 643, 649

Parliamentary History. 39, 44, 51, 53, 57, 94, 95, 118, 126, 139, 153, 155, 164, 168, 172, 178, 179, 180, 186, 194, 213, 215, 218, 256, 258, 264, 271, 274, 277, 279, 280, 283, 285, 286, 287, 289, 291, 296, 303, 304, 312, 314, 317, 318, 321, 327, 328, 338, 343, 349, 352, 355, 383, 384, 387, 399, 400, 401, 404, 405, 408, 410, 412, 415, 438, 459, 460, 470, 486, 490, 494, 500, 509, 529, 541, 544, 548, 550, 562

Parnell, Sir H. *On Financial Reform* (1830). 668

Pashley, R. *Pauperism and Poor Laws* (1852). 495

Pearson, J. B. *A biographical sketch of the Chaplains to the Levant Company, maintained at Constantinople, Aleppo and Smyrna* 1611 —1706 (1883). 108

Pearson, J. B. *On the theories on Usury adopted in Europe during the period* 1100—1400 A.D. (1877). 82

Peckard, P. *Memoirs of the Life of Mr Nicholas Ferrar* (1790). 144

Pellew, G. *The Life and Correspondence of the Right Honourable Henry Addington, First Viscount Sidmouth* (1847). 612

Penn, W. *The benefit of Plantations or Colonies,* in *Select Tracts relating to Colonies* (edited by J. R. Macculloch, 1856). 153

Pennant, T. *A Journey from London to the Isle of Wight* (1801). 37, 284, 286, 288, 373, 374, 380, 467

Pennington, W. *Reflections on the various Advantages resulting from the Draining, Inclosing, and Allotting of Large Commons and Common Fields* (1769). 371

Peters, S. *A general history of Connecticut* (1781). 108

Petition of Margaret Walker. 129

Petition of the Lord Mayor &c. of London to the Parliament for the Reducing of all Forein Trade under Government (1662). 47

Petty Bag Depopulation Returns (Record Office). 52, 53

Petty, Sir W. *The Political Anatomy of Ireland* (1691). 133, 136, 139, 143, 248, 295

Petty, Sir W. *An Essay concerning the Multiplication of Mankind* (1689). 248

Petty, Sir W. *Several Essays in Political Arithmetick* (1699). 248, 255, 342

Petty, Sir W. *The History of the Survey of Ireland, commonly called the Down Survey* (1655—6), (edited by T. A. Larcom for the Irish Archaeological Society, 1851). 138

Petty, Sir W. *Quantulumcunque concerning Money* (1682), in *Select Collection of scarce and valuable Tracts on Money* (edited by J. R. Macculloch, 1856). 250, 253, 255

Petty, Sir W. *A Treatise of Taxes and Contributions* (1667). 231, 232, 234, 235, 239, 240, 245, 249, 253, 418

Philips, Sir T. *A letter from Sir Th. Philips, to King Charles I. concerning the Plantations of the Londoners.* 135

Phillips, J. *A general History of Inland Navigation, Foreign and Domestic* (1803). 379

Philopoliticus. *Memorialls for the government of the Royall-Burghs in Scotland* (1685). 334, 353

Plat, Sir H. *The Jewell House of Art and Nature* (1594). 183, 185

Plato. *Hipparchus* in *Opera* IV. (edited by G. Stallbaum, 1821). 70

Playfair, W. *Inquiry into the Permanent Causes of the Decline and Fall of Powerful and Wealthy Nations* (1805). 437, 513

Pococke, R. *Tour in Ireland in 1752* (edited by G. T. Stokes, 1891). 137, 143, 295, 306, 341, 459, 523

Pollexfen, Sir H. *A Discourse of Trade, Coin, and Paper Credit* (1697). 126, 130, 154, 160

Population Tables. Accounts and Papers 1852—3, LXXXV. 695

Porder, R. *A Sermon of Gods fearefull threatnings for Idolatrye, mixing of religion, retayning of Idolatrous remnaunts, and other wickednesse: with a Treatise against Usurie* (1570). 76

Porter, G. R. *The Progress of the Nation* (1836—1843). 514, 519, 522, 596, 598, 601

Porter, Sir James. *Observations on the Religion, Law, Government and Manners of the Turks* (1771). 282

[Postlethwayt, M.] *The African Trade, the great Pillar and Support of the British Plantation Trade in America* (1745). 315

Postlethwayt, M. *The Universal Dictionary of Trade and Commerce* (1774). 290, 400

Postlethwayt, M. *Great Britain's True System* (1757). 260, 420

Povey, C. *A discovery of indirect practices in the coal trade* (1700). 175

Povey, C. *English Inquisition* (1718). 226

Povey, C. *The Unhappiness of England, as to its Trade by Sea and Land* (1701). 179, 343, 353, 421

[Pownall, T.] *Considerations on the scarcity and high prices of Bread-Corn and Bread at the Market* (1795). 498

Pownall, T. *A Letter from Governor Pownall to Adam Smith, LL.D., F.R.S.* (1776). 437, 438, 439

Prendergast, J. P. *The Cromwellian Settlement of Ireland* (1870). 109, 133, 135, 138, 224

Prendergast, J. P. *Ireland from the Restoration to the Revolution, 1660 to 1690* (1887). 139

Price, L. L. *A Short History of Political Economy in England, from Adam Smith to Arnold Toynbee* (1891). 574

Price, R. *An Essay on the Population of England from the Revolution to the present time* (1780). 505

Prior, T. *A List of the Absentees of Ireland and the yearly value of their Estates and Incomes spent abroad* (1729), in *Collection of Tracts and Treatises illustrative of the Natural History, Antiquities and the Political and Social State of Ireland* II. (1861). 299

Proposals and Reasons for constituting a Council of Trade (1701). 412

Proposals for uniting the English Colonies on the Continent of America so as to enable them to act with Force and Vigour against their Enemies (1757). 327

Proposals set forth by the Company of London Insurers (1710). 227

Prothero, R. E. *The Pioneers and Progress of English Farming* (1888). 476, 479, 484, 489, 572, 657, 658

Purchas, S. *His Pilgrimes* (1625). 128, 144, 145, 149, 152

Pynnar, N. *Survey of Ulster* (1619). 133, 134

Quarter Session Records (edited by J. C. Atkinson, in North Riding Record Society Publications, 1883—4). 199

Quesnay, F. *Œuvres économiques et philosophiques* publiées avec une introduction et des notes par A. Oncken (1888). 435, 436

R., L. *A second letter to his honoured Friend, Mr M. T.* 225

Radcliffe, W. *Origin of the New System of Manufacture, commonly called "Power-Loom Weaving," and the purposes for which this system was invented and brought into use, fully explained in a narrative* (1828). 473, 482, 514

[Raleigh, Sir W.] *Observations touching Trade and Commerce with the Hollander, and other Nations*, in J. R. Macculloch's *Select Collection of scarce and valuable Tracts on Commerce* (1859). 224

[Raleigh, Sir W.] *Observations touching Trade and Commerce with the Hollander, and other Nations*, in *Works* VIII. (edited by W. Oldys and Birch, 1829). 102

Ranke, L. von. *History of England, principally in the seventeenth century* (1875). 113

Raynal, W. T. *A Philosophical and Political History of the Settlements and Trade of the Europeans in the East and West Indies* (1777). 268, 270, 272, 276

Reasons for a limited exportation of Wool (1677). 335

Reasons for renewing the Office for finding out and punishing the Abuses in Silk Dyeing. 166

Reasons humbly offered for passing the Bill for encouraging and improving the Trade to Russia. 122

Reasons humbly offered for permitting Rice of the Growth of the British Plantations, to be transported to Spain, Portugal, and other Places to the Southward of Cape Finisterre, without being first brought to England. 330

Reasons humbly offered to consideration (167–). 121

Reasons offered by the Merchant Adventurers of England and Eastland Merchants residing at Hull, for the preservation of their Societies and Regulations. 69

Reflections on the Importation of Bar-Iron from our own Colonies of North America (1757). 329, 330

Reflections on the Prohibition Act (1708). 132

Reflections upon Naturalizations, Corporations and Companies; supported by the Authorities of both Ancient and Modern Writers (1753). 352

Reinhard, C. *A concise history of the present state of the Commerce of Great Britain* (translated by J. Savage, 1805). 513, 515, 522

Relation, short and true, concerning the Soap-business (1641). 167

Relation strange and true, of a Ship of Bristol named the Jacob of 120 Tunnes (1622). 217

Remarks on the Present State of the Poor. Oswestry (1826). 587

Report from the Select Committee on Agriculture. Reports, 1833, v. 479, 482, 652, 656

Reports of Special Assistant Poor Law Commissioners on the Employment of Women and Children in Agriculture. Reports, 1843, XII. 482, 650, 653

Report from the Select Committee, to whom the several Petitions, complaining of the depressed state of the Agriculture of the United Kingdom, were referred. Reports, 1821, IX. 654, 656, 657

Reports from the Select Committee on Artizans and Machinery. Reports, 1824, v. 608, 609, 645, 648

from 1801—1841. *Also of gross receipts of Revenue for Great Britain and Ireland in the same period.* Accounts and Papers, 1841, XIII. 698

Return showing the Total amount of Money levied for Poor Rate and County Rate in England and Wales, and expended thereout, for the relief of the Poor, for the years ended Lady Day, 1813—1844, *both inclusive.* Accounts and Papers, 1845, XLI. 699

Return showing the Population, the Annual value of Property rated to the Poor's Rate, Expenditure for the Relief of the Poor, &c. &c. in England and Wales, Scotland and Ireland. Accounts and Papers, 1847, XLIX. 699

Return showing the Population, the Annual value of Property rated to the Poor's Rate, Expenditure for the Relief of the Poor, &c. &c. in England and Ireland and Scotland. Accounts and Papers, 1849, XLVII. 699

Returns showing the Population, the Annual Value of Property rated to the Poor's Rates, Expenditure for the Relief of the Poor, &c. in England and Wales, Ireland and Scotland. Accounts and Papers, 1847—8, LIII. 699

Reynel, C. *The True English Interest* (1674). 115, 153

Ricardo, D. *Letters of David Ricardo to T. R. Malthus,* 1810—1823 (edited by J. Bonar, 1887). 599

Ricardo, D. *On the Principles of Political Economy and Taxation* (1817). 571

Ricardo, D. *Principles of Political Economy and Taxation* (edited by E. C. K. Gonner, 1891). 571

[Richardson.] *An Essay on the Causes of the Decline of the Foreign Trade, consequently of the value of the Lands of Great Britain and on the means to restore both* (1744). 298, 387, 388, 409, 420, 561

Rickman, J. *Observations on the Results of the Population Act* 41 Geo. III. appended to *An Abstract of the Answers and Returns made pursuant to an Act, passed in the forty-first year of his Majesty King George III.* (1802). 476

Rivers, M. J., and Foyle, O. *England's Slavery* (1659). 109

Roberts, L. *The Treasure of Traffike* (1641). 301, 345

Robertson, W. *The History of America* (1808). 109, 314

Robinson, H. *England's Safety, in Trades Encrease* (1641). 112, 115, 128

Robinson, H. *Libertas, or Relief to the English Captives in Algier* (1642). 217

Robson, J. *An account of six years residence in Hudson's Bay* (1752). 603

Roe, Sir T. *Speech in Parliament* (1641), in *Harleian Miscellany* IV. (1809). 171

Rogers, J. E. T. *A History of Agriculture and Prices in England*

neighbourhood from the Earliest Period down to the Present Time (1823). 177

Sharp, T. *A Dissertation on the Pageants or Dramatic Mysteries anciently performed at Coventry by the Trading Companies of that City* (1835). 45

Shaw, P. *Digest of Cases decided in the Supreme Courts of Scotland* 1800—1842 (1843). 353

Sheppard, W. *Of Corporations, Fraternities and Guilds* (1659). 90, 160

Sheppard, W. *The whole office of the Country Justice of Peace* (1656). 200

Sherlock, W. *An Exhortation to the redeemed Slaves* (1702). 115

Sinclair, Sir J. *The history of the Public Revenue of the British Empire* (1790). 698

Sinclair, Sir J. *The Statistical Account of Scotland* (1791—1799). 461

Smiles, S. *The Huguenots, their Settlements, Churches, and Industries in England and Ireland* (1889). 349

Smith, A. *An Inquiry into the Nature and Causes of the Wealth of Nations* (edited by J. S. Nicholson, 1887). 151, 208, 212, 262, 263, 264, 265, 293, 294, 353, 361, 417, 418, 431, 432, 434, 437, 438, 511, 545, 547, 548, 550, 552, 557, 564, 565, 581

Smith, C. *Ancient and present state of the County of Kerry* (1756). 341

Smith, C. *Three Tracts on the Corn-Trade and Corn Laws* (1766). 356, 359, 364, 371, 372

Smith, H. *Examination of usury* (1592). 80

Smith, Captain J. *Advertisements for the unexperienced Planters of New England, or anywhere* (1631), in E. Arber's *English Scholar's Library* XVI. (1884). 145, 147, 152

Smith, Capt. J. *The generall History of Virginia, New England and the Summer Isles* (1624) (edited by E. Arber, in *the English Scholar's Library* XVI. 1884). 151, 155

Smith, Capt. J. *Works* (edited by E. Arber in *the English Scholar's Library*, 1884). 145, 147, 151, 152, 155

Smith, J. *Chronicon Rusticum-Commerciale; or, Memoirs of Wool* (1747). 141, 194, 264, 265, 335, 424, 561

Smith, J. *The Case of the English Farmer, and his Landlord* (N. D.). 560

Smith, John. *England's Improvement revived* (1673). 115

Smith, J. T. *The Parish* (1857). 61, 93

Smith, S. *America*, in *Edinburgh Review*, XXXIII. (1820). 666

Smith, S. *Works* (1839). 666

Smith, W. *An Essay for Recovery of Trade* (1661). 51

Some Considerations relating to the Enlarging the Russia Trade. 122

Some Remarks on a late Pamphlet, intituled, Reflections on the Expediency of opening the Trade to Turkey (1753). 282

Soto, D. de. *Libri decem de justitia et jure* (1569). 109

Spectator (1712). 396

Spedding, J. *The Letters and the Life of Francis Bacon* (1861—1874). 53, 165

Spenser, E. *Works* (edited by H. J. Todd, 1805). 18, 19

Stanhope, Earl. *History of England, comprising the reign of Queen Anne until the Peace of Utrecht* (1870). 264

Stanley. *Stanleyes Remedy* (1646). 201

State of the Revenues and Forces by sea and land of France and Spain compared with those of Great Britain (1740). 331

State Papers. Domestic, Elizabeth CXLVII. Record Office. 22

Statutes at large, passed in the Parliaments held in Ireland:

       17 and 18 C. II. *c.* 15. 142, 357

       2 Anne *c.* 2. 525

       1 Geo. II. *c.* 10. 525

       25 Geo. II. *c.* 10. 527

       19 and 20 Geo. III. *c.* 17. 525

       21 and 22 Geo. III. *c.* 47. 526

       23 and 24 Geo. III. *c.* 19. 527

Statutes of the Realm (1810):—

   7 H. IV. *c.* 17. 42

   4 H. VII. *c.* 19. 52, 53

   11 H. VII. *c.* 27. 345

   19 H. VII. *c.* 7. 46

   3 H. VIII. *c.* 15. 34

   7 H. VIII. *c.* 1. 52

   14 and 15 H. VIII. *c.* 2. 173, 178

   22 H. VIII. *c.* 4. 46, 178

   24 H. VIII. *c.* 4. 22, *c.* 10. 56

   27 H. VIII. *cc.* 22, 28. 52

   28 H. VIII. *c.* 5. 46

   34 and 35 H. VIII. *c.* 4. 92

   35 H. VIII. *c.* 17. 341

   1 Ed. VI. *c.* 14. 45

   2 and 3 Ed. VI. *c.* 15. 46, 47, 90

   3 and 4 Ed. VI. *c.* 20. 47, 91

   5 and 6 Ed. VI. *c.* 14. 91, *c.* 18. 20, *c.* 20. 75, 80, *c.* 22. 456, *c.* 25. 169

   1 and 2 P. and M. *c.* 5. 49, 54

   2 and 3 P. and M. *c.* 3. 56, *c.* 8. 377

   4 and 5 P. and M. *c.* 5. 49

   1 Eliz. *c.* 13. 21, *c.* 14. 50, *c.* 21. 65

   5 Eliz. *c.* 2. 52, *c.* 3. 58, *c.* 4. 38, 41, 46, 56, 611, *c.* 5. 21, 23, 54, 287, *c.* 6. 92, *c.* 7. 33, *c.* 8. 48, *c.* 12. 91

   8 Eliz. *c.* 3. 34, *c.* 6. 34, *c.* 7. 49, *c.* 11. 48, *c.* 15. 56, *c.* 22. 35

   13 Eliz. *c.* 7. 92, *c.* 8. 48, 75, *c.* 11. 23, *c.* 13. 21, 55, *c.* 19. 34, *c.* 25. 56

   14 Eliz. *c.* 5. 59, 60, *c.* 12. 49

   18 Eliz. *c.* 3. 60, *c.* 15. 48, *c.* 16. 50

   23 Eliz. *c.* 11. 23

Statutes of the Realm (1810):—
  35 Eliz. *c.* 6. 174, *c.* 7. 52, 54
  39 Eliz. *c.* 3. 59, *c.* 4. 61, *c.* 5. 61, *c.* 10. 23, *c.* 14. 33
  43 Eliz. *c.* 2. 61, *c.* 11. 57, *c.* 12. 289
  1 J. I. *c.* 6. 43, 200, *c.* 9. 169, *c.* 15. 209, *c.* 24. 36
  3 J. I. *c.* 6. 88, *c.* 18. 173
  4 J. I. *c.* 5. 170, *c.* 11. 204
  7 J. I. *c.* 4. 206, *c.* 9. 169, *c.* 18. 185, *c.* 21. 186
  21 J. I. *c.* 3. 164, *c.* 7. 170, *c.* 17. 75, *c.* 31. 159
  3 C. I. *c.* 4. 43, 170
  16 C. I. *c.* 4. 43, *c.* 26. 287
  17 C. I. *c.* 21. 158, *c.* 31. 114
  12 C. II. *c.* 13. 252, *c.* 18. 330, 671, *cc.* 23, 24. 221, *c.* 32. 177, 335,
     c. 34. 155, 156, *c.* 35. 222
  13 and 14 C. II. *c.* 12. 207, *c.* 13. 338
  13 C. II., II. *c.* 2. 210
  14 C. II. *c.* 7. 177, *c.* 10. 221, *c.* 13. 176, *c.* 15. 169, *c.* 18. 177,
     c. 19. 176, *c.* 23. 289
  15 C. II. *c.* 7. 180, 190, 212, *c.* 34. 155
  17 and 18 C. II. *c.* 15. 142
  18 and 19 C. II. *c.* 2. 180, *c.* 4. 177, *c.* 8. 175
  22 and 23 C. II. *c.* 8. 169, *c.* 20. 210, *c.* 26. 155, 156
  25 C. II. *c.* 6. 179, *c.* 7. 122, 284
  29 C. II. *c.* 3. 186
  30 C. II. *c.* 3. 177, *c.* 4. 210
  1 W. III. and M., I. *c.* 12. 371
  4 W. III. and M. *c.* 17. 284
  4 and 5 W. III. and M. *c.* 15. 407
  5 and 6 W. III. and M. *c.* 7. 399, *c.* 10. 95, *c.* 20. 395, *c.* 21. 407,
     c. 24. 286
  7 and 8 W. III. *c.* 10. 341, 525, *c.* 18. 407, *c.* 21. 286, *c.* 33. 284,
     c. 39. 302
  8 and 9 W. III. *c.* 20. 525, *c.* 21. 408, *c.* 23. 286, *c.* 29. 288, *c.* 30.
     361, *c.* 36. 350
  9 W. III. *c.* 26. 279, *c.* 44. 271
  9 and 10 W. III. *c.* 23. 405, *c.* 43. 350
  10 W. III. *c.* 6. 123
  10 and 11 W. III. *c.* 2. 338, *c.* 10. 303
  11 and 12 W. III. *c.* 10. 131, 337, 351, *c.* 11. 337
  12 and 13 W. III. *c.* 12. 223
  1 Anne II. *c.* 18. 357, 358, 397
  2 and 3 Anne *c.* 6. 287
  3 and 4 Anne *c.* 8. 292, 302, *c.* 10. 285, 330
  4 Anne *c.* 20. 287
  5 Anne *c.* 17. 337
  6 Anne *c.* 8. 335, *c.* 17. 272

Statutes of the Realm (1810):—

8 Anne *c.* 6. 338, *c.* 9. 408, *c.* 10. 285, *c.* 13. 330, *c.* 17. 287, *c.* 18. 355, *c.* 19. 352

9 Anne *c.* 15. 286, *c.* 17. 285, 330

10 Anne *c.* 19. 351, *c.* 23. 272, *c.* 27. 286

12 Anne *c.* 9. 285, 330, *c.* 13. 355

12 Anne, II. *c.* 7. 305, *c.* 9. 351, *c.* 15. 288, *c.* 18. 336

5 Geo. I. *c.* 4. 305, *c.* 12. 378, *c.* 21. 272, *c.* 27. 362

6 Geo. I. *c.* 14. 283, *c.* 18. 290

7 Geo. I. *c.* 5. 271, *c.* 7. 351, *c.* 13. 360, *c.* 21. 271

8 Geo. I. *c.* 12. 413, *c.* 15. 335, 339, 413, *c.* 18. 336

9 Geo. I. *c.* 7. 381, 491, *c.* 26. 272, *c.* 27. 357

12 Geo. I. *c.* 34. 360

13 Geo. I. *c.* 23. 357, 358, *c.* 24. 354, *c.* 25. 592

1 Geo. II. *c.* 11. 378, *c.* 19. 359

2 Geo. II. *c.* 7. 286, *c.* 35. 330, *c.* 36. 287

3 Geo. II. *c.* 28. 330, *c.* 36. 288

5 Geo. II. *c.* 7. 317, *c.* 8. 350, *c.* 22. 329, *c.* 24. 330

6 Geo. II. *c.* 13. 312, 313

7 Geo. II. *c.* 18. 592

8 Geo. II. *c.* 29. 286

9 Geo. II. *c.* 4. 346, 351, *c.* 37. 339, 358

11 Geo. II. *c.* 22. 356

12 Geo. II. *c.* 21. 335

13 Geo. II. *c.* 3. 287, *c.* 8. 397, *c.* 28. 339

14 Geo. II. *c.* 36. 282, 592, *c.* 39. 288, *c.* 41. 344, *c.* 42. 378

15 Geo. II. *c.* 31. 292

17 Geo. II. *c.* 17. 273

18 Geo. II. *cc.* 24, 25. 358, *c.* 31. 286, *c.* 36. 338

19 Geo. II. *c.* 19. 200, 359, *c.* 22. 288, *c.* 27. 339

20 Geo. II. *c.* 38. 287

21 Geo. II. *c.* 2. 415, *c.* 26. 338, *c.* 30. 330

22 Geo. II. *c.* 27. 357, 358, 360, *c.* 40. 288

23 Geo. II. *cc.* 9, 20. 336, *c.* 31. 279, *c.* 34. 336

26 Geo. II. *c.* 11. 335, *c.* 18. 283, *c.* 22. 354, *c.* 25. 288, *c.* 26. 283

27 Geo. II. *c.* 1. 283, *c.* 18. 335

28 Geo. II. *c.* 19. 373

29 Geo. II. *c.* 36. 370

31 Geo. II. *c.* 8. 288, *c.* 10. 286, 287, *c.* 12. 335, *c.* 29. 355, *c.* 38. 288

2 Geo. III. *c.* 18. 288, *c.* 87. 288

3 Geo. III. *c.* 11. 356, *c.* 14. 288

4 Geo. III. *c.* 20. 280, *c.* 37. 350

5 Geo. III. *c.* 18. 335, *c.* 29. 336, *c.* 38. 378, *c.* 48. 336, *c.* 51. 357

6 Geo. III. *c.* 25. 357, *c.* 31. 288, *c.* 49. 312

7 Geo. III. *c.* 52. 288, *c.* 58. 302

Statutes of the Realm (1810) :—
  6 and 7 W. IV. *c.* **71.** 655
  1 and 2 Vict. *c.* **113.** 597
  3 and 4 Vict. *c.* **36.** 591
  5 and 6 Vict. *c.* **99.** 590, 644
  7 and 8 Vict. *c.* **32.** 673, *c.* **110.** 678
  9 and 10 Vict. *c.* **17.** 353, *c.* **22.** 654, 670
  12 and 13 Vict. *c.* **29.** 671
  17 and 18 Vict. *c.* **104.** 671

Stephen, J. *War in Disguise; or, the Frauds of the Neutral Flags* (1805). 289, 514, 518, 519, 543

Steuart, Sir J. *Works* (1805). 419, 422, 429, 430, 431, 502, 559, 561

Stevens, H. *The dawn of British Trade to the East Indies* (1886). 24, 25, 27, 28, 29

Stith, W. *The History of the First Discovery and Settlement of Virginia* (1747). 144, 145, 146

Story, J. *Commentaries on the Constitution of the United States* (1873). 146, 147

Stow, J. *A Survey of the cities of London and Westminster* (edited by J. Strype, 1720). 25, 35, 36, 38, 45, 46, 47, 48, 49, 50, 66, 67, 89, 93, 94, 95, 122, 124, 125, 208, 225, 254, 289, 352

Strype, J. *Life of the learned Sir Thomas Smith* (1820). 32, 33

Strype, J. *The Life and Acts of John Whitgift, D.D.* (1822). 114

Swift, J. *Works* (edited by J. Hawkesworth, D. Swift, and J. Nichols 1765—1775). 402

Sydney, W. C. *England and the English in the eighteenth century* (1891). 374

Sympson, A. *A short, easy and effectual Method to prevent the running of Wool, &c. from Great-Britain and Ireland to foreign parts* (1741). 335

Table of all terms of years from one to thirty-one inclusive (1681). 225

Table of the Insurance Office at the Back-side of the Royal Exchange (1682). 225

Tables of the Revenue, Population, Commerce, &c. of the United Kingdom and its Dependencies. Accounts and Papers, 1833, XLI. 695

Taylor, S. *Common-Good* (1652). 181, 182, 184, 193, 205, 206

[Temple, W.] *Considerations on Taxes, as they are supposed to affect the Price of Labour in our Manufacturies* (1765). 358, 458, 560, 688

[Temple, W.] *An Essay on Trade and Commerce: containing Observations on Taxes, as they are supposed to affect the Price of Labour in our Manufactories, together with some interesting Reflections on the Importance of our Trade to America* (1770). 383, 420, 560, 600, 689

Temple, Sir W. *Miscellanea* (1681). 301

Temple, Sir W. *Works* (1814). 102, 139

Thoughts on the pernicious consequences of borrowing money (1759). 409

Young, A. *A six months' Tour through the North of England* (1771).
284, 363, 364, 365, 366, 367, 368, 369, 373, 374

Young, A. *A six weeks' Tour through the Southern Counties of England and Wales* (1772). 366, 367, 370, 377, 378

Young, A. *Political Arithmetic* (1774). 489

Young, A. *The expediency of a free exportation of Corn at this time: with some observations on the Bounty and its effects* (1770). 489

Young, A. *The Farmer's Letters to the People of England* (1768).
337, 359, 367, 373, 377, 381, 383, 384, 387, 388, 389, 428

Young, A. *Tour in Ireland* (1780). 306

Young, Sir W. *The West-India Common-Place Book* (1807). 316, 544

Zimmern, H. *The Hansa Towns* (1889). 596

INDEX.

Lightning Source UK Ltd.
Milton Keynes UK
UKHW012145180219
337529UK00012B/1287/P